MOON HANDBOOKS

BIG ISLAND OF HAWAI'I

ROBERT NILSEN

BIG ISLAND OF HAWAI'I

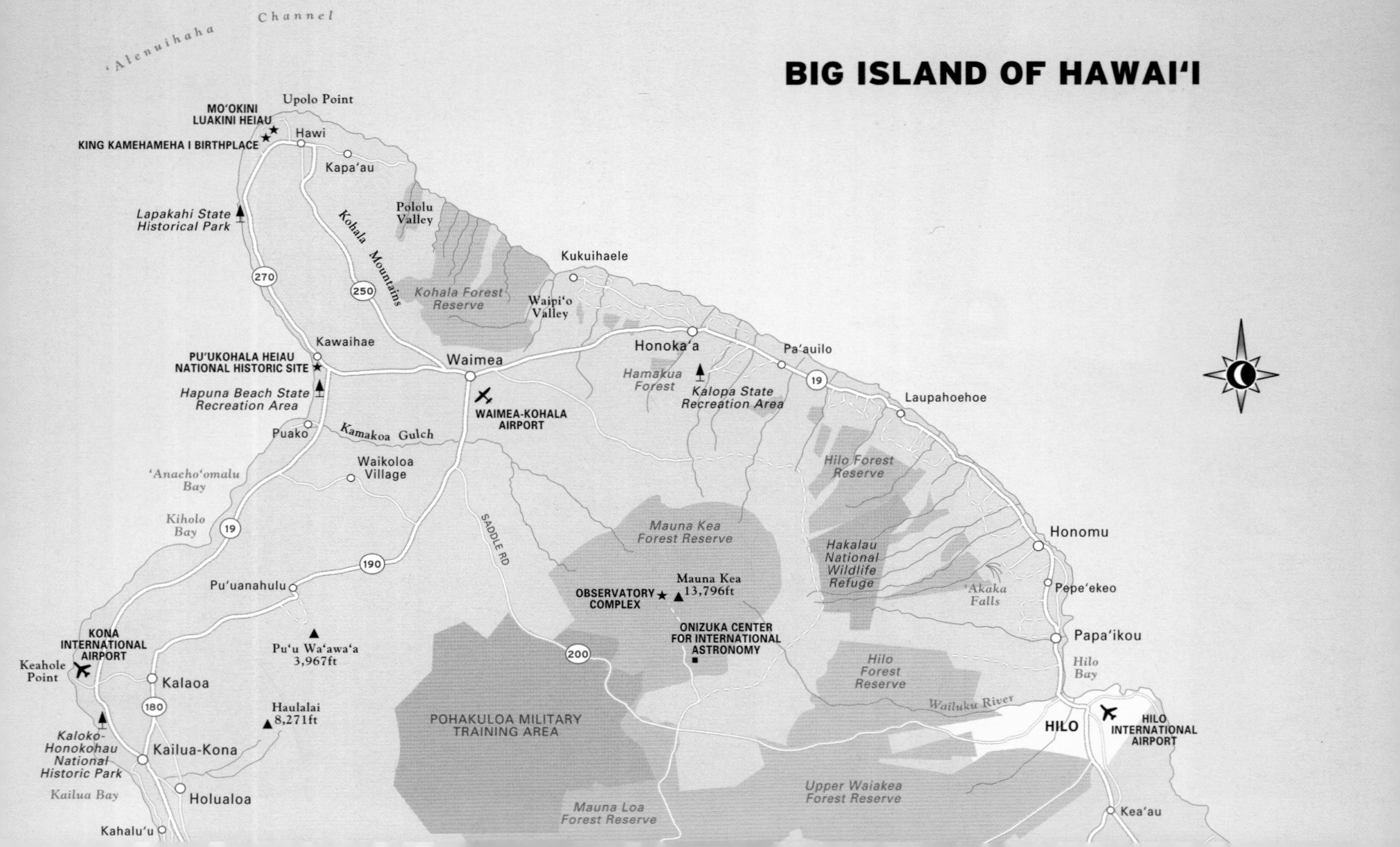

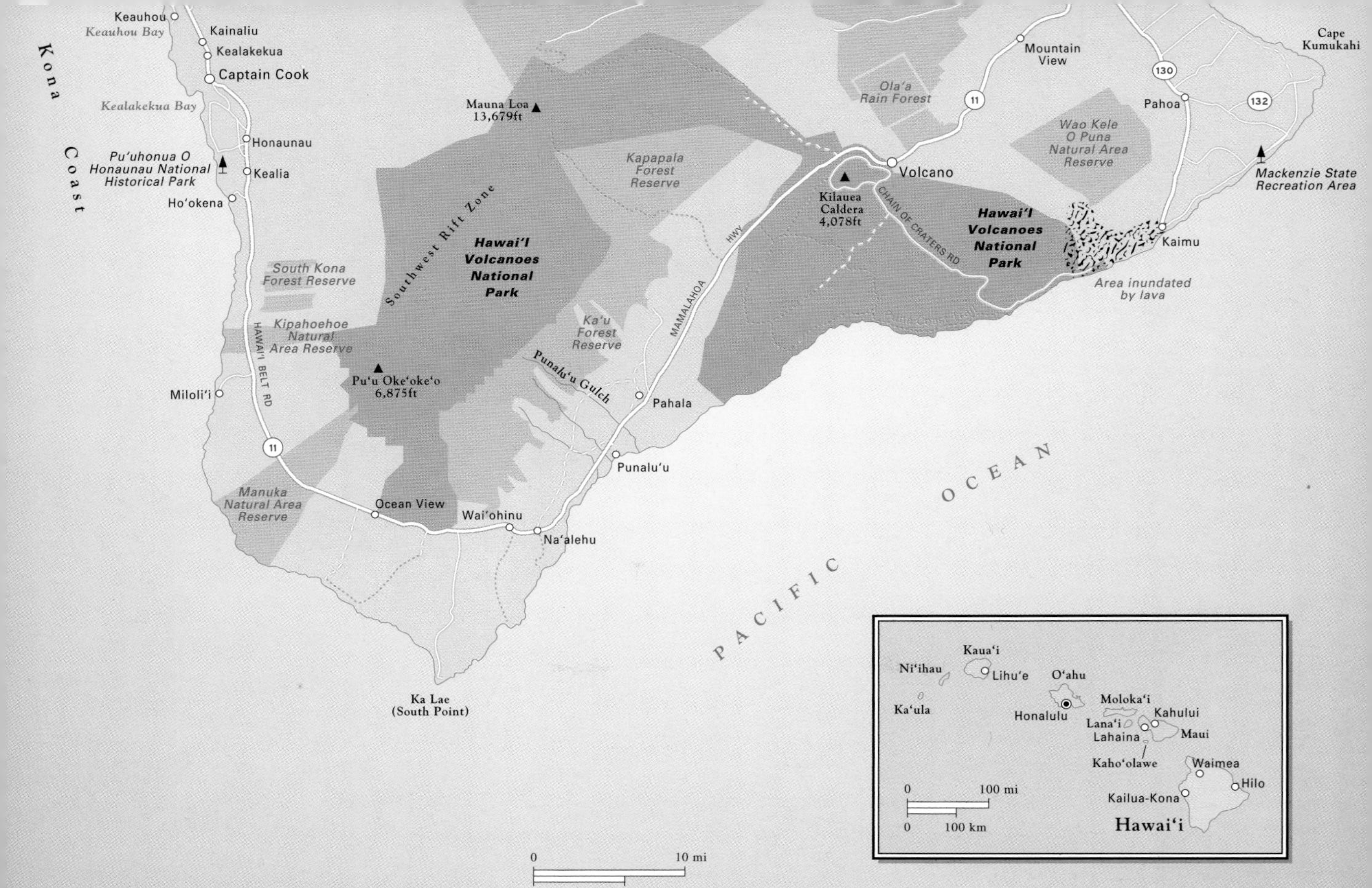

Kona Coast
Keauhou
Keauhou Bay
Kainaliu
Kealakekua
Captain Cook
Kealakekua Bay
Honaunau
Pu'uhonua O Honaunau National Historical Park
Kealia
Ho'okena
South Kona Forest Reserve
Kipahoehoe Natural Area Reserve
HAWAI'I BELT RD
11
Miloli'i
Manuka Natural Area Reserve
Ocean View
Wai'ohinu
Na'alehu
Ka Lae (South Point)
Mauna Loa 13,679ft
Southwest Rift Zone
Hawai'I Volcanoes National Park
Pu'u Oke'oke'o 6,875ft
Kapapala Forest Reserve
Ka'u Forest Reserve
Punalu'u Gulch
MAMALAHOA HWY
Pahala
Punalu'u
Kilauea Caldera 4,078ft
CHAIN OF CRATERS RD
Volcano
Ola'a Rain Forest
Mountain View
Wao Kele O Puna Natural Area Reserve
Hawai'I Volcanoes National Park
Area inundated by lava
Kaimu
130
Pahoa
132
Mackenzie State Recreation Area
Cape Kumukahi
PACIFIC OCEAN
0
10 mi
0
10 km
Kaua'i
Ni'ihau
Lihu'e
Ka'ula
O'ahu
Honalulu
Moloka'i
Kahului
Lana'i
Lahaina
Maui
Kaho'olawe
Waimea
Hilo
Kailua-Kona
Hawai'i
0
100 mi
0
100 km

DISCOVER THE BIG ISLAND OF HAWAI'I

The Big Island must have filled the first Polynesian settlers with awe as they approached the island from the south after traveling for weeks through the broad expanse of the Pacific Ocean. Immense in size, the island with its black volcanic shore, green-forested mountainsides, fertile valleys, and snow-capped peaks surely must have looked like heaven to them. Those early settlers knew they had found something special. Visitors today – whose trip is much swifter and less laborious – will be similarly enchanted by the raw beauty of the island, its dominant size, the uncrowded openness, and its varied nature.

The Big Island is formed by five volcanoes. The dynamism of Kilauea, its most active, draws the adventurous to the island. While peering over the precipitous edge into the maw of this huge caldera is of interest in and of itself, greater thrills await those who hike

multicolor plumeria

to an active lava flow, where rivers of red lava course over cliffs and spew into the sea, creating new land in clouds of steam and gas. This dynamic process is the act of birth itself – the island of Hawai'i grows under your feet. In such a way the island formed, and these broad, black rivers of frozen stone are a dominant feature throughout the island.

However inspiring the volcanoes are, the island has much more to offer. Head north along the Hamakua Coast to its sheer sea cliffs and survey the island's grandest valley, where its mile-long black-sand beach, its thousand-foot cliffs, and its silvery strands of waterfalls create a tropical Eden. Imagine yourself, as ancient Hawaiian royalty did, at home in the embracing arms of this sanctuary.

Early Hawaiians lived throughout the island, and its dry western side preserves many of their remnants and artifacts. Travel the windswept northern tip of the island to pay your respects at a *heiau* that is nearly as old as the Hawaiian culture itself, or stop to unravel

lava flow

PURESTOCK

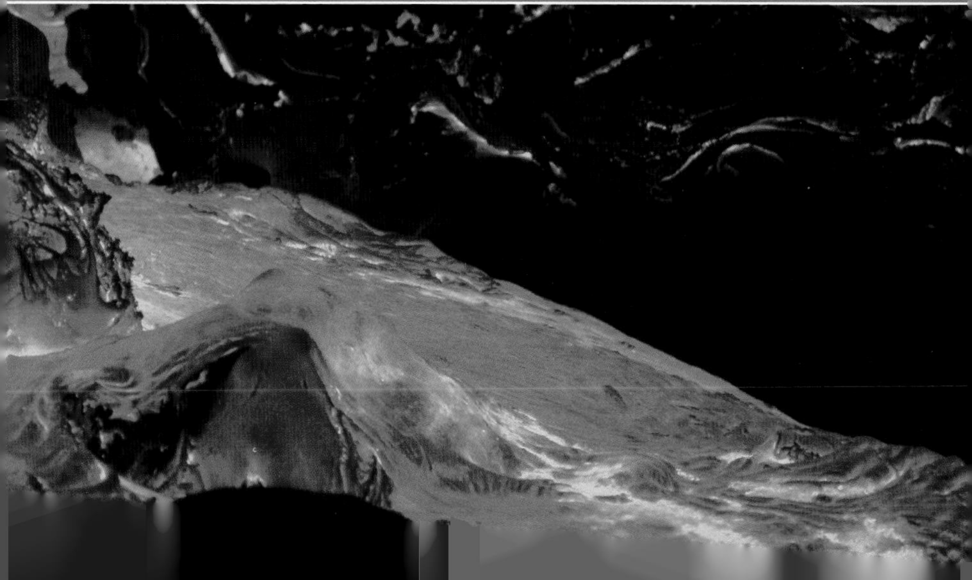

the meaning behind the enigmatic petroglyph carvings that sprinkle desolate landscapes. As you explore the island's ancient temple of refuge, imagine the relief of a vanquished warrior of old as he desperately reached its perimeter, knowing that he could return home again safely, free and unapproachable to his foes.

The Big Island is not just about the historical and cultural. Visitors flock here for fun and pleasure, knowing the sun is guaranteed to shine. As the sugar economy faded, tourism grew, and with it came a shift in prominence from the windward to the leeward side of the island, where dry Kona offers plenty of adventure for all who come. There, you can experience the dazzling colors of tropical fish while snorkeling the aquarium-like waters of Kealakekua Bay or feel the fight at the end of a line that's hooked a giant blue marlin. Enjoy the opportunity to play the emerald green of some of the best golf courses in the nation or skim the black coastline by sleek catamaran to explore little-visited coves.

While now eclipsed by Kona, the Hilo side of the island refuses to be forgotten. To visit the island without seeing the wet side would

sea turtles

PHOTO COURTESY OF HVCB/RON DAHLQUIST

be to miss the colorful floral abundance of fragrant tropical gardens and deep coastal valleys sporting cascading waterfalls. Once you've arrived, you won't be able to resist a dip in its warm thermal pools as you explore the steamy jungle shoreline.

Those willing to stray from the coast will find even more variety in the island's interior. Feel free to canter across upland pastures where cowboy life is the norm or stop in artists' communities along an upland road through America's most famous coffee-producing region. After pacing yourself through an endurance-busting triathlon, you can reward yourself by luxuriating in lush valleys, where countless waterfalls break through the rock faces of thousand-foot-high chasms. All these adventures and more await those willing to explore.

The mountains also beckon, and it's their immensity that gives this island its presence. While a sunset along the coast can be romantic, you won't forget the evening you make the drive to the top of Mauna Kea. As you snuggle into the lee of shelter at one of the world's most outstanding locations for astronomical observatories,

konane game board at Pu'uhonua O Honaunau

you'll watch the sun dip into a fleecy sea of clouds and drop below the horizon. The chill of the night air brings you back to reality – you are standing at over 13,000 feet in elevation in the middle of the vast Pacific Ocean. Pause and watch the sky light up with a show of stars that's almost impossible to comprehend.

The island of Hawai'i is grand in so many ways. The island is broad and unpretentious, open like petals on a spring morning flower. Its two nicknames, "The Orchid Island" and "The Volcano Island," are both excellent choices: the island produces more of the delicate blooms than anywhere else on earth; and Pele, the fire goddess who makes her mythological home here, regularly sends rivers of lava from the world's largest and most active volcanoes. However, to the people who live here, Hawai'i has had only one real nickname, "The Big Island." Bigger isn't necessarily better, but when combined with beautiful, uncrowded, and varied, it's hard to beat. So embrace the many wonders of this grand paradise. As you journey through the Big Island, let them inspire and arouse you like the early Polynesian settlers of old.

Rainbow Falls

Contents

MAP CONTENTS

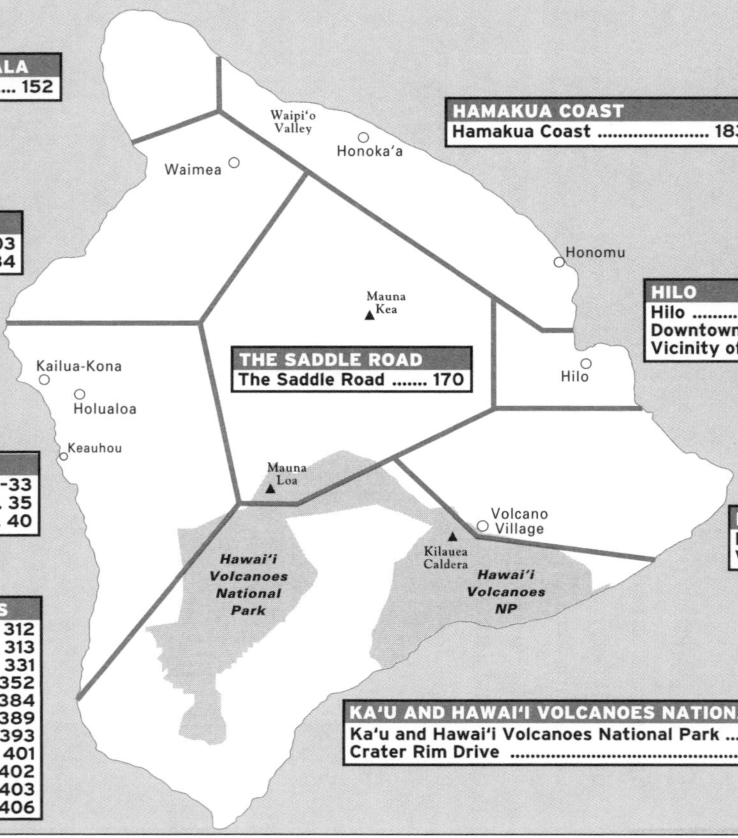

The Lay of the Land

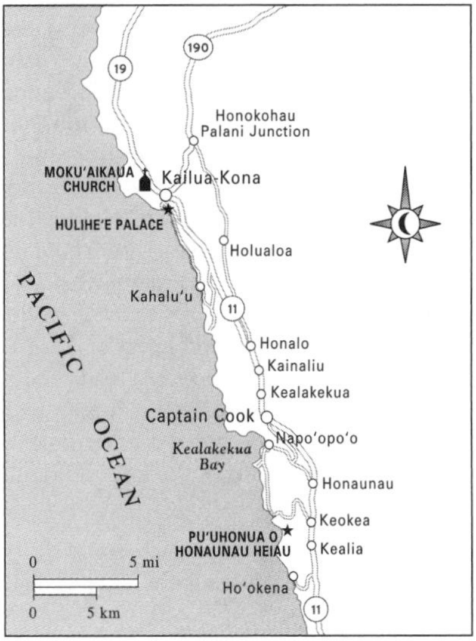

KONA

Kona is dry, sunny, and brilliant—most visitors' introduction to the island. When watered, the rich soil blossoms, as in the small artists' enclave of Holualoa and South Kona, renowned for its diminutive **coffee plantations.** As the center of this region, Kailua-Kona boasts an array of art and designer shops, economical accommodations, great restaurants, and plenty of historical and cultural sites like **Moku'aikaua Church,** a legacy of the very first packet of missionaries to arrive in the islands, and **Hulihe'e Palace,** vacation home of the Hawaiian royalty. **Kealakekua Bay,** one of the first points of contact with foreigners, is also one of the best snorkel sites that Hawaii has to offer. Nearby is the restored **Pu'uhonua O Honaunau Heiau,** a traditional Hawaiian safe refuge. World-class triathletes come here to train, and charter boats depart in search of billfish and other denizens of the deep.

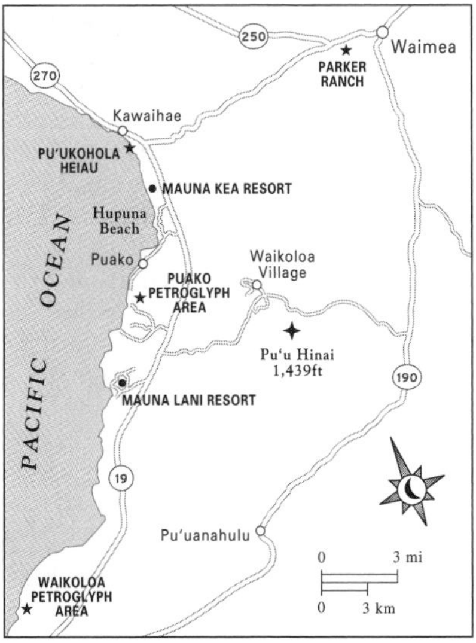

SOUTH KOHALA

Lying north of Kailua, otherworldly black lava bleeds north into South Kohala. Up the coast is **Hapuna Beach,** one of the best on the island. In 1965, Laurance Rockefeller opened the Mauna Kea Resort near there. Since then, other expansive resorts and golf courses have been added, making this the island's luxury resort area. These resorts have turned barren lava into oases of green and playgrounds of the well-to-do, accompanied only by the soothing music of the surf and by the not-so-melodious singing of "Kona nightingales"—wild donkeys that frequent this area. Peppered among these resorts are petroglyph fields left by old Hawaiians, and farther north is the magnificent Pu'ukohola Heiau. Upcountry is **Waimea,** center of the enormous **Parker Ranch,** the epitome of Hawaiian cowboy country where *paniolo* still ride herd in time-honored tradition.

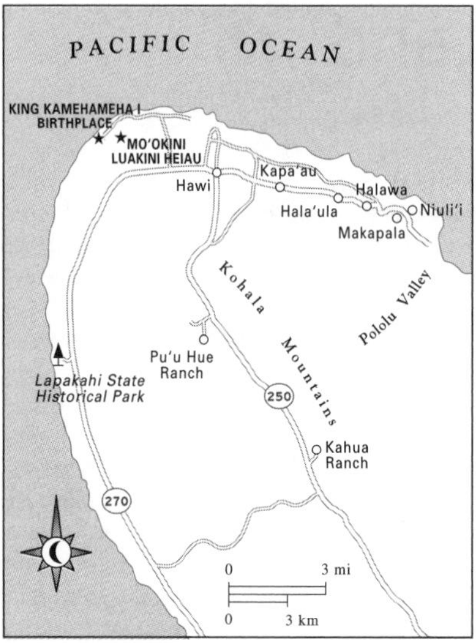

NORTH KOHALA

North Kohala is the hilly peninsular thumb at the northern extremity of the island. The **Kohala Mountains** sweep down to the west to a warm and largely uninhabited coast, and to the east tumble into deep valleys cut by wind and rain. Several isolated beach parks dot the coast, and here and there are cultural sites, including the remnants of a fishing village at **Laupakahi State Historical Park,** the **birthplace of Kamehameha the Great,** and the nearby and much older **Mo'okini Luakini Heiau.** The main town up this way is sleepy **Hawi,** holding on after sugar left. Down this little-traveled road is **Kapa'au,** where Kamehameha's statue resides in fulfillment of a *kahuna* prophecy and artists offer their crafts in small shops. At road's end is the overlook of **Pololu Valley,** where a steep descent takes you to a secluded beach in an area once frequented by some of the most powerful sorcerers in the land.

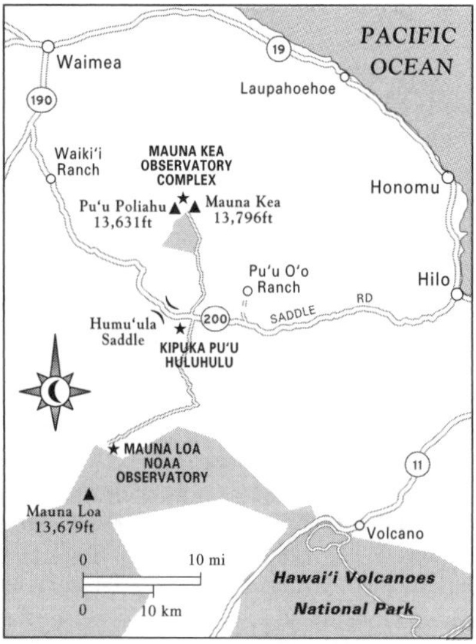

THE SADDLE ROAD

This cross-island road slices through a most astonishing high valley or "saddle" separating the mountains of **Mauna Loa** and **Mauna Kea.** Along the Saddle Road are long stretches of native forest, barren lava flow, and rangeland, plus a number of worthy spots for a stretch. Perhaps the most convenient is **Kipuka Pu'u Huluhulu,** a low forested hill surrounded by stark lava flows that offers a good short hike for birders. From the Saddle Road, a spur road heads up to a **visitors information center** at 9,300 feet, where you can learn about the mountain and the science going on at the top of Mauna Kea, where, at 13,796 feet, a group of **observatories** peer into the heavens through the clearest air on earth. Heading south, another road zigzags up the slope to an atmospheric observatory, from where a hiking trail for the hale and hearty heads to the top of Mauna Loa.

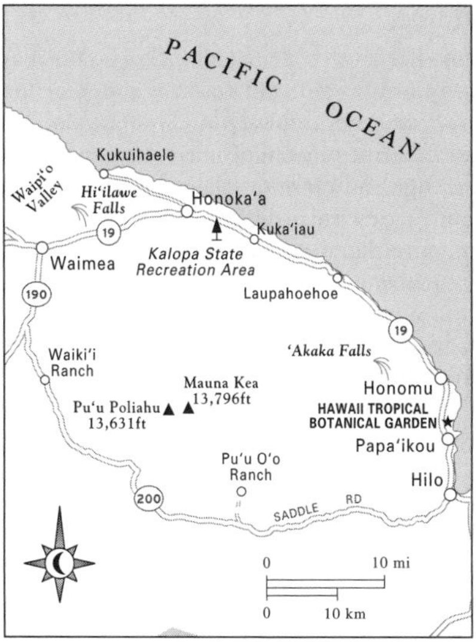

HAMAKUA COAST

Hamakua refers to the northeast coast above Hilo, where streams, wind, and pounding surf have chiseled the lava into cliffs and precipitous valleys. The road north from one-street Honoka'a dead-ends at the lookout pavilion on the ridge at the top of **Waipi'o Valley,** the most spectacular and enchanted valley on the island. Once a burial ground of Hawaiian *ali'i,* where *kahuna* came to commune with spirits, this verdant valley now supports a handful of families who live simply within its embrace. South are **Laupahoehoe Point,** with its memorial to victims of the terrible tsunami of 1946; the native and introduced forests at **Kalopa;** mesmerizing '**Akaka Falls,** inland from the forgotten sugar town of Honomu; and **Hawaii Tropical Botanical Garden,** one of the best such gardens in the state.

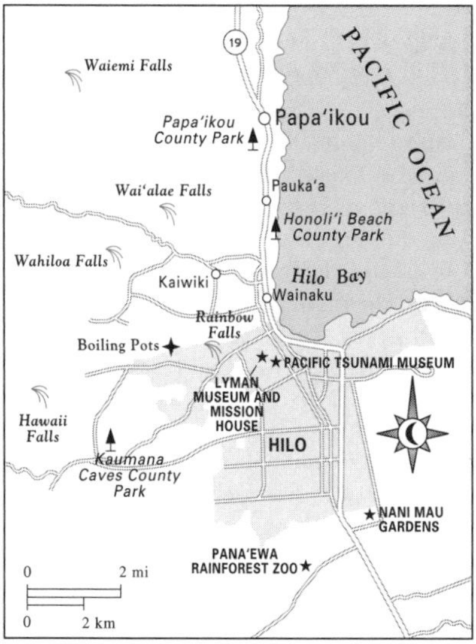

HILO

Hilo is the county seat, the oldest port of entry, the most tropical town on Hawai'i, and the only major city on the island's windward coast. The city is one tremendous greenhouse where exotic flowers and tropical plants are a normal part of the landscape, and entire blocks canopied by adjoining banyans are taken for granted. The town, which hosts the yearly **Merrie Monarch Festival,** boasts Japanese gardens, several **tropical gardens,** the **Lyman Museum and Mission House,** the **Pacific Tsunami Museum,** and a profusion of natural phenomena, including **Rainbow Falls** and **Boiling Pots.** Even the animals are happy in their tropical paradise at **Pana'ewa Rainforest Zoo.** The best way to see historic downtown Hilo and its buildings of yesteryear is on a walking tour. For the rest of town, you'll need a car. As the focus of tourism has shifted to the Kona side, Hilo has become easy on the pocketbook.

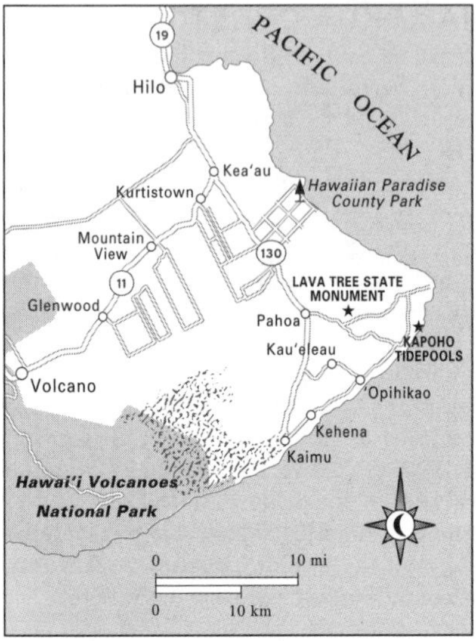

PUNA

Puna lies south of Hilo and makes up the majority of the southeast coast. It is one of the last bastions of tropical old Hawaii, a place of independent-minded people willing to live on the edge and make do from the land. While it once grew sugarcane, it's now best known for anthuriums, orchids, and papayas. Recent **lava flows** cover this region. One embraced a forest in its fiery grasp, entombing trees that stand like sentinels today in **Lava Tree State Monument.** Another formed Cape Kumukahi in 1868, becoming the easternmost point in Hawaii. The Kapoho **tidepools** anchor the eastern end of this coast, and from there a string of **ebony-black beaches** dot the shoreline. The coastal road dead-ends where it's been covered by lava at the small village of **Kaimu,** and there you come face to face with a raw, but now stilled, show of nature. Inland are a string of frontier towns that run up to Kilauea Volcano.

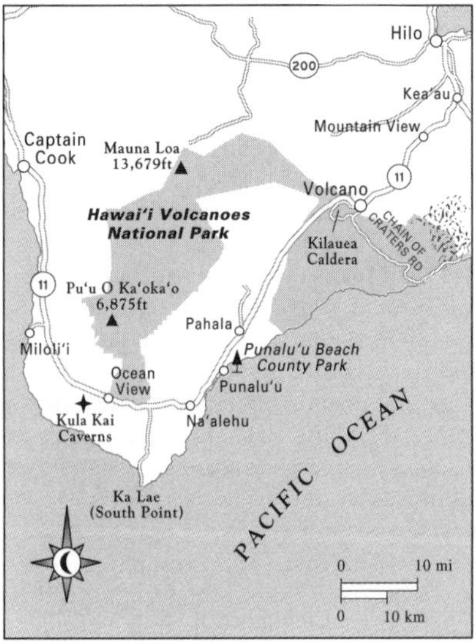

KA'U AND HAWAI'I VOLCANOES NATIONAL PARK

The greatest lava fields that have spewed from **Kilauea** dominate the heart of Hawai'i Volcanoes National Park. While miles of **hiking trails** crisscross the park, most see it by car along the rim drive that brings you up close to sights like the impressive **Halema'uma'u Crater,** the mythical home of Madame Pele. **Chain of Craters Road** spills off the *pali* through a forbidding yet vibrant wasteland of old and new lava to where this living volcano fumes and throbs. The park is just one portion of Ka'u, the southernmost region of the island, primarily an arid coastal region with few towns at the base of Mauna Loa. Below the ranches, macadamia nut farms, and coffee fields are some lovely beaches and verdant coves that you'll have virtually to yourself, and a lonely narrow ribbon of road leads to windswept **Ka Lae,** the most southerly piece of real estate in the United States.

Planning Your Trip

WHEN TO GO

As with all of the Hawaiian Islands, the prime tourist season for the Big Island starts two weeks before Christmas and lasts until Easter. It picks up again with summer vacation in early June and ends once more in late August. Everything is more heavily booked and prices are higher. Hotel, airline, and car reservations are a must at this time of year. You can generally save substantially and avoid a lot of hassle if you travel in the "off-season"—September to early December and mid-April (after Easter) until late May. Recently, the drop in numbers of tourists during the off-season has not been nearly as substantial as in years past, indicating the increasing popularity of the island at all times of the year, but you'll still find the prices better and the beaches, trails, activities, and even restaurants less crowded.

The weather in Hawai'i is moderate all year round, and any time can be pleasant. Rains come and go—more so in winter—and are seldom sustained, so usually you can move a few miles down the coast to a sunny spot or wait for the warm breezes to blow away the clouds and dry things up.

While nearly all activities are available throughout the year, there are some exceptions. For instance, if you intend to see humpback whales, you must visit from late winter through spring, as these lovable giants of the sea are in Hawaiian waters only from December through April. Plenty of coffee is grown on the Big Island, and if you intend to view its harvesting and processing, it's best to go from September through January when the bulk of that job is done.

HOW LONG TO STAY

The average visitor to Hawaii spends 6–8 days on his or her vacation, most often on one island but sometimes split between two. The Big Island is relatively large, and it takes hours to drive straight around. The island can be "seen" in a few days, but there is much more to see and do than even a week or 10 days will give you time for. At a minimum for sightseeing, spend one day each in Kona and Hilo, another day at Hawai'i Volcanoes National Park, a day up the Hamakua Coast, and a day in Waimea and the North Kohala area. For those with more time, a trip up to the top of Mauna Kea would be rewarding, or a cultural tour of historical sites up and down the Kona-Kohala coast might be worth your time. Then there are the activities, most of which are half-day or full-day affairs. Soon you're at a full week. Remember that some activities should not be coupled with others on the same day, like scuba diving and a helicopter ride. Leave them for different days. If you spend less than a week on the island, you may leave feeling like you didn't give yourself enough time. The Big Island is indeed big, so you'll have many opportunities for exploration and adventure when you return.

WHAT TO TAKE

It's a snap to pack for a visit to the Big Island. Everything is on your side. The weather is moderate and uniform on the whole, and the style of dress is delightfully casual. The rule of thumb is to pack lightly: few items, and clothing light in both color and weight. If you forget something at home, it won't be a disaster. You can buy everything you'll need in Hawaii.

Even for those who have traveled to warmer climates previously, a few points are worthy of note. While shorts and T-shirts or short-sleeve shirts and blouses might be your usual daily wear, jeans or other long pants and closed-toe shoes are best and sometimes required if you plan on taking a horseback ride or dusty ATV tour. Remember to bring a billed or brimmed hat for the rain and sun, and, if you forget, inexpensive baseball caps and straw or woven hats are found easily throughout the island. Only a few classy restaurants in the finest hotels require men to wear a sport coat for dinner.

If you don't have one, those hotels can supply you with one for the evening. For women, a dress of the "resortwear" variety will suffice for most any occasion. By and large, "resort casual" is as dressy as you'll need to be in Hawaii.

One occasion for which you'll have to consider dressing warmly is a visit to the mountaintop. If you intend to visit Mauna Kea or Mauna Loa, it'll be downright chilly. In a pinch, a jogging suit with a hooded windbreaker/raincoat will do the trick, although you'll be more comfortable in warmer clothing like a wool sweater or thick jacket, cap, and gloves. If your hands get cold, put a pair of socks over them.

Tropical rain showers can happen at any time, so you might consider a fold-up umbrella. Nighttime winter temperatures may drop into the lower 60s or upper 50s, even on the coast, so be sure to have a light sweater and long pants along.

Dressing your feet is hardly a problem. You'll most often wear zori slippers (rubber thongs) for going to and from the beach, leather sandals for strolling and dining, and jogging shoes for hiking and sightseeing. Tevas and other types of outdoor strap sandals are good for general sightseeing and beach and water wear, plus they're great in the rain. Some people prefer *tabi,* a type of rubberized slipper, for crossing streams or wet trails. If you plan on heavy-duty hiking, you'll definitely want your hiking boots: the lightweight version is usually sufficient. Lava, especially ʻaʻa, is murderous on shoes. Most backcountry trails are rugged and muddy, and you'll need those good old lug soles for traction and laces for ankle support. If you plan moderate hikes, jogging shoes should do.

Two specialty items that you might consider bringing along are binoculars and snorkel gear. A pair of binoculars really enhances sightseeing—great for viewing birds and sweeping panoramas, and almost a necessity if you're going whale-watching. Flippers, mask, and snorkel can easily be bought or rented in Hawaii but don't weigh much or take up much space in your luggage. They'll save you a few dollars in rental fees and you'll have them when you want them.

Explore the Big Island

BEST OF THE BIG ISLAND

The Big Island is big—at least in relation to the other Hawaiian Islands. While it's possible to "do" the island in a few days, it is preferable to go at a more leisurely pace. As the average visitor from the Mainland spends eight days on a vacation in Hawaii, this time frame is a good choice for an all-encompassing "Best of the Big Island Tour," while leaving plenty of time for your own interests.

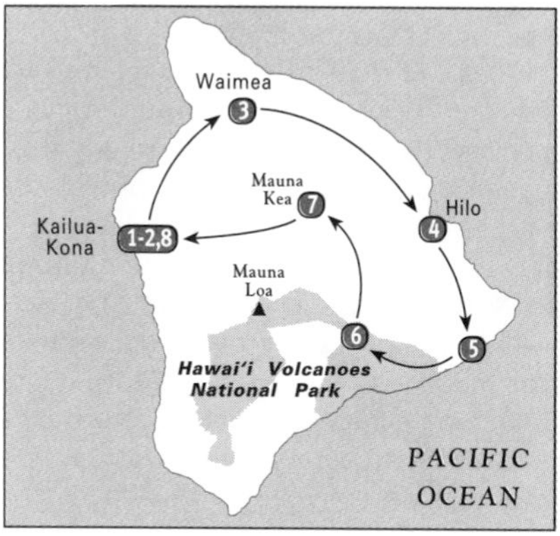

DAY 1

Fly into Kailua-Kona, knowing that the bleak, black lavascape that you come in over will not be how the entire island looks. Pick up your rental car and if you are staying in Kailua or Keauhou, head into town and take the shoreline route down **Ali'i Drive** to your hotel. If you're staying up in the resorts of South Kohala, leave Kailua for tomorrow and take the highway north to your hotel. Settle in, have a look around the property, and take a leisurely stroll along the beach in the moonlight after dinner.

DAY 2

Head into Kailua for a look at its historical sites. **Ahu'ena Heiau, Hulihe'e Palace,** and **Moku'aikaua Church** are all conveniently clustered near the center of town at Kamakahonu Beach. The old town lines the shore, so spend some time perusing the shops along this street before heading up above town to Holualoa for a few hours of wandering through its **art galleries.** Most Holualoa galleries are closed on Mondays, so it's not worth the drive on that day of the week.

DAY 3

There are several old Hawaiian sites along the Kohala Coast, so today leave early and head north as there is some walking to do. First, make a stop at either the **Waikoloa** or **Puako petroglyph field sites** before continuing on to **Pu'ukohola Heiau,** the last large *heiau* to be constructed on the island, and the old fishing village site at **Lapakahi State Historical Park,** which requires about a mile-long walk. From there, head to the artist towns of Hawi and Kapa'au on your way to the end of the road at **Pololu Valley.** Return by the route over the mountain to Waimea, where you can enjoy an upcountry sunset and a wonderful meal in one of the town's several fine restaurants.

DAY 4

Take Mamalahoa Highway around the flank of the mountain from Kailua to Waimea and cross over to the wet side. In Honoka'a, turn north and take the road to its end at

Waipi'o Valley, the greatest of all Hawaiian valleys. The Hamakua Coast is deeply cut by "gulches," and many waterfalls and scenic points abound along the way. As you get closer to Hilo, turn off the main highway and take the **Onomea Scenic Route.** In a few minutes you are in Hilo. Stay the night and enjoy an evening in this old town. Otherwise, it's a long drive back around to Kona.

DAY 5

Spend the morning on a walking tour of downtown Hilo. Visit the **Lyman Museum and Mission House** and don't miss the **Pacific Tsunami Museum,** as it tells the story of the two deadly tsunamis that wreaked havoc on this city during living memory. Visit the **Nani Mau Gardens,** stroll along **Banyan Drive,** or walk through the bayside **Lili'uokalani Park.** Natural sites only a few minutes from the center of town are **Rainbow Falls** and **Boiling Pots.** If you want to stretch the day, take a quick roundtrip through Puna. Head first to Pahoa, turn down toward Cape Kumukahi, then drive the long languid coastal road to Kaimu where lava stops your way.

DAY 6

This is the day for **Hawai'i Volcanoes National Park.** From Hilo it's an hour's drive; from Kona, perhaps twice that. Make your first stop at the **visitors center** for a quick introduction to the wonders of the park. For the best overall tour, head around the **Crater Rim Drive,** stopping at all the marked sites. Be sure to spend time at the **Thomas A. Jaggar Museum** to learn more about the geology of the park. Pay your respects at **Halema'uma'u Crater,** the home of the Hawaiian goddess Pele, before heading down the **Chain of Craters Road** to the ever-changing landscape at the shore. Return to Kona.

DAY 7

After many days of travel, take most of the day off to catch up on sleep, do a little shopping for gifts and mementos, or spend some time along one of the superb beaches along the Kona-Kohala coast. In the afternoon, take a (prearranged) guided tour to the top of **Mauna Kea** for a sunset spectacle and for stargazing after sundown.

DAY 8

This will be your last day on the Big Island and your last chance for another dip in the ocean or to pick up gifts before heading to the airport for your trip home.

KONA-KOHALA CULTURAL AND HISTORICAL TOUR

While the entire island was inhabited by the Hawaiians, most of the readily accessible precontact and early postcontact historical remains are found on the dry side of the island. A number of these have been turned into state and national historical parks and monuments. All are easily reached from either Kailua or the resorts of South Kohala. Visiting all these sites in one day would be too much. Better to take it in three trips—the northern three parks, the middle one park, and the southern two parks, combining your visits with other cultural and historical sights of the region.

DAY 1

The remote northern tip of the Big Island has two remarkable sites that are drawn together as the **Kohala Historical Sites State** Monument. These two lonely sites are the **Birthplace of King Kamehameha I** and the ancient **Mo'okini Luakini Heiau.** Of royal birth, Kamehameha I used windswept North Kohala as his base from which to consolidate power on this island and to force unification on the entire Hawaiian Island chain. While the exact site of his birth is not known for certain, the marked spot is assumed to be that where Hawaii's most well-known historical figure was born. A short stride away and much, much older is Mo'okini Heiau, a sacrificial temple, certainly one of the oldest *heiau* on the island and one which has been overseen by a hereditary *kahuna* since its founding. Family genealogical chants say that the temple was erected in 480 A.D., and if so, it is in surprisingly good shape today. It was to Mo'okini Heiau where Kamehameha I was taken for his birth rites.

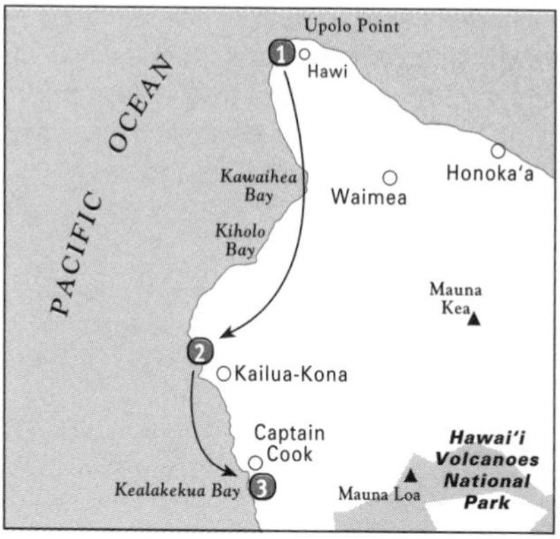

The North Kohala coast was inhabited by scattered fishing communities. The site of Lapakahi is one of these, and it contains numerous home sites and other stone remains that have been partially restored to better give the visitor a sense of the place. The entire site is now preserved as **Lapakahi State Historical Park.** It's not surprising that offshore is a Marine Life Conservation District.

As part of a prophesy regarding his domination of the islands, King Kamehameha I was told to built a temple to his war god Ku. Requiring about one year to construct, **Pu'ukohola Heiau,** now a National Historical Site, is the result. Sitting high on the hill overlooking Kawaihae Harbor, Pu'ukohola Heiau is a commanding stone structure and the last large *heiau* built before the dissolution of the Hawaiian religious system.

DAY 2

Just north of Kailua along the dry coastal plain near the Honokohau Harbor is **Kaloko-Honokohau National Historical Park.** This park contains many scattered relics of the old Hawaiian community that occupied this site and is one of the largest concentrations of such relics in the state. Rather spread out, it will require some walking over dry and brushy coastal land and along the beach to see its sights. Approach it from the new visitors center or from the marina parking lot. Among other interests in the park are a *heiau,* home sites, petroglyphs, and fishponds. Additional **petroglyph fields** are located up the coast at Ka'upulehu, Waikoloa, and Puako.

Numerous individual historical sites lie between Kailua and Keauhou. Start at Kamakahonu Beach in Kailua-Kona, where **Ahu'ena Heiau** protrudes into the water. King Kamehameha lived the last few years of his life near this complex and used this *heiau* for governing purposes. Later rulers built **Hulihe'e Palace,** an escape from the affairs of state in Honolulu. Land had been given to the first missionaries to put up a church across the street from the palace, and the structure that rose from their labor is **Moku'aikaua Church.** Down the coast next to the diminutive St. Peter's Catholic Church are the remains of **Ku'emanu Heiau,** a surfing temple. A few steps away are the remains of **Kapuanoni, Hapai Ali'i,** and **Ke'eku *heiau*.** Taken together, these *heiau* indicate that this was an important area and one of large settlement. Even King Kamehameha III was born near here at Keauhou Bay. Following the death of Kamehameha I, the old ways fell. Not everyone was happy with this new turn of events, and some tried to uphold the old customs. The last resistance to this new social direction took place near **Leke Leke Burial Grounds** at the end of Ali'i Drive, where the fallen warriors were buried.

DAY 3

Follow Napo'opo'o Road from the highway down to Kealakekua Bay. This lovely crescent bay was the site of the first significant and sustained contact between Hawaiians and Europeans and is now designated **Kealakekua Bay State Historical Park.** While it started off well, the relationship deteriorated, ending in the death of many Hawaiians, Captain Cook, and several of his crewmembers. Near the end of the road is **Hikiau Heiau,** a temple at which the first European to pass away in Hawaii was buried. Across the bay is a white obelisk memorial to Cook, marking the spot where he fell. The bay itself, also a Marine Life Conservation District, is arguably the best place on the island to snorkel.

A few short miles south of Kealakekua Bay is the best-known **temple of refuge** in the state. Within the precint of **Pu'uhonua O Honaunau National Historical Park** is the refuge that functioned as a safe haven for wrongdoers, *kapu*-breakers, and defeated warriors for at least two hundred years before the demise of the Hawaiian religious system. A huge wall surrounds the sacred area, and in it are three temple ruins, plus a *heiau* dedicated to Keawe, a legendary Hawaiian king. Outside its walls is a royal village site, reconstructed to give visitors an idea of what it might have looked like when used by Hawaiians centuries ago.

HILO SIDE BOTANICAL AND NATURAL TOUR

The Hilo Side is the wet side of the island, and the abundant rainfall makes for lush vegetation, thickly forested hillsides, and deeply scoured valleys. South of Hilo, the rains are less and the effects of the island's volcanic activity more apparent. This little tour will take you to some of the best natural and botanical sites on the east side of the island as a tour down the coast from north to south, but feel free to see these sites in an order that is more convenient to you as you travel. All sites are easily reached by car, with only a few requiring a short walk. It is possible to see them in one long day, but it's best to give it two so you can travel more slowly, have more opportunities to take photographs, and savor the beauty on this side of the island.

Waipi'o Valley: In Honoka'a, head north on Route 240 to the end of the road. Before you spreads the island's largest and most majestic valley. Notice the incredibly steep sides, the flat valley bottom, and the black-sand beach at its mouth. This and other valleys to the north score the long sheer sea cliffs of this coastline with deep cuts.

'Akaka Falls: Get back on the highway and travel south, turning inland at Honomu, an old sugar plantation town that still looks a bit like the old days. Drive for about three miles uphill to a parking lot, from where a circular walk of about 40 minutes takes you to 'Akaka Falls and the shorter but equally lovely Kahuna Falls.

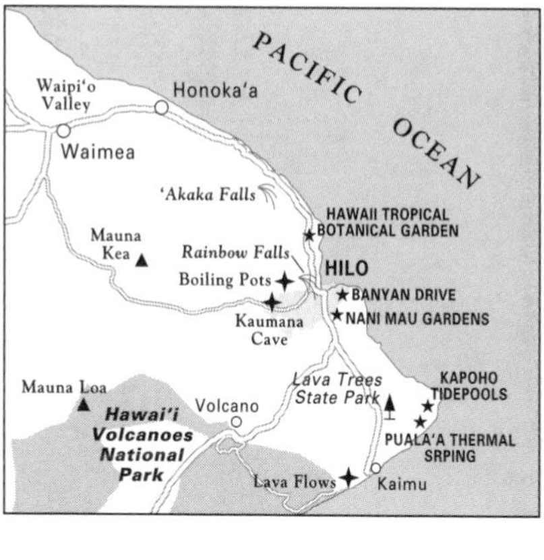

Hawaii Tropical Botanical Garden: Before entering Hilo, turn off the highway and take the Onomea Scenic Drive. This older and slower road starts through fallow sugarcane fields and shortly enters a steep wooded valley. One of the best examples in the state, this large botanical garden is a profusion of tropical plants set in amongst the surrounding jungle vegetation.

Rainbow Falls: Just after you cross the Singing Bridge on the north edge of Hilo, turn and head uphill, following signs to Rainbow Falls. This waterfall is nearly picture perfect as it tumbles over a wide lava ledge into a large circular pool below.

Boiling Pots: Farther up is Boiling Pots, a series of natural potholes and cascades in the riverbed that churn and "boil" the water as it rushes swiftly to the sea.

Kaumana Cave: A short way inland along the Saddle Road, set almost directly at roadside, is Kaumana Cave. Open for exploration, this cave is a fine example of a lava tube for one who has never seen such a thing before. Quite young, it was formed in the eruption of 1881 and the subsequent flow that threatened the city of Hilo.

Nani Mau Gardens: Now for a more formal botanical exhibit. Take the new shortcut across the back of town to get to these gardens. Nani Mau Gardens are the city's premier landscaped floral garden, with some 20 acres arranged by type of flower, level walkways, and other decorative touches as a bonus.

Banyan Drive: When the tsunamis of 1946 and 1960 destroyed much of downtown Hilo, most of the structures in Waiakea were also tumbled like matchsticks. However, a long line of banyan trees survived and now canopies the circular drive that skirts this peninsular thumb where it pushes into the bay. Have a stroll there, and be sure to spend some time walking through the quiescent Lili'uokalani Park.

Lava Trees State Park: Head south into Puna. Decades ago, when a flow of lava came pushing through the forest at what is now this park, the trees were engulfed by hot lava. After most of the lava drained away and the tree trunks burned out, hollow lava tubes remained.

Kapoho Tidepools: When lava reaches the sea, it sometimes creates tidepools, inlets, and other similar formations great for snorkeling. Some of the best of these are at Kapoho. Recently, a section just offshore was designated Wai'opae Tidepools Marine Life Conservation District.

Puala'a Thermal Spring: A short way down Puna's coastal "red road" is a natural but somewhat altered thermal spring that is now part of a state park. While not unique, this spring is one of few along this coast whose waters are heated by the volcano below.

Lava Flows at the End of the Road: Follow the coastal road to its end. Lava from the 1990s has covered the road, blocking any further progress along the coast. Here you come face to face with the unstoppable force of the volcano. Kilauea Volcano has been oozing lava almost continually at different locations since 1983, burning hillsides of trees, covering villages, destroying homes, and adding new surface area to this island, making it – literally – the youngest land on the planet.

HEAVEN AND EARTH: A GEOLOGIC AND CELESTIAL TOUR

The Big Island of Hawai'i was created by volcanic action over the past million years or so. The primary geologic features are volcanic in nature. However, the forces of wind and rain and other nature action have sculpted and changed the template, leaving the island that we experience today. Set up as a modified S-curve through the island, this tour features some of the most outstanding geologic features that you will see as you make your way around the island, with the addition of a peek at the stars from the mountain heights. It would be near impossible to travel this entire route in one day, so take this tour at your leisure.

Hamakua Coast Cliffs and Valleys: Head north to the end of the road at Pololu Valley. From there south to Waipi'o Valley are a series of medium to large valleys that cut through the steep coastal cliff. These sheer cliffs were created when large chunks of land broke off the mountainside and slid into the sea. The valleys formed when the sea level was much lower than it is today and the mountain was worn away in deep V grooves by erosion. When the sea level rose, soil was deposited on the valley floor, leaving flat bottoms. These features can also be observed from the south end at the Waipi'o Valley overlook.

Kohala Mountains: Head back up the road and over the mountain shoulder to Waimea. The Kohala Mountains at this north nub are the oldest on the island. The passage of time has worn these peaks into gentle slopes and rounded tops, where forests cover the uplands. Much of the upper slopes there, as well as the middle elevations of adjacent Mauna Kea, were cleared as pastureland, and this region of wide open places remains Hawaii's cattle country.

Western Mountain Slopes: The bulk of the island is formed by lava deposited from the mountains Mauna Kea, Mauna Loa, and Hualalai. Mauna Kea is presumed extinct; however, the other two are only dormant. As you travel south along the highway you pass over lava flows of various ages and can see others on the slopes above. Two of the most recent flows were from 1801 and 1859. Generally, the more barren the flow, the younger its age.

Saddle Road: Turn inland and take the Saddle Road, but only if your vehicle is allowed to traverse this highway. Rising to 6,500 feet, this road takes you through miles of barren lavascape. Cinder cones and secondary vents dot the slopes of Mauna Kea, while large sections of Mauna Loa look like huge scree slopes. Here and there, island-like *kipuka* poke up through surrounding lava flows, maintaining an established forest cover and wildlife population. Stop and appreciate this high-elevation environment before heading up the Mauna Kea access road to the astronomic observatories at its lunar-like top and a view of the stars through telescopes at the visitors center on the slope below. As it is one of the clearest places on earth, searching the heavens from here cannot be beat.

Kilauea Volcano: Head down the rugged Hamakua Coast, around and past Hilo to the many wonderful natural features at Kilauea Volcano. Features along Crater Rim Drive are a microcosm of what the area offers: fumaroles, steam vents, sulfur banks, broad lava flows, and jagged cracks in the earth. Dominant here is Kilauea Caldera itself. Several miles across and several hundred feet deep, it is impressive in its breadth. Lying on the floor of this hardened lava lake is Halema'uma'u Crater, the mythical home of Madame Pele, the Hawaiian goddess of fire. Until it hardened over in 1942, Halema'uma'u Crater was a seething mass of molten lava. Heading down Chain of Craters Road leads you over the *pali* to the coast. Here, the cliff steps down to the littoral plain, having slumped away in stages due to violent volcanic activity. Beyond the end of the road, steam rises at water's edge, marking the location of the current lava entry point into the ocean. While you can walk out to see the action close-up, it is a difficult hike and you must be well prepared.

Black and Green Sand Beaches: New lava begins to wear down as soon as waves break against it. Slowly, this lava turns to granules of sand, and in this way new black-sand beaches and shoreline are formed. One of these new beaches can be approached from the end of the coastal road at Kaimu in Puna. Older black-sand beaches are also dotted here and there along the coast but are largely unapproachable except to hikers and boaters. Farther south in Ka'u, you are able to visit what is arguably the most famous of these beaches, Punalu'u Black Sand Beach. Just a short drive off the main highway, it snuggles into a small bay against low dunes under coconut trees and is a favorite of green sea turtles. Farther along at South Point is the olive green-sand beach of Papakolea. With generally clear air and few lights, Ka'u offers some of the best stargazing on the island for the night sky sparkles with heavenly light.

SEVEN-DAY ADVENTURE

Adventure activities listed below are a sampling of some of the most exciting the island has to offer. This tour represents a full week's worth of activities, but you may want to pick and choose those that suit you best. In most cases, you will have to choose among tour operators for the type of tour that best fits your needs, wants, and physical abilities. Generally, organized tours must be reserved in advance; it is best to do so soon after you arrive on island. Contact numbers for various tour operators are listed in the destination chapters.

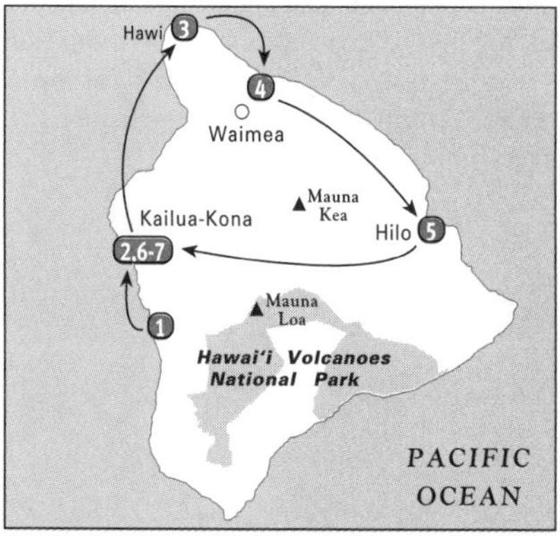

DAY 1

Start your tour with a morning snorkel trip to **Kealakekua Bay.** While you can just head to the water at any number of good snorkel spots along this coast, an organized boat trip to Kealakekua Bay not only gets you to the best snorkel location on the island but gives you a tour of this largely undeveloped and inaccessible coast.

Rest and relax a bit for most of the afternoon. Later, head north to **'Anaeho'omalu Beach** on the Kohala Coast for a sunset catamaran cruise.

DAY 2

This is another day on the water, but it will take you farther out. Head for **Honokohau Harbor** and hop aboard that **deep-sea fishing** boat for a day of pursuing the big one. The waters off the Kona Coast are some of the best sport fishing waters in the world and a half-day fishing trip (or full-day, if your pocketbook is willing) will make for great memories – even if you don't catch any fish.

DAY 3

Continue farther north today to North Kohala. Today's activity is **kayaking the ditch,** where you float a specially designed kayak down several miles of former sugar plantation flume, in and out of tunnels and across ravines.

In the afternoon, head farther along the coast to your next activity, an **ATV tour** of the rocky coast and inland forest in the area.

DAY 4

This morning, drive around to the wet side of the island for a hike along the ridge above **Waipi'o Valley.** While not the longest or most difficult on the island, this hike gives you wonderful views into the most wonderful valley on the island.

In the afternoon, head down into the valley for a **horseback ride** that ambles through this wet and steamy vale.

DAY 5

Take the lovely drive down the Hamakua Coast to Hilo and hop on a **helicopter** for a flight over **Kilauea Volcano** and the current lava flow. While helicopters also fly to the volcano from the Kona side, it's shorter and less expensive from Hilo, and these flights usually include views of some of the wet side waterfalls. If you have the means, take a circle-island helicopter flight for a more encompassing view of the Big Island.

From Hilo, head back across the island via Ka'u to Kona.

DAY 6

Back in Kona, take a morning **submarine tour.** The Big Island is just as fine underwater as above. Your tour leaves from the Kailua pier. Relax for the rest of the day.

DAY 7

This morning is for an **ocean kayak tour.** You can rent a kayak and go on your own or arrange a tour with one of several companies that offer this activity. Most are located near Kealakekua Bay, but other equally good spots are at Keauhou Bay and Puako.

You've got the afternoon off. Get some rest because you'll be up late tonight. Late in the afternoon, hop on a van that takes you on a sunset and stargazing tour on **Mauna Kea.** While coastal sunsets can be beautiful, a sunset from the top of the mountain is awe-inspiring. After sunset, telescopes are set up for viewing the heavens. Return is near midnight.

KONA

Kona is long and lean and takes its suntanned body for granted. This district *is* the west coast of the Big Island and lies in the rain shadows of Mauna Loa and Mauna Kea. You can come here expecting brilliant sunny days and glorious sunsets, and you won't be disappointed; this reliable sunshine has earned Kona the nickname "The Gold Coast." Offshore, the fishing grounds are legendary, especially for marlin that lure game-fishing enthusiasts from around the world. There are actually two Konas, north and south, and both enjoy an upland interior of forests, ranches, and homesteads while most of the coastline is low, broad, and flat. If you've been fantasizing about swaying palms and tropical jungles dripping with wild orchids, you might be in for "Kona shock," especially if you fly directly into the Kona Airport. Around the airport the land is raw black lava that can appear as forbidding as the tailings from an old mining operation. Don't despair. Once in town, trees form a cool canopy and flowers add color at every turn.

The entire Kona district is old and historic. This was the land of Lono, god of fertility and patron of the Makahiki Festival. It was also the spot where the first missionary packet landed and changed Hawaii forever, and it's been a resort since the 19th century. In and around **Kailua** are restored *heiau,* a landmark lava church, and a royal summer palace where the monarchs of Hawaii came to relax. The coastline is rife with historical sites: lesser *heiau, petroglyph* fields, fishponds, and a curious sporting slide dating from the days of the *makahiki.* Below the town of Captain Cook is

PHOTO COURTESY OF HVCB/HAWAII TOURISM JAPAN

HIGHLIGHTS

Ahu'ena Heiau: This is the spot where King Kamehameha I spent his last days ruling over a peaceful and united land (page 36).

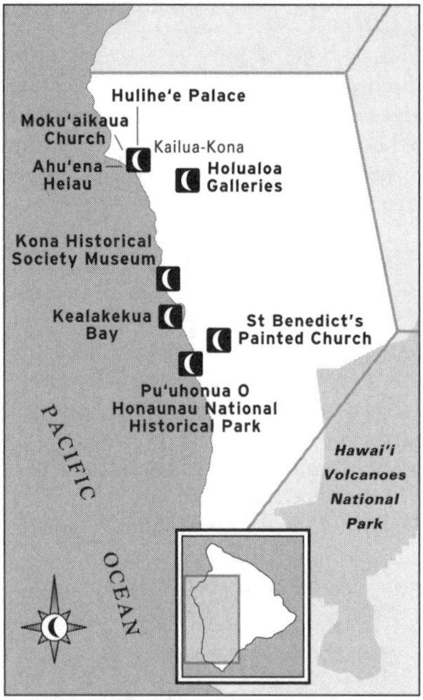

Moku'aikaua Church: This first Western-style church on the island is a fine representation of early missionary architecture (page 37).

Hulihe'e Palace: Used by king and royal family alike, this was a fine getaway retreat from the hubbub of the capital at Honolulu and is now a repository of royal furnishings and memorabilia (page 38).

Holualoa Galleries: These galleries are a center of island art (page 79).

Kona Historical Society Museum: This museum and the nearby D. Uchida Coffee Farm offer fine introductions to the cultural history and legacy of this region (page 87).

St. Benedict's Painted Church: Illustrating stories from the Bible on its wood plank walls, St. Benedict's is a unique testament to the inventive ways missionaries taught their flock (page 90).

Kealakekua Bay: Site of glory and tragedy for Captain Cook, this is also one of Hawaii's most superb snorkel spots (page 91).

Pu'uhonua O Honaunau National Historical Park: This re-creation of a royal village site and place of refuge provides a visual connection with old Hawaii (page 92).

LOOK FOR TO FIND RECOMMENDED SIGHTS, ACTIVITIES, DINING, AND LODGING.

Kealakekua Bay, the first and main *haole* anchorage in the islands until the development of Honolulu Harbor. This bay's historical significance is overwhelming, alternately being a place of life, death, and hope from where the spirit of Hawaii was changed for all time. Here on the southern coast is a Hawaiian temple of refuge, restored and made into a National Historical Park. The majority of Kona's sights are strung along Route 11. Except for Kailua-Kona, where a walking tour is perfect, you need a rental car to visit the sights; the Big Island's Hele-On Bus runs too infrequently to be feasible. If you're walking, pick up a copy of the pamphlet *Walking Tour of Historic Kailua Village,* produced by the Kona Historical Society.

Kailua-Kona is the heart of North Kona, by far the most developed area in the district. Its **Ali'i Drive** is lined with shops, hotels, and condos, and by and large, the shoreline vista peeks out between them. To show just how fertile lava can be when tended, miles of multihued bougainvillea and poinsettias line Ali'i Drive like a lei. Above Kailua is the former coffee town and now artists' community of **Holualoa.** This upcountry village sits on the lower slope of **Mount Hualalai** (8,271 feet), and it's here that local people still earn a living growing vegetables and taro on small truck farms high in the mountain coolness. But it has been—and still is—coffee that is the most famous agricultural product of the upcountry region and its dominant economic force. Just a few miles north of Kailua, the land turns dry, and huge swaths of black lava interspersed with arid scrubland become characteristic of the terrain from here through South Kohala to Kawaihae.

South Kona begins near the town of **Captain Cook.** Southward continues a region of diminutive coffee plantations where bushes grow to the shoulder of the road and the air is heady with the rich aroma of roasting coffee. South Kona is rural and far less populated. It's a rugged region, and the road stays high above the coastline. Farther south, rough but passable roads branch from the main highway and tumble toward hidden beaches and tiny fishing villages where time just slips away. From north to south, Kona is awash in brilliant sunshine, and the rumble of surf and the plaintive cry of seabirds create the music of peace.

PLANNING YOUR TIME

Kona is where most tourists fly into when they visit the Big Island. The weather is superb, the food and accommodations plentiful, the water inviting, and many sites close at hand. Often travelers will spend their entire vacation along this coast, but using this as a base from which to see the rest of the island is a better idea. Kailua is a bustling town that at one time was the capital of Hawaii and was the first place that missionaries came to preach the Good News to Hawaiians who had recently had the underpinnings of their native beliefs swept out from under them. Spend at least one day delving into the past by visiting **Ahu'ena Heiau, Moku'aikaua Church,** and **Hulihe'e Palace,** all in the center of town, and go farther afield by visiting the **Birthplace of Kamehameha III** and the **Leke Leke Burial Grounds** in Keauhou, as well as the historical remains at **Kaloko-Honokohau National Historical Park.**

It's rather dry on the Kona side and the beaches are few and far between, but there are several that will prove perfect for a snorkel trip or a relaxing day on the sand. Kailua and the Keauhou Resort area to its south have the great majority of shopping and restaurants in the area, so save time for those activities. However, don't spend your whole time in town. Head up the hill to spend a day in the cooler climate of **Holualoa,** where art galleries will tease your eyes and the smell of roasting coffee will tempt your taste buds. If you have an extra hour, tour a coffee roasting facility to learn about coffee growing, harvesting, and processing.

South Kona also holds many fascinations, and most people spend at least one day snorkeling at **Kealakekua Bay,** site of Captain Cook's death, and at the well-restored royal village site and "place of refuge," **Pu'uhonua O Honaunau,** now a National Historical Park. Kealakekua and Keauhou bays, plus the strip of coastline between, is prime kayaking territory.

PHOTO COURTESY OF HVCB/HAWAII TOURISM JAPAN

Pu'uhonua O Honaunau

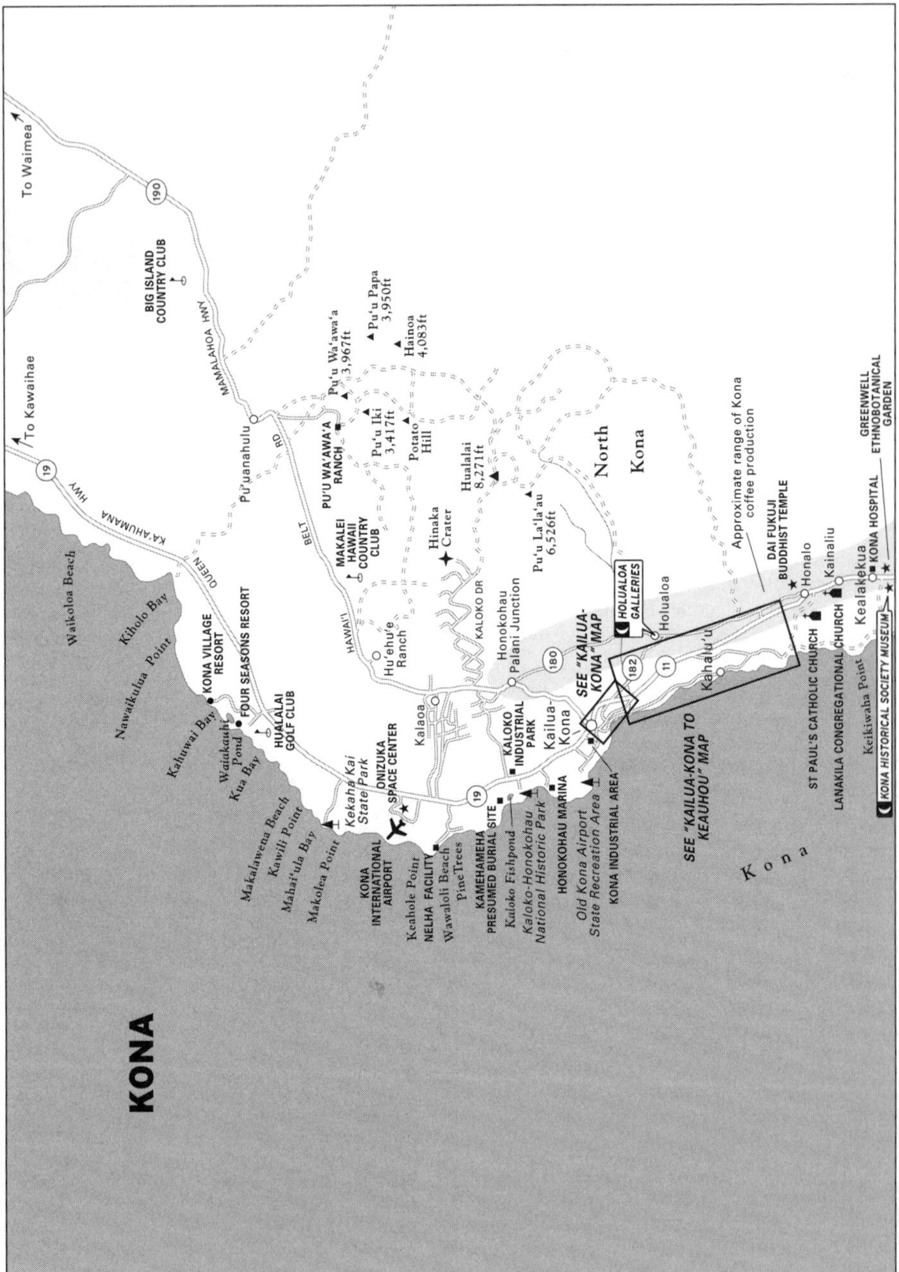
KONA
To Waimea
To Kawaihae
BIG ISLAND COUNTRY CLUB
MAMALAHOA HWY
KA'AHUMANU HWY
QUEEN
HAWAI'I BELT RD
Pu'uanahulu
Waikoloa Beach
Kiholo Bay
Nawaikulua Point
KONA VILLAGE RESORT
FOUR SEASONS RESORT
HUALALAI GOLF CLUB
Kahuwai Bay
Waiakauhi Pond
Kua Bay
Makalawena Beach
Kawili Point
Mahai'ula Bay
Makolea Point
Kekaha Kai State Park
ONIZUKA SPACE CENTER
KONA INTERNATIONAL AIRPORT
Keahole Point
NELHA FACILITY
Wawaloli Beach
Pine Trees
KAMEHAMEHA PRESUMED BURIAL SITE
Kaloko Fishpond
Kaloko-Honokohau National Historic Park
HONOKOHAU MARINA
Old Kona Airport State Recreation Area
KONA INDUSTRIAL AREA
KALOKO INDUSTRIAL PARK
Kalaoa
Kailua-Kona
Hu'ehu'e Ranch
MAKALEI HAWAII COUNTRY CLUB
PU'U WA'AWA'A RANCH
Pu'u Wa'awa'a 3,967ft
Pu'u Papa 3,950ft
Hainoa 4,083ft
Pu'u Iki 3,417ft
Potato Hill
Hinaka Crater
Hualalai 8,271ft
Pu'u La'la'au 6,526ft
KALOKO DR
Honokohau
Palani Junction
North Kona
SEE "KAILUA-KONA" MAP
HOLUALOA GALLERIES
Holualoa
Kahalu'u
SEE "KAILUA-KONA TO KEAUHOU" MAP
Approximate range of Kona coffee production
DAI FUKUJI BUDDHIST TEMPLE
Honalo
Kainaliu
ST PAUL'S CATHOLIC CHURCH
LANAKILA CONGREGATIONAL CHURCH
Kealakekua
KONA HOSPITAL
GREENWELL ETHNOBOTANICAL GARDEN
KONA HISTORICAL SOCIETY MUSEUM
Keikiwaha Point
Kona
19
190
180
182
11

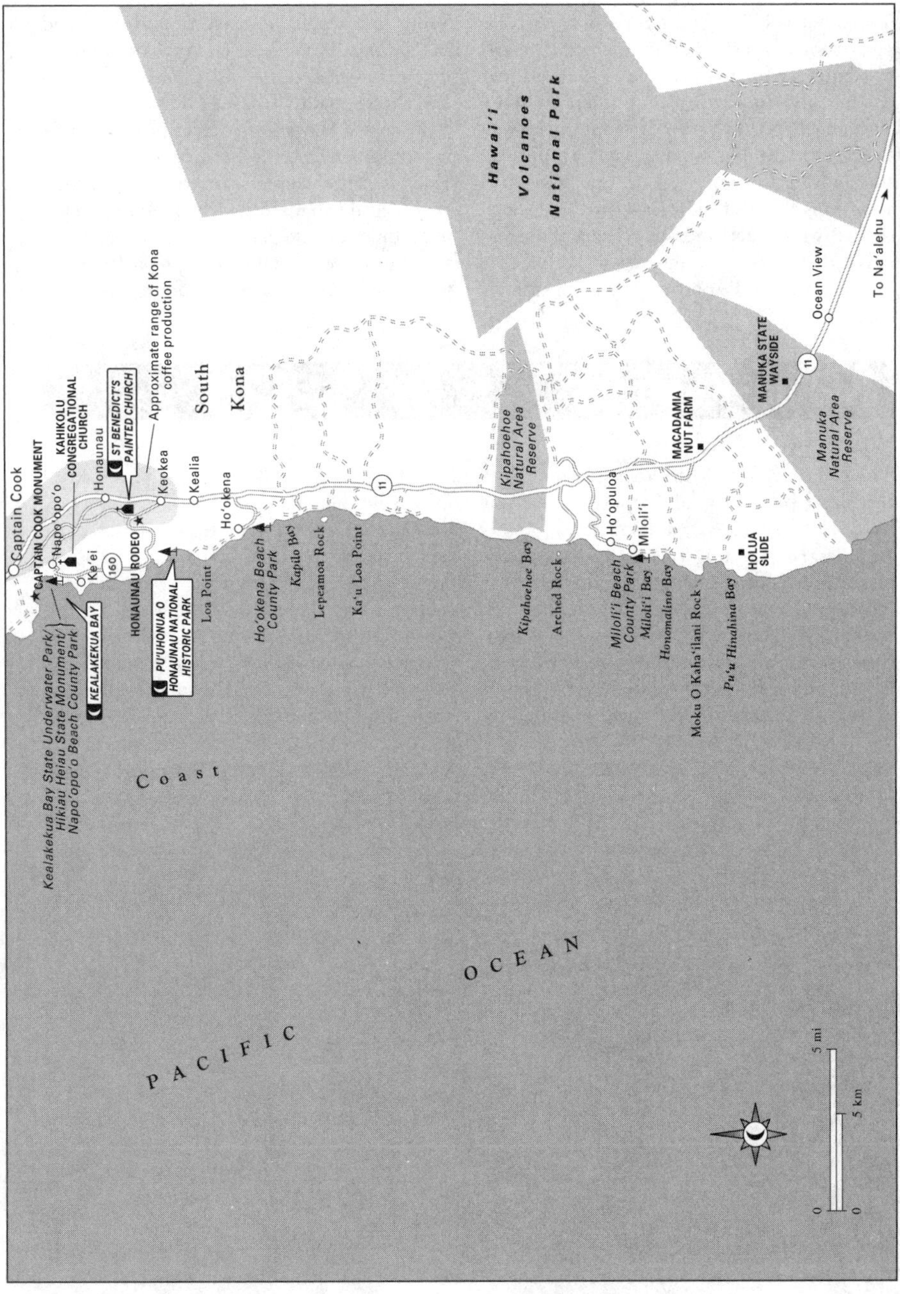
Captain Cook
CAPTAIN COOK MONUMENT
Napo'opo'o
Ke'ei
160
Kealakekua Bay State Underwater Park/
Hikiau Heiau State Monument/
Napo'opo'o Beach County Park
KEALAKEKUA BAY
KAHIKOLU CONGREGATIONAL CHURCH
Honaunau
ST BENEDICT'S PAINTED CHURCH
Approximate range of Kona coffee production
HONAUNAU RODEO
PU'UHONUA O HONAUNAU NATIONAL HISTORIC PARK
Keokea
Kealia
South Kona
Ho'okena
Loa Point
Ho'okena Beach County Park
Kapilo Bay
Lepeamoa Rock
Ka'u Loa Point
11
Kipahoehoe Natural Area Reserve
Kipahoehoe Bay
Arched Rock
Ho'opuloa
Miloli'i
Miloli'i Beach County Park
Miloli'i Bay
Honomalino Bay
Moku O Kaha'ilani Rock
Pu'u Hinahina Bay
HOLUA SLIDE
MACADAMIA NUT FARM
Manuka Natural Area Reserve
MANUKA STATE WAYSIDE
Ocean View
To Na'alehu
Hawai'i Volcanoes National Park
Coast
PACIFIC OCEAN
0
5 mi
0
5 km

The water is generally smooth and there are plenty of sea caves and other interesting physical shoreline features to explore, so save a half day for this trip. Farther south, there are some isolated villages with their own out-of-the-way beaches that might make a day's trip for the more adventurous.

Kona is a fine location for day trips north to the classy resort area and fine beaches of the Kohala Coast, to the cowboy town of Waimea, or farther north to the northern tip of the island. While it is possible to drive around the island in one long day, it's best to reserve two or more days for longer trips across the island to Hilo and the Hamakua Coast or down to Kilauea Volcano and Hawai'i Volcanoes National Park. As convenient as Hilo but not quite as close, Kona is still a wonderful starting point for a very special trip up to the observatories on top of Mauna Kea or for a hike to the top of Mauna Loa, but these will take more preparation and planning because of the altitude and cold.

Kailua-Kona

The greater Kailua-Kona area stretches from the Kona International Airport all the way south to Keauhou Bay, a distance of roughly 10 miles. Most of this built-up urban area lies on the oceanside of Queen Ka'ahumanu Hwy. North of downtown Kailua includes light industrial areas, beach and historical parks, the major commercial fishing harbor for the island, and a few new residential neighborhoods that line the sinuous roads running upland. Downtown Kailua lies along Kailua Bay and pushes inland. This is the heart of town, with its old historical buildings and sites, older residential and commercial areas, and a recreational pier, as well as a gaggle of shopping centers. From downtown Kailua, Ali'i Drive runs south for about five miles following the waterfront, passing a long series of condo complexes interspersed with a few small, well-established neighborhoods and a couple of beaches,

© ROBERT NILSEN

The renovated Ahu'ena Heiau lies on a small island at Kamakahonu Beach in Kailua Bay.

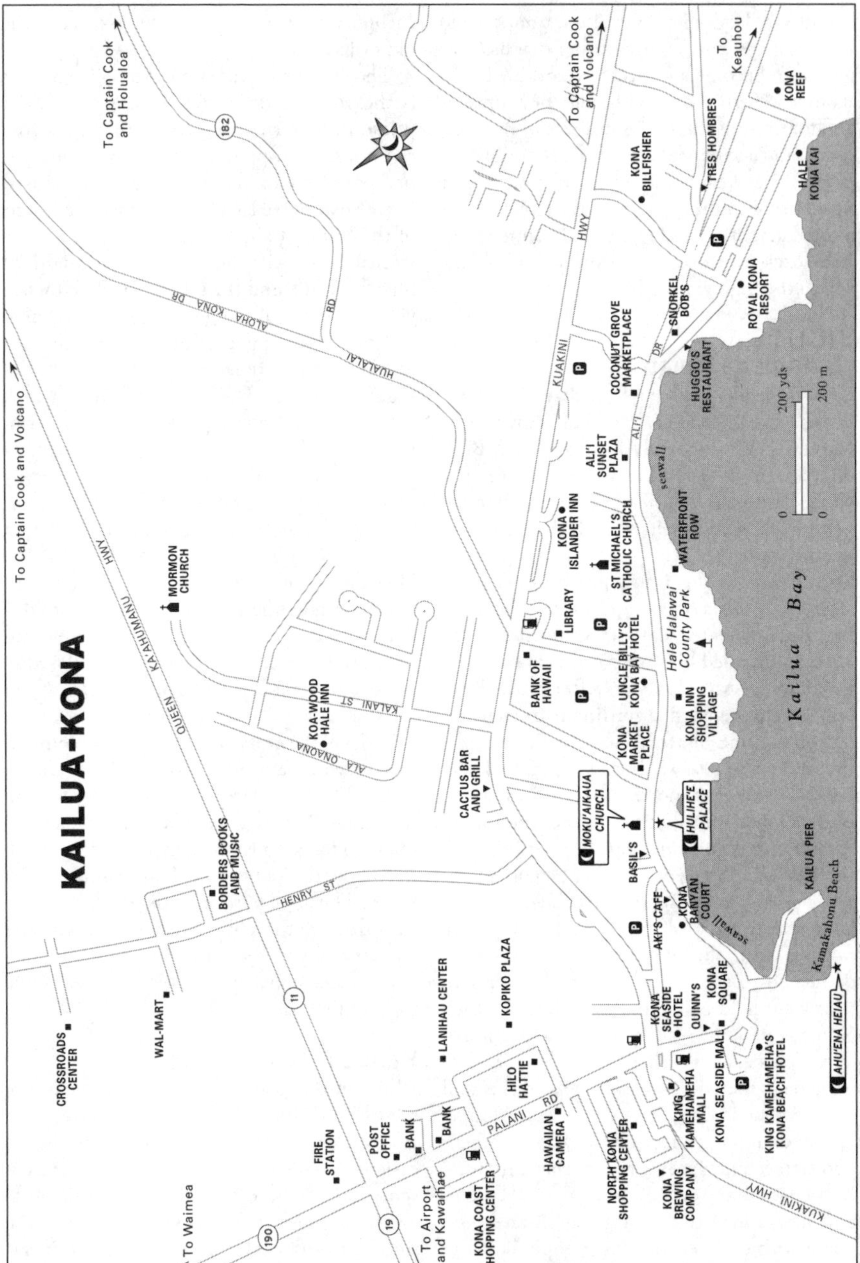
KAILUA-KONA
To Captain Cook and Holualoa
182
To Captain Cook and Volcano
To Keauhou
KONA REEF
HALE KONA KAI
TRES HOMBRES
KONA BILLFISHER
ROYAL KONA RESORT
SNORKEL BOB'S
HUGGO'S RESTAURANT
COCONUT GROVE MARKETPLACE
KUAKINI HWY
ALI'I DR
ALOHA KONA DR
HUALALAI RD
200 yds
200 m
0
ALI'I SUNSET PLAZA
seawall
KONA ISLANDER INN
ST MICHAEL'S CATHOLIC CHURCH
WATERFRONT ROW
LIBRARY
MORMON CHURCH
To Captain Cook and Volcano
QUEEN KA'AHUMANU HWY
Kailua Bay
Hale Halawai County Park
UNCLE BILLY'S KONA BAY HOTEL
BANK OF HAWAII
KALANI ST
KOA-WOOD HALE INN
ALA ONAONA
KONA INN SHOPPING VILLAGE
KONA MARKET PLACE
CACTUS BAR AND GRILL
MOKU'AIKAUA CHURCH
HULIHE'E PALACE
BASIL'S
KAILUA PIER
Kamakahonu Beach
BORDERS BOOKS AND MUSIC
HENRY ST
AKI'S CAFE
KONA BANYAN COURT
seawall
KONA SQUARE
KOPIKO PLAZA
LANIHAU CENTER
WAL-MART
CROSSROADS CENTER
11
KONA SEASIDE HOTEL
QUINN'S
AHU'ENA HEIAU
KING KAMEHAMEHA'S KONA BEACH HOTEL
KONA SEASIDE MALL
KING KAMEHAMEHA MALL
HILO HATTIE
PALANI RD
HAWAIIAN CAMERA
NORTH KONA SHOPPING CENTER
KONA BREWING COMPANY
KUAKINI HWY
FIRE STATION
POST OFFICE
BANK
BANK
KONA COAST SHOPPING CENTER
To Airport and Kawaihae
19
190
To Waimea

eventually leading to Keauhou, another old historical area with a small harbor that has now grown to become a respected resort area with its own refurbished fine hotels, new upscale condominiums, high-end residential communities, and a variety of eating and shopping opportunities. Keauhou is, in essence, a separate upscale community with a lovely bay, recreational activities, and good road connections, both back up the coast to Kailua and up the hill to the highway.

SIGHTS

Ahu'ena Heiau

Directly seaward of King Kamehameha's Kona Beach Hotel, at the north end of "downtown" Kailua, is the restored Ahu'ena Heiau. Built on an artificial island in Kamakahonu (Eye of the Turtle) Beach, it's in a very important historical area. Kamehameha I, the great conqueror, came here to spend the last years of his life settling down to a peaceful existence after many years of war and strife. The king, like all Hawaiians, reaffirmed his love of the *'aina* and tended his own royal taro patch on the slopes of Mt. Hualalai. After he died, his bones were prepared according to ancient ritual on a stone platform within the temple, then taken to a secret burial place, which is believed to be just north of town somewhere near Wawahiwa'a Point—but no one knows for sure. It was Kamehameha who initiated the first rebuilding of Ahu'ena Heiau, a temple of peace and prosperity dedicated to Lono, god of fertility. The rituals held here were a far cry from the bloody human sacrifices dedicated to the god of war, Kuka'ilimoku, that were held at Pu'ukohola Heiau, which Kamehameha had built a few leagues north and a few decades earlier. At Ahu'ena, Kamehameha gathered the sage *kahuna* of the land to discourse in the Hale Mana (main prayer house) on topics concerning wise government and statesmanship. It was here that Liholiho, Kamehameha's son and heir, was educated, and it was here that as a grown man he sat down with the great queens, Keopuolani and Ka'ahumanu, and broke the ancient *kapu* of eating with women, thereby destroying the old order.

The tallest structure on the temple grounds is the *'anu'u* (oracle tower), where the chief priest, in deep trance, received messages from the gods. Throughout the grounds are superbly carved *kia akua* (temple image posts) in the distinctive Kona style, considered some of the finest of all Polynesian art forms. The spiritual focus of the *heiau* was humanity's higher nature, and the tallest figure, crowned with an image of the golden plover, was that of Koleamoku, a god of healing. Another interesting structure is a small thatched hut of sugarcane leaves, Hale Nana Mahina, which means "house from which to watch the farmland." Kamehameha would come here to meditate while a guard kept watch from a nearby shelter. The commanding view from the doorway affords a sweeping panorama from the sea to the king's plantations on the slopes of Mt. Hualalai. Though the temple grounds, reconstructed under the auspices of the Bishop Museum, are impressive, they are only one-third their original size. The *heiau* itself is closed to visitors, but you can get a good look at it from the shore.

Tours of the *heiau* are offered by the community-based organization, Kulana Huli Honua (808/327-0123), caretakers of the *heiau,* and run 9:30–10:30 A.M. weekdays for $25 per person ($10 for King Kamehameha Hotel guests), starting in the lobby of the King Kamehameha Hotel. The hotel portion of the tour includes a walk through the lobby, where various artifacts and artworks are displayed. Don't miss this excellent educational opportunity, well worth the time and effort!

Kailua Pier

While in the heart of downtown, make sure to visit the Kailua Pier, which is set directly in front of Ahu'ena Heiau. Tour boats and the occasional fishing boat use this facility, so there is some activity on and off all day. Shuttle boats also use this pier to ferry passengers from cruise ships to town for land excursions. While it varies throughout the year, more of these large ships make Kailua a port of call during the late spring and autumn months than the rest of the year, and interisland cruise ships make regular stops here throughout the week. When periodic canoe races and the swimming portion of the Ironman Triathlon competition are held in the bay, the pier is crowded with plenty of onlookers.

Moku'aikaua Church

Kailua is one of those towns that would love to contemplate its own navel if it could only find it. It doesn't really have a center, but if you had to pick one, it would be the 112-foot steeple of Moku'aikaua Church. This highest structure in town has been a landmark for travelers and seafarers ever since the church was completed in January 1837. Established in 1820, the church claims to be the oldest house of Christian worship in Hawaii. The site was given by King Liholiho to the first Congregationalist missionaries, who arrived on the brig *Thaddeus* in the spring of that year. Taking the place of two previous grass structures, the construction of this building was undertaken in 1835 by the Hawaiian congregation under the direction of Rev. Asa Thurston. Much thought was given to the orientation of the structure, designed so the prevailing winds blow through the entire length of the church to keep it cool and comfortable. The walls of the church are fashioned from massive, rough-hewn lava stone, mortared with plaster made from crushed and burned coral that was bound with *kukui* nut oil. The huge cornerstones are believed to have been salvaged from a *heiau* built in the 15th century by King Umi that had occupied this spot. The masonry is crude but effective—still sound after more than 170 years.

Inside, the church is extremely soothing, expressing a feeling of strength and simplicity. The resolute beams are native 'ohi'a, pegged together and closely resembling the fine beamwork used in barns throughout 19th-century New England. The pews, railings, pulpit, and trim are all fashioned from koa, a rich

© ROBERT NILSEN

Moku'aikaua Church was the first Christian Church built on the island of Hawai'i.

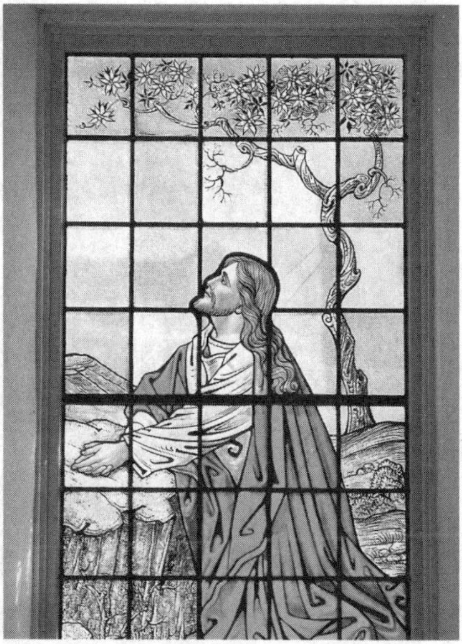

PHOTO COURTESY OF HVCB/HAWAII TOURISM JAPAN

stained glass behind the altar at the front of Moku'aikaua Church

brown, lustrous wood that begs to be stroked. Although the church is still used as a house of worship, it also has the air of a museum, housing paintings of historical personages instrumental in Hawaii's Christian past. The crowning touch is an excellent model of the brig *Thaddeus,* painstakingly built by the men of the Pacific Fleet Command in 1934 and presented to the church in 1975. The church is open daily from sunrise to sunset.

Hulihe'e Palace

Go from the spiritual to the temporal by walking across the street from Moku'aikaua Church and entering Hulihe'e Palace. This two-story Victorian structure commissioned by Hawaii's second governor, John Kuakini, dates from 1838. A favorite summer getaway for all the Hawaiian monarchs who followed, especially King Kalakaua, it was used as such until 1914. At first glance, the outside is unimpressive, but the more you look the more you realize how simple and grand it is. The architectural lines are those of an English country manor, and indeed Great Britain was held in high esteem by the Hawaiian royalty. Inside, the palace is bright and airy. Most of the massive furniture is made from koa. Many pieces were constructed by foreigners, including the German Wilhelm Fisher. The most magnificent pieces include a huge formal dining table, 70 inches in diameter, fashioned from one solid koa log. Upstairs is a tremendous four-poster bed that belonged to Queen Kapi'olani, and two magnificent cabinets built by a Chinese convict serving a life sentence for smuggling opium. King Kalakaua heard of his talents and commissioned him to build the cabinets. They proved to be so wonderfully crafted that after they were completed the king pardoned the craftsman.

Prince Kuhio, who inherited the palace from his uncle, King Kalakaua, was the first Hawaiian delegate to Congress. He decided to auction off all the furniture and artifacts to raise money, supposedly for the benefit of the Hawaiian people. Providentially, the night before

Hulihe'e Palace was a home away from home for the Hawaiian royalty who desired to escape the hustle and bustle of government at Honolulu.

the auction each piece was painstakingly numbered by the royal ladies of the palace, and the name of the person bidding for the piece was dutifully recorded. In the years that followed, the **Daughters of Hawai'i,** who now operate the palace as a museum, tracked down the owners and convinced many to return the items for display. Most of the pieces are privately owned, and because each is unique, the owners wish no duplicates to be made. It is for this reason, coupled with the fact that flashbulbs can fade the wood, that a strict *no photography* policy is enforced. The palace was opened as a museum in 1928. In 1973, Hulihe'e Palace was added to the National Register of Historic Sites.

Historical artifacts are displayed in a downstairs room. Delicate and priceless heirlooms on display include a tiger-claw necklace that belonged to Kapi'olani. You'll also see a portrait gallery of Hawaiian monarchs. Personal and mundane items are on exhibit as well—there's an old report card showing a 68 in philosophy for King Kalakaua—and lining the stairs is a collection of spears reputedly belonging to the great Kamehameha himself.

Hulihe'e Palace (75-5718 Ali'i Dr., 808/329-1877, www.huliheepalace.com) is on the *makai* side of the road and is open 9 A.M.–4 P.M. Monday–Saturday and 10 A.M.–4 P.M. Sunday, except major holidays. You can look around on your own or ask the staff for a tour, which usually lasts 45 minutes. Admission is $6 adults, $4 seniors, $1 students. A hostess knowledgeable in Hawaiiana is usually on duty to answer questions, and the Palace Gift Shop is open daily for gift sales. Once a month, free concerts are given on the palace grounds starting at 4 P.M. and are open to everyone.

Historical Walking Tour

The Kona Historical Society offers a leisurely 1–1.5-hour guided walking tour of the Ahu'ena Heiau, Moku'aikaua Church, Hulihe'e Palace, and other nearby sights at 9 and 11 A.M. Monday–Friday, for $20 per person. Advance reservations are necessary (808/323-3222 or 808/938-8825). You can tour each of these sites on your own, but you can learn so much more from a knowledgeable guide. Be sure to wear comfortable shoes and a hat.

Sadie Seymour Botanical Gardens

At the intersection of Kuakini and Queen Ka'ahumanu Highways, on the grounds of the Kona Outdoor Circle Education Center (808/329-7286, www.konaoutdoorcircle.org) is a landscaped sliver of land called the Sadie Seymour Botanical Gardens. Grouped and planted on nearly a dozen terraces are typical plants that grow in Hawaii that are originally from other areas of the world. Small but well landscaped, this garden is a quiet retreat in the otherwise dry and hot upper Kona area. Open 9 A.M.–5 P.M. daily for self-guided tours; there is no admission to the garden, but donations are accepted. For those interested in in-depth botanical material, the center's well-stocked library is open to the public 9 A.M.–3 P.M. Monday–Friday, while the gift shop operates 10 A.M.–2 P.M. Monday–Saturday.

Adjacent to the botanical gardens is **Kealakowa'a Heiau,** an ancient sacred site dedicated to blessing canoes. This blessing was done after the rough shape had been cut from a log in the upland forest but before the final work of shaping the canoe was completed at the beach. Consisting of four separate platforms, this *heiau* was reputedly built around 1600 by King Umi. The *heiau* is easily seen when looking over the surrounding stone wall.

Ali'i Drive

Ali'i Drive heads south from Kailua, passing the majority of Kona's accommodations on its way to Keauhou. On the mountain side of the road, a continuous flow of flowers drapes the shoulder like a femme fatale's seductive boa, while seaside the coastline slips along, rugged and bright, making Ali'i Drive a soothing sight.

At your first stop, near White Sands Beach, look for the historic **Hale Halawai O Holualoa Congregational Church** built in 1855 by Rev. John D. Paris. Services are still held every Sunday at 9 A.M. The base of the church is mostly original lava rock topped with a new roof. The

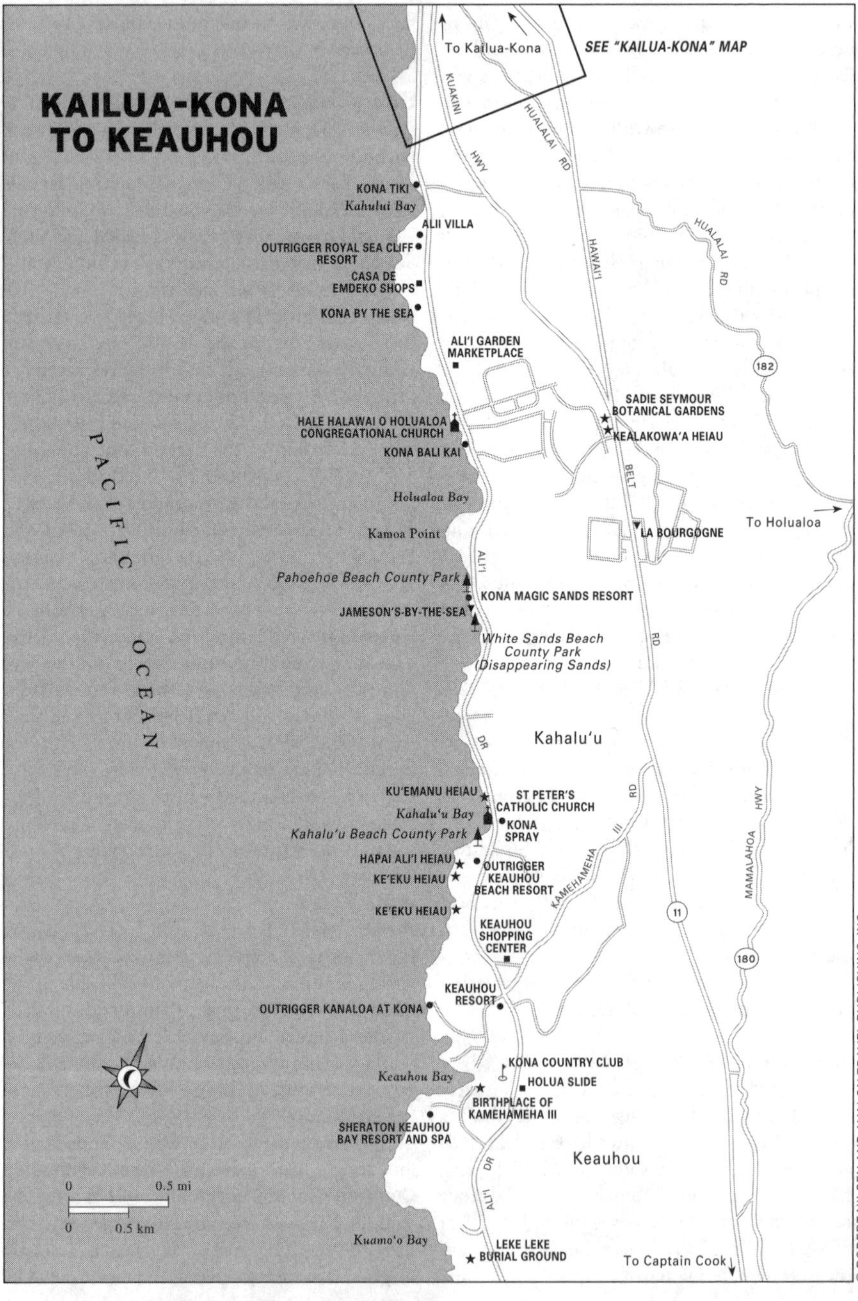
KAILUA-KONA TO KEAUHOU
To Kailua-Kona
SEE "KAILUA-KONA" MAP
KUAKINI
HWY
HUALALAI
RD
HAWAI'I
BELT
RD
HUALALAI
RD
182
KONA TIKI
Kahului Bay
ALII VILLA
OUTRIGGER ROYAL SEA CLIFF RESORT
CASA DE EMDEKO SHOPS
KONA BY THE SEA
ALI'I GARDEN MARKETPLACE
SADIE SEYMOUR BOTANICAL GARDENS
KEALAKOWA'A HEIAU
HALE HALAWAI O HOLUALOA CONGREGATIONAL CHURCH
KONA BALI KAI
PACIFIC
OCEAN
Holualoa Bay
Kamoa Point
LA BOURGOGNE
To Holualoa
ALI'I
Pahoehoe Beach County Park
KONA MAGIC SANDS RESORT
JAMESON'S-BY-THE-SEA
White Sands Beach County Park (Disappearing Sands)
DR
Kahalu'u
KU'EMANU HEIAU
ST PETER'S CATHOLIC CHURCH
Kahalu'u Bay
KONA SPRAY
Kahalu'u Beach County Park
HAPAI ALI'I HEIAU
OUTRIGGER KEAUHOU BEACH RESORT
KE'EKU HEIAU
KE'EKU HEIAU
KAMEHAMEHA
III
RD
MAMALAHOA
HWY
11
180
KEAUHOU SHOPPING CENTER
KEAUHOU RESORT
OUTRIGGER KANALOA AT KONA
KONA COUNTRY CLUB
HOLUA SLIDE
Keauhou Bay
BIRTHPLACE OF KAMEHAMEHA III
SHERATON KEAUHOU BAY RESORT AND SPA
Keauhou
0
0.5 mi
0
0.5 km
ALI'I
DR
Kuamo'o Bay
LEKE LEKE BURIAL GROUND
To Captain Cook

cemetery area is peaceful and quiet and offers a perfect meditative perch from which to scan the shore.

Back on the road, look for signs to Kahaluʻu Beach Park; pull in and park here. On the rocky northern shore of this bay is **St. Peter's Catholic Church.** Its diminutive size, capped by a blue tin roof that winks at you from amidst the lava like a bright morning glory in an ebony vase, has earned it the nickname Little Blue Church. Built in 1889 on the site of an old, partially reclaimed *heiau,* the church is a favorite spot for snapshots. Inside, simplicity reigns with bare wood walls and a plain crucifix. The only splash of color is a bouquet of fresh flowers on the altar. To the right of the church as you face it are the remains of **Ku'emanu Heiau,** a temple where chiefs would pray for good surfing conditions. Their prayers must have worked, as surfers today still gracefully ride the waves offshore within sight of this rock platform.

On the grounds of the Outrigger Keauhou Beach Resort, a 10-minute walk south along the coast, are the remains of **Kapuanoni Heiau** and **Hapai Ali'i Heiau.** Just beyond that, at water's edge and fronting the abandoned Kona Lagoons hotel property, is the **Ke'eku Heiau.** All are unrestored historical sites that still show signs of being used, and all offer vantage points from which to view the coast. Plans for a cultural park on the old Kona Lagoons property, said to be a spot where the old Hawaiians would gather for Makahiki events, are in the works; it will be a fine cultural addition to the Keauhou area. The old hotel buildings have been torn down, but it may be years before the cultural park becomes a reality. A better vantage point for viewing part of the coast and Keauhou Bay is from a roadside rest stop, a short way farther up along Aliʻi Drive and across from the Keauhou Shopping Center.

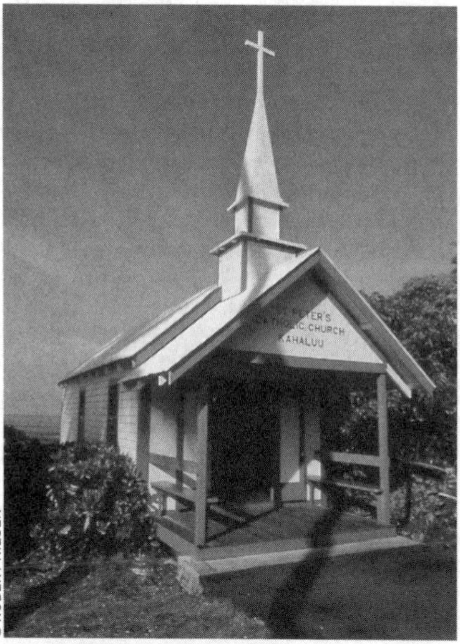

tiny St. Peter's Catholic Church

Near the end of the road is **Keauhou Bay.** Here you'll find a cluster of historical sites, and the small harbor and boat ramp. Look for a monument marking the **Birthplace of Kamehameha III** in 1814. Local people come to fish from the pier around 5 P.M. for *halalu,* a tough little fish to catch. Along the shoreline are a number of partially developed *heiau* sites. A small home stuck on a point of land on the edge of the bay is where John Wayne married his wife Pilar in 1954, and it marks the site of the first modern house built on the bay. Opposite the harbor, at the end of King Kamehameha III Road is **Keauhou Park** and beach access, an area of lawn, pavilion, sand volleyball court, and restrooms.

At the very end of the Aliʻi Drive, where the road curves down around the Kona Country Club golf course toward the water, is the **Leke Leke Burial Grounds.** Laid to rest here are troops that fought under the leadership of Kekuaokalani, keeper of the war god Ku after the death of King Kamehameha I, in an attempt to sustain the traditional religious and social order of the Hawaiian people. More than 300 died near here in 1819 at the Kuamoʻo Battle site, using firepower obtained from the foreigners. This battle was the violent end to the old ways and symbolized the shaky introduction of the Western overlay on Hawaiian society.

ANCIENT SPORT OF HOLUA

In principle, *holua* was similar to snow sledding, and mostly a "chiefly" sport of the *ali'i*. Sleds were long two-runner affairs, perhaps six inches wide and eight feet long or longer, stabilized by cross bracing and grab bars on which the person would lie. These sleds were launched down a slope that was up to one mile in length and ended at or near the ocean. Only a few of these slopes remain, largely fallen into disrepair or taken apart to make way for modern constructions.

Most prominent on the Big Island, the largest known sledding course was Kaneaka in Keauhou, the remains of which lie on the Kona Country Club *makai* golf course. Look for it across the road from the clubhouse. These slopes were constructed of volcanic rock and filled in with small pebbles to make a flat top. It is believed that this flat top was then covered with layers of large leaves (maybe banana or ti) or thatching to provide a slippery surface for sledding.

Once on the runway, there was no stopping until the sled got to the bottom – or went over the side. The danger associated with this sport must have been an important component of its thrill. With no steering mechanism, the chance of disaster seems large.

Holua seems to have slowly died out through the 1800s, perhaps, as some have suggested, after the Makahiki Festival – which may have been its principle forum – ceased to be a central component of the Hawaiian cultural tradition. No one in living memory is purported to have actually seen the sport in action. Only recently has there been much attention turned to its understanding. Few examples of a *holua* sled have survived – the best is displayed at the Bishop Museum in Honolulu – and few accounts relate anything about the sport. Aside from a few brave, modern souls who have tried short sections of slope for the thrill, this sport has not yet been brought back by the resurgence of ancient Hawaiian culture. Perhaps its time is still to come.

Where Ali'i Drive ends, the Kahului-Keauhou Parkway begins. This new road, built to connect the coast at Keauhou with the highway near the town Captain Cook, is finished as far as the planned community of Hokulia. This controversial, large-scale, private development of housing lots, golf course, and a shoreline park has for years has caused a bitter dispute between some local residents and the developers. At issue, among other items, are the alleged disturbance of archeological sites and sacred grounds of the ancient Hawaiians and the use of agricultural land for housing. Although a golf course and several homes have been built, further development has been stalled due to lawsuits.

North of Town

Honokohau Harbor, three miles north of Kailua-Kona, is a huge small-boat harbor and deep-sea fishing facility that has eclipsed the old Kailua Pier. This is the premier fishing harbor on the island—it is used by other water-sport activity companies and sailboats and is frantic with energy during the various "billfish tournaments" held throughout the year. The harbor area is full of fishing-oriented shops, including Kona Marine for nautical charts, and is also home to the Harbor House Restaurant, where you can hear a yarn from Kona's old salts. Primarily, this is where you come to see huge fish caught that day and talk to the skippers of the deep-sea fishing boats that go after them. When you pull into the marina, you'll see a road that goes off to the left. Head that way toward the tan building, to where the pier, fuel dock, and the weigh-station are located. There fish will be hoisted, measured, and photographed while the skippers and their crews clean and prepare the boats for the next day's outing. Although an activity that doesn't command the interest that it once did even a few years ago, partially due to the more frequent trend of catch-and-release fishing, **weigh in** is every day around 11:30 A.M. and 3:30 P.M., basically when the boats return from their half-day and full-day trips. If you are fascinated by deep-sea fishing, this is your chance to pick a likely boat and to get acquainted with the crew.

Dedicated to Kona's own Col. Ellison S. Onizuka and to the men and women who tragically perished aboard the space shuttle *Challenger* on January 28, 1986, the **Onizuka Space Center** (808/329-3441, www.planet-hawaii.com/astronautonizuka, 8:30 A.M.–4:30 P.M. daily except Thanksgiving, Christmas, and New Year's Day, $3 adults, $1 children.) is located at Kona International Airport. From this tragedy, a living memorial and space education facility was erected. Inside the modern, well-appointed building children and adults alike can marvel at human exploration of space by viewing exhibits like a moon rock, a scale model of a space shuttle and space station, an interactive staffed maneuvering unit, a real space suit, and a theater showing educational videos throughout the day. There is a gift shop with plenty of fascinating reading material, toys, and collectible items concerning the international effort to explore the heavens. Stop in before flying out.

BEACHES AND PARKS

If Kona is short on anything, it is beaches. The ones it has are adequate, some quite striking in their own way, but they tend to be small, few, and far between. People expecting a huge expanse of white sand will be disappointed. These beaches do exist on the Big Island's west coast, but they are north of Kailua-Kona in the Kohala district. Kona does, however, have beaches alive with marinelife, providing excellent and safe snorkeling and top-notch tidepool exploration opportunities.

All along Ali'i Drive and at each beach, you will find Beach Access signs pointing you to official shoreline entry points. If there is no parking lot near where you want to get to the water, be sure to park off the roadway and stay out of No Parking areas.

The following are the main beaches in and around Kailua-Kona.

Kamakahonu Beach

You couldn't be more centrally located than at

NELHA

The future is now at the amazing Ocean Technology facilities, located just south of the airport between mile markers 95 and 94, where you'll find a turnoff heading toward the sea. This is the **Natural Energy Laboratory of Hawaii Authority (NELHA)** (www.nelha.org, 7:45 A.M.–4:30 P.M. Mon.–Fri.).

The NELHA access road is open 6 A.M.–8 P.M. Incredible things are being done here. For example, cold water from 2,000 feet below the surface of the ocean is placed in a turbine with warm surface water from a 35–89-foot depth, a process that generates electricity and also provides desalinated water. In addition, the cold water is used for raising very un-Hawaiian things such as alpine strawberries, lobsters, abalone, sea cucumbers, commercial black pearls, and Japanese flounder, as well as for raising *limu,* a local edible seaweed, and oysters, clams, and shrimp.

More than 30 companies use this nutrient-rich deep-sea water to make fish jerky, grow shiitake mushrooms, create and use salt products, and even to raise tropical fish and coral that will become living bouquets of color in fish tanks around the world. Cyanotech, a leading manufacturer of marine products for worldwide nutrition and pharmaceutical markets, uses the facilities to make spirulina, available in health food stores, as well as numerous other products and ingredients. More recently, several firms have begun to bottle this desalinated deep-sea water as drinking water, while others are experimenting with solar energy technology.

Tours are offered at 10 A.M. Wed. and Thurs.; call 808/329-7341 for reservations. Tours run about two hours in length; donations of $5 are accepted. If you choose to take a tour, don't be overwhelmed by the size of the complex; the products are brought to a central area for your viewing. A short self-guided tour of an open-air outdoor display area will introduce you to the basics of what is done here, some of the products produced here, and a sample of the huge pipe used to bring the water to the surface.

"Eye of the Turtle" Beach. Find it in downtown Kailua-Kona next to Kailua Pier, in front of King Kamehameha's Kona Beach Hotel. Local people refer to it as "Kids' Beach" because it is so gentle and safe, perfect for a refreshing dip. Big kids come here to play too, when every year world-class athletes churn the gentle waters into a fury at the start of the Ironman Triathlon. Rent snorkel gear, kayaks, and other water gear for reasonable prices from the beach shack located in front of the hotel, or from other shops nearby. Restrooms and telephones are located at the inland end of the pier.

Ali'i Drive Beaches

White Sands Beach County Park (a.k.a. **Magic Sands** or **Disappearing Sands**) is an excellent spot for a dip—if the sand is there. Every year, usually in winter, the sands are stripped away by heavy seas and currents, exposing rough coral and making the area too rugged for the average swimmer. People still come during those months because it's a good vantage point for observing migrating humpback whales. The sands always come back, and, when they do, the beach is terrific for all kinds of water sports, including bodysurfing and snorkeling. White Sands is known locally as a great boogie boarding and bodysurfing spot. The best board surfing is just north of the beach in a break the locals call "Banyans." White Sands' amenities include drinking water, showers, restrooms, and lifeguard, making the beach a favorite spot with local people and tourists. Traditionally, this beach was known as La'aloa (Very Sacred); on the rise at the north of the beach sits a *heiau* within a small archeological preserve.

Just before White Sands park is the small and narrow **Pahoehoe Beach County Park.** With its seawall, lawn, palm trees, and walkways, it's a good place to suntan on the grass or picnic in the shade, but the rocky shoreline is not a place to swim.

Kahalu'u Beach Park on Kahalu'u Bay has always been a productive fishing area. Even today, fishermen come to "throw net." You'll occasionally see large family parties surround-

© ROBERT NILSEN

White Sands Beach, known as La'aloa Beach, is one of the best in the area for boogie boarding.

ing their favorite fish with a huge *hukilau* net, then sharing their bounty among all participants. Because of this age-old tradition, the area has not been designated a marine conservation district. Kahalu'u became a beach park in 1966. This ensured that the people of Kona would always have access to this favorite spot, which quickly became surrounded by commercial development. Outrigger Keauhou Beach Resort occupies the land just to the south. Amenities at the park include picnic tables, showers, restrooms, a lifeguard, and even a basketball court. Often a *kaukau* wagon and snorkel rental truck are also there for those who didn't prepare well enough, and across the street is Kahalu'u Bay Surf and Sea for a wide variety of water rental gear. The swimming is very good, but the real attraction is snorkeling. The waters are very gentle, and Kahalu'u is a perfect place for families or beginning snorkelers, as the water is generally only six to eight feet deep. However, stay *within* the reef of the bay, known locally as the "Menehune Breakwater," because a powerful and dangerous rip current lurks outside. The shoreline waters are alive with tropical fish: angelfish, parrotfish, unicorn fish, the works. Unfortunately, Kahalu'u is often crowded, but it is still worth a visit. The reef offshore makes great waves, and this bay has been a great surfing spot for centuries.

Old Kona Airport State Recreation Area

In 1970 the old Kona Airport closed and the state of Hawaii turned it into a beach park. Take Kuakini Highway north from downtown until it ends. Often used on weekends by families for picnics and other gatherings, facilities include showers, restrooms, and a picnic area near the water, plus athletic fields, a gymnasium and aquatic center, and a children's playground near the entrance. Parking is nearly unlimited along the old runway, where you can also walk, bike, in-line skate, or jog. The park gate closes at 8 P.M. The white-sand beach is sandwiched between the black lava at water's edge and the runway. You can enter the water at some shallow inlets, but the bottom is often rocky (be sure to wear water shoes) and the waters can be treacherous during high surf. The safest spot is a little sandy cove at the southern end of the beach. Swimming is generally not good here, but sunbathing is great. Tidepooling is good when the water is low. Snorkeling is fine at the northern end of the park, and offshore a break at "Shark Rocks" makes the old airport popular with Kona surfers. The waters in front of the park are a 217-acre marinelife conservation district open to surfers, scuba divers, and snorkelers, with a section protected from motorized boat usage.

Kaloko-Honokohau National Historical Park

Dedicated in 1978, the 1,160-acre Kaloko-Honokohau National Historical Park (808/329-6881, www.nps.gov/kaho) lies on the ocean side of the highway across from Kaloko Industrial Park. This area was heavily populated during old Hawaiian days, and plenty of archaeological sites—mostly fishponds, ruins of houses, *heiau,* a small *holua* slide, and a few petroglyphs—are found along the shoreline. These sites are protected; if you come to an archaeological area, obey all posted signs and approach with great care and respect. Remember, it is imperative that you do not touch, disturb, or remove any historical artifacts.

The park can be entered either from the Honokohau Small Boat Harbor north parking lot, via Kaloko Gate, which is just off Hwy. 19 near Hina Lani Street, or at the new visitors center. The visitors center and parking lot is open 8:30 A.M.–4 P.M. daily. From the visitors center and the Kaloko Gate entrance, trails lead down across the sparsely vegetated lava to the ocean. The easiest and quickest way to the water is from the small boat harbor dirt parking lot near the Kona Sailing Club. Follow the well-worn path into the vegetation on the far side of the berm, and keep walking for a few minutes to Honokohau Beach, several small anachaline ponds, the 'Ai'opio Fishtrip, and a *heiau.* In the past, all types of people came to Honokohau Beach, including fishermen, surfers, and snorkelers, but it was primarily known to many as a clothing-optional beach. That status drastically changed when the area became part of the park; nudity is officially illegal within the park. Camping and open fires, also illegal, are citable offenses under federal regulations. The coarse, gray sand of Honokohau Beach offers safe swimming in somewhat shallow water. Kaloko Beach, some distance up the coast, also has great snorkeling in only 10–20 feet of water. Before Kaloko Beach and over a natural sand rise is 'Aimakapa Fishpond. This fishpond, along with Kaloko Fishpond and its engineered seawall, have been rehabilitated to a more natural environment and are home to several endangered water birds that include the *ae'o* (stilt) and the *alae ke'oke'o* (Hawaiian coot). Swimming in the pond is prohibited. The entire area is a favorite with green sea turtles, which make their presence known mainly in the evenings.

North Kona Beaches

The next beach you come to heading north is the famous **Pine Trees** surfing beach, located near the NELHA facility just south of the airport. Where the long access road turns abruptly to the right, look for a well-worn dirt road leading to the left away from NELHA, and follow it to Pine Trees. Although famous with surfers and the site of many competitions, Pine Trees (none of which are in evidence) is not a good swimming beach. There are a few one-towel coves along the rocky shoreline where you can gain access to the water, but mostly it's a place from which to observe the action. You can also follow the road toward the NELHA facility a short way to **Wawaloli Beach,** a small public beach of sand and crushed coral, fronted by plenty of rock near the south end of the airport runway. There are a few restrooms and some picnic tables. The gate on the access road to these beaches is closed 8 P.M.–6 A.M.

Kekaha Kai State Park

North of the airport, Kekaha Kai State Park encompasses several sandy secluded beaches in its 1,642-acre domain. The first is about two miles north of the airport between mile markers 91 and 90. Follow the very rugged but passable dirt road (4WD vehicles, trucks, and other vehicles with high clearance highly recommended; open 9 A.M.–7 P.M. daily except Wed.) for about 1.5 miles to one of the better beaches close to Kailua-Kona. Here, the land rises slightly before getting to the coarse, salt-and-pepper-sand beach. The swimming is usually safe here except in winter, and some come to snorkel, but always be careful. The semi-improved area just back from the sand has toilets and picnic tables built around palm trees.

Before you get to the official parking area, notice a walking path off to the right. It is a 10-minute walk to Mahai'ula Bay and its magnificent **Mahai'ula Beach.** This crescent of tan sand stretches for about 200 yards, with shade trees coming down almost to the water's edge. Completely unimproved and fairly secluded, it's a great beach to "get away from it all" for the day. Back from the water here are the remains of an abandoned red beach house that once belonged to the Magoon family, longtime island residents and major stockholders in Hawaiian Airlines. These buildings have appeared as a movie set over the years. Walk north from Mahai'ula Beach along an arrow-straight path across a hot stretch of rough lava for about 15 minutes to the smaller and more secluded white-sand **Makalawena Beach.** Local boys love to bodysurf here in winter. At the north end of this beach is a small brackish but mostly freshwater pond, the domain of *nanini* fish and a harmless brine shrimp. Makalawena and other small beaches beyond are frequented by green sea turtles. Be sure to bring water, especially if you intend to spend the day.

A few minutes farther north by car, just inland of the Pu'u Ku'ili cinder cone, whose vegetation has been given a crew cut by the trade winds, you'll find a road leading through a new residential area to **Kua Bay,** a famous swimming and boogie boarding beach, now part of the Nanini'owali section of Kekaha Kai State Park. Kua Beach is a white-sand beach bordered by black lava and some crushed coral that eases out into inviting aquamarine-colored water. Look for the turnoff between mile markers 88 and 89 and follow the road down to the parking lot and restrooms.

ENTERTAINMENT

The most memorable evening experience for most is free: watching the sunset from Kailua Pier and taking a leisurely stroll along Ali'i Drive. Otherwise, Kona nights come alive mainly in the restaurants. The lu'au have "Polynesian Revues" of one sort or another, which are generally good clean fun, but of course these shows are limited only to the lu'au guests. For those who wish to spend the evening listening to live music, there's a small but varied selection from which to choose.

Music

Huggo's Restaurant, with its romantic waterfront setting along Ali'i Dr., and the attached Huggo's on the Rocks, feature music 8:30 P.M.–midnight. The entertainment changes nightly: blues, smooth Jawaiian, other mellow contemporary sounds, or a touch of rock or jazz now and again.

For other music over the dinner hour and beyond, try **Durty Jake's** at the Coconut Grove Marketplace or the **Kona Brewpub,** which has live music on Sunday.

At the Royal Kona Resort's open-air **Windjammer Lounge,** sip a flavorful tropical concoction while watching the sun melt into the Pacific. Entertainment is offered several evenings a week, featuring hula at sundown.

The **Billfish Bar** at King Kamehameha's Kona Beach Hotel has live entertainment, *pu pu,* and sushi 6–9 P.M. Friday and Saturday, featuring mellow Hawaiian music.

There are also a few nice options in Keauhou, like the **free hula show** 6–7 P.M. on Fridays at the Keauhou Shopping Center.

Set over the broad tidepool at shoreline so you can look over the railing and see fish and turtles swimming in the water below, the **Verandah Lounge** (3–10:30 P.M.) does cocktails and has a solid *pu pu* menu until mid-evening. It offers soothing, easy-listening, Hawaiian-style music nightly and is a great spot for sunset.

The open-air **Crystal Blue Cocktail Lounge** at the Sheraton Keauhou Bay Resort also swings with the sounds of the islands every evening and offers a sophisticated setting for drinks and Hawaiian tapas. Set almost over the water, it's a superb place for sunsets and manta ray watching in the evening.

Lu'au

Tihati's **Lava, Legends and Legacies** lu'au and Polynesian revue at the Royal Kona Resort (808/329-3111), held every Monday, Wednesday, and Friday, offers an evening of entertainment and feasting, Hawaiian style. The lu'au begins at 5 P.M. and is followed by an open bar, lavish buffet, and thrilling entertainment for three fun-filled hours. Many supposedly authentic lu'au play-act with the *imu*-baked pig, but here it is carved and served to the guests. Prices are $62 adults, $28 children ages 6–11, free for children age five and under. Reservations are strongly recommended.

King Kamehameha's Kona Beach Hotel sways with Hawaiian chants during its famous **Island Breeze Lu'au** (800/329-8111, www.islandbreezeluau.com), held every Sunday, Tuesday, Wednesday, and Thursday on the beach and grounds of King Kamehameha's last residence, Ahu'ena. The pig is placed into the *imu* every morning at 10:15 A.M. and the festivities begin in the evening with a lei greeting at 5 P.M., followed by a crafts demonstration, torch-lighting, and an *imu* ceremony at 6 P.M. Cocktails flow 6–8 P.M.; the 22-course lu'au dinner is served 6:30–8:30 P.M., with the Polynesian show starting at 7:30 P.M. Prices are $62.50 adults, $26.50 children 5–12, free for children four and under. Limited cocktail and show seating runs $37 adult and $26.50 children. Reservations are required; stop by the lu'au desk in the lobby of the hotel.

In Keauhou you will find the newest of the lu'au and Polynesian shows in the area. **Origins** is staged at the Sheraton Keauhou Bay Resort (808/930-4828, 6 P.M. Mon. and Thurs.) on the lawn overlooking Keauhou Bay. Special family-style seating runs $79, while buffet service is $65; children are half price. Dinner is a scrumptious meal of all the usual island favorites, and the show is hosted by Na Hoku winner Danny Couch.

Movies

In Kailua, see movies at the 10-screen multiplex **Makalapua Stadium Cinemas** (808/327-0444), located up in the Makalapua Center by Kmart, and the **Hualalai Cinema** (808/327-0444), at the corner of Hualalai and Kuakini Highway. The **Keauhou 7 Cinemas** (808/324-7200) at the Keauhou Shopping Center in Keauhou shows first-run movies. Tickets run $8–8.50 for adults and $5–6 for seniors and kids.

SHOPPING

The Kailua-Kona area has an abundance of two commodities near and dear to a tourist's heart: sunshine and shopping malls. Most of the small malls crowd together along Ali'i Drive in what is the heart of town. You won't have any trouble finding these little complexes, as they stand cheek to jowl and sport shops that carry everything from swimsuits to jewelry, tiki bowls to works of art. Less than a mile down the road is the new "cluster shop"–style Coconut Marketplace with a variety of upscale shops, restaurants, and activity vendors. You'll need a car to get to the newer and more typical strip malls and larger neighborhood malls that line Palani Road, which heads away from the water, starting at the King Kamehameha Hotel, or those located along Queen Ka'ahumanu Highway running as far north as the Kaloko Industrial area near the airport. If this is not enough, Keauhou also has a large shopping center that hosts a wide variety of stores. Below is a brief selection of shops that might be of interest to the tourist and traveler, but keep in mind that there are plenty more where these shops are found.

Ali'i Drive

The fully air-conditioned **King Kamehameha's Kona Beach Hotel Mall** features a cluster of specialty shops that include the **Kailua Village Artists Galleries** (808/329-6653), a local artist-owned art emporium, and the **Made on the Big Island** store (808/326-4949), with its large sampling of local crafts and gifts, one of the best general gift shops of local wares on the island.

Kitty-corner to King Kamehameha's Hotel is the **Kona Seaside Mall,** where you'll find **Neptune's Garden** (808/326-7490) creating rainbows with its display of stained glass art fashioned into lamps, creative hangings, and vases, plus a few paintings.

The **Kona Square Shopping Center,** next to the Kona Seaside Mall, features **Island Silversmiths** (808/329-1195), Kona's oldest modern-day shop, in business since 1973, so you know it's doing something right; and **Maui Divers Jewelry** (808/329-9560) for a wide selection of attractive jewelry made from things that come from the sea.

Just down the way, the **Kona Banyan Court** has a dozen shops with a medley of goods and services. The most impressive shop in the complex is **Big Island Jewelers** (808/329-8571), owned and operated by brothers Flint and Gale Carpenter, master goldsmiths. The shop motto, "Have your jewelry made by a Carpenter," applies to custom-made jewelry fashioned to their or your personal design. Big Island Jewelers, in business since 1983 and open daily, does repairs and also carries a full line of pearls and loose stones that you can have mounted into any setting you wish.

Kitty-corner from Hulihe'e Palace is **Kona Marketplace,** which offers a variety of shops in several adjacent buildings selling everything from diamonds to inexpensive bathing suits. Stuck in the back is the **Kona Flea Market** (808/320-9296) with its stock of inexpensive travel bags, shells, beach mats, suntan lotion, and all the junk that you could want.

One of the largest malls along Ali'i Drive is the **Kona Inn Shopping Village.** It spreads south from Hulihe'e Palace in a long meandering series of buildings, taking the place of much of the old Kona Inn Hotel. This shopping village boasts more than 40 shops selling fabrics, fashions, T-shirts, art, gems and jewelry, food, bicycles, souvenirs, and gifts. One intriguing shop in this mall is **Hula Heaven** (808/329-7885), which specializes in vintage Hawaiian shirts and modern reproductions, plus some Hawaiiana collectibles. Prices for these fashionable shirts range from $50 for the look-alikes to $1,000 for the rarest of the classics. Because many of the items on display date from the 1940s and 1950s, the shop is like a trip back in time.

Waterfront Row is a newer art and food complex on the south side of Hale Halewai County Park. Built of rough-cut lumber, it's done in period architecture reminiscent of an outdoor promenade in a Boston shipyard at the turn of the 20th century. Here, **Crazy Shirts** (808/326-2285) sells unique island creations that are wearable memories of your trip, and **Wyland Galleries of Hawaii** (808/334-0037) displays island-inspired paintings and sculpture.

Newest to the Kailua strip, located at the Royal Kona Resort end and just across from the seawall, is **Coconut Grove Marketplace.** This shopping plaza, with its sand volleyball court, half a dozen independent buildings, and plenty of parking, has about a dozen shops that include **Kane Malia** and **Tropics** for clothing, **Pai Moana** (808/334-9863) for pearls, and **Jack's Diving Locker** (808/329-7585), which can set you up with snorkel gear and send you on a scuba tour. Hungry? You'll find half a dozen local and chain eateries here to fill your belly.

Palani Road

There are several malls on both sides of Palani Road, which heads away from the water, starting at the King Kamehameha Hotel.

Backing up against King Kamehameha's Kona Beach Hotel is the small **King Kamehameha Mall,** where you will find, among other shops, the **Kona Wine Market** (808/329-9400), with the town's largest selection of wines and champagne, liqueurs, a good selection of domestic and imported beers, a variety of cheeses, chocolate, crackers, and other gourmet foods, plus premium cigars and natural tobacco. If you're nearby, stop by on Friday afternoon for the free wine-tasting.

In the **Kona Sports Center** on the south side of Palani Road is **B&L Bike and Sports** (808/329-3309). The official Ironman store, it has one of the largest selections of sporting equipment in town. A few steps away is the Kona location of **Hilo Hattie** (808/329-7200, 9:30 A.M.–5:30 P.M.), where you can find right pricing for family fashions, gifts, souvenirs, music, and packaged island foods. Hilo Hattie offers free transportation to and from hotels in the area.

Just up from the Hilo Hattie store are the **Kopiko Plaza** and the **Lanihau Center.** Both have a great variety of shops and restaurants, but at the Lanihau Center you can also find **Longs Drugs** (808/329-1380, 8 A.M.–9 P.M.), for sundries, snacks, and photo supplies, a **Sack 'n Save** supermarket, three banks, and the Kailua-Kona post office.

Another of the large supermarkets in town, the **KTA Super Store** is across Palani Road in the **Kona Coast Shopping Center.** Here too you'll find several inexpensive eateries, a handful of fashion shops, and a Blockbuster Video (808/326-7694, 10 A.M.–11 P.M. Sun.–Thurs., 10 A.M.–midnight Fri.–Sat.), where you can rent a movie for the evening.

Queen Ka'ahumanu Highway

At the corner of Queen Ka'ahumanu Highway and Henry Street is the **Crossroads Center.** The two big stores there are **Wal-Mart** (808/334-0466) for general merchandise and Safeway (808/329-2207) for food.

The new **Makalapua Center** above the old Kona Industrial Area has a huge **Kmart** (808/326-2331, 7 A.M.–10 P.M.) for all general shopping needs, camping and athletic supplies, photo supplies, and medicines, while **Macy's** (808/329-6300) is open for family fashions.

For those with a membership, **Costco** (808/334-0770) is located at the back of the Kaloko Industrial Park, north of town on the way to the airport.

Keauhou Shopping Center

If, heaven forbid, you haven't found what you need in Kailua, or if you suddenly need a "shopping fix," the Keauhou Shopping Center is at the corner of Ali'i Drive and Kamehameha III Road in Keauhou. Look for flags waving in the breeze high on the hill marking the entrance. This mall houses over 40 shops in two sections and is one of the newest in the area. You can find all your food and prescription needs at **KTA Super Store** (808/322-2311, 7 A.M.–10 P.M.), the largest in the area, and mail your postcards at a branch post office. Head to **Longs Drugs** (808/322-5122, 8 A.M.–9 P.M.) for everything from foot care products to photo developing, and **Ace Hardware** (808/322-3336, 7 A.M.–7 P.M.) for nuts and bolts. Other shops include the **Showcase Gallery** (808/322-9711), for glassware, paintings, ceramics, and local crafts; and **Paradise Found Boutique** (808/324-1177) for eclectic apparel.

Art, Craft, and Specialty Shops

The small **Palace Gift Shop** is located on the grounds of Hulihe'e Palace. Open daily except Sunday, it has a fine selection of quality Hawaiian craft items nice enough for gifts or memorabilia and a good collection of postcards and books on Hawaiiana. Here as well are koa sculptures of fish, sharks, and even a turtle, other handmade artwork, along with Hawaiian music CDs. Just outside is a saltwater pond with tropical fish.

Alapaki's Hawaiian Gifts (808/322-2007) for a fine sampling of quality island gifts, crafts, artwork, and souvenirs from black coral jewelry to koa bowls, prints and paintings to musical instruments and hula implements, and a replica of a Hawaiian double-hulled canoe made of coconut and cloth with traditional crab-claw sails to *tutu* dolls bedecked in colorful mu'umu'u. Alapaki's represents about a hundred artists and craftspeople from all the major islands.

One of the few fine art galleries in Kailua is **RiftZone** (808/331-1100), located in the Coconut Grove Marketplace. This "Hawaiian Style Gallery" displays the whole spectrum of artwork, almost exclusively from Big Island artists, including ceramics by Robert Joiner, bronze sculpture, paintings, wood art, furniture, and art glass. If you're looking to purchase art made in Hawaii, this is an excellent place to start, as it has an intriguing collection in many media.

Two other shops to look at for island art are **Wyland Galleries** (808/334-0037) at Waterfront Row, which carries marine, landscape, and environmental paintings and sculpture from such well-known island artists as Wyland, Steven Power, John Pitre, William DeShazo, James Colman, Neolito, and Walfrido Garcia; and **Kailua Village Artists Galleries** (808/329-6653), a co-op gallery of lesser-known Big Island artists at the King Kamehameha Hotel mall and its sister gallery at the Outrigger Keauhou Beach Resort.

Hawaii Forest and Trail (74-5035B Queen Ka'ahumanu Hwy., 808/331-8505 or 800/464-1993, info@hawaii-forest.com, www.hawaii-forest.com, 7 A.M.–5:30 P.M. Mon.–Fri., until 5 P.M. weekends) is a tour company that leads wonderful bird-watching, hiking, and mule ride eco-adventures around the island. Its retail store is located just up from the entrance to Honokohau Harbor and carries a small selection of hiking and outdoor gear and supplies, adventure clothing, first-aid supplies, outdoor books, and USGS maps. While you're there, inquire into the company's tours. They are excellent.

Kailua Candy Company (808/329-2522, www.kailua-candy.com, 8 A.M.–6 P.M. Mon.–Sat., 8 A.M.–4 P.M. Sun.), has relocated to the upper edge of the Kaloko light industrial area near the entrance to Home Depot. All the chocolates are made of the finest ingredients available, and all would try the willpower of Gandhi, but the specialty is the macadamia nut *honu,* Hawaiian for turtle. Shipping of all boxed candy is available at the cost of postage plus a handling fee. Have a peek through the plate glass windows into the kitchen to watch the work being done on weekdays and nibble samples of the products any day. The

Kailua Candy Company may be the only store of interest for the traveling public in this light industrial park.

Bookstores

In the North Kona Shopping Center, around back behind Kona Business Center, is **Bargain Books** (808/326-7790, 10 A.M.–6 P.M.), a shop with shelves stacked full of used books at half the cost of new books. If you're looking for a cheap read or just like browsing, have a look here.

The largest bookstore in town, however, is **Borders Books and Music** (808/331-1668, 9 A.M.–9 P.M.) at the corner of Queen Ka'ahumanu Highway and Henry Street. As at all Borders, you have a huge selection of paperbacks and hardcover books in all genres, plus a great Hawaiiana section and a wide selection of maps, postcards, magazines, newspapers, and CDs. Special readings and musical events are held throughout the month, and Cafe Espresso is there for you when you get thirsty.

Photo Needs

Most gift shops and many other stores, like ABC Store, carry ordinary print film.

For a wider selection of films, as well as sales of cameras and accessories, and limited service and repair, head to **Hawaiian Camera Supply** (74-5614 Palani Rd., 808/326-7355, 9 A.M.–5 P.M. Mon.–Fri., 10 A.M.–3 P.M. Sat.), just up from the North Kona Shopping Center. Look for the building that carries the sign Lighthouse Camera.

Longs Drugs' photo departments at both the Lanihau Center and Keauhou Shopping Center have excellent prices on film and camera supplies. Both **Kmart** in the Makalapua Center and **Wal-Mart** in the Crossroads Shopping Center have one-hour photo finishing departments.

RECREATION

Snorkeling

Snorkel cruises can be booked through the various activity centers along the Kona coast and at your hotel travel desk. Snorkeling excursions are also provided by the following. **Fair Wind** (808/322-2788 or 800/677-9461, www.fair-wind.com), a well-established company with the 60-foot catamaran *Fair Wind II,* has a great reputation and is sure to please. Its boat leaves daily from magnificent Keauhou Bay and stops at Kealakekua Bay in front of the Captain Cook monument. This boat has a diving platform and water slide, sunning deck, and easy access steps into the water. All equipment is on board, and snuba is an option for an additional fee. The 4.5-hour morning cruise runs $105 for adults, $65 for children 4–12; the 3.5-hour afternoon tour is $69 and $43, respectively. The Fair Wind's new hydrofoil catamaran, the ***Hula Kai,*** runs a five-hour morning snorkel and scuba tour for $139. A continental breakfast and/or lunch and snacks and beverages are served on all trips.

Departing from the Kailua pier and sailing north to Pawai Bay, **Body Glove Cruises** (808/326-7122 or 800/551-8911, www.bodyglovehawaii.com) is a full-fledged snorkel and scuba company offering a bar and lunch aboard their trimaran. Costs for the morning and afternoon snorkel sails on the 51-foot *Body Glove* run $94 adult/$54 child and $59 adult/$39 child, respectively. In season, whale-watching trips may take the place of the afternoon snorkel sail for $59 adult and $39 kids. Introductory scuba dives and dives for certified divers are also an option for an additional fee.

Kamanu Charters (808/329-2021 or 800/348-3091, www.kamanu.com), Kona's original snorkel sail, in business over 30 years, provides a full day of fun with beer and snacks included in the price. It pilots a true sailing catamaran and takes fewer passengers—a maximum of 24. Sails leave from the Honokohau Marina for Pawai Bay at 9 A.M. and 1:30 P.M., $75 adults and $45 kids 12 and under. Kamanu Charters is a good choice for a fun-filled sail and snorkel experience.

For the "do-it-yourself" snorkeler who doesn't care to take an organized tour, there are a number of options in the Kona area. Some visitors and locals snorkel at Kamakahonu Beach in the heart of Kailua and

Kahalu'u Beach Park is one of the easiest snorkel sites to reach along the Kona Coast.

others try at Disappearing Sands Beach Park or along the coast at the Old Kona Airport Beach Park—all decent except during winter storms. However, the best snorkel spot that is close to town and also very easy to get to is at Kahalu'u Beach Park, just as you near Keauhou. In South Kona, Kealakekua Bay is the premier snorkel area, but the best spots are usually reached by boat or kayak as they are on the far side of the bay from the Napo'opo'o. You can, of course, hike down to the Captain Cook monument and enter the water there, but the hike is long and steep, and the trail is not all that easy to locate at the upper end. Easier and also quite satisfying is to snorkel the bay adjacent to Pu'uhonua O Honaunau. Enter at the boat launch area of the tiny village next to the national historical park. Stay clear of the kayaks as you swim out to see the fish and turtles.

If you're lily white or have just come from a Mainland winter, it's perhaps better to snorkel at mid-morning or later in the afternoon to avoid the scorching sun, but anytime seems to be fine for viewing fish and other marinelife.

For some of the best prices, equipment, and service for snorkeling equipment rental on the island, try **Snorkel Bob's** (808/329-0770, www.snorkelbob.com, 8 A.M.–5 P.M. daily), located across from Huggo's Restaurant. Gear, which includes mask, snorkel tube, and fins, is rented for a 24-hour day or by the week and can be taken interisland and turned in at any Snorkel Bob's location. Depending on the quality, a snorkel set runs $2.50–9 a day or $11–44 a week. Rental boogie boards are also available for $6 a day or $22 a week, and Bob and his crew can arrange tours as well.

The **Kalani Beach Boys** (9 A.M.–5 P.M. daily), on the beach at the King Kamehameha's Kona Beach Hotel, not only rents snorkel gear, it also rents kayaks, paddleboats, boogie boards, and other beach and water equipment.

The 1940 Pontiac woody wagon out front points you to **Kahalu'u Bay Surf and Sea** (78-6685 Ali'i Dr., 808/322-4338, 8:30 A.M.–5 P.M. daily), located just down the road and across the street from Kahalu'u Bay and beach park. This shop can set you up with snorkel gear, surfboards, kayaks, and other water equipment at a fair price. Snorkel gear runs $6.74 a day or $19.25 a week.

Miller's Snorkeling (76-6246 Ali'i Dr., 808/326-1772, 8 A.M.–5 P.M. daily) at the Kona Bali Kai condo, rents complete snorkeling gear for $7 per day or $15 per week and also rents surfboards, boogie boards, and beach accessories.

Many dive shops also rent snorkel gear at competitive prices.

Snuba

Part scuba, part snorkeling, snuba is a fairly recent underwater concept that is perfect for an introductory underwater adventure. Tethered to a flotation raft bearing a scuba tank, the only apparatus you wear is a regulator, weight belt, mask, and flippers. Your descent is limited to 25 feet, but the fun isn't. For those who feel timid about scuba diving or who just want a new, fun-filled adventure, snuba might be the answer.

Snuba Big Island, Inc. (808/326-7446, www.snubabigisland.com) can set you up for this new adventure. Shore dives take place four times every day at the beach in front of King Kamehameha's Kona Beach Hotel and boat dives go twice a day from the Honokohau Harbor to sites on the Kohala Coast. The basic snuba experience from shore costs about $79 per person, while the boat dives run $120. Alternatively, you can snuba (and snorkel) at Kealakekua Bay on the twice-daily sail with the Fair Wind sailing boat for the cost of the sail plus $65 per person.

Scuba

There are about two dozen companies on the Big Island, mostly on the Kona side, that offer scuba instruction, escorted dives, and rental scuba equipment.

An excellent diving outfit is **Jack's Diving Locker** (75-5819 Ali'i Dr., 808/329-7585 or 800/345-4807, www.jacksdivinglocker.com), a responsible outfit that does a good job of watching out for its customers and taking care of the reef. Owners Teri and Jeff Leicher,

© ROBERT NILSEN

Kailua Bay

along with their crew, run diving and snorkeling excursions along the Kona Coast from Kealakekua Bay to Keahole Point, which takes in over 50 dive sites (most of which have permanent moorings to protect the reef from damage by anchoring). Jack's also specializes in snorkel sales and rentals, scuba equipment rentals, a kids' program, and various certification classes. It has a new and expanded shop at the Coconut Grove Marketplace with a dedicated diving pool with viewing windows. Dives run the gamut from a one-tank beach dive at $55 to a multi-day, multi-dive arrangement for $265. Its most popular dive is a two-tank boat dive that runs $99, while advanced dives are $145–195, and night dives run $85–195. Jack's has plenty of options.

Associated with Jack's Diving Locker, **Kona Coast Divers** (808/329-8802 or 800/562-3483, www.konacoastdivers.com) is located at the fuel dock at the Honokohau Harbor. This outfit is efficient and to the point. There are many dive options, including a two-tank boat dive, $99; night dive, $99; a manta ray dive, $65; and an introductory dive, $145. Full underwater gear is sold and rented.

Big Island Divers (75-5467 Kaiwi St., 808/329-6068 or 800/488-6068, www.bigislanddivers.com), departing from Honokohau Harbor on a custom-built 35-foot dive boat, offers various regular dive tours, like a two-tank, two-location dive for $99, an introductory dive for $149, and night dives for $80. Also offered are inexpensive scuba certification courses. The normal four-day course costs about $500.

Sandwich Isle Divers (808/329-9188, www.sandwichisledivers.com), located in the Kona Marketplace, is owned and operated by longtime Kona Coast divers who know all the spots. They have a custom, six-passenger dive boat, great for small, personalized trips for avid divers. Sandwich Isle Divers offers competitive rates for instruction and day and night dives: certified diver with all gear for $105, introductory dive at $130, and a night dive for $75.

Bottom Time (74-5590 Luhia St., 808/331-1858 or 866/463-4836, www.bottomtimehawaii.com) offers similar tours. Two-tank introductory dives run $130, two-tank day dives are $110, and an evening manta dive (when available) is $76.

A twist on the usual snorkel adventure is offered by **Torpedo Tours Hawaii** (808/938-0405, www.torpedotours.com), which does shore and boat dives as well as certification and night manta ray dives. Small groups are important here. To provide a little extra power, this company provides "torpedo" scooters, battery-powered motors that pull you through the water at two mph. Some rates include $59–149 for shore dives or $129 for a torpedo dive from a boat.

Leaving from the Honokohau Harbor, **Ocean Eco Tours** (808/324-7873, www.oceanecotours.com) specializes in beginners. Introductory dives run $125, shore dives $85, and two-tank boats dives $95. Certification courses are also taught.

Honu Sports (808/327-3483, www.honusports.com), near Lava Java, offers several shore and boat dives for $79–99, an introductory boat dive for $139, and a variety of certification courses.

Located at the Keauhou Bay pier, **Sea Paradise** (808/322-2500 or 800/322-5662, www.seaparadise.com) offers dives at the south end of Kona. Introductory dives run $140, two-tank boat dives $105, and night manta ray dives (best seen May–October) $89.

For those still dancing to the primordial tune of residual DNA from our one-celled, ocean-dwelling ancestors, ***Kona Aggressor II*** (808/329-8182 or 800/344-5662, www.aggressor.com or www.pac-aggressor.com) is a live-aboard dive boat that departs Kona every Saturday for six days of diving along the Kona Coast toward South Point. Passengers dive up to five times per day and night, as the *Aggressor* completely fulfills its motto of "Eat, Sleep, and Dive." This is the Cadillac of dive cruises, and everything on board is taken care of. Rates run $2,195 per person.

You can shore dive from any of the beach snorkel sites with your own or rented equipment, but unless you are *very* familiar with

Hawaiian waters, it's best to let the pros guide you to their favorite sites.

Surfing

Surfing is not as significant a sport on the Big Island as on the other islands. Proportionally for the size of the island and in terms of real numbers, there are fewer good surfing spots on this island and many of the traditional surfing sites are just not easy to access. Whether this is due to the lack of the underwater environment necessary to create the right kind of waves or for some other reason, conditions seem to be lacking for great surf that the other islands have in abundance. However, there are a few local sites on the Kona side that do draw the faithful. Perhaps the most popular is the break along the reef at Kahalu'u Bay in front of the beach park. Two alternate spots are "Banyans" near Disappearing Sands Beach Park and "Pine Trees," north of town near the airport. Any of the shops that sell or rent boards can give you current information about surfing conditions and sites, so be sure to ask.

If you're thinking about buying a surfboard in Kona, try **Honolua Surf Co.** (808/329-1001) at the Kona Inn Shopping Village in Kailua-Kona for starters. For renting, try **Millers Surf and Sport** (76-6246 Ali'i Dr., 808/326-1772, 8 A.M.–5 P.M. daily) at the Kona Bali Kai condominiums or **Kahalu'u Bay Beach Rentals** (78-6685 Ali'i Dr., 808/322-4338, 8:30 A.M.–5 P.M. daily), near Kahalu'u Beach Park in Keauhou. Kahalu'u Bay Beach Rentals also arranges lessons. For other surf lessons, try **Ocean Eco Tours** (808/324-7873, www.oceanecotours.com) or **Hawaii Lifeguard Surf Instructors** (808/324-0442, www.surflessonshawaii.com). Expect to find two-hour group lessons for about $100–110 or private lessons for $150–165. Be sure to ask any of these places about what's happening with the water when you're on-island.

Parasailing and Jet Skiing

UFO Parasail (808/325-5836 or 888/359-4836, flykona@ufoparasail.netwww.ufoparasail.net) offers boat platform takeoff and

© ROBERT NILSEN

Ku'emanu Heiau was and still is known for good surfing conditions.

landing parasail flights that are safe and easy for young and old alike. A "400 feet for seven minutes" atmospheric ride runs $60 and the "800 feet for 10 minutes" stratospheric ride is $70. For those tempted to leave orbit, they'll let out 1,200 feet of rope for $80. Tandem riders are welcome, but are limited to 350 pounds. Single riders have to be at least 130 pounds. From the end of the rope, you can see not only the coast and mountains, but also coral and dolphins. It's surprisingly quiet. Reduced rates are available for early birds, and boat ride-alongs are $30. You, too, can dangle from a parachute and put your life in the hands of these fun-filled Kona guys who will streak you through the air. The boat leaves from the Kailua pier; check in at the office across the street from the pier in the Kona Square Shopping Center. Parasailing on the Big Island is done year-round.

If you want speed but know that staying on the water is more your style, try **Pacific Jet Sports** (808/329-2745 or 866/667-2001, www.mauiwatersports.com/pacificjetsports.html) for jet-ski fun. To take a powerful Kawasaki for a spin around the bay, you must be 18 years old to drive and at least 12 to ride. Up to three persons are allowed on each machine. Rates run $60 for a half hour, $95 an hour ($85 for early birds), and $18 for a second person. No experience necessary.

Kayaking

Kayaking along the Kona Coast can be good any time of year, but it's best to stay out of the water when the winds kick up and blow a Kona storm in from the south during winter. Kahalu'u Bay is a decent place to launch a kayak to head south along the Keauhou coastline. Keauhou Bay also provides a good place to put in your watercraft and you are closer to a less developed shoreline. Farther south, both Kealakekua Bay and the small bay adjacent to Pu'uhonua O Honaunau National Historical Park are the most popular kayak launch sites as they are right where the great snorkel sites are located.

While most kayak rental companies are located farther south near Kealakekua Bay, there are several options available in Kailua and Keauhou. With a shop at the Keauhou Bay pier, the foremost of these is **Ocean Safaris Kayak Adventures** (808/326-4699, www.oceansafariskayaks.com), which offers half-day guided sea cave tours in the Keauhou area for $64 and an early bird tour for $35, or you can make your own route for the price of a kayak rental.

Sailing

Sailing is a year-round adventure, and boats take advantage of the steady breezes and fine weather along the Kona Coast.

One of the only true monohull charter sailing ships on the island, the *Honu* is put in the water by **Honu Sail Charters** (808/896-4668, www.sailkona.com), which runs half-day, full-day, and sunset sailing tours on its sleek sailboat from Honokohau Marina. Half-day tours, including snorkeling and snacks, run $86, full-day tours run $128, and the sunset tour with *pu pu* is $67; maximum of six guests.

Also leaving out of Honokohau Marina is the catamaran **Kamanu** (808/329-2021 or 800/348-3091, www.kamanu.com). Kamanu runs morning and afternoon snorkel and whale-watch (in season) sails Monday through Saturday and provides snacks and drinks at $75 adults and $45 for children. Maximum 24 guests.

Leaving out of Keauhou Bay, **Sea Paradise** (808/322-2500 or 800/322-5662, www.seaparadise.com) sends its catamaran *Hokuhele* down the coast to Kealakekua Bay for morning, afternoon, and night snorkel trips. The four-hour morning trip runs $95 adult and $59 for children under 12, a three-hour afternoon excursion is $65 adult and $59 kids, while the special nighttime snorkeling with manta rays trip is $79 adult and $59 children.

Whale-Watching

Three-hour whale-watching tours on the 40-foot boat *Lady Ann* are offered by **Captain Dan McSweeney's Whale Watching Adventures** (808/322-0028 or 888/942-5376,

PURESTOCK

whale tail

www.ilovewhales.com). While many are interested in looking only for the humpback whales, Dan, a marine biologist and whale researcher, takes visitors year-round so they can also learn about different kinds of whales and other ocean mammals that inhabit this coast. This is an educational trip, the best the island has to offer. If you want to see whales and learn about these beautiful mammals in the process, go with Dan. The *Lady Ann* leaves from the Honokohau Marina every day from mid-December through mid-April, and Tuesday, Thursday, and Saturday the rest of the year. Tours run $69.50 adults and $59.50 children.

From December through May, most of the Zodiac, snorkel, scuba, catamaran, and sailing boats also run whale-watching tours in addition to or in place of their other activities.

Deep-Sea Fishing Charters

The fishing around the Big Island's Kona Coast ranges from excellent to outstanding! It's legendary for marlin fishing, but there are other fish in the sea. The best time of year for big blues is July–September; August is the optimum month. Rough seas can keep boats in for a few days during December and early January, but by February all are generally out. A large fleet of charter boats with skilled captains and tested crews is ready, willing, and competent to take you out. Most of the island's 80 charter boats are berthed at Honokohau Harbor off Route 19, about midway between downtown Kailua and Kona Airport. When the big fish are brought in, they're weighed in at the fuel dock, usually around 11:30 A.M. and 3:30 P.M. Honokohau Harbor has far eclipsed Kailua pier, which is now tamed and primarily for swimmers, triathletes, and body-boarders.

You can hire a boat for a private or share charter. Boat size varies, but four anglers per midsize boat is average. No matter the size, most boats will take no more than six anglers. The range of rates generally fall into the following parameters: private, full day $400–900, half day $300–600; share, full day $150–200, half day $80–125. Full days are eight hours, half days four, with three-quarter days and overnighters available on some boats. No licenses are required, and all gear is provided. It is customary for the captain to keep the catch, but arrangements for you to keep or mount your fish can be made. Catch and release is encouraged by many boats and is happening more and more each year. Bring your own lunch (no bananas), beverages, and camera.

To charter a boat contact the individual captains directly, check at your hotel activities desk, or book through one of the following agencies. **Charter Services Hawaii** (808/334-1881 or 800/567-2650, charterservices@konazone.com, www.konazone.com), operated by Ed Barry, offers boats in all sizes and price ranges. If you're after a company that's knowledgeable about getting you onto a boat and that will bring you to waters where you'll have the opportunity to catch one of the twirling and gigantic "big blues," this is one of the best places to come.

Located on the fuel dock at Honokohau Harbor, **The Charter Desk** (808/329-5735 or

888/566-2487, charter@aloha.net, www.charterdesk.com) represents some 50 boats in the harbor. This is another well-respected and competent company that works hard at matching clients to boats.

The **Kona Charter Skippers Association** (808/329-3600 or 800/762-7546, konafish@hawaii.rr.com, www.konabiggamefishing.com) is another agency that tries to match you and your desires with the right boat and captain.

Cruises and Boat Tours

Zodiac Tours: A Zodiac is a very tough, motorized rubber raft, sometimes with a rigid fiberglass bottom. It looks like a big, horseshoe-shaped inner tube that bends itself and undulates with the waves like a floating water bed. These seaworthy craft, powered by twin Mercury 280s, have five separate air chambers for unsinkable safety.

Captain Zodiac (808/329-3199, www.captainzodiac.com) will take you on a fantastic ocean odyssey beginning at Honokohau Small Boat Harbor just north of Kailua-Kona, from where you'll skirt the coast south all the way to Kealakekua Bay. Skippers take you and up to 15 others for a thrilling ride down the Kona Coast, pausing along the way to whisk you into sea caves, grottoes, and caverns, and if it's the right time of year you have the added benefit of seeing whales. The Kona Coast is also marked with ancient ruins and the remains of villages, which the captains point out, and about which they relate historical anecdotes as you pass by. You stop at Kealakekua Bay, where you can swim and snorkel in this underwater conservation park. Round-trips departing at 8 A.M. and 1 P.M. take about four hours and cost $82 adults, $67 children 4–12. During winter, Captain Zodiac also runs a whale-watching tour for $65 adults or $56 for kids. Captain Zodiac also provides a light tropical lunch of fresh exotic fruit, taro chips, fruit juice, iced tea, and sodas. All you need are a bathing suit, sun hat, towel, suntan lotion, camera, and sense of adventure.

Sea Quest (808/325-7238 or 888/732-2283, www.seaquesthawaii.com) runs a similar inflatable raft snorkel tour to Kealakekua Bay from Keauhou Bay with numerous stops along the way to explore sea caves and other coastline features. Morning and afternoon departures are available and cost $85 and $64, respectively, while in season a whale-watching tour runs $53; it's always less for children. These smaller rafts take only six to twelve guests.

Using a smaller inflatable raft for more intimate groups, **Dolphin Discoveries** (808/322-8000, www.dolphindiscoveries.com) also offers raft and snorkel trips to Kealakekua Bay from Keauhou Bay boat ramp. Morning and afternoon trips are given daily. The four-hour morning tour runs $83 adult and $62 kids 5–15; the three-hour afternoon tour is $62 per person. These folks are very focused on the study and research of dolphins, whales, and other sea animals, so your trip will be educational. Part of your fee goes to support marine conservation programs.

Sunset Dinner Cruises: A Kona institution, **Captain Beans' Polynesian Cruise** (808/329-2955 or 800/831-5541, www.robertshawaii.com) will take you aboard its glass-bottom bargelike boat, departing Kailua Pier at 5:15 P.M. daily except Monday and returning about two hours later. If you are after a pleasant but not adventurous sunset cruise, take this one, but keep in mind that this is the boat equivalent of a bus tour. During the very tame cruise you'll spot fish, listen to island music, and enjoy a sunset dinner. On board, you are entertained while the deck groans with an all-you-can-eat buffet. The best part—after the sunset—is that you get a terrific panorama of the Kona Coast from the sea. You can't help having a good time on this cruise. The adult fare is $58, children 4–11 $36 (slightly more for guests from the Kohala Coast hotels), and this includes dinner, one drink, and transportation from area hotels. Reservations suggested.

A twist to the evening sunset sail is offered by **Body Glove** (808/326-7122 or 800/551-8911, www.bodyglovehawaii.com), which entertains its guests with tropical music, *pu pu*, and plenty of island drinks. This trip, $59 for adults and $39 for youth, is only offered several times a week, so call for the current schedule.

Running out of Keauhou Bay, *Hokuhele* offers an adults-only champagne sunset dinner cruise for $95. Contact **Sea Paradise** (808/322-2500 or 800/322-5662, www.seaparadise.com) for reservations.

Glass-Bottom Boats: The 36-foot *Marian* of the **Kailua Bay Charter Company** (808/324-1749, www.konaglassbottomboat.com) does glass-bottom boat tours from the Kailua pier, daily on the hour 10 A.M.–2 P.M. Taking only 24 passengers, this cruise runs $25 adults or $10 for kids ages 5–12. Sunset cruises are also available.

Submarine Tours: One company in Kailua offers a once-in-a-lifetime, below-the-surface-of-the-water experience to view undersea life at the fish-eye level. **Atlantis Submarine** (808/329-6626 or 800/548-6262, www.altantisadventures.com) allows everyone to live out the fantasy of Captain Nemo on a silent cruise under the waves off Kailua-Kona. After checking in at the office at the King Square Shopping Center, you board a launch at Kailua pier that takes you on a 10-minute cruise to the waiting submarine tethered offshore. You're given all of your safety tips on the way there. The underwater portion lasts about a half hour. As you descend to 120 feet, notice that everything white, including teeth, turns pink because the ultraviolet rays are filtered out. The only colors you can see clearly beneath the waves are blues and greens because water is 800 times denser than air and filters out the reds and oranges. You cruise in air-conditioned comfort and have great viewing out the two-foot-diameter windows. There's not a bad seat in this 48-passenger submarine, so you don't have to rush to get on. Don't worry about being claustrophobic, either—the sub is amazingly airy and bright, with aircraft-quality air blowers above the seats. Although the schedule may vary somewhat according to the time of year, these one-hour cruises generally run three times a day, 10 A.M.–1:30 P.M.; the price is $80 adults and $42 children. Atlantis offers a number of combination packages that include lu'au, snorkel or whale-watching trips, and helicopter rides.

Air Tours

Tropical Helicopters (808/961-6810, www.tropicalhelicopters.com) flies one round-island tour from Kona, heading south to the Kilauea volcano, then up the Hamakua Coast to Waipi'o and Waimanu valleys, before heading back down the Kohala Coast past the luxury resorts to Kailua. This two-hour flight runs $335 per person and might be the highlight of your visit. Tropical Helicopters uses six-passenger Bell 407 and four-passenger Hughes 500 aircraft. It also runs several flights from the Hilo Airport.

Leaving from the Kona Airport, **Paradise Helicopters** (808/329-6601, www.paradisecopters.com) flies a two-hour round-island tour for $364 and 3.5-hour volcano, waterfall-landing flight for $514 per person. Like Tropical Helicopters, Paradise Helicopters uses six-passenger Bell 407 and four-passenger Hughes 500 aircraft. Paradise Helicopters also offers flights from the Hilo Airport.

For fixed-wing air tours, try one of the following. **Big Island Air** (808/329-4868 or 800/303-8868) offers small-plane flights from Kona Airport, with a two-person minimum. A 1.5-hour round-island/volcano flight in a nine-passenger turbo jet prop Cessna costs $275 adult and $180 for children ages 2–18. Every seat is a window seat, and the wings in the new plane are set above the windows. Generally, five flights go every day starting at 7 A.M.

For a smaller and more intimate plane, also with wings above the windows, try **Island Hopper** (808/329-0018), which offers flights in a six-seat plane from Kona Airports. The sunset volcano tour runs $227, while the circle-island flight is $267 per person. Island Hopper also flies out of the Hilo Airport for a volcano tour. This company has been doing aerial tours for longer than any other on the island.

With similar flights and prices is **Mokulele Flight Service** (808/326-7070 or 866/260-7070, www.mokulele.com), but Mokulele flies five- and nine-passenger twin prop planes. The circle-island tour from Kona side runs $269. Air taxi service is also offered to Maui, with charter service to Moloka'i and Lana'i.

For the daring, **WingOver Hawaii** (808/936-1809) offers aerobatic tours that combine three, six, or nine maneuvers.

Bus and Van Tours

Most tour companies run vans, but some larger companies also use buses. Though cheaper, tours on full-sized coaches are generally less personalized. Wherever a bus can go, so can your rental car—but on a tour you can relax and enjoy the scenery without worrying about driving. Also, tour drivers are very experienced with the area and know many stories and legends with which they annotate and enrich your trip. Tours generally run $50–80 per person and either circle the island or have Kilauea volcano as their main feature. Narrated and fairly tame bus tours are operated by **Roberts Hawaii** (808/329-1688 in Kona, 808/966-5483 in Hilo, 800/831-5541, www.robertshawaii.com) and by **Polynesian Adventure Tours** (808/329-8008 or 800/622-3011, www.polyad.com). **Jack's Hawaii** (808/961-6666 or 800/442-5557, www.jackshawaii.com) also runs various group bus tours to major sights on the island.

Mauna Kea Summit Adventures (808/322-2366 or 888/322-2366, www.maunakea.com), owned and operated by Pat Wright, has been taking visitors on high-adventure trips around the Big Island for more than 20 years. Your comfort and safety as you roam the Big Island are ensured as you ride in sturdy turbo diesel Ford vans with 4WD, air-conditioning, sound system, first-aid kit, and oxygen! The premier tour is an eight-hour journey to the top of Mauna Kea. Pat and his drivers not only fill your trip with stories, anecdotes, and fascinating facts during the ride, they top off the safari by setting up an eight-inch telescope not far from the Onizuka Center so you can get a personal view of the heavens through the rarefied atmosphere atop the great mountain. Mauna Kea Summit Adventures will pick you up at your hotel in Kailua-Kona at about 4 P.M. If you're staying on the Hilo side, a driver will meet you at a predetermined spot along the Saddle Road. The price is $175, with hot savory drinks, soup and sandwiches, and good warm parkas included. Special trips for photography, hiking, astronomy, and shore fishing can also be tailored to your needs.

Hawaii Forest and Trail (74-5035B Queen Ka'ahumanu Hwy., 808/331-8505 or 800/464-1993, info@hawaii-forest.com, www.hawaii-forest.com) offers much the same summit and stargazing tour at $165 per person.

There are some restrictions for this trip, including a minimum age of 16, good physical condition, and a proper time lapse after scuba diving. Check with your tour company for other safety tips.

Hiking

There are no hiking trails as such in Kailua except for the short trails in the national historical parks. Sections of the historical King's Trail run through Kona, but it's not maintained as an established hiking trail. The few hiking trails in the mountains above Kailua run over private land, so it is best to hike with one of the established hiking companies or groups that have access. See below for those in Kona.

If you're not familiar with good bird-watching spots on Hawai'i, contact Rob or Cindy Pacheco at **Hawaii Forest and Trail** (74-5035B Queen Ka'ahumanu Hwy., 808/331-8505 or 800/464-1993, info@hawaii-forest.com, www.hawaii-forest.com). This well-established naturalist company uses powerful 4WD vans to get you to where the less common birds are found. Its two exclusive bird-watching tours take you to the rainforests and dry forests of the Hakalau National Wildlife Refuge on the eastern slope of Mauna Kea, and the forests on the leeward slope of Mauna Kea plus some on the northeastern slope of Mauna Loa. Other tours include the Valley Waterfall Adventure to the spectacular Pololu Valley of North Kohala, the Kohala Country Waterfall Adventure, a tour to Hawai'i Volcanoes National Park, and a rainforest walk around volcanic features on Mt. Hualalai. All tours are kept to a maximum of 10 people, are guided by knowledgeable naturalists, include food and beverage, provide all necessary equipment, and include pickup and drop-off from specified locations on the Kona side. The waterfall and Hualalai hikes are half-day affairs and run $99–125 adult or $79–99 for children ages 8–12. The birding hikes are full-day tours that run $155 adult, while the Kilauea Volcano trip is $149 for adults and $115 children. Any of these tours will certainly be a highlight of your vacation.

The **Kona Hiking Club** is a fairly loosely organized group of individuals that offers no-cost hikes usually on the third Saturday of the month. Outings are advertised in the West Hawaii newspaper the Sunday before the hike. Hikes run to various destinations, some to private land that cannot be accessed any other way. Bring your own lunch.

Bicycling

By and large, bicycling in Kailua means peddling your beach cruiser on a leisurely ride along Ali'i Drive. Watch for traffic as there are plenty of cars and the shoulders are narrow or nonexistent in sections. Some riders prefer road bikes and head out along the highway for a workout. The highway running north is gentle in gradient and has wide shoulders. This road is hot and can be windy. It has broad vistas with no shade and is noisy, as traffic speeds by on the way to the Kohala resorts. Running south, the highway heads gradually up the hill to Honalo. This section also is wide and it, too, has plenty of traffic. Mamalahoa Highway south from Honalo to Captain Cook and beyond as well as north from Honalo through Holualoa to the Palani Junction, is narrow and winds through this upcountry coffee growing region, so be much more careful of cars even though the speed limit is slower. Perhaps the toughest workouts for a biker in the Kona area would be to take any of the steep roads that connect Queen Ka'ahumanu Highway and Mamalahoa Highway, such as Hualalai Road or Ka'iminani Drive. For other biking options and information on established mountain biking trails, check with the bike shops listed below.

Dave's Bike and Triathlon Shop (808/329-4522), owned and pedaled by triathlete Dave Bending, is located just a long stride or two from the beginning of the Ironman Triathlon across from King Kamehameha's Kona Beach Hotel in the Kona Square Shopping Center. Dave rents mountain bikes, hybrids, full-suspension bikes, and a few road bikes from $15 a day to $60 a week. Prices include helmet, water bottles, map, bicycle lock, and, most importantly, road advice. Dave is a font of information, one of the best bicycle men on the island. He knows his stuff, so pay heed! If you want to do more than just pedal along the beach, come see Dave.

Hawaiian Pedals (808/329-2294, www.hawaiianpedals.com, 9 A.M.–9 P.M. daily), at the Kona Inn Shopping Village, rents basic mountain bikes and hybrids. A sister store, **HP Bike Works** (74-5599 Lehua St., Ste. F-3, 808/326-2453, 9 A.M.–6 P.M. Mon.–Sat.), located in the old industrial area just off Queen Ka'ahumanu Hwy., rents suspension mountain bikes and road bikes but also does sales and repair. Rates for 24 hours are $20 for mountain bikes and hybrids, $35 for road and front-suspension bikes, and $40–45 for full-suspension mountain bikes. Five-hour and multi-day rates can also be arranged. Rentals include helmet, lock, pump, and patch kit. Various bike racks are also available for $5–15 a day.

Located in the Kaloko Light Industrial Park above Home Depot, **Cycle Station** (73-5619 Kauhola, #105, 808/327-0087, www.cyclestationhawaii.com) does sales, service, and rental of bikes and offers multi-day bike tours. A daily rate for hybrids is $20, and it's $25–35 for road or mountain bikes. A helmet, water bottle, pump, and patch kit come with your rental, but car racks are extra at $5 a day. Staff can provide great information about rides appropriate for your riding level and the type of riding you want to do.

Kona Coast Cycling Tours (808/327-1133 or 877/592-2453, www.cyclekona.com) offers six different tours—some half-day rides, some full-day trips—a few for the beginner, some for advanced riders, and all for the enthusiastic. Two of the rides concentrate on the coffee country in Kona, while the rest head to the less-traveled byways of the Kohala district for waterfall, downhill, and back-road adventures. Tours rates vary from $70 to $190. Call for reservations.

Tennis

The **Royal Kona Tennis Club** (808/334-1093) has four latexite courts, three of which are lighted for night play, that are open to resort guests and nonguests alike. Court fees are a reasonable $10 per day. Avid tennis players should check the weekly rates. Instruction can be arranged and rackets rented. Call the pro shop to reserve court times, particularly for night play, as well as for round robins and other organized play.

Island Slice Tennis (808/322-6112) at the Outrigger Keauhou Beach Resort, offers reserved tennis play on six lighted courts (until 9 P.M.) for $5 for the first hour and $10 for as long as you want to play after that if courts are open. Round robins are held at various times throughout the week and instruction runs $20 an hour. Racket rental runs $3–5. Call for reservations.

Golf

The **Kona Country Club** (808/322-2595, www.konagolf.com) is a lovely golf course near the end of Ali'i Drive in Keauhou that has 18-hole ocean and mountain courses, with grand views over this eminently rocky coast. Greens fees run $140 for the mountain course and $155 for the ocean course, $89 and $99, respectively, after noon. The pro shop is open daily, and the adjacent Vista Restaurant at the clubhouse serves breakfast and lunch daily and dinner Wednesday to Saturday.

A little farther afield but still close enough to Kailua to make a good play date are Big Island Country Club and Makalei Hawaii Country Club—both are located along Mamalahoa Hwy. heading toward Waimea. The **Big Island Country Club** (808/325-5044) is a rolling, challenging course with wonderful vistas over the Kohala Coast. Greens fees run $99 for morning play and $69 in the afternoon. Carved from ranchland up on the steep hillside closer to Kailua is the equally challenging **Makalei Hawaii Country Club** (808/325-6625), where play costs $110 before 12:30 P.M. or $50 after that.

© ROBERT NILSEN

Kona Country Club Golf Course

If the local golf courses are just too expensive or if you're just not sure enough about your game, spend some time first at the **Swing Zone** (808/329-6909, 8 A.M.–8 P.M. daily) 18-hole grass miniature putting course that's shaped like the Big Island itself. One round runs $6.75 and includes a putter and balls. No players under age 12 are allowed; golf rules apply. This pint-size course has no lights, so it's daytime play only. If you need more than putting practice, try the six holes of golf for $13 on its standard course. Also at the Swing Zone is a full-size driving range that's lit at night; a bucket of 60 balls costs $6.75. If these two aren't enough to wear you out, try the batting cage, also lit, where $1 buys 10 pitches. On occasion, the Swing Zone will host a music event on its lawns. The Swing Zone is located across the street from the Old Airport Beach Park at the end of Kuakini Highway.

ACCOMMODATIONS IN KAILUA

Almost all of Kona's accommodations lie along the six miles of Ali'i Drive from Kailua-Kona to Keauhou. Most hotels/condos fall in the moderate to expensive range. A few inexpensive hotels are scattered here and there along Ali'i Drive, and back up in the hills are a "sleeper" or two, cheap but decent. The following list should provide you with a good cross section.

It's sad but true: except for the limited beach parks at Ho'okena and Miloli'i, south of Kailua-Kona, there is no official camping in all of the Kona district. Campers wishing to enjoy the coast must go north to the Kohala district to find a campground, or south to Ka'u.

Hostel

The most affordable place to stay in Kailua is at **Koa-Wood Hale Inn** (75-184 Ala Ona Ona St, 808/329-9663), a small four-unit apartment complex turned into rental rooms. Rooms are shared ($35) or private ($55–65), and there is one two-bedroom unit with a kitchen for $130. Everyone must leave a security deposit. The place is kept as neat as the proverbial pin and is well run. A kitchen and laundry facilities can be utilized, and there is free TV and parking, but there is no phone or Internet service. Office hours are 8 A.M.–noon and 4:30–10 P.M. only.

$50-100

For a reasonable and homey hotel, try the **Kona Tiki Hotel** (75-5968 Ali'i Dr., 808/329-1425, fax 808/327-9402, www.konatiki.com), one of the first accommodations south of "downtown." At more than 50 years old, this is one of the oldest vacation hotels along the coast, and although of an old style without the luxury, the place is kept up. Sandwiched between the ocean and the road, it's a bit noisy during the day but quiets down at night except for the lullaby of the rolling surf. The Kona Tiki features refrigerators in all rooms, some kitchenettes, a complimentary continental breakfast daily, and a small guest pool. The 15 refurbished rooms are clean, with ceiling fans but no phones or televisions, and all units face the ocean so everyone gets a view. Prices are $65–79 for a standard room with queen or queen and twin bed, and $88 for a kitchenette; extra adult $10; three-night minimum; no credit cards.

Uncle Billy's Kona Bay Hotel (75-5744 Ali'i Dr., 808/329-1393 or 800/367-5102, resv@unclebilly.com, www.unclebilly.com) is a locally owned hotel right in the center of town, run by Uncle Billy and his Kona family. Its best feature is the friendly and warm staff. The hotel is a remaining wing of the old Kona Inn, most of which was torn down to accommodate the shopping center across the road. The semicircular hotel is built around a central courtyard and garden containing Kimo's Family Buffet, a bar, and a swimming pool. Free parking is in the rear. Uncle Billy's is a bit of a throwback to Kona's earlier days; still, it's comfortable, clean, and convenient, but not plush. The rooms are a combination of moderate and superior with a/c, TV, and mini-fridge. Rates run $94–99, with $99 kitchenettes; many discounts and package rates are available.

$100-150

Kona Seaside Hotel (75-5646 Palani Rd.,

808/329-2455 or 800/560-5558, fax 808/329-6157, www.konaseasidehotel.com) is a basic but well-cared-for downtown hotel just up the street from the Kailua pier. Part of the island-owned Sand and Seaside Hotel chain, most rooms here have a/c, cross ventilation, and lanai, and there's self-service laundry on the premises. A sundeck and central courtyard surround one swimming pool; a second pool is located near the front entrance. Prices range from $118 standard to $150 deluxe, with AAA, Internet, and *kama'aina* discounts and room and car packages available. The Kona Seaside operates three adjacent restaurants and the Seaside Shopping Center next door.

$150-250

King Kamehameha's Kona Beach Hotel (75-5660 Palani Rd., 808/329-2911 or 800/367-6060, fax 808/329-4602, reservations@hthcorp.com, www.konabeachhotel.com) in downtown Kailua-Kona is one of the only Kona hotels that has its own beach and is located on a spot favored by Hawaiian royalty. Kamehameha the Great spent the last days of his life here and at the adjacent and restored Ahu'ena Heiau. The walls of the hotel lobby are lined with historical artifacts; portraits of the Kamehameha royal family beginning with the great chief Kamehameha are displayed in the reception area; two *kahili* stand nearby as signs of royalty; and a feather cape and hat adorn one wall. Other displays make up this mini-museum, and it's worth a look even if you are not staying here. Pick up a brochure about these artifacts at the front desk. In addition, weekly events introduce guests to aspects of Hawaiian art and culture. Rooms each feature a lanai with a sweeping panorama of the bay or Mt. Hualalai. Prices for the 460 rooms are $170–250 for standard to oceanfront rooms and up to $600 for a three-bedroom suite, additional person $30, and children under 18 stay free when sharing their parents' room. The hotel features the Kona Beach Restaurants, Billfish Bar, Island Breeze lu'au, tennis courts, a plethora of shops in its indoor air-conditioned mall, a freshwater pool, and a beach, as well as an activities desk, Internet access for guests, and self-service laundry. The King Kamehameha's Kona Beach Hotel is an older property, but it's well run by a proud staff, well maintained to keep a high standard, and good value for your money.

The **Royal Kona Resort** (75-5852 Ali'i Dr., 808/329-3111 or 800/222-5642, www.royalkona.com) has become a Kona landmark. The hotel, built like rising steps with the floor below larger than the one above, commands a magnificent view from its perch atop a beautiful promontory of black lava that anchors the south end of downtown Kailua. All 450 rooms are spacious, and each includes a lanai. Standard rates run from $210 for a garden view to $280 for an ocean view and $350 for an oceanfront room, with the oceanfront corner king rooms costing $385. Many packages are available. On the property, you can dine for breakfast or dinner at Don the Beachcomber Restaurant, which has a lovely sun-soaked veranda with a sweeping view of the surrounding coastline. The Windjammer Lounge next door, which serves light lunches during the day, becomes an open-air lounge featuring entertainment several evenings each week. The hotel pool has an upper kiddies' pool and a lower, re-tiled main pool adjacent to the rolling surf, and an ocean-fed beach lagoon is sheltered from the force of the waves by huge black lava boulders. Between the main building and the beach tower is the small coconut grove. Here, the *imu* is fired up every Monday, Wednesday, and Friday evening, creating delectable morsels for the famous Kona sunset lu'au that comes complete with island entertainment that fills the grounds with music and laughter. The tennis courts, attended by a professional staff, are lit for nighttime play. Other full-service amenities include a small clutch of shops, a business center, massage center, a self-serve laundry, free parking, exercise spa classes, baby-sitters, and no charge for children less than 17 years of age sharing a room with their parents. Some public areas of the hotel were renovated in 2005. Like King Kamehameha's Kona Beach Hotel, the Royal Kona Resort is an older hotel that keeps alive the tradition of quality service in an aging yet well-cared-for facility.

Condominiums

Kona Islander Inn (75-5776 Kuakini Hwy., 808/329-3333) has hotel-style condominium apartments, well appointed for a reasonable price. Conveniently located within walking distance of downtown Kailua-Kona, they're tucked into a tight but well-landscaped garden next door to St. Michael's and Kealoakamalamalama Churches and are one of the first condo properties along Ali'i Drive. The style is "turn-of-the-20th-century plantation" shaded by tall palms. All rental units have phone, off-road parking, a/c, TV, and refrigerators. Rates are $70–100.

A few steps down the road, the **Kona Billfisher** (808/329-3333) offers apartment-style condos with full kitchens, pool, barbecues, limited maid service, and gazebo. One-bedroom units cost $90 daily for up to four persons, two-bedroom units $135 for up to six guests. Weekly and monthly rates and discounts are available; minimum three days.

Set next to the Royal Kona Resort is the small and quiet **Hale Kona Kai** (75-5870 Kahakai Rd., tel./fax 808/329-2155 or 800/421-3696, www.halekonakai-hkk.com). These one-bedroom, oceanfront apartments are fully equipped condo units with lanai, and a swimming pool and laundry facilities are on the premises. Room rates for this basic, older-style complex are $135–155 a night, three-night minimum, $10 for each additional person over two.

Located very close to "downtown" Kailua and a few steps from the Royal Kona Resort at the start of "condo row" is the Castle Resort property **Kona Reef** (75-5888 Ali'i Dr., 808/329-2959 or 800/367-5004, www.castleresorts.com/KRH). Finely appointed units look out over the central garden and pool to the sea beyond. Each unit is set up with full kitchen, washer and dryer, and all you need for an easy stay. One-, two-, and three-bedroom suites run $240–565 high season, slightly less during low season, and can sleep four to eight people.

On a narrow property that slides down to the sea, the contemporary-style **Alii Villa** (75-6016 Ali'i Dr., 808/329-1288) looks as if it came out of the 1960s with its straight lines and architectural concrete blocks. Set amidst plentiful vegetation, with a swimming pool and two barbecue grills in the middle of the property, these condos run up to $150 during high season.

The **Outrigger Royal Sea Cliff Resort** (75-6040 Ali'i Dr., 808/329-8021 or 800/688-7444), winner of the AAA Three-Diamond Award, offers classy condo apartments. The alabaster contemporary building features rooms fronting a central garden courtyard. The unobstructed views of the black lava coast from most rooms are glorious, and a perfect day-ending activity is sunset enjoyed on your private lanai. Amenities include free tennis, daily maid service, cable color TV, freshwater and seawater swimming pools, jet spa and sauna, and activities desk. Units here are spacious, and regular season rates start with a studio at $233, one bedroom $263–318, and two bedrooms $298–393. The "family plan" allows children under 18 to stay at no charge when using existing beds; otherwise there's a $20 daily extra person charge.

Managed by ResortQuest Hawaii, **Kona by the Sea** (75-6106 Ali'i Dr., 808/327-2300 or 866/774-2924, www.RQKonaByTheSea.com) is a beautifully situated condominium with extraordinary coastal views; it went through exterior renovation in 2004. Like many of Kona's properties, it has no beach, but there is a pool on the premises, outdoor cooking grills, and an activities desk. From the balcony of your suite overlooking a central courtyard, you can watch the aqua-blue surf crash onto the black lava rocks below. Each spacious one- or two-bedroom unit has two bathrooms, tiled lanai, full modern kitchen, living room with foldout couch, dining room, color cable TV, and central air-conditioning. Regular season prices are $270–385 for one-bedroom units and $335–445 for two-bedroom units. Like the neighboring Royal Sea Cliff Resort, this property is also a AAA Three-Diamond Award winner. Kona by the Sea and the Royal Sea Cliff Resort are two of the nicest properties in Kailua.

A Castle Resorts and Hotels property, **Kona Bali Kai** (76-6246 Ali'i Dr., 808/329-9381 or 800/367-5004, fax 808/326-6056, www.castleresorts.com/KBK) is a very decent, comfortable place with a swimming pool, activities desk, concierge, and sundries shop on property. The studio, one-, and two-bedroom units have a fully equipped kitchen, TV and VCR, and phone for local calls. All apartments are individually owned so the decor differs, but most have muted colors and a tropical feel. Rates run $200–350, with plenty of specials and discounts. While some units are directly on the ocean, others are on the mountain side of Ali'i Drive, so they may or may not have an ocean view. This is a good choice for being close to town but not in the center of the hubbub.

Kona Magic Sands Resort (77-6452 Ali'i Dr., 808/329-3333) couldn't get closer to the water. It sits on oceanside lava directly adjacent to White Sands Beach. Here, you can lounge poolside and eat at Jameson's Restaurant without leaving the property. The studios have full kitchens, color TV, and phones. Rates run $135 during high season or $105 during low season; three nights minimum.

Small in comparison, **Kona Seaspray** (78-6665 Ali'i Dr., 808/322-2403, fax 808/322-0105, seaspraykona@aol.com, www.konaseaspray.com) rents 12 condo units in its two-building complex, with an exceptional setting across from Kahalu'u Bay and St. Peter's Church. Spacious and well-kept with all amenities and a small pool on property, these one-bedroom, one-bath and two-bedroom, two-bath units run $599–1,000 a week. Interior remodeling was done on all units in 2005. Kona Seaspray is popular, so call well in advance.

ACCOMMODATIONS IN KEAUHOU

$150–250

The **Outrigger Keauhou Beach Resort** (78-6740 Ali'i Dr., 808/322-3441 or 800/688-7444) is built on a historic site that includes the remains of three *heiau,* a reconstruction of King Kamehameha III's summer cottage, two freshwater springs, and several fishponds. Kahalu'u Bay Beach Park is adjacent with its white-sand beach and famous surf break, and the entire area is known for fantastic tidepools. This famous Kona hotel underwent an extensive renovation in 1999 and the result is a wonderful feeling of old-fashioned Hawaii. Rates range from $199 for a garden view up to $289 for deluxe oceanfront room, with suites at $579; rates are lower during value season and many special discounts are available all year. Each of the 309 rooms has a/c, TV, phone, private lanai, and small refrigerator. For food, the hotel has the open-air Kama'aina Terrace restaurant open for breakfast and dinner; the Kalanikai Bar and Grill near the water serves wraps, sandwiches, and other light fare for lunch; and the Verandah Lounge offers drinks throughout the day and free music every evening. The resort also has a swimming pool, activities desk, the Lamont's sundries store, Kailua the Village Artists Inc. gallery, Kolona salon and day spa, and a fitness center. In keeping with the new outlook, the hotel is offering daily activities and presentations in Hawaiian dance, music, arts and crafts, and a torch lighting ceremony. A free cultural tour is offered daily that takes you around to the historical sites on the hotel grounds. For the tennis player, Island Slice Tennis is on the property. Although not the largest, the Outrigger Keauhou Beach Resort is one of two fine hotel properties in Keauhou. Like the newly remodeled Sheraton down the road, the Outrigger Keauhou Beach Resort serves the mid- to upper-range travelers, as the King Kamehameha Kona Beach Hotel and Royal Kona Resort in Kailua aim for the economy travelers.

$250 and Above

Sitting on the black lava seashore south of Keauhou Bay, the 521-room **Sheraton Keauhou Bay Resort and Spa** (78-128 Ehukai St., 808/930-4900 or 888/488-3535, www.sheratonkeauhou.com) has risen like a phoenix from the old Kona Surf Hotel, greatly transforming the bones of the hotel and opening up the property to the water. The grounds have been extensively landscaped to add color and some formality to this otherwise black and forbidding coastline. The resort has three separate multistory buildings that face the water and one that looks inland for mountain views. These buildings surround a large courtyard swimming pool with a long and twisting water slide. Comfortable, with good views, all rooms and public areas have been totally redone and all amenities are new. Rooms rates are $325–425, with suites twice that. On property are the Keiki Club children's program, a business center, fitness center, tennis courts, basketball court, the full-service Ho'ola Spa, a large convention center, and a lu'au and Polynesian show that's held on the lawn twice a week. On-site shops include Maui Divers Jewelry, Lamont's Sundries, and Kohala Bay Collections, Kilauea Clothing Company, and Victoria's Floral Elegance for casual resortwear. As a destination resort, the Sheraton prepares food and drink at the fine-dining Restaurant Kai, the poolside and very casual Manta Ray Bar and Grill, the more stylish Crystal Blue Lounge, and the ground-level Caffé Hahalua. The Kona Coast is known for manta rays, and the resort shines a light on the water each evening hoping to attract the rays as they come to feed on fish. Manta ray viewing is best May–October, even though these sea creatures live along the coast all year long. The Sheraton is a real winner, the only five-star hotel in the Keauhou-Kailua strip, and it intends to lure visitors looking for luxury at a less-than-luxury price.

Condominiums

Set kitty-corner to the Keauhou Shopping Center and backed up against the Kona Country Club Golf Course is the **Keauhou Resort** (78-7039 Kamehameha III Rd., 808/322-9122 or 800/367-5286, fax 808/322-9410, keauhouresort@konanet.net), a town house complex of low-rise units in a garden of bougainvillea and other tropical plants. One- and two-bedroom units have electric kitchens, washers and dryers, telephones, and color TV, and there are two pools on the property. Reasonable rates run around $100–120 a day for a one-bedroom garden unit to $120–160 for a two-bedroom ocean-view unit; five-night minimum stay.

The **Outrigger Kanaloa at Kona** (78-261 Manukai St., 808/322-9625 or 800/688-7444) is situated in a quiet upscale residential area away from traffic at the southern end of Kailua-Kona in Keauhou. The one- and two-bedroom units are enormous. Bigger isn't always better, but in this case it is. Each individually owned and decorated unit comes with a modern kitchen, two baths, a lanai with comfortable outdoor furniture, a wet bar, and a washer and dryer. Rates range from $250 for one-bedroom, fairway-view villas to $390 for two-bedroom units with loft on the ocean; the rooms can accommodate four and six people, respectively, at no extra charge. Two nights minimum. Many package rates and discounts are available. A security officer is on duty at all hours, and on the grounds you'll find three swimming pools and whirlpool spas, two lighted tennis courts for guest use only, gas barbecue grills, an activities desk with free morning coffee, and even a fine-dining restaurant and cocktail lounge overlooking the black rocky shore. The complex itself consists of some three dozen low-rise units that lie between the Kona Country Club and the water, and the grounds are finely landscaped. This is a place that feels like vacation. If you would like to escape the hustle and bustle but stay near the action, the Kanaloa at Kona is the place. It's a winner.

Vacation Rental Agencies

With the multitude of condos and rental houses along this coast, there are plenty of agencies to do the looking for you. It's often better the first time around to let one of the agencies find one to fit your needs and then look for something else for next time while you're on the island. Try one of the following for condominium units or rental homes.

Reservations for several hundred units in about 20 mostly economy and moderate condos and a handful of vacation homes along the coast in Kailua can be made through Hawaii Resort Management (808/329-3333 or 800/244-4752, www.konahawaii.com), which has its office at the Kona Islander Inn.

SunQuest Vacations (77-6435 Kuakini Hwy., 808/329-6438 or 800/367-5168 in the U.S., 800/800-5662 in Canada, fax 808/329-5480, www.sunquest-hawaii.com) manages over 200 units in some 30 condo properties in the Kona area, with nearly two dozen homes. By and large, these units are mid- to upper-range. They also arrange car rentals, tours, and activities. This company is one of the "big boys" and has a well-deserved good reputation.

Century 21 All Islands (75-5759 Kuakini Hwy., Suite 200, 808/326-2121 or 800/546-5662, fax 808/329-6768, www.hawaiimoves.com) handles mostly economy to midrange condo units in Kailua and Keauhou.

Property Network (75-5799 Ali'i Dr., 808/329-7977 or 800/358-7977, fax 808/329-1200, vacation@hawaii-kona.com, www.hawaii-kona.com) handles the full range of condos along the Kona Coast in about two dozen different economy to midrange properties plus a handful of homes.

For mostly upper-end condo units in the Keauhou area, try **Keauhou Property Management, Inc.** (76-6225 Kuakini Hwy., Ste. C-105, 808/326-9075 or 800/745-5662, fax 808/326-2055, kona@kpmco.com, www.konacondo.net).

Knutson and Associates (75-6082 Ali'i Dr., Ste. 8, 808/329-6311 or 800/800-6202, fax 808/326-2178, www.konahawaiirentals.com) manages midrange condo units and a few vacation homes mostly in the central Kona area.

With roughly 150 properties, of which about two dozen are homes, **West Hawaii Property Services, Inc.,** (78-6831 Ali'i Dr., Ste. 234A, 808/322-6696 or 800/799-5662, fax 808/324-0609, makereservations@konarentals.com, www.konarentals.com) has a good range of places from economy to deluxe.

A smaller company with about half condo units and half homes is **C. J. Kimberly Realtors** (75-5875 Kahakai Rd., 808/329-7000 or 888/780-7000, fax 808/329-5533, cjkimberly@aloha.net, www.cjkimberlyrealtors.com).

ATR Properties, Inc. (75-5660 Kopiko St., Ste. A4, 808/329-6020 or 888/311-6020, www.konacondo.com) handles many condo units in about two dozen properties, as well as a number of individual homes in Kona.

FOOD IN KAILUA

Local Style

Kimo's Family Buffet (808/329-1393, 7–10 A.M., 5:30–8 P.M., Sunday brunch 7:30 A.M.–1 P.M.), located in the heart of Kailua in the courtyard of Uncle Billy's Kona Bay Hotel, serves very reasonably priced breakfast and dinner buffets. The breakfast buffet runs $6.95, dinner buffet is $10.95, and a Sunday brunch is $6.95. These prices can't be beat, but don't expect a lavish layout or a gourmet production—just plenty of good local food.

In the Kopiko Plaza, along Palani Raod, you'll find several places to eat, including **Kona Mix Plate** (808/329-8104, open 10 A.M.–8 P.M. Mon.–Sat.), a no-frills counter restaurant serving standard Japanese, Korean, and local breakfasts, sandwiches, and plate lunches like teriyaki beef, *kalbi* ribs, loco moco, and shrimp platters, with most sandwiches under $6 and plate lunches for about $10. While not special, the food is plentiful and inexpensive, and there always seems to be a line at lunch—a good sign.

Fusion

Aki's Cafe (75-5699 Ali'i Dr., 808/329-0090), located across from the seawall, is a moderately priced Japanese/American restaurant offering breakfast, lunch, and dinner. Breakfast can be three-egg omelettes, an eggs Benedict scramble, pancakes, or a Japanese breakfast with eggs, miso soup, rice, and your choice of meat. Lunch can be California-roll sushi, fried noodles with chicken or shrimp, or curry with rice. The dinner menu offers marinated New York steak, chicken teriyaki, garlic pasta, and its well-known fish and chips. Aki's is a centrally located, simple restaurant that adds a nice touch to ordinary food.

Up in the Crossroads Shopping Center on Henry Street is **O's Bistro** (808/327-6565, 10 A.M.–9 P.M.), a wonderful gourmet bistro that serves meals at moderate prices. Don't be put off by the shopping center location—the food is great and the rich colorful decor, low light, and dark tile floor are conducive to a fine meal. O's serves standard breakfast items and bistro sandwiches and plates during the day and a fusion of East and West for dinner,

FISH FOR DINNER

Waters around the Big Island produce great quantities of excellent fresh fish. Unless you know the captain of a fishing boat or have good luck on a fishing tour, you'll probably have to get your fish from a fish market. Several around the island have good selections and reputations to match. Have a good look in the deli case for the many and varied fish, seafood, and seaweed preparations, many that you won't find elsewhere. Still, most visitors will get their fish experience at a restaurant.

Anyone who loves fresh fish and seafood has come to the right place. Island restaurants specialize in seafood, and it's available everywhere. Pound for pound, seafood is one of the best dining bargains on the Big Island. You'll find it served in every kind of restaurant. The following is a sampling of the best.

Mahimahi is an excellent eating fish, one of the most common, most popular, and least expensive on Hawai'i. It's referred to as Dorado or "dolphin fish" but is definitely a fish, not a mammal. The flesh of mahimahi is moderately firm, light, flaky, and moist. While different preparations are available, this mild-flavored fish is perhaps best seared, sautéed, baked, or broiled. You will find it served as a main course and as a patty in a fish sandwich. This fish is broadest at the head. When caught it's a dark olive color, but after a while the skin turns iridescent shades of blue, green, and yellow.

The ***a'u,*** a broadbill swordfish or marlin, is a true island delicacy. It's expensive even in Hawaii because the damn thing's so hard to catch. The meat is moist and light – truly superb – and the flavor is definitely pronounced. If it's offered on the menu, order it. It'll cost a bit more, but you won't be disappointed.

Ono means delicious in Hawaiian, so that should tip you off to the taste of this wahoo, or king mackerel. An open-ocean fish, *ono* is regarded as one of the finest eating fishes, and its mild, sweet meat lives up to its name. Its white, delicate, and lean flesh can be done in almost any preparation.

Ulua, a bottomfish and member of the jack crevalle family, has white flesh with a steak-like texture. Delicious when baked, sautéed, or broiled.

Opakapaka is a pink snapper, the most preferred of the bottomfish. It has light pink, clear, and firm flesh that has a delightfully delicate flavor. Whole fish with the head on are often baked or steamed; larger fillets can be baked, poached, or sautéed.

Cousin to the *opakapaka,* ***uku*** is a gray snapper that is a favorite with local people for its moderately firm and slightly flaky flesh. It can be prepared like its relative but is often steamed.

'Ahi, a yellowfin tuna with distinctive firm, pinkish meat, is a great favorite cooked or served raw in sushi bars but can be prepared in almost any way.

Two moderately firm, open-ocean fish that sometimes appear on menus are ***opah,*** or moonfish (as it's shape is nearly that round when seen from the side), and ***monchong.*** *Opah* is more moist and tender, while *monchong* is denser, but both have full flavor.

Moi is the Hawaiian word for "king," and this fish was traditionally considered the privilege of royalty. This fish has large eyes and a shark-like head. Considered one of the finest eating fishes in Hawaii, it's best during the autumn months. It doesn't often show up at restaurants, but try it when it does.

For the uninitiated, **sushi** is a finger-size block of sticky rice, topped with a slice of (usually) raw fish or other sea creature. A delicacy in Japan, it has become very popular and much appreciated in Hawaii as a fine food.

with such items as steamed island fish, crispy half of Peking duck, double cut lamb chops, and a variety of pasta and noodle dishes. Most lunch entrées cost under $14, dinners $14–25. Food here is a treat for the taste buds. O's is an excellent choice.

Thai

Orchid Thai Cuisine (74-5563 Kaiwi, Suite 27, 808/327-9437, 11 A.M.–9 P.M. Mon.–Fri.), located in a small strip mall in the old Kona industrial area, has a plain pedestrian ambience but better than average food. Here, you'll find all your usual favorite Thai dishes, like chicken *satay;* papaya salad; pad Thai noodles; red, green, and yellow curries; plus a host of other items. Most main dishes run under $10; takeout is available on all orders.

With a menu that's at least twice as long as you might expect to find, **Bangkok House** Thai restaurant (75-5626 Kuakini Hwy., 808/329-7764, 11 A.M.–3 P.M. and 5–9 P.M. Mon.–Fri., 5–9 P.M. Sat.–Sun.) serves plentiful food in a pleasing setting in the King Kamehameha Mall. Your choices include standard Thai fare, with soups, curries, rice, noodles, and vegetarian dishes, plus many surprises. Most entrées run $8–12, with specials a few dollars more. The lunch menu is a few bucks cheaper.

Italian

Basil's Pizzeria and Restaurante (75-5707 Ali'i Dr., 808/326-7836, 11 A.M.–9:30 P.M.) in downtown Kailua-Kona, is a place that makes its own pizza dough. Individual gourmet pizzas are $9.95–10.95, depending upon your choice of toppings; New York–style pizza, 14-inch and 16-inch, is $12.95–13.95. Besides pizza, Basil's offers soup of the day, various salads, fettucine primavera, shrimp marinara, eggplant parmigiana, chicken cacciatore, and an assortment of other fine Italian foods mostly for $8–16. Or you can order any number of sandwiches for under $8. Pizza by the slice is available 11 A.M.–5 P.M. only, and you can do takeout. If you don't care to come down, Basil's offers free delivery of any menu item in the Kailua area. So go ahead, recline on your condo lanai and call Basil's, and they'll be over *molto rapido.*

Greek

Cassandra's Greek Taverna (75-5669 Ali'i Dr., 808/334-1066, 11 A.M.–10 P.M.), on the second floor directly across from the Kona pier, is decorated in a predominantly blue and white motif reminiscent of the Greek Isles. Lunch is served until 4 P.M., with most items under $11. Dinner expands the lunch menu and includes such offerings as traditional appetizers like dolmades (grape leaves stuffed with meat and rice) and *keftedes* (pan-fried Greek meatballs), and savory entrées like a gyro plate, Greek-style baby-back pork ribs, shrimp *posidonian,* or souvlaki made with chicken, beef, or lamb. Prices are usually $15–28; there is a full bar. This is the place to come for eastern Mediterranean food and earthy, vibrant Greek music to stir the soul.

Mexican

Cool down with a frosty margarita and watch life go by as you perch on a stool at the upstairs location of **Pancho and Lefty's Cantina and Restaurante** (75-5719 Ali'i Dr., 808/326-2171, 8 A.M.–10 P.M.), kitty-corner across from Hulihe'e Palace. Poncho and Lefty's covers the whole gamut of fine Mexican foods with a dash of good old American thrown in to round out the menu. The menu selections begin with appetizers such as buffalo wings, skinny dippers (potatoes covered with bacon and cheese, and nachos. Full dinners include taco salad, enchiladas, and fajitas, while specials are enchiladas rancheros, *carne asada,* seafood Vera Cruz, or a tamale dinner. Most everything is in the $12–16 range, with some fajitas for two over $25. Put the food together with the late afternoon happy hour and you'll know that Pancho and Lefty's is a good-time place with satisfying food that's easy on the budget.

Looking over the Royal Kona Tennis Club toward the sea is **Tres Hombres** (75-5864 Walua Rd., 808/329-2173, 11:30 A.M.–9 P.M.), a Mexican steak and seafood restaurant with a strong island influence. Taquitos, tostadas, burritos, chiles rellenos, fajitas, and all the usual offerings are on the menu, as are steak, fresh fish, and seafood items. Lunch and dinner have roughly the same menu, with few items more than $18. Before dinner, stop at the bar for a cool one and watch the sunset. This is a good choice for Mexican.

More authentic Mexican food and flavor can be found at **Cactus Bar and Grill** (75-5711 Kuakini Hwy., 808/329-4686), at the corner of Hanama Place. You have to come for the food, not the views. It's open for lunch and dinner, with music and dancing on Sunday. Mexican music fills the restaurant while fans blow the air around. The short but adequate menu includes tacos, quesadillas, chiles rellenos, and carne asada—in short, all your favorites, plus a full bar. Chips and tangy homemade salsa are complimentary. The owner is from the Nayar Province, and the food reflects that area.

American and Seafood

Harbor House (808/326-4166, 11 A.M.–7 P.M. Mon.–Sat., 11 A.M.–5:30 P.M. Sun.) at the Honokohau Small Boat Harbor features one of Kona's longest bars. Harbor House is more or less an open-air pavilion, but it is actually quite picturesque as it overlooks the harbor. If you are interested in a charter fishing boat, this is the best place to come to spin a yarn with the local skippers who congregate here daily in the late afternoon. Over the bar hangs a gigantic 1,556-pound marlin, almost as big as the Budweiser sign. Strategically placed TVs make it a good sports bar, and the jukebox has a great selection of oldies and contemporary tunes. You can not only quaff a variety of draft beers here, you can order off the bill of fare for grilled bacon cheeseburgers with fries, shrimp and chips, crab-salad sandwiches, clam chowder, and the like. Harbor House is one of the truly *colorful* places in Kailua-Kona, and one of the best places to relax and have a hassle-free brew. It's also a place where the fish stories you tell might easily become exaggerated with the number of beers you drink.

The **Kona Brewing Company** (808/334-2739, www.konabrewingco.com, 11 A.M.–10 P.M. Sun.–Thurs. and 11 A.M.–11 P.M. Fri.–Sat.) has been creating quality beer since the mid-1990s and sponsors the annual Kona Brewers Festival in March. It produces nearly a dozen varieties from a light lager to a dark porter, perhaps the best known of which are Pacific Golden Ale, Fire Rock Pale Ale, and Longboard Lager, with additional seasonal brews. Bar beer is brewed on the premises at a rate of about 80 kegs a week, but retail bottled beer is brewed in California according to Kona Brewing Company's recipe. Free brewery tours and tastings are given weekdays at 10:30 A.M. and 3 P.M. (no need for a reservation), but if you miss the tour, stop by the brewpub anyway to try a beer or two. The café serves mostly handcrafted pizza, salads, and sandwiches—nothing elegant, but a good complement to the brew. This busy place is popular with both locals and visitors, so expect lots of people and plenty of noise. A seat at the bar gets you up close to all the action there, or you may choose a booth inside or a table out on the lanai where you can watch the sun go down as easily as the beer in your tall, cool glass. Periodic live music is performed, mostly on Sundays. Located behind Kona Business Center in the North Kona Shopping Center, Kona Brewpub is open for lunch and dinner daily.

Quinn's (75-5655A Palani, 808/329-3822, 11 A.M.–11 P.M.), located across from King Kamehameha's Kona Beach Hotel, is Kona's socially eclectic bar and grill where everyone from local bikers to pink-roasted tourists and tournament anglers are welcomed. It's also a roost for night owls who come here to munch and have a beer or mixed drink when everything else in town is closed. The inside bar is cozy, friendly, and sports-oriented. For lunch, a gigantic mound of shrimp and crab salad is wonderful. The fresh catch-of-the-day sandwiches with salad or charbroiled burgers are a deal. Fill up for under $10. Dinner entrées are juicy filet mignon, chicken stir-fry, and fresh catch sautéed or broiled. Main entrées are $19–23 and all include soup or dinner salad, vegetable, rice, and Quinn's home-fried potatoes. For the less hearty eater, reasonably priced specialties include tenderloin tips sautéed in brandy with onions, shrimp and chips, and fish and chips, all for less than $10.50.

One of several restaurants at the Coconut Marketplace is **Durty Jake's** (808/329-7366). Open all day, food here is easy and the atmosphere is casual. Breakfast brings eggs Benedict (or variations), griddle items, and omelettes; lunch is mostly burgers, sandwiches, and salads. Dinner gets a bit more sophisticated with choices like Thai fresh catch, fish and chips, steak and shrimp, fajitas, and pasta, and there are always dinner specials. A long list of *pu pu* are on the menu for those who don't care for a full meal. As it's on the sidewalk level looking out across the road to the water, Durty Jake's has plenty of walk-by traffic. There is happy hour daily, live music on the weekends, and other music every evening except Monday. While the kitchen closes at 10 P.M., the bar stays open until 2 A.M.

The Kona Inn Restaurant (808/329-4455, 11:30 A.M.–9:30 P.M.) at the Kona Inn Shopping Village is a lovely but lonely carryover from the venerable old Kona Inn. On entering, notice the marlin over the doorway and a huge piece of hung glass through which the sunset sometimes forms prismatic rainbows. The bar and dining area are richly appointed in native koa and made more elegant with a mixture of turn-of-the-20th-century wooden chairs, polished hardwood floors, and sturdy open-beamed ceilings. If you want to enjoy the view, try a cocktail and some of the *pu pu* served until closing. Lunch is reasonable at the café grill, serving mostly light foods, sandwiches, burgers, soups, and salads. Dinner is served from 5:30 P.M., reservations recommended. The menu is heavy on fish and meat but offers a few Asian stir-fry dishes and pastas. Expect dinner entrées to run $16–30. The Kona Inn Restaurant epitomizes Kona beachside dining, and the view is simply superb.

The **Kona Beach Restaurant** (808/329-2911) at King Kamehameha's Kona Beach Hotel is open daily for breakfast and dinner and is especially known for its Sunday champagne brunch served 9 A.M.–1 P.M., $29.95 for adults. The long tables are laden with fruit, vegetables, pasta salad, peel-and-eat shrimp, omelettes, waffles, hot entrées, fresh catch, sashimi, and desserts so sinful you'll be glad that someone's on their knees praying at Sunday services. Friday and Saturday nights are very special because of the prime rib and seafood buffet at $27.95, which brings hungry people from around the island. Served 6–10 A.M., the breakfast buffet for $13.95 is a deal, and there are children's prices for all meals. The Kona Beach Restaurant is sure to please. The restaurant itself is tasteful, but the best feature is an unobstructed view of the hotel's beach, especially fine at sunset.

Bakeries, Delis, Coffee, and Cafés

You can't get "hotter" than **Island Lava Java** (808/327-2161, 6 A.M.–10 P.M.), one of Kona's popular coffeehouse/restaurants, located in the Ali'i Sunset Plaza across from the seawall. Here, local people and tourists alike come to kick back, read the papers, and actually engage in the lost art of conversation. Sandwiches, soups, and salads are major menu items, with most under $8. Try the turkey and ham, a veggie burger, Polish dog, Greek wrap, chicken salad, or chips and salsa. Island Lava Java has a counter offering muffins, cookies, and other delectable sweets, root beer floats, Kona coolers made with tropical fruit sorbet, Italian sodas, ice cream, and bulk 100 percent Kona coffee by the pound. Reasonable Internet access is available.

Buns in the Sun (808/326-2774, 5 A.M.–4 P.M. weekdays, 5 A.M.–3 P.M. weekends) bakery, sandwich, and coffee shop is located in the back corner of the Lanihau Center. Buns not only sells fresh-brewed gourmet coffee, pastries, and bread, it also makes right-price American-standard and Hawaiian-style breakfasts, unique lunch sandwiches, tasty wraps, and more. If you're out and about, this is a good stop.

The **French Bakery** (74-5467 Kaiwi, #6, 808/326-2688, 5 A.M.–2 P.M. weekdays, 5 A.M.–1 P.M. Sat.), in the Old Kona Industrial Area, is a budget gourmet deli/restaurant where the food is great and the prices are low. Not only does it have the full range of pastries, breads, and other goodies you would expect, it has wonderful and inexpensive sandwiches and coffee.

Nearby is **Pot Beli Deli** (74-5543 Kaiwi, Suite A115, 808/329-9454, 7:30 A.M.–3 P.M. weekdays). The refrigerated deli case holds such things as chicken, ham, or tuna salad sandwiches, spinach pie, and bagels with cream cheese. The shelves hold all the condiments and extras you need for a terrific picnic lunch. You can get your order to go or eat at one of the few booths inside.

Hawaiian Awa Bar and Restaurant (808/327-1660) in the Coconut Grove Marketplace is the only bar in town selling organic fresh kava as well as *'awa* root and *noni* fruit products. Fresh kava goes for $3 a bowl, but the bar also has Yerba Mate, coffee, and juice and sells simple plate lunches for $10–16 and appetizers to have with your kava.

Sweet Treats

Palazzo Aikalima Gelato (808/327-338, 10:30 A.M.–9 P.M. weekdays, 10:30 A.M.–10 P.M. weekends) in the Kona Coast Shopping Center serves up sinfully rich gelato in all its intense fruit and dairy flavors, plus grilled panini and crepes. This is a great place for a quick, cool treat.

Fine Dining

At **Huggo's** restaurant (75-5828 Kahakai Rd., 808/329-1493, 11:30 A.M.–2:30 P.M. Mon.–Fri., 5:30–10 P.M. daily), next door to the Royal Kona Resort, it's difficult to concentrate on the food because the setting is so spectacular. If you were any closer to the sea, you'd be in it, and of course the sunsets are great. Because it's built on a pier, you can actually feel the floor rock. Lunch is reasonable, with tasties like Huggo's club, a pizza with your choice of toppings, or a classic Huggo's burger. The dinner menu is superb and starts with fresh sashimi and seafood chowder made from clams and fresh fish and seasoned with sherry, cream sauce, and butter. The best entrées come from the sea just outside the door and are priced daily at around $31. Also worth trying is shrimp scampi, spiny lobster tail, Huggo's teriyaki steak, and chicken with ginger-orange sauce. Huggo's has been in business for more than 35 years and is consistently outstanding. Enjoy free *pu pu* 4–6 P.M. Mon.–Fri. while sipping a cocktail as the red Kona sun dips into the azure sea. Huggo's is fine dining indoors. To its side is its more casual half, Huggo's on the Rocks, which does lunch, a late-lunch service, and dinner under umbrellas. There is a bar for drinks and evening entertainment every night in both halves.

Oui oui, Monsieur, but of course we have zee restaurant *Français.* It is **La Bourgogne French Restaurant** (77-6400 Nalani, Suite 101, 808/329-6711, 6–10 P.M. Tues.–Sat.), located at the corner of Nalani St., about three miles south of downtown Kailua-Kona along Route 11. For those who just can't live without escargot or real French onion soup, you've been saved. How much will it set you back? Plenty, *mon petit!* Cold and hot appetizers include *pâté du chef,* and escargots de Bourgogne, while scrumptious French onion soup or homemade lobster bisque will follow. For salads, order greens with local goat cheese or greens with mango and lobster. Titillating seafood and poultry entrées ($25–32) feature fresh catch of the day; Maine lobster braised with shallots, tomato, brandy, and cream; and roast duck breast with raspberries and pine nuts, and a slow-roasted rabbit. Meat courses ($27–32) include delectable roast rack of lamb with creamy mustard sauce, tenderloin of venison with sherry and pomegranate sauce, and osso bucco veal shank in red wine. Top off your gourmet meal with fresh, made-in-house desserts like crème brûlée or a lemon tartlet. This restaurant—small, somewhat out of the way, and in a fairly nondescript building—is definitely worth a visit for those who enjoy exceptional food and a memorable gastronomic experience. Definitely call for reservations, perhaps a couple of days in advance.

Jameson's By The Sea (77-6452 Ali'i Dr., 808/329-3195, 11 A.M.–2 P.M. weekdays,

5–9:30 P.M. nightly) is small and popular, so reservations are necessary for dinner. Jameson's makes a good attempt at elegance with high-backed wicker chairs, crystal everywhere, white linen table settings, and a back-lit fish tank in the entry. The sea foams white and crashes on the shore just outside the restaurant's open windows. The quality of food and service here is excellent. While there are other items on the menu, people come here for fish, and they are never disappointed. The lunch menu lists appetizers like sashimi, salmon pâté, and fried calamari, a variety of sandwiches, and cajun blackened ***'ahi.*** The dinner menu offers the same appetizers but adds fried calamari and crab-stuffed mushrooms. The dinner entrées range from fresh catches like *opakapaka, ono,* and mahimahi to baked stuffed shrimp and lobster tail. Other full meals include filet mignon with béarnaise sauce, ocean scallops, and shrimp curry with mango chutney, mostly $25–40. Save room for the assortment of homemade chiffon pies and other desserts.

Food Markets

KTA Super Stores (808/329-1677, 5 A.M.–midnight daily) are generally the cheapest markets in town and are located at the Kona Coast Shopping Center along Palani Road and at the Keauhou Shopping Center. They're well stocked with sundries; an excellent selection of Asian foods, fresh veggies, fish, and fruit; and a smattering of health food. The market also contains a full-service pharmacy.

You'll also find a **Sack 'n Save** supermarket (808/326-2729, 5 A.M.–midnight) in the Lanihau Center, and a **Safeway** (808/329-2207, open 24 hours a day) in the newer Crossroads Center up on Henry Street.

Kona Wine Market (75-5626 Kuakini Hwy., 808/329-9400, 9 A.M.–8 P.M. Mon.–Sat., 10 A.M.–6 P.M. Sunday, in the small King Kamehameha Mall, is the best wine shop on the Kona Coast. It features an impressive international selection of wine and a large cooler holds a fine selection of beer, both domestic and imported, and liquor. Store shelves also hold wonderful gourmet munchies like Indian chutney, Sicilian olives, mustards, dressings, marinades, smoked salmon, hearty cheeses, pasta imported from Italy, and locally produced packaged foods. Cigar smokers will also appreciate the humidor filled with fine cigars from around the world.

Kona Reef Liquor and Deli (808/326-5475, 6 A.M.–10 P.M. Mon.–Sat., 7 A.M.–8 P.M. Sun.) is located south of downtown at the Casa De Emdeko condominium. It's well stocked with drinks, packaged groceries, and alcoholic beverages at convenience-store prices, and the deli does simple food items.

Outdoor Markets

You'll find the **Kona Farmers Market** held 7 A.M.–3 P.M. every Wednesday, Friday, Saturday, and Sunday at the parking lot across from Hale Halawai County Park and Uncle Billy's Kona Hotel. A limited selection of locally grown fruits, flowers, and crafts, this market has many booths that sell nonfood items.

About two miles south of the pier on the *mauka* side of Ali'i Drive is the well-maintained outdoor **Ali'i Gardens Marketplace** (75-6129 Ali'i Dr., 808/334-1381, 9 A.M.–5 P.M. Wed.–Sun.). Vendors sell crafts, jewelry, and some island clothing and beachwear. There is a food stall, and sometimes someone will have produce and flowers.

Health Food Stores

Kona keeps you healthy with **Kona Natural Foods and Deli** (808/329-2296, 8:30 A.M.–9 P.M. Mon.–Sat., 8 A.M.–7 P.M. Sun., with the deli open only until 4 P.M.) in the Crossroads Shopping Center on Henry Street. Besides a good assortment of health foods, there are cosmetics, books, and dietary and athletic supplements. Vegetarians will like the ready-to-eat and inexpensive sandwiches, salads, soups, smoothies, and juices. Shelves are lined with teas, organic vitamins and herbs, and packaged foods. A cooler is filled with organic juices, cheeses, and soy milk. A refrigerator holds organic produce, while bins are filled with bulk grains. Overall it's a good store; there seems to be a greater emphasis on nutrition than natural organic foods.

FOOD IN KEAUHOU

Bakery and Café

If you're looking for doughnuts, pastries, sandwiches, or ice cream while at the Keauhou Shopping Center, head for **Daylight Donuts and Deli** (808/324-1833; 6 A.M.–8 P.M.).

Peaberry & Galette (808/322-6020, open 9:30 A.M. daily, until 8 P.M. Mon.–Thurs., 10 P.M. Fri.–Sat., and 6 P.M. Sun.) in the Keauhou Shopping Center near the cinema offers a trendy and tasty menu of crepes, dessert crepes, sandwiches, quiche, pastries, and a variety of coffee, tea, chai, and Italian sodas in a shop of contemporary decor.

Italian

Rocky's (808/322-3223, 11 A.M.–9 P.M. daily), at the Keauhou Shopping Center, not only serves pizza ($11–27), but also a variety of Italian pasta and meat dishes, barbecued chicken, ribs, sandwiches, and salads that mostly run under $17. This is a friendly, family-style place that does takeout.

Japanese

A new addition to the Keauhou Shopping Center food options and a sign that even quality food is available at a mall is **Kenichi Pacifico** (808/322-6400, 11:30 A.M.–1:30 P.M. Mon.–Fri., 5–9:30 P.M. nightly), where master chef and owner Kenichi Marada creates a fusion of Japanese and Pacific Rim cuisine. Kenichi has a full-service sushi bar and its tempura has become well known. Some highlights from the menu, aside from the many sushi, sashimi, and tempura options, are duck confit, pan-roasted mahimahi, bamboo salmon, and New York steak, with most entrées $19–29. Save room for the signature dessert, molten cake (flourless cake with kona coffee chip ice cream and espresso crème anglaise), for $11. Kenichi Pacifico has patio seating as well as its pleasing inside dining room.

American

Located in the Keauhou Shopping Center is the breezy, easygoing **Drysdale's Too** restaurant (808/322-0070, 11 A.M.–11:30 P.M.), where you can get burgers, sandwiches, hot dogs, gyros, and any number of meat and meatless dishes, plus soups, salads, tropical drinks, and beer. A friendly, comfortable, indoor/outdoor place with sports theme decorations, full bar, and views of the ocean, it's somehow familiar, and you'll be happy that it won't cost an arm and a leg. Burgers and sandwiches run $6–10, while most entrées are less than $15.

If you're staying in Keauhou, rather than driving into town, reserve a seat at the casually elegant **Kama'aina Terrace Restaurant** (808/322-3441, 6:30–10:30 A.M. daily, 9:30 A.M.–12:30 P.M. for Sunday brunch, and 5:30–9 P.M. nightly), the main dining room at the Outrigger Keauhou Beach Resort. This is an open-air restaurant with a perfect view over the rocky shoreline to Kahalu'u Bay. Breakfast is standard American à la carte or buffet menu. Sunday brunch ($24.95) is special, as are the Friday night prime rib and seafood buffet ($29.95) and Saturday lobster night ($19.95). While the restaurant is open for breakfast, it's perhaps best in the evening. For an island-style dinner entrée, choose from such items as chili-crusted *'ahi,* seafood pasta, oven-roasted chicken, marinated rib eye steak, or a lamb chop, all in the $18–25 range.

The **Kalanikai Bar and Grill** (808/322-3441, 11 A.M.–3 P.M.) also at the Outrigger Keauhou Beach Resort is open at lunch for large-portion, good-value light fare under $10 that includes salads, wraps, and sandwiches, and serves cocktails and smoothies until 4 P.M.

Fine Dining

Located at the Outrigger Kanaloa at Kona condominium in Keauhou is **Edward's at Kanaloa** (808/322-1434, last seating is 8:30 P.M.). Edward's provides outdoor seating under a covered arbor at the oceanside, nearly on the rocks. This is a perfect spot for a sunset dinner: small, intimate, and romantic. The staff is attentive, there is an extensive wine list, and the bar can set you up with any drink that you wish. While American-style breakfasts and light lunches are served, the restaurant is best known for dinner. Start your evening meal with a baked oyster appetizer and move on to a ginger chicken orzo soup and salad. With most in the $24–35 range, the short menu has pork tenderloin with tarragon sauce, rack of lamb, veal chop au champignons, Cornish hen, mussels Provençal, and a variety of local fresh fish. Choosing dessert is a difficult task, as your choices might include praline chocolate mousse cake, crème brûlée, roasted Kea'au banana tiramisu, and the like. This is an excellent choice for a night out; reservations are strongly suggested as there is limited seating and a guest pass to the property is necessary.

The **Restaurant Kai** (808/322-3411, 6:30–10:30 A.M., 6–9:30 P.M.), located on the ground floor at the Sheraton Keauhou Bay Resort, is the apex of fine resort dining in the Keauhou area. Reservations are requested, and "upper end of casual" resort attire is expected. Morning brings an extensive breakfast buffet for $17.95 and an à la carte menu with lots of tropical fruits. In the evening, the soft lighting and floor-to-ceiling windows that open to the moonlight lend the restaurant a romantic atmosphere. The evening menu showcases Hawaiian regional cuisine with an emphasis on seafood. Entrées, in the $21–29 range, include roasted island chicken brined in saltwater, marinated grilled pork chops, steamed *moi,* kiawe-smoked Hawaiian sea bass, and grilled *'ahi* steak. The full salad bar accompanies each meal or can be ordered alone. Save room for dessert, as lilikoi crème brûlée, warm Hawaiian chocolate brownies, seven-layer cream cheese carrot cake, and others adorn the list.

INFORMATION AND SERVICES

Emergencies and Health

The **Kona Community Hospital** (79-1019 Haukapila St., 808/322-9311) is located in Kealakekua, about 10 miles south of central Kailua-Kona. Along with its many other departments, it offers 24-hour emergency care.

For minor emergencies and urgent care, try **Hualalai Urgent Care** (808/327-4357) at the Crossroads Medical Center on Henry Street.

For pharmacies, try **Longs Drugs** in Kailua (808/329-1632) and Keauhou (808/322-6627), **KTA Super Stores** in Keauhou (808/322-254110), and **Kmart** (808/326-1707) at the Makalapua Center.

Post Office

The Kailua-Kona post office is located at 74-5577 Palani Rd., at the Lanihau Center.

Banks

The **First Hawaiian Bank, Bank of Hawaii,** and the **American Savings Bank** all have branches and ATM machines at or next to the Lanihau Center on Palani Road. Bank of Hawaii also maintains a store office at the KTA Super Stores in Keauhou and at the Safeway supermarket in the Crossroads Shopping Center.

Library

The **Kailua-Kona Public Library** (75-140 Hualalai Rd., 808/327-4327) is up the road from Hale Halawai Park in downtown Kailua. Open 11 A.M.–7 P.M. Tues., 9 A.M.–5 P.M. Wed. and Thurs., 11 A.M.–5 P.M. Fri., and 9 A.M.–5 P.M. Sat.; closed Sunday and Monday.

Business Center

Kona Business Center (808/329-0006, 8:30 A.M.–5:30 P.M. Mon.–Fri.) is a full-service business, computer, Internet access, shipping, and printing shop at the North Kona Shopping Center.

Mailboxes, The Business Center (808/329-0038) in the Crossroads Shopping Center also does packing, shipping, copies, and Internet access.

The **UPS Store** (808/331-2285) in the Kopiko Plaza offers many of the same packing and shipping services.

Internet Access

Internet Island Lounge.com (808/329-8555, 8:30 A.M.–8 P.M. Mon.–Sat.) in King Kamehameha Mall offers high-speed internet access at $2.50 for 15 minutes or $8 for one hour, plus espresso, cappuccinos, lattes, and other drinks.

Ep!topia business and Internet center

(808/331-8999, 9 A.M.–1 P.M. and 5–8 P.M. Mon.–Fri., and 9 A.M.–1 P.M. Sat.) is located in the Royal Kona Resort main building lobby for basic Internet, fax, and copy service. Internet access runs $3.75 for 15 minutes.

Kona Business Center (808/329-0006, 8:30 A.M.–5:30 P.M. Mon.–Fri.) in the North Kona Shopping Center has Internet access at $2.75 for 15 minutes or $5.25 for 30 minutes.

Island Lava Java (75-5799 Ali'i Dr., 808/327-2161) is a coffee shop/deli that generally charges $2–3 for 15 minutes or $7–8 an hour.

Laundry

For a self-service laundry, try **Hele Mai Laundromat** (808/329-3494, 6 A.M.–10 P.M. daily) at the rear of the North Kona Shopping Center, or **Tyke's Laundromat** (14-5483 Kaiwi, Bay 135, 808/326-1515, 6:30 A.M.–9:30 P.M. daily) in the old Kona Industrial Area. Each has drop-off service.

GETTING AROUND

Motorcycles and Mopeds

DJ's Rentals (808/329-1700 or 800/993-4647, http://harleys.com, 7:30 A.M.–6 P.M. daily), located directly across from King Kamehameha's Hotel in Kailua-Kona in an outdoor booth, rents scooters and motorcycles. One-person scooters (capable of attaining 35 mph) run $25 half day or $45 daily. A Road King Classic rents for $150 a day or $95 half day; Big Twin Harleys run $145 daily or $90 half day; and smaller Harley-Davidsons and Honda cruisers run about 20 percent less. A half day is 7:30 A.M.–12:30 P.M. or 12:30–5:15 P.M. Drivers must be 16 years old for scooter rentals and 21 for the big machines.

Located up along Queen Ka'ahumanu Hwy., the **Big Island Harley-Davidson Rentals** (75-5615 Luhia St., 808/326-9887, www.bigislandHDrentals.com) is an authorized Harley rental center. Big Harleys here rent for $125 for an 8:30 A.M.–5:30 P.M. day or $155 for 24 hours. Half-day rates of $100 and two-day rates of $250 are also available. Each rental requires a $2,000 insurance deposit. Riders must be 23 years old, have a motorcycle endorsement on their driver's license, and wear eye protection. Helmets are available if you want them but are not required.

Shuttle

The once ever-running Ali'i Shuttle seems now to be a thing of the past, so low-cost, public transportation along Ali'i Drive is more problematic. However, the free Keauhou Shuttle, which once just ran between points in Keauhou, now makes some runs up Ali'i Drive into downtown Kailua, stopping at many of the well-known spots along the coast. Check with your hotel front desk for exact information. Within the Keauhou resort area, the Keauhou Shuttle runs on a periodic basis between the Keauhou hotels, Kahalu'u Beach, and Keauhou Shopping Center.

Hele-On Bus

Hawaii County operates the public Hele-On bus on several routes along this coast, in and around Hilo, and between the west and east sides of the island, yet buses run infrequently so are not very convenient for the traveler. There is no bus terminal in Kailua, yet most buses travel up and down the length of Ali'i Drive and make a stop at the Lanihau Center on their routes. For more information, contact the county Mass Transit Agency (808/961-8744, www.co.hawaii.hi.us/mass_transit/transit_main.htm).

One intra-Kona route connects Kailua and Keauhou to Captain Cook in South Kona, but only on weekdays. This schedule runs buses four times a day in each direction, two in the morning and two in the afternoon. Once a day Monday–Saturday, a bus runs all the way from Kealia, through Kailua, up to Waimea, and down the Hamakua Coast to Hilo. This bus leaves the Lanihau Center at 6:45 A.M. The return bus from Hilo leaves the Mo'oheau in Hilo at 1:30 P.M. and gets to the Lanihau Center at 4:25 P.M. Buses also run from Pahala and Ocean View in Ka'u to the South Kohala resorts, but these buses make few stops and do not drop down into Kailua.

As of October 2005, the county has instituted "no-fare" rides for all bus routes on the island, so all Hele-On bus transportation is free.

Taxis

Taxis will also do the trick for getting around town but can be quite expensive when going long distances. Several companies that operate in Kona are: C&C Taxi (808/329-6388), Kona Airport Taxi (808/329-7779), and Paradise Taxi (808/329-1234).

An alternative that works particularly well with groups is **Speedi Shuttle** (808/329-5433 or 877/521-2085, kona@speedishuttle.com, www.speedishuttle.com, 7 A.M.–10 P.M. daily), which runs door-to-door service between the Kona airport and your accommodation. Speedi Shuttle mainly services Kailua, Keauhou, and Kohala resort areas but will go farther for a price. It has a courtesy phone at the airport for your convenience. Rates for single travelers on a shared basis from the airport to downtown Kailua run about $19 or $27 as far south as the Sheraton Keauhou Bay Resort. Going north, shared rates are about $33 to the Waikoloa Beach Resort, $42 to the Mauna Lani Resort area, and $50 to the Mauna Kea Resort Rates. Farther afield, rates to Ocean View in the south run about $82 while it is roughly $60 up to Waimea. Private shuttle rates run about three times as much.

Holualoa

Holualoa (The Sledding Course) is an undisturbed mountain community perched high above the Kailua-Kona Coast with many of the island's most famous artists creating art in galleries that line up paintbrush to easel along its vintage main street. Prior to its transformation to an art community, Holualoa had another history. In days past, general stores, hotels, restaurants, bars, and pool halls lined its streets. Before Hawaii found its potential for tourism and started to develop its coastal areas, rural Hawaii was primarily agricultural, and the farms, and consequently most of the people, were located on the mountainsides. Large agricultural areas sustained working communities, and Holualoa was one such population center. While agriculture is still a big part of the local economy, it has been bolstered by tourism and the arts. Get there by taking the spur Route 182, known as **Hualalai Road,** off Route 11 (Queen Ka'ahumanu Hwy.) from Kailua-Kona, or by taking Route 180 (Mamalahoa Hwy.) from Honalo in the south or from Palani Junction in the north (where Route 190 and Route 180 meet). Nine-mile-long Route 180, a narrow mountain road that parallels Route 11, gives you an expansive view of the coastline below. Climbing Hualalai Road also affords glorious views of the coast. Notice the immediate contrast of the lush foliage against the scant vegetation of the lowland area. On the mountain side, bathed in tropical mists, are tall forest trees interspersed with banana, papaya, and mango trees. Flowering trees pulsating in the green canopy explode in vibrant reds, yellows, oranges, and purples. This is coffee country, so you'll see acres of coffee trees at numerous plantations and several coffee stands along Route 180, with more along Route 11 farther to the south. If you want to get away from the Kona heat and dryness, head up to the well-watered coolness of Holualoa at 1,400 feet in elevation. When leaving Holualoa for points south, stay on Route 180, the Mamalahoa Highway, a gorgeous road with great views from the heights. Going north, take Route 180 until it meets Route 190, which leads around the western flank of Mt. Hualalai and very gradually uphill to Waimea. For the coast, Kaiminani Drive cuts down through the residential area of Kalaoa just north of Kailua-Kona, or, farther north, take Waikoloa Road to the South Kohala coastal region. For more history on the Holualoa area and the stretch of Mamalahoa Highway between Palani Road and Kuakini Highway, pick up a copy of *A Driver's Guide to the Kona Heritage Corridor and Historic Holualoa.*

For the past one hundred years or so, a string of small dry goods and general merchandise stores dotted what are now Route 180 and Route 11 south of Honalo. Many of these stores were built by new immigrants to cater to the then-growing number of coffee workers and small-time farmers. Along this 20-mile stretch were some 90 stores. Most are now gone, some have been converted to other uses, but a few still function as they have for decades. Some are still operated by the original family, but most have different names, different owners, or different uses. Some of the best known are Komo Store, Kimura Lauhala Shop, Ushijima Store, Oshima Store, Kamigaki Market, and Fujihara Store. As you drive this road, stop in to get a sense of what these stores were like and consider what impact they had on the economy of the area. To help you along, pick up a copy of the *Guide to Kona Heritage Stores.*

SIGHTS

Holualoa Galleries

After you wind your way up Hualalai Road through this verdant jungle area, you suddenly enter the village at Mamalahoa Highway and are greeted by the **Kimura Lauhala Shop** (808/324-0053, 9 A.M.–5 P.M. weekdays, 9 A.M.–4 P.M. Sat.). The shop, still tended by the Kimura family, has been in existence since 1915. In the beginning, Kimura's was a general store, but it always sold *lau hala* and became famous for its hats, which local people would make to barter for groceries. Famous on, and later off, the island, only **Kona-side hats** have a distinctive pull-string that makes the hat larger or smaller. The older generation Kimuras, and most of the friends who helped manufacture the hats, are getting on in age and can no longer keep up with the demand. Many hatmakers have passed away, and few young people are interested in keeping the art alive. Kimura's still has handmade hats, but the stock is dwindling. All *lau hala* weavings are done in Kona, while some of the other gift items are brought in. Choose from authentic baskets, floor mats, handbags, slippers, and of course an assortment of the classic sun hats. Also for an authentic souvenir, look for a round basket with a strap, the original Kona coffee basket.

After Kimura's, follow the road for a minute or so to enter the actual village, where the library, post office, and a cross atop a white steeple welcome you to town. The tiny village, complete with its own elementary school, is well kept, with an obvious double helping of pride put into this artists' community by its citizens. Next to Holualoa Library is **Cinderella's** (808/322-2474, noon–5 P.M. Tues.–Sat.), an antiques and collectibles shop where you'll find furniture, art, knickknacks, jewelry, and much from estate sales.

At the upper end of town is the **Shelly Maudsley White Gallery** (808/322-5220, www.shellymaudsleywhite.com, 10 A.M.–5 P.M. Tues.–Sat.). The gallery displays the works of accomplished watercolorist Shelly Maudsley White. Tropical flora and fauna is the theme, and the hibiscus, exotic birds, plumeria-dotted forests, and hilarious yet pointed marine works confirm her philosophy that "there is more happening on this earth than what meets the eye." Also shown are meticulous and artistic fine woodwork by the local furniture maker Tai Lake.

Across the road you'll find a display of decorative gourds at **Ipu Hale** (808/322-9069, 10 A.M.–4 P.M. Tues.–Sat.). Once a common container for ancient Hawaiians, these gourds in everyday life have all but disappeared, but Ipu Hale works to put life back into crafting these practical containers.

A premier gallery in town, **Studio 7** (808/324-1335, open 11 A.M.–5 P.M. Tues.–Sat.) is owned and operated by Hiroki and Setsuko Morinoue. The shop showcases Setsuko and Hiroki's work, along with that of about two dozen other Big Island artists. Most of what's displayed is abstract in character, and much is wood, metal, and pottery. Hiroki works in many media but primarily does large watercolors or woodblock prints. Setsuko, Hiroki's wife, is a ceramicist and displays her work with other potters. Strolling from room to room in Studio 7 is like following a magic walkway where the art is displayed simply but elegantly, a legacy of the owners' very Japanese sense of style.

"He's a potter, I'm a painter," is the understatement uttered by Mary Lovein, the female half of the artistic husband-and-wife team of Mary and Matthew Lovein. They produce and display their lovely and inspired artwork at **Holualoa Gallery** (808/322-8484, www.lovein.com, 10 A.M.–5 P.M. Tues.–Sat.) Mary uses acrylics and airbrush to create large, bold, and bright seascapes and landscapes of Hawaii. Matthew specializes in *raku:* magnificent works of waist-high vases, classic Japanese-style ceramics glazed in deep rose, iridescent greens, crinkled gray, and deep periwinkle blue. Mary and Matthew collaborate on some of the larger pieces. Matt creates the vessel and, while it is still greenware, Mary paints its underglaze. Other artists featured in the shop are Cecilia Faith Black, who does delicate jewelry; Patricia Van Asperen-Hume, who creates fused glassworks; Frances Dennis, who hand-paints romantic Hawaiian imagery on porcelain, and multimedia artist Charles Corda, who creates metal sculpture and acrylic images. Also displayed are works in ceramic, glass, wood, and carved Plexiglas; most of the inspiring works are done in a contemporary or modernist style.

Down and across the street is **Hawaii Color Fine Art** gallery (808/324-1590, 10 A.M.–4 P.M. Mon.–Fri.), which features impressionist paintings mostly by owners Darrell and Pat Hill.

Holualoa's original post office, toward the south end of the community, houses both **Hale O Kula Goldsmith Gallery** (808/324-1688) and the **Holualoa Ukulele Gallery** (808/324-4100, 10:30 A.M.–4:30 P.M. Tues.–Sat.). Sam, the goldsmith, doesn't need much room, so he has the back. He works mostly in gold, silver, and precious stones; he also creates ceramics and bronze sculptures...very, very small sculptures. As he does mostly commission work, his shop is only open by appointment, but he does display a few other island jewelers' works outside his door. Sam also owns the ukulele gallery and displays and sells these fine musical instruments that he has made. If you're at all interested in this island instrument, stop in and talk with Sam.

Around back are the **L. Capell Fine Arts** (808/937-8893, 11 A.M.–4 P.M. Tues.–Sat.), where you are treated to original works by the owner—*plein air* oil paintings of tropical scenes, some of contemporary style, and multiple-block, wood block prints, and **Dovetail Gallery** (808/322-4046, 10 A.M.–4 P.M. Tues.–Sat.) which displays and sells wonderfully designed and intriguing woodwork and furniture.

A side road, easily spotted along Holualoa's main street, leads you up to **Koyasan Daishiji Shingon,** a Japanese Buddhist mission with distinctive red-orange buildings and a stone-lantern lined entrance that was a century old in 2002. The mission is basic, simple, and unpretentious, combining Japanese Buddhism with a Hawaiian air. The roof has the distinctive shape of a temple, but unlike those found in Japan, which are fashioned from wood, this is corrugated iron. Getting to the temple takes only a few minutes, and coming back down the road rewards you with an inspiring vista of Kona and the sea.

Note: Keep in mind that it is customary for most of the galleries to be *closed on Monday.*

Coffee Plantation and Outlets

Holualoa and the mountainside south of here is prime coffee-growing area. Literally hundreds of small farms produce beans to be turned into America's most favorite drink. The farms in this region produce about one third of the state's total coffee production, and there are several mills along the strip that process the beans. Everyone knows Kona coffee, and those who drink this black brew hold it in high esteem for its fine character. Every year in November, the Kona Coffee Cultural Festival is

KONA COFFEE

A coffee belt runs like a band through Kona. Generally speaking, it's a swath of mountainside 800-1,400 feet in elevation, about two miles inland from the coast, from one to two miles wide, and perhaps 25 miles long. In this warm upland region, watered by cool morning mists and rains, warmed by the afternoon sun, and cooled by evening breezes, coffee trees have an ideal climate in which to grow. Within this band, about 2,500 acres are planted in coffee, producing about 2.5 million pounds of the beans, which amounts to about one-third of the state's production. Most coffee estates here are small, in the 3-20 acre range, and there are about 600 individual growers. Kona has been known for decades as a region that produces exceptional coffee. Until a few short years ago, it was the only area in the state (and country) that grew coffee. Now, farms on each of the main Hawaiian Islands also produce the bean.

While coffee was introduced to Hawaii in the early 1800 and grown first on O'ahu, it wasn't until about 1840 that it began to be grown commercially, mostly by large plantation owners on the Big Island. For economic and market-driven reasons, by the 1880s most of these large plantations were divided into small five- to 10-acre farms, many of which were tended by tenant farmers, many of whom were newly arrived Portuguese immigrants. In the early 1900s, when the Portuguese began to move on to other businesses, the Japanese took over and expanded the farms and the coffee-growing acreage. With greater stability in the coffee market, many others have gotten into the business but the farms remain relatively small.

PURESTOCK

Arabica coffee trees are grown in Kona. Trees will produce beans at a young age and keep producing until at least 80 years old if properly tended. Newly formed, coffee "cherries" are green. Most contain two flat beans, but a small portion have single, more or less round beans called peaberries. When the cherries ripen they turn red. Kona coffee beans are picked by hand – a tough and tedious job, but one that produces quality fruits. Harvest generally takes place for the five months from September through January, with the lower elevation fields starting earlier and the higher elevation fields ending later. After picking, the beans are brought to the mill to be processed. The first step is wet milling, where the outer covering is removed and the slimy inner liquid released. The beans are then rinsed and dried to a specific moisture content, and the silver skin-like "parchment" covering is taken off. Beans are then separated according to their shape and size by a shaker, graded by quality and substance, bagged, and weighed before they are certified for bulk shipping. Roasting is another matter. Most roasting is done either the traditional way in a drum roaster or by a newer hot air method. Various roasts include light, medium, and dark; the result is determined primarily by the temperature, while the length of roasting time is less of a factor. After waiting a few hours for carbon dioxide to off-gas, roasted coffee is packaged. Roughly seven pounds of hand-picked coffee cherries are required to make one pound of roasted coffee.

About a dozen Kona coffee plantations are open for year-round visitation of their property and mills. A few are listed in the text; others have signs along the road you will see as you drive through this region. To help you on your way, pick up a copy of the *Kona Coffee Country Driving Tour* brochure, put out by the Kona Coffee Cultural Festival.

coffee mill

held to celebrate coffee, the importance this agricultural crop has had on the region for some 175 years, and the people of the area who make it possible.

One mile south of Kimura's is the **Holualoa Kona Coffee Company** plantation and mill (77-6261 Mamalahoa Hwy., 808/322-9937 or 800/334-0348, www.konalea.com, 7:30 A.M.–4 P.M. weekdays). This mill is open to visitors for a free tour of the milling and roasting process and coffee tasting. If you haven't ever been introduced to how coffee gets from tree to cup, this would be a good opportunity to discover how it's done. Although a small operation, this mill handles coffee beans from dozens of area farmers. A retail shop on-site sells estate coffee; it can also be ordered by mail.

In this upland area, other coffee producers that have retail shops are UCC Hawaii (www.ucc-hawaii.com), which has a stand a couple of miles north of the village; Ferrari (www.ferraricoffee.com), with an outlet shop in the village of Holualoa; and Kona Blue Sky Coffee (www.konablueskycoffee.com), situated along Hualalai Road just below Mamalahoa Highway. Blue Sky also offers tours of its mill weekdays and Saturdays.

ACCOMMODATIONS

Under $50

The shocking pink **Kona Hotel** (808/324-1155) along Holualoa's main street primarily rents its 11 units to local people who spend the workweek in Kailua-Kona's seaside resorts and then go home on weekends. They are more than happy, however, to rent to any visitor passing through and are a particular favorite with Europeans. The Inaba family opened the hotel in 1926, and it is still owned and operated by Goro Inaba and his wife Yayoko, who will greet you at the front desk upon arrival. A clean room with bare wooden floors, a bed and dresser, no phone or television in the room, and shared baths down the hall goes for $25 single, $30 double, and $35 with twin beds. Call ahead for reservations. No meals are served, but Mrs. Inaba will make coffee in the morning if you wish. The hotel is simple, clean, and safe, and while not stupendous, the view from the back rooms is more than worth the price.

Bed-and-Breakfast

A wooden jewel box nestled in velvet greenery waits to be opened as it rests on the edge of Holualoa high above the wide, rippling, cerulean Pacific. **The Holualoa Inn Bed and Breakfast** (76-5932 Mamalahoa Hwy., P.O. Box 222, Holualoa, HI 96725, 808/324-1121 or 800/392-1812, fax 808/322-2472, inn@aloha.net, www.holualoainn.com) was the retirement home of Thurston Twigg-Smith, CEO of the *Honolulu Advertiser* and member of an old *kama'aina* family. Twigg-Smith built the original home in 1978, but, tragically, it burned to the ground. Undaunted, he rebuilt, exactly duplicating the original. After living here a few years Twigg-Smith decided it was too quiet and peaceful and went back to live in Honolulu. In 1987 it was converted into a bed-and-breakfast. The home is a marvel of taste and charm—light, airy, and open. Top to bottom, it is the natural burnished red of cedar and eucalyptus. Here the Hawaiian tradition of removing your shoes upon entering a home is made a pleasure with cool, smooth eucalyptus floors. The front lanai is pure relaxation, and stained glass puncturing the walls here and there creates swirls of rainbow light. A pool table holds king's court in the commodious games room, as doors open to a casual yet elegant sitting room where breakfast is served. A back staircase leads to a gazebo, floored with tile and brazenly open to the elements, while the back lanai is encircled by a roof made of copper. From here, Kailua-Kona glows with the imaginative mistiness of an impressionist painting, and, closer by, 50 acres are dotted with coffee trees and cattle raised by the family. Just below is the inn's swimming pool, tiled in blue with a torch ginger motif, and off to the side is the hot tub. The six island-theme rooms, each with private bathroom and superb views of the coast, run $195–265, including breakfast, and all differ in size and decor. There is a two-night minimum and discounts for stays longer than seven days. No preteen children, please. Some years back, Twigg-Smith was offered $7 million for the home. Much to our benefit, he declined. This is a gem.

FOOD

The enticing aroma of rich coffee has been wafting on the breeze in this mountain community ever since the **Holuakoa Cafe** (808/322-2233, 6:30 A.M.–3 P.M. Mon.–Fri.) opened its doors in 1992. Just up the hill from the Kona Hotel, the café serves wonderful coffee, juices, and herbal teas, as well as salads, sandwiches, and smoothies. The café also serves as a revolving art gallery for local artists and displays a few boutique, souvenir, and craft items. You can sit inside at a table or enjoy your coffee and pastry alfresco on the veranda, from where the two-block metropolis of Holualoa sprawls at your feet.

In the center of town is **Paul's Place** (808/324-4702, 7 A.M.–8 P.M. weekdays, 8 A.M.–8 P.M. weekends), a reasonably well-stocked country grocery store with an ATM.

South Kona

Kailua-Kona's Ali'i Drive eventually dead-ends in Keauhou. Before it does, King Kamehameha III Road turns up the mountainside and joins Route 11, which in its central section is called the Kuakini Highway. This road, heading south, quickly passes the towns of **Honalo, Kainaliu, Kealakekua,** and **Captain Cook,** and farther on whisks through the smaller communities of **Honaunau, Keokea,** and **Kealia.** These mountainside communities lie along a 10-mile strip of Route 11, and if it weren't for the road signs, it would be difficult for the itinerant traveler to know where one village ends and the next begins. You'll have ample opportunity to stop along the way for gas, food, or sightseeing. These towns have some terrific restaurants, fine bed-and-breakfast accommodations, specialty shops, and unique boutiques. If you are up for some off-the-beaten-track sightseeing, you won't be disappointed. At Captain Cook, you can dip down to the coast and visit Kealakekua Bay, or continue south to **Pu'uhonua O Honaunau,** a reconstructed temple of refuge—the best in the state. Farther south still, little-traveled side roads take you to the sleepy seaside villages of **Ho'okena** and **Miloli'i,** where an older, slower lifestyle is still the norm.

HONALO AND KAINALIU

This dot on the map is at the junction of Routes 11 and 180. Not much changes here, and the town is primarily known for the red and white **Dai Fukuji Soto Mission** Buddhist temple at the beginning of town. This temple is open during the day for those who care for a

© ROBERT NILSEN

Honalo's Dai Fukuji Soto Mission

look. Inside are two ornate altars, one enshrining Shakyamuni, the Historical Buddha, and the other, Kwan Yin, the Bodhisattva of Compassion. Feel free to meditate or to take photos but please remember to remove your shoes before entry. A Sunday morning service and various other services throughout the week are open to anyone who desires to attend.

A short distance down a side road is the older **St. Paul's Catholic Church** (1864). Also up the way, again on the ocean side of the highway, is **Lanakila Congregational Church,** erected in 1867.

Kainaliu is larger and more of a town, with a choice of shopping, restaurants, and a theater. It's just a mile or less up the road from Honalo, and it seems as if these two communities mesh into one.

One of the coffee mills in the area, **Capt. Cook Coffee Co.** (808/322-3501) does roasting and offers free tastings at its dry mill facility in Kainaliu. Look for the big red building on the mountain side of the highway.

Entertainment

The **Aloha Theater** (808/322-2323, www.alohatheatre.com) in Kainaliu hosts productions of the local, amateur repertory company, Aloha Performing Arts Company, which puts on about six plays per year that run for about three weeks each. Check the local newspaper or HVB office, or look for posters here and there around town. The theater periodically hosts other types of stage performances, live music, dance, and art films, and is a venue for the Hawaii International Film Festival in November. Show times and ticket prices differ for all performances in this completely refurbished and well-appointed theater (built 1929–32).

Shopping

There is not much in the way of shopping in Honalo except for a gas station and kayak shop. You'll have much better luck in Kainaliu.

The **Blue Ginger Gallery** (808/322-3898, 9 A.M.–5 P.M. Mon.–Sat.) showcases the art of owners Jill and David Bever, as well as over 100 artists' works from all over the island. David creates art pieces in stained glass, fused glass, and wood. Jill paints on silk, creating fantasy works in strong primary colors. Using her creations as base art, she then designs one-of-a-kind clothing items that can be worn as living art pieces. The small but well-appointed shop brims with paintings, ceramics, sculptures, woodwork, fiber art, and jewelry. As a complement to the local artwork, about half the gallery holds imported Asian art and craft items, including Polynesian masks, carved elephants, Buddha heads, and batiks from Indonesia. The Blue Ginger Gallery is a perfect place to find a memorable souvenir of Hawaii.

A wonderful assemblage of paintings, line drawings, and other forms of art are on display at **Lavender Moon Gallery** (808/324-7708). Along with the works of owners Patricia and Dux Missler, you'll find the captivating pencil sketches of Kathy Long, the contemporary paintings of Megan Long (Kathy's daughter), and the renderings of Hawaiian children by Mary Koski (Kathy's mother).

In the Basque Building across from Kimura's is the **Eternal Wave Gallery** (808/322-3203), which displays pottery, prints, photography, jewelry, candles, woodwork, and more, done mostly by local artists. An intriguing collection, it has perhaps more common quality pieces than the works in other galleries in town.

Paradise Found (808/332-2111) has "clothing for the adventurous." This shop is an eclectic mix of women's and men's clothing, alohawear, accessories, and some furniture and art objects. All are new, but some are reproduction pieces of masterful older designs.

Surfin' Ass Coffee Company (808/324-7733, 7 A.M.–9 P.M. daily), is a coffee and espresso bar (with chocolate-covered or salted macadamia nuts—"donkey balls" and "donkey nuts," respectively) where they roast their own beans on the premises in a Royal No. 4 Roaster manufactured in 1910, probably the last operational roaster of its type left in the state. This was the original Bad Ass coffee shop. From here, the revolution spread—and the name changed.

Oshima Dry Goods (808/322-3885) is well stocked with drugs, fishing supplies, magazines, a huge collection of fabric, and some wines and spirits. Also in town is **Kimura Market** a general grocery store with sundries, and **H. Kimura Store** (808/322-3771) for bolts of fabric. Oshima's and H. Kimura's are two of the stores along this road that still function pretty much the same as they have for decades.

As you are leaving the built-up area of Kainaliu, look for the **Island Books** (79-7360 Mamalahoa Hwy., 808/322-2006, 9 A.M.–7 P.M. daily—usually) sign reading Used Books Bought and Sold. This shop stocks a general mix of titles, but history, geography, Hawaiiana, and a good selection of used travel books are the specialty. Here's a great place to purchase some casual reading material and save money at the same time.

At the south end of town in the Mango Court is **Hemp and Glass** (9 A.M.–7 P.M.), a shop selling hemp products: clothing, oils, magazines, posters, pipes, and other items. All clothing and accessories are imported due to the U.S. prohibition on the production of hemp fiber. Stop in to have a look at the items for sale and to learn about this, one of Mother Nature's most versatile and useful natural gifts.

Recreation

Located across from Teshima's Restaurant in Honalo, **Aloha Kayak Co.** (808/322-2868 or 877/322-1444, www.alohakayak.com) handles rental kayaks and runs kayak tours. Daily rental rates are $28 single and $50 double. Its four-hour tour for $75 per person runs out of Keauhou Bay and on it you explore a sea cave, snorkel, and are able to jump from a cliff into the ocean. The longer six-hour trip for $129 per person goes for a day of adventure at Kealakekua Bay to the best snorkeling spot on the island.

Food

Teshima's Restaurant (79-7291 Mamalahoa Hwy., 808/322-9140, 6:30 A.M.–1:45 P.M., 5–9 P.M.) is one of the old-style eateries along the highway. Here, in unpretentious surroundings, you can enjoy a full American, Hawaiian, or Japanese lunch for about $7 and dinner for $10–15. A lunch specialty is the bento box lunch that includes rice balls, luncheon meat, fried fish, teriyaki beef, kamaboku (fish cake), and Japanese roll. Evening meals include fresh catch, tempura, donburi, udon noodles, and a teishoku full meal. Since 1940, Teshima's has been a mom-and-pop (and kids) family restaurant. If you're interested in a good square meal, you can't go wrong here. No credit cards.

Aloha Angel Café (79-7384 Mamalahoa Hwy., 808/322-3383), 7:30 A.M.–2:30 P.M. and 5–8 P.M. daily, until 9 P.M. on event nights) is part of the lobby of the Aloha Theater in Kainaliu. The enormous yet economical breakfasts feature locally grown eggs, cornbread, and potatoes. Lunchtime sandwiches, around $10, are super-stuffed with varied morsels, from turkey and avocado to fresh island fish. There are also a variety of soups, salads, and wraps. For a snack choose from an assortment of homemade baked goods that you can enjoy with an espresso or cappuccino. Order at the counter and then sit on the lanai that overlooks a bucolic scene. There is table service for dinner inside the dining room to the side. The dinner menu changes periodically, and there is a special menu on event nights, but entrées may include items like taro-crusted fresh *'ahi,* Cajun spice chicken, coconut lemongrass yellow curry, and linguine pasta with shrimp, all of which run $15–23. This is an excellent place for food any time of the day and gets high marks from residents and visitors alike.

People in the know give the **Ke'ei Cafe** (808/322-9992, 10:30 A.M.–2 P.M. Mon.–Fri., 5–9 P.M. Tues.–Sat.) rave reviews. The Ke'ei Cafe has made a name for itself and is very popular, so you'll need a dinner reservation. Bring cash, too, as no credit cards are accepted. Set above the highway, the café's new building has high ceilings with fans, warm colors, and large windows to let in the breezes. Lunch is mostly salads, wraps, and sandwiches, most for under $12, but the dinners are more elegant and sophisticated. In fact, this is the last gourmet, Hawaiian Regional restaurant going south until you reach Volcano Village. Start dinner with a Greek salad or Brazilian seafood chowder. Most entrées run $13–20 and include seafood pasta with heady herbs and spices, roast half chicken in white wine peppercorn gravy, pan-seared rib eye steak, and fresh catch prepared with red Thai curry or pan seared in lemon-caper butter. Follow this with a coconut flan or tropical bread pudding dessert. Yum! You will find entrée and dessert specials every evening. While the menu is short, the preparation is superb and your meal should be memorable.

At the south end of Kainaliu in the Mango Court is **Evie's Natural Foods** (808/322-0739, open 9 A.M.–9 P.M. weekdays, 9 A.M.–5 P.M. weekends) Evie's stocks plenty of coffee, herbs, supplements, some fresh produce, packaged natural foods, and an assortment of bulk grains, and also has "grab and go" items in a cooler. This full-range health food store serves freshly made, organic, and wholesome sandwiches, soups, and other delicious foods at its deli and now serves wholesome, organic entrées on weekday evenings. There's a small eating area out back.

The **Standard Bakery** (808/322-3688) in Kainaliu has breads, baked goods, and wonderful hot *malasadas* to take for the road.

Services

Located behind Sandy's Restaurant in Kainaliu is **KC Washerette** (808/322-2929, 5:30 A.M.–9 P.M. daily), a well-run, full-service laundry with attendant and drop-off service. This is the only launderette in the area.

KEALAKEKUA

Kealakekua is one of the old established towns along the road, but it has a newer look with more modern buildings and small subdivisions. In town are a post office and library, a small shopping center, gas station, several eateries, a few gift shops, and an antiques store. Just south of town on the road up to the schools is **Christ Church Episcopal,** established in 1867 as the first Episcopal church in the islands. Newer is the **Kona Hongwanji Mission.**

As coffee farms do in other areas of Kona, the **Greenwell Farm Coffee Mill** grows and

PURESTOCK

coffee for sale

roasts its own estate coffee. Located downhill from the Kona Historical Society Museum, the mill runs tours of its orchard and processing facility 8 A.M.–4 P.M. Mon.–Sat., and its retail stand is happy to sell half-pound, one-pound, and five-pound packages of its best roast.

Kona Historical Society Museum

The main building of the Kona Historical Society Museum was originally a general store built around 1875 by local landowner and businessman H. N. Greenwell using native stone and lime mortar made from burnt coral. Now on both the Hawaii and National Registers of Historic Places, the building served many uses, including the warehousing and packaging of sweet oranges raised by Greenwell, purported to be the largest, sweetest, and juiciest in the world. The museum (open 9 A.M.–3 P.M. weekdays, $2 donation for admission) is located 0.25 mile south of Kealakekua. The main artifact is the building itself, but inside, you will find a few antiques like a surrey and glassware, and the usual photographic exhibits with themes like coffee growing and ranching—part of the legacy of Kona. The basement of the building houses archives filled with birth and death records of local people, photographs both personal and official, home movies, books, and maps, most of which were donated by the families of Kona. The archives are open to the public by appointment only. To the rear is the Kona Historical Society office.

The **Kona Historical Society** (P.O. Box 398, Captain Cook, HI 96704, 808/323-3222, www.konahistorical.org) is a nonprofit organization whose main purpose is the preservation of Kona's history and the dissemination of historical information. Sometimes the society sponsors lectures and films, which are listed in the local newspapers. They also offer 4WD tours of the Kona area three times per year, usually in March, July, and November, and a historical boat tour in late January that takes you from Kailua-Kona south along the coast. There is no fixed schedule, but if you are in the area during those times of year, it would be well worth the trouble to contact the museum to find out if these excellent tours are being offered. A Captain Cook lecture tour at Kealakekua Bay and an archaeological tour of Keauhou can also be arranged by appointment only, with a minimum of three people. However, walking tours of the historical district of Kailua are regularly scheduled at 9 A.M. and 11 A.M. Monday–Friday; a 24-hour advance reservation is required.

Another excellent tour is the walking tour conducted at the historic **D. Uchida Coffee Farm,** now listed on the National Register of Historic Places, but begun by Japanese immigrants in the early years of the 1900s. The Living History Farm guided tour (808/323-2006, on the hour 9 A.M.–1 P.M. weekdays, $15) takes you to a working farm with original authentic buildings, machinery, and live animals, and explains how the farm and its workers fit into the multiethnic Kona community. With groups of 12 or more, costumed interpreters will perform chores typical of such a farm from that era, so the tour is a representation of what daily life was like when the farm operated from 1925 to 1945. Look for it at mile marker 110.

Although not up and running yet, future plans of the historical society call for the reconstruction of a ranching homestead and the establishment of a living history museum there.

Amy B. H. Greenwell Ethnobotanical Garden

You can not only smell the flowers but feel the history of the region at the Amy B. H. Greenwell Ethnobotanical Garden (808/323-3318, www.bishopmuseum.org/exhibits/greenwell/greenwell.html, suggested donation $4), along Route 11 south of Kealakekua at mile marker 110. The garden is open 8:30 A.M.–5 P.M. Monday–Friday, with guided tours for $5 on Wednesday and Friday at 1 P.M. and free on the second Saturday of every month at 10 A.M. Greenwell died in 1974 and left her lands to the Bishop Museum, which then opened a 12-acre interpretive ethnobotanical garden, planting it with indigenous Hawaiian plants, Polynesian introduced plants, and Hawaiian medicinal plants. At the beginning of the walking path through the lower section of the garden, take a fact sheet that describes the garden, complete with self-guided tour map. Represented here are four zones: coastal, agricultural, lowland dry forest, and upland wet forest. Within these sections are plants typical of the zone. The garden contains remnants of the Kona field system, dating from precontact times when a broad network of stone ridges delineated intensive agriculture fields that were spread over some 30 square miles and sustained a large population.

Shopping

The Grass Shack (808/323-2877, 9 A.M.–5 P.M. Mon.–Sat., sometimes noon–5 P.M. Sunday), a.k.a. The Little Grass Shack, is an institution in Kealakekua, owned and operated by *kama'aina* Lish Jens and located at the intersection of the highway and Konawaena Road. This tiny shop looks like a tourist trap, but don't let that stop you from going in and finding some authentic souvenirs, most of which come from the area or from Jens's many years of traveling and collecting. The items *not* from Hawaii are clearly marked so. But the price is right. There are plenty of trinkets and souvenir items, as well as a fine assortment of artistic pieces, especially wooden bowls, hula items, exquisite Ni'ihau shellwork, and Hawaiian masks. A shop specialty is items made from curly koa. Each piece is signed with the craftsperson's name and the type of wood used. Others are made from Norfolk pine and *milo.* A showcase holds jewelry and tapa cloth imported from Fiji, and a rack holds tapes of classic Hawaiian musicians from the 1940s and 1950s. The shop is famous for its distinctive *lau hala* hats, the best hat for the tropics.

Next door to the Peacock House Chinese Restaurant is the **Collectible Shop** (open 10 A.M.–5 P.M. Mon.–Sat., from 11 A.M. on Sun.), with its large and varied collection of antiques and Hawaiiana, as well as its Tropical ice cream counter.

Recreation

Horseback riding is available at **Kings' Trail Rides O'Kona** (808/323-2388, www.konacowboy.com), located along the highway at mile marker 111. From here, wranglers lead you down a Jeep and hiking trail to Kealakekua Bay and the Captain Cook monument. The four-hour trip includes two hours of riding followed by snorkeling in the bay (bring your swimsuit—change in the bushes) and a picnic lunch. The price is $135 per person weekdays and $150 on weekends, limited to six riders. No riders over 250 pounds or under age seven, please. The ride office doubles as a retail tack and gift shop and is open 7:30 A.M.–5 P.M. daily. There you can purchase koa boxes, plantation coffee, and Tropical Temptation chocolates like chocolate-covered coffee beans, along with cowboy items like spurs, western belts, and a full assortment of tack.

Kayakers should head to is **Kona Boys** kayak rental and tour outfit (79-7539 Mamalahoa

Hwy., 808/328-1234, www.konaboys.com), located just before Kealakekua. Rental kayaks run $27–32 single, $47–52 double, or a clear bottom craft for $79. Kona Boys offers morning guided tours of Kealakekua Bay for $135 per person and a sunset tour for $79. If you're just after rental snorkel gear, they have it for $6 a day. Surfboard rentals, surf lessons, and guided scuba shore dives are also available.

Food

The **Korner Pocket Bar and Grill** (808/322-2994, 11 A.M.–10 P.M. weekdays) is a family-oriented restaurant and friendly pool bar where you can get excellent food and drink at very reasonable prices. The Korner Pocket sits below the highway in the small shopping center on Haleki'i Street. Grill selections are a poolroom burger, fresh catch, or scrumptious bistro burger of grilled beef on crusty sourdough topped with fresh mushrooms sautéed in wine garlic sauce. Dinners are items like fresh catch, top sirloin, and its encore entrée, baby back ribs, mostly for under $15. The complete bar is well stocked with wines and spirits, or you can wash down your sandwich with an assortment of draft beers. The Pocket rocks with live music on weekends and hosts a pool tournament on Tuesdays. The Korner Pocket looks as ordinary as a Ford station wagon, both inside and out, but the food is surprisingly good.

Near the south end of town is the **Peacock House** Chinese restaurant (808/323-2366). Open Mon.–Sat. for lunch and dinner and Sunday for dinner only, this is a local eatery with a typically long list of menu selections with not much on the menu over $8. No MSG upon request.

On your way out of town going south, stop by **Chris' Bakery** (81-6596 Mamalahoa Hwy., 808/323-2444, 6 A.M.–1 P.M. Mon.–Fri.) and pick up a snack for the road. A variety of pastries are available here, but Chris' is best known for hot *malasadas,* made fresh daily. Don't come by too late, as they close early.

The full-service grocery store **Kamigaki Market** (808/323-3505) is open most days 7 A.M.–9 P.M. and from 8:30 A.M. on Sunday.

CAPTAIN COOK AND VICINITY

Captain Cook is the last of the big towns along this highway. You can get gas, food, and lodging here, and shop for some arts and crafts. Captain Cook is the gateway to the sights on the coast. In town is the Greenwell County Park with its numerous athletic fields, and next door is the county administration sub-office. Beyond this, the smaller towns are each but a few houses that create wide spots in the road.

If you're in the area in March, have a look at the yearly **Kona Stampede Rodeo** at the Honaunau Rodeo Grounds, one of the largest in the state, located at the big bend in the road going down to Pu'uhonua O Honaunau, and watch the local cowboys rope steers, mug calves, and ride bulls.

Coffee Mills and Candy Factory

South of Captain Cook, you can't help noticing the trim coffee bushes planted along the hillside. On the highway almost to Honaunau, you find the **Royal Kona Coffee Mill and Visitors Center** (83-5427 Mamalahoa Hwy., 808/328-2511, www.royalkonacoffee.com, open for self-guided tours 8 A.M.–5 P.M. daily) The tantalizing smell of roasting coffee and the lure of a "free cup" are more than enough stimulus to make you stop. Mark Twain did! The visitors center displays some old black-and-white prints of the way Kona coffee country used to be and some heavy machinery used in coffee processing. The most interesting item is a homemade husker built from an old automobile. More or less integrated is a small gift shop where you can pick up the usual souvenirs, but the real treats are gourmet honeys, jellies, jams, candies, and of course coffee. You can't beat the freshness of getting it right from the source. Refill anyone? Be sure to have a look at the mill while you are here, particularly during coffee processing season. You can witness the entire process from harvest to roast.

Other coffee farms in the area that also offer tours of their mills are: **Bayview Farm** (808/328-9658, www.bayviewfarmcoffees.com, 9 A.M.–5 P.M.), a half mile north of St. Benedict's Church along Painted Church Road;

and **UCC Hawaii** (808/328-5662, www.ucc-hawaii.com, 9 A.M.–5 P.M.), which has a mill and coffee outlet/gift shop on the way down to Napo'opo'o. UCC Hawaii offers tours and tastings throughout the day. Bayview Farm also has an outlet for its coffee, gifts, and craft items up on the Hawaiian Belt Road highway. **Kona Pacific Farmers Cooperative** (808/328-2411, www.kpfc.com) sells its coffee and other gift items to the public and holds a farmers market on Friday. There are numerous other small coffee farms with outlets and tasting rooms that also line the byways of this area. Look for them as you cruise through this region.

Is that sweet tooth of yours starting to crave a little attention? Stop for a visit to the **Kona Coast Macadamia Nut and Candy Factory** (808/328-8141, 8 A.M.–4 P.M. Mon.–Sat., 10:30–4 P.M. Sun.), near the intersection of the belt road and Middle Ke'ei Road, where you can slake the craving with roasted macadamia nuts, chocolate-covered nuts, and macadamia cookies and candy. For something not so sinful, go for the Kona coffee or other gift items.

Lion's Gate (84-0719 Mamalahoa Hwy., 808/328-2335 or 800/955-2332, fax 808/328-1123, www.coffeeofkona.com, 9 A.M.–5 P.M.), owned by Diane and Bill Shriner, offers free tours of their 10-acre working macadamia nut and Kona coffee farm. Samples of both are offered for sale but there is no hard sell. Only minutes from the Pu'uhonua O Honaunau National Historical Park turnoff on the highway, the house is down the long row of tall palm trees.

St. Benedict's Painted Church

Whether going to or coming from Pu'uhonua O Honaunau, make sure to take a short side trip off Route 160 to St. Benedict's Painted Church. Located on Painted Church Road, this small house of worship is fronted by latticework, and with its gothic-style belfry looks like a little castle. Inside, a Belgian priest, John Berchman Velghe, took house paint and, with a fair measure of talent and religious fervor, painted biblical scenes on the walls and tropical skies and palm fronds on the ceiling. Some panels and parts of others are left unfinished. His masterpiece is a painted illusion behind the altar that gives you the impression of being in the famous Spanish cathedral in Burgos. Father John was pastor here 1899–1904, during which time he did these paintings, similar to others that he did in small churches throughout Polynesia. Before leaving, visit the cemetery to see its petroglyphs and homemade pipe crosses, and make your way up past the stations of the cross to a statue that's a representation of the "Pieta" by Michelangelo.

© ROBERT NILSEN

interior of St. Benedict's Painted Church

Napo'opo'o

In the town of Captain Cook, Napo'opo'o Road branches off Route 11 and begins a roller-coaster ride down to the sea, where it ends at Kealakekua Bay. Many counterculture types once took up residence in semi-abandoned "coffee shacks" throughout this hard-pressed economic area, but the cheap, idyllic, and convenience-free life isn't as easy to arrange as it once was. The area has been "rediscovered." Near the bottom, you pass **Kahikolu Congregational Church** (1852), the burial site of Henry Opukaha'ia, a young native boy taken to New England, where he was educated and converted to Christianity. Through impassioned speeches begging for salvation for his pagan countrymen, he convinced the first Congregationalist missionaries to come to the islands in 1820.

Continue down Napo'opo'o Road to the once-thriving fishing village of Napo'opo'o (The Holes), now just a circle on the map with a few houses fronted by neat gardens. During much of the last century, Napo'opo'o was a thriving community and had an active port where commodities and animals were shipped. Now only remnants of the old pier remain. When Napo'opo'o Road nears the water, turn right for Kealakekua (Pathway of the God) Bay. At the end of this short road is **Kealakekua Bay State Historical Park,** near the parking lot with a new pavilion and bathrooms. The beach here is full of cobbles with a little sand strip along the water. Fronting the beach is Hikiau Heiau. Taking a side road around the south side of the bay will bring you to the more secluded **Manini Beach Park.**

Just south of Napo'opo'o, down a narrow and very rugged road is the sleepy seaside village of **Ke'ei.** This side trip ends at a canoe launch area and a cozy white-sand beach good in spots for swimming. The wide reef here is a fine snorkeling spot and a favorite of surfers. A channel to an underwater grotto has been sliced through the coral. On the shore are the remains of Kamaiko Heiau, where humans were once sacrificed. In 1782, on the flats beyond this village, the **Battle of Moku'ohai** was fought, the first battle in King Kamehameha I's struggle to consolidate power not only over the island of Hawai'i but eventually all the islands.

Kealakekua Bay

Kealakekua Bay has been known as a safe anchorage since long before the arrival of Captain Cook and still draws boats of all descriptions. The entire bay is a 315-acre **Marine Life Conservation District,** and it lives up to its title by being an excellent scuba and snorkeling site and an area that attracts spinner dolphins. Give the dolphins wide berth. Organized tours from Kailua-Kona often flood the area just off the Captain Cook monument with boats and divers, but the bay is vast and you can generally find your own secluded spot to enjoy the underwater show. The area between Napo'opo'o and Manini Beach, an area at the southern tip of the bay, is also excellent for coral formations, lava ledges, and fish. If you've just come for a quick dip or to enjoy the sunset, look for beautiful, yellow-tailed tropicbirds that frequent the bay.

Relax a minute and tune in all your sensors because you're in for a treat. The bay is not only a Marine Life Conservation District with top-notch snorkeling, but it drips with history. *Mauka,* at the small **Kealakekua Bay State Historical Park,** is the well-preserved **Hikiau Heiau,** dedicated to the god Lono, who had long been prophesied to return from the heavens to this very bay to usher in a "new order." Perhaps the soothsaying *kahuna* were a bit vague on the points of the new order, but it is undeniable that at this spot of initial contact between Europeans and Hawaiians, great changes occurred that radically altered the course of Hawaiian history.

The *heiau* lies at the base of a steep *pali* that forms a well-engineered wall. From the temple, priests had a panoramic view of the ocean to mark the approach of Lono's "floating island," heralded by tall white tapa banners. The *heiau* platform was meticulously backfilled with smooth, small stones; a series of stone footings, once the bases of grass and thatch houses used in the religious rites, is still very much intact. The *pali* above the bay is pocked with numerous burial caves that still hold the bones of the ancients.

Captain James Cook, leading his ships *Resolution* and *Discovery* under billowing white sails, entered the bay on the morning of January 17, 1778, during the height of the Makahiki Festival, and the awestruck natives were sure that Lono had returned. Immediately, traditional ways were challenged. Shortly after their arrival, an old crew member, William Watman, died, and Cook was invited to bury him and perform

This monument to Captain Cook sits on the site at which he was slain on the edge of Kealakekua Bay.

a Christian burial atop the *heiau.* This was, of course, the first Christian ceremony in the islands, and a plaque at the *heiau* entrance commemorates the event. On February 4, 1778, a few weeks after open-armed welcome, the goodwill camaraderie that had developed between the English voyagers and their island hosts turned sour, due to terrible cultural misunderstandings. The sad result was the death of Captain Cook. During a final conflict, this magnificent man, who had resolutely sailed and explored the greatest sea on earth, stood helplessly in knee-deep water, unable to swim to rescue boats sent from his waiting ships. Hawaiians, provoked to a furious frenzy because of an unintentional insult, beat, stabbed, and clubbed the great captain and four of his mariners to death. A 27-foot obelisk of white marble erected to Cook's memory in 1874 "by some of his fellow countrymen" is at the far northern end of the bay.

The land immediately surrounding the monument is actually under British rule, somewhat like the grounds of a foreign consulate. Once a year, an Australian ship comes to tend it, and sometimes local people are hired to clear the weeds. The monument fence is fashioned from old cannons topped with cannonballs. Here too is a bronze plaque, often awash by the waves, that marks the exact spot where Cook fell. You can see the marble obelisk from the *heiau,* but actually getting to it is tough. Most people kayak across or take a tour boat from up the coast. Expert swimmers have braved the mile swim to the point, but be advised it's through open water. A rugged Jeep/foot trail leads down the hill to the monument, but it's poorly marked and starts way back near the town of Captain Cook, almost immediately after Napo'opo'o Road branches off from Route 11. Behind the monument are the ruins of the Ka'awaloa village site, some of which can be seen in the trees. Ruins of a lighthouse and a boat launch are nearby.

Pu'uhonua O Honaunau National Historical Park

This historical park, the main attraction in the area, shouldn't be missed. Though it was once known as City of Refuge Park, the official name of Pu'uhonua O Honaunau is now used in keeping with the strong reemergence of Hawaiian culture and heritage. One way to get there is to bounce along the narrow four miles of coastal road from Kealakekua Bay. The other more direct and much better road is Route 160, where it branches off Route 11 at Keokea around mile marker 104, a short distance south of Honaunau.

The setting of Pu'uhonua O Honaunau couldn't be more idyllic. It's a picture-perfect cove with many paths leading out onto the sea-washed lava flow. The tall royal palms surrounding this compound shimmer like neon against the black lava so prevalent in this part of Kona. Planted for this purpose, these beacons promised safety and salvation to the vanquished, weak, and war-tossed, as well as to the *kapu*-breakers of old Hawaii. If you made it to this "temple of refuge," scurrying frantically ahead of avenging warriors or leaping into the sea to swim the last desperate miles, the attendant *kahuna,* under pain of their own death, had to offer you sanctuary. *Kapu*-breakers were particularly pursued because their misdeeds could anger the always-moody gods, who might send a lava flow or tsunami to punish all. Only the *kahuna* could perform the rituals that would bathe you in the sacred mana and thus absolve you from all wrongdoing. This *pu'uhonua* (temple of refuge) was the largest in all Hawaii, and be it fact or fancy, you can feel its power to this day.

The temple complex sits on a 20-acre finger of lava fronting the sea. A massive, 1,000-foot-long mortarless wall, measuring 10 feet high and 17 feet thick, borders the site on the landward side and marks it as a temple of refuge. Archaeological evidence dates use of the temple from the mid-16th century, and some scholars argue that it was a well-known sacred spot as much as 200 years earlier. Actually, three separate *heiau* are within the enclosure. In the mid-16th century, Keawe, a great chief of Kona and the great-grandfather of Kamehameha, ruled here. After his death, his bones were entombed in Hale O Keawe Heiau at the end

canoe shed at Pu'uhonua O Honaunau

© ROBERT NILSEN

carved wooden images at Pu'uhonua O Honaunau

of the great wall, and his mana re-infused the temple with cleansing powers. For 250 years the *ali'i* of Kona continued to be buried here, making the spot more and more powerful. Even the great Queen Ka'ahumanu came here seeking sanctuary. As a 17-year-old bride, she refused to submit to the will of her husband, Kamehameha, and defied him openly, often wantonly giving herself to lesser chiefs. To escape Kamehameha's rampage, she made for the temple. Ka'ahumanu chose a large rock to hide under, and she couldn't be found until her pet dog barked and gave her away. Ka'ahumanu was coaxed out only after a lengthy intercession by Capt. George Vancouver, who had become a friend of the king. The last royal personage buried here was a son of Kamehameha who died in 1818. Soon afterward, the "old religion" of Hawaii died and the temple grounds were abandoned but not entirely destroyed. The foundations of this largest city of refuge in the Hawaiian Islands were left intact.

On the landward side of the refuge wall was the "palace grounds" where the *ali'i* of Kona lived. Set here and there around the sandy compound are numerous buildings that have been re-created to let you sense what it must have been like when *ali'i* walked here under the palms. The canoe shed, set directly back from the royal canoe landing site on the beach, was exceedingly important to the seagoing Hawaiians, and the temple helped sustain the mores and principles of the highly stratified and regimented society. Several fishponds lie in this compound that raised food for the chiefs, and a *konane* stone set next to the water—*konane* is a game similar to checkers—is a modern version of one of the games the old Hawaiians played. It is easy to envision this spot as one of power and prestige. Feel free to look around, but be respectful and acknowledge that Hawaiians still consider this a sacred spot.

In 1961, the National Park Service opened Pu'uhonua O Honaunau after a complete and faithful restoration was carried out. Careful consultation of old records and vintage

KONANE

Konane is a traditional board game played by Hawaiians that is similar to checkers. Old boards have been found at various locations around the islands, often close to the water. The "board" is a flat rock with small depressions ground into it. These depressions usually number around 100, but may be as many as 200. Each of the depressions is filed with an alternating white and black stone or shell. Although there are many variations to the game, one is as follows. Each of two players removes one of his stones, creating two blank spots. One of the two players starts by jumping an opponent's stone, capturing it and taking it off the board. Play then moves to the other person, who in turn jumps the opposite color stone, removing it. The game continues like this, each person alternately jumping the opponent's stones, until one player is no longer able to make a jump, which ends the game.

© ROBERT NILSEN

Keawe Heiau at Pu'uhonua O Honaunau

sketches from early ships' artists gave the restoration a true sense of authenticity. Local artists used traditional tools and techniques to carve giant 'ohi'a logs into faithful renditions of the temple gods. They now stand again, protecting the *heiau* from evil. All the buildings are painstakingly lashed together in the Hawaiian fashion, but with nylon rope instead of traditional cordage, which would have added the perfect touch.

Stop at the visitors center (808/328-2288, 8 A.M.–4:30 P.M. daily, www.nps.gov/puho, $5 per person) to pick up a map and brochure for a self-guided tour. Exhibits line a wall, complete with murals done in heroic style. Push a button and the recorded messages give you a brief history of Hawaiian beliefs and the system governing daily life—or stay for one of the ranger talks.

The beach park section of this 180-acre park is open at 6 A.M. and closes at 8 P.M. Monday–Thursday and at 11 P.M. Friday–Sunday and holidays. Swimming, sunbathing, and picnicking are allowed there, while snorkeling and kayaking can be done in the bay right in front of the refuge. Kayaks and small boats can be launched from the boat ramp in the village just to the north and adjacent to the refuge.

A trail from the 1870s cuts across another section of the park and along it are a number of historic and geologic points of interest. A hike along this trail takes you to the Ki'ilae Village site, over land that was given by King Kamehameha I to John Young. Along this trail are several old stone walls and constructions, both animal pens and heiau, as well as the remains of a small *holua* course and *konane* board carved into a rock slab. You pass a couple of partially collapsed lava tubes on the way to a point and the remains of a home site from where you have a good view back along the coast. The visitors center may have a map of the trail with descriptions of these sites. About two miles round-trip, this trail starts about 200 feet toward the beach from the main parking lot. A second trailhead is at the beach/picnic parking lot.

Every year on the weekend closest to July 1

carved wooden images at Keawe Heiau

(the first was held in 1971), the free two-day Pu'uhonua O Honaunau Cultural Festival is held here, featuring traditional Hawaiian arts and crafts, music and dance, canoe rides, and food. Be sure to stop by for a peek into the past if you are in the area during this time.

Shopping

Along the highway as you enter town is the **Antiques and Orchids** (81-6224 Mamalahoa Hwy., 808/323-9851) collectibles shop. With a wide selection of furniture and housewares (many small items too) and an amazing variety of potted orchids, this is a great shop for any discriminating shopper.

A few steps away is the much smaller and more eclectic **Grandma's Attic** antique shop (808/323-8282).

Just south of the turnoff for Ho'okena is the **Kealia Ranch Store** (808/328-8744), the last chance store for jewelry, T-shirts, country-oriented gifts, ice cream, and cowboy hats.

Recreation

In Captain Cook, **Adventures in Paradise** (81-6367 Mamalahoa Hwy., 808/323-3005 or 888/371-6035, www.bigislandkayak.com) is the company to see for kayak rentals and kayak and snorkeling tours, as well as hiking trips. Kayak rentals are $25 single and $50 double; snorkel gear is $8 a day. Kayak tours run $60–100 per person.

Kayak Central (808/323-2224), located at the Pineapple Park hostel on the highway, rents kayaks but does not do guided tours. Rental rates are $20–30 single, $40–50 double, and $60–80 triple.

Hostel

The least expensive place to stay in the area is **Pineapple Park** (808/323-2224 or 877/800-3800, fax 808/323-2086, ppark@aloha.net, www.pineapple-park.com). This clean and commodious hostel accommodation is in a converted plantation-era house along the main highway. Running $25 a bed, the dorm rooms are located in the converted walk-out basement, which also has a TV lounge and inexpensive Internet access. A private room runs $65. All guests share baths, have use of laundry facilities and a large kitchen, and can rent kayaks and snorkel gear on-site for minimal fees.

Bed-and-Breakfasts

Areca Palms Estate Bed and Breakfast (808/323-2276 or 800/545-4390, arecapalms@konabedandbreakfast.com, www.konabedandbreakfast.com) is considered, even by other B&B owners, to be one of the best on the island. Innkeepers Janice and Steve Glass are more than happy to share their home with you. The house is always perfumed by fresh-cut flowers, and Hawaiian music plays in the background to set the mood. Bedspreads are thick, the quilts in floral designs, and carpets cover the bedroom floors. Set in a broad manicured lawn surrounded by tropical flowers and areca palms, the outdoor hot tub and deck is the premier spot on the property. Rates for the four rooms range $95–130, inclusive of the sumptuous breakfast feast; two nights minimum.

Just a few steps from the Royal Kona Coffee Mill is **Affordable Hawaii at Pomaika'i "Lucky" Farm B&B** (83-5465 Mamalahoa Hwy., 808/328-2112 or 800/325-6427, innkeeper@hawaii.rr.com, www.luckyfarm.com). This B&B is part of a working coffee and macadamia nut farm that has views of the coast from the back lanai of the main house. The front bedroom in the restored farmhouse runs $60 a night, has its own bathroom, and lies off the sitting room with its TV and library. This room is a little close to the road and so may be a bit noisy during the day, but it all quiets down at night. The greenhouse, a newer addition down below, runs $70 a couple for each of its two rooms. Both have queen-size beds, futons for an extra two people, private entrances, and private baths. Then there's the coffee barn. Converted to a bedroom, it's been left with its rough-hewn framing and bare walls, but a half-bath has been added inside and a shower set up just outside the door. Renting for $75, it's just right for a romantic honeymoon couple. All rooms have a two-night minimum stay. Guests are served a farm-healthy, homemade breakfast each morning, and you can pick fruit from the trees on the property. Pomaika'i Farm offers relaxation, affordability, and great food. For reservations, contact Nita Isherwood, innkeeper.

Also on a working coffee and macadamia nut farm is **Rainbow Plantation B&B** (808/323-2393 or 800/494-2829, fax 808/323-9445, sunshine@aloha.net, www.rainbowplantation.com), a peaceful country place where chickens, potbellied pigs, and peacocks rule the yard, the koi pond adds a touch of elegance, and the sounds of nature surround you. Most views are of the garden, but you can get a glimpse here and there of the ocean in the distance. Each of the rooms in the main house and detached cottages has a private entrance and bathroom. Two rooms in the main house run $79–89, while the two rooms in the multistory converted macadamia nut husking building are $89–99. The most unusual unit here is a converted fishing boat, which also runs $89 a night. These rooms have a two- to three-night minimum stay. Breakfast is served each morning on the lanai, and all may use the "gazebo" kitchen. The Rainbow Plantation is set up for the eco-friendly traveler and nature lover. German and French spoken.

The Dragonfly Ranch (808/328-2159 or 800/487-2159, reservations@dragonflyranch.com, www.dragonflyranch.com), owned and operated by Barbara Moore, offers "tropical fantasy lodging" set amongst thick vegetation on the way down to Pu'uhonua O Honaunau. Rooms are intriguing and range from the Honeymoon Suite featuring a king-size bed in a screened outdoor room, the airy Lomi lomi suite, and more private Writer's studio, to the smaller Dragonfly and Dolphin rooms. All rooms include a small refrigerator and basic cooking apparatus, indoor bathroom, private outdoor shower, cable TV, stereo, and small library. Rates run $100–250, two nights minimum, with discounts for longer stays, and breakfast is included. This is an open, airy place, where the outside and inside boundaries begin to blur. For those who might think the touted tropical fantasy may be a "tropical nightmare," the Dragonfly Ranch is not for you, although the nearby Dragonfly Cottage, which rents for $300 a night, might fit the bill as it's a standard two-bedroom, two-bath house with full kitchen and amenities. The hosts are very friendly and inviting, indeed, but definitely have an alternative, counter-culture, new-age leaning. Occasionally, alternative healing arts and wellness workshops are given. Free-spirited adventurers will feel comfortable here; others may not. Rainbow streamers and a Buddha in a butterfly banner greet you as you turn in the drive.

Just a few hundred yards up the road and inland above Napo'opo'o and set in a manicured lawn with good views down onto the bay and the bay edge *pali* is the **Kealakekua Bay Bed and Breakfast** (82-6002 Napo'opo'o Rd., 808/328-8150 or 800/328-8150, www.keala.com). This comfortable, contemporary, island-inspired, Mediterranean-style house offers guests two ground-floor rooms, one second-floor suite, and the two-bedroom, 1,300-square-foot "cottage" next door. Each has its own entrance and bathroom, and all share common space. The rooms run $120–140 and the suite $190 a night including breakfast (two nights minimum); the full-house cottage is $250 with a three-night minimum.

Hotel

The **Manago Hotel** (808/323-2642, fax 808/323-3451, www.managohotel.com) has been in the Manago family since 1917, and anyone who puts his name on a place and keeps it there that long is doing something right. The Manago Hotel is clean and unpretentious with an old-Hawaii charm. There is nothing fancy going on there, just a decent room for a decent price. The old section of the hotel along the road is clean but a little worse for wear. The rooms are small with wooden floors, double beds, and utilitarian dressers, no fans, and shared bathrooms. Walk through to find a bridgeway into a garden area that's open, bright, and secluded away from the road. The new section features rooms with wall-to-wall carpeting, private baths, louvered windows, ceiling fans, and private lanai. Although the new section is away from the road, those with a noise sensitivity may hear conversations of other guests through the thin walls and across balconies. The rates are $28 single or $31 double for a room with a shared bath, $48–53 single and $51–56 double in the new section, plus $3 for an extra person. There is also one Japanese room that goes for $67 single or $70 double. Weekly and monthly discounts are available on all rooms. The views of the Kona Coast from the hotel grounds are terrific. Downstairs in the old building, the restaurant serves breakfast, lunch, and dinner every day except Monday.

Vacation Rentals

In Napo'opo'o there are several options. On the inland side of the road to the *heiau* is the multistory **McConnell House** (604/942-4148 or 604/462-8315, www.hawaiibaybeach.com), split into two suites. Each suite has a queen-size bed, an extra bed, a full bathroom, and a kitchen. Both share a rooftop lanai from which your views of Kealakekua Bay are tops. Rates run $1,000 a week for the suites or $1,200–1,600 a week for the entire house, which can sleep up to six. With a reservation, there is a $300 damage deposit due and a $75 out-cleaning fee.

Across the road and directly on the water are **The Dolphin Retreat** and **Hale Naia** (808/247-3637, fax 808/235-2644, hibeach@lava.net, www.hibeach.com). The Dolphin Retreat is a three-bedroom, three-bath house with full modern kitchen that sleeps up to 12; it goes for $2,650–2,950 a week, plus there is a substantial out-cleaning fee. Not cheap, but the location can't be beat. Next door is Hale Naia, a four-bedroom, three-bath house with full kitchen and equally great views out onto the bay. This is a more modern house with a slight Asian touch that rents for $2,950–3,450, plus an out-cleaning fee.

Food

Locals say to try the pork chop dinner served at the large and airy, old-style **Manago Hotel Restaurant** (808/323-2642, 7–9 A.M., 11 A.M.–2 P.M., 5–7:30 P.M. Tues.–Sun.) in downtown Captain Cook. This meal and other offerings on the menu are plain old American food with a strong Hawaiian overlay. Other items are New York steak, the most expensive item at $13.50, beef teriyaki, teri chicken, and four or five fish selections. All come with three side dishes and rice. This food won't set your taste buds on fire and it won't make everyone happy, but you won't be complaining about being hungry or not having a wholesome meal.

A local stop for a quick meal like a plate lunch, loco moco, fish, bento, or standard American breakfast, where most everything is under $8, is the **Capt. Cook Grill** (81-6224 Mamalahoa Hwy., 808/323-8344, 7 A.M.–8 P.M. weekdays, 7 A.M.–7 P.M. weekends). Order at the window and sit under the canopy to eat.

Señor Billy's Cantina (82-6123 Mamalahoa Hwy., 808/323-2012, 11 A.M.–9 P.M. daily) is the place to head for a carne asada plate, nachos, veggie quesadilla, pork enchilada, burritos, or other fresh Mexican dishes while in Captain Cook or the vicinity. Most meals will set you back less than $11 per person. Takeout available.

Located across from the police and fire station in Captain Cook is **Paparoni's** (82-6127 Mamalahoa Hwy., 808/323-2661, 11 A.M.–9 P.M. Mon.–Sat., 4–9 P.M. Sun.), which—not surprisingly—serves up pizza, pasta, and deli sandwiches. Paparoni's homemade pizzas run $7–12 plus extra for toppings, and pasta is $7–11. Sit inside or out on the back lanai.

Perhaps the best view down onto the Napo'opo'o/Kealakekua Bay area is from under the mango tree on the back lanai of **The Coffee Shack** (83-5799 Mamalahoa Hwy., 808/328-9555, 7 A.M.–5 P.M. daily), and, aside from its superb view, it has delicious treats at a fair price. The Coffee Shack has a full list of coffee and cold drinks, simple breakfasts, soup, salads, hot sandwiches, and pizza, but best of all, a wide variety of luscious cakes, pies, pastries, and a host of other sweet treats all made fresh daily here in the kitchen. Most everything is under $8, except the pizzas, which run a few dollars more. Eat in or takeout. The views! The views!

Also in Honaunau but farther down the road is **H.Y.** mini-mart (83-5487 or 808/328-2262) for takeout Korean barbecue.

Food Markets

The **Kealakekua Ranch Center** in Captain Cook is a two-story utilitarian mall with a few small shops, an Ace Hardware store, and a Choice Mart supermarket. **Choice Mart** (808/323-3994, 6 A.M.–9 P.M. Mon.–Sat., until 8:30 P.M. on Sunday) is the last of the large markets along this road going south, so pick up supplies here. This full-service grocery store also has a small deli section with surprising variety.

Bong Brothers and Sistah (84-5227 Mamalahoa Hwy., 808/328-9289, 8:30 A.M.–6 P.M. Mon.–Fri., 10 A.M.–6 P.M. Sunday) is on the *makai* side of the road near mile marker 106 and is housed in a coffee mill complex circa 1920, one of the oldest in Honaunau. This shop sells not only coffee but organic produce and health food deli items. The shelves hold dried mango, candied ginger, bulk coffee, chocolate-covered coffee beans, Puna honey, dried pineapple, apples, bananas, special sauces, and—no shop is complete without them—T-shirts. Also look for a stack of burlap coffee bags, some bearing the Bong Brothers logo, that make a nifty souvenir. Adjacent is **Gold Mountain Mill,** a functional roasting mill tended by Tom Bong and his dog Bear. Coffee from the surrounding area comes in to be roasted in the still-functional, vintage 1930s roaster.

A short way past the Route 160 turnoff, look for **Higashi Store** (808/328-2394) for basic supplies of food and snack items.

A few minutes farther is the **South Kona Fruit Stand** (84-4770 Mamalahoa Hwy., 808/328-8547, 9 A.M.–6 P.M. Mon.–Sat., 11 A.M.–5 P.M. Sun.), which sells one of the widest selections of fruit on the island, much of it home-grown on the family farm nearby.

In Kealia, the **Fujihara Store** (808/328-2224) has a slightly wider selection and is the last chance for packaged food and drinks until you get to Ocean View.

FARTHER SOUTH

Ho'okena

If you want to see how the people of Kona still live, visit Ho'okena. A mile or two south of the

Pu'uhonua O Honaunau turnoff, or 20 miles south of Kailua-Kona, take a well-marked spur road *makai* off Route 11 and follow it to the sea. The village is somewhat in a state of disrepair, but a number of homey cottages line the coast. Ho'okena boasts the **Ho'okena Beach County Park** with pavilions, restrooms, and picnic tables, but no potable water. Camping is allowed with a county permit. Even as remote as this is, you'll likely see the ranger checking on permits in the evening—be sure to have one. For drinking water, a tap is attached to the telephone pole near the beginning of your descent down the spur road. The gray-sand beach is broad, long, and probably *the* best in South Kona for both swimming and body surfing. If the sun gets too hot, some palms and other trees lining the beach provide not only shade but a picture-perfect setting. Until the road connecting Kona to Hilo was finally finished in the 1930s, Ho'okena shipped the produce of the surrounding area from its bustling wharf. At one time, Ho'okena was the main port in South Kona and even hosted Robert Louis Stevenson when he passed through the islands in 1889. Part of the wharf still remains. The surrounding cliffs are honeycombed with burial caves.

If you walk a short quarter mile north along the shore, you'll find the vacant walled remains of **Maria Lanakila Church,** built in 1860 but leveled in an earthquake in 1950. The church was another "painted church" done by Father John Velghe in the same style as St. Benedict's.

Miloli'i

This active fishing village is approximately 15 miles south of Pu'uhonua O Honaunau. Again, look for signs to a spur road off Route 11 heading *makai.* The long and winding road, leading through bleak lava flows, is narrow but worth the detour. Much of the old village of Miloli'i was covered by a lava flow in the early 1900s but the village survived and even has a relatively new, but stark, subdivision sprouting on the lava. Miloli'i (Fine Twist) earned its name from times past when it was famous for producing *'aha,* a sennit made from coconut-husk fibers; and *olona,* a twine made from the *olona* plant and mostly used for fishnets. This is one of the last villages in Hawaii where traditional fishing was the major source of income and where old-timers are heard speaking Hawaiian. Some fishermen may still use small outrigger canoes powered by outboards to catch *opelu,* a type of mackerel that schools in these waters. The method of catching the *opelu* has remained unchanged for centuries. Boats gather and drop packets of chum made primarily from poi, sweet potatoes, or rice. No meat is used so sharks won't be attracted.

The **Miloli'i Beach County Park** is a favorite with local people on the weekends; camping is allowed by permit. Tents are pitched in and around the parking lot, just under the ironwoods at road's end. There are flushing toilets, a basketball court, and a brackish pond in which to rinse off, but no drinking water, so bring some. Swimming is safe inside the reef, and the tidepools in the area are some of the best on the south coast. Across the parking lot is the yellow Huoli Kamanao Church. A few steps back up the road, the small, understocked Miloli'i Grocery Store has little more than drinks and snacks, but it does hamburgers and a few other hot items and the price is right for being so far out.

A 15-minute trail leads south to the coconut tree–fringed **Honomalino Bay,** where there's a secluded gray-sand and black-pebble beach great for swimming or spending the day in the shade—beware of falling coconuts.

Macadamia Nut Farm

When back on the highway heading south, you'll notice a long stretch of macadamia nut trees on both sides of the road. Mac Nut Farms of Hawaii is the largest macadamia nut farm in the state. Unfortunately, the company offers no tours of its facility, nor do they have an outlet to sell their products. You'll just have to satisfy yourself with the view of acre after acre of trees and wait until you get to town to make that nutty purchase.

SOUTH KOHALA

The **Kohala District** is the peninsular thumb in the northwestern portion of the Big Island. At its tip is Upolu Point, only 40 miles from Maui across the 'Alenuihaha Channel. Kohala was the first section of the Big Island to rise from beneath the sea. The long-extinct volcanoes of the Kohala Mountains running down its spine have been reduced by time and the elements from lofty, ragged peaks to rounded domes of 5,000 feet or so. Kohala is divided into North and South Kohala. North Kohala, an area of dry coastal slopes, former sugar lands, a string of sleepy towns, and deeply incised lush valleys, forms the northernmost tip of the island. South Kohala boasts *the* most beautiful swimming beaches on the Big Island, along with world-class hotels and resorts.

South Kohala is a region of contrast. It's dry, hot, tortured by wind, and scored by countless old lava flows. The predominant land color here is black, and this is counterpointed by scrubby bushes and scraggly trees, a seemingly semi-arid wasteland. This was an area that the ancient Hawaiians seemed to have traveled through to get somewhere else, yet Hawaiians did live here—along the coast—and numerous archaeological sites dot the coastal plain. Still, South Kohala is stunning with its palm-fringed white-sand pockets of beach, luxury resorts, green landscaped golf courses, a proliferation of colorful planted flowers, and its deep blue inviting water. You don't generally travel here to appreciate the stunning landscape, although it too has its attraction. You come here to settle into a sedate resort community, to be pampered and pleased by the finer things that

PHOTO COURTESY OF HVCB/HAWAII TOURISM JAPAN

HIGHLIGHTS

Puako Petroglyphs: These are perhaps the best and one of the most varied examples of petroglyph fields on this coast, while being easily accessible to the public (page 106).

Pu'ukohola Heiau: The last large *heiau* created before the abandonment of the traditional Hawaiian religion, this was the most important construction performed by King Kamehameha I on his quest for control of the Big Island (page 107).

'Anaeho'omalu Bay: This classic Kohala beach, one of the best on the island, is a perfect playground for water sports. In addition, it links the old Hawaii of royal fishponds and *heiau* with the modern luxury hotels and amenities on the surrounding Waikoloa Resort (page 109).

Hilton Waikoloa Village: The Hilton is more than a resort hotel. It's like three hotels in one, with restaurant and activity opportunities, an astounding art collection, and boat and tram transportation (page 118).

Parker Ranch Historic Homes: These homes in Waimea serve as bookends – humble beginning to lavish manor – for the Parker family homestead and its immense influence over this upcountry cowboy region (page 135).

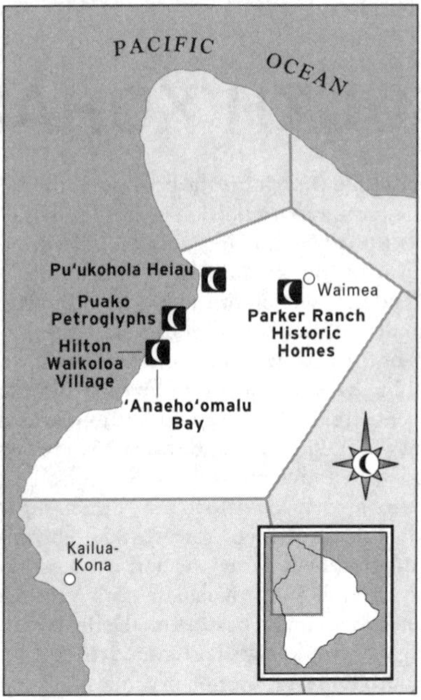

LOOK FOR TO FIND RECOMMENDED SIGHTS, ACTIVITIES, DINING, AND LODGING.

await at luxury resorts that are destinations in and of themselves. Of the many scattered villages that once dotted this coast, only two remain: Puako, now a sleepy beach hideaway, and Kawaihae, one of the principal commercial deepwater ports on the island. Inland is Waimea (Kamuela), the *paniolo* town and center of the massive Parker Ranch. Between the coast and Waimea lies the newer planned community of Waikoloa, with its clusters of condominiums and family homes, a shopping center and school, and a golf course.

PLANNING YOUR TIME

The luxury resorts of the Kohala Coast have been designed as destinations in and of themselves so it's not difficult to head right there after landing on the island and spend your entire vacation partaking of what the resort communities offer. And they offer a lot, from accommodations and food to basic cultural events and a plethora of sporting activities. However, unless you want to spend all your free time on the beach or relaxing on your lanai, save some time to head up to the cowboy country of Waimea, back down the coast to Kailua-Kona, or farther afield. If you are fond of cultural and historical sites, visiting all the petroglyph fields of South Kohala, plus a trip to Pu'ukohola Heiau will take most of a day. Reserve half a day for getting to and from, with plenty of time to look around

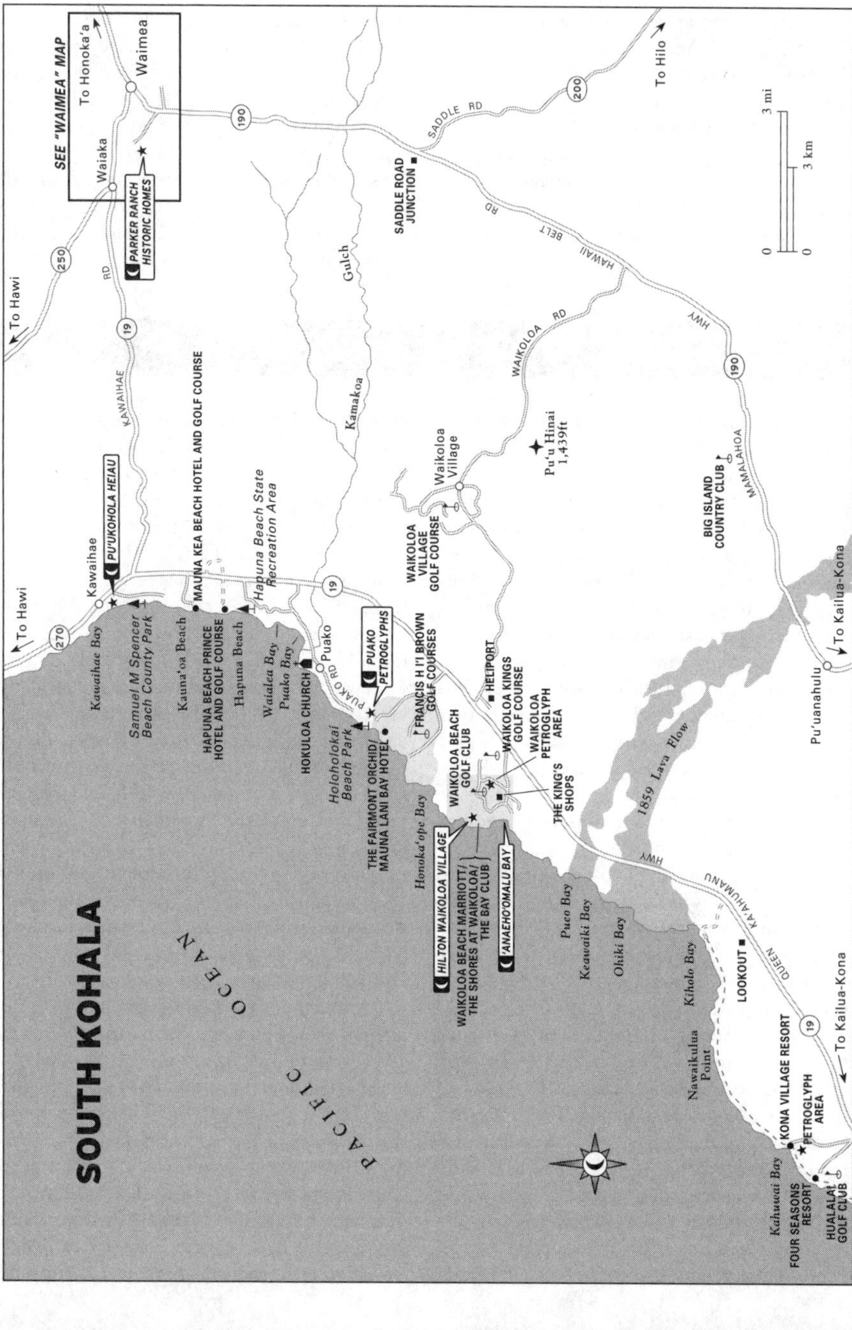
SOUTH KOHALA
PACIFIC
OCEAN
SEE "WAIMEA" MAP
To Honoka'a
Waimea
Waiaka
PARKER RANCH HISTORIC HOMES
To Hawi
To Hilo
SADDLE RD
SADDLE ROAD JUNCTION
HAWAII BELT RD
Gulch
Kamakoa
KAWAIHAE RD
PU'UKOHOLA HEIAU
Kawaihae
Kawaihae Bay
Samuel M Spencer Beach County Park
Kauna'oa Beach
MAUNA KEA BEACH HOTEL AND GOLF COURSE
HAPUNA BEACH PRINCE HOTEL AND GOLF COURSE
Hapuna Beach
Hapuna Beach State Recreation Area
Waialea Bay
Puako Bay
Puako
PUAKO RD
HOKULOA CHURCH
PUAKO PETROGLYPHS
Holoholokai Beach Park
THE FAIRMONT ORCHID/ MAUNA LANI BAY HOTEL
FRANCIS H I'I BROWN GOLF COURSES
HELIPORT
WAIKOLOA KINGS GOLF COURSE
WAIKOLOA PETROGLYPH AREA
WAIKOLOA BEACH GOLF CLUB
THE KING'S SHOPS
Honoka'ope Bay
HILTON WAIKOLOA VILLAGE
WAIKOLOA BEACH MARRIOTT/ THE SHORES AT WAIKOLOA/ THE BAY CLUB
'ANAEHO'OMALU BAY
WAIKOLOA VILLAGE GOLF COURSE
Waikoloa Village
WAIKOLOA RD
Pu'u Hinai 1,439ft
BIG ISLAND COUNTRY CLUB
MAMALAHOA HWY
To Kailua-Kona
Pu'uanahulu
1859 Lava Flow
QUEEN KA'AHUMANU HWY
Pueo Bay
Keawaiki Bay
Ohiki Bay
Kiholo Bay
LOOKOUT
Nawaikulua Point
KONA VILLAGE RESORT
PETROGLYPH AREA
Kahuwai Bay
FOUR SEASONS RESORT
HUALALAI GOLF CLUB
0 3 mi
0 3 km
270
19
250
190
200

SOUTH KOHALA

Pua Mau Place, an arid zone botanical garden. Unless you're staying in the village of Waikoloa, chances are that you will just blow by on your way up to Waimea, which, with its fine shopping opportunities and restaurants, can occupy the better part of a day. As the uplands of Waimea is still *paniolo* cowboy country, reserve half a day for a horseback ride at one of the several stables that offer rides. If you're staying along the coast in South Kohala or up in Waimea you're already close to North Kohala. Unless you just don't have time, plan on spending a full day exploring the lovely north end of the island, for it's a different world than the dry coast region of South Kohala or the green pasture land of Waimea. In the same manner, as you are near, arrange an afternoon and early evening for a drive up to the top of Mauna Kea for sunset, a very memorable way to cap off a day.

The Coast

The shoreline of South Kohala, from 'Anaeho'omalu Bay north to Kawaihae Bay, is rich with some of the finest super-deluxe resorts in the state. This coast's fabulous beaches are known not only for swimming and surfing, but for tidepooling and awe-inspiring sunsets as well. Also, two of the coast's main beaches offer camping and one even has rental cabins. There are little-disturbed and rarely visited archaeological sites, expressive petroglyph fields, and the educational **Pu'ukohola Heiau.** No "towns" lie along the coast, in the sense of a laid-out community with a main street and attendant businesses and services. The closest facsimile is Kawaihae, with a small cluster of restaurants, shops, a gas station, boat landing, and commercial harbor, but it's just an oversized village. More of a laid-back beach community, Puako is just a string of homes along a road paralleling the water.

As you begin heading north from Kailua-Kona on coastal Route 19 (Queen Ka'ahumanu Hwy.), you leave civilization behind. There won't be a house or any structures at all, and you'll understand why they call it the "Big Island." Perhaps to soften the shock of what's ahead, magnificent bushes loaded with pink and purple flowers line the roadway for a while. Notice too that friends and lovers have gathered and placed white coral rocks on the black lava along the road, forming pleasant graffiti messages.

Suddenly you're in the midst of enormous flows of old 'a'a and pahoehoe as you pass through a huge and desolate lava desert. At first it appears ugly and uninviting, but the subtle beauty begins to grow. On clear days you can see Maui floating on the horizon, and *mauka* looms the formidable presence of Mauna Kea streaked by sunlight filtering through its crown of clouds. Along the roadside, wisps of grass have broken through the lava. Their color, a shade of pinkish gold, is quite extraordinary and made more striking juxtaposed with the inky-black lava. Caught by your headlights at night, or especially in the magical light of dusk, the grass wisps come alive, giving the illusion of wild-haired gnomes rising from the earth. In actuality, it's fountain grass imported from Africa. This is also where you might catch a glimpse of the infamous "Kona nightingales," wild jackasses that roam throughout this area and can be road hazards, particularly at dawn and twilight. Watch for Donkey Crossing road signs.

Around mile marker 70, the land softens and changes. The lava is older, carpeted in rich green grass appearing as rolling hills of rangeland. These long, flat stretches of road can give you "lead foot." Be careful! The police patrol this strip heavily, using unmarked cars, looking for unsuspecting tourists who have been "road hypnotized." From Kailua-Kona to the Waikoloa Beach Resort is about 25 miles, with another five miles to the Mauna Kea Beach Resort near Kawaihae. If you're day-tripping

PHOTO COURTESY OF HVCB/HAWAII TOURISM JAPAN

Many names and messages written with pieces of white coral are seen along the road from Kohala to Kona.

to the beaches, expect to spend an hour traveling each way.

If you're approaching Kohala from Hilo or the east side of the island, you can take one of two routes. The Saddle Road (Rt. 200) comes directly west from Hilo and passes between Mauna Kea and Mauna Loa. This very scenic road has the alluring distinction of being the least favorite route of the car-rental agencies, which may forbid their cars to travel this route. The Saddle Road intersects Route 190, where you can turn north and drive for six miles to Waimea, south for 33 miles to Kailua-Kona, or take the 13-mile shortcut Waikoloa Road to the coast. Route 19, the main artery connecting Hilo with the west coast, changes its "locally known" name quite often, but it's always posted as Route 19. Directly north from Hilo as it hugs the Hamakua Coast, it's called the Hawaii Belt Road. When it turns west in Honoka'a, heading for Waimea, it's called the Mamalahoa Highway. From Waimea directly west to Kawaihae on the coast Route 19 becomes Kawaihae Road, and when it turns due south along the coast heading for Kailua-Kona, its moniker changes again to Queen Ka'ahumanu Highway.

HISTORICAL SIGHTS

The following sights and beaches are listed from south to north. All lie along coastal Route 19.

Ka'upulehu Petroglyphs

Located just back from the ponds at the Kona Village Resort is a cluster of approximately 440 lava rock carvings, near where the ancient Kings Highway must have passed. This group of petroglyphs contains designs, many of them different from others along this coast. There are numerous human figures, some with paddles and fishing lines held in their hands, a turtle figure, and dozens that illustrate the lines of crab-claw sails of sailing canoes. While some of these carvings are speculated to be as much as 900 years old, others are obviously newer, as you can discern the date 1820 and some Western script—

obviously done after contact with early white sailors. In 1998, the resort constructed a wooden boardwalk around the majority of these carved figures in order to protect the integrity of these fine works of art. As this field lies on Kona Village property, you will need to contact the hotel in order to get permission to enter the property for a guided tour. Tours can be arranged through the resort activities department (808/325-5555), where printed information and a map of the site are available.

Waikoloa Petroglyphs

Set along a reconstructed section of the Kings' Trail and surrounded by the Beach Course golf course is the Waikoloa Petroglyph field. Unlike others nearby, this grouping is done in an undulating area and also includes remains of temporary structures. While many and varied designs are seen here, a circular pattern is much in evidence. Cinder rock paths have been constructed throughout this petroglyph field. Stay on the paths; do not walk on the carvings. Approach this area from the Kings' Shops for a self-guided tour or take one of the free guided tours conducted by the shopping center at 10:30 A.M. daily. Wear sturdy shoes and a hat, and bring drinking water.

Puako Petroglyphs

These rock carvings, approximately 3,000 individual designs, are considered some of the finest and oldest in Hawaii, but carvings of horses and cattle signify ongoing art that happened long after Westerners appeared. Circles outlined by a series of small holes belonged to families who placed the umbilical cords of their infants into these indentations to tie them to the *'aina* and give them strength for a long and good life. State archaeologists and anthropologists have reported a deterioration of the site due to vandalism, so please look but don't deface, and stay on established paths. Access is by a well-marked, self-guiding trail starting from Holoholokai Beach Park, located on the north side of the Fairmont Orchid hotel in the Mauna Lani Resort.

© ROBERT NILSEN

Various images, including stick human figures, are found at the Waikoloa Petroglyph sites.

© ROBERT NILSEN

Pu'ukohola Heiau lies on the hilltop overlooking Kawaihae Harbor.

SOUTH KOHALA

Pu'ukohola Heiau

Don't miss this restored Hawaiian temple, a National Historical Site located one mile south of Kawaihae where coastal Route 19 turns into Route 270 heading into North Kohala. This site, covering 86 acres, includes **Mailekini Heiau,** an old *heiau* of unknown date and usage, and the **John Young's Homestead** site. Below the *heiau,* in the trees near the sea, Kamehameha I kept a royal household, and a short way offshore in the bay is an older **Hale O Kapuni Heiau** dedicated to the shark god. The shark god *heiau* silted over in the 1950s due, at least in part, to construction of the harbor facilities nearby, but to this day an inordinate number of black-tip reef sharks can be spotted near where this site was. Administered by the National Park Service, this sacred ground is open daily and has free admission (808/882-7218, www.nps.gov/puhe, 7:30 A.M.–4 P.M.). As you enter, pick up a map highlighting the points of interest. It's worthwhile checking out the visitor center (2006), where there are displays and cultural exhibits and good views of the *heiau.* The rangers provide excellent information and pertinent, informative books are available. The one trail through the park leads to its notable sites, and from it, a short section of a coastal trail runs to Spencer Beach County Park nearby. It's hot and dry at this site, so bring water and wear a hat. Pu'ukohola (Whale Hill) received its name either because the hill itself resembles a whale, or because migrating whales pass very close offshore every year. It was fated to become a hill of destiny. For the best views of the *heiau,* enter the Kawaihae Small Boat Harbor and take an immediate left down a crushed coral drive to the flats alongside the bay opposite the park land.

Kamehameha I built Pu'ukohola Heiau in 1790–1791 on the advice of Kapoukahi, a prophet from Kaua'i who said that Kamehameha would unify all the islands only after he built a temple to his war-god Kuka'ilimoku. Kamehameha complied, building this last of the great Hawaiian *heiau* from mortarless stone that when finished measured 100 by 224 feet. The dedication ceremony of the *heiau* is fascinating history. Kamehameha's last rival was his cousin, Keoua Kuahu'ula. This warlike chief realized that his *mana* had deserted him and that it was Kamehameha who would rise to be sovereign of all the islands. Kamehameha invited him to the dedication ceremony, but en route Keoua, in preparation for the inevitable outcome, performed a death purification ceremony by circumcising his own penis. When the canoes reached the beach, they were met by a hail of spears and musket balls. Keoua was killed and his body laid on Kuka'ilimoku's altar as a noteworthy sacrifice. Kamehameha became the unopposed sovereign of the Big Island and, within a few years, of all Hawaii.

Every August on the weekend closest to Establishment Day, a free two-day Hawaiian Cultural Festival is held on the *heiau* grounds, including arts and crafts exhibitions, games, hula demonstrations, music and dance, and re-creation of ancient ceremonies in traditional dress.

Near the *heiau,* but on the upland side of the highway, is the house site of John Young, an English seaman who became a close adviser to Kamehameha. Young, dubbed 'Olohana (All Hands) by Kamehameha, taught the Hawaiians how to use cannons and muskets and fought alongside Kamehameha in many battles. He turned Mailekini Heiau into a fort, and over a century later the U.S. Army used it as an observation area during World War II. Young became a respected Hawaiian chief and grandfather of Queen Emma. Only he and one other white man have the honor of being buried at the Royal Mausoleum in Nu'uanu Valley on O'ahu. Little remains of the house itself, but it was certainly one of the first Western-style homes and plastered structures in the islands. Apparently, John Young's wife didn't like the house too much; she had traditional-style structures built to the side for her use.

BOTANICAL GARDEN

Pua Mau Place (10 Ala Kahua Dr., 808/882-0888, www.puamau.org, 9 A.M.–4 P.M. daily, $10 adults, $8 seniors and students) botanical and sculpture garden has an unlikely location here in arid Kohala, just north of Kawaihae, but that's one of its drawing cards. Two decades in the making and still a work in progress, about 12 acres of Pua Mau (Ever Blooming) Place opened to the public in 2000. The focus here is on flowering plants, ones that thrive and flourish in a windy and arid environment. While many plants have established, some of the showiest are the hibiscus, plumeria, and date palm. With so much sunshine and so little rain, this is a harsh environment, and only certain types of plants survive. A greater challenge for the plants is that no pesticides are sprayed and brackish water is used for irrigation. Only the hearty make it, and those that do seem to love it. Heavy mulch guides you along the well-signed paths; plant numbers correspond to a book you take on your self-guided tour. A bit of whimsy is added by a fair number of giant bronze sculptures of insects that dot the garden here and there, the aviary, and the Magic Circle, a circle of stones reminiscent of megalithic stone monuments like Stonehenge. Payable at the gift shop, the entrance fee helps to support the nonprofit foundation that maintains the Pua Mau Place garden.

BEACHES AND PARKS

There are a number of excellent beaches along this coast, most with good to excellent facilities. In addition, all resorts offer access to their beaches with (limited) public parking.

Kahuwai Beach and Kuki'o Beach

The picturesque Kahuwai Bay has a sandy bottom bounded by rocky shorelines on either side. It is a spot often chosen by green sea turtles to relax on the sand or to lay their eggs. Give them wide berth. Kona Village Resort fronts this bay and creates a fine Polynesian village background. Offshore is a fine reef for snorkeling and scuba. Next door, the Four Seasons Resort sits on a narrow strip of sandy beach and one swimming lagoon. Anchialine ponds here have been set aside as a fish management area. South of the Four Seasons is Kuki'o Beach, reachable by public access between the Four Seasons Resort and the private Kuki'o development. Public access to Kahuwai Beach is via a long path that runs between the Kona Village and the Four Seasons resorts, but you'll have to get permission from the resort front gate to use the public parking lot for visitors. Taking the beachside resort pathway (please stay off of the resort property), you can easily go between Kahuwai Beach and Kuki'o Beach.

Kuki'o Beach is bounded by rocky points. The aquamarine water pushes the steep and narrow brown sand beach up the dune, beyond which are more anchialine ponds. At the far end of this beach and tucked into the rocks is a much more protected and much smaller beach, just right for kids. Beyond this is a larger rocky cove. If you're adventurous, follow the very rough path across the 'a'a cobbles and around the point over broken coral. The path is not distinct and not easy, but once you get a ways around (it may take half an hour) you're rewarded with a fine view of the more isolated Kua Bay.

Kiholo Bay

Near mile marker 81 on the highway is a pull-off and overlook that offers a good glimpse of this stark lava-covered coast. Down on the coast just north of the pull-off you'll see Kiholo Bay and Luahinewai Pond. The pond was a favorite stop for Hawaiian sailors going up the coast, who would have a swim in its cool turquoise waters before continuing on. Look for a stand of royal palms marking the spot, and follow the rough but passable 4WD road down to the rocky beach (or follow a hiking trail for about 20 minutes that starts near mile marker 82), where you will find several homes hidden in the trees, including a large round wooden house that once belonged to Loretta Lynn. There is public access to this beach, but please stay off the private property that fronts the water. While you will find seclusion here, there are no amenities and no white sand beach. For a better spot to swim and sunbathe, head to a more convenient location.

'Anaeho'omalu Bay

After miles of the transfixing monochrome blackness of Kohala's lava flows, a green standout of palm trees beckons in the distance. Turn

SOUTH KOHALA

© ROBERT NILSEN
Anchialine ponds front the Marriott hotel on 'Anaeho'omalu Beach.

near mile marker 76 at the Waikoloa Beach Resort entrance, and follow the access road to historic 'Anaeho'omalu Bay, referred to locally as "A-Bay." Set back from the beach here is the Waikoloa Beach Marriott. The bay area, with its freshwater springs, coconut trees, blue lagoon, and white-sand beach, is a picture-perfect seaside oasis. Between the large coconut grove and the beach are two well-preserved fishponds where mullet was raised for consumption only by the royalty who lived nearby or were happening by in seagoing canoes. Throughout the area along well-marked trails are petroglyphs, a segment of the cobblestoned Kings' Highway, and numerous archaeological sites including house sites and some hard-to-find burial caves. The white-sand beach is open to the public, with access, parking (6 A.M.–8 P.M.), picnic tables, and beautiful lava stone showers/bathhouses. Although the sand is a bit grainy, the swimming, snorkeling, scuba diving, windsurfing, and just about any water sport are great. A walk north along the bay brings you to an area of excellent tidepools and waters heavily populated by marinelife.

Mauna Lani Beaches

Public access to the Mauna Lani resort beaches is via a walkway that runs through a cave complex and petroglyph historic preserve from a parking lot near the Mauna Lani Spa. This walkway continues past a series of historic fishponds to the water. To the left is the small beach that fronts the Beach Club on the south side of Makaiwa Bay; right is the wider beach that fronts the Mauna Lani Bay hotel. The shoreline path leads beyond the Mauna Lani Bay hotel to Pauoa Beach, which fronts the Fairmont Orchid.

Located adjacent to the Fairmont Orchid hotel on a well-marked access road, the tiny Holoholokai public beach park is open to the public 7 A.M.–6:30 P.M. daily and is improved with a bathroom, running water, picnic tables, and resort-quality landscaping. Unfortunately, the beach itself is mostly coral boulders with only tiny pockets offering very limited water access. However, the park is used very little and is perfect for relaxing under a palm tree or for a leisurely stroll to explore the many tidepools. From the back side of the parking lot at this beach park, a trail heads into the *kiawe* and leads to Puako Petroglyphs.

Waialea Bay Marine Life Conservation District

Between the community of Puako and Hapuna Beach State Recreation Area just up the coast is Waialea Bay Marine Life Conservation District, a 35-acre preserve. Turn off Puako Road onto Old Puako Road and then turn down a rough road near pole number 69 to reach the shore. The white sand beach is best in summer. The reef is wonderful for snorkeling, better at its southern end. Although a bit hard to get to, it's a favorite for the local community.

Hapuna Beach State Recreation Area

Approximately seven miles north of 'Anaeho-'omalu is the *second*-best (some rate this the best), but most accessible, white-sand beach on the island. Hapuna Beach is wide and spacious, almost 700 yards long by 70 wide in summer, with a reduction by heavy surf in winter. A lava finger divides the beach into almost equal halves. During good weather the swimming is excellent and lifeguards are on duty. During heavy weather, usually in winter, the rips are fierce, and Hapuna has claimed more lives than any other beach park on all of Hawaii! At the north end is a small cove almost forming a pool that is usually safe, a favorite for snorkeling with families and children. Many classes in beginning scuba and snorkeling are held in this area, and shore fishing is good throughout. At the south end, good breaks make for tremendous body surfing (no boards allowed), and those familiar with the area make spectacular leaps from the sea cliffs. Picnic tables, pavilions, restrooms, a beach rental kiosk and snack bar, and plenty of parking are available in this nicely landscaped park. Hapuna beach is open 7 A.M.–8 P.M. daily.

Camping is available in six A-frame screened shelters that rent for $20 per night and accom-

Hapuna Beach is arguably the best all-around beach on the island.

modate up to four. Provided are sleeping platforms (you bring your own bedding), electric outlets, cold-water showers, and toilets in separate comfort stations, plus a shared range and refrigerator in a central pavilion. Although the spot is a little run-down, the A-frames are very popular, so reservations and a deposit are required. You can receive full information from the Division of State Parks, P.O. Box 936, Hilo, HI 96721, 808/974-6200; or visit the office at 75 Aupuni St., Room 204, in Hilo.

Kauna'oa Beach

Better known as Mauna Kea Beach because of the nearby luxury hotel of the same name, Kauna'oa is less than a mile north of Hapuna Beach and is considered the best beach on the Big Island by not only the local population, but also by those who judge such things from a broader perspective. In times past, it was a nesting and mating ground for green sea turtles, and although these activities no longer occur because of human pressure on the habitat, turtles still visit the south end of the beach. Mauna Kea Beach is long and wide, and the sandy bottom makes for excellent swimming within the reef. It is more sheltered than Hapuna but can still be dangerous. Hotel beach boys, always in attendance, are unofficial lifeguards who have saved many unsuspecting tourists. During high surf, the shoreline is a favorite with surfers. Like all beaches in Hawaii, this one is public, but to keep the number of nonguests down, only 10 parking passes are handed out each day on a first-come, first-served basis. Pick up a pass at the guardhouse as you enter the hotel grounds. This entitles you to spend the day on the beach, but on weekends they're gone early. Alternately, park at Hapuna Beach and return via an easy mile-long trail connecting Hapuna and Mauna Kea Beaches.

Spencer Beach County Park

The entrance for this park is the same as that for Pu'ukohola Heiau on Route 19 just south of Kawaihae. A coastal trail leads from the beach park up to the *heiau,* so you can combine a day at the beach with a cultural education. The park is named after Samuel Mahuka Spencer, a longtime island resident who was born in

Waimea, served as county mayor for 20 years, and died in 1960 at Honoka'a. The park provides pavilions, restrooms, cold-water showers, electricity, picnic facilities, and even tennis courts. Day use is free, but tent and trailer camping are by county permit only. Spencer Beach is protected somewhat from wind and heavy wave action by an offshore reef and by breakwaters built around Kawaihae Bay. These make it the safest swimming beach along South Kohala's shore and a favorite with local families with small children. The wide, shallow reef is home to a wide spectrum of marinelife, making the snorkeling entertaining. The shoreline fishing is also excellent.

ENTERTAINMENT

Entertainment in South Kohala is limited but generally means soft Hawaiian vocal and instrumental music performed at the restaurants and lounges of the luxury resorts along this coast, movies and hula performances at the Kings' Shops, and the sporadic dinner music at restaurants in Kawaihae.

Music at the Resorts

Each resort provides music at one or more of its restaurants or lounges. Remember that some of the hotels will not even let you on their grounds unless you are a guest or have a reservation at one of their restaurants, so the following is a short list of some of the options along this coast that will be open to everyone.

Live entertainment happens each night 5–11:30 P.M. at the **Clipper Lounge** at the Waikoloa Beach Marriott. This soothing music complements the evening breezes, light bar menu, and smooth tropical drinks from the bar.

The sweet sounds of Hawaiian music precede the edgier strands of jazz every evening 5 P.M.–midnight at the 1920s steamship-era **Mololo Lounge** near the front entrance of the Hilton. The hotel's Kamuela Provision Company has evening musical entertainment for restaurant diners.

The **Atrium Lounge** fills the inner courtyard of the Mauna Lani Bay Hotel with traditional Hawaiian music and the swaying hula dance in the early evening, entertainment put on by the members of the Lim family for more than 23 years. On some nights, the hotel's Bay Terrace restaurant offers piano music, while the Honu Lounge often has live vocal duos on the weekend.

Both the **Reef Lounge** at the Hapuna Beach Hotel and the **Copper Bar** at the Mauna Kea Beach Hotel have light Hawaiian music around sunset and later, a perfect recipe to slip into the quiet evening.

At the Kings' Shops

Although the schedule changes periodically, **free entertainment** is offered at the Kings' Shops every weekday afternoon at 6 P.M. and on weekends at 4 P.M. when a local *hula halau* comes to perform or local musicians play traditional and contemporary Hawaiian music. Daily at 11:30 A.M. or 12:30 P.M., some hands-on cultural activity is presented, like ukulele lessons, fiber crafts, or hula lessons. These events are popular with both tourists and locals and are an excellent chance to have fun Hawaiian style.

Every Tuesday evening when the sun goes down the outdoor movie screen, the Kings' Keaka, on the lawn next to the lake at the Kings' Shops lights up with a full-length **movie.** Every week brings a different film, and many are kid-oriented. Admission is $5, free for children 5 years old or younger. The show starts at 7 P.M. Bring something to sit on.

SHOPPING

Waikoloa Resort

The Waikoloa Beach Resort community has its own very adequate shopping center. The **Kings' Shops,** open 9:30 A.M.–9:30 P.M. daily, feature more than 50 different shops and restaurants, along with entertainment, special events, a Hawaiian Visitors Bureau office, and a gas station. A number of Hawaiian artifacts and exhibits are displayed here and there around the center. Many shops carry clothing, from couture fashions to resortwear, aloha shirts, and T-shirts. Buy camera film at **Zac's Photo** or **Whaler's General Store,** which is the place for light groceries and sundries. **Pacific Rim Collections** is where you will find Hawaiian quilts, masks from throughout the South Pacific, and carved whales and dolphins. For artwork, try either **Dolphin Galleries** or **Genesis Galleries,** where you'll see pieces by Roy Tabora, Lau Chun, and glasswork by Dale Chihuly; and **Under the Koa Tree** showcases Hawaiian artists who have turned their hands to koa woodwork and fine jewelry. **Indochine** has jewelry, gifts, and art from the Orient, and you can find an amazing collection of stringed musical instruments at **The Ukulele House. Na Hoku** and **Maui Divers** carry local jewelry. If all this shopping hasn't worn you out, head for **Macy's** or the **Galleria,** where its many departments carry goods from around the world. The center wouldn't be complete without a place to eat, and you can find everything from fast food to a fine meal. There's something for everyone.

A full complement of free entertainment and cultural events are planned throughout the day and low-cost movies are shown on an outdoor movie screen on Tuesday evenings.

Free **guided tours** of native Hawaiian plants are offered at 11:30 A.M. on weekdays from in front of the food pavilion. Additionally, a petroglyph tour also runs at 10:30 A.M. daily. These petroglyphs offer a link to the mythology and lore of ancient Hawaii. Wear comfortable clothing and bring water for this two-hour walk.

A new addition to the existing shops, the larger Waikoloa Queens' Marketplace, is planned for the space inland and kitty-corner across the resort access road. Not only will it have retail clothing, gift, and art shops, but a performance venue and cultural exhibits are planned.

Mauna Lani

Under construction at the time of this book revision, the Shops at Mauna Lani will add retail shopping space, restaurants, and an entertainment venue for the expanding Mauna Lani Resort and surrounding area and will provide an alternative to the upscale Kings' Shops down the coast at the Waikoloa Resort.

RECREATION

Golf

The resorts in South Kohala offer half a dozen of the best golf courses in the state, and they are all within a few miles of each other.

One of the most recent constructed along the coast is the Four Seasons' **Hualalai Golf Club** (808/325-8480). This Jack Nicklaus course seems to be set in the starkest surroundings. Starting inland, you wind over the tortured lava, finally returning to the water. This course is open only to residents of the Hualalai community and to resort guests. The neighboring beach club community of Kukio has two courses designed by Tom Fazio, a 10-hole short course and an 18-hole course, both of which are open to community members only.

Like rivers of green, the Waikoloa Scottish-links **Kings' Golf Course** (808/886-7888), designed by Tom Weiskopf and Jay Morrish, and **Beach Golf Course** (808/886-6060), a Robert Trent Jones Jr. creation, wind their way around the hotels and condos of Waikoloa Beach Resort. Both have plenty of water and lava rock hazards, and each has its own clubhouse. Lessons, a golf clinic, and a half-day golf school can be arranged through both courses.

Surrounding the Mauna Lani Bay Hotel are the marvelous **Francis H. I'i Brown North Course** and **Francis H. I'i Brown South Course,** whose artistically laid out fairways, greens, and sand traps make it a modern landscape sculpture. The 18-hole courses are carved from lava, with striking ocean views in every direction. Call the Pro Shop (808/885-6655) for information, tee times, clinics, and lessons.

The Mauna Kea's classic, trend-setting **Mauna Kea Golf Course** (808/882-5400) was designed by the master, Robert Trent Jones Sr., has been voted among America's 100 greatest courses and one of Hawaii's finest. Deceptive off the tee, it's demanding at the green. It lies near the ocean and has been joined by the more spread out **Hapuna Golf Course** (808/880-3000), designed by Arnold Palmer and Ed Seay, which has been cut into the lava up above the hotels and highway. Both 18-hole courses give even the master players a challenge.

If you are on vacation without your golf clubs and plan to play more than a round or two, consider renting clubs from **Island Discount Golf** (74-5583 Luhia St., Suite A-5, in Kailua-Kona, 808/334-1771), open daily. Rental rates start at $18 per day but go down for longer rental periods. These rental rates are cheaper than those at the golf courses.

Tennis

Virtually every hotel and condominium has at least a couple of tennis courts on its property. Most are for use by guests only, but a few tennis centers are open to the public, and these can always arrange lessons, clinics, round robins, and other match play.

For guests only, the Hualalai tennis club offers eight courts (four lit for night play) with lessons and arranged play. Court fees run $15 per person per day. The Waikoloa Beach Marriott tennis center (808/886-6666) has six day-use courts with a $10 per hour court fee. At $25 for 1.5 hours, the eight plexi-cushion hard courts at the Hilton Waikoloa Village Resort (808/886-2222) are also open to the public. Court time on one of the six plexi-pave courts (three lighted) at the Mauna Lani Fitness Club tennis courts (808/885-7765) runs $12.50; daily clinics and lessons are extra. The Tennis Pavilion at the Fairmont Orchid (808/887-7532) has 10 courts (seven lit) at $15 per person a day, teaches lessons, and arranges match play. With 13 courts, the largest court complex is the Seaside Tennis Club at the Mauna Kea Beach Resort (808/882-5420). Play for $15 per person a day, or sign up for lessons, a clinic, or round robin play.

Outrigger Canoe Ride

A 35-foot replica double-hull outrigger sailing canoe takes guests for rides along the Kohala Coast on morning and early-afternoon sails. Be part of the crew for a voyage and learn about the old sailing ways of the Hawaiians, snorkel in a quiet bay, put a line out for fish, and perhaps spot a whale. The *Halalua Lele* (808/885-2000, www.hawaiiankineadventures.com) leaves from the beach in front of the Fairmont Orchid; rides cost $95 per person.

A 28-passenger rigid-hull raft has joined the company and is an option for a faster and more modern means of cruising the coast. Snorkel adventures on it run $75–95 per person.

Water Sports

For general water sports activities including scuba dives, snorkel gear rental and tours, catamaran or mono-hull sailing cruises, kayak rental, hydro bikes, boogie boards, windsurfing, and more, check with either **Ocean Sports** (808/886-6666, www.hawaiioceansports.com) or **Red Sail Sports** (808/886-2876 or 877/733-7245, www.redsailhawaii.com). These companies operate from 'Anaeho'omalu Beach. Red Sail also has activities happening at the Hapuna Beach Prince Hotel and the Hilton Waikoloa Village, while Ocean Sports runs activities from the Mauna Kea Hotel.

At the Four Seasons Resort, **Hualalai Water Sports** (808/325-8222, www.divesail.com) can put you onto a snorkel cruise, into the water for scuba diving, or aboard a catamaran for a sunset sail. Snorkel gear rental is available, as is scuba instruction and certification. This company also offers various dive trips from and certification courses at Kona Village Resort next door.

At the Mauna Bay Lani Hotel, **Mauna Lani Sea Adventures** (808/885-7883) offers sailing, snorkel, and scuba tours from the white-sand beach in front of the hotel. Sunset sails run $50, snorkel trips $55, and scuba excursions $75–100.

Helicopter Tour

Flying out of the Hapuna Heliport on Astar machines, **Sunshine Helicopters** (808/882-1233 or 800/622-3144, www.sunshinehelicopters.com) runs a 45-minute Kohala Mountain and Hamakua Valley tour at $170 and a two-hour circle-island flight for $360. This company also offers a unique in-house flight from Kona Village Resort to the "Red Roof House," the sole remaining home not destroyed by lava in the Royal Garden subdivision in Puna. Sunshine offers packages with Atlantis Submarine and Body Glove snorkel trips for reduced rates on activities. Sunshine also operates helicopter flights from Hilo and on Maui.

With its spotless safety record and large operation, **Blue Hawaiian Helicopters** (808/961-5600 in Hilo, 808/886-1768 in Waikoloa, 800/786-2583, www.bluehawaiian.com) operates several A-Star helicopters from the Waikoloa Heliport on the Kona side and additional A-Stars from the Hilo Airport. From Waikoloa, a two-hour circle-island flight costs $368 and a shorter Kohala Mountain and valley tour goes for $190. Blue Hawaiian also offers flights on Maui and Kaua'i.

LUXURY RESORT ACCOMMODATIONS

The South Kohala Coast has four resort areas, all providing luxury accommodations, fine dining, golf courses, full-service resort amenities, the best beaches on the island, and a smattering of historical and cultural sites. They are, in effect, self-sufficient mini-villages. The first north of Kailua-Kona is not referred to by one name, but encompasses the adjacent properties of the **Four Seasons Resort** at Hualalai and the **Kona Village Resort** at Ka'upulehu. A huge new 700-acre, private and gated home-site property with two golf courses is rising from the lava fronting Kuki'o Beach, wrapping around both the Four Seasons and Kona Village Resorts and the Hualalai resort community, and encompassing land on the inland side of the highway. These resorts are actually situated in the North Kona district but are discussed here as they are more similar to the South Kohala luxury resorts than to any hotel complex in Kailua or Keauhou to the south. Kona Village Resort, the oldest resort along this coast, is designed like a Polynesian village: low-slung, thatch roofs, palm trees, white-sand beach, and shoreline ponds. It's a welcome oasis in a land of stark black lava and as it has kept up with the times, it still offers one of the best getaway destinations in the state. The Four Seasons Resort is the island's newest, a modern complex of tasteful low-slung buildings, a counterpoint to Kona Village, where you will find golf, tennis, and water sport opportunities. It's new and fresh, a delight for the senses.

Next up the way is **Waikoloa Resort,** the largest, busiest, and most commercial of the resort complexes. Here you have the Waikoloa Beach Marriott, a redesigned hotel that reflects the grandeur of Hawaii from the 1930s and 1940s, the gargantuan Hilton Waikoloa Village, several high-class condominium properties, a number of time-share properties, and very exclusive, private oceanfront estates in the new Kolea development. Here as well are the Kings' Shops, two superb golf courses, a multitude of tennis opportunities, a petroglyph field, remnants of the ancient Kings' Trail, anchialine ponds, and one of the best beaches on the coast. Just across the highway from the resort access road is a commercial heliport. To ease getting around between shops and hotels, the free Waikoloa Shuttle runs every 15 minutes between 10 A.M. and 10 P.M.

Mauna Lani Resort comes next, also big but not as commercial. Here too you find two magnificent hotels, five (and counting) condominiums, two golf courses, two tennis centers, several small beaches, historic fishponds, two petroglyph fields, and a long history. A new shopping complex is rising at the main resort rotary, and each hotel also has a bevy of retail shops. This is a quality high-end resort, without glitz or hype.

Farthest to the north is the **Mauna Kea Resort.** Smaller and more intimate, it contains the grande dame of Kohala hotels, the Mauna Kea Beach Hotel, and its more recent addition, the Hapuna Beach Prince Hotel. Like bride and groom, these two hotels with their golf courses are sufficient unto themselves, and they sit on two of the finest beaches on the island. While there are no major historical sites on the property, they lie a mile or two south of one of the most significant and well-kept *heiau* on this island.

Four Seasons Resort

The **Four Seasons Resort, Hualalai** (100 Ka'upulehu Drive, 808/325-8000 or 888/340-5662, www.fourseasons.com/hualalai), at

© ROBERT NILSEN

formal pool at the Four Seasons Resort

historic Ka'upulehu, opened in late 1996. This 243-room AAA Five-Diamond resort is split into 36 low-rise bungalows in four crescent groups that front a half-mile beach and several natural lagoons adjacent to the Kona Village Resort. Located in among old lava flows from the Hualalai volcano, 32 of these units have ocean views, while four are located along the 18th green of the accompanying golf course. Authentic Hawaiian art pieces from the late 1700s to the present are displayed throughout the hotel. There is no skimping on space, furnishings, or amenities in any of the rooms or suites. Large as well are the bathrooms, each of which looks out onto a private garden, lanai, or patio. An exceptional place, this all-inclusive destination resort is not cheap. Rooms run $560–810 per night, suites $975–7,320, $150 for a third adult in a room. Numerous attractive packages are always offered, so inquire. To help keep all the guests fed and happy, the resort has three on-site restaurants and two bars.

On the ocean side of the meeting room building and the outdoor Hoku stage theater is Kids for all Seasons, the hotel's service of supervised care for five- to 12-year-olds that provides a wide variety of fun-filled and indoor and outdoor activities. For teens (and their parents), Hale Kula is the activity center for indoor games. Hualalai Tennis Club is open for resort guests only. Located adjacent to the tennis courts is the Sports Club and Spa, a full-service facility that offers a variety of instructional classes, a 25-meter lap pool, exercise machines, massage and spa therapies, and sand volleyball and half-court basketball courts. For the duffer, the private Hualalai Golf Club offers 18 holes of challenging play along the ocean for resort guests. Be sure to check out the Cultural Center with its 1,200-gallon reef aquarium just downstairs from the lobby, where you can learn about the surrounding waters, the Ka'upulehu area, and the life and lifestyle of ancient Hawaiians. In addition to the natural lagoons, the resort has both freshwater and saltwater swimming pools set just back from the beach. For those interested, a water sport kiosk on the beach can fix you up with needed gear or water activities.

Kona Village Resort

So you want to go "native," and you're dreaming of a "little grass shack" along a secluded beach? No problem! The **Kona Village Resort** (One Kahuwai Bay Drive, 808/325-5555 or 800/432-5450 in Hawaii, 800/367-5290 Mainland, kvr@aloha.net, www.konavillage.com) is a once-in-a-lifetime dream experience. Located on Kahuwai Bay, a picture-perfect cove of black and white sand dotted with coconut palms, the village lies seven miles north of the Kona Airport, surrounded by acres of seclusion. The accommodations are 125 distinctive "hales," individual renditions of thatch-roofed huts found throughout Polynesia and Hawaii. They are simple but luxurious, and in keeping with the idea of getting away from it all, have no TVs, radios, or telephones. All, however, do have ceiling fans and louvered windows to let the tropical breezes blow through. Each hut features a wet bar, refrigerator, coffeemaker, and extra-large bathroom, and is either located along the water, around the lagoon, or back in a garden setting. At one time you had to fly into the hotel's private airstrip, but today you arrive by car. Almost exactly at mile marker 87, turn in, make a right within 100 yards, and follow the access road that leads through coal-black lava fields. Don't despair! Down by the sea you can see the shimmering green palm trees as they beckon you to the resort. Kona Village gives you your money's worth, with a lei greeting, free valet service, a private tennis center, water sports, numerous cultural activities, and a lu'au. Guided tours (reservations required) are also offered to the petroglyph field on property, complete with history and legends of the area.

© ROBERT NILSEN

The proverbial "grass shack" is real at the Kona Village Resort.

Except for the lu'au, meals at Kona Village are served only for resort guests and are included in room rates. Hale Moana is the main dining room, and the adjacent Hale Moana Terrace serves the famous luncheon buffet daily. Hale Samoa is the fine dining restaurant, open daily except Wednesday and Friday for dinner only. Upon entering Hale Samoa, your spirits rise immediately with the sweep of cathedral ceiling. On the walls is an original painting by Herb Kane, Hawaii's foremost artist, that depicts *The Fair American,* a tiny ship commandeered by King Kamehameha that was instrumental in changing the history of old Hawaii. The walls also hold portraits of the hotel's original owner, Johnno Jackson, an oil geologist from Texas, who in 1960 sailed in with his wife Helen, their Labrador dog, a monkey, and a parrot—all in a 42-foot schooner—landed on these shores and declared, "This is the spot!" Also on the grounds are Hale Ho'okipa "House of Hospitality," where a lu'au is held on Friday nights as it has for over 30 years. Back by popular demand is the Wednesday Paniolo Night buffet. Drinks and tropical libations are offered throughout the afternoon at the Shipwreck Bar next to the beachfront pool, at the beachside Talk Story Bar over lunch, and all day at the Bora Bora Bar next to Hale Moana, where soft musical entertainment soothes guests every evening.

Rates per night start at $530 per couple with full American plan (includes three meals), and go up to $940. Two-room units for three adults run $875–1,160. Add $38 for children 3–5, $143 for children 6–12, and $193 for an extra adult. Several honeymoon and celebration packages are also available. There is a strict reservations and refund policy, so check. These rates also include all scheduled activities, use of the tennis and fitness centers, water sports equipment, and all activities except scuba, snuba, massage, and the Friday night lu'au. The hotel's Na Keiki in Paradise is a children's program included in the room price that will entertain and educate children ages six and up throughout the day (except May and September). The beach shack is open every day for your pleasure, as are the jewelry store and gift shop. For those with interests beyond the village, a new helicopter trip from the resort property flies to the only house in the Royal Gardens subdivision in Puna that was not destroyed by lava since the eruptions began at Kilauea in 1983. Now owned by Ty Warner Hotels and Resorts, some small changes are taking place at Kona Village Resort, but most of the highly professional and seasoned staff remain. They take pride in the hotel and do everything to help you have a rewarding, enjoyable, and relaxing stay at this premier resort. The Kona Village is a serene Hawaiian classic that deserves its well-earned reputation for excellence, and as a consequence gets 65 percent repeat visitors and 25 percent honeymooners.

Waikoloa Beach Marriott

Following a $25 million renovation and facelift in the early 2000s, the former Royal Waikoloan re-emerged as an artful Outrigger property known as the Waikoloa Beach Marriott, an Outrigger Resort (69-275 Waikoloa Beach Dr., 808/886-6789 or 800/922-5533, www.waikoloabeachmarriott.com). On a perfect spot fronting the palm-fringed 'Anaeho'omalu Bay, the hotel looks out over ponds that once stocked fish for passing *ali'i.* The hotel lobby is a spacious open-air affair that lets the trade winds blow through across its cool sandstone floor. Six floors of rooms extend out in wings on both sides, flanking the landscaped courtyard with swimming pool and water slide. Greeting you as you enter the lobby is a marvelous old koa outrigger canoe set in front of a three-part mural by renowned Hawaiian artist Herb Kane of a royal canoe and Western frigate meeting off the Kona coast. The renovation has bequeathed a look and feel reminiscent of the 1930s and 1940s with its decorative artistic touches. The Waikoloa Beach Marriott is a class act.

All 545 hotel rooms and suites are tastefully decorated in light soothing colors, with king-size beds, rattan furnishings, custom quilts, and island prints of a mid-20th century art deco style. Each room has air-conditioning, color TV, high-speed Internet access, *yakuta* robes, in-room safe, small refrigerator, marble vanities, and a private lanai. Rooms are reasonably priced at $325–485, while suites run $965–3,100 per night; the separate "cabanas" go for $535. Hotel services and amenities include an activities desk for all on-site and off-property excursions and several retail shops and boutiques, and a Kahn Galleries shop for fine art. You can take part in daily Hawaiian cultural programs, use the business center, or have your kids properly cared for at the Waikoloa Keiki Club children's program. Enjoy the garden swimming pool, spa and fitness center, six plexi-pave tennis courts, and a grand beach with plenty of water activities. The hotel is just a few minutes' stroll past the royal fishponds to the beach or to the remains of a nearby ancient but now restored *heiau.* For a self-guided walk through the historical, cultural, and natural points of note from the hotel property down to the beach, pick up a copy of *A Walking Tour of Our Hawaiian Treasures* at the guest service desk in the lobby of the hotel.

Hilton Waikoloa Village

At the Hilton Waikoloa Village (425 Waikoloa Beach Dr., 808/886-1234 or 800/445-8667, fax 808/886-2900, www.hiltonwaikoloavillage.com), the idea was to create a reality so beautiful and naturally harmonious that anyone who came here, sinner or saint, would be guaranteed a glimpse of paradise. The three

© ROBERT NILSEN

At the Hilton, taking a launch is one of the easiest ways to get around the property.

main towers, each enclosing a miniature fern-filled botanical garden, are spread over the grounds almost a mile apart and are linked by pink flagstone walkways, canals navigated by hotel launches, and a quiet, space-age tram. Attention to the smallest detail is immediately apparent, and everywhere sculptures, art treasures, and brilliant flowers soothe the eyes. The museum promenade displays choice artworks from Hawaii, Oceania, and Asia—pick up a brochure from the sundries shops at the hotel explaining this $7 million collection or choose one of the twice-weekly art tours—and here and there around the property are brilliant artistic flourishes. Nearly everywhere you look you delight in beauty. Songs of rare tropical birds and the wind whispering through a bamboo forest create the natural melody that surrounds you. The beach fronting the property offers excellent snorkeling, while two gigantic pools and a series of lagoons are perfect for water activities and sunbathing. You can swim in a private lagoon accompanied by reef fish, help feed the dolphins, dine at any one of the nine first-rate restaurants, delight in the food and extravagant dinner show of the twice-weekly Legends of the Pacific lu'au, relax to a soothing message after a game of tennis at the Kohala Sports Club and Spa, leave your kids for the day in the experienced hands of the Camp Menehune staff, follow the self-guiding botanical and wildlife tour booklet for a naturalist's view of the property, peruse the in-house art gallery, pick up a memento at the retail shops, participate in a plethora of other daily activities, or just let your cares slip away as you lounge in perfect tranquility.

This resort is definitely a distinctive undertaking, a step apart from any other resort complex in the state. It has cut its own path and gone its own way. Yet with all the grandeur, beauty, and expansiveness, somehow it seems a bit overblown and incongruous with its surroundings. Forget intimacy—you don't come here to get away, you come here to participate. With 1,240 rooms (it's like three hotels in one) on a 62-acre property, it's so big that entering

DOLPHIN QUEST

With all the splendor at the Hilton Waikoloa, one of the most talked-about features at the hotel is Dolphin Quest (www.dolphinquest.org). A specially constructed saltwater pond is home to Atlantic bottlenose dolphins from Florida's Gulf Coast. Daily, but with reservations up to two months in advance, guests are allowed to interact with the dolphins. Dolphin Quest is an educational experience. Here you don't ride the dolphins and they don't do tricks for you. In half-hour to four-hour sessions that range $105-320 per person, guests wade in chest-deep water with the dolphins gliding by while a staff member imparts information concerning not only dolphins but all marinelife and human interdependence with it. Participants help with training, feeding, and games. The experience is voluntary on the dolphins' part – *they* choose to swim with *you* as a guest in their domain. Much of the proceeds from the program go toward marine research.

the lobby can be like walking into Grand Central Station, and navigating certain walkways, particularly at dinnertime, is like pushing through throngs at a fair. The Hilton is so big and complex that it employs over 1,200 people, serves over 12,000 meals a day, and uses 7 percent of the island's electricity. You be the judge: is this paradise or something else? For all that, the Hilton still offers plenty for everyone, gives you unlimited options for a great vacation, treats families well, and does that at a fair and very competitive price, making a stay at this resort the best bet for many visitors who desire to experience this wonderful Kohala Coast. As with everything else, Hilton offers a variety of room options. Rates are $199–539 for garden/mountain rooms, $209–509 for golf view rooms, $244–609 for partial ocean views, $264–719 for deluxe ocean rooms, $359–869 for cabanas, and $1,060–6,150 for suites! Ask about discounts, packages, and special offers.

Mauna Lani Bay Hotel and Bungalows

As soon as you turn off Route 19, the entrance road, trimmed in purple bougainvillea, sets the mood for Mauna Lani Bay Hotel and Bungalows (68-1400 Mauna Lani Dr., 808/885-6622 or 800/367-2323, www.maunalani.com), a 350-room hotel that opened in 1983. A short stroll beyond the central courtyard leads you past the swimming pool and through a virtual botanical garden to a white-sand beach perfect for island relaxation. From here, any number of water sports activities can be arranged. Nearby are convoluted lagoons, and away from the shore you find the Sports and Fitness Club with tennis courts, a lap pool, and weights, the full-service Mauna Lani Spa, and exclusive shops. Jogging and walking trails run throughout and a cave complex and petroglyph field lies right in the middle of the resort complex. Surrounding the hotel is the marvelous Francis I'i Brown Golf Course, whose artistically laid-out fairways, greens, and sand traps make it a modern landscape sculpture.

Rooms at the AAA Five-Diamond award-winning Mauna Lani Bay Hotel run $430 mountain view to $920 for corner oceanfront, suites are $980–1,800. Rooms are oversized; the majority come with an ocean view, and each includes a private lanai, remote color TV and VCR, honor bar, in-room safe, and all the comforts of home. The very exclusive 4,000-square-foot, two-bedroom bungalows rent for $4,800–5,900 a night but each comes complete with a personal chef, butler, and swimming pool. In addition, one-, two-, and three-bedroom home-like villas go for $620–1,180, three-night minimum required. Weekly rates are available on the villas and bungalows, and there are always many different special and packages. Guest privileges include complimentary use of snorkeling equipment, Hawaiian cultural classes and activities, hula lessons, complimentary morning coffee, and resort and historic tours. Five restaurants and lounges cater to the culinary needs of resort guests, from quick and casual to classic island fare. For parents with young children who have come to the realization that "families who want to stay together don't always play together," the hotel offers a break from those little bundles of joy with Kids' Club of Mauna Lani for children ages 5–12. While you play, the kids are shepherded through games and activities. One of the favorite evening activities at the hotel, Twilight at Kalahuipua'a, takes place once a month at the Eva Parker Woods cottage. For this free event, Hawaiian musicians, dancers, and storytellers gather to share their cultural talents with community and resort guests. Ask the concierge for particulars and for information about the numerous daily activities.

The Fairmont Orchid

In a tortured field of coal-black lava made more dramatic by pockets of jade-green lawn rises ivory-white The Fairmont Orchid (One N. Kaniku Dr., 808/885-2000 or 800/845-9905, www.fairmont.com/orchid). A rolling drive lined with *haku lei* of flowering shrubs entwined with stately palms leads to the open-air porte cochere. Nature, powerful yet soothing, surrounds the hotel in a magnificent free-form pool and trimmed tropical gardens of ferns and flowers. Walls are graced with Hawaiian quilts and excellent artwork on view everywhere; every set of stairs boasts a velvety smooth koa banister carved with the pineapple motif, the Hawaiian symbol of hospitality. The Fairmont Orchid is elegant in a casual European sense, a place to relax in luxury and warm *aloha*.

Located in two six-story wings off the main reception hall, the 539 hotel rooms, each with private lanai and sensational view, are a mixture of kings, doubles, and suites. Done in neutral tones, the stylish and refined rooms feature handcrafted quilts, twice-daily room attendance, an entertainment center, fully stocked honor bar, in-room safe, and spacious marble bathrooms. Room rates begin at $329 for a garden view to $759 for a deluxe oceanfront room. One-bedroom executive suites run $959 and the two magnificent Presidential Suites are... well, very expensive. Rates run substantially higher during the Christmas and New Year's holiday. Some special packages are available.

In addition to several restaurants and lounges, the hotel offers first-rate guest services, amenities, and activities that include a small shopping mall with everything from sundries to designer boutiques, complimentary shuttle to and from Mauna Lani's famous championship golf courses, golf bag storage, 11 tennis courts (with seven lit for evening play), a fitness center, snorkel equipment, the full-service Spa Without Walls for massage, body treatments, and exercise, an enormous swimming pool and sun deck, double-hulled canoe sailing, Hawaiian crafts, a property botanical tour, safe-deposit boxes, on-property car rental, baby-sitting, the Keiki Aloha instructional day camp program for children ages 5–12, and much, much more. The Fairmont has even gone "green," using many ways of being more environmentally sensitive throughout its facility and grounds.

Hapuna Beach Prince Hotel

Opened in 1994, the Hapuna Beach Prince Hotel (62-100 Kauna'oa Dr., 808/880-1111 or 800/882-6060, www.hapunabeachprincehotel.com) fronts Hapuna Beach about one mile down the coast from the Mauna Kea Hotel. These two hotels are separate entities but function as one resort, joined as if in marriage. The princess, Mauna Kea, has finally found her prince. Long and lean, the AAA four-Diamond Prince hotel steps down the hillside toward the beach in eight levels. A formal portico fronts the main entryway, through which you have a splendid view of palm trees and the ocean. Lines are simple and decoration subtle. An attempt has been made to simplify and let surrounding nature become part of the whole. As at the Mauna Kea, visitors are not overwhelmed with sensory overload. A free periodic shuttle connects the Hapuna Beach to the Mauna Kea, and all services available at one are open to guests of the other.

Carpeted bedrooms are spacious, allowing for king-size beds, and the bathrooms have marble floors. Each of the 350 large and well-appointed rooms has an entertainment center, comfy chairs, live plants, prints on the walls, and a lanai. Although rooms are air-conditioned, they all have louvered doors, allowing you to keep out the sun while letting breezes flow through. Rates for the 350 guest rooms start at $360 and go up to $650 a night; suites run $1,200. In addition, there is an 8,000-square foot estate on property that rents for $7,000 a night for the party that just needs its privacy and seclusion. Four restaurants serve a variety of food for all meals during the day, and the lounges stay open for evening drinks.

The Prince Keiki Club at the Hapuna offers a reprieve to parents who desire some time away from their energetic kids. Children 5–12 years old can fill their time with fun activities and educational projects. For Mom and Dad are the links-style Hapuna Golf Course and the hotel's physical fitness center. While the spa and fitness center has weights, its main focus is on dance, yoga, stretching, and alignment techniques, with various massage therapies and body treatments also available. Set in the garden below the lobby, the swimming pool is great recreation during the day and reflects the stars at night. Speaking of the stars, four nights a week, the hotel hosts a stargazing program for hotel guests (reservations required, $25), and numerous other activities are scheduled through the week. A few shops whet the appetite of those needing sundries or resortwear, and, if one has to use it, the business center can help with all business, packaging, shipping, and electronic needs.

The Mauna Kea Beach Hotel

This hotel has set the standard of excellence along Kohala's coast ever since former Hawaii Governor William Quinn interested Laurance Rockefeller in the lucrative possibilities of building a luxury hideaway for the rich and famous. Beautiful coastal land was leased from the Parker Ranch, and the **Mauna Kea Beach Hotel** (62-100 Mauna Kea Beach Drive, 808/882-7222 or 800/882-6060, www.maunakeabeachhotel.com) opened in 1965. The Mauna Kea was the only one of its kind for a few years, until others saw the possibilities, and more luxury hotels were built along this coast. Over the years, the Mauna Kea aged a bit and suffered stiff competition from newer resorts nearby. After an extensive one-year restoration, the Mauna Kea reopened with youthful enthusiasm in December 1995 and shines again as the princess it always was. Class is always class, and the landmark Mauna Kea again receives very high accolades as a fine resort hotel.

The Mauna Kea fronts the beautiful Kauna'oa Beach, one of the best on the island. Million-dollar condos also grace the resort grounds, and hotel guests tend to come back year after year. The hotel itself is an eight-story terraced complex of simple, clean-cut design. The grounds and lobbies showcase more than 1,000 museum-quality art pieces from throughout the Pacific (pick up a brochure from the front desk and take a self-guided tour), and more than a half million plants add greenery and beauty to the surroundings. The award-winning Mauna Kea Golf Course surrounds the grounds, and on a bluff overlooking the water, the 11 courts of the tennis center (plus an additional two by the golf clubhouse) vie for use. Swimmers can use the beach or the round courtyard swimming pool, set just off the small fitness center, and horseback riding is available at the Parker Ranch up in Waimea. A host of daily activities are scheduled, including a twice-weekly stargazing program, but perhaps the most unusual activity at the hotel is the evening manta ray viewing off Lookout Point.

The 310 beautifully appointed rooms, starting at $370, feature an extra-large lanai and specially made wicker furniture. From there, rates rise to $575–620 for beachfront units, $590–650 for deluxe ocean view rooms, and suites run $975–1,600. Numerous packages are available. The rooms are, like the rest of the hotel, the epitome of understated elegance. A television-free resort at its inception, the hotel now has TVs in most of the rooms as part of the recent restoration. The Mauna Kea has four restaurants and several lounges, but a resort shuttle operates between here and the Hapuna Beach Prince Hotel, where Mauna Kea guests have signing privileges.

CONDOMINIUMS

Waikoloa Condominiums

The **ResortQuest Shores at Waikoloa** (69-1035 Keana Place, 808/885-5001 or 800/321-2558 in Hawaii, 886/774-2924 Mainland and Canada, www.RQShoresatWaikoloa.com) are secluded luxury condominiums nestled away in the planned community of Waikoloa along the 18th fairway of the Beach Course. Enter through a security gate to see the peaceful and beautifully manicured grounds of these white-stucco and red-tile-roof condominiums. A few minutes away are the best beaches on Hawai'i and all of the activities offered by the large luxury hotels, if you wish to participate. The condominium offers an activities desk where your outings can be arranged, a swimming pool and hot tub, two complimentary tennis courts, a small exercise facility, and outdoor barbecues. The condos are decorated by the individual owners so each room is unique, but there are guidelines and standards so every unit is tasteful and comfortable. All units are extremely spacious, with many boasting marble and terra cotta floors. All have huge bathrooms, full modern kitchens, laundry facilities, and light and airy sitting rooms complete with state-of-the-art entertainment centers. Rates range

$285 for a one-bedroom to $700 for a three-bedroom golf villa. Low season brings a 10 percent reduction, and a number of packages are available. ResortQuest's newest Hawaii property is the contemporary-style **ResortQuest Waikoloa Colony Villas** (69-555 Waikoloa Beach Drive, 808/886-8899). Located along the 15th fairway of the Beach Course, one-, two-, and three-bedroom villas run $330–550. If you are after a luxury vacation within a vacation where you can get away from it all after you've gotten away from it all, either of these ResortQuest properties is a superb choice.

The attractive three-story **Outrigger Fairway Villas** (69-200 Pohakulana Pl., 808/886-0036 or 800/688-7444, www.outrigger.com) is located across the lake and opposite the Kings' Shops. Deluxe two- and three-bedroom units have all top-of-the-line amenities as well as a private pool, exercise center, and guest service center. Rates run $325–550 a night.

Lying next to golf links and the clubhouse, the Mediterranean white **Vista Waikoloa** (69-1010 Waikoloa Beach Drive, 808/886-0412 or 800/822-4252) has an ideal location. Like all other accommodations in this planned community, Vista Waikoloa is luxury living in a secure environment. On the property are a lap pool and barbecue pavilions. You can partake in as much as you like or just lounge to your heart's content. Two-bedroom units run $150–280 while those with three bedrooms go for $395.

Mauna Lani Condominiums

Sitting in the lap of luxury are two secure, private, modern, and very high-end condo properties. They are **Mauna Lani Point,** which is surrounded by golf fairways at oceanside, and **The Islands at Mauna Lani,** also surrounded by golf links but set away from the water. Each has superbly built, spacious units that leave nothing lacking. The Mauna Lani Point has one- and two-bedroom units that run $340–650 a night, while The Island rents two- and three-bedroom, two-story homes for $575–725; three-night minimum. All guests can make use of the activities and amenities located within the Mauna Lani Resort complex. For reservations and information about either, contact Classic Resorts (68-1050 Mauna Lani Point Dr., 808/885-5022 or 800/642-6284, fax 808/885-5015, info@classicresorts.com, www.classicresorts.com).

Nearby and surrounding one of the lagoons with wonderful views of the ocean is the older but very well-maintained, three-story **Mauna Lani Terrace** condominium. The one- and two-bedroom condo units run $285–580 a night and the three-bedroom town homes are $420–975.

VACATION RENTAL AGENCIES

Along with a few high-end condos, luxury resorts are the mainstay of accommodations in coastal South Kohala. There are, however, a number of vacation rental homes and individual condo units available for those who want more privacy but still want the sun. Try the following agencies for options.

For exclusive condo units and mansion-style homes at various resort complexes along the South Kohala Coast, try **South Kohala Management** (P.O. Box 384900, Waikoloa, HI 96738, 808/883-8500 or 800/822-4252, fax 808/883-9818, info@southkohala.com, www.southkohala.com). From its office at the Vistas Waikoloa condo complex, it handles premium properties only, with prices to match. Minimum stays are three nights for condos and five nights for homes, seven nights during Christmas.

MacArthur & Company (65-1148 Mamalahoa Hwy., Kamuela, HI 96743, 808/885-8875 or 877/885-8285, info@letsgohawaii.com, www.letsgohawaii.com), with an office in Waimea at the Historic Spencer House, manages numerous rental homes mostly in the Kohala resort area, Puako, North Kohala, and Waimea with a few others south in Kona, that range mostly $350–1,000 a night, with several under $150 and a few that you have to call for a quote!

FOOD

Except for a few community-oriented restaurants in Waikoloa Village, a handful of reasonably priced roadside restaurants in Kawaihae, and a gaggle of eating establishments in the Kings' Shops, all of the food in South Kohala is served in the elegant but expensive restaurants of the luxury resorts.

Four Seasons Resort

This first-class resort's three restaurants will fill your every culinary need for all three meals of the day. Both the elegant AAA Four-Diamond **Pahu i'a Restaurant** and the casual **Beach Tree Bar and Grill** are set oceanside. With seating inside and out, Pahu i'a opens in the morning with local and international favorites, buffet or à la carte, and transforms in the evening into a more formal eatery with an emphasis on cuisines of the Pacific and the imaginative combinations of food and flavorings. Some items that you might find on the menu are steamed Hawaiian snapper, prime shutome (swordfish) steak, grilled veal tenderloin, and peppercorn steak; most entrées fall in the $36–46 range. Resortwear is required and reservations are necessary (808/325-8000). Serving lunch and less-expensive dinners, the Beach Tree offers grill items near the main pool. Several evenings a week, this restaurant offers theme nights with regional foods of the world. Nightly music is also a part of this venue, with a hula dancing performance several nights of the week. In addition, the **Hualalai Grille** at the golf clubhouse across the main entrance drive serves lunch and fine-dining dinners in a sophisticated but informal setting. Entrées from the sea and land, like ginger-crusted onaga and Kobe beef, are generally in the mid-$30 range. For drinks and convivial late-night companionship there are several options. The Lava Lounge at the Pahu i'a is open evenings only and offers light music most nights. Set as close as you can get to the water without being in it, the Beach Tree bar dispenses libations throughout the day under its canopy roof and is an easygoing place to sit and watch the sun set. Both the Lava Lounge and the Beach Tree Bar have a simple bar menu for appetizers.

Waikoloa Beach Marriott

Harking back to the days when Hawaiian music and news of the islands was transmitted to the world by radio and when Pan Am Clipper Ships flew travelers to the islands, is **Hawaii Calls Restaurant,** the hotel's main dining room. Open for breakfast and dinner, the decor says yesteryear but the menu is thoroughly modern with a mix of Continental and Asian cuisine. A special seafood and prime rib buffet is presented on Saturdays. Breakfast is standard American fare but dinner brings such entrées as baby back ribs, black pepper roasted salmon, crab-crusted opakapaka, and pasta, with entrées in the $22–37 range. As part of this open-air restaurant, the **Clipper Lounge** serves tropical drinks as smooth as a Clipper's landing on a mirror lagoon. This lounge serves up a late bistro menu and nightly entertainment 5–11:30 P.M., while the more casual poolside **Nalu Bar and Grill** is open 10 A.M.–sunset for snacks, fill-'er-ups, and drinks. Fit for the royalty who once called this bay their home, the twice-weekly Royal Lu'au draws appreciative guests for food and entertainment.

Hilton Waikoloa Village

Like the grandness of the hotel in general, the Hilton's nine restaurants are culinary powerhouses, and every taste is provided for. Of the nine, four stand out as the finest. **Donatoni's** features classic Northern Italian cuisine for dinner only in a romantic and formal setting; **Imari** serves traditional Japanese dinners prepared at your table and sushi from the bar; the Chinese **Kirin** restaurant offers dim sum lunches and dinner entrées from various regions of the country; and, set closest to the ocean, the **Kamuela Provision Co.** specializes in steak and seafood prepared in a Hawaiian Regional style. Entrées at Donatoni's, Imari, and the Kamuela Provision Company generally run in the $25–48 range, while those at Kirin are $15–24. Reservations are recommended for each of these fine restaurants, and evening resort attire is best. Other more casual and less expensive restaurants at the hotel include the

Palm Terrace, which presents breakfast and dinner buffets, with a different theme nightly; the outside **Orchid Cafe** provides light breakfasts, deli lunches, and a soda fountain; the **Lagoon Grill** has casual lunches and tropical drinks all afternoon; and the **Boat Landing Pavilion Food Court** offers casual foods, snacks, and takeout orders all day, along with a sushi bar and drinks. The hotel's bars and lounges are other options, the Kamuela Provision Co.'s wine bar has become a hit, while twice weekly the **Legends of the Pacific** lu'au delights guests with fine food and an extravagant dinner show.

Mauna Lani Resort

The Mauna Lani offers superb dining options. The **Bay Terrace,** open daily for breakfast and dinner, offers casual, gardenside dining, with an emphasis on fish and seafood. Its weekend seafood dinner buffet shouldn't be missed, and a Sunday brunch draws visitors and locals alike. Set within the arms of a lagoon and overlooking the ocean is **Canoe House,** the hotel's signature restaurant. Open daily for dinner only, it delights you with exciting Pacific Rim cuisine. Resortwear is required at the Canoe House, and reservations (808/881-7911) are highly recommended at either. Dinner reservations are also recommended at **The Gallery** (808/885-7777), a fine dining "upscale chophouse" serving lunch and dinner Tues.–Sat. up at the golf clubhouse overlooking the fairways. Also at the clubhouse is **Knickers Bar and Lounge** for libations, sandwiches, and snacks into the evening except Sunday and Monday. For lunch and cocktails, try the informal **Ocean Grill,** set between the pool and beach, where you'll be comfortable in a bathing suit and cover-up. On the far side of Makaiwa Bay, the **Beach Club** (808/885-5910) also serves light lunches in an open-air environment until mid-afternoon. And for a perfect place to relax after a day of golf or tennis, seek out the **Honu Bar,** just off the atrium, where you will find a pool table and dance floor, an excellent selection of liqueurs, wine, and fine cigars, and a bar menu of sushi and light late-night meals and desserts. For the Canoe House, The Gallery, and the Bay Terrace, expect entrées in the $25–40 range, substantially less for the other restaurants and lounges.

Fairmont Orchid

Dining at The Fairmont Orchid can be everything from poolside casual to haute cuisine, prepared in various styles, using locally grown produce, herbs, meats, and seafood. The culinary results are not only mouth-watering but healthy and wonderfully nutritious. The Orchid's fine-dining signature restaurant is **The Grill,** where crystal and dark koa wood set the scene and most dishes are either steak or fish; entrées fall in the $34–49 range. The Grill is open for dinner only; evening clothes or alohawear requested. The **Orchid Court,** a casual restaurant, is the hotel's main breakfast dining room, offering either à la carte or buffet menus. The fine-dining, evening-only **Norio's Restaurant and Sushi Bar** gives guests a choice of sushi, fish, or other traditional Japanese favorites. Reservations are necessary. Poolside, **Brown's Beach House** is the most casual restaurant, where you dine alfresco in a garden setting for lunch and dinner, and where dinner entrées are inspirations of the islands and the Orient. Soft Hawaiian music accompanies a hula dancer in the evening. For a relaxing evening of drinks, a cigar, or billiards, and periodic live entertainment, lower yourself into an overstuffed leather chair at the Paniolo Lounge and Polo Bar.

Hapuna Beach Prince Hotel

Of the hotel's four restaurants (808/880-3192 for reservations), the oceanfront **Coast Grill** is its signature establishment. It specializes in fresh seafood, mixing flavors and preparations from the Pacific and Asia as fresh Hawaiian Regional Cuisine. Main dishes generally run $23–38. The Oyster Bar here, with its oyster bar sampler, oysters on the half shell, and steamed clams, is renowned, and Monday night sushi is always top notch. Open only for dinner, reservations are recommended and resort attire is required. Priced at the upper end, sushi, Japanese-inspired meat dishes, and complete Japanese dinners are available on Friday, Saturday, and Sunday at the **Hakone Steakhouse and Sushi Bar.** On Friday and Saturday, this restaurant features a Japanese buffet for $48 adult and $24 children. For a more economical buffet and à la carte breakfasts, head for the alfresco **Ocean Terrace** overlooking the pool and ocean. Located just off the lobby, **Cafe Hapuna** also serves many standard breakfast items, as well as a light lunch, snacks, and food items to go. Located in the clubhouse and catering mainly to the golfers, **Arnie's** serves standard American and health-conscious food with a few Oriental touches. Open for lunch only, with cocktails until late afternoon. In addition, you can get lunch and afternoon snacks and drinks at the **Beach Bar** down by the pool. Snuggled into a lower lobby level, the **Reef Lounge** is the perfect spot for sunset viewing while relaxing with a tropical drink and enjoying the nightly entertainment of hula and vocal music.

Mauna Kea Beach Hotel

Exceptional food is served in this exceptional environment. Serving classic Euro-Asian cuisine for dinner only Wednesday–Friday is the **Batik,** the hotel's finest restaurant. Dining here is truly a treat, and some specialties are curries and the dessert soufflé; entrées range $32–56. Reservations are necessary, and dressy resortwear is the norm. For buffet or à la carte breakfast or more formal dinner in an open-air setting with grand views of the coast, try the somewhat less expensive **Pavilion** restaurant, which is legendary for the selection and quality of its Sunday brunch at $39 adults and $20 children. Near the beach, the **Hau Tree** does salads and sandwiches for lunch daily, and the **19th Hole** is a more casual spot at the golf course clubhouse that serves food from the East and West through midday. Three lounges also grace the grounds, each with its own entertainment. At the Saturday evening **Clambake** at the Hau Tree, you can feast buffet-style on Maine lobster, garlic shrimp, sumptuous steamed clams, and much, much more. Tuesday evenings are extra special as a lu'au is performed at the Lu'au Gardens at North Pointe. Both the lu'au and the Clambake run $79 adult and $38 children. Call for dining reservations (808/882-5810) at the Batik, Pavilion, Clambake, and lu'au.

The Kings' Shops

Hama Yu Japanese Restaurant (808/886-6333, daily 11:30 A.M.–3 P.M., 5:30–9 P.M.) serves authentic Japanese cuisine in a restaurant with strikingly contemporary decor. Choose appetizers like soft-shell crab, yakitori, and a variety of sashimi and sushi. Dinners, mostly $20 and up, include tempura, Japanese steak, *tonkatsu,* and tempura. Sit at western-style tables or choose the sushi bar. Lunches are simpler with less expensive soups, noodles, donburi, sushi, and other similar dishes that generally run $10–20.

The **Grand Palace Chinese Restaurant** (808/886-6668, daily 11 A.M.–9:30 P.M.) serves appetizers ranging from deep-fried won ton to a cold platter, and soups from the ordinary pork with mustard cabbage to the very expensive shark's fin soup with shredded crabmeat. There are also your standard beef, pork, seafood, poultry, and vegetable dishes, with some specialties like whole Peking duck, hot pot dishes, and sizzling platters. With over 150 items on the menu and prices that are only marginally above average, this is not your ordinary Chinese restaurant but a dining experience.

The **Big Island Steakhouse** (808/886-8805) is open daily for all three meals. Breakfast is standard American, lunch mostly sandwiches, while dinner (5:30–10 P.M.) has a much broader menu of meats and fish. The *pu pu* plates are good for those with a smaller appetite, but the other entrées, mostly $20–33, include New York strip steak, filet mignon, prime rib, teriyaki pork chops, coconut prawns, and fresh fish. While not outstanding, the Big Island Steakhouse provides a filling meal in somewhat familiar surroundings.

Roy's Waikoloa Bar and Grill (808/886-4321, 5:30–9:30 P.M.) is well known throughout the islands for blending ingredients from East and West. Roy's produces imaginative cuisine that will titillate your taste buds. The menu changes daily and always features nightly specials, but you might expect to find cassoulet of escargot appetizers and romaine and watercress salad. For main entrées, look for caramel rum-glazed rack of lamb, kabayaki grilled black tiger shrimp, and lemon-thyme steamed shellfish pasta. Most entrées are in the $21–29 range. Reservations are definitely recommended.

With inside and courtyard dining, and a delicatessen that stocks fresh fish, meats, cheeses, and more, **Merriman's Marketplace** (808/886-1700, 11 A.M.–9 P.M.) is an ideal spot to eat in or buy food to prepare at your condominium. From the restaurant, lunch items include a grilled eggplant and fresh basil sandwich, a lamb pita, and Portuguese bean soup. For dinner, the mostly Italian menu has plenty of small dishes to share, fresh fish like Tuscan-style opakapaka, various pasta dishes, and meat entrées in the $22–25 range.

A separate area called **The Food Pavilion** will satisfy anyone on the run with everything from a sub sandwich to pizza and espresso coffee.

Waikoloa Beach Grill

More than just a clubhouse eatery, the Waikoloa Beach Grill restaurant at the Waikoloa Beach Course golf clubhouse (69-1022 Keana Pl., 808/886-6131, daily 11 A.M.–9 P.M.) is a diverse dining establishment with an exquisite list of pies, fresh-baked bread, and a full wine selection. Lunch items are mostly light sandwiches and salads, with a few surprises, but dinner is a more sophisticated affair with candlelight and linens. The changing menu, which might include an Asian-style fresh fish, lamb kabobs, and smoked pork ribs, has entrées mostly in the $16–28 range. The Waikoloa Beach Grill is conveniently located for all guests at Waikoloa Resort and is open for lunch until 4 P.M., with appetizers until dinner starts at 5 P.M. Save room for pie, as one of the owners/chefs is a former hotel pastry chef who loves to create an array of these traditional and seasonal desserts.

Lu'au

A sumptuous old-style ***'Aha'aina*** feast is held at the Kona Village Resort (808/325-5555). It's worth attending this lu'au just to visit and be pampered. Adults pay around $84, children 6–12 $50, children 2–5 $26. This lu'au is held every Friday by reservation only and as it's so popular you should call well in advance, perhaps even when you make your room reservation. Seating begins at 5:30 P.M., the *imu* ceremony is at 5:30 P.M., followed by cocktails, and the entertainment gets going at 7 P.M. The Kona Village Resort lu'au has been happening every Friday night for over 30 years, making it the longest-running lu'au on the island.

The **Royal Lu'au** at the Waikoloa Beach Marriott (808/886-6789) is offered on Sunday and Wednesday from 5:30 P.M., with the *imu* ceremony beginning at 6 P.M., followed by an open bar, dinner, and Polynesian entertainment of song and dance from islands of the Pacific that ends about 8:30 P.M. Prices are adults $75, children 6–12 $36.50, free for children five and under.

Legends of the Pacific (808/886-1234) at the Hilton Waikoloa Village is performed by Tihati Productions each Friday evening 6–9 P.M. A full buffet dinner, one cocktail, and a rousing show of Tahitian music and dance is performed at the Kamehameha Court on the resort grounds. Tickets are $74 adults, $37 kids 5–12.

The Mauna Kea **Old Hawaii *'Aha'aina* Lu'au** (808/822-5810) is presented every Tuesday at the North Pointe Lu'au Grounds. While dinner and entertainment start at 6 P.M., you may watch the *imu* preparation at 9 A.M. and the *imu* opening ceremony at 5:30 P.M. Dinner is a veritable feast, followed by entertainment by Nani Lim and her award-winning *hula halau*. Adults pay $79, children 6–12 are $38.

HAWAIIAN LU'AU

The lu'au is an island institution. For a fixed price, you get to gorge yourself on a tremendous variety of island foods, sample a few island drinks, and have a night of entertainment as well. Generally, lu'au run from about 5 or 5:30 P.M. to 8:30 or 9 P.M. On your lu'au day, eat a light breakfast, skip lunch, and do belly-stretching exercises! Lu'au food is usually served buffet-style, although a few do it family-style. All lu'au have pretty much the same format, although the type of food and entertainment differ somewhat.

To have fun at a lu'au you have to get into the swing of things. Entertainment is provided by local performers in what is usually called a "Polynesian Revue." This includes the tourist's hula, the fast version with swaying hips and dramatic lighting, a few wandering troubadours singing Hawaiian standards, and someone swinging swords or flaming torches. Although individual lu'au vary, some also offer an *imu* ceremony where the pig is taken from the covered oven, traditional games, arts and crafts, or a *hukilau* (pulling in a fishnet) demonstration. All the Hawaiian standards like poi, *haupia, lomi* salmon (a salad of salmon, tomatoes, and onions with garnish and seasonings), *laulau* (a package of meat, fish, and veggies wrapped in ti leaves), and *kalua* (*imu*-baked) pig are usually served. If these don't suit your appetite, various Asian dishes, plus chicken, fish, and roast beef are often also on the table. If you leave a lu'au hungry, it's your own fault!

The lu'au master starts the *imu* on the morning of the gathering; stop by and watch if it's permitted. He lays the hot stones and banana stalks so well that the underground oven maintains a perfect 400°F temperature. In one glance, the lu'au master can gauge the weight and fat content of a succulent porker and decide just how long it should be cooked. The water in the leaves covering the pig steams and roasts the meat so that it falls off the bone. Local wisdom has it that "all you can't eat in the *imu* are the hot stones."

Lu'au range in price about $60-80 for adults and about half that for children, including entertainment. This is the tourist variety – a lot of fun, but definitely a show. The least expensive, most authentic, and best lu'au are often put on by local churches or community groups. If you ask locals which is the best you won't get two to agree. It's literally a matter of taste.

PHOTO COURTESY OF HVCB/KIRK LEE AEDER

INFORMATION AND SERVICES

The **Big Island Visitors Bureau** (808/886-1655) maintains their West Side office at the Kings' Shops. It's open regular hours for brochures and inquiries.

There are **no banks** or branch offices along the South Kohala coast, but you will find ATMs at Kings' Shops.

The Kings' Shop also has the only **gas station** along the coast between the Kona airport and Kawaihae, but there is a gas pump for guest use at the Four Seasons Resort.

See **Zac's Photo and Copy Center** at Waikoloa Resort for camera film, print film developing, Internet access, and all your copying needs.

South Kohala Towns

The South Kohala Coast was generally a place where people passed through. Yet this hot and arid region did support a number of communities where water was adequate and fishing was good. Few of these villages transitioned from the old to the new, but Puako survived as a tiny and all-but-forgotten cluster and Kawaihae, once the site of a royal compound, lives on as a small port and the island's second commercial harbor. Inland and upslope is a different story with its plentiful rain, productive soil, and wide open range land. There, the town of Waimea dominates, surrounded by cattle country. As if caught between the dry and the wet, Waikoloa has been scratched from the marginal hillside, a community separate, self-sufficient, and unto its own.

The coastal villages of Puako and Kawaihae and the upland town of Waikoloa are discussed here. Because of its size and complexity, Waimea will be discussed separately.

PUAKO

Puako and its environs receive about 10 inches of rain a year, making it one of the driest, if not the driest, areas of the state. This alluring area is located *makai* on a side road off Route 19 about four miles south of Kawaihae. Hawaiians lived here in times past, but a modern community has been building along the three-mile road past Puako Bay since the 1950s. This quiet, no-frills community is a mixture of working-class homes, beach cottages, rental properties, and discreet vacation hideaways that is slowly becoming more desirable and definitely more upscale with the conversion of older homes and the construction of new and expensive beachfront mini-mansions. Services amount to one reasonably well-stocked general store, a public telephone, and a vacation rental agency. A thin ribbon of white sand runs the length of the beach near the boat ramp that provides fair swimming. Sunsets here are magnificent, and you'll usually have the beach to yourself. The remainder of the shoreline through this community is mostly rock shelf with inlets and tidepools, for good fishing, snorkeling, and some surfing. Near-shore scuba diving is excellent, with huge caverns and caves to explore, and a colorful concentration of coral and marinelife. There are half a dozen shoreline access routes with parking along this strip road.

Along Puako Road is **Hokuloa Church,** built by Rev. Lorenzo Lyons in 1859. This musically talented reverend mastered the Hawaiian language and composed lovely ballads such as "Hawaii Aloha," which has become the unofficial anthem of the islands. The church is a thick-walled structure with a plain, simple interior. Sunday service is held at 9 A.M.

Shopping

As the only store in town, the diminutive **Puako General Store** (808/882-7500, 8 A.M.–7 P.M. daily) carries a limited but sufficient assortment of groceries and sundries for those staying in this coastal community. For other items, you must head into Kawaihae, up to Waimea, or back down to the Kings' Shops in Waikoloa.

Accommodations

Hawaii Vacation Rentals (7 Puako Beach Dr., 808/882-7000 or 800/332-7081, fax 808/882-7607, seaside@aloha.net, www.vacationbigisland.com) handles properties almost exclusively in Puako, with a few others up and down the coast, that range from a seaside cottage for $130 a night to a multi-bedroom oceanfront mansion for over $1,000 a night. A five- to 10-night minimum stay applies. This company also represents three units in Puako Beach Condominium, the only condo in this residential neighborhood and the only moderately priced, multiple-unit accommodation in this diamond-studded neck of the woods. These two- and three-bedroom units run $125–195 a night, three nights minimum, with a kitchen, laundry, TV, and swimming pool.

Puako Bed and Breakfast (25 Puako Beach Dr., 808/882-1331 or 800/910-1331, puakobb@hawaii.rr.com, www.bigisland-bed-breakfast.com) is a modest home with plenty of comfort. Island-furnished rooms are located off the living and dining rooms, each with its own king-size bed, private bathroom, and entrance. The Garden room runs $130, the Ocean View room is $140, while the two-room Suite is $160. A simple, wholesome breakfast is served to all guests each morning.

KAWAIHAE

This port town marks the northern end of the South Kohala Coast. Here, Route 19 turns eastward toward Waimea, or turns into Route 270 heading up the coast into North Kohala. Not really more than a village, Kawaihae town is basically utilitarian, with a deep draft commercial harbor, wharves, fuel tanks, and a boat ramp for a small-boat harbor. A service cluster has a handful of shops, restaurants, and a 76 gas station. Unless you're stopping to eat, you'll probably pass right through.

Shopping

The small **Kawaihae Shopping Center** can take care of your rudimentary shopping needs. There's a 7-Eleven convenience store, a couple of clothing shops, Mountain Gold Jewelers, Black Pearl Gallery jewelers, and the Harbor Gallery art and gift shop. The Harbor Gallery, which represents over 100 Big Island artists, largely painters, woodworkers, and ceramicists, has a second shop up on the highway below the Seafood Bar restaurant.

Recreation

Kohala Divers (808/882-7774, www.kohaladivers.com, open 8 A.M.–5 P.M. daily) is a full-service dive shop on the lower level of the Kawaihae Shopping Center that takes up to six people on each trip. This company offers open-ocean certification for $575, two-tank morning boat dives for $115, one-tank afternoon or manta ray viewing night dives for $89–99, an introductory dive for $169, scuba package rentals for $30, and snorkeling gear rentals for $10. If there's room on the boat, Kohala Divers will take snorkelers along for $59. Kohala Divers is also a retail shop where you can buy boogie boards, fins, masks, snorkels, and scuba equipment. If you are a scuba enthusiast, you can come here to get your tanks refilled or overhaul your diving gear. It's a bit far to go from Kailua-Kona—much closer from the Kohala resorts—but rates are competitive. Divers are taken up the coast from Kawaihae Harbor.

Mauna Kea Divers (808/882-1544, www.maunakeadivers.com) also rents scuba and snorkel gear in Kawaihae and offers comparable scuba tours. Mauna Kea Divers will work with you to give you the experience that you want.

The ***Maile,*** berthed at Kawaihae Harbor (808/326-5174 or 800/726-7245, www.adventuresailing.com), is a 50-foot Gulfstar sloop that can take up to six passengers. It's available for luxury sailing and whale-watching charters, sunset sails, half- or full-day charters, multi-day rentals, as well as interisland runs. Rates are $590 for four hours, $990 for eight hours, and up to $5,000 for five days. A one-way interisland charge is $1,000, and there is an extra fee for all lunches and special dinners served onboard. Sailing on *Maile* is an exercise in comfort and adventure.

Accommodations

Hale Ho'onanea bed-and-breakfast (P.O. Box 44953, Kamuela, HI 96743, 808/882-1653 or 877/882-1653, melanie@houseofrelaxation.com, www.houseofrelaxation.com) is up at about 900 feet in elevation, just a few miles north of Kawaihae. Turn onto Ala Kahua Drive at mile marker 6 and head uphill. Modern in design, all three detached suites on this three-acre property have private entrances and baths, a small kitchenette, some local art on the walls, a lanai for relaxation, and perhaps best of all, plenty of privacy. A continental breakfast will be waiting for you each morning when you get up. Just over 1.5 miles from the coast, there are great ocean views out over the surrounding ranch land, whale-watching in season, and unbeatable stargazing any time of the year. The Bamboo Suite, with its king-size bed and queen-size sofa sleeper, runs $130. The Tranquility Suite, with its king-size bed and trundle bed, goes for $110. The smallest, with a queen-size bed and queen-size futon, is the Palm Suite; it rents for $100. All three have a two-night minimum.

Food

Who'd expect an upscale yuppie restaurant in the sleepy village of Kawaihae? **Café Pesto** (808/882-1071, 11 A.M.–9 P.M. Sun.–Thurs., 11 A.M.–10 P.M. Fri.–Sat.) has a chic interior design with black-and-white checkerboard flooring and black tables trimmed with wood, similar to its sister café in Hilo. The bold gourmet menu tantalizes you with starters like fresh basil crostini and a host of freshly made salads. Pasta and seafood dishes are scrumptious and mostly under $25, and the less-costly calzones and sandwiches are just as filling. Café Pesto is perhaps best known for creating hand-tossed gourmet pizza with crust and sauces made fresh daily, ranging in price $9–18. Among its best pizzas are shiitake mushrooms and artichokes with rosemary Gorgonzola sauce, but you can also create your own. Save room for one of the well-appreciated desserts, or stop at the attached bar before or after your meal. Café Pesto is a perfect place to stop for a civilized meal as you explore the Kohala Coast.

Pancho Villa in aloha shirt and sombrero and riding a surfboard (!) would be instantly at home in **Tres Hombres Beach Grill** (808/882-1031) located on the upper level of the Kawaihae Center and open 11:30 A.M.–9 P.M. Sunday–Thursday, until 10 P.M. on weekends. Besides being a south-of-the-border restaurant, Tres Hombres is an unofficial surfing museum filled with a fine collection of surfboards and surfing memorabilia donated by such legendary greats as Dewey Weber, Greg Knoll, and Jack Wise. The bamboo-appointed interior has a relaxed tropical effect. The extensive menu offers antojitos such as nachos and calamari. Substantial meals include all the Mexican favorites for $9–15, plus the grill also offers fish in tomato, pepper, and onion sauce, shrimp basted in lime butter, honey-mustard chicken, and more unusual items like crab enchiladas, for up to $21. For families, the kids' menu helps make the bill easier on Mom and Dad. The full bar serves not only a range of beers and all the island favorites, but adds special concoctions like the Kawaihae Sunsets that will help you go down for the evening, and Mauna Kea Sunrises that, with a great deal of wishful thinking, will pop you back up. *Pu pu* are served 3–6 P.M. daily. Relax with an ice-cold margarita on the lanai of this casual restaurant, and experience an excellent change of pace from the luxury hotels just down the road.

Kawaihae Harbor Grill (808/882-1368, 11:30 A.M.–2:30 P.M., 5:30–9:30 P.M.) is located along the highway a short distance before you get into town. Climb the steps to the large veranda from where you have, unfortunately, an unobstructed view of the petrochemical tanks across the road. Focus on the food! Dinners include fresh catch, strip steak, tandoori chicken, red Thai seafood curry, and rack of ribs, all $19–27. Lighter dining options are also offered. Inside, the one-time village store is quite tasteful, with *lau hala* mats, lava lamps, and a glass partition that has been etched with an octopus and tropical fish. Food at the Kawaihae Harbor Grill is tasteful and presented with pride.

The owners of the Kawaihae Harbor Grill have opened the **Seafood Bar** on the upper level of the neighboring two-story green building; the Harbor Gallery's second space is below. The Seafood Bar has a more casual, open-air atmosphere with an extra long bar; its menu is primarily fish, seafood, burgers, and salads, with lunches mostly under $10 and dinners under $15.

Set at the edge of town along Route 270 is the **Blue Dolphin Restaurant** (808/882-7771, 5–10 P.M. Wed.–Sat., until 11:30 P.M. Friday) Seating is all outdoors, but in the dry climate of Kawaihae that hardly matters. Dinner, mostly $13–22, might be crispy macadamia nut pork loin, *pulehu* (broiled) chicken breasts, nori-wrapped tempura *'ahi,* or fresh catch. While the food is OK, the Blue Dolphin is perhaps best known for its music, which is live jazz or other on Friday and Saturday.

For ice cream, shave ice, and pizza to go, try the **Anuenue Ice Cream** takeout window counter on the upper level of the shopping center.

For groceries, sundries, and deli items, head for **Kawaihae Market and Deli** (808/880-1611, 4:30 A.M.–9 P.M. Mon.–Fri., 5:30 A.M.–8 P.M. Sat. and Sun.) on the upper level of the Kawaihae Shopping Center.

If you're cooking for yourself, you can stop across the highway for fresh fish from local fishing boats at **Laau's Fish Market** (808/882-1052, 6 A.M.–6 P.M. Mon.–Sat.).

WAIKOLOA VILLAGE

If you're interested in visiting Waimea as well as seeing the South Kohala coast, you might consider turning right off Route 19 near mile marker 75 onto Waikoloa Road. This route cuts inland for 13 miles, connecting coastal Route 19 with inland Route 190, which leads to Waimea. About halfway up, you pass the planned and quickly growing community of Waikoloa Village about six miles inland from Waikoloa Resort. Try to overlook the condo complexes along the road and head into the village itself, which is low-rise and quite tasteful. Waikoloa Village is a mixture of condominiums and single-family homes that is also home to Waikoloa Village Golf Club, whose course is open to the public.

Waikoloa sits below the saddle that runs between Mauna Kea and the North Kohala Mountains. When the trade winds blow from the northeast, they funnel over this saddle and race down the slope, creating windy conditions that challenge golfers. For the dubious distinction of being a windy community, Waikoloa is sometimes jokingly called "Waiko-blow-a."

Shopping

The village is serviced by the **Waikoloa Highlands Shopping Center,** a small but adequate shopping mall with a gas station, a full-service supermarket, First Hawaiian Bank, postal service store, small medical center, a health food shop, a few restaurants, and numerous other types of shops. This is the only place on the mountainside between the coast and Waimea to get supplies and, aside from the restaurant at the golf course, the only stop for a bite to eat.

Recreation

Occupying the lower portion of this community is **Waikoloa Village Golf Club** (68-1792 Melia St., 808/883-9621). No slouch for difficulty, with the added challenge of the wind, this Robert Trent Jones Jr. course gives the pricier golf courses along the coast a run for their money. This and the Waimea Country Club golf course up in Waimea are by far the most economical in South Kohala.

Accommodations

Paniolo Greens (808/883-0600 or 888/450-

4646), a time-share property with office at the Waikoloa Highlands Shopping Center rents units when space is available. Each two-bedroom, two-bath unit runs $260 a night and comes with a complete kitchen, washer and dryer, and entertainment center. Tennis courts, exercise gym, and swimming pool are on the property.

Waikoloa has at least eight other condo/apartment properties that offer rental units, most in the economy and mid-range, with one-bedroom units that start as low as $110 a night during low season. For information about some of what is available, contact **Aldridge Associates** (68-1897 Puu Melia St., 808/883-8300 or 800/662-5642, www.waikoloa.net).

Food

Skarkey's Bar & Grill (808/883-0020) at the Waikoloa Highlands Shopping Center is one of the few restaurants in town. A casual bar/restaurant mix, you'll find sandwiches, teriyaki chicken, burgers, and such on the menu and a full bar for drinks. Food is served from noon to 9 P.M., drinks until later. If you're killing time, try the pool table or dartboard. Evenings bring DJ or karaoke music and sometimes dancing to live bands.

The **Waikoloa Village Market** (6:30 A.M.–9 P.M.) is a full-service supermarket with a good deli and bakery section. It is the only place here to stock up on supplies without heading out of town.

Waimea

Waimea is in the South Kohala district, but because of its inland topography of high mountain pasture on the broad slope of Mauna Kea, it is vastly different than the long Kohala coastal district. It also has a unique culture inspired by the range-riding *paniolo* of the expansive **Parker Ranch.** This spread, founded early in the 19th century by John Palmer Parker, dominates the heart and soul of the region. Waimea revolves around ranch life and livestock. Herds of rodeos and "Wild West shows" are scheduled throughout the year. But a visit here isn't one-dimensional. In town are homey accommodations, inspired country dining, and varied shopping opportunities. The town supports arts and crafts in fine galleries, has the island's premier performance venue, and hosts a scientific community to staff a number of the observatories high on the mountain above. For fun and relaxation there's a visitors center and ranch center; Pu'opelu, the Parker mansion and art collection; a litany of historic shrines and churches; and an abundance of fresh air and wide-open spaces, the latter not so easily found in the islands.

The town, at elevation 2,670 feet, is split almost directly down the center—the east side is the wet side, and the west is the dry side. Houses on the east side are easy to find and reasonable to rent; houses on the dry side are expensive and usually unavailable. You can literally walk from verdant green fields and tall trees to semi-arid landscape in a matter of minutes. This imaginary line also demarcates the local social order: upper-class ranch managers (dry), and working-class *paniolo* (wet). However, the air of Waimea, refreshed and cooled by *kipu'upu'u* (fine mists) and wind, combines with only 20 inches of rainfall a year into the best mountain weather in Hawaii. Waimea is also known as Kamuela, the Hawaiianized version of Samuel, after one of John Parker's grandsons. Kamuela is used as the post office address, so as not to confuse this town of Waimea with towns of the same name on the islands of O'ahu and Kaua'i.

For decades, Waimea was a sleepy insular ranch community. World War II brought an end to its isolation as thousands of GIs descended on the town when Camp Tarawa was built for training. To cater to all these eager young men, the town had to gear up to provide services, which it did in a rousing way. After the war, the town settled back to

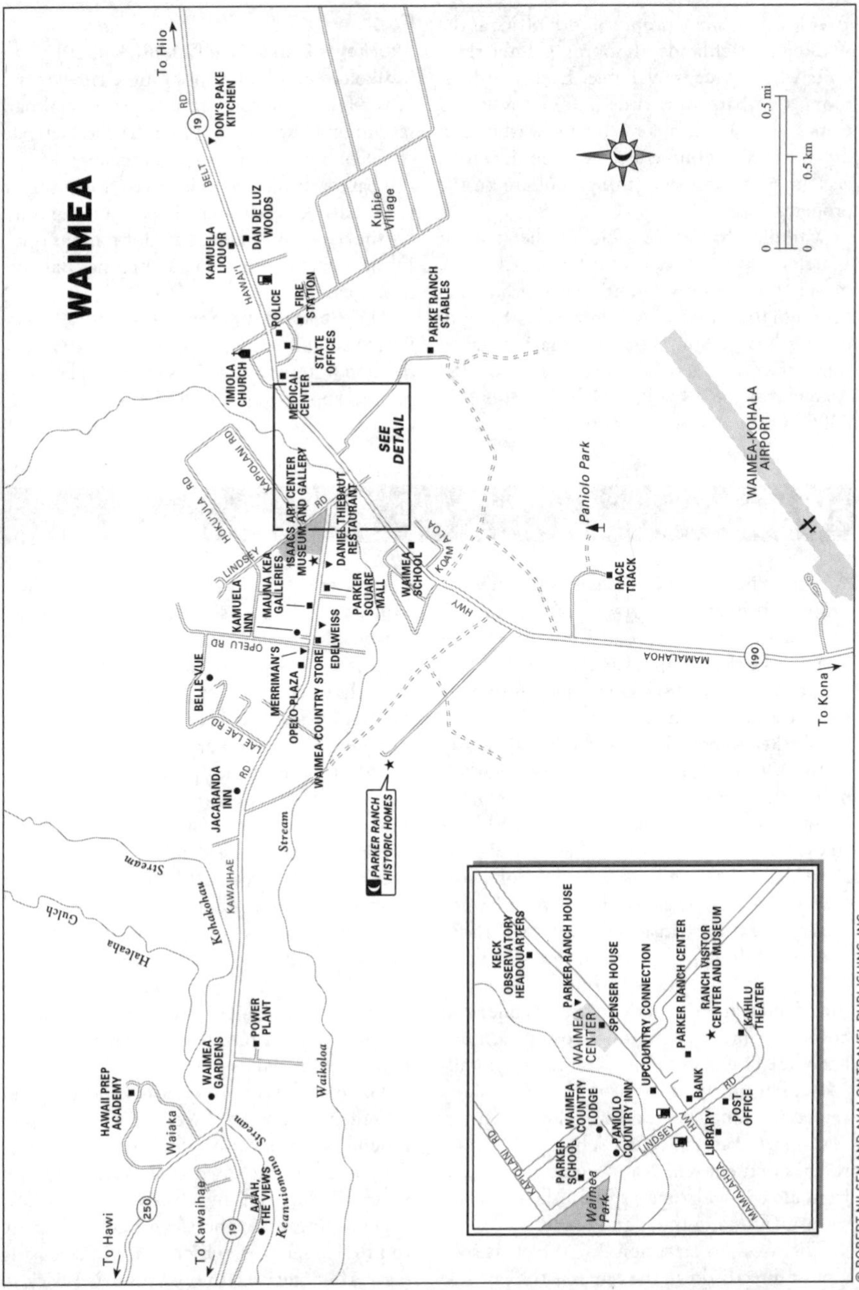
WAIMEA
To Hilo
DON'S PAKE KITCHEN
19
BELT RD
KAMUELA LIQUOR
DAN DE LUZ WOODS
Kuhio Village
HAWAI'I
POLICE
FIRE STATION
STATE OFFICES
'IMIOLA CHURCH
MEDICAL CENTER
PARKE RANCH STABLES
SEE DETAIL
ISAACS ART CENTER MUSEUM AND GALLERY
DANIEL THIEBAUT RESTAURANT
KAPIOLANI RD
HOKU'ULA RD
LINDSEY
KAMUELA INN
MAUNA KEA GALLERIES
PARKER SQUARE MALL
EDELWEISS
WAIMEA COUNTRY STORE
OPELO PLAZA
MERRIMAN'S
OPELU RD
BELLE VUE
LAE LAE RD
JACARANDA INN
RD
WAIMEA SCHOOL
ALOA
HWY
MAMALAHOA
190
Paniolo Park
RACE TRACK
WAIMEA-KOHALA AIRPORT
To Kona
0
0.5 mi
0
0.5 km
PARKER RANCH HISTORIC HOMES
Stream
KAWAIHAE
Kohakohau
Haleaha Gulch
Stream
POWER PLANT
WAIMEA GARDENS
HAWAII PREP ACADEMY
Waiaka
Waikoloa
Stream
250
To Hawi
To Kawaihae
19
AAAH, THE VIEWS
Keanuiomano
KECK OBSERVATORY HEADQUARTERS
PARKER RANCH HOUSE
SPENSER HOUSE
WAIMEA CENTER
UPCOUNTRY CONNECTION
PARKER RANCH CENTER
RANCH VISITOR CENTER AND MUSEUM
KAHILU THEATER
WAIMEA COUNTRY LODGE
PANIOLO COUNTRY INN
BANK
PARKER SCHOOL
KAPIOLANI RD
LINDSEY
HWY
RD
LIBRARY
POST OFFICE
MAMALAHOA
Waimea Park

© ROBERT NILSEN

cattle on Waimea ranch land

its quieter times. More recently, Waimea has experienced real and substantial growth. In 1980 it had no traffic lights and was home to about 2,000 people. Now the population has grown more than threefold, there are three lights along the main highway, and there are occasional traffic jams. Waimea is modernizing and gentrifying, and its cowboy backwoods character is rapidly changing.

Waimea is at the crossroads of the main east coast road (Rt. 19) from Hilo and Route 190 from Kailua-Kona. Route 19 continues west through town, reaching the coast at Kawaihae, where it turns south and cuts along the barren Kohala Coast to Kailua-Kona. The main artery connecting Waimea and Kailua-Kona is Route 190, also known as the Hawaii Belt Road. This stretch is locally called the Mamalahoa Highway. From Kailua-Kona, head out on Palani Road until it turns into Route 190. As you gain elevation heading into the interior, look left to see the broad and flat coastal lava flows. Seven miles before reaching Waimea, Saddle Road (Rt. 200) intersects this road from the right, and now the highlands, with grazing cattle amidst fields of cactus, look much more like Marlboro Country than the land of aloha.

SIGHTS

Parker Ranch Historic Homes

Richard Smart, last heir to the gigantic Parker Ranch, opened **Pu'opelu** (808/885-5433), a century-old family mansion, to the public just a few years before he passed away on November 12, 1992. On the grounds, the ranch's reconstructed original home is also open to visitors. Pu'opelu is located off Route 190 a few minutes southeast of town and is open 10 A.M.–5 P.M. daily, admission $8.50 adults, $8 seniors, $7 children.

A formal drive lined with stately eucalyptus trees leads to the mansion. The home was begun in 1862 by an Englishman but bought by John Palmer Parker II in 1879. In 1910, Richard Smart's grandmother, Aunt Tootsie, added the living room, kitchen, and fireplace. In 1960, Richard Smart, who inherited the ranch lands and home from Aunt Tootsie, replaced

A BRIEF PARKER FAMILY HISTORY

John Palmer Parker was a seaman who left Newton, Massachusetts, on a trading vessel in 1809 and landed in Kealakekua, becoming a fast friend of Kamehameha the Great. Parker, then only 19, jumped ship and in 1816 married Kipikani, the granddaughter of King Kamehameha. Domesticated cattle, a present from Captain George Vancouver to Kamehameha, had gone wild due to neglect and were becoming a dangerous nuisance all over the Big Island. Parker was hired to round up the best of them and exterminate the rest. While doing so, he chose the finest head for his own herd. In 1847 King Kamehameha III divided the land by what was known as the Great Mahele, and John Parker was granted Royal Deed No. 7, for a two-acre parcel on the northeast slopes of Mauna Kea. His wife, being royal born, was entitled to 640 acres, and with these lands and tough determination, the mighty Parker Ranch began.

Unfortunately, many members of the Parker family died young. The firstborn, John Palmer Parker II, married Hanai. His brother, Ebenezer, married Kilea, an *ali'i* woman from Maui, who bore him four children. The oldest boy was Samuel Parker, known in Hawaiian as Kamuela, the co-name of Waimea town. Samuel married Napela, and together they had nine children. Samuel's father Ebenezer died at age 26. Kilea could never get over his death and visited his grave daily. Finally, she decided that she wanted to return to her family on Maui. She was advised by the people of the island not to go because of rough seas. Kilea did not heed the advice and, along with her entourage, was lost at sea.

John Palmer Parker II moved the family and ranch's central operation from the original homestead to Waimea in 1879. His wife, Hanai, gave birth to only one boy, who died within 12 months. Childless, they adopted one of their nephew Samuel's nine children as a *hanai* child, in a practice that continues to this day. He was Samuel's fifth child, John, who became John Palmer Parker III and who later married Elizabeth Dowsett, known as Aunt Tootsie. They had one girl, Thelma Parker, before John III died of pneumonia at age 19. Aunt Tootsie raised Thelma as a single parent and somehow managed to purchase Samuel Parker's and his eight children's half of the ranch. Thelma Parker married Gillian Smart. They had one boy, Richard Smart, before Thelma died at age 20 of tuberculosis. Aunt Tootsie literally took the bull by the horns to keep the ranch going, and when she passed away in 1943, she left everything to her grandson Richard. The ranch prospered under his ownership. After his death, the ranch became a charitable trust called the Parker Ranch Foundation Trust that

the living room and raised its ceiling to 16 feet to accommodate his art collection, and he landscaped the grounds. He added elegant French doors and skylights, and the koa doorways were installed to match. Smart grew up in San Francisco and became enamored with the theater at a young age. He studied at the Pasadena Playhouse in the late 1920s and later appeared on Broadway with such famous names as Carol Channing and Nanette Fabray. Smart performed in plays all over the United States, and recordings of his singing provide the background music as you tour the house.

Enter an elegant sitting room illuminated by a crystal chandelier to begin your tour. Inside this living museum, the works of prominent European artists are displayed, but since Smart's death, some artworks have been sold off and the collection diminished. The tour is self-guided, with all art pieces named. Besides paintings by famous artists, there are magnificent pieces of wooden furniture, tall cabinets holding yellow Chinese Peiping glass from the 19th century, silver tea sets, glassware, figurines, and magnificent chandeliers. Make sure to see the little side bedroom, called the Venetian Room, aptly decorated with paintings of gondolas and appointed with treasures from Venice. Lighting the room are two chandeliers, one pink and the other turquoise. Here, benefits the people of Waimea and local communities long associated with its operation. When Richard Smart was alive, the Parker Ranch was the largest privately owned, single-owner ranch in the United States. Although the ranch at one time was a huge 500,000 acres, it is now down to 175,000 acres, with about 400 horses and 35,000 head of cattle. The Parker Ranch Foundation Trust is the second-largest landowner in the state, following the Bishop Estate. Find more information about the ranch and family at www.parkerranch.com.

PHOTO COURTESY OF HVCB/HAWAII TOURISM JAPAN

Parker Ranch

the filigreed art deco mirrors are also fabulous. The feeling is of genteel elegance, but notice that the walls are rather rough board-and-batten covered with beautiful artwork. Richard Smart's bedroom is loaded with memorabilia from his stage performances and mementos given by the people he knew on Broadway. You get the feeling of class, but it's obvious that you are on a ranch. In the emerald-green kingdom that is the Parker Ranch, Pu'opelu is the crown jewel.

Just outside Pu'opelu is the reconstructed New England "saltbox" **Mana Hale,** the original Parker Ranch homestead. The home was built in 1847 by family patriarch John Palmer Parker from the durable native koa found at high elevations on the ranch lands. The sons, who were by then married, built two homes, and as children came, added more rooms in the sprawling New England tradition. They also built one large community kitchen, in which the entire family cooked and dined. A replica shows how the home grew over the years, and it is a good indicator of how the Parker fortunes grew along with it. As the children's children got older, they needed a schoolhouse, so they built one at the corner of the original site. It still stands and is maintained by a *paniolo* and his family who live there. The exterior of the original home, covered by a heavy slate roof, was too brittle to move from its original site 12 miles away, but the interior was removed, numbered, and put back together again like a giant jigsaw puzzle in the reconstructed home. A model in the living room shows you what the original site looked like back in the 1800s. To preserve the rich wood interior of the home, all that's required is to wipe it down once a year with lemon oil. At first the home seems like a small cabin, just what you'd expect from the 1850s, but in actuality it's a two-story home with one bedroom downstairs and three upstairs.

Parker Ranch Visitor Center and Museum

This is the first place to stop while in town if you want an overview of the evolution of this upcountry domain. The visitors center (808/885-7655) at the Parker Ranch Center, is open 9 A.M.–5 P.M. daily (last tickets sold at 4 P.M.); admission is $6.50 adults, $6 seniors, $5.50 children. Tickets for joint admission to the visitors center, museum, and historic homes are $14, $13, and $11.50, respectively.

After spending an hour at the center's museum and taking in the slide presentation, you'll have a good overview of the history of the Parker Ranch and, by extension, Waimea. Exhibits at the John Palmer Parker Museum depict the history and genealogy of the six generations of Parkers who have owned the ranch. In the museum, old family photos include one of Rev. Elias Bond, who presided over the Christian marriage of John Palmer Parker and his Hawaiian wife in 1820. Preserved also are old Bibles, clothing from the era, and an entire koa hut once occupied by woodcutters and range riders. There are fine examples of quilting, stuffed animals, an arsenal of old weapons, and even a vintage printing press. The 15-minute video in the comfortable Thelma Parker Theater begins whenever enough people have assembled after going through the museum. The video presents a thorough and professional rendition of the Parker Ranch history, along with sensitive

DAVID DOUGLAS HISTORICAL MONUMENT

South from Waimea along the very rugged Mana Road and 10 miles inland from Laupahoehoe Point on the Hamakua Coast is the David Douglas Historical Monument. This stone monument marks the spot where the naturalist, after whom the Douglas fir is named, lost his life under mysterious circumstances. Douglas, on a fact-gathering expedition on the rugged slopes of Mauna Kea, never returned. His body was found at the bottom of a deep pit that was used at the time to catch feral cattle. Douglas had spent the previous night at a cabin occupied by an Australian who had been a convict. Many suspected that the Australian had murdered Douglas in a robbery attempt and thrown his body into the pit to hide the deed. No hard evidence of murder could be found, and the death was officially termed accidental.

© J.D. BISIGNANI

Waimea is cattle country: The broad grasslands support large numbers of cows and horses.

glimpses of ranch life of the still very active *paniolo.* To the rear of the shopping center is an old wood-and-stone corral.

'Imiola Church

Head east on Route 19 to "church row," a cluster of New England–style structures on the left, a few minutes past the Parker Ranch Visitor Center. Most famous among these old structures is 'Imiola (Seeking Life) Congregational Church. It was built from 1855 to 1857 by the Rev. Lorenzo Lyons, who mastered the Hawaiian language and translated some of the great old Christian hymns into Hawaiian, as well as melodic Hawaiian chants into English. Restored in 1976, the yellow clapboard church with white trim would be at home along any New England village green. When you enter, you'll notice an oddity: the pulpit is at the near side and you walk around it to face the rear of the church. Nearly all inside surfaces are of rich brown koa. The hymnals contain many of the songs translated by Father Lyons. Outside is a simple monument to Rev. Lyons, along with a number of his children's gravesites. Have a look inside or stop by for one of the two Sunday worship services.

Also along this row are the Ka Ola Mau Loa Hawaiian Church, the Kamuela Hongwanji Mission, the First Baptist Church, and the Waimea Chapel of the Church of Jesus Christ of Latter-Day Saints.

Isaacs Art Center Museum and Gallery

Located in a renovated elementary school building that was moved to the site from elsewhere in town, the Isaacs Art Center (65-1268 Kawaihae Rd., 808/885-5884, http://isaacsartcenter.hpa.edu, 10 A.M.–5 P.M. Tues.–Sat.) is a fine new addition to the cultural scene in Waimea. This gallery displays many pieces of art, some owned by the Hawaiian Preparatory Academy, which runs the museum, and some that are donated. A few of the well-known artists displayed are Huc Luquiens, Jean Charlot, Madge Tennent, Martha Greenwell, and Albrect Durer, but many lesser known artists also appear. Paintings predominate, but there are some wood furniture pieces, ceramics, and pieces in other media.

'Imiola Church

At the entrance, a small gift shop sells artwork. Donations are accepted.

W. M. Keck Observatory Headquarters

The Keck Observatory has its main offices and a small visitors center (65-1120 Mamalahoa Hwy., 808/885-4464, weekdays 8 A.M.–4:30 P.M.) in a bright white building along the highway, east of the Waimea Center. In the visitors center, basically just the main entrance foyer of the building, are a handful of small displays and some printed information about the Keck telescopes and the work being done by the scientists who use them and analyze the data collected from them.

While the Canada-France-Hawaii Telescope Corporation also has its office in Waimea, it does not have any visitors center or information for the public.

ENTERTAINMENT

Periodically throughout the year, movies, plays, music, and a variety of other first-rate domestic and international events are held at the **Kahilu Theater** (808/885-6868, www.kahilutheatre.org) at the rear of the Parker Ranch Center. The events produced at this theater are a huge cultural draw for the community, and the fact that this community of 7,000 supports such a wonderful center is a blessing.

Sunday afternoon 4–6 P.M. brings a music jam session with local musicians at the Daniel Thiebaut restaurant. Everyone is welcome.

SHOPPING

Waimea's accelerated growth can be measured by the shopping centers springing up around town. These mostly small malls house boutiques that add to the shopping possibilities in Waimea's established centers.

Parker Ranch Center

This long-established mall was totally rebuilt in 2002, completely changing the face of the center of town. With more of a country look, the mall now has more store space than it originally held and many new upscale vendors. Anchoring the center is a new Foodland grocery store, but the alternative food store, Healthways II, also has a spot. There is a food court in the center of the complex and many fast-food joints. The **Parker Ranch Store** (808/885-5669), in its prominent spot up front, focuses on its country cowboy heritage; the shop sells boots, cowboy hats, shirts, skirts, and buckles and bows, and many handcrafted items are made on the premises. Also up front is **Reyn's** (808/885-4493) for island fashions and alohawear, and the children's toy, game, and clothing store **Giggles** (808/885-2151). Located in the rear section is **The Quilted Horse** (808/887-0020), a fun shop full of household items, gifts, prepared food items, Christmas ornaments, knickknacks, and one of the best selections of quilts on the island. Reasonably priced, the quilts are made in the Philippines but designed in Hawaii. Also in the back is the Parker Ranch Visitor Center and Museum.

Waimea Center

Well marked along the Mamalahoa Highway behind McDonald's, most Waimea Center stores are open 9 A.M.–5 P.M. weekdays and 10 A.M.–5 P.M. Saturday. Among its shops you will find a **KTA Super Store** with everything from groceries to pharmaceuticals; **Leilani Bakery** (808/885-2772) with pastries and breads; **Pack, Ship and Copy Depot** (808/885-8810), for copies, shipping, Internet access, and other business needs; and a number of eateries.

Parker Square

Located along Route 19, heading west from town center, this small mall has a collection of fine boutiques and shops. Here, like an old trunk filled with family heirlooms, the **Gallery of Great Things** (808/885-7706) really is loaded with great things. Inside you'll find novelty items like a carousel horse, silk dresses, straw hats, koa paddles, Ni'ihau shellwork, vintage kimonos, an antique water jar from the Chiang Mai area of northern Thailand, Japanese woodblock prints, and less expensive items like shell earrings and koa hair sticks. The Gallery of Great Things represents about 200 local artists on a revolving basis, and the owner, Maria Brick, travels throughout the Pacific and Asia collecting art, some contemporary, some primitive. With its museum-quality items, the Gallery of Great Things is definitely worth a browse. But remember, most items are one of a kind—"now you see them, now you don't."

Sweet Wind (808/885-0562, 9:30 A.M.–5:30 P.M. Mon.–Fri.) is packed with books, beads, videos, and unique gifts. This "alternative thought and resource center" also sells incense, aromatherapy tinctures, crystals, and some religious accessories. The beads come from the world over, and a display case holds Native American rattles, drums, and silver and amber jewelry. Visiting Sweet Wind is soothing for body and soul; the smells and sounds envelop you as you enter and put you in a peaceful mood.

The **Silk Road Gallery** (808/885-7474, open daily except Sunday) is resplendent with an exceptional collection of Asian antiques and craft items, specializing in creations from Japan and China. In this tasteful shop you will discover such treasures as carved ivory *netsuke,* a favorite of the well-dressed samurai; ornate silk kimonos; Sung Dynasty vases; and Satsumayaki painted pottery from Japan. As you look around you may spot lacquered tables and bowls, ornate *tansu* (chests), straw sandals, an actual water wheel, sacred scrolls that hang in a place of honor in Japanese homes, a Chinese jade bowl with elaborate dragon handles, and an 18th-century Chinese mogul lotus bowl. The owners make frequent trips to Asia, where they personally pick all the items in their shop, at which the artistic wonders of the ancient Silk Road are still on display.

The **Waimea General Store** (808/885-4479, 9 A.M.–5:30 P.M. Mon.–Sat., 10 A.M.–4 P.M. Sun.) sells mostly high-end sundries with plenty of stationery, kitchen items, children's games, stuffed toys, books on Hawaiiana, and gadgets—overall, lots of neat and nifty gifts.

Other stores in the center include **Bentley's Home and Garden Collection,** with crockery, glassware, books, *lau hala* bags, and ceramics; **Imagination Toys,** hung with kites, Hawaiian dolls, stuffed gorillas, parrots, puzzles, and other great toys for kids; and **Kamuela Goldsmiths,** where custom-made jewelry or stones can be procured.

Other Shops

Who would have thought that one of the best wine and liquor stores on the island would be in a country town like Waimea? Look for **Kamuela Liquor Store** (64-1010 Mamalahoa Hwy., 808/885-4674, 8 A.M.–7:30 P.M. Mon.–Sat., 9 A.M.–5 P.M. Sun.) east along the highway just past the Police Station. It's been in business since 1946. This shop not only has a great selection of wines and liqueurs, it has many select bottled beers.

Across from the liquor store is **Dan De Luz's Woods** (64-1013 Mamalahoa Hwy., 808/885-5856), a fine shop and showroom in a nondescript warehouse-type building along the highway, selling large bowls and small boxes made from native woods. These pieces are roughed out in Mountain View, where De Luz has another workshop, and the blanks are finished in Waimea after a year of drying.

Perhaps the best place in town, and one of the best of the island, to see authentic Hawaiian antiques and collectibles is **Mauna Kea Galleries** (65-1298 Kawaihae Rd., 808/887-2244 or 877/969-4852). Line drawings from the early years, prints from the 1930s, Aloha shirts from the 1950s, jewelry, old books, vintage artifacts, period furniture, and more are all here, but don't expect to pinch pennies. These fine-quality items may cost a bundle.

A few doors away is **Waimea Antiques and Collectibles** (65-1290 Kawaihae Rd., 808/887-0024), a varied collection with average prices.

Up the road is **Antiques by...** (65-1275 Kawaihae Rd., 808/887-6466), a co-op shop where one room is filled with Hawaiiana and the rest of the house has more ordinary collectibles. Good pricing and plenty to look at.

Near the main intersection in town is the **Upcountry Connection** art gallery (808/885-0623). Open daily except Sunday, this gallery

Rangeland near Waimea offers many opportunities for horseback riding adventures.

focuses on two basic themes, cultural Hawaiiana and cowboy art and crafts, and has a very decent collection of both. Well worth a stop.

RECREATION

Horseback Riding

Paniolo Adventures (808/889-5354, www.panioloadventures.com) offers horseback riding on the 11,000-acre working Ponoholo Ranch along Route 250 (near mile marker 13) in the Kohala Mountains north of Waimea. With your comfort in mind, they offer chaps, rain slickers, cowboy hats, and boots. Prices vary according to the ride, from novice to cowpoke. The most popular 2.5-hour Paniolo Ride goes out twice every morning for $96. On it you walk, trot, and canter your horse where appropriate. Also in the morning is the four-hour Wrangler Ride for well-seasoned horse riders only, at $149. The three-hour Picnic Ride runs in the afternoon and costs $124, while the one-hour Sunset Ride at $79 leaves about an hour before the sun goes down and makes a great end to the day. Generally, riders eight years old and older and those less than 230 pounds are accommodated. Private and custom rides can also be arranged, and the full-day Upcounty Horsemanship Program and Open Range Ride at $299 is designed for those who want to polish their riding skills. After your guide matches you with an appropriate steed, you head out onto the open range where you'll likely see some of the 6,000 cattle on the ranch.

Using horses from its own working ranch east of Waimea, **Dahana Ranch** (808/885-0057 or 888/399-0057, www.dahanaranch.com) gives riders free-range rides on its own property. The 1.5-hour range rides leave four times a day and are $60. For those with lots of experience, a two-hour advanced rider only ride runs $100. Want to work the cattle? Try the 2.5-hour Range Station Ride at $130 (minimum of four persons), where you take part in driving cattle from one pasture to another and learning about the history and culture of ranching on the Big Island. These are all open-range rides with native Hawaiian ranchers. Experienced or not, no problem; riders age three and up, and up to 300 pounds are OK. Good upcountry range landscape.

Kohala Na'alapa Stables (808/889-0022, www.naalapastables.com) offers open-range rides on the historic, 8,500-acre Kahua Ranch, high in the Kohala Mountains near mile marker 11 along Route 250. A 2.5-hour morning ride at 9 A.M. runs $89, and the 1.5-hour afternoon ride at 1:30 P.M. is priced at $68. All riders should be at least eight years old and no more than 230 pounds. Na'alapa Stables also offers rides down in Waipi'o Valley.

Enjoyable rides are also offered by the **Parker Ranch Stables** (808/882-7655). Turn between K. M. Seeds and Ace Hardware and follow the signs. Parker Ranch cowboys guide you over open rangeland on the slopes of Mauna Kea. There are two-hour morning and afternoon rides, as well as a 1.5-hour sunset ride, all available for $79 per person. Seven years old is the minimum age for riders; 210 pounds is the maximum weight. All rides are guided, but this is open-range riding.

Kohala Carriages offers a tame 45-minute ranch wagon tour on Parker Ranch land, every hour on the hour 10 A.M.–2 P.M. Tuesday–Saturday, leaving from the Parker Ranch Visitor Center. Rides cost $15 adult, $12.50 seniors over 60, and $12 ages 4–11. The "Hitching Up" ride offers guests a chance to have a ride after getting to know the horse a bit as they are hitched to the wagon for the day. Rates are $20 adult, $18 seniors, $17 children. Reserve a seat by calling 808/885-7655.

Every Fourth of July, the Parker Ranch hosts a **rodeo** that is one of the best in the state.

ATV Rides

Riding on the open range or along one of the ranch's back roads, you can experience the history and scenery of the Parker Ranch while astride your ATV. Morning, afternoon, and sunset rides are scheduled for $95 per person; you must be at least 16 years old. Contact Cowboys of Hawaii (808/885-5006) to reserve a ride.

Biking

The best place in town to rent quality mountain bikes is **C & S Outfitters** (808/885-5005). Located kitty-corner across from the police station, C & S can set you up for $35 a day and put you on the right road or trail according to your skill level and interests.

Mauna Kea Mountain Bikes (888/682-8687) rents mountain bikes (delivered to your accommodation) for about $25–30 a day and periodically offers bike tours, including the Kohala Downhill, a 21-mile ride down Highway 250 over the shoulder of the Kohala Mountains to Hawi, and a Mana Road ride, a back roads jaunt that lets you get a feel for upcountry Waimea rangeland.

Golf

Several miles east of town on the way to Honoka'a is the **Waimea Country Club** golf course (47-5220 Mamalahoa Hwy., 808/885-8053, www.waimeagolf.com), a pleasantly rolling Scottish links–style course carved from rangeland at over 2,000 feet in elevation. Enter between mile markers 51 and 52.

Tennis

The Hawaii Preparatory Academy has the first-class, lighted, indoor, four-court **Rutgers Tennis Center** (808/881-4037) on its campus, open to the public for $5 per person. While the courts are often open, it's best to call ahead to verify if they are available.

Waipi'o Ridge Hike

It is possible to hike a portion of the Hamakua Ditch Trail, constructed a century ago when water was needed to irrigate the Hamakua sugar plantations. Drive along Hwy. 19 to the eastern outskirts of Waimea and turn left onto White Road. Proceed to the end of the road and park as much off the roadway as possible. This is a narrow road, and residents dislike cars parked on the roadway. If the way is not blocked, head through the gate—you are crossing Hawaiian Homelands property. A gravel track leads around a water reservoir and on to the flume, which is in the forest reserve and open to the public. Follow the flume and hiking trail about an hour upstream, where it eventually skirts the edge of the upper reaches of the Waipi'o Valley and from where there are superb vistas (on a clear day) into the valley and a long thin waterfall. About a half hour farther along the trail, you can look back down the valley to the ocean and beach. This area often clouds in by late morning, so hit the trail early. Periodically, this trail is closed, so if there are any signs indicating a closure, be respectful and do not enter.

ACCOMMODATIONS

$50-100

The **Kamuela Inn** (808/885-4243 or 800/555-8968, kaminn@aloha.net, www.hawaii-bnb.com/kamuela.html), a onetime basic cinder block motel, has been transformed into a bright and airy 31-unit boutique hotel. It is located down a short cul-de-sac off Route 19 just before Opelu Road. The owner takes personal pride in the hotel and offers each guest a complimentary continental breakfast each morning in the small art gallery on premises. The pleasant grounds are appointed with flowers and manicured trees, and you'll find a swing to lull you into relaxation. The basic motel rooms are small, neat, and tidy with twin or double beds with wicker headboards, private bathrooms, and color TV, but no a/c (not needed) or phones. About one-third of the units have kitchens. The deluxe Penthouse is upstairs in the old wing and breaks into two joinable units that can accommodate up to five guests. The newer wing has larger rooms with hardwood floors and king-size or twin beds, and it features deluxe Executive Suites with full kitchens. Prices range $59–85 for a room, $89–99 for suites with kitchenettes. The Penthouse suites, when sleeping five, and the Executive suites are $185. Smoking and nonsmoking rooms are available. Reserve well in advance.

$100-150

The **Waimea Country Lodge** (65-1210 Lindsey Rd., 808/885-4100 or 800/367-5004, www.castleresorts.com) is located in "downtown" Waimea, but don't let "downtown" fool you—it's very quiet. Renovated in 1997, the rooms, many with kitchenettes and vaulted ceilings, have full baths and are well appointed with knotty pine furnishings, two double-, king-, or queen-size beds with turned pine lamps, wicker easy chairs, fans and portable heaters, phones, and TVs. The barn-red board-and-batten inn sits off by itself and lives up to its place in *paniolo* country by giving the impression of a gentleman's bunkhouse. The view out the back toward the mountain is an added bonus. Rates are $105 standard, $115 superior, $125 with a kitchenette.

Bed-and-Breakfasts

Appropriately named, **Aaah, The Views** (66-1773 Alaneo St., 808/885-3455 or 866/885-3455, info@aaahtheviews.com, www.aaahtheviews.com) is a bed-and-breakfast located in a quiet residential neighborhood just downhill from central Waimea, with unimpeded views of Mauna Kea, Mauna Loa, and Mt. Hualalai to the south, and, of course, the ocean off the Kohala Coast to the west. It's fine for the sunrise over the mountains, the sunsets on clear days are stupendous, and clear nights illuminate a star-studded sky. Aaah, The Views sits along a seasonal stream next to Parker Ranch land, so you may see cattle grazing nearby. The Stream Room and Sunset Room, the two upper rooms of the main house, can be booked individually or together. Each has a sleeping room with a cozy loft and a small deck, and they share a good-sized bathroom with tub and shower. New and modern, these rooms are tastefully appointed and laid with Berber carpet. Each room has a small refrigerator, microwave, and coffeemaker. The lower level of this house is the apartment-size Dream Room, with king-size bed, single bed in a skylight alcove, full kitchen, and lanai. The Garden Cottage is a tidy, compact studio with queen-size bed and a double bed in the loft, separate bathroom, and small kitchen. A continental breakfast with plenty of fruits, pastries, cereals, and coffee is served each morning for all guests in the detached house dining area or on the lanai that overlooks the stream, also a perfect place to use the wireless Internet access. Room rates are $70–155, add $20 for an additional person; two-night minimum stay. Aaah, the Views is a nonsmoking establishment.

Tucked back off the highway in a little oasis of green alongside a gently cascading stream near where Route 250 splits from Route 19 is **Waimea Gardens** (808/885-8550, fax 808/885-0473, contact@waimeagardens.com, www.waimeagardens.com). This lovely B&B is a quality professional place with all the modern amenities of home and then some, and a style that speaks of yesteryear with wainscoting, antique furniture, hardwood floors, and French doors leading to garden lanai. There's even a computer available to check your email. Two cottages in the detached building are suitable for couples or for families with one small child. You enter the Kohala Cottage through a century-old wash house, but inside the studio is completely modern, with a full kitchen and dining room with a large bank of windows that look out onto the back lawn, and a large bathroom with its own private garden lanai. The Waimea Cottage has a fireplace for those chilly nights, plus an efficiency kitchen. Both units have queen-size beds, TV, stereo with plenty of music selections, shelves full of books, and light daily room cleaning. The Kohala Cottage runs $160 and the Waimea Cottage $150; $15 for one additional person in a room; three nights minimum. Plentiful breakfast treats are left in your room for you to fix at your leisure in the morning. The affable and charming owners have been in the hospitality business for more than three decades, so they know how to treat their guests right. Overall, this is a very homey place, with many repeat guests.

With great views over the long and broad Kohala Coast and up to Mauna Loa, Mauna Kea, and Hualalai, **Belle Vue** (1351 Konokohau Rd., 808/885-7732 or 800/772-5044, bellvue@aloha.net, www.hawaii-bellevue.com) has a location above town that's just right. A spacious suite with living room, kitchenette, queen-size bed, and garden patio, and the upper floor penthouse with living room, kitchenette, king-size bed and queen-size sofa bed, and lanai rent for $95–175 including a fine breakfast; $25 for an additional person. French and German spoken.

Built in 1897 as the Parker Ranch manager's house, this plantation estate has gone through several metamorphoses and most recently been renovated, expanded, and turned into **The Jacaranda Inn** (65-1444 Kawaihae Rd., 808/885-8813, fax 808/885-6096, tji@ilhawaii.net, www.jacarandainn.com). This estate, with its raspberry-colored roof, dominates a broad lawn. A white ranch fence and bougainvillea hedge separate it from the road. Set amidst towering trees, the main house retains the original Hawaii Victorian flavor, with rich koa wood and numerous antiques. Enter the huge living room with its imposing fireplace, and from there you can move to the dining rooms, library, billiard room, bar, or terrace. Separate oversized suites have also been constructed to the rear as guest rooms. They are all decorated according to different themes and colors, and while each shows individual character and style, they all have a similar romantic feel. These are not ordinary rooms; they are designed to pamper guests in luxury. The eight guest rooms, with pretty flower names like White Lily, Iris, Orchid, and Passion Flower, rent for $159–225, and this includes a hot meal prepared each morning. In addition, a three-bedroom, three-bath cottage that can sleep up to six goes for $450 a night with a five-night minimum.

Vacation Rental Agency

With an office at the Historic Spencer House in the Waimea Center, **MacArthur & Company** (65-1148 Mamalahoa Highway, 808/885-8875 or 877/885-8285, fax 808/885-00569, mary@letsgohawaii.com, www.letsgohawaii.com) handles several rental homes in Waimea, with prices $95–200 a night, three- or five-night minimum stay. This company also manages other rental properties in Puako, Kawaihae, Kohala Ranch, and in the Kohala resort communities along the coast.

FOOD

While Waimea is small and set apart and has a strong cowboy flavor, it has become known for its great mix of fine restaurants.

Local Style

The cafeteria-style **Kamuela Deli** (808/885-4147) offers foods all day like sirloin steak, boneless spicy chicken, seafood, and other mixed plates, all less than $7. They also have breakfasts like omelettes, corned beef hash, or hamburger patties with eggs and hash browns. Deli sandwiches are also available. The good price and good food make this a favorite spot for locals.

The **Hawaiian Style Café** (808/885-4295, 7 A.M.–1:30 P.M. Mon.–Fri., closed Saturday, 7 A.M.–noon Sunday, but closed the last Sunday and Monday of the month), located in a modest building across from Parker Square, offers local and American standard food at very reasonable prices. Inside the blue-painted interior, chairs line a low counter where the menu offers breakfasts of two eggs with Spam or bacon, a three-egg omelette with a side of pancakes, Hawaiian-style loco moco, and Belgian waffles with whipped butter, strawberries, and maple syrup. Plate lunches, around $9, served with rice and potato or macaroni salad include curry stew, *lau lau,* chicken, pickled veggies, or a steak plate. This is the kind of food that's tasty as can be but gives cholesterol watchers shaky knees. A little short on Martha Stewart panache but long on pride, the Hawaiian Style Café will fill you up while being easy on your wallet.

Chinese

Don's Pake Kitchen (808/885-5828, 10 A.M.–8:30 P.M., closed Sunday), about one mile east of town on Route 19, is a Chinese family restaurant that has a good reputation for food at reasonable prices, even though most of its selections are of the steam-table variety. Some items are ginger beef, oyster chicken, and roast duck, but many people come for the saimin. Don's has a second place in the Parker Ranch Center that has the same menu and hours but is open on Sunday.

Thai

Don't be fooled by the name or the plain decor. **Charley's Thai Cuisine** (808/885-5591, 11 A.M.–3 P.M. and 5–9 P.M.) in the Waimea Center does tasty Thai food that's some of the best on the island. Come for Tom Kha Gai soup, shrimp green curry, pad Thai noodles, Thai chicken larb, or any of the many other traditional dishes on the menu. Most dishes are priced under $10, with a few up to $14.

Korean

A no-nonsense place, clean but somewhat sterile, is **Yong's Kalbi** (808/885-8440) in the Waimea Center. Open daily except Sunday, this Korean restaurant serves dishes like kalbi chicken, shrimp tempura, and spicy pork, all priced under $10.

American

Stop at the casual **Waimea Coffee Company** (808/885-2100, 7 A.M.–5 P.M. weekdays, 8 A.M.–5 P.M. Sat., 9 A.M.–4 P.M. Sun.) in the Parker Square, for small estate Kona coffee and light and healthy soups, salads, sandwiches, and wraps. Order inside and sit outside on the covered wooden walk.

When visiting the Parker Ranch Museum at the rear of the Parker Ranch Center, stop by the **Little Juice Shack** (808/885-1686, 7 A.M.–4 P.M. Mon.–Fri., 9 A.M.–4 P.M. Sat.) for juice, smoothies, salad, homemade soup, or other quick fill-'er-ups. Hardly anything on the menu is over $7.

Paniolo Country Inn (808/885-4377, open daily for breakfast, lunch, and dinner until 8:45 P.M.) on Lindsey Street, just a few steps from the main intersection in town, specializes in full country-style and inexpensive breakfasts, burgers, lunch platters, and flame-broiled steaks. Breakfast selections include omelettes, hotcakes, waffles, huevos rancheros, loco moco, and the *wiki wiki* breakfast of English muffin, banana bread, or wheat toast, coffee, and small fruit juice. For the rest of the day, sandwiches and burgers, cowboy-size pizzas, and more substantial Paniolo Platters like teriyaki short ribs, top sirloin, or porterhouse steak are on the menu for $10–18, with a selection of Mexican dishes thrown in for good measure. Prime rib dinners are served Friday, Saturday, and Sunday evenings. The food is wholesome, the atmosphere American country, and the service prompt and friendly. Don't miss having a look at the cattle brands hanging on the walls.

Aioli's Restaurant (808/885-6325, 11 A.M.–8 P.M. Tues.–Thurs., 11 A.M.–9 P.M. on Fri. and Sat.) is a simple, unpretentious place at Opelo Plaza that serves quick but tasty soups, salads, and sandwiches for lunch. The dinner menu changes every three weeks, and there is always a vegetarian entrée or two on the menu. Items you might find on the short menu include herb-crusted prime rib, seared scallops in a lime cream sauce, pan-seared duck, and eggplant pasta. Most dinner entrées run less than $20. BYOB if you want—there's no corkage fee. Definitely make dinner reservations, as Aioli's is popular and there are only about a half dozen tables.

Located adjacent to the Waimea Center is **Parker Ranch House** (808/885-2088, 11 A.M.–1:30 P.M. and 5–8:45 P.M., closed Tues.), a well-liked casual place for Parker Ranch steak and ribs, lamb, and chicken. This is good standard American food, served in good portions at moderate prices. While a variety of sandwiches, pasta, and pizza make up the lunch menu, dinner entrées branch out from pasta to include braised duck, Abruzzi-style seafood stew, osso bucco, rack of lamb with mint pesto and balsamic syrup, and rib eye steak, mostly in the $22–30 range. Lighter food is served all day at the bar on weekdays.

German/Swiss

The **Edelweiss** (808/885-6800, 11:30 A.M.–1:30 P.M. and 5–9 P.M. Tues.–Sat.), on Route 19 across from the Kamuela Inn, is Waimea's established gourmet restaurant, where chef Hans-Peter Hager, formerly of the Mauna Kea Beach Hotel, serves gourmet food in rustic but elegant surroundings. Inside, heavy posts and beams and dark wood plank paneling exude that "country feeling," but fine crystal and pure white tablecloths let you know you're in for some superb dining. The wine cellar is extensive, with selections of domestic, French, Italian, and German wines. Affordable lunches include offerings like soup, turkey sandwiches, and chicken salad in papaya. Dinner starts with appetizers such as melon with prosciutto, escargot, onion soup, and Caesar salad. Some Edelweiss specialties are sautéed veal, lamb, beef, and bacon with pfefferling; roast duck braised with a light orange sauce; half spring chicken diablo; and of course Swiss and German favorites like Wiener schnitzel and roast pork and sauerkraut, mostly $20–25. In addition to the short standard evening menu, there are often over a dozen specials. The cooking is rich, robust, and creamy, somewhat salty and saucy. The same for years, the food is always consistent (Hans-Peter is the only chef), and you get large portions for your money. The real proof is the loyal clientele who return again and again.

Hawaiian Regional

Merriman's (808/885-6822, 11:30 A.M.–1:30 P.M. weekdays, 5:30–9 P.M. daily), in the Opelo Plaza, has received a great deal of well-deserved praise from travelers and residents alike for its excellent food and stylish table settings. Many guests of the luxury hotels on the coast make their way up to Merriman's for dinner; others stop for a savory lunch at half the dinner prices. Here, chefs create fusion cuisine from local organic ingredients when available. The menu changes every few months, but perennial appetizer and salad favorites are sweet corn and shrimp fritters and vine-ripened Lokelani tomatoes with Maui onions. Lunch fare includes coconut curry grilled chicken with peanut dipping sauce and rice; grilled eggplant sandwich with Puna goat cheese, basil, and hot sauce; and Chinese short ribs. Dinner entrées from $21 to $38 are superb and might be panko- and Kefir lime–crusted scallops, wok-charred *'ahi,* butter-poached shrimp, and prime New York steak. Vegetarians always have a selection or two. Some of the most delicious offerings, however, are the fresh catch, prepared in various gourmet styles including herb-grilled and macadamia nut–crusted. Owned and operated by Peter Merriman, one of Pacific Rim cuisine's originators, Merriman's is a Big Island classic, so call to reserve a seat. In addition to his food, Chef Merriman does a farm tour on Tuesday afternoons that gives you a peek at some of the great agricultural treasures of the island and culminates in a farm-fresh meal at the restaurant; it costs $125 per person and reservations are required.

Great food in a fine setting can also be had at the **Daniel Thiebaut Restaurant** (808/887-2200, 11:30 A.M.–2 P.M. Mon.–Sat., 5:30–9 P.M. nightly), located along Route 19 near the Parker Square Mall in the renovated and rambling plantation-era Chock In Store building; reservations are usually necessary. Chef Daniel and his attentive staff serve a fusion of French and Asian cuisine with excellent flavors and textures. While the lunch menu is much simpler, dinner entrées, mostly in the $20–30 range, might include such items as Hunan-style rack of lamb, hoisin-glazed pork tenderloin, macadamia-crusted tofu with fresh vegetable stir-fry, and Chinese five-spice duck breast with Asian pear chutney. There is a long wine list to accompany each different entrée, and save room for one of the scrumptious desserts or an after-dinner liqueur. Special to the restaurant are the Tuesday–Sunday evening sushi bar and the much appreciated Sunday Brunch. There is live music during the Sunday brunch and each Sunday afternoon 4–6 P.M. in the restaurant lounge.

Barbecue

The Kahua Ranch does an upcountry *paniolo* version of the lu'au twice a week at its **Evening at the Ranch Bar-B-Que** (808/987-2108, www.eveningatkahua.com). Activities include an introduction to the ranch and cowboy culture, songs by cowboy musicians, pitching horseshoes, roping, roasting marshmallows around the campfire, and stargazing, but the heart of the evening is the outdoor hearty meal of ranch steak, chicken, Portuguese beans, corn on the cob, potatoes, and much more. At over 3,000 feet in elevation, it's cooler up on the ranch than at the coast, so be sure to bring along a sweater or light jacket. The rate for the evening is $89 per person.

Food Markets

For food shopping try the **KTA Super Store** (808/885-8866, 6 A.M.–11 P.M.) at the Waimea Center, for everything from groceries to pharmaceuticals. Across the highway at the Parker Ranch Center, the newer and larger **Foodland** (808/885-2022, 5 A.M.–11 P.M.) also has a full range of options and a pharmacy, plus **Healthways II** (808/885-6775) offers "alternative" groceries, packaged and bulk foods, and nutritional supplements.

On the west end of town across from Merriman's is the **Waimea Country Store** (4 A.M.–10 P.M. Mon.–Sat., 5 A.M.–9 P.M. Sun.). This small mini market–type shop, which also sells gas, carries an assortment of packaged foods and drinks and, surprisingly, a fairly good selection of wines.

The **Hawaiian Homestead Farmers Market** is held 7 A.M.–noon every Saturday, when local farmers come to sell their produce, much of which is organic. Flowers, baked goods, and crafts are usually available. Look for the stalls in front of the Hawaiian Homelands office located along Route 19, about two miles east of town center heading toward Honoka'a.

Alternately, try the **I Ka Pono Farmers Market** held 7:30 A.M.–noon Saturday at the Parker School.

SERVICES

The **post office** is located in the Parker Ranch Center, at the main intersection in town. The

U.S. Postal Service designates Waimea as Kamuela, so as not to confuse it with the Waimeas on Oʻahu and Kauaʻi.

The **Police and Fire** departments and district court are located in the civic center complex across Mamalahoa Highway from Church Row.

Gas is available at two stations at the main intersection in town, near the fire station on the way toward Honokaʻa, and at the small Waimea Country Store along the highway going west out of town toward Kawaihae.

Health

The full-service **North Hawaii Community Hospital** (808/885-4444) is located across from the Keck Observatory Office along Route 19. Physicians are available at the **Kaiser Permanente Waimea Clinic** (808/881-4500) in the Parker Ranch Center.

Laundry

Laundry can be done at the new and clean **Emma's Waimea Washerette** (5:45 A.M.–9 P.M.), located on the highway next to the Shell station on the way to the Honokaʻa. Emma's has change and soap machines. For drop-off laundry service at about $6 a load, head a bit farther up the road to the **Swiss Laundry** (8 A.M.–6 P.M.), a little building on the right.

Camera and Film

For the photographer, **Waimea Photo and Imaging Center** (808/885-0006) sells print film and does photo developing. Just around the corner and along the highway, **Positive Image Photo** (808/885-0488) also carries and develops film. Both shops are open Monday through Saturday only. The KTA Superstore in the Waimea Center also sells and develops film.

Airport

The **Waimea-Kohala Airport** (808/887-8126) is along Route 190 just a mile or so before you enter town from Kailua-Kona. This airport is used by private planes and a few daily flights by Pacific Wings, a small commuter airline that flies to Kahului, Maui, and to Honolulu. Facilities amount to a waiting lounge and basic restrooms. Unless a flight is scheduled, nothing will be happening at the terminal.

NORTH KOHALA

In North Kohala, jungle trees with crocheted shawls of hanging vines stand in shadowed silence as tiny stores and humble homes abandoned by time melt slowly back into the muted earth. This secluded region changes very little, and very slowly. It also has an eastward list toward the wetter side of the island, so if you're suffering from "Kona shock" and want to see flowers, palms, banana trees, and Hawaiian jungle, head for the north coast. Here the island of Hawai'i lives up to its reputation of being not only big, but bold and beautiful as well.

North Kohala was the home of Kamehameha the Great. From this fiefdom he launched his conquest of all the islands. The shores and lands of North Kohala are rife with historical significance, and with beach parks where only a few local people ever go. Here cattle were introduced to the islands in the 1790s by Captain George Vancouver, an early explorer and friend of Kamehameha. Among North Kohala's cultural treasures is Lapakahi State Historical Park, a must-stop offering a walk-through village and "touchable" exhibits that allow you to become actively involved in Hawaii's traditional past. Northward is Kamehameha's birthplace—the very spot—and within walking distance is Mo'okini Luakini, one of the oldest *heiau* in Hawaii and still actively ministered by the current generation of a long line of *kahuna.*

Hawi was a sugar town whose economy turned sour when the last of the seven sugar

HIGHLIGHTS

Lapakahi State Historical Park: The best-preserved precontact fishing village in the state, this park presents a glimpse into the world of everyday Hawaiian life on this dry and seemingly inhospitable coast (page 154).

Mo'okini Luakini Heiau: This is one of the oldest *heiau* in the islands, reputedly built around the year A.D. 480, and continuously cared for by members of the Mo'okini family (page 155).

Kamehameha's Birthplace: This is a lonely, wind-swept spot only a short distance from Mo'okini Luakini Heiau. From here, the "lonely one" grew to prominence and eventually united the Hawaii Island chain (page 157).

King Kamehameha's Statue: This was the original statue of two that were produced in the 1880s to commemorate Hawaii's greatest ruler; it now graces the rural community of Kapa'au (page 162).

Pololu Valley: Once an abode of a thriving community, the large valley has since reverted to a more natural state. This beautiful vale is one of several that open to the dramatically rugged North Kohala coastline, and from the overlook on its ridge, you can imagine what it must have been like when cultivated and full of people (page 164).

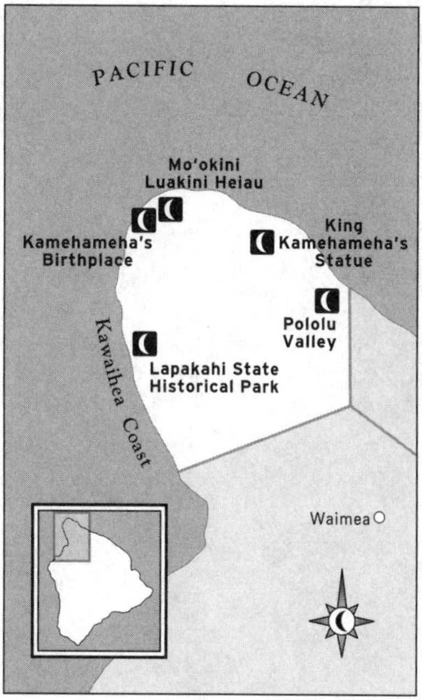

LOOK FOR TO FIND RECOMMENDED SIGHTS, ACTIVITIES, DINING, AND LODGING.

mills in the area stopped operations in the mid-1970s. Hawi is making a slow comeback, along with this entire northern shore, which has seen an influx of small, boutique businesses and art shops. In **Kapa'au,** a statue of Kamehameha I peering over the chief's ancestral dominions fulfills an old *kahuna* prophecy. On a nearby side road stands historic Kalahikiola Church, established in 1855 by Rev. Elias Bond. On the same side road is the old Bond Homestead, one of the most authentic missionary homes in all of Hawaii. The main coastal road ends at Pololu Valley Lookout, where you can overlook one of the premier taro-growing valleys of old Hawaii. A walk down the steep *pali* into this valley is a walk into timelessness, with civilization disappearing like an ebbing tide.

In Kawaihae, at the base of the North Kohala peninsula, Route 19 turns east and coastal Route 270, known as the Akoni Pule Hwy., heads north along the coast. It passes through both of North Kohala's two major towns, Hawi and Kapa'au, winding in and out of numerous small gulches and crossing some one-lane bridges, ending at the *pali* overlooking Pololu Valley. All the historical sites, beach parks, and towns in the following sections are along this route.

Route 250, the back road to Hawi, is a delightful country lane that winds through

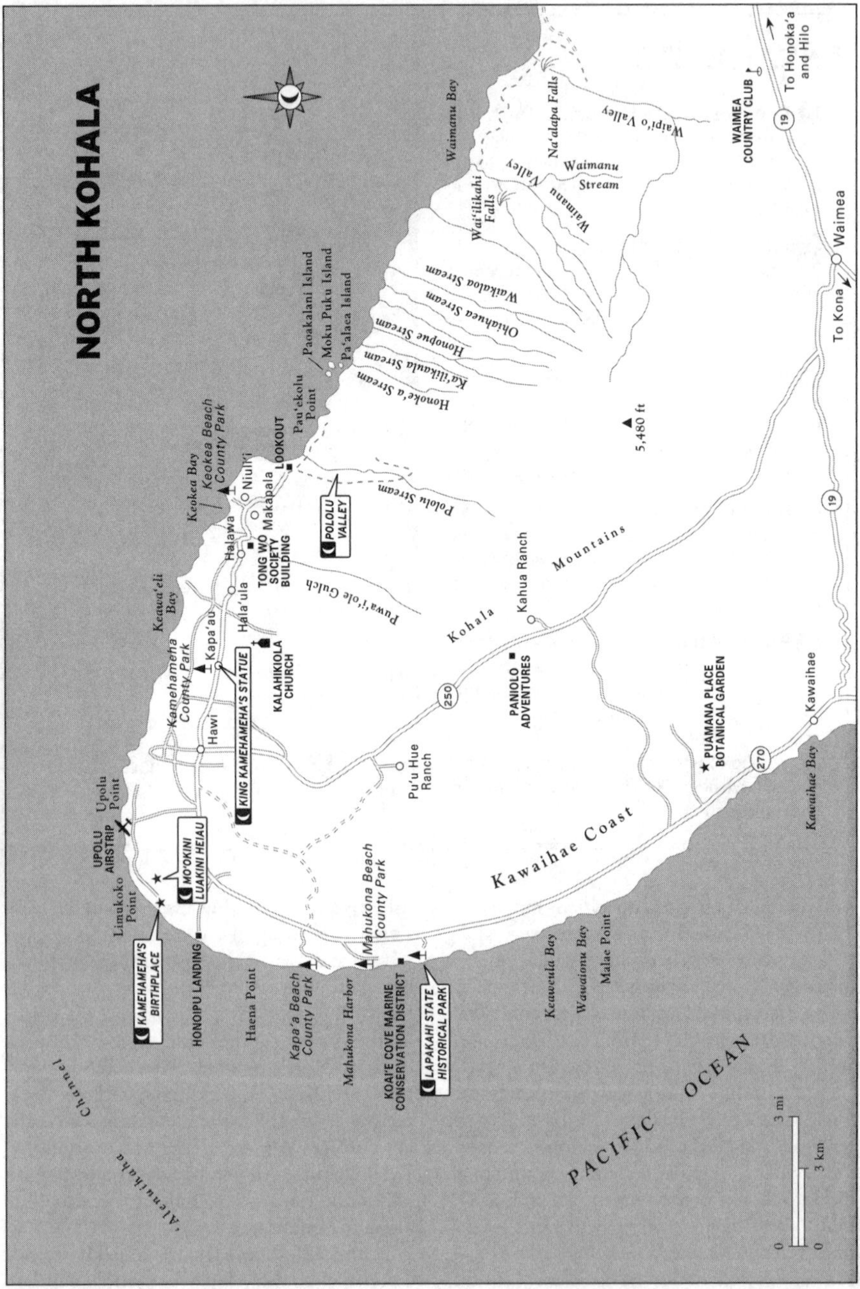
NORTH KOHALA
Waimanu Bay
Na'alapa Falls
Waipi'o Valley
Waimanu Stream
Waimanu Valley
Wai'ilikahi Falls
WAIMEA COUNTRY CLUB
To Honoka'a and Hilo
19
Waimea
To Kona
Paoakalani Island
Moku Puku Island
Pa'alaea Island
Waikaloa Stream
Ohiahuea Stream
Honopue Stream
Ka'ilikaula Stream
Honoke'a Stream
Pau'ekolu Point
5,480 ft
Keokea Bay
Keokea Beach County Park
Niuli'i
LOOKOUT
Makapala
Pololu Stream
POLOLU VALLEY
Halawa
TONG WO SOCIETY BUILDING
Mountains
Kahua Ranch
Keawa'eli Bay
Hala'ula
Puwa'i'ole Gulch
Kohala
Kamehameha County Park
Kapa'au
KALAHIKIOLA CHURCH
KING KAMEHAMEHA'S STATUE
250
PANIOLO ADVENTURES
PUAMANA PLACE BOTANICAL GARDEN
Kawaihae
Hawi
Upolu Point
UPOLU AIRSTRIP
MO'OKINI LUAKINI HEIAU
Pu'u Hue Ranch
270
Kawaihae Bay
Kawaihae Coast
Limukoko Point
KAMEHAMEHA'S BIRTHPLACE
HONOIPU LANDING
Haena Point
Kapa'a Beach County Park
Mahukona Beach County Park
Mahukona Harbor
KOAI'E COVE MARINE CONSERVATION DISTRICT
LAPAKAHI STATE HISTORICAL PARK
Keaweula Bay
Wawaionu Bay
Malae Point
'Alenuihaha Channel
PACIFIC OCEAN
0
3 mi
3 km

gloriously green grazing lands for almost 20 miles along the leeward side of the Kohala Mountains. It begins in the western outskirts of Waimea and ends in Hawi. One of the most picturesque roads on the island, it's lined with ironwood trees and dotted with mood-setting cactus, and herds of cattle graze in the pastures of the several ranches along the way. Vistas open to the west, and far below are expansive panoramas of rolling hills tumbling to the sea. Just outside Hawi, Route 250 splits; going right takes you to Kapa'au, left to Hawi. If you're coming along coastal Route 270 from Kapa'au toward Hawi, look for the H. Naito Store, and make a left there at Kynnersley Road to get back to Route 250 for Waimea; you don't have to go all the way to Hawi to catch Route 250.

Upolu airstrip is a lonely runway at Upolu Point, the closest spot to Maui. A sign points the way at mile marker 20 along coastal Route 270. Here, you'll find only a bench and a public telephone. The strip is serviced only on request for small propeller planes; it has no commercial service.

PLANNING YOUR TIME

North Kohala is tiny, and most people who visit usually take in its sites in a day. While it's certainly feasible to do so in one quick trip, you might think about several days to get a more in-depth look, especially if you decide to try one of the outdoor activities available in this area. Many people stop at Lapakahi State Historical Park for an hour's walk along its trail, but because of the hiking involved and their remoteness, Mo'okini Luakini Heiau and Kamehameha's Birthplace are just as often passed by. If you go, set aside two to three hours. Generally, visitors just blast by and make a beeline for Pololu Valley. While a great goal, it doesn't take long to get a view of the valley and appreciate its beauty. Those who want to hike down to the beach and spend some time should plan on a couple of hours. On your way back down the road, set aside a few hours to peruse the art galleries and gift shops, making sure to spend a few minutes at King Kamehameha's statue in Kapa'au, and perhaps make a short side trip off the highway. ATV, flume riding, and hiking

Pololu Valley beach and the rugged Kohala cliffs

excursions are fun both in the morning and afternoon. If you're able to make it up for a morning departure, do so, as you'll then have the rest of the day for sightseeing. If not, come back for a second day. In any case, stop for a meal in Hawi before you leave the district, for either the road along the coast back down to Kawaihae and the South Kohala Coast or the meander over the mountain to Waimea are pleasant routes to depart.

Kawaihae Coast

Unlike the rest of the North Kohala region, the Kawaihae Coast is long, hot, and dry. The lack of rainfall on the lower slopes made it poor for growing fruits and vegetables, but some were grown in the upper elevations. Much of the land was used for cattle grazing as it is today, and a railroad line once snaked along the coast from the sugar plantations farther north to the ports of Mahukona and Kawaihae. In olden days, this area was one of the least populous parts of the island. Today it still supports few people, but as elsewhere on the island, developers have begun to nibble away at its edges. As desolate as it may seem, this coast does preserve numerous very important historical and cultural sites, and it was literally from this wind-swept shoulder of the island that the winds of change blew to unite all the Hawaiian Islands under one ruler.

SIGHTS

Lapakahi State Historical Park

This 600-year-old Hawaiian fishing village, combined with adjacent **Koai'e Cove Marine Conservation District,** is a standout hunk of coastline 12 miles north of Kawaihae, just before mile marker 14. The park is open

© ROBERT NILSEN

Visit the Lapakahi site for an introduction to old Hawaiian coastal living.

8 A.M.–4 P.M. (gate closes at 3:30 P.M.) daily except holidays for a self-guided tour, but the ranger's knowledgeable anecdotes make a guided tour much more educational, when offered. Arrive at least by 3 P.M. so you have enough time to fully appreciate this site before the gate is locked.

The small hut at the end of the entrance road may stock annotated brochures. As you walk clockwise around the numbered stations, you pass canoe sheds and a fish shrine dedicated to Ku'ula, to whom the fishermen always dedicated a portion of their catch. A salt-making area demonstrates how the Hawaiians evaporated seawater by moving it into progressively smaller "pans" carved in the rock. There are numerous home sites along the wood-chip trail. Particularly interesting to children are exhibits of games like *konane* (Hawaiian checkers) and *'ulu maika* (a form of bowling using stones) that the children are encouraged to try. Throughout the area, numerous trees, flowers, and shrubs are identified, and as an extra treat, migrating whales come close to shore December–April. Don't leave without finding a shady spot and taking the time to look out to sea. In an otherwise forbidding coastal region, Lapakahi was home to generations of Hawaiians. A stop here is great for the opportunity to glimpse the remnants of this precontact fishing village and to imagine just what it took to sustain a community in this environment. For additional information, write Lapakahi State Historical Park, P.O. Box 100, Kapa'au, HI 96755, 808/889-5566.

Mahukona and Kapa'a Beach County Parks

Mahukona Beach County Park is a few minutes north of Lapakahi down a well-marked side road. As you approach, notice a number of abandoned warehouses and a Hawaii Railroad Company office building from 1930. Mahukona was once an important port from which the Kohala Sugar Co. shipped its goods. Still there is a pier with a hoist used by local fishermen to launch their boats. The harbor is filled with industrial debris, which makes for some good underwater exploring, and snorkeling the offshore reef rewards you with an abundance of sealife. Only 150 yards offshore (follow the anchor chain from the landing) in only 20 feet of water lie the remains of a wrecked steamboat, the only wreck in Hawaii that's accessible from shore. The wooden boat has almost completely deteriorated, but you will find a huge boiler, engine, shaft, and propeller. Swimming off the pier is also good, but all water activities are dangerous during winter months and high surf. Picnic facilities include a large but somewhat run-down pavilion and tables, but no drinking water. There are also cold-water showers and restrooms, and electricity is available in the pavilion. Both tent and trailer camping are allowed with a county permit near the parking lot.

Kapa'a Beach County Park is five minutes farther north. Turn *makai* on a side road and cross a cattle grate as you head toward the sea. As you head down to the coast, you also cross a cut in the slope that was used as the rail bed for the rail line that brought sugarcane and cattle to the harbor at Mahukona from farther north. This park is even less visited than Mahukona. The rocky beach makes water entry difficult. It's primarily for day use and fishing, but there is a pavilion, some barbecue grills, and a restroom, but, again, no potable water. Camping is allowed with a county permit. Neither of these two beaches is spectacular, but they are secluded and accessible. If you're interested in a very quiet spot to contemplate a lovely panorama of Maui in the distance, this is it.

Mo'okini Luakini Heiau

At mile marker 20, turn down a one-lane road to Upolu airstrip. Follow it until it reaches the dead end at the runway. Turn left here on a *very* rough dirt road to Mo'okini Luakini—this road may not be passable. This entire area is one of the most rugged and isolated on the Big Island, with wide windswept fields, steep sea cliffs, and pounding surf. Pull off at any likely spot along the road and keep your eyes peeled for signs of cavorting humpback whales, which frequent this coast November–May. After

Lichen-covered walls of Mo'okini Heiau rise from the wind-swept North Kohala coast.

bumping down the road for about two miles (count on at least 45 minutes if you walk), turn and walk five minutes uphill to gain access.

Only *ali'i nui* were allowed to come to the *heiau* to purify themselves and pray, sometimes offering human sacrifices. In 1963, Mo'okini Luakini was the first Hawaiian site to be listed in the National Historical Sites Registry. Legend says that the very first temple at Mo'okini was built as early as A.D. 480. This incredible date indicates that Mo'okini must have been built immediately upon the arrival of the first Polynesian explorers, who many scholars maintain arrived in large numbers a full two centuries later. According to oral tradition, this original *heiau* was enlarged by the Tahitian high priest Pa'ao, who came with conquering warriors from the south in the 12th century, bringing the powerful *mana* of the fierce wargod Kuka'ilimoku. The oral tale relates that the stones for the temple were fitted in a single night, passed hand to hand by a human chain of 18,000 "little people" for a distance of 14 miles from Pololu Valley. They created an irregular rectangle measuring 125 by 250 feet, with 30-foot-high and 15-foot-thick walls in some sections. Regardless of its age, the integrity of the remaining structure is remarkable and shows great skill in construction.

When you visit the *heiau,* pick up a brochure from a box at the entrance (often empty); if none are available, a signboard nearby gives general information. The entire *heiau* is surrounded by a stone wall erected for its protection in 1981. In one corner of the enclosure is a traditional Hawaiian structure used in some of the temple ceremonies. On occasion, this building is blown down by the strong winds that lash this coast. Be aware of the integration of its stone platform and notice how perfectly suited this thatched structure is to provide comfort against the elements in Hawaii. Look through the door at a timeless panorama of the sea and surf. Notice that the leeward stones of the *heiau* wall are covered in lichens, giving them a greenish cast and testifying to their age. A large, flat stone outside the wall was used to prepare victims for the sacrificial altar. Next to it and embedded in the ground is Kapakai, the guardian god in stone of the nearby King Kamehameha birthsite. This stone was removed here in the mid-1900s for protection but will be returned to its original place when the time is right. The only entrance to the *heiau* itself is in the wall roughly facing southwest. Inside is an enclosure used by the *Mu,* the person responsible for finding and catching the human sacrifices that were offered at the temple. Once a closed temple only for the *ali'i,* the *kapu* of restriction was lifted in 1977 so that others may visit and learn. However, please be respectful as you walk around, as this temple is still in use, and stay on the designated paths that are cordoned off by woven rope. Along the short wall closest to the sea is a "scalloped" altar, reputedly set up and used by Pa'ao, but where recent offerings of flowers are often seen. When you visit, bring a lei to place in respectful offering on the altar. Inside the *heiau* are remnants of enclosures used by the *ali'i* and space set aside for temple priests. The floor of the temple is carpeted with well-placed stones and tiny green plants that give a natural mosaic effect. By oral tradition, members of the Mo'okini family have been the priests and priestesses of the temple for at least 15 centuries, with the family line and duties of maintaining temples for the Polynesian rulers as they moved throughout the Pacific region that go back to the mists of time. Today, the inherited title of *kahuna nui* rests with Leimomi Mo'okini Lum, who has gone to great lengths to offer visitors information about the temple and particularly to instruct schoolchildren about its historical and religious significance. If you desire an accompanied tour of the *heiau* for a further explanation of its importance, please call the Mo'okini Preservation Foundation (808/373-8000) to arrange a visit at least two weeks in advance.

Kamehameha's Birthplace

A few minutes' walk south of the *heiau* along this coastal dirt track is Kamehameha's birthplace, **Kamehameha 'Akahi 'Aina Hanau.** Rather unpretentious for being of such huge significance, the entrance to the area is at the back side, away from the sea. Inside the low stone wall, which always seems to radiate heat, are some large boulders believed to be the actual "birthing stones" where the high chieftess Kekuiapoiwa, wife of the warrior *ali'i* Keoua Kupuapaikalananinui, gave birth to Kamehameha sometime around 1758. There is much debate about the actual year and place of Kamehameha's birth, and some place it elsewhere in 1753, but it was to the Mo'okini Heiau nearby that he was taken for his birth rituals and it was there that he performed his religious rituals until he completed Pu'u Kohola Heiau down the coast at Kawaihae around 1791. This male child, born as his father prepared a battle fleet to invade Maui, would grow to be the greatest of the Hawaiian chiefs—a brave, powerful, but lonely man, like the flat plateau upon which he drew his first breath. The temple's ritual drums and haunting chants dedicated to Ku were the infant's first lullabies. He would grow to accept Ku as his god, and together they would subjugate all of Hawaii. In this expansive North Kohala area, Kamehameha was confronted with unencumbered vistas and sweeping views of neighboring islands, unlike most Hawaiians, whose outlooks were held in check by the narrow, confining, but secure walls of steep-sided valleys. Only this man with this background could rise to become "The Lonely One," high chief of a unified kingdom.

Together, Mo'okini Heiau, King Kamehameha's birthplace, and several other nearby historical sites make up the seven-acre **Kohala Historical Sites State Monument.** In 2005, Kamehameha Schools bought a large tract of land surrounding Kamehameha's Birthplace and Mo'okini Luakini Heiau in order to protect the environs from residential and commercial development that might disturb the sacred nature of these cultural sites.

North Coast Towns

During the sugar heyday, this lush and very productive coast was chockablock with one small town after another until they stopped abruptly at the edge of Pololu Valley. Work was tough but life was simple. When the plantations closed, many drifted away to look for work elsewhere. Those who stayed, along with others who have come, have begun to transform the remaining towns into centers of arts and crafts, with a burgeoning recreational component.

HAWI

As you come into Hawi along Route 270, you'll see a line of false-front buildings leaning shoulder-to-shoulder like patient old men knowing that something *will* happen—and it has! Introducing you to the town are Sacred Heart Church, Hawi Jodo Buddhist Mission, and the Kohala Seventh-Day Adventists Church, lovely temples of worship and symbols of Hawaii's diversified spirituality. In the middle of town at the gas station, Route 250, crossing the Kohala Mountains from Waimea, intersects the main road.

Hawi was once a bustling sugar town that in its heyday boasted four movie theaters and four sugar mills. In 1975, the Kohala Sugar Co. pulled up stakes, leaving the one-industry town high and dry. Still standing is the monumental stack of the sugarworks, a dormant reminder of what once was. The people of Hawi have always had grit, and instead of moving away they toughed it out and have revitalized their town. Spirit, elbow grease, and paint were their chief allies. Hawi has risen from its slumber and is now making a comeback with new restaurants, galleries, and recreational activities. Here, too, are a handful of local shops selling food and fashions, some remarkable craft stores, and the only functioning hotel in North Kohala.

A glowing example of Hawi's modern restoration and revitalization is the old Takata building, now occupied by the Bamboo Restaurant and Gallery. This venerable old building was built by the Harada Family sometime before 1915 and served as a hotel for contract workers on their way to plantation work camps in the area. As the sugar trade took root, merchants came to town, and the hotel began catering to this more upscale clientele. These traveling salesmen were the epitome of the stereotype, and they desired evening entertainment. "Ladies of the night" took up residence in a few back rooms. The fortunes of the Harada family took a turn for the worse, and the building was bought in 1926 by the Takata family, who converted it to a grocery and dry goods store that served the community until 1991, when they moved shop, building a new store about one mile down the road. The old building fell into disrepair but was reopened as a restaurant after 16 months of restoration. New touches were added, like the old wicker chairs that once rocked wealthy vacationers into a light slumber at Waikiki's Moana Hotel, but they left the best alone, preserving the original feel of the building. Upon entering, notice the floor, heavily trodden over the decades, every nick marking a memory. The original wavy window glass is intact and still bears the original painted signs reading Fruits, Groceries, Cigars, Candy, Meats, and Coca Cola. The restaurant section, to the left as you enter, is perfect for an evening of dining; to the right is a gallery selling artworks. Browse before or after dinner and appreciate that this little community is finding a way to restore itself.

Shopping

The **Nakahara Store** (808/889-6359) has been serving the people of Hawi for decades, near the main intersection in town. One part of the store has groceries, while the other is a basic dry goods shop selling general merchandise and gifts.

In Hawi as well is the **H. Naito Store** (808/889-6851) another general grocery, dry goods, and fishing supplies store.

Proof that two establishments can occupy the same place at the same time, the **Gallery**

at Bamboo (808/889-1441) shares the vintage Takata Building with the Bamboo Restaurant. The gallery is lustrous with all types of artwork: koa furniture, covered photo albums, jewelry boxes, and sculptures, representing the work of many island artists. The furniture includes rocking chairs that beg to be sat in and fine koa dining room tables. Works of other well-known artists on display include lovely boxes, creamy white hand-thrown crystalline-glazed ceramics with flower or fish motifs, tapa-covered notebooks, replicas of sailing canoes, a smattering of aloha shirts, hand-painted silk clothing, jewelry with an ocean motif, and bright prints.

Across the street and down a bit in the renovated Toyama Building is **As Hawi Turns** (808/889-5023), a small but intriguing shop for fashions and distinctive gifts. Women will find dresses, skirts, wraps, sarongs, hats, slippers, jewelry, and accessories here, and men have a selection of aloha shirts. Most everything is brightly colored with wild or distinctive designs. Other neat novelty items, gifts, crafts, and postcards are also carried.

The **L. Zeidman Gallery** (808/889-1400) shows an amazing collection of turned wooden bowls. If you haven't seen the work of Hawaiian woodturning craftsmen or a sampling of native and introduced Hawaiian woods, this is a good place to stop for a look.

Also worth a stop is **Swift Gallery** (808/889-6995) for its paintings and painted ceramic tiles, **Mother's Antiques and Fine Cigars** (808/889-0496) for collectibles and burnables, and **Passion Flower** (808/889-0866), which sells art, antiques, and collectibles.

Recreation

There is little in the way of organized recreation along the north coast, but what there is can be exciting. Perhaps the most unusual activity is a kayak ride down a section of the Kohala Ditch. Completed in 1906 and considered a feat of engineering, this 22-mile-long irrigation system, with its 57 tunnels, supplied the Kohala sugar mills with a steady supply of water until the last plantation ceased business in 1975. Specially designed five-person inflatable kayaks put in above Makapala and drift down the flume, into and out of tunnels and over gullies for about three miles. Prepare to get wet. Tours go at 8:30 A.M. and 12:30 P.M. daily and run $99 for adults and $68 for children ages 5–18. Make reservations with **Flum'in da Ditch** (808/889-6922 or 877/449-6922, www.flumindaditch.com), or stop by the office at the back of the old sugar mill headquarters, up from the banyan tree in the center of Hawi.

HMV Tour (808/889-6922 or 877/449-6922) also takes you into the back mountain areas of the Kohala district, but you ride in the relative luxury of a formidable four-wheel drive Hummer. Morning and afternoon rides are offered Tuesday through Saturday, last about three hours, and run $120 for adults and $68 for children 5–15.

Accommodations

The 18-room **Kohala Village Inn** (55-514 Hawi Rd., 808/889-0404, www.kohalavillageinn.com) has always catered to local working people or island families visiting the area, as well as passing tourists. Located just up from the intersection in Hawi, the inn is an old plantation-style building, white with blue trim and a blue roof, that has a quiet central courtyard encircled by a wide and airy lanai, along with a remodeled two-story plantation-style building next to it. All rooms have been renovated and spiffed up with new amenities. Each has a shower and television, but none have phones, although there is one in the lobby. The standard rooms with single, double, or queen-size beds run $65–75. The Ohana suites, two connecting rooms that share a bath, are $100–120, and the larger deluxe rooms in the adjoining building with queen-size or king-size beds run $85–95. Clean, comfortable, economic, and somewhat spartan in the older rooms, the hotel has a friendly, quiet atmosphere and evokes the spirit of the past. Check in 3–8:30 P.M. please.

Vacation Rentals

Just a short walk from the center of town is **Hawi Guest House** (808/896-4169), a studio unit with kitchenette and bath that rents for $95 a day.

Overlooking horse pastures and out across the channel toward Maui is **Cabin in the Treeline** (P.O. Box 190591, Hawi, HI 96719, 808/884-5105, cwej@vacationhi.com, www.vacationhi.com). Cabin in the Treeline has two buildings literally set at treeline at the edge of a pasture. These modern buildings with all modern amenities and conveniences have been designed in a rustic *paniolo* or mountain cabin style. The main house has a large living room, kitchen, two bathrooms, a master bedroom downstairs, and an upstairs bedroom. The barn-like loft has one large bedroom upstairs with a queen-size bed and futon, television, and refrigerator. The bathroom with shower is downstairs with laundry facilities. Rates start at $180 per night depending upon the number of guests.

For a variety of vacation rental properties in North Kohala, contact **Kohala Pacific Realty** (808/889-5181, www.kohalapacificrealty.com).

Food

Occupying the renovated old Takata building is the **Bamboo Restaurant** (808/889-5555, 11:30 A.M.–2:30 P.M. and 6–9 P.M. Tues.–Sat., 11 A.M.–2 P.M. Sun.), with live music on Friday and Saturday evenings—sometimes by well-known local boy John Keawe. Lunch at the Bamboo can be a salad, sandwich, or one of the many entrées, like *kalua* pork and cabbage, herb-grilled fresh fish, or a Kohala quesadilla with your choice of main ingredient. Dinner begins with *pu pu* such as coconut prawns and calamari strips, but the restaurant is best known for its pot stickers, which are Thai seasoned chicken pieces with herbs and peanuts served with a sweet chili mint sauce. From the land comes pork ribs or beef tenderloin. However, as you're so close to the sea, why not try the fish, which comes in several different preparations? Sesame-nori-crusted shrimp, shrimp Alfredo, flame-broiled tiger shrimp, local-style stir-fry noodles, and teriyaki chicken are also options. Sunday brunch is a crowd-pleaser, with the regular lunch menu plus platters like eggs Bamboo—poached egg on a toasted English muffin with a slice of smoked ham or vegetables and topped with *lilikoi* hollandaise sauce and served with fried potatoes or rice. While moderately expensive, the Hawaiian Regional–style food at the Bamboo Restaurant is the finest and most sophisticated on the north coast. Reservations are often necessary, and while you wait, try one of their famous passion fruit margaritas.

For a south-of-the-border taste treat, stop at **Hula La's Mexican Kitchen** (808/889-5668, 11 A.M.–8 P.M., until 5 P.M. on Sat.), located at the back of the Kohala Trade Center building. Hula La's is known for its gut-filling burritos, tasty concoctions with beans, pork, chicken, or fish, fresh greens, other tasty morsels, and homemade salsa, $5.50–7.50. The Mexican-style plate lunches are also filling. If a burrito or plate lunch sounds like too much, choose a quesadilla, fish taco, an order of nachos, or one of the menu specials. At this neat little eatery with seating in the hallway or out on the back lanai, you can fill up for under $10 including a drink and be on your way in no time.

Sushi Rocks (808/889-5900, noon–3 P.M. and 5:30–8 P.M. daily), housed in the same shop as a gift and housewares shop just east of the main intersection, not only serves sushi but also puts several Japanese-inspired dishes, soups, and salads on its menu. The hot dinners run about $14 and sushi mostly $7–10. There may be music on Friday evenings.

In tiny Hawi, you can find island-style food with an Asian touch, Japanese delicacies, and Mexican treats, so why not German food? On the *mauka* side of the main road is **Aunty's Place** (808/889-0899, 11 A.M.–10 P.M. Mon.–Fri., noon–4 P.M. Sun.), where you can enjoy Wiener schnitzel, jager schnitzel, schweinbraten, and bratwurst, along with a few selections from elsewhere, like chicken Cordon Bleu, lasagna, ribs, Reuben sandwiches, and pizza. For those with less of an appetite, Caesar, Greek, chef, and Chinese chicken salads are also on the menu. Most entrées run $10–

14, so it goes easy on the wallet. Pizzas, served from 4 P.M., are more expensive. Aunty's bar is at the front of this tiny, easygoing restaurant. Happy hour is 4–6 P.M., and occasionally there will be live music in the evenings.

Open from early morning until mid-evening, except Wednesday, at the front of the Kohala Trade Center building, the **Hawi Bakery** (808/990-1444) puts out plenty of bread and pastries, but also does sandwiches made from their own bread, salads, and pizza.

Sun, surf, and the trek to Hawi made you a

MEAL MONEYSAVERS

Only one thing is better than a great meal: a great meal at a reasonable price. The following are island institutions and favorites that will help you eat well and keep prices down.

KAUKAU WAGONS

These are lunch wagons, but instead of slick, stainless-steel jobs, most are old delivery trucks converted into portable kitchens. Some say they're a remnant of World War II, when workers had to be fed on the job; others say that the meals they serve were inspired by the Japanese *bento,* a boxed lunch. You'll see these wagons parked along beaches, in city parking lots, or on busy streets. Usually a line of local people will be placing their orders, especially at lunchtime – a tip-off that the wagon serves delicious, nutritious island dishes at reasonable prices. They might have a few tables, but basically they serve food to go. Kaukau wagons specialize in the "plate lunch."

PLATE LUNCH

One of the best island standards, these lunches give you a sampling of authentic island food that can include teriyaki chicken, mahimahi, *laulau,* and *lomi* salmon, among others. They're on paper or Styrofoam plates, are packed to go, and usually cost less than $7. Standard with a plate lunch is "two-scoop rice" and a generous dollop of macaroni or other salad. Full meals, they're great for keeping down food costs and for instant picnics. Available everywhere, from *kaukau* wagons to restaurants.

BENTO

Bento are the Japanese rendition of the box lunch. Aesthetically arranged, they are full meals. They are often sold in supermarkets and in some local eateries with takeout counters.

SAIMIN

Special saimin shops as well as restaurants serve this hearty, Japanese-inspired noodle soup. Saimin is a word unique to Hawaii. In Japan, these soups would be called *ramen* or *soba,* and it's as if the two were combined into "saimin." A large bowl of noodles in broth, stirred with meat, chicken, fish, shrimp, or vegetables, costs only a few dollars and is big enough for an evening meal. The best place to eat saimin is in a local hole-in-the-wall shop run by a family.

EARLY BIRD SPECIALS

Even some of the island's best restaurants in the fanciest hotels offer "early bird specials" – regular menu dinners offered to diners who come in before the usual dinner hour, which is approximately 6 P.M. You pay as little as half the normal price and can dine in luxury on some of the best foods. The specials are often advertised in free tourist magazines, which might also include coupons for two-for-one meals or limited dinners at much lower prices.

BUFFETS

Buffets are also quite common in Hawaii, and like lu'au are all-you-can-eat affairs. Offered at a variety of restaurants and hotels, they usually cost $12 and up, but will run $25–35 in the better hotels. The food ranges considerably from passable to quite good. At lunchtime, they're priced lower than at dinner, and breakfast buffets are cheaper yet. Buffets are always advertised in free tourist literature, which often include discount coupons.

bit droopy? Salvation is at hand at the **Kohala Coffee Mill** (808/889-5577) in downtown Hawi; open daily. Inside the remodeled vintage building, order Kona coffee, espresso, cappuccino, pastries, and soft drinks, or a Tropical Dreams ice cream cone. Shelves hold T-shirts, herbal teas, fruit jelly and jam, honey, and other packaged food and gifts. Whether you sit inside in the cool of the shade or out on the sidewalk, this is a perfect place to watch the slow life of Hawi amble by.

For something a little more potent, head around the side and up the driveway to the **Hawi Health Hut and 'Ava Bar** (808/990-0277, 10 A.M.–5 P.M. Mon.–Fri., 11 A.M.–5 P.M. Sat.) to try the traditional island beverage, kava *('awa)*. While here, you can pick up some organic nutritional supplements, personal care products, and flowers.

If you're looking for something not as healthy, head across the street to **Kohala Spirits** and their stock of beer, wine, liquor, and snack items.

Food Market

K. Takata Store (808/889-5413, 8 A.M.–7 P.M., 8 A.M.–1 P.M. on Sun.) is the best-stocked full-service grocery store in Hawi. It's located along the highway about one mile east of the town center.

For fruits and vegetables grown in the area, head to the farmers market under the banyan tree in the center of town, each Saturday from 7:30 A.M.

Services

Even thought a post office substation is located near the Nakahara Store in the center of Hawi, the area's main **post office** is a large new facility about a mile east of town near the intersection of Route 270 and Kynnersley Road.

At the main intersection in town is a Shell **gas station.** At the intersection of highway 270 and Kynnersley Road is a second gas station.

KAPA'AU

Kapa'au is a sleepy community, the last town for any amenities on Route 270 before you reach the end of the line at Pololu Valley Overlook. In town are a library, bank, police station, and the historic and renovated Nambu Building (1898). Some distance outside of town in either direction are the Union Market and the Arakawa Store. Most young people have moved away seeking economic opportunity, but the old folks remain, and macadamia nuts are bringing some vitality back into the area. Here too, but on a smaller scale than in Hawi, local artists and some new folks are starting shops and businesses catering to tourists.

Kamehameha County Park, down a marked side road, has a full recreation area, including an Olympic-size pool open to the public, basketball courts, and weight rooms in the main building along with outside tennis courts with night lighting and a driving range. There are restrooms, picnic tables, and a kiddie area, all free to use.

King Kamehameha's Statue

The main attraction in town is Kamehameha's statue, set right in front of the old Kapa'au Courthouse, now a senior citizen's center. The statue was commissioned by King Kalakaua in 1878, at which time an old *kahuna* said that the statue would feel at home only in the lands of Kamehameha's birth. Thomas Gould, an American sculptor living in Italy, was hired to do the statue, and he used John Baker, part Hawaiian and a close friend of Kalakaua, as the model. Gould was paid $10,000 to produce the remarkable and heroic sculpture, which was sent to Paris to be cast in bronze. It was freighted to Hawaii, but the ship carrying the original statue sank just off Port Stanley in the Falkland Islands, and the nine-ton statue was thought lost forever. With the insurance money, Gould was again commissioned and he produced another statue that arrived in Honolulu in 1883, where it still stands in front of the Judiciary Building. About the same time, however, a British ship arrived in Honolulu, carrying the original statue, which had somehow been salvaged and unceremoniously dumped in a Port Stanley junkyard. The English captain bought it there and sold it to King

© ROBERT NILSEN

the original King Kamehameha statue in Kapa'au

Kalakaua for $850. There was only one place where the statue could be sent: to the then-thriving town of Kapa'au in the heart of Kamehameha's ancestral homelands. Every year for Kamehameha Day, the statue is hung with many strands of lei.

Kalahikiola Church

A few minutes east of town, a county lane leads uphill to Kalahikiola Congregational Church. The road is delightfully lined with palm trees, pines, and macadamias like the formal driveway it once was. Pass the weathering buildings of the Bond Estate and follow the road to the church. This church was built by Rev. Elias Bond and his wife Ellen, who arrived at Kohala in 1841 and dedicated the church in 1855. Rev. Bond and his parishioners were determined to overcome many formidable obstacles in building Kalahikiola (Life from the Sun) Church, so that they could "sit in a dry and decent house in Jehovah's presence." They hauled timber for miles, quarried and carried stone from distant gulches, raised lime from the sea floor, and brought sand by the jarful all the way from Kawaihae to mix their mortar. After two years of backbreaking work and $8,000, the church finally stood in God's praise, 85 feet long by 45 feet wide. The attached bell tower, oddly out of place, looks like a shoebox standing on end topped by four mean-looking spikes. Note that the doors don't swing, but slide—some visitors leave because they think it's locked. Inside, the church is dark and cool and, inexplicably, the same type of spikes as on the bell tower flank both sides of the altar. There is also a remarkable koa table.

The Bond Estate

The *most* remarkable and undisturbed missionary estate extant in Hawaii is the old Bond Homestead and its attendant buildings, including the now defunct but partially renovated Kohala Girls' School up the road and the Kalahikiola Church. All three of these wonderful structures are on the National Historical Register. No tours are given, but you can have a look at the outside of the buildings on the homestead grounds from the road and at the girls' school if the gate on the drive in is not locked.

Tong Wo Society Building

Behind the Rankin Fine Art Gallery in Halawa is the lovely and historically significant Tong Wo Society building (1886) and cemetery—well worth a visit. As the third Chinese Triad hall in Hawaii, Tong Wo Kung Ssu, as it was called and as the placard over the door still reads, was one of the early formal meeting places for the Chinese immigrant workers, a place to push for the overthrow of the Manchu government in China, an organizational force for community action and mutual support, and a social center. Around 1970, work was done to restore the building to its former splendor, and it now stands as a shining example, not only of the renovation of a structure, but also of the reinvigoration of a social organization, and the will of the community to remake one of its own.

Keokea Beach County Park

Two miles past Kapa'au toward Pololu you pass a small fruit stand and an access road heading *makai* to secluded Keokea Beach County Park. The park, on the side of the hill going down to the sea, is a favorite spot of North Kohala residents, especially on weekends, but it receives little use during the week. The rocky shoreline faces the open ocean, so swimming is not advised except during summer calm, yet there is a protected cove for the little ones. Amenities include a pavilion, restrooms, showers, and picnic tables. No camping is permitted.

Pololu Valley

Finally you come to Pololu Valley Overlook. It's about 12 miles from Pololu Valley to Waipi'o Valley, with five deep-cut valleys in between, including the majestic Waimanu, the largest. There are better views down the coast from this overlook than up the coast from the Waipi'o overlook. From this end-of-the-road lookout, it takes about 20 minutes to walk down to Pololu beach. The trail is well maintained as you pass through a heavy growth of *lau hala,* but it can be slippery when wet. **Kohala Ditch,** a monument to labor-intensive engineering, runs along

© ROBERT NILSEN

The Tong Wo Society building reminds us of the simpler days of the Kohala sugar plantation era.

NORTH KOHALA

© ROBERT NILSEN
Pololu Valley

the walls at the rear of this valley and carried precious water to the Kohala sugar plantations. Pololu and the other valleys were once inhabited and were among the richest wet taro plantations of old Hawaii. Today, abandoned and neglected, they have been taken over by introduced vegetation. The black sand and pebble beach fronting Pololu is backed by a tall dune that's crisscrossed by trails that run through a thick cover of trees. The rip current here can be very dangerous, so enter the water only in summer months. The rip fortunately weakens not too far from shore; if you're caught, go with it and ride the waves back in. Many people come to Pololu Valley for the solitude, seclusion, and an undisturbed day at the beach. For the most peace and quiet, go early or remain late in the day.

Shopping

In Kapa'au, across from the Kamehameha statue, is **Ackerman Gift Gallery** (808/889-5971, 9 A.M.–5:30 P.M. daily), owned and operated by artist Gary Ackerman. Displayed are local paintings, pottery, carvings, woven baskets and other natural fiber works, and one-of-a-kind jewelry. He also carries a smattering of artwork from throughout the Pacific. You can choose a reasonably priced gift item, especially from the handmade jewelry section. Make sure to check out the display of beautiful hand-blown glass. The distinctive, iridescent glaze is achieved by using volcanic cinders—you can bring home a true island memento that includes a bit of Madame Pele herself.

Ackerman has a second shop just down the street, the **Ackerman Fine Art Gallery** (808/889-5971, www.ackermangalleries.com, 9 A.M.–5:30 P.M. daily). This lovely gallery, housed in a renovated turn-of-the-20th-century building, showcases only his paintings (mostly still lifes, landscapes, and seascapes, but now some abstracts), known for their dramatic colors and textures, giclé and lithographs of his work. It is a testament to the man and his enduring popularity.

Occupying another renovated old building along the highway is the **Sue Swerdlow Art Gallery** (808/889-0002, www.sueswerdlowart.com). Swerdlow, "a colorist," displays her own works of bold and bright colors, plus a selection of pieces by other artists.

In the renovated Nambu Building is **Kohala Book Shop** (808/889-6400, fax 808/889-6344, shop@kohalabooks.com, www.kohalabooks.com), reputedly the largest used bookstore in the state. It handles fiction and nonfiction, rare and unusual books, books on Hawaii and the Pacific, and even some cards and other gift items. Thousands of volumes line the shelves, and if you can't find what you're looking for, the owners will try to locate a copy by searching their sources for it. Many of their books are sold online. If you want to visit the shop, stop by 11 A.M.–5 P.M. Monday–Saturday.

Also in the same building are the **Nambu Galleries** (808/889-0997), **Elements** jewelry and crafts shop (808/889-0760), and **Victoria Fine Arts** gallery (808/889-1711). Nambu Galleries shows landscapes by the owner and other paintings by artists from diverse places like California, China, and Colombia. Elements, which displays jewelry by local artist John Flynn, is more gift-oriented with a diverse collection of pottery, wind chimes, jewelry, prints, painted scarves, Christmas ornaments, and much more. Victoria explores colorful fantasy worlds in her paintings.

The **Rankin Fine Art Gallery** (808/889-6849, 11 A.M.–5 P.M. Tues.–Sat., 1–4 P.M. Sun.), occupies the historic Wo On (Harmony and Peace) general store in Halawa, which served the Chinese community during plantation days. This gallery displays a wide range of island-inspired paintings, turned wooden bowls, prints, and some American Southwest art. Around the side and in the back is the Tong Wo Society building.

Recreation

ATV Outfitters Hawaii (808/889-6000 or 888/288-7288, www.outfittershawaii.com) will take you to out-of-the-way places along the coast and up into the rainforest on former Kohala sugar plantation land on its rugged four-wheel motorcycles. You'll ride over back roads and fields, through lush gullies to waterfalls, come to the edge of ocean cliffs, or dip down to a pebble beach. These fully equipped machines let you get to places that you wouldn't be able to otherwise. Safe and reliable, the four-wheelers are easy to operate even for those who have had no experience on a motorcycle. Helmets, gloves, and goggles are supplied and instruction is given. Wear long pants and closed-toe shoes. Riders must be 16 years old or older and 90–300 pounds. Children can go along but must ride with the guide. Several daily rides are offered: a 1.5-hour ocean view ride for $109, a 2.5-hour waterfall ride for $169, and the 22-mile, deluxe three-hour ride that sees it all for $249.

© ROBERT NILSEN

At the back of Pololu Valley, Kapaloa Falls can be reached only by an organized hiking tour.

Hawaii Forest and Trail (808/331-8505 or 800/464-1993, www.hawaii-forest.com) offers a hiking experience along the Kohala Ditch trail to Kapoloa Waterfall at the back of the Pololu Valley and another hiking trek to other waterfalls in the area. It also takes guests on its six-wheel Pinzgauer vehicle into rugged former sugarcane lands for views of waterfalls and the coast.

Accommodations

Located 0.25 mile above Kapa'au is the **Kohala**

Country Adventures Guest House (808/889-5663 or 866/892-2484, getaway@pixi.com, www.kcadventures.com), an island home with three units that could be your base for exploring North Kohala. The Sundeck Suite, with its large deck and panoramic views, has a living area with king-size and double beds upstairs and a combination dining area and bath with shower downstairs. It rents for $160 a night, multiple-night rentals preferred. Basically a room with a double bed and a bathroom, the Cozy Bedroom rents for $85 and can be adjoined to the suite for a larger family. The downstairs Garden Bedroom, with its queen-size bed and single bed, kitchenette, and full bath with spa tub, also has a deck off the bedroom and rents for $125. Each unit has its own private entrance and views of the garden. All guests receive a light continental breakfast in the morning to have at their leisure. Two nights minimum requested. For reservations, call proprietor Bobi Moreno.

Located near Kapa'au, *mauka* of the highway in a residential neighborhood, is **Cook's Cottage** (808/889-0912), a studio with a full kitchen and bath, TV, laundry facilities, and separate entrance, available for $65 a night or $350 a week. It sleeps up to four. Contact Sue Cook for information or reservations.

In the village of Niuli'i, on the road down to Keokea Beach Park is **Kohala's Guest House** (P.O. Box 172 Hawi, HI 96719, 808/889-5606, fax 808/889-5572, www.kohalaguesthouse.com), where you have a choice of a studio or either half of a duplex. The studio comes with a queen-size bed and bath, kitchenette, color TV, and private entrance. Both halves of the duplex are fully contained houses with a full kitchen, living and dining areas, three bedrooms, two bathrooms, TV, and laundry facilities. The studio rents for $49 a night. The houses run up to $125 a night or $600 a week, depending upon the number of bedrooms you need.

Food

Nambu Courtyard Café (808/889-5546, 6:30 A.M.–4 P.M. Mon.–Fri.) is located in the historic Nambu Building. This little café offers such items as bagels and English muffins with various toppings for breakfast. Grilled sandwiches like stuffed focaccia, spicy Italian, and Swiss beef, plus a salad, are best for lunch, or you could try one of the fresh-baked pastries or ice cream with any number of coffees or other drinks. Hardly anything on the menu is over $8. Have your food inside or out back in the garden. The Nambu Courtyard Café is a great spot for a morning pick-me-up or a tasty bite during the day.

Kohala Rainbow Cafe (808/899-0099, 10 A.M.–5 P.M. weekdays, 11 A.M.–5 P.M. weekends), located across the street from the Kamehameha Statue in Kapa'au, is the place to stop for wraps, sandwiches, burgers, soups, smoothies, and pies, with most everything under $9.

J&R's Place (808/889-5500), on the *mauka* side of the highway, offers plate lunches for around $6.25, pizza for around $14, and coffee. You can't go wrong at this simple, clean, good, and inexpensive eatery.

Markets

The **Union Market** (808/889-6450) along Route 270 coming into Kapa'au sells not only general merchandise and meats, but also a hefty assortment of grains, nuts, fruits, and locally made pastries and breads.

To the east of town is the **A. Arakaki Store** (808/889-5262), also with a combination of groceries, general merchandise, and dry goods.

Near mile marker 27 in Makapala is the tiny **Pololu Valley Store** (808/884-5686). You can stop here for an assortment of gifts and souvenirs, but for most, it is the last stop before the valley for something cool and refreshing to drink or for a quick bite to eat.

Services

The **Kamehameha Pharmacy** (808/889-6161) in Kapa'au is a full-service pharmacy.

Those with a little extra time on their hands should stop at the **Bond Memorial Public Library** in Kapa'u to check out books relating to the area. This library is open noon–8 P.M. Monday, 9 A.M.–5 P.M. Tuesday–Thursday, and 9 A.M.–4 P.M. Friday.

THE SADDLE ROAD

Slicing across the midriff of the island in a gentle arch from Hilo to the Mamalahoa Highway near Waimea is Route 200, the Saddle Road. Everyone with a sense of adventure loves this bold cut across the Big Island through a broad high valley separating the two great mountains, Mauna Loa and Mauna Kea. Along this stretch of some 55 miles you pass rolling pastureland, broad swaths of lava flows, arid desert-like fields that look a bit like Nevada, a *nene* sanctuary, trailheads for several hiking trails, mist-shrouded rainforests, an explorable cave, and spur roads leading to the tops of Mauna Kea and Mauna Loa. Here as well is the largest military training reserve in the state, with its live firing range, and the Bradshaw Army Airfield. What you won't see is much traffic or many people. It's a great adventure for anyone traveling between Hilo and Kona. Keep your eyes peeled for convoys of tanks and armored personnel carriers as they sometimes sally forth from the Pohakuloa Training Area, and also watch out for those who make this a high-speed shortcut from one side of the island to the other.

Road Conditions

The Saddle Road was constructed in 1942 and left as gravel until about 30 years ago. While the road up both sides is at a good incline, the saddle itself is reasonably flat and at about 6,000–6,500 feet. Car-rental companies cringe when you mention the Saddle Road. Most still do not allow their cars on this road even though it is reasonably well paved through most of its length. Check your rental agreement, as it'll

© ROBERT NILSEN

HIGHLIGHTS

Kipuka Pu'u Huluhulu: This small hill of mostly native vegetation and birds is surrounded by barren lava flows. Several trails offer short hikes through this preserve (page 171).

Onizuka Center for International Astronomy Visitors Information Center: Located at the 9,300-foot level along the Mauna Kea Access Road, this is the first stop for all visitors heading up to the observatories at the top of the mountain. Not only does this center provide useful information about astronomy, it offers guided stargazing opportunities in the evening and also gives visitors needed time to acclimatize on their way up the mountain (page 173).

Mauna Kea Observatory Complex: More than one dozen large and small telescopes cap the sacred mountain Mauna Kea. This is the largest gathering of telescopes in the world and, atmospherically, one of the best spots on the globe (page 174).

LOOK FOR [icon] TO FIND RECOMMENDED SIGHTS, ACTIVITIES, DINING, AND LODGING.

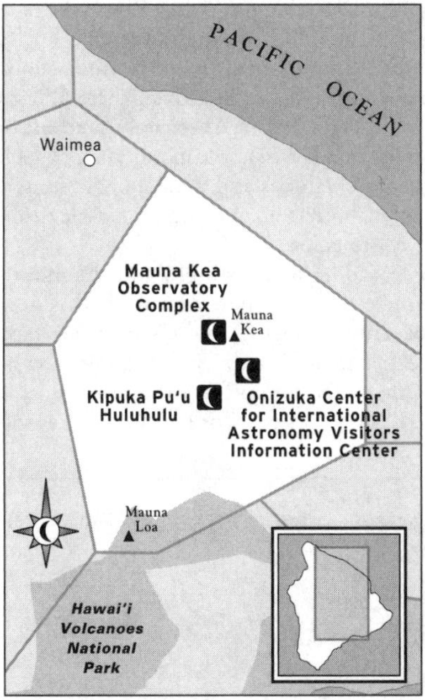

be very specific on this point. They're terrified you'll rattle their cars to death. For the most part, these fears are groundless, as there are only short sections that are rough, due mostly to military use, and with little or no solid shoulder. The road is very curvy, though, with several one-lane bridges and sections that do not have good sight lines. Plus, it is known to have a higher accident rate than other two-lane roads on the island. Drive defensively at a reasonable speed and do not pass. The Hilo side is wider, has better shoulders, and has seen more repair than the Kona side. Department of Transportation plans call for widening and new pavement, adequate shoulders, better drainage, and some rerouting over the next several years. However, one cannot escape the fact that this road *is* isolated, and there are no facilities whatsoever along its length. If you do have trouble, you'll need to go a long way for assistance, but if you bypass it, you'll miss some of the best scenery on the Big Island. On the Kona side, the Saddle Road turnoff is about six miles south of Waimea along Route 190, about halfway between Waimea and Waikoloa Road. From Hilo, follow Waianuenue Avenue inland. Saddle Road, Route 200, also signed as Kaumana Drive, splits left after about a mile and is clearly marked. Passing Kaumana Caves County Park, the road steadily gains elevation as you pass into and then out of a layer of clouds. Expect fog or rain.

PLANNING YOUR TIME

As there are no accommodations in this high mountain region except for a few state park cabins, travel along the Saddle Road is strictly a day-trip affair. Most standard rental vehicles are not allowed on this road, so find a four-wheel drive that can be driven there and go with a full tank of gas. Alternately, take one of the tours that heads up the mountain for a look at the observatories and a memorable sunset, or one that offers hikes through mid-elevation native forests for birders.

The Saddle Road is high, and the mountains are much higher. Approach this area respectfully. Start early and give it a day. It's easier to acclimatize if you go up slowly. Whether heading up from the Kona side or the Hilo side, it's perhaps best to make a stop where the side roads turn off Route 200 to stretch your legs and get used to the thinner mountain air. The goal for the vast majority of visitors who pass this way is the top of Mauna Kea, and that's reasonably easy as you can drive there. A few hearty souls head for the top of Mauna Loa, but this requires much more preparation and physical endurance. Don't try the hike unless you've done serious planning. If you do want to go to the end of the Mauna Loa Road and hike a bit, do that first before heading up the Mauna Kea access road. However much time you allow yourself, make sure that you're at the top of Mauna Kea *before* sunset and plan to spend some time after sunset looking at the stars from the visitors center below. As you plan your time to this region, know that you'll

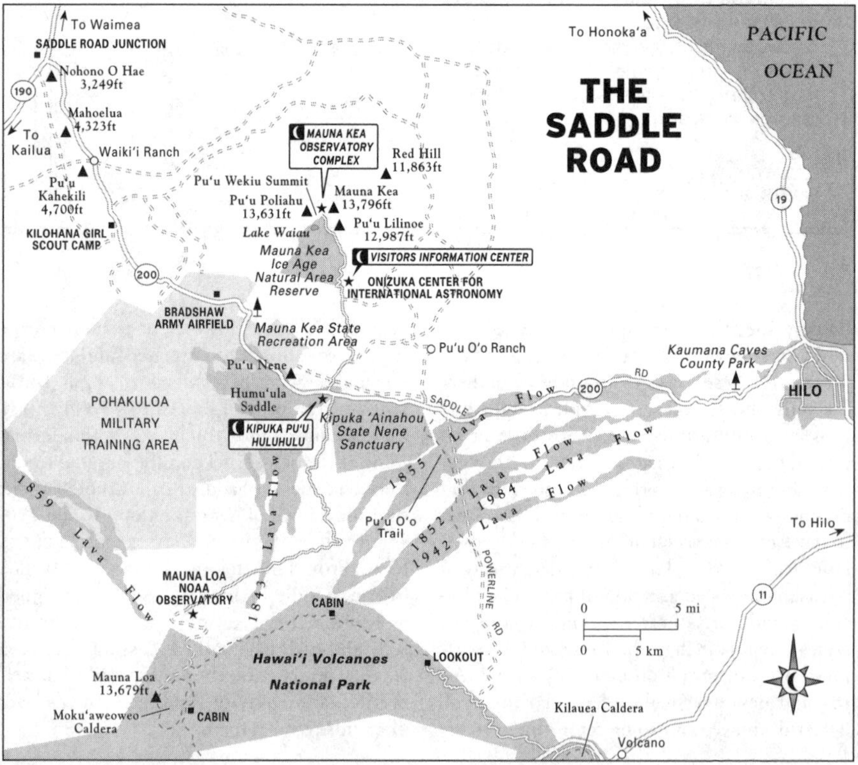

have a late evening so make no early plans for the following day.

SIGHTS ALONG ROUTE 200

Pu'u O'o Trail

Just after mile marker 24 on the way up from Hilo is the trailhead for Pu'u O'o Trail. From the small parking lot along the road, this trail heads to the south about four miles where it meets Powerline Road, a rough four-wheel drive track, and returns to the Saddle Road. This area is good for bird-watching, and you might have a chance to see the very rare *'akiapola'au* or *'apapane,* and even wild turkeys. This area is frequently shrouded in clouds or fog, and it could very well rain on you. You may want to walk only part way in and return on the same trail, rather than making the circle.

Kipuka Pu'u Huluhulu

Bird-watchers or nature enthusiasts should turn into the Kipuka Pu'u Huluhulu parking lot across the road from the Mauna Kea Access Road turnoff. A *kipuka* is an area that has been surrounded by a lava flow, but never inundated, that preserves an older and established ecosystem. The most recent lava around Pu'u Huluhulu is from 1935. At the parking lot you'll find a hunters' check-in station. From there, a hiking trail leads into this fenced, 38-acre nature preserve. One loop trail runs through the trees around the summit of the hill, and there is a trail that runs down the east side of the hill to a smaller loop and the two exits on Mauna Loa Observatory Road, on its eastern edge. Pu'u Huluhulu means Shaggy Hill, and this diminutive hill (about 200 feet high) is covered in a wide variety of trees and bushes, which include *mamane, naio, 'iliahi* (sandalwood), koa, and 'ohi'a. Some of the birds most often seen are the greenish-yellow *'amakihi,* the red *'i'iwi* and *'apapane,* the dull brown and smoky-gray *'oma'o.* In addition, you may be lucky enough to spot a rare *'io,* Hawaiian hawk, or the more numerous *pueo,* short-eared owl. Even if you are not particularly drawn to the birds or the trees, this is a good place to get out of the car, stretch your legs, and get acclimatized to the elevation.

Pohakuloa

The broad, relatively flat saddle between Mauna Kea and Mauna Loa is an area known as Pohakuloa (Long Stone). At an elevation of roughly 6,500 feet, this plain alternates between lava flow, grassland, and semi-arid desert pockmarked with cinder cones. About seven miles west of the Mauna Kea Road, at a sharp bend in the road, you'll find a cluster of cabins that belong to the Mauna Kea State Recreation Area. This is a decent place to stop for a picnic and potty break. No camping is allowed, but housekeeping cabins uhat sleep up to six can be rented for $45 a night for 1–4 people and $5 per person for the fifth and sixth. Bedding is provided, and there is electricity, but you must bring your own cooking utensils and water. Permits are required for these cabins. For additional information and reservations, contact the State Park Office (75 Aupuni St. #204, Hilo, HI 96721, 808/974-6200). Nearby is a game management area, so expect hunting and shooting of wild pigs, sheep, and birds in season. A few minutes west is the Pohakuloa Training Area, where maneuvers and bomb practice can sometimes disturb the peace in this high mountain area. If the military is on maneuvers while you're passing through, be very attentive to vehicles on or crossing the road.

MAUNA KEA

There is old lava along both sides of the road as you approach the broad tableland of the saddle. Much of the lava here is from the mid-1800s, but some is from a more recent 1935 flow. About 28 miles out of Hilo and 25 miles up from the Kona side, a clearly marked spur road to the north, officially called the John A. Burns Way, but most often referred to as the Mauna Kea Access Road, leads to the summit of 13,796-foot Mauna Kea (White Mountain). You can expect wind, rain, fog, hail, snow, and altitude sickness. Intrigued? Proceed—it's not as bad as it sounds. In fact, the road, while steep, is well paved for the first six miles to the **Onizuka Center for International Astronomy and Visitor Information Center** at 9,300 feet,

MAUNA KEA OBSERVATORIES' WEBSITES

University of Hawaii 2.2-meter Telescope: www.ifa.hawaii.edu/88inch
NASA Infrared Telescope Facility: http://irtfweb.ifa.hawaii.edu
Canada-France-Hawaii Telescope: www.cfht.hawaii.edu
United Kingdom Infrared Telescope: www.jach.hawaii.edu/UKIRT/
James Clerk Maxwell Telescope: www.jach.hawaii.edu/JCMT/
Caltech Submillimeter Observatory: www.submm.caltech.edu/cso
Very Long Baseline Array: www.vlba.nrao.edu
W. M. Keck Observatory: www.keckobservatory.org
Subaru: www.subarutelescope.org
Gemini Northern 8.1-meter Telescope: www.gemini.edu
Submillimeter Array: sma-www.harvard.edu

visitors ready for the sunset at the observatory complex atop Mauna Kea

where there are restrooms and drinking water. Just beyond the visitors center is **Hale Pohaku** (House of Stone), which looks like a ski resort; many of the scientists from the observatory atop the mountain live here. From here, the road is graded gravel, banked, and usually well maintained but sometimes like a washboard, with the upper four miles paved so that dust is kept to a minimum to protect the sensitive "eyes" of the telescopes. A four-wheel drive vehicle is required beyond the visitors center, and if there's snow, the road may not be passable at all. For current road conditions, call 808/935-6268.

As you climb, you pass through the clouds to a barren world devoid of vegetation. The earth is a red, rolling series of volcanic cones. You get an incredible vista of Mauna Loa peeking through the clouds and what seems like the entire island lying at your feet. In the distance the lights of Maui flicker. Off to your right is Pu'u Kahinahina, a small hill whose name means Hill of the Silversword. It's one of the only places on the Big Island where you'll see this very rare plant. The mountaintop was at one time federal land, and funds were made available to eradicate feral goats, one of the worst destroyers of the silversword and many other native Hawaiian plants.

Lake Waiau (Swirling Water) lies at 13,020 feet, making it the third-highest lake in the United States. For some reason, ladybugs love this area. This lake is less than two acres in size and quite shallow. Oddly, in an area that has very little precipitation and very dry air, this lake never dries up or drains away, as it apparently is fed by a bed of melting permafrost below the surface.

Here and there around the summit are small caves, remnants of ancient quarries where Hawaiians came to dig a special kind of fired rock that is the hardest in all Hawaii. They hauled roughed-out tools down to the lowlands, where they refined them into excellent implements that became coveted trade items. These adze quarries, Lake Waiau, and a large triangular section of the glaciated southern slope of the mountain have been designated **Mauna Kea Ice Age Natural Area Reserve.**

A natural phenomenon is the strange thermal properties manifested by the cinder cones that dot the top of the mountain. Only 10 feet or so under their surface is permafrost that dates back 10,000 years to the Pleistocene Epoch. If you drill into the cones for 10–20 feet and put a pipe in, during daylight hours, air will be sucked into the pipe. At night, warm air comes out of the pipe with sufficient force to keep a hat levitating.

Mauna Kea was the only spot in the tropical Pacific thought to be glaciated until recent investigation provided evidence that suggests that Haleakala on Maui was also capped by a glacier when it was higher and much older. The entire summit of Mauna Kea was covered in 500 feet of ice. Toward the summit, you may notice piles of rock—these are terminal moraines of these ancient glaciers—or other flat surfaces that are grooved as if scratched by huge fingernails. The snows atop Mauna Kea are unpredictable. Some years it is merely a dusting, while in other years, such as 1982, there was enough snow to ski from late November to late July.

Evening brings an incredibly clean and cool breeze that flows down the mountain. The Hawaiians called it the Kehau Wind, whose source, according to ancient legend, is the burning heart of the mountain. To the Hawaiians, this inspiring heavenly summit was the home of Poliahu, The Goddess of Snow and Ice, who vied with the fiery Pele across the way on Mauna Loa for the love of a man. He could throw himself into the never-ending embrace of a mythical ice queen or a red-hot mama. Tough choice, poor fellow!

Onizuka Center for International Astronomy Visitors Information Center

The entire mountaintop complex, plus almost all of the land area above 12,000 feet, is managed by the University of Hawaii. Visitors are welcome to tour the observatory complex and stop by the visitors information center at the Onizuka Center for International Astronomy (808/961-2180, www.ifa.hawaii.edu/info/vis) at the 9,300-foot level. Named in honor of astronaut Ellison Onizuka, born and raised on the Big Island, who died in the *Challenger* space shuttle tragedy in 1986, this center is a must-stop for stargazers. Inside are displays of astronomical and cultural subjects, informational handouts, computer links to the observatories on the hill above, and evening videos and slide shows, as well as a small bookstore and gift shop. At times, 11- and 16-inch telescopes are set up outside during the day to view the sun and sunspots; every evening they are there to view the stars and other celestial objects. The visitors center is about one hour from Hilo and Waimea and about two hours from Kailua-Kona. A stop here will allow visitors a chance to acclimatize to the thin, high-mountain air—another must. A stay of one hour here is recommended before you head up to the 13,796-foot summit. The visitors center provides the last public restrooms before the summit and is a good place to stock up on water, also unavailable higher up. The visitors center is open 9 A.M.–10 P.M. daily. Free stargazing is offered 6–10 P.M. daily and a summit tour 1–5 P.M. every Saturday and Sunday (weather permitting). These programs are free of charge. For either activity, dress warmly. Evening temperatures will be 40–50°F in summer and might be below freezing in winter, and winds of 20 miles per hour are not atypical. For the summit tour, you must provide your own four-wheel drive transportation from the visitors center to the summit. For information on the Internet about the mountaintop observatories or the individual telescope installations, log onto the University of Hawaii Institute for Astronomy website (www.ifa.hawaii.edu) and follow the links from there.

Going Up the Mountain

If you plan on continuing up to the summit, you must provide your own transportation and it must be a four-wheel drive vehicle. Because of the high altitude and the remoteness of the mountaintop from emergency medical facilities, children under age 16 are prohibited from venturing to the summit. People with cardiopulmonary or respiratory problems or with physical infirmities or weakness, women who are pregnant, and those who are obese are also discouraged from attempting the trip. In addition, those who have been scuba diving should not attempt a trip to the top until at least 24 hours have elapsed. As the observatories are used primarily at night, it is requested that visitors to the top come during daylight hours and leave by a half hour after sunset to minimize the use of headlights and reduce the dust from the road, both factors that might disrupt optimum viewing. It's suggested that on your way down you use flashing warning lights that let you see a good distance ahead of you while keeping bright white lights unused. However, as one security person has stated, safety is their primary concern for drivers, so if you feel you must use your headlights to get yourself down without an accident, by all means do so. For rental vehicles, contact **Harper Car and Truck Rentals** in Hilo (808/969-1478), which offers four-wheel drive rentals certified for driving to the mountaintop. Alternately, make arrangements for a **guided tour** to the top. These tours usually run seven to eight hours and run about $165–185 per person. Tour operators supply the vehicle, guide, food, snacks, and plenty of warm clothing for your trip. They also supply telescopes for your private viewing of the stars near the visitors center after seeing the sunset from the top. From the Kona side, try **Mauna Kea Summit Adventures** (808/322-2366 or 888/322-2366, www.maunakea.com) or **Hawaii Forest and Trail** (808/331-5805 or 800/464-1993, www.hawaii-forest.com). In Hilo, contact **Arnott's Hiking Adventures** (808/969-7097, www.arnottslodge.com). Take extra layers of warm clothing and your camera. Photographers using fast film get some of the most dazzling shots *after* sunset. During the gloaming, the light show begins. Look down upon the clouds to see them filled with fire. This heavenly light is reflected off the mountain to the clouds and then back up like a celestial mirror in which you get a fleeting glimpse of the soul of the universe. Most visitors head to the highest point of the complex to huddle on the leeward side of the Gemini telescope building for a windbreak, with the Keck Observatory and Subaru telescopes in the foreground. However, the Keck Observatory, while sitting on the summit peak, Pu'u Wekiu (Pu'u Kukahau'ula) or on Pu'u Poliahu, the lower peak to the west of the complex, are other wonderful locations to watch the sunset but require more of a walk.

Mauna Kea Observatory Complex

Atop the mountain is a mushroom grove of astronomical observatories, as incongruously striking as a futuristic earth colony on a remote planet of a distant galaxy. The crystal-clear air and lack of dust and light pollution make the Mauna Kea Observatory site *the* best in the world. At close to 14,000 feet, it is above 40 percent of the earth's atmosphere and 98 percent of its water vapor. Temperatures generally hover around 40–50°F during the day,

© ROBERT NILSEN

Gemini Northern and the Canada-France-Hawaii telescopes stand near the high point of the observatory complex.

and there's only 9–11 inches of precipitation annually, mostly in the form of snow. The astronomers have come to expect an average of 325 crystal-clear nights per year, perfect for observation. The state of Hawaii leases plots at the top of the mountain, upon which various institutions from all over the world have constructed telescopes. Those institutions in turn give the University of Hawaii up to 15 percent of their viewing time. The university sells the excess viewing time, which supports the entire astronomy program and makes a little money on the side. Those who work at the top must come down every four days because the thin air makes them forgetful and susceptible to making calculation errors. Scientists from around the world book months in advance for a squint through one of these phenomenal telescopes, and institutions from several countries maintain permanent outposts there.

The second telescope that you see on your left is the United Kingdom's **James Clerk Maxwell Telescope** (JCMT), a radio telescope with a primary reflecting surface more than 15 meters in diameter. This unit was operational in 1987. It was dedicated by Britain's Prince Philip, who rode all the way to the summit in a Rolls Royce. The 3.6-meter **Canada-France-Hawaii Telescope** (CFHT), finished in 1979 for $33 million, was the first to spot Halley's Comet in 1983.

A newer eye to the heavens atop Mauna Kea is the double **W. M. Keck Observatory.** Keck I was operational in 1992 and Keck II in 1996. The Keck Foundation, a philanthropic organization from Los Angeles, funded the telescopes to the tune of over $140 million; they are among the world's most high-tech, powerful, and expensive. Operated by the California Association for Research in Astronomy (CARA), a joint project of the University of California and Cal Tech, the telescopes have an aperture of 400 inches and employ entirely new and unique types of technology. The primary reflectors are fashioned from a mosaic of 36 hexagonal mirrors, each only three inches thick and six feet in diameter. These "small" mirrors have been very carefully joined

Cal Tech observatory, open and ready to start work for the night

together to form one incredibly huge, actively controlled light reflector surface. Each of the mirror segments is capable of being individually positioned to an accuracy of a millionth of an inch; each is computer-controlled to bring the heavenly objects into perfect focus. These titanic eyeballs have already spotted both the most distant known galaxy and the most distant known object in the universe, 12 and 13 billion light years from earth, respectively. The light received from these objects today was emitted not long after the "Big Bang" that created the universe theoretically occurred. In a very real sense, scientists are looking back toward the beginning of time!

In addition to these are the following: The **NASA Infrared Telescope Facility** (IRTF), online since 1979, does only infrared viewing with its three-meter mirror. Also with only infrared capabilities, the **United Kingdom Infrared Telescope** (UKIRT), in operation since 1979 as well, searches the sky with its 3.8-meter lens. Directly below it is the **University of Hawaii 0.6-meter Telescope.** Built in 1968, it was the first on the mountaintop and has the smallest reflective mirror. Completed in 1970, the **University of Hawaii 2.2-meter Telescope** was a huge improvement over its predecessor but is now the second smallest telescope at the top. The **Caltech Submillimeter Observatory** (CSO) has been looking into the sky since 1987 with its 10.4-meter radio telescope. **Subaru** (Japan National Large Telescope) is a monolithic 8.3-meter mirror capable of both optical and infrared viewing. It is the most recently completed telescope on the mountain, fully operational since 2000. The **Gemini Northern 8.1-meter Telescope,** also with both optical and infrared viewing, is run by a consortium from the United States, United Kingdom, Canada, Chile, Argentina, and Brazil. Its southern twin is located on a mountaintop in Chile, and together they have been viewing the heavens since 1999. Situated to the side and below the rest is the **Submillimeter Array,** a series of eight six-meter-wide antennae. About two miles distant from the top is the **Very Long Baseline Array,** a 25-meter-wide, centimeter wavelength radio dish that is one in a series of similar antennae that dot the 5,000-mile stretch between Hawaii and the Virgin Islands.

While the state is considering expansion of the complex to include additional telescopes and support facilities, a number of groups, including The Hawaiian-Environmental Alliance, are calling upon the state to proceed in a culturally and environmentally friendly manner or to not proceed at all.

Visiting the Telescopes

At present, only the Subaru telescope allows visitors on organized tours. These free, 30-minute tours are given at 10:30 A.M., 11:30 A.M., and 1:30 P.M. only on weekdays that they are offered. Tours are run in English and Japanese, with the first and last tours of the day usually in English. The tour schedule is posted three months in advance on the telescope website (www.subarutelescope.org), and tours must be booked at least a week in advance. Transportation to the telescope is the visitor's responsibility. This tour is a brief introduction to the telescope itself and the work being performed. There is no opportunity to actually view anything through the telescope. All safety precautions pertaining to visiting the summit also apply to visiting this telescope for the tour. For addition information, check the website or call (808/934-5056 or 808/934-7788).

While the Keck telescopes do not offer tours, the visitors gallery at the telescope base is open 10 A.M.–4:30 P.M. weekdays for a 12-minute video, information about the work being done, and a "partial view of the Keck I telescope and dome." Two public restrooms are also available to visitors. For those who cannot visit the summit, the same information and video are available in the lobby at the Keck headquarters in Waimea.

Hiking on the Mountain

Hiking on Mauna Kea means high altitude hiking. Although the height of the mountain is not necessarily a problem, the elevation gain in a short hour or two of getting to the top is. It takes time for the body to acclimatize, and when you drive up from the ocean you rob yourself of the chance to acclimatize easily. What you may expect to experience normally are slight dizziness, a shortness of breath due to reduced oxygen levels, and reduced ability to think clearly and react quickly. Some people are more prone to elevation problems, so if you experience more severe symptoms, get to a lower elevation immediately! These symptoms include prolonged or severe headache, loss of appetite, cramped muscles, prolonged malaise or weakness, dizziness, reduced muscle control and balance, and heart palpitations. Use your head, know your limits, and don't push yourself. Carry plenty of water (more than you would at a lower elevation) and food. Wear a brimmed hat, sunglasses, sunscreen, and lip balm, a long-sleeved shirt and long pants, and sturdy hiking boots or shoes. Carry a windbreaker, sweater, and gloves, as it can be cold and windy at and near the top. Don't alter the natural environment and stay on established trails. As always, please carry out all that you take in.

There are a few good trails on the mountain. About six miles above the visitors center, a dirt track heads off the access road to the west and downhill to a parking lot. From the parking area, it's about one mile farther west, over the saddle between two small cones, to Lake Waiau and its placid waters. This should take less than 30 minutes. On the way, you cross the Mauna Kea Humu'ula Trail, which starts at the third parking lot near the T intersection above and heads down the mountain to the visitors center. Taking the Humu'ula Trail to Lake Waiau should also take less than 30 minutes. Continuing on down the Humu'ula Trail a couple of miles brings you past an ancient adze quarry site. If you are planning to hike from Lake Waiau to the visitors center, please fill out a Mauna Kea trail hiker registration form and leave it at the visitors center. Perhaps the most convenient hike is that to the true summit of the mountain. Start from the roadway across from the University of Hawaii 2.2-meter Telescope, cross over the guardrail, and follow the rough path down into the saddle and steeply up the hill, a distance of less than half a mile.

MAUNA LOA

The largest mass of mountain to make up the Big Island is Mauna Loa (Long Mountain). It lies to the south of Mauna Kea and dominates the southern half of the island. At 13,677 feet, it is about 100 feet shorter than Mauna Kea. The top of this mountain is the huge **Moku'aweoweo Caldera,** virtually as big as Kilauea Crater near Volcano. Connected to this caldera are the smaller but equally impressive North and South Pits, each about as big as Halema'uma'u, which is within Kilauea Crater. Unlike Mauna Kea, Mauna Loa has had some recent volcanic activity, spilling lava in 1949, 1950, 1975, and 1980. The top of this mountain is within the Hawai'i Volcanoes National Park boundary. One of the longest and perhaps the most difficult hiking trail in the park runs up the south side of Mauna Loa from the Mauna Loa Lookout above Volcano to the rim of Moku'aweoweo Caldera.

Mauna Loa Road near the top

Going Up

Mauna Loa Observatory Road, a one-lane paved road with long stretches of potholes and rough patches, turns south off Route 200 between mile marker 27 and 28 and leads about 17 miles in a big zig and zag and gentle incline up to the **Mauna Loa NOAA Atmospheric Observatory** at 11,140 feet, which you can see high on the hillside above as you progress along this road. According to the signboard below this small complex, measurements are gathered here for CO2, CO, CH4, CFCs, ozone, solar radiation, atmospheric dust, stratospheric aerosols, and temperatures, among other items. Even a two-wheel drive vehicle could handle this road without problems, but driving it would abrogate your rental car contract. Use a four-wheel drive rental vehicle that is approved for this road. Although it could be done faster, give yourself an hour to take in the surroundings, check out the distant sights, and reach the end of the road. Use your vehicle lights, particularly if there are low clouds, and straddle the reflective white line that runs down the center of this single-lane road all the way up to the observatory, pulling over only to let vehicles from the other direction get by. The atmospheric observatory is not open to the public, but you can park in a small parking lot below it at the end of the pavement.

About two miles in from the turnoff is a rock formation at the side of the road that, at a certain angle, looks remarkably like Charles deGaulle, former president of France—and you don't have to use your imagination much at all. As you continue, you get a fine, distant look at the observatories on top of Mauna Kea across the saddle, Pu'u Huluhulu below at the turnoff, and the military reservation beyond to the west. About four miles in, at a turn in the road, there is a gravel road that heads over the horizon to the west, an abandoned attempt at a highway shortcut to Kailua-Kona. About eight miles up, at a point where there are a number of telephone and television transmitter towers, the road makes

SKIING ON MAUNA KEA

Bored with sun and surf? Strap the "boards" to your feet and hit the slopes of Mauna Kea for one of the most unusual ski adventures in the world. Most skiers careen down what's known as the "poi bowl," an area inside the ring of observatories, but they will try wherever there is enough snow to run. Numerous popular runs have been named by those who ski the mountain often. Skiing here is done the old-fashioned way – no lifts and no services. Because of the altitude, the task of skiing and walking back up the hill are more laborious than down below. You must be in top physical condition, yet nearly everyone suffers from some sort of altitude sickness. Remember that there is just rock below the snow – no grass and no cushioning – and the snow may end abruptly, so you must be very careful and mindful of where you're going and when to stop. Yet, the experience can be otherworldly as you are surrounded by stark white snow, black volcanic rock, a deep blue sky, an amazing quiet, and surreal shapes of the observatories topping the hill.

There are no ski rental shops on the island, so you must bring your own ski equipment. What's more, you'll need your own four-wheel drive vehicle to get there. You can bring your skis and rent four-wheel drives, but if that seems like too much hassle, contact **Ski Guides Hawaii** (P.O. Box 1954, Kamuela, HI 96743, 808/885-4188, www.skihawaii.com). Here you can rent skis, and they'll provide the "lifts" to the top. Skis, boots, and poles (or snowboards and shoes) rent for $50 a day; the popular full-day ski/snowboard tour with equipment, ride and driver, ski guide, and lunch goes for $250 per person (minimum three people). Other ski packages and cross-country ski tours are available and priced on request. For additional information about skiing the mountain, check the Hawaii Ski Club website (www.hawaiisnowskiclub.com).

You can expect snow December–May, but you can't count on it. It's most probable during February and March, and occasionally it stays as late as June or July. Generally speaking, your chances for skiable snow are better the few days after a moisture-laden front has moved across the island, blanketing the top with a white covering. More snow comes in La Niña years and less during El Niño.

a big zag and heads almost in a straight-line shot, following power poles to the observatory. Notice the different colors of lava that the road crosses and the amount of vegetation on each type. The older brown lava has some grasses and small bushes growing from it, while the newer black lava is almost totally barren. There are large areas of red lava as well, and some of that has been used as road base and paving material. You will see several collapsed lava tubes near the road as you make your way up. Still farther on, areas of ropy pahoehoe lava stick up through newer 'a'a lava. Around mile 15, new pavement has been laid so your ride gets smother even as the road goes through a series of roller coaster waves as you approach the end of the road. Beyond the end of the pavement, an extremely rough Jeep track continues—best used as a hiking trail. This track zig-zags up the mountainside, eventually ending near the crater rim after about seven miles.

Hiking

A hiking trail leaves the gravel Jeep track several hundred yards beyond the end of the pavement and heads almost straight up the mountainside, crossing the Jeep trail several times. This observatory trail is a rigorous 3.8 miles long and rises some 2,500 feet to the caldera rim. Follow the cairns. If you intend to hike the observatory trail, be aware that this is a very remote area. There are no services, restrooms, or water along the way. It can be cold and moist, snow and winter conditions can happen at any time of year, and there is virtually no protection from the weather until you get to the cabin on the eastern rim. Stay away when there's inclement weather or the clouds embrace the mountain. Park officials estimate that about half of all hikers taking this trail get some degree of altitude sickness. If you are planning on hiking more than a short distance, get an early start. The air is noticeably thin and dry. Go slowly, take your time, and notice how quiet it is. The only noises you hear might be the beating of your own heart and your own labored breathing. Bring plenty of water and snacks to eat. Wear a long-sleeved shirt, long pants, sturdy hiking boots, and a brimmed hat, and use sunscreen and lip balm. This trail meets the Mauna Loa Trail, which comes up the south side of the mountain. From this junction, a 2.6-mile trail skirts the western edge of the caldera to the actual summit. About two miles long, a second trail runs to the Mauna Loa cabin, perched on the eastern edge of the rim, directly across from the summit.

From the hiking trail above the Mauna Loa NOAA atmospheric observatory, you can see across the saddle and, if the clouds are not blocking the view, the observatory complex at the top of Mauna Kea.

HAMAKUA COAST

Along the shore, cobalt waves foam into razor-sharp valleys where cold mountain streams meet the sea at lonely pebbled beaches. Inland, the Hamakua Coast, once awash in a rolling green sea of sugarcane, is now being put to some other uses. Along a 50-mile stretch of the Hawai'i Belt Road (Rt. 19) from Waipi'o to Hilo, the Big Island grew its cane for 100 years or more. Water was needed for sugar—a ton to produce a pound—and this coast has plenty. Huge flumes once carried water to the fields and the cut cane to the mills. In the 19th century so many Scots worked the plantations hereabouts that Hamakua was called the "Scotch Coast." Now most residents are a mixture of Scottish, Japanese, Filipino, and Portuguese ancestry. Side roads dip off Route 19 into one-family valleys where the modest, weather-beaten homes of plantation workers sit surrounded by garden plots on tiny, hand-hewn terraces. These valleys, as they march down the coast, are unromantically referred to as "gulches." From the Belt Road's many bridges, you can trace silvery-ribboned streams that mark the valley floors as they open to the sea. Each valley is jungle, lush with wildflowers and fruit trees transforming the steep sides to emerald-green velvet. This is a spectacular drive, and the coast shouldn't be missed.

This stretch of the island has recently been named the "Hilo-Hamakua Heritage Coast" in an effort to draw attention to its historic and cultural significance. Pick up a copy of *A Driver's Guide to the Hilo-Hamakua Heritage Coast* pamphlet and look for brown and white

HIGHLIGHTS

Waipi'o Valley: The largest such valley on the island, Waipi'o Valley is a magnificent place – wide, deep, and verdant, and once home to the kings of Hawai'i (page 191).

Laupahoehoe Point County Park: A flat nub of land pushing into the ocean, the park occupies a site of disastrous loss during the 1946 tsunami. This is an appropriate place to contemplate natural disaster and human loss (page 199).

Laupahoehoe Train Museum: It captures the essence of what coastal living was like until 1946 and why the rail line was so integral to the development of the sugar industry along the Hamakua Coast. It's a good rest stop and point of education for a drive up or down this coast (page 200).

'Akaka Falls State Park: One of Hawaii's tallest single falls, this is one of the most impressive and easily accessible waterfalls along this coast, which seems to have one in every valley (page 202).

Hawaii Tropical Botanical Garden: This is a little slice of paradise, a well-tended tropical valley full of native and imported flowers, bushes, bamboo, and birds (page 206).

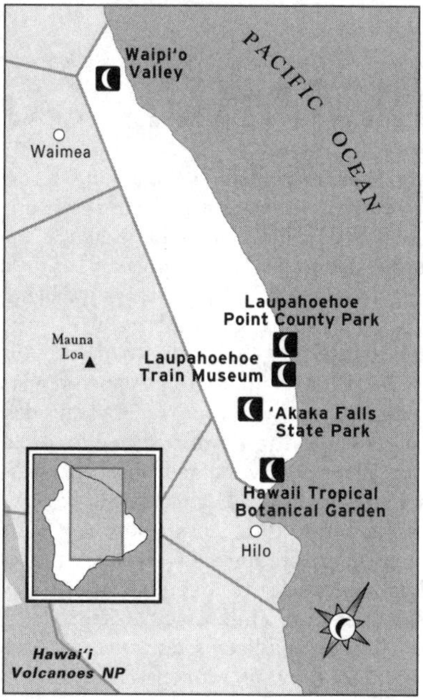

LOOK FOR TO FIND RECOMMENDED SIGHTS, ACTIVITIES, DINING, AND LODGING.

road signs indicating points of interest as you proceed along Route 19.

In continuing the clockwise coverage of the island, sites along this coast will be noted from north to south, starting in Honoka'a, where Route 19 deposits you as you come over the hill from Waimea. If coming up the highway from Hilo, use this chapter in reverse.

PLANNING YOUR TIME

It can easily take a full day to travel the 50 miles from Waipi'o Valley overlook to Hilo. Count on an extra half day or more if you want to walk down into the valley to the beach, and add a day if you're *much* more energetic and desire to hike part of the Muliwai Trail toward Waimanu Valley. Set aside at least half a day for any of the horseback riding, hiking, or ATV adventures in the valley or up on the ridge. Any of these activities is time well spent. Take this coast leisurely, as there are plenty of side roads and old byways that can occupy your time. While the tiny community of Kukuihaele won't take much of your time, you could spend a few hours in the shops of Honoka'a and Honomu looking for art, crafts, and antiques. But it's the natural sights that should pull you along the

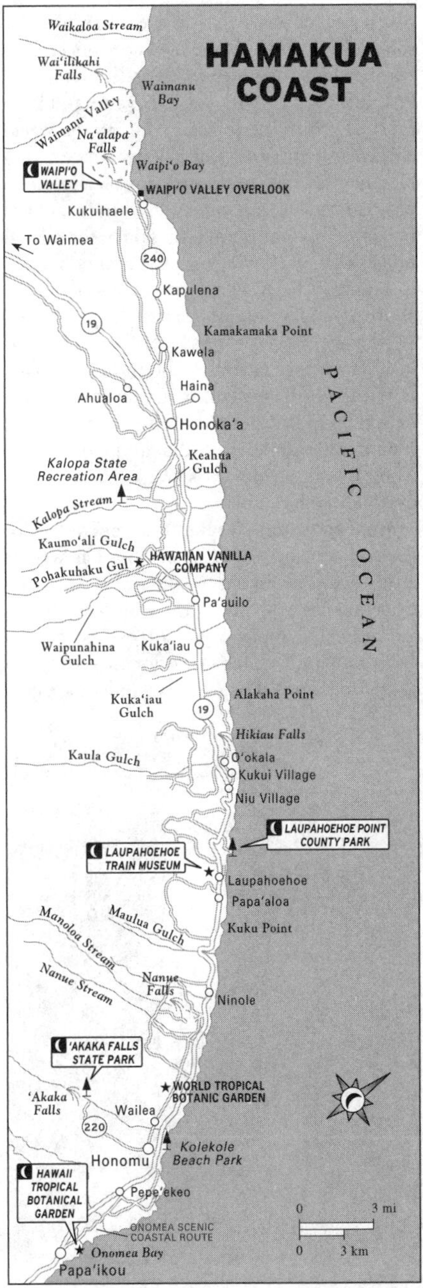

coast. Dip down to Laupahoehoe Point, stop at the train museum, make the drive up to 'Akaka Falls, and walk at least one of the trails in Kalopa State Park. If you have even half an interest in riotous tropical plants, plan to spend an hour or two in the Hawaii Tropical Botanical Garden along the Onomea Scenic Drive. Soon enough you'll be down in the big city of Hilo. Most people take this drive in a day, but there are several places to stay and eat to savor the beauty of the coast and let the spirit of Hamakua embrace you.

Honoka'a to Waipi'o Valley

The small town of Honoka'a is the gateway to the north Hamakua Coast. It's a place for food and antiques, a stop for the night, and a community that's managed to find life after sugar. Turn north there and drift along the slow highway where eucalyptus has taken the place of cane. This road offers fine vistas of the ocean, but the real treat is at the end of the road where the broad and majestic Waipi'o Valley rents the sheer sea cliffs, creating an unforgettable coastal scene.

HONOKA'A

With a population of around 2,300, Honoka'a (Rolling Bay) is the major town on the Hamakua Coast. In the past, it was a center for cattle, sugar, and macadamia nut industries and a place where GIs stationed at Camp Tarawa in Waimea would come for R&R. Now it's mainly a tourist town and a center for controversy about land use issues, since sugar is no longer the economic behemoth of the region. One issue that has caused some uproar is the 18,000 acres of former cane land, now owned by the Bishop Estate after the Hamakua Sugar Mill went bankrupt in the mid-1990s, that's been turned into a huge eucalyptus tree farm. From Honoka'a, Route 19 slips down the long Hamakua Coast to Hilo and Route 240 heads north for nine miles to the edge of Waipi'o Valley, which you should not miss. First, however, stroll the main street of Honoka'a, Mamane Street, where there are a number of shops specializing in locally produced handicrafts, several galleries, local-style restaurants, clothing and gift shops, and general merchandise stores next to antiques shops. Also in town are a small health center, a post office, two banks, a movie theater, public library, and a nine-hole golf course. It's also the best place to stock up on supplies or gasoline. If you are proceeding north along Route 240, the coastal route heading to Waipi'o Valley, just past mile marker 6 on the left, keep an eye peeled for a lava-tube cave right along the roadway. This is just a tease of the amazing natural sights that follow.

Entertainment and Events

The **Hamakua Music Festival** (P.O. Box 1757 Honoka'a, HI 96927, 808/775-3378, www.hamakuamusicfestival.org), held yearly in early October and lasting two weekends, attracts not only island musicians but musicians of national and international fame. While there is always jazz, classical, and Hawaiian music on the schedule, other genres of music are sometimes also performed. Major concerts are performed on the weekends at the Honoka'a People's Theater, with related events and local musical groups performing during the week. Tickets usually run about $20 per concert, very reasonable for big name performers, and excess profits from the festival are used to fund local music scholarships and the salary for a local music teacher. Other musical events happen in January and May and may also take place at other venues around the island.

The annual **Taro Festival** is held in November and it celebrates the most cherished of traditional Hawaiian foods. Events include Hawaiian music, hula, chanting, taro exhibits, food made from taro, crafts, and games. The whole town gets into the swing of things—this daylong event is a hit.

Western Days Weekend is scheduled for the end of May. Genuine cowboys as well as city slickers from the Mainland pretending to be *paniolo* will throw their Stetsons in the air and yell "yippie yi yo kai yea!" when this event rolls around. It's a time for all cowboys to gather for fun and games. Two rodeos are held

© ROBERT NILSEN

Local horseback riders take to main street during Honoka'a's Western Days parade.

during the weekend at the Honoka'a Arena for those who like that sort of rough and tumble affair—and for those who just like to watch. Aside from a lively but homespun parade that makes its way through town, there's horseshoe pitching, craft displays, a dinner and dance, and—everyone's favorite—the Saloon Girl contest. For information about either the Western Days Weekend or the Taro Festival, contact the Honoka'a Business Association (P.O. Box 474, Honoka'a, HI 96727, www.alternative-hawaii.com/hba).

The once run-down but classic "Last Picture Show" **Honoka'a People's Theater** (808/775-0000), along the main drag, has been renovated to its old 1930s splendor. It's a big-screen theater that seats about 500 and has a high-tech sound system that generally shows both first-run movies and some art movies. Showtime is 7 P.M. and tickets run $6 for adults, $4 for seniors, and $3 for children. This theater is also used as a venue for the yearly Hawaii International Film Festival, for the autumn Hamakua Music Festival, and for other community events throughout the year. Call to hear what's happening or check the signboard out front.

Shopping

There is never a shortage of antiques and collectibles in Honoka'a. **The Honoka'a Trading Company** (808/775-0808, 10 A.M.–5 P.M. daily) is a discovery shop owned and operated by Denise Walker. Items come and go, but you can expect to find classic artwork from the Matson Steamship Lines, hula dolls, Japanese netsuke, poi bowls, costume jewelry, pots and pans, bottles, and old crockery. Denise has also filled this rambling building with a good selection of old books, Hawaiian instruments, Japanese fans, and vintage signs. Denise focuses not only on things *from* Hawaii, but on things brought *to* Hawaii. Much of the furniture and many of the antique items were brought to Hawaii by *kama'aina* and GI families.

Toward the east end of the downtown row is **Seconds To Go** (808/775-9212, 9:30 A.M.–5 P.M. daily except Sunday). Owned and operated by Elaine Carlsmith, this collectibles and antiques shop specializes in Hawaiian artifacts; it brims with classic Hawaiian ties and shirts from the 1950s, dancing hula-doll lamps, antique hardware and building materials, claw-foot bathtubs, old books, Japanese bowls, a good collection of plates and saucers, and an ukulele. Elaine also sells used fishing gear in case you want to try your luck. If you like collectibles of any sort, you'll love it here.

For something newer and brighter, make a stop at **Honoka'a Market Place** (808/775-8255, 9:30 A.M.–5:30 P.M. Mon.–Fri., 9:30 A.M.–4:30 P.M. Sat.–Sun.), where you can find a great selection of colorful (imported) quilts, pillows, clothing, and accessories for the home.

Perhaps the best shops in town for gift items, crafts, clothing, and accessories are **Taro Patch Gifts** (808/775-7228, 9:30 A.M.–5 P.M. daily) and the nearby **Maya's Clothing and Gifts** (808/775-1016, 9 A.M.–5:30 P.M. Mon.–Fri., 9 A.M.–5 P.M. Sat.–Sun.). If you have an interest in beads and gems, head for **Starseed** (808/775-9344, 10 A.M.–5 P.M. Mon.–Sat.), a longtime feature of town located at the east end of the main downtown section.

The **Bamboo Gallery** (808/775-0433) is a spacious showroom on the main drag where you will find an eclectic mix of wood, bamboo, fiber, canvas, multimedia, and glass art, all displayed in a sparse Asian style. One other gallery to check out along Mamane Street houses both the **Big Island Glass Gallery** (808/775-7715) and **Clytie Mead Watercolors** (1–5 P.M. Tues.–Sat.).

Kama'aina Woods (808/775-7722, 9 A.M.–5 P.M. Mon.–Sat.) is located a hundred yards down the hill from the post office in the old soda works factory building. The shop is owned and operated by Bill Keb, a talented woodworker who specializes in fabulous bowls turned from native woods like koa, *milo,* extremely rare *kou,* and a few introduced woods like mango and Norfolk Island pine. Boxes, platters, and other items are made by different island craftsmen. All of the wooden art pieces, priced from affordable to not-so-affordable, are one of a kind and utilitarian. Less expensive items are koa or *milo* bracelets, letter openers, rice paddles, and hand-like salad grabbers.

Farther down toward the ocean, in the old macadamia nut factory, is **Live Art Gallery** (808/775-1214, 10 A.M.–5 P.M. Mon.–Sat.), a large showroom with work space that displays work by local artists. Of particular interest is the glass-blowing studio at one end of the building. An assortment of gifts is sold at the gift counter and coffee is roasted for the snack bar, where you also can have ice cream or other tasty treats.

Recreation

A well-established and reputable hiking company that will help you stretch your legs in the great outdoors yet have minimal impact on the land is **Hawaiian Walkways** (808/775-0372 or 800/457-7759, hiwalk@aloha.net, www.hawaiianwalkways.com). Run by Hugh Montgomery, his wife Kaulana, and family, this company will teach you about the land you walk through and help you appreciate its diversity and sanctity. Hikes are easy to moderate and generally last three to five hours. Four basic hikes take you to the rim of Waipi'o Valley for a peek into the Valley of Kings, into Hawai'i Volcanoes National Park to discover the secrets of Kilauea volcano, up on the mist-shrouded slopes of Mount Hualalai, and to the many *kipuka* along the Saddle Road. Custom hikes can also be arranged. The Waipi'o rim hike is offered daily, while the others can be arranged and customized to the guests' needs. Both the Waipi'o Waterfall Adventure and the Kona Cloud Forest Botanical Walk run $95 per person; children on the Waipi'o Waterfall Adventure go along for $75. The Kilauea Volcano Discovery and Saddle Road Exploration hikes are $135 adults and $95 for children. A small day pack, walking stick, rain gear, lunch, and drinks are provided, as is expert commentary by the knowledgeable guides. A hike with Hawaiian Walkways is not only good physical exercise; it's an excellent introduction to the natural world of the Big Island. Two thumbs up.

Tired of those big fancy golf courses? Want a real down-home rural course? Head to the Hamakua Country Club (808/775-7244). This nine-hole course lies on sloped ground below Route 19; because of its limited space, its fairways cross. There is no sign on the highway, so turn off near the gas station and take an immediate left onto the driveway that leads to the small clubhouse. Greens fees run $20, and you can play all day for that price. Bring your own clubs, as there are none to rent, but you can use one of the pull carts. If you have any questions, just ask any one of the duffers who hang out at the clubhouse and they'll put you right.

Accommodations

Centrally located along Route 240 in downtown Honoka'a is **Hotel Honoka'a Club** (P.O. Box 247, Honoka'a, HI 96727, 808/775-0678 or 800/808-0678, www.hotelhonokaa.com). Built in 1908 as the plantation manager's club, it's still infused with the grace and charm of the old days. What it lacks in elegance it makes up for in cleanliness and friendliness. The hotel, mostly used by local people, is old and well used but clean and comfortable, and it's the only hotel right in town. From the back rooms, you get a view over the tin roofs of residential Honoka'a and the ocean. There are more spartan but very clean rooms downstairs. Rooms run $95 for a two-room suite; $68–75 for an ocean-view room with TV, private bath, and queen-size bed; and $50–60 for an economy room with a private bath. Rates include a simple continental breakfast. Hostel rooms, located in the basement, all with shared bath and kitchen facilities, are separated into three private rooms at $38 and two communal rooms (one sleeping three people and the other six people) that rent for $28 and $18. The basement hostel rooms, although a bit dungeonesque, are clean, with windows to catch the breeze.

Set in a quiet neighborhood below the library off the main road in town is **Luana Ola B&B Cottages** (808/775-1150 or 800/357-7727, luanacottages@yahoo.com, www.island-hawaii.com). The two neat and trim, single-wall construction, cedar wood cottages are set amongst trees but have views of the ocean.

Modern in amenities, with kitchenette, bath, breakfast nook, and lanai, these cottages rent for $125 a night, two nights minimum, and $15 per extra person up to four. A continental breakfast of fruits and pastries is left in your refrigerator to have when you decide to start your day.

About four miles up above town in the pasture and forest land of Ahualoa is **Mountain Meadow Ranch B&B** (P.O. Box 1697, Honoka'a, HI 96727, tel./fax 808/775-9367, bill@mountainmeadowranch.com, www.mountainmeadowranch.com). Perfect for peace and quiet, the lower level of the ranch home has a living room with TV and VCR, sitting room with microwave and small refrigerator, two bedrooms, a dry sauna, tub, shower, and its own entrance. A light continental breakfast left on the sideboard is included in the room price. This unit with one room runs $95, or $135 for the two bedrooms. A separate guest cottage with full kitchen, two bedrooms with queen-size beds, bath, wood stove, full entertainment center, and laundry room is also available, but no breakfast is included. There is a three-night minimum, and the rate is $135 a night or $800 a week. No smoking is permitted inside either unit.

The **Log Cabin** guesthouse in Ahualoa (P.O. Box 1994, Kamuela, HI 96743, 808/885-4243 or 800/555-8968, kaminn@aloha.net, www.hawaii-bnb.com/kamuela.html) is associated with Kamuela Inn in Waimea. It sits on a five-acre forested property in a cool mountain setting at about 2,500 feet. The log-style walls and framing and barn roof give this large house a welcoming country feel. This house has a large living room with fireplace, upstairs library, full kitchen, five cozy guest bedrooms, and a hot tub stuck in a garden gazebo. Room rates are $59 with shared bath, $99 with private bath, or $375 a night for the whole house, continental breakfast included.

Food

Local people thought Jolene was such a good cook, they talked her into opening **Jolene's Kau Kau Corner Restaurant** (808/775-9498, 10 A.M.–3 P.M. weekdays, until 8 P.M. Mon., Wed., and Fri.) in downtown Honoka'a. Most tried-and-true recipes were handed down by her extended family, who lends a hand in running the restaurant. The restaurant, located in a vintage storefront, is trim and neat, and the menu includes a variety of plate lunches like beef teriyaki and breaded shrimp, a steaming chili bowl or saimin, other meals like a chicken basket and seafood platter, and burgers and fries, almost all under $9. Jolene's is as down-home and local as you can get, with friendly service, hearty dishes, and reasonable prices. This is one of the best places to eat along the northern Hamakua Coast!

Follow the comforting aroma of fresh-baked bread to **Mamane Street Bakery & Café** (45-3625 Mamane St., 808/775-9478, 6 A.M.–5 P.M. Mon.–Sat.), owned and operated by Eliahu "Ely" Pessah. Ely bakes goodies including coconut turnovers, Danish pastries, and ensemada, a special type of cinnamon roll, but the local people come in the honey-nut bran muffins, crunchy with chunks of macadamia nuts. Ely oven also turns out ham and cheese croissants, mozzarella or marinara focaccia, or three-cheese focaccia. Eat in or takeout while enjoying your purchase with a cup of steaming coffee or tea.

Simply Natural (808/775-0119, 8 A.M.–5 P.M. Mon.–Fri., 8:30 A.M.–1:30 P.M. Sat.–Sun.) is next door to the Mamane Street Bakery. Besides ice cream in tropical and standard flavors, a variety of smoothies and drinks, this shop offers a full sandwich menu, including veggie mushroom, ginger tempeh patty, and spicy tuna melt, with plenty of soups, salads, and other vegetarian items. Simply Natural tries to be as organic as possible, so the menu may change based upon what is available.

Across the street is **Cafe Il Mondo** (808/775-7711, 11 A.M.–8 P.M. Tues.–Sat.), an Italian pizzeria and coffee bar that's the best Honoka'a has to offer. This is a cheery place with Italian music on the sound system and Hawaiian prints on the walls. Here you feel the spirit of Italy. While handmade pizzas, mostly $11–13, are the main focus, you can also get tasty calzones, pasta dishes, sandwiches, and salads for under $10, as well as ice cream and gourmet coffee. If you're on the road, ask for your pizza to go. When having dinner, it's OK to bring your own bottle of wine. As small as this cafe is, it puts aside space for live musicians on some evenings.

Tex Drive In (808/775-0598, 6 A.M.–8 P.M. daily) is an institution in town. Everyone knows it and everyone's been there—many times. The long-established Hamakua restaurant is known for its fresh malasadas (sugared, holeless Portuguese donuts), production of which is showcased behind plate glass windows inside. Get some! They're a treat. But ask before 7 P.M. or they'll probably be sold out. Every month, 15,000 of these tasty treats are sold—sometimes many more. Tex has a fast-food look, a drive-up window, walk-up counter, and inside and outside tables, but the cavernous dining room in the back is still there and the food is still as filling and reasonable as ever. Serving "Ono Kine" local food, it specializes in *kalua* pork, teriyaki chicken and beef, hamburgers, and fresh fish, and there are many ethnic items on the menu. Prices are very reasonable, with most dinners around $9 and sandwiches less. Local people and (an even better sign) the local police come here to chow down on good, easy-on-the-wallet food in a clean atmosphere. Tex Drive In is located along Route 19, at the corner of Pakalana Street.

Clean, white, and bright, **Blaine's Drive Inn** (5 A.M.–9 P.M. Mon.–Sat., 6 A.M.–9 P.M. Sun.) is the new fast food restaurant in town. Blaine's offers American-style breakfasts, and typical Hawaiian-style plate lunches, burgers, bento, loco moco, and sandwiches the rest of the day, with almost nothing on the menu over $7. Order at the window to takeout or sit in one of the few tables to the side and front. Look for it on Mamane Street as you enter downtown.

Markets: For groceries and even a few health food items, stop at **T. Kaneshiro Store** (808/775-0631, 7:30 A.M.–8 P.M. Mon.–Sat., 7:30 A.M.–6 P.M. Sun.), a well-stocked market at the intersection of Mamane and Lehua Streets. A short way farther along the highway toward Kukuihaele is the much smaller **K.K. Super-Mart** (808/775-0666). Next to Tex Drive In up on the highway is **Honoka'a Stop 'N Shop** (808/775-0808), a convenient convenience store for drinks, sundries, and snacks. A small selection of mostly local and organic produce, fruits, packaged and canned health foods, supplements, and vitamins is available at **Nutrition Niche Natural Foods** (10:30 A.M.–6 P.M. Mon.–Fri., 10 A.M.–4:30 P.M. Sat.) on the south end of town.

On Saturday mornings, pick up home-grown vegetables and flowers at the small **Honoka'a farmers market** (7:30 A.M.–2 P.M.) in front of the old Bothelo Building along main street.

Services

Both Bank of Hawaii and First Hawaiian Bank have branch **bank** offices on the main street in town. The **post office** is located just downhill of the main intersection in town along Lehua street. Located along the main drag across from the school athletic field is the **public library** (45-3380 Mamane St., 808/775-8881, 11 A.M.–7 P.M. Mon. and Thurs., 9 A.M.–5 P.M. Tues. and Wed., 9 A.M.–3 P.M. Fri.). Steps away are the **police** and **fire stations.** The town's two small **launderettes** are located behind Blaine's restaurant and across the street from Tex Drive In. There are three **gas stations** in town, one along Route 19 and two in town on the main drag, Route 240.

KUKUIHAELE

For all of you looking for the "light at the end of the tunnel," Kukuihaele (Traveling Light) is it. A small plantation town, Kukuihaele now subsists on tourism. The new highway bypasses town. Take the old road down and in; it pops out again on the other side. At the far edge of town, on the cusp of the valley wall, is the **Waipi'o Valley Overlook,** an exceptional location for peering into this marvelous, mysterious, and legend-filled valley. For most tourists, this is as close as you'll get to the "Valley of Kings." But, oh, what a sight! Stand a while and soak in the surroundings: the valley and ocean, the black-sand beach, the coastal cliffs, and the ever-changing clouds. During winter months you might be treated to a special sight when mama humpbacks bring their newborn babies to the bay below to teach them how to be whales. If you intend to hike down to the valley, use the restrooms here, as there are none below.

Upper Rim Adventures

The valley itself doesn't get all the attention. Recently, several other opportunities have opened for people to explore the east rim of the valley. You have your choice of hiking, horseback riding, ATV, and four-wheel drive van exploration. Each adventure takes a different route, although some may overlap trails. All include a trip through former sugarcane land, and each brings you to wonderful vistas that overlook the broad expanse of the Waipi'o Valley from a height of over 1,000 feet. As you go, you'll be told stories and legends of the valley and vignettes of the culture and history of the area; some tours may even include a dip in a secluded pool under a tumbling waterfall.

Hiking: Tours with **Hawaiian Walkways** (808/775-0372 or 800/457-7759, hiwalk@aloha.net, www.hawaiianwalkways.com), led by Hugh Montgomery or one of his able staff, guide you through the rim-edge forest and over a long-abandoned former flume construction trail to the very edge of the valley. Here you can sneak up on and look down upon Hi'ilawe Waterfall and get to spots overlooking the valley that cannot be reached any other way. This is not just good physical exercise but also an education in the flora and fauna of the region, as Hugh is a proverbial font of knowledge about the area. This hike is moderate, takes about four hours, and goes daily for $95 per adult or $75 per child. Lunch, drinks, and all necessary equipment are supplied. Meet at their office in Honoka'a.

Horseback Riding: For a ride up on Waipi'o's rim, looking down into Hawai'i's largest and most spectacular valley, try **Waipi'o Ridge Stables** (808/775-1007 or 877/757-1414, www.waipioridgestables.com). This outfit offers a 2.5-hour rim ride to valley vistas through former sugarcane land for $85. The five-hour, $165 ride adds a side trip to a waterfall where you stop for lunch and a swim. Rides leave at 8:45 A.M. and 12:45 P.M. from Waipi'o Valley Artworks in Kukuihaele.

ATV Tours: Aside from its horse rides in Waipi'o Valley, **Waipi'o On Horseback** (808/775-7291 or 877/775-7291) also offers ATV rides across its working ranch up top above the valley, going to the valley rim, along a stretch of the old Hamakua Ditch, and to spots for good views down onto the coast. Riders should be in good shape and at least 16 years old. Tours depart at 9:30 A.M. and 1:30 P.M. and last about 2.5 hours. The cost of $100 per person includes transportation from the Last Chance Store in Kukuihaele to the ranch. Make reservations 24 hours in advance and inquire about specific details. **Kukui ATV Adventures** (808/775-1701, www.kukuiatv.com) also offers two-hour tours through former sugarcane land that take you over back roads and dirt trails to the edge of the valley and on to a refreshing waterfall and pool. Tours depart twice daily at 9:30 A.M. and 1 P.M. from Waipi'o Valley Artworks. No riders under 100 pounds or over 300 pounds, please.

Adventure Van Tours: Starting at 9:30 A.M., a three-hour four-wheel drive van tour is offered by **Waipi'o Rim Backroad Adventures** (808/775-1122 or 800/492-4746, www.topofwaipio.com/4x4.htm) that takes you in comfort to many of the same spots for exceptional vistas into the Waipi'o Valley. This catered ride runs $85 per adult or $40 for kids 12 and under and is less physical but just as rewarding as the other adventures. Meet at Waipi'o Valley Artworks.

Shopping

Waipi'o Valley Artworks (808/775-0958 or 800/492-4746, 9 A.M.–5:30 P.M. daily, www.waipiovalleyartworks.com) is an excellent shop in which to pick up an art object. There are plenty of offerings in wood by some of the island's best woodworkers, but the shop also showcases various Hawaii-based artists working in different media. Definitely check out inspired prints, paintings, line drawings, pottery, and jewelry. You'll also find crafts, a smattering of souvenir items, a fairly extensive collection of books mostly on Hawaiiana, designer T-shirts, and other wearables. This is one of those wonderful finds, an out-of-the-way place that carries a good selection of excellent artwork—and they'll ship. The shop also features a counter serving ice cream, sandwiches, and soft drinks. Waipi'o Valley Artworks is the meeting place for Waipio Valley Shuttle, which will take you down to the valley, and for the horseback and van tours that explore the valley rim. All in all, Waipi'o Valley Artworks is the hub of activity in this not so bustling town.

Bed-and-Breakfast

A vintage home of a one-time plantation manager, **Waipio Wayside** (P.O. Box 840, Honoka'a, HI 96727, 808/775-0275 or 800/833-8849, wayside@ilhawaii.net, www.waipiowayside.com), is owned and operated by Jacqueline Horne as a congenial B&B Inn. Look for the Waipio Wayside sign hung on a white picket fence exactly two miles toward Waipi'o from the Honoka'a post office. You enter through double French doors onto a rich wooden floor shining with a well-waxed patina. The walls are hand-laid vertical paneling, the prototype that modern paneling tries to emulate. Here is a formal dining area and an informal seating area with books, a television, videos, and music. The home contains five bedrooms, each with private bathroom, ranging in price $95–185, $25 extra for an additional person beyond two. The Bird's Eye Room has a three-night minimum and the Library Room a two-night minimum, with a $10 surcharge for single-night stays. Spacious and airy, all rooms are individually decorated by theme and hung with beautiful Battenburg lace curtains. The back deck, where you will find hammocks in which to rock away your cares, overlooks manicured grounds that gently slope to a panoramic view of the coast. Jackie, whose meticulous and tastefully appointed home is straight from the pages of a designer magazine, is also a gourmet cook. Breakfast is sometimes waffles with strawberries and whipped cream, sometimes omelettes and biscuits, with fresh fruit from the property. Beverages are pure Hamakua coffee, juices, and gourmet teas from around the world, and there is always an assortment of snacks. A stay at Waipio Wayside is guaranteed to be civilized, relaxing, and totally enjoyable. As a benefit, Jackie will gladly arrange island activities for her guests.

Vacation Rentals

Hale Kukui (P.O. Box 5044, Honoka'a, HI 96727, 808/775-7130 or 800/444-7130, retreat@halekukui.com, www.halekukui.com) is owned and operated by Bill and Sarah McCowatt. This is a secluded vacation rental on four acres that's perched high on the *pali,* from where you get a sweeping view over the tropical fruit orchard up the rugged coast and out to the wide Pacific. Follow the road *through* Kukuihaele and look for a sign pointing you down a private drive that leads about 200 yards to the finely landscaped yard and two comfortable cottages and a studio. The rental units are separate from the main house, lending guests privacy and quiet, and each has an open-beam ceilings and a jetted tub on the lanai. Inside, these spacious units are tastefully decorated with comfy furniture and ceiling fans, and there are large windows on the lanai side that provide the exceptional views. Efficiency kitchens contain all you'll need to cook a meal, and that's good as all meals are your responsibility. The studio has a queen-size bed and a queen-size fold-down futon sofa. The two-bedroom cottage has two queen-size beds and a queen-size fold-down futon sofa. The deluxe cottage has a king-size bed with a queen-size fold-down futon sofa. Rates run $145 for the studio and $180 or $195 for the cottages; two nights minimum, and the seventh night is free. No children, please. For the use of guests, a simple trail leads down to a semiprivate stream where you'll find a small but refreshing pool.

Enjoy the privacy of **Hamakua Hideaway** (P.O. Box 5104, Kukuihaele, HI 96727, 808/775-7425 or 808/775-0995 weekdays, jhunt@gte.net, http://home1.gte.net/jhunt). This rental is only a 15-minute walk from the Waipi'o Valley overlook, tucked into trees with a lush garden surrounding. With living room, kitchenette, bath, television, and phone, the "treehouse" runs $95 a night or $85 a night for two nights or more, with reduced weekly and monthly rates available.

Surrounded by green acres of pasture on the edge of the sea cliff next to the Waipi'o Valley Overlook is the **Cliff House** (P.O. Box 5045, Kukuihaele, HI 96727, 808/775-0005 or 800/492-4746, www.cliffhousehawaii.com). This two-story, two-bedroom house has a living room, full kitchen, laundry room, one bathroom, and lanai that looks over the ocean and coastal cliffs. This house runs $195 a night for a couple, two nights minimum, with an extra per person charge of $35 for up to four. No credit cards. Check-in is at the Waipi'o Valley Artworks shop.

With its ridgeside location, **Waipio Ridge Vacation Rental** (808/775-0603) has an exceptional spot. From the front lawn, you can peer down onto the valley and out to the blue ocean with unobstructed views. This little studio has one bedroom, one bath, and two queen-size beds and rents for $95 a night or $85 a night for two or more nights, with a $15 extra person charge. While the studio is fine, it's for the views that you come.

WAIPI'O VALLEY

Waipi'o is the way the Lord would have liked to fashion the Garden of Eden, if he hadn't been on such a tight schedule. You can read about this incredible valley, but you really can't believe it until you see it for yourself. Route 240 ends a minute outside of Kukuihaele at an overlook, and 900 feet below is Waipi'o (Curving Water), the island's largest and most southerly valley of the many that slice the harsh Kohala Mountains. The valley is a mile across where it fronts the sea at a series of sand dunes, and six miles from the ocean to its back end. It's vibrantly green, always watered by Waipi'o Stream and lesser streams that spout as waterfalls from the *pali* at the rear and to the side of

Waipi'o Valley from north side cliff trail

the valley. The green is offset by a wide band of black-sand beach. The far side of the valley ends abruptly at a steep *pali* that is higher than the one on which you're standing. An eight-mile trail leads over it to Waimanu Valley—smaller, more remote, and more luxuriant.

Travelers have long extolled the amazing abundance of Waipi'o. From the overlook you can make out the overgrown outlines of garden terraces, taro patches, and fishponds in what was Hawai'i's largest cultivated valley. Every foodstuff known to the Hawaiians once flourished here; even Waipi'o pigs were said to be bigger than pigs anywhere else. In times of famine, the produce from Waipi'o could sustain the populace of the entire island (estimated at 100,000 people). On the valley floor and alongside the streams you'll still find avocados, bananas, coconuts, passion fruit, mountain apples, guavas, breadfruit, tapioca, lemons, limes, coffee, grapefruit, and pumpkins. The old fishponds and streams are alive with prawns, wild pigs roam the interior, as do wild horses, and there are abundant fish in the sea. Carrying on the traditions of farmers of old, some farmers in the valley still raise taro, and this has once again become one of the largest taro-producing regions on the island and one of the principal production centers in the state.

But the lovingly tended order, most homes, and the lifestyle were washed away in the tsunami of 1946. Now Waipi'o is largely unkempt, a wild jungle of mutated abundance. The valley is a neglected maiden with a dirty face and disheveled, windblown hair. Only love and nurturing can refresh her lingering beauty.

Recorded History

The remains of **Paka'alana Heiau** is in a grove of trees on the right-hand side of the beach as you face the sea. It dates from the 12th century and was a temple of refuge where *kapu* breakers, vanquished warriors, and the weak and infirm could find sanctuary. Paka'alana was a huge *heiau* with tremendous walls that were mostly intact until the tsunami of 1946. The tsunami sounded like an explosion when the waters hit the walls of Paka'alana, according to firsthand accounts. The rocks were scattered, and all was turned to ruins. Nearby, **Hanua'aloa** is another *heiau* in ruins. Archaeologists know even less about this *heiau,* but all agree that both were healing temples of body and spirit, and the local people feel that their positive *mana* is part of the protection in Waipi'o.

Great chiefs have dwelt in Waipi'o. King Umi planted taro just like a commoner and fished with his own hands. He went on to unite the island into one kingdom in the 15th century. Waipi'o was the traditional land of Kamehameha the Great and in many ways was the basis of his earthly and spiritual power. It was here that he was entrusted with the war god, Kuka'ilimoku, as King Kalani'opu'u was dying. Kamehameha came here to rest after heavy battles, and offshore was the scene of the first modern naval battle in Hawaii. Here, Kamehameha's war canoes faced those of his nemesis, Keoua. Both had recently acquired cannons bartered from passing sea captains. Kamehameha's artillery was manned by two white sailors, Davis and Young, who became trusted advisors. Kamehameha's forces won the engagement in what became known as the "Battle of the Red-Mouthed Gun."

When Captain Cook came to Hawaii, 4,000 natives lived in Waipi'o; a century later only 600 remained. At the turn of the 20th century many Chinese and Japanese moved to Waipi'o and began raising rice and taro. People moved in and out of the valley by horse and mule, and there were schools, stores, a post office, churches, and a strong community spirit. Waipi'o was painstakingly tended. The undergrowth was kept trimmed and you could see clearly from the back of the valley all the way to the sea. World War II arrived, and many people were lured away from the remoteness of the valley by a changing lifestyle and a desire for modernity. The tsunami in 1946 swept away most of the homes, and the majority of the 200 people who lived there then pulled up stakes and moved away. For 25 years the valley lay virtually abandoned. The Peace Corps considered it a perfect place to build a compound in which to train volunteers headed for Southeast Asia. This too was later abandoned. Then in the late 1960s and early 1970s a few "back to nature" hippies started trickling in. Most only played Tarzan and Jane for a while and moved on, especially after Waipi'o served them a "reality sandwich" in the form of the flood of 1979.

Waipi'o is still very unpredictable. In a three-week period from late March to early April of 1989, 47 inches of rain drenched the valley. Roads were turned to quagmires, houses washed away, and more people left. Part of the problem is the imported trees in Waipi'o. Until the 1940s, the valley was a manicured garden, but now it's very heavily forested. All of the trees you will see are new; the oldest are mangroves and coconuts. The trees are both a boon and a blight. They give shade and fruit, but when there are floods, they fall into the river, creating logjams that increase the flooding dramatically. Waipi'o takes care of itself best when humans do not interfere. Taro farmers, too, have had problems because the irrigation system for their crops was washed away in the last flood. But, with hope and a prayer to Waipi'o's

LEGENDS OF WAIPI'O VALLEY

Waipi'o is a mystical place. Inhabited for more than 1,000 years, it figures prominently in old Hawaiian lore. In the primordial past, Wakea, progenitor of all the islands, favored the valley, and oral tradition holds that the great gods Kane and Kanaloa dallied in Waipi'o, intoxicating themselves on *'awa*. One oral chant relates that the demigod Maui, that wild prankster, met his untimely end here by trying to steal baked bananas from these two drunken heavyweights. One flung Maui against the rear valley wall, splattering blood everywhere, hence the distinctively red color of the earth at the far back reaches of the valley. Lono, god of the Makahiki, came to Waipi'o in search of a bride. He found Kaikilani, a beautiful maiden who lived in a breadfruit tree near **Hi'ilawe Waterfall,** which tumbles 1,000 feet in a cascade of three drops to the valley below and is the island's tallest waterfall.

Nenewe, a shark-man, lived near a pool at the bottom of another waterfall on the west side of Waipi'o. The pool was connected to the sea by an underwater tunnel. All went well for Nenewe until his grandfather disobeyed a warning never to feed his grandson meat. Once Nenewe tasted meat, he began eating Waipi'o residents after first warning them about sharks as they passed his sea-connected pool on their way to fish. His constant warnings aroused suspicions. Finally, the cape he always wore was ripped from his shoulders, and there on his back was a shark's mouth! He dove into his pool and left Waipi'o to hunt the waters of the other islands.

Pupualenalena, a *kupua* (nature spirit), takes the form of a yellow dog that can change its size from tiny to huge. He was sent by the chiefs of Waipi'o to steal a conch shell that mischievous water sprites were constantly blowing, just to irritate the people. The shell was inherited by Kamehameha and is now in the Bishop Museum. Another dog-spirit lives in a rock embedded in the hillside halfway down the road to Waipi'o. In times of danger, he comes out of his rock to stand in the middle of the road as a warning that bad things are about to happen.

Finally, a secret section of Waipi'o Beach is called **Lua o Milu,** the legendary doorway to the land of the dead. At certain times, it is believed, ghosts of great *ali'i* come back to earth as Marchers of the Night, and their strong chants and torch-lit processions fill the darkness in Waipi'o. Many great kings were buried in Waipi'o, and it's felt that because of their *mana,* no harm will come to the people who live here. Although the horrible tsunami of 1946 and a raging flood in 1979 filled the valley with wild torrents of water, and in both cases, the devastation to homes and the land was tremendous, not one life was lost. Everyone who still lives in Waipi'o will tell you they feel protected.

spirits, they rebuild, knowing full well that there will be a next time. And so it goes.

Waipi'o Now

Many of the old people have died or moved topside (above the valley) with relatives. Those who live in the valley learned to accept life in Waipi'o and genuinely love the valley, while others come only to exploit its beauty. Fortunately, the latter underestimate the raw power of Waipi'o. Developers have eyed the area for years as a magnificent spot in which to build a luxury resort. But even they are wise enough to realize that nature rules Waipi'o, not humankind. For now the valley is secure. A few gutsy families with a real commitment have stayed on and continue to revitalize Waipi'o. The valley now supports perhaps 40 residents. More people live topside but come down to Waipi'o to tend their gardens. On entering the valley, you'll see a lotus-flower pond, and if you're lucky enough to be there in December, it will be in bloom.

In the summer of 1992, the Bishop Museum requested an environmental impact survey on Waipi'o Valley because the frequency of visitors to the valley had increased tremendously. Old-time residents were complaining not only about the overuse of the valley but about the loss of their quiet and secluded lifestyle. Some tour operators cooperated fully and did their best to help in the preservation and reasonable use of one of Hawaii's grandest valleys; others did not. Because of the impact study, commercial tours are not allowed to go to the beach area on the far side of the stream, which is now open to foot traffic only, and the valley is closed on Sunday to commercial tours.

A type of socio-ethnic battle has evolved in the valley. Long-term residents, mostly but not exclusively of Hawaiian descent, have largely withdrawn the spirit of *aloha* from the melanin-challenged visitors to their wonderful valley. Their dissatisfaction is not wholly without basis, as some who have come to the valley have been quite disrespectful, trespassing on private property, threatening to sue landowners for injuries caused by themselves, or finding themselves

Waipi'o Valley from the valley overlook

© ROBERT NILSEN

taro fields in Waipi'o Valley

stuck in a river that no one in their right mind would try to cross in a vehicle. Many wonderful, open, and loving people still live in the valley, but don't be too surprised to get the "stink face" treatment from others. Be respectful and stay on public property. If the sign says *Kapu* or Keep Out, believe it. It is everyone's right to walk along the beach, the switchback that goes to Waimanu, and generally waterways. These are traditional free lands in Hawaii open to all people, and they remain so. It's really up to you. With proper behavior from visitors, Waipi'o's mood can change, and *aloha* will return.

Driving

The road leading down to Waipi'o is outrageously steep and narrow, averaging a 25 percent gradient! If you attempt it in a regular car, it'll eat you up and spit out your bones. More than 20 fatalities have occurred since people started driving it, and it has only been paved since the early 1970s. You'll definitely need four-wheel drive to make it; vehicles headed downhill yield to those coming up. There is very little traffic on the road except when surfing conditions are good. Sometimes Waipi'o Beach has the first good waves of the season, and this brings out the surfers en masse.

Waipio Valley Shuttle (808/775-7121, www.waipiovalleytour.com) makes a 90-minute descent and tour of Waipi'o Valley ($45 adults, $20 children under 11) in air-conditioned, four-wheel drive vans that leave from Waipi'o Valley Artworks in Kukuihaele, at 9 A.M., 11 A.M., 1 P.M., and 3 P.M. Monday–Saturday. Along the way, you'll be regaled by legends and stories and shown the most prominent sights in the valley by drivers who live in the area. This is the easiest way into the valley, and the guys know what they're doing as they've been at it since 1970. Sometimes drivers of this shuttle will give hikers a ride down to the valley floor or up the road to the overlook parking lot for a few bucks, if there's room in the vehicle.

Hiking

If you have the energy, the hike down the paved section of the road is just over one mile, but it's a tough mile coming back up! Once you're down in the valley, make a hard right and follow the dirt road to the beach or head straight ahead and plunge into the heart of the valley. You should remember before you go too far that you will have to cross one or more of the valley streams. There are no bridges; you'll have to wade through. None are deep or wide and they are not usually a problem, but when steady rains swell the streams, stay out for your own sake, as you could easily be swept downstream.

The Waipi'o Overlook has a 24-hour parking limit. That's good for day use of the valley, but not sufficient for those attempting the hike across to Waimanu Valley to camp. Check with Waipi'o Valley Artworks in Kukuihaele for longer-stay parking arrangements. There are no public restrooms in the valley, so use those at the Waipi'o Overlook before you head down.

Waipi'o Beach

Stretching over a mile, this is the longest black-sand beach on the island. A tall and somewhat tangled stand of trees and bushes fronts this beach, capping the dune. The surf here can be very dangerous, and there are many riptides. If there is strong wave action, swimming is not advised. It is, however, a good place for surfing and fishing. The road to the beach leads along the east wall of the valley and opens onto plenty of space to picnic under the trees. In order to get to the long expanse of beach across the mouth of the stream, you have to wade across it. It's best to try closer to where it enters the ocean as there are fewer slippery boulders there. To compound matters, waves sometimes wash water up the mouth of the stream. Be advised, be careful, and if possible go at low tide. Alternately, walk into the valley and find a public path that leads to the beach on the far side of the stream.

While it once was possible, camping is no longer legal in the valley.

Horseback Riding in the Valley

For a fun-filled experience guaranteed to please, try horseback riding with **Waipi'o Na'alapa Stables** (808/775-0419, www.naalapastables.com). Sherri Hannum, a mother of three who moved to Waipi'o from Missouri, and her husband own and operate the trail rides. The adventure begins at Waipi'o Valley Artworks in Kukuihaele, where you begin a four-wheel drive ride down to the ranch, which gives you an excellent introduction to the valley. Sherri puts you in the saddle of a sure-footed Waipi'o pony and spends two hours telling you legends and stories while leading you to waterfalls, swimming holes, gravesites, and finally a *heiau.* She knows the trails of Waipi'o intimately. If the fruits of Waipi'o are happening, Sherri will point them out and you can munch to your heart's delight. Tours lasting 2.5 hours cost $89 and start at 9:30 A.M. and 1 P.M. Riders need to be at least eight years old and no more than 230 pounds. Go prepared with long pants, shoes, and swimsuit.

Waipi'o On Horseback (808/775-7291 or 877/775-7291) also offers horseback riding through fabulous Waipi'o Valley. These sightseeing rides for all skill levels start at 9:30 A.M. and 1:30 P.M. and last about 2.5 hours. The cost of $75 per person includes transportation from the Last Chance Store in Kukuihaele to the valley floor. Make reservations 24 hours in advance.

WAIPI'O VALLEY WILD HORSES

The lineage of the horses of Waipi'o dates from the late 1700s. They were gifts to the *ali'i* from Capt. George Vancouver. Waipi'o was especially chosen because the horses were easy to corral and could not escape. Today, more than 150 semi-wild progeny of the original stock roam the valley floor. If you meet them on the roads or trails in the valley, let them go on their way or walk around their nose end so you don't spook them from behind. They have been known to be aggressive, so leave them alone.

© ROBERT NILSEN

the road into the Waipi'o Valley from the trail on the north cliff

Wagon Tour

Waipio Valley Wagon Tours (808/775-9518) is one of the most fun-filled ways of exploring Waipi'o. This surrey-type wagon, which can hold about a dozen people, is drawn by two Tennessee mules. The fascinating 90-minute tours depart four times daily at 9:30 A.M., 11:30 A.M., 1:30 P.M., and 3:30 P.M.; cost is $45, or $22.50 for children under 12. To participate, make reservations 24 hours in advance, then check in 30 minutes before departure at the Last Chance Store up top, where a four-wheel drive vehicle will come to fetch you. Lunch is not included, but if you bring your own, you can walk down to the beach and have a great picnic. The original wagon was built from parts ordered from the Mainland. Unfortunately, every part broke down over a nine-month trial period. All new parts were made at a local machine shop, three times thicker than the originals! After the wagon was "Waipi'onized," the problems ceased. As you roll along you get regaled with entertaining commentary about the history, biology, and myths of Waipi'o.

WAIMANU VALLEY

The hike down to Waipi'o and over the *pali* to Waimanu Valley is considered by many one of the top three treks in Hawaii. You must be fully prepared for camping and in excellent condition to attempt this hike. Also, water from the streams and falls is not good for drinking due to irrigation and cattle grazing topside; hikers should bring purification tablets or boil or filter it to be safe. To get to Waimanu Valley, a switchback trail locally called the Z trail but otherwise known as the **Muliwai Trail,** leads up the 1,200-foot *pali,* starting about 100 yards inland from the west end of Waipi'o Beach. Although not long, this is by far the most difficult section of the trail. Waimanu was bought by the State of Hawaii some years ago, and it is responsible for trail maintenance. The trail ahead is decent, although it can be muddy, but you go in and out of more than a dozen gulches before reaching Waimanu. In the third gulch, which is quite deep, a narrow cascading waterfall tumbles into a small pool right at trailside, just right for a quick dip or to dangle your feet. Another small pool is found in the fifth gulch. After the ninth gulch is a trail shelter. Finally, below is Waimanu Valley, half the size of Waipi'o but more verdant, and even wilder because it has been uninhabited for a longer time. Cross Waimanu Stream in the shallows where it meets the sea. The trail then continues along the beach and back into the valley about 1.5 miles, along the base of the far side, to Wai'ilikahi Falls, some 300 feet high. For drinking water (remember to treat it), walk along the west side of the *pali* until you find a likely waterfall. The Muliwai Trail to the Waimanu Valley floor is about 15 miles round-trip from the trailhead at the bottom of the *pali* in Waipi'o Valley, or 19 miles round-trip from Waipi'o Lookout.

To stay overnight in Waimanu Valley you must have a (free) camping permit available through the Division of Forestry and Wildlife (P.O. Box 4849, Hilo, HI 96720, 808/974-4221, open 8 A.M.–4 P.M. Mon.–Fri.). Apply not more than one month in advance. Your length of stay is limited to seven days and six nights. Each of the nine designated campsites along the beach has a fireplace, and there are three composting outhouses in the valley for use by campers. Carry out what you carry in!

Early in the 19th century, because of economic necessity brought on by the valley's remoteness, Waimanu was known for its *'okolehau* (moonshine). Solomon, one of the elders of the community at the time, decided that Waimanu had to diversify for the good of its people. He decided to raise domesticated pigs introduced by the Chinese, who roasted them with spices in rock ovens as a great delicacy. Solomon began to raise and sell the pigs commercially, but when he died, out of respect, no one wanted to handle his pigs, so they let them run loose. The pigs began to interbreed with feral pigs, and after a while there were so many pigs in Waimanu that they ate all the taro, bananas, and breadfruit. The porkers' voracious appetites caused a famine that forced the last remaining families of Waimanu to leave in the late 1940s. Most of the trails you will encounter are made by wild-pig hunters who still regularly go after Solomon's legacy.

According to oral tradition the first *kahuna lapa'au* (healing doctor) of Hawaii was from Waimanu Valley. His disciples crossed and recrossed Waipi'o Valley, greatly influencing the development of the area. Some of the *heiau* in Waipi'o are specifically dedicated to the healing of the human torso; their origins are traced to the healing *kahuna* of Waimanu.

Honoka'a to Honomu

The ride alone, as you head south on the Belt Road, is gorgeous enough to be considered a sight. But there's more! You can pull off the road into sleepy one-horse towns where dogs are safe snoozing in the middle of the road. If you want solitude, you can go inland to a forest reserve and miles of trails. Take a cautious dip at one of the seaside beach parks, or visit plantation stores in Honomu on your way up to 'Akaka Falls.

Kalopa State Recreation Area

This spacious natural area is five miles southeast of Honoka'a, 12 miles north of Laupahoehoe, three miles inland on a well-marked secondary road, and 2,000 feet in elevation. Little used by tourists, it's a great place to get away from the coast and up into the hills. Hiking is terrific throughout the park and adjoining forest reserve on a series of nature trails where some of the flora has been identified. Most of the forest here is endemic, with few alien species. Some of what you will see are 'ohi'a, koa, the *hapu'u* tree fern, and *kopiko* and *pilo,* both species of the coffee tree family. Near the entrance and camping area is a young arboretum of Hawaiian and Polynesian plants. Beyond the arboretum is an easy

0.75-mile nature loop trail through an 'ohi'a forest, and a three-mile loop trail takes you along the gulch trail and back to camp via an old road. All trails are well marked and vary widely in difficulty. Birdlife here may not be as varied as high up the mountainside, but still you can catch sight of *'elepaio, auku'u* (a night heron), the white-eye, cardinal, and the Hawaiian hoary bat. The park provides an excellent opportunity to explore some of the lush gulches of the Hamakua Coast, as well as day-use picnicking, tent camping, and furnished cabins (state permit required) that can house up to eight people. Camping and cabin use is limited to five consecutive days per party. The bunk-style cabins, each with a bathroom and shower, rent for $55 for one to eight campers. Linens and blankets are provided, and you may cook in the recreation hall. For reservations, contact the State Park office (75 Aupuni St. #204, Hilo, HI 96721, 808/974-6200).

Pa'auilo

About seven miles south of Honoka'a is Pa'auilo, a ghost of a sugar town. Set close to the highway, the town has a post office, several schools, and a former plantation manager's house. In business for about 100 years, **Paauilo Store** carries sundries, a few groceries, and from a window at its front, serves plate lunches and sandwiches. Down toward the sea were plantation workers' camps that are now just quiet neighborhoods, and on the coast are the old abandoned mill site and docks where raw sugar was once loaded for transport.

About three miles above Pa'auilo—head up Pohakea Road—you'll find the **Hawaiian Vanilla Company** mill and gift shop (808/776-1771 or 877/771-1771, 1–5 P.M. Mon.–Fri., www.vanillavineyard.com). Established in 1998, this company is the only one in the country that grows vanilla commercially. It uses its Hawaiian-grown vanilla beans, which are derived from a specific variety of hand-pollinated orchid flower, to produce extracts and vanilla-flavored food and healthcare products. Vanilla beans are also sold individually or by the pound. At about $200 per pound, natural vanilla is bested only by saffron as the most expensive flavoring. By reservation only, tastings are held every Monday and Tuesday afternoon at 3 P.M. for $10 per person; luncheons at $39 per person take place at 12:30 P.M. on Wednesdays and Thursdays; and an upcountry tea at $29 per person is given on the second Saturday of each month.

LAUPAHOEHOE

As you proceed down the coast, the road moves a little closer to the cliffs above the water and runs into and out of several large and scenic valleys, the largest and most impressive of which is **Maulua Gulch,** located south of Laupahoehoe. Along the way you pass the small communities of O'okala, Niu, Laupahoehoe, and Papa'aloa, now just shrunken memories of what they were during the plantation days. Although now silent, you can almost imagine the hubbub of activity when these towns, and others like them on the coast, were alive with sugar production. There's little happening here these days, but turn down the road to the **Papaaloa Store,** where local people go to buy the area's *best* smoked meats and fish, and *laulau* made right at the store; macaroni salad and meals to go are also available. The largest community here is Laupahoehoe. Located about halfway between Honoka'a and Honomu, the Laupahoehoe valley at one time supported farmers and fishermen who specialized in catching turtles. Laupahoehoe was the best boat landing along the coast, and for years canoes and, later, schooners would stop here. In town along the old highway you'll find schools, a post office, police station, the remains of a small business district, a local restaurant and a small gallery. A mini-mart and gas station are located on the highway. New to town is a large gourmet mushroom–growing operation.

Laupahoehoe Point County Park

This wave-lashed peninsula is a finger of smooth pahoehoe lava covered in grass that juts into the bay and is a popular place for weekend family outings. A plaque at water's edge commemorates the tragic loss of 20 schoolchildren and their teacher, who were taken by the great tsunami of 1946. Afterward, the village was moved to the high ground overlooking the point. Laupahoehoe Point County Park now occupies the low peninsula; it has picnic tables, showers, electricity, and a county camping area. The sea is too rough to swim in, except perhaps by the boat launch ramp, but many anglers come here, along with some daring surfers. Laupahoehoe makes a beautiful rest stop along the Belt Road. Turn near mile marker 27, on the north side of the valley. The road down to the park is narrow and winding and runs past several rebuilt homes and a restored Jodo Mission. Alternately, walk down the old roadway from the train museum, crossing the highway, passing a handful of homes, and continuing down the track as it hugs the steep wall of the hillside.

Laupahoehoe Train Museum

Near the Laupahoehoe scenic overlook, the **Laupahoehoe Train Museum** (36-2377 Mamalahoa Hwy., www.thetrainmuseum.com, 808/962-6300, 9 A.M.–4:30 P.M. weekdays, 10 A.M.–2 P.M. weekends, $4 adult, $3 seniors) treats you to a taste of the olden days when trains hauled sugarcane, commercial goods, and people up and down this rugged coast. The museum once was the home of the superintendent of maintenance for this division, and it is now filled with train memorabilia, photographs, books, and furniture either from the house or typical of the era. Two videos give insight into the train line and sugar era. The house itself has been lovingly restored as has the track "wye" on the grounds, and you can

THE HAKALAU FOREST NATIONAL WILDLIFE REFUGE

The Hakalau Forest National Wildlife Refuge was acquired with the help of the Nature Conservancy but is administered solely by the U.S. Fish and Wildlife Service. This 33,000-acre tract of land lies in the uplands above the Hamakua Coast north of the Saddle Road that borders the Department of Hawaiian Home Lands land. It's upland forest and former ranch land that drifts down into solid rainforest and is the home of such birds as the endangered *'akiapola'au*, *'akepa*, *'io*, Hawaiian creeper, and *nene*, and the common *i'iwi*, *'oma'o*, *'apapane*, *'amakihi*, *'elepaio*, and *pueo*. The U.S. Fish and Wildlife Service is working hard to allow the upper abandoned pastures of this refuge to regenerate with native forests; efforts include fencing, snaring, and hunting to rid the area of feral pigs and cattle, and replanting with koa, 'ohi'a, *opeka*, *pilo*, and other native species while removing introduced and exotic foliage. It's a tremendous task being shouldered mainly by U.S. Fish and Wildlife Service manager Dick Wass and his staff. The refuge is not adequately staffed to accept visits by the general public at all times, but the Maulau Tract, the northernmost section of the refuge, is open for hiking and birding – with prior permission – every weekend. This area is a two-hour drive from Hilo, half of which is over a rugged dirt road traversable only by a four-wheel drive vehicle! Numerous volunteer opportunities are available for various ongoing projects, either in the field or at the greenhouse, for a weekend or weeklong stint. If you *truly* have a dedication to help and aren't afraid to get your hands dirty, contact Dick Wass for a very rewarding experience. To enter the refuge for any reason, contact the office at least three weeks in advance to make arrangements; call 808/933-6915, fax 808/933-6917, write to the Refuge Manager, Hakalau Forest NWR, 32 Kino'ole St., Suite 101, Hilo, HI 96720, or email at richard_wass@fws.gov. The refuge is a very beautiful diamond in the rough, encompassing an incredible rainforest.

© ROBERT NILSEN

restored caboose at the Laupahoehoe Train Museum

see remnants of a loading platform out front. Biding its time, one train car waits to be rebuilt as two others have already been brought back to life. This museum is a worthy enterprise that gives you a glimpse into late-19th-century and early-20th-century coastal culture and is a fine place to stop on your way up the road. This line was part of the railroad that ran down to Hilo and beyond to Pahoa and up to Mountain View, but this rail system came to an abrupt halt on the first day of April 1946, when a tsunami washed ashore and destroyed track, bridges, and other property. The railroad company never recovered.

Food

Back to the 50's Highway Fountain, (35-2074, Government Main Rd., 808/962-0808) in a white and turquoise converted gas station, along the old road in Laupahoehoe Village, is as vintage a burger joint as you can get, with decorations of the era on the walls and a real jukebox in the corner. Stroll in and sit at the low diner bar or one of the small tables. Breakfast is hotcakes and omelettes, while lunch can be burgers and plate lunches, and everything is very moderately priced. Any time is right for a scoop of ice cream, a float, shake, sundae, or banana split. Open until early evening, it closes at 1 P.M. on Sunday, and is closed on Monday.

While in the village, look for the **M. Sakado Store** (808/962-6014, 9 A.M.–7 P.M. Mon.–Fri., until 6 P.M. on weekends), an old-fashioned convenience store. This tiny shop sells basic items like milk, bread, and soft drinks—enough for a picnic.

HONOMU

During its heyday, Honomu (Silent Bay) was a bustling center of the sugar industry boasting saloons, a hotel/bordello, and a church or two for repentance. It was even known as "Little Chicago." Now Honomu mainly serves as a stop as you head elsewhere, but you should definitely take the time to linger. Honomu is 10 miles north of Hilo and about a half mile or so inland on Route 220, which leads to 'Akaka

Falls. On entering, you'll find a string of false-front buildings doing a great but unofficial rendition of a "living history museum." The town has recently awoken from a long nap and is now bustling—if that's possible in a two-block town—with a gaggle of art galleries, craft shops, and small cafés. At the south end of town, just at the turn to 'Akaka Falls, notice the Plantation-style **Odaishisan,** a beautifully preserved Buddhist Temple. Beyond it are the Honomu Hongwanji Buddhist mission and the United Church of Christ and Good Shepard Catholic Mission Christian churches. It takes only minutes to walk the main street, but those minutes can give you a glimpse of history that will take you back 100 years. There is no gas station in Honomu, but there is a post office.

'Akaka Falls State Park

Follow Route 220 uphill from Honomu past former sugarcane fields for three miles to the parking lot of 'Akaka Falls, at a little more than 1,000 feet in elevation. From here, walk counterclockwise along a paved "circle route" that takes you through everybody's idea of a pristine Hawaiian valley. For the 40-minute hike, you're surrounded by heliconia, *ti,* ginger, orchids, azaleas, ferns, and bamboo groves as you cross bubbling streams on wooden footbridges. Many varieties of plants that would be in window pots anywhere else are giants here, almost trees. An overlook provides views of **Kahuna Falls** spilling into a lush green valley below. The trail becomes an enchanted tunnel through hanging orchids and bougainvillea. In a few moments you arrive at **'Akaka Falls.** The mountain cooperates with the perfect setting, forming a semicircle from which the falls tumble 442 feet in one sheer drop, the tallest single-tier waterfall in the state. After heavy rains, expect a mad torrent of power; during dry periods marvel at liquid-silver threads forming mist and rainbows. The area, maintained by the Division of State Parks, is one of the most easily accessible forays into Hawaii's beautiful interior. There is no gate that blocks access to the parking lot here but you are limited by daylight hours for seeing the falls.

bamboo and stream along trail to 'Akaka Falls

Kolekole Beach Park

Look for the tall bridge (100 feet high) a few minutes north of Honomu, where a sign points to a small road that snakes its way down the valley to the beach park below. Slow down and keep a sharp eye out, as the turnoff is right at the south end of the bridge and easy to miss. Amenities include restrooms, grills, electricity, picnic tables, pavilions, and a camping area (county permit required); no drinking water is available. Kolekole is very popular with local people, who use its pavilions for all manner of special occasions, usually on weekends. A pebble beach fronts a treacherous ocean. The entire valley was inundated with more than 30 feet of water during the great 1946 tsunami. The stream running through Kolekole comes from 'Akaka Falls, four miles inland. From here, you might take the old road back through the village of Wailea to the highway.

World Tropical Botanical Gardens

With such an impressive name, this garden promises to be good. But wait, the gardens are only in their infancy! Created on land that was sugarcane just a few short years ago, the gardens, which opened in 1995, are destined to be a wonderful sight. So far, however, and until the collection starts to mature and many more plants are put in, there are only small sections worth seeing near the entrance of this 300-acre tract, along with a newer children's maze. By far, the most impressive sight on the property is the three-tier **Umauma Waterfall**—and it is sure to please. The plan is to cultivate some 30,000 species—arranged in evolutionary grouping—and every year the gardens grow a little more toward that goal. Follow the signs up from the highway near mile marker 16, three miles north of Honomu, to the visitors center (808/963-5427, www.worldbotanicalgardens.com, 9 A.M.–5:30 P.M. Mon.–Sat., $9.50 adults, $5 teens, $2.50 kids 5–12).

Shopping

All of the town's shops and galleries lie along its short main street. The **Woodshop Gallery/Café** (808/963-6363 or 877/479-7995, www.woodshopgallery.com, 10:30 A.M.–6 P.M. daily) offers a wonderful opportunity for browsing among fine tropical wood furniture and artworks. This is one of the island's finest collections of arts and crafts. Shelves shine with the lustrous patina of bowls, mirrors, and furniture fashioned from koa, mango, *milo,* and macadamia wood, as well as from Norfolk pine, which can be turned to a translucent thinness. All pieces can be shipped, as can wood planks if you desire to create your own furniture or art piece. Jeanette and Peter McLaren, the shop owners, create glass works and furniture, respectively. Other artists produce additional furniture, art glass, ceramics, pottery, prints, paintings, photographs, and a great selection of turned bowls. Less expensive items include chopsticks, wooden spoons made of coconut and wood, combs, barrettes, and lovely vanity mirrors that come in a velvet bag.

More craftsy is the **Honomu Plantation Gallery** (808/963-5022, 9:30 A.M.–5:30 P.M.), which has a whole host of arts and crafts that make perfect gifts from your trip. Quilts are a specialty.

© ROBERT NILSEN

Umauma Waterfall

© ROBERT NILSEN

"main street" Honomu

The **'Ohana Gallery** (808/963-5467, 10 A.M.–4 P.M. Tues.–Sat.) operates with the philosophy that Hawaii's culture, history, and beauty are alive in the art of its people. This shop is a combination fine arts cooperative gallery and gift shop. Gracing the shelves and walls of the two-story gallery are works of wood, clay, pottery, paint, paper, glass, stone, and other media, all by island artists.

Showing jewelry and creations in wood, **Circle A Gifts** (808/963-6687) does much of the work on the premises.

Honomu Teddy Bear Emporium (808/963-6769), like its name implies, is where you'll find almost anything connected to teddy bears, as well as dolls and toys.

Another establishment worth a visit is **Glass From the Past** (808/963-6440) with vintage bottles, dug locally, and a variety of antiques, clothing, other collectibles.

Bed-and-Breakfasts

Nestled into three oceanfront acres of fruit and nut trees, with the driveway lined in palms, is the luxuriant, neo-Victorian **The Palms Cliff House** (28-3514 Mamalahoa Hwy., 808/963-6076, fax 808/963-6316 or 866/963-6076, palmscliffhouse@aol.com, www.palmscliffhouse.com). Overlooking a small bay where you can see whales in the winter and spinner dolphins year-round, this bed-and-breakfast caters to the discriminating crowd. The eight rooms, all done in individual themes (Orchid, Bombay Nights, Bellisimo, and Tropical Splendor, for example), are decorated with antique beds, custom-made Italian sheets, coordinated furniture, and artwork on the walls. Marble entryways and bathrooms, fireplaces in four rooms, whirlpool tubs in several rooms, a wide private lanai facing the ocean for each room, an entertainment center, and all plush amenities are what you might expect from such a high-end establishment. The upper rooms have air-conditioning, but it's hardly necessary. And to ensure a peaceful and uninterrupted getaway, there are no phones in the rooms and a separate hot tub sits in the garden. Gourmet breakfast specialties are cooked every morning in addition to fruits, juice, and other drinks. With all this luxury, room rates are not cheap. Set up for no more than two individuals in a room, they run $255–395 a night with four nights minimum; six rooms have king-size beds, one has a queen-size bed, and one has twins. No children under 12, please. With prior arrangement, special dinners, Saturday high tea, cooking classes, weddings, massage, yoga, and other activities can be arranged. This is a no-smoking establishment.

In the sleepy former sugar town of Wailea, a few short miles north of Honomu along the old road, is the easygoing and casual **Akiko's Buddhist Bed and Breakfast** (P.O. Box 272, Hakalau, HI 96710, tel./fax 808/963-6422, msakiko@aloha.net, www.alternative-hawaii.com/akiko). You need not be a Buddhist to stay, but you should come with an open mind and open heart. The bright yellow main house clues you in to the cheeriness and energy inside. Akiko's offers four Japanese-style rooms in the main building, a common kitchen, and bathroom with shower. This building is called the Monastery and is set aside for silence 6:30 P.M.–6:30 A.M. The adjacent two-story plantation house, Pu'uhonua, also has five rooms, plus a living room, kitchen, and a basic bathroom with shower. Breakfast is a group affair in the main house with fruits from the garden, yogurt, oatmeal, nuts, fresh-baked bread, and other goodies created by the talented Akiko. While it is not required, you may want to attend one of the informal meditations held every morning at 5 A.M. or in the evening 7–8 P.M. on Monday, Wednesday, and Friday in the main house meditation room, or tag along on one of the morning walks when they are held. Yoga may be offered on Sunday morning. The rooms in the main house have folding futons on the floor; the plantation house has beds. Rates for either house are $40 single or $55 double per night, two nights minimum; weekly and monthly rates are an option. Recently, Akiko has created two very basic solar cottages next door. These one-room buildings with screens as windows have a separate and simple propane-powered kitchen and bathhouse to share. The Mango Tree Cottage is good for one or two people and rents for $85 a night, while the Banana Patch Cottage is made for a single person and is $65 a night; three nights minimum for both. An easy place with good vibes and always plenty going on, you can rest and relax, participate or not, or head out to explore the countryside yourself. Check the website for an activity calendar.

Food

Before entering town proper you'll spot **Jan's** (808/963-6062), a convenience store run by members of the Muneno family since 1949 that's open until 6 P.M., selling cold beer, groceries, and sundries.

On the left as you drive along the main street are several shops for sit-down or takeout food. First up is **Akaka Cafe** (808/963-6701), a little eatery serving saimin, sandwiches, and plate lunches, all for easy-on-the-pocketbook prices. The interior of the old building holds a few tables with chairs salvaged from Honomu's defunct theater and a counter with little red stools. Akaka Cafe is clean, friendly, and caught in a time warp harkening back to the days when a burger was the treat of the week! This little shop has been run by the same extended family since the 1930s.

The **Woodshop Gallery/Café** (808/963-6363) has a more modern and artsy atmosphere. After perusing the fine artwork, sit down for a sandwich, burger, smoothie, ice cream, or coffee. Choose a table inside, or head for the lanai where you can watch the "action" in the two-block downtown of Honomu.

At the very upper end of town in a section of the Ishigo Building, the oldest building in Honomu, is **Ed's Bakery** (808/963-5000, 6 A.M.–6 P.M. Mon. –Sat., 7 A.M.–6 P.M. Sun.), with its display of bread, pastries, cookies, and ice cream. Attached to Ed's is a small grocery store.

ONOMEA SCENIC DRIVE

Route 19 heading south from Honoka'a to Hilo has magnificent inland and coastal views one after another. From Honomu, the Hawaii Belt Road pushes inland a bit and slides by Pepe'ekeo, popping out to the coast again at Papa'ikou, from where it's just a few minutes to the outskirts of Hilo. But even this section has good coastal views—if you follow the old coastal road, Mamalahoa Highway, also named Onomea Scenic Drive. From the north, you can find this four-mile-long scenic drive near mile marker 11. Turn in toward the ocean and skirt around the back side of Pepe'ekeo, a workers' village. Like much of the coast, this is former sugarcane land; if you take Sugar Mill Road down the hill, it will bring you to the remains of the old Pepe'ekeo sugar mill. This area and similar spots both above and below the highway along this coast have become prime land for housing, ranches, and hobby farms.

Most people find the Onomea Scenic Drive when coming north from Hilo. Only five minutes from the city, you'll come to Papa'ikou town. Just past mile marker 7 and across the road from the Papa'ikou School, a road posted as the scenic drive dips down toward the coast. Take it. Almost immediately, signs warn you to slow your speed because of the narrow winding road and one-lane bridges, letting you know what kind of area you're coming into. Start down this meandering lane past some very modest homes and into the jungle that covers the road like a living green tunnel. Prepare for tiny bridges crossing tiny valleys. Stop, and you can almost hear the jungle growing. Along this route are sections of an ancient coastal trail and the site of a former fishing village. Drive defensively, but take a look as you pass one fine view after another. This road runs past the Hawaii Tropical Botanical Garden and a couple of places for quick eats before heading up to higher ground to rejoin Route 19 at Pepe'ekeo.

If you have time, turn at Pinky's store and take Mill Road down to its end (one long block), passing a line of plantation houses in various states of repair. Park at the end and enter through the gate to find a path that runs through the old sugar mill property. This is a decent place to see remnants of old sugar plantation buildings. Almost immediately, head down to the right to the rather small and confined black-pebble beach and surfing spot on Papa'ikou Bay, once the landing site for ships that hauled sugar away for refining. Unless the surf is happening, you'll have the place to yourself.

Hawaii Tropical Botanical Garden

Just a few minutes along the Onomea scenic coastal route is the Hawaii Tropical Botanical Garden (808/964-5233, www.hawaiigarden.com, 9 A.M.–5 P.M. daily, adults $15, children 6–16 $5). Remember that the entrance fee not only allows you to walk through the best-tamed tropical rainforest on the Big Island but helps preserve this wonderful area in perpetuity. The gardens were established in 1978 when Dan and Pauline Lutkenhouse purchased the 25-acre valley and have been open for viewing since 1984. Mr. Lutkenhouse, a retired San Francisco businessman, personally performed the work that transformed it into one of the most exotic spots in all of Hawaii. The locality was amazingly beautiful but inaccessible because it was so rugged. Through personal investment and six painstaking years of toil aided by only two helpers, he hand-cleared

© ROBERT NILSEN

Onomea Bay, at the bottom of Hawaii Tropical Botanical Garden the land, built trails and bridges, developed an irrigation system, acquired more than 2,000 different species of trees and plants, and established one mile of scenic trails and a water lily lake stocked with *koi* and tropical fish. Onomea was a favorite spot with the Hawaiians, who came to fish and camp for the night. The valley was a fishing village called Kahali'i in the early 1800s. Later on it became a rough-water seaport used for shipping sugarcane and other tropical products.

Start at the visitors center along the road, where you'll find a gift shop, the tiny Onomea Museum, self-guided tour maps, drinking water, restrooms, umbrellas for your convenience, and jungle perfume—better known as mosquito repellent! Cross the road to the garden entrance and descend into this lush valley. The steep trail into the valley is about 500 feet long; once into the heart of the garden, the trails are more level. Plants from the four corners of the globe are named with a full botanical description. Native plants from Hawaii are included. As you walk, listen for the songs of the native birds that love this ancient spot. Choose one of the aptly named trails and lose yourself in the beauty of the surroundings. You are in the middle of a tamed jungle, walking along manicured paths. Stroll the Ocean Trail down to the sea, where the rugged coastline is dramatically pummeled by frothy waves, a sea arch provides dramatic sculpture, and turtles swim the bay. You can hear the waves entering submerged lava caves, where they blow in and out like a giant bellows. Away from the sea you'll encounter screened gazebos filled with exotic birds. Walk the inland trails past Onomea Waterfall, streams, ponds, a bamboo grove, palms, and innumerable flowers. For at least a brief time you get to feel the power and beauty of a living Garden of Eden.

Onomea Trails

The botanical garden trails are not the only ways to reach Onomea Bay. Short walks from the road head down the hill on both sides of the botanical garden. These are free trails, part of the statewide Na Ala Hele trail system. On the south side, you can take an old Jeep trail of crumbling pavement for five minutes to the water, where you can cross a section of the botanical garden between privacy fences to the stream. Please don't sneak in to the botanical garden, but pay your entrance fee and go in the main entrance if you want a look. Alternately, you can head down the steeper Donkey Trail on the north side, a rocky and muddy footpath that starts just north of the garden visitors center and goes through a canopy of trees to the water—about 10 minutes. These two trails connect over the shallow stream. Be careful to pull all the way off the roadway when you park your car to walk either of these trails, as there is no parking lot and very little room along this winding section of road.

Shopping

Just before you pop out to the highway from the Onomea Scenic Drive in Papa'ikou, you come across **Hawaiian Artifacts** (808/964-1729, 9 A.M.–5 P.M. daily), a shop owned and operated by Paul Gephart. Paul creates small wood boxes and ornaments, mainly from koa and 'ohi'a, poi bowls, and sculptures of whales, dolphins, and birds. He also has a small collection of tasteful jewelry and seashells, all at decent prices. Most intriguing perhaps are his reproductions of old Hawaiian weapons.

Food

In Papa'ikou, look for **Pinky's** convenience store (5 A.M.–7 P.M. Mon.–Fri., 6 A.M.–6 P.M. Sat.–Sun.) in the pink building on the ocean side of the road. Catercorner across the street is **Baker Tom's** (808/964-8444) for various types of hot malasadas and other tasty treats.

What's Shakin' (808/964-3080, 10 A.M.–5 P.M. daily) is a fine pit stop along the Onomea Scenic Drive. Stop here for juice or smoothies, or a more substantial veggie burger, chicken wrap, tuna sandwich, or teriyaki-ginger tempeh burger. Most items on the menu are under $8. Also along this scenic route is **Low Store** (808/964-1390, 6 A.M.–6 P.M. daily), where you can pick up fresh fruits and smoothies for the road.

HILO

Hilo is a blind date. Everyone tells you what a beautiful personality she has, but...But? It rains—130 inches a year. Mostly the rains come in winter and spring and are limited to predictable afternoon showers, but they do scare some tourists away, keeping Hilo reasonably priced and low-key. In spite of, and because of, the rain, Hilo is gorgeous. Hilo's weather makes it a natural greenhouse; botanical gardens and flower farms surround Hilo like a giant lei. To counterpoint this tropical explosion, Mauna Kea's winter snows backdrop the town. Hilo is one of the oldest permanently settled towns in Hawaii, and the largest on the windward coast of the island. Don't make the mistake of underestimating Hilo, or of counting it out because of its rainy reputation. For most, the blind date with this exotic beauty turns into a fun-filled love affair.

At just under 40,000, Hilo has the second-largest population in the state after Honolulu. It is the county seat, has a bustling commercial harbor, has a long tradition in agriculture and industry, boasts a branch of the University of Hawaii, and is home to the Hawai'i Community College. Hilo is a classic tropical town. Some preserved historical buildings, proud again after new face-lifts, are a few stories tall and date from the turn of the 20th century when Hilo was a major port of entry to Hawaii. Sidewalks in older sections are covered with awnings because of the rains, which adds a turn-of-the-20th-century gentility. You can walk the central area comfortably in an

HIGHLIGHTS

Lyman Museum and Mission House: This attraction offers visitors a glimpse into the life of early missionaries to Hawaii, a look at the natural history of the island, and snippets of the cultural makeup of those who have made the Big Island their home (page 211).

Pacific Tsunami Museum: To better understand the natural force of destruction that periodically has swept through the city of Hilo, stop at this informative museum (page 213).

Downtown Walking Tour: Hilo has a good number of well-maintained historical buildings in a range of styles and ages (page 213).

Around Banyan Drive: This area was destroyed during the last major tsunami, yet the giant banyan trees, picturesque Lili'uokalani Gardens, and culturally significant Coconut Island are still there to be appreciated (page 215).

Rainbow Falls and Boiling Pots: Two of the city's best known natural features are both in the Wailuku River State Park (page 216).

Pana'ewa Rainforest Zoo: Check out the zoo to see tropical animals in their natural habitat (page 218).

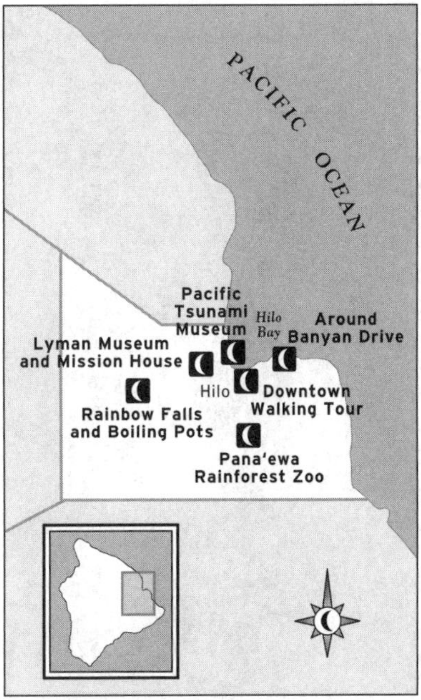

LOOK FOR ☾ TO FIND RECOMMENDED SIGHTS, ACTIVITIES, DINING, AND LODGING.

afternoon, but the town does sprawl some due to the modern phenomena of large shopping malls and residential subdivisions in the outlying areas. Hilo is the opposite of Kailua-Kona both spiritually and physically. There, everything runs fast to a new and modern tune. In Hilo the old beat, the old music, that feeling of a tropical place where rhythms are slow and sensual, still exist. Hilo nights are alive with sounds of the tropics and the heady smell of fruits and flowering trees wafting on the breeze. Slow down and relax; you'll start to feel at home. Hilo remains what it always was—a town, a place where people live, work, and love.

PLANNING YOUR TIME

While many visitors to the Big Island stay only on the Kona side, those that know the island well and appreciate its diversity split their time between the Kona and Hilo sides. Hilo, being the largest city and main hub on the east side is the logical place to use as a base. The city is bite-size, but you'll need a rental car to visit most of the sights around town. Hilo itself has

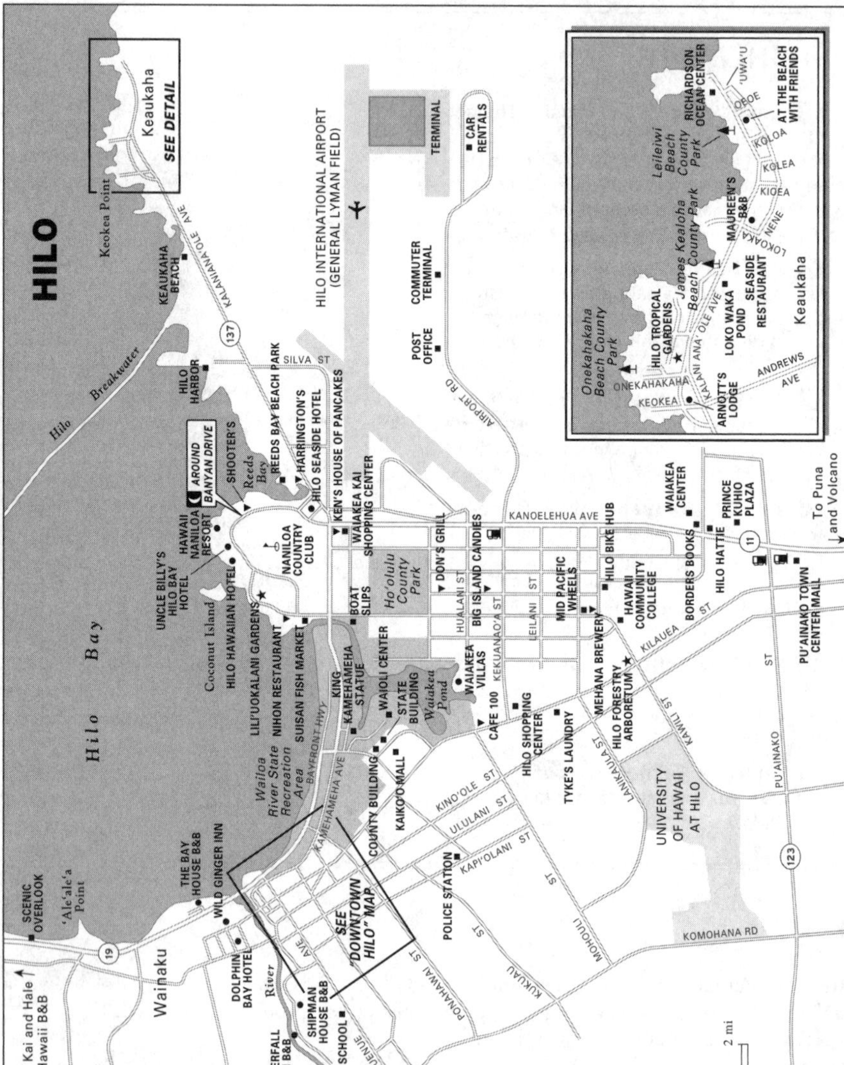
HILO
Hilo Bay
Hilo Breakwater
Keokea Point
Keaukaha
SEE DETAIL
KEAUKAHA BEACH
KALANIANA'OLE AVE
137
HILO INTERNATIONAL AIRPORT (GENERAL LYMAN FIELD)
TERMINAL
CAR RENTALS
COMMUTER TERMINAL
POST OFFICE
AIRPORT RD
HILO HARBOR
SILVA ST
REEDS BAY BEACH PARK
HARRINGTON'S
HILO SEASIDE HOTEL
KEN'S HOUSE OF PANCAKES
WAIAKEA KAI SHOPPING CENTER
SHOOTER'S
Reeds Bay
AROUND BANYAN DRIVE
HAWAII NANILOA RESORT
UNCLE BILLY'S HILO BAY HOTEL
NANILOA COUNTRY CLUB
HILO HAWAIIAN HOTEL
Coconut Island
LILI'UOKALANI GARDENS
NIHON RESTAURANT
SUISAN FISH MARKET
BOAT SLIPS
Ho'olulu County Park
DON'S GRILL
HUALANI ST
BIG ISLAND CANDIES
LEILANI ST
MID PACIFIC WHEELS
HILO BIKE HUB
KANOELEHUA AVE
WAIAKEA CENTER
PRINCE KUHIO PLAZA
BORDERS BOOKS
HILO HATTIE
11
To Puna and Volcano
HAWAII COMMUNITY COLLEGE
KILAUEA ST
PU'AINAKO TOWN CENTER MALL
MEHANA BREWERY
HILO FORESTRY ARBORETUM
KAWILI ST
WAIOLI CENTER
KING KAMEHAMEHA STATUE
WAIAKEA VILLAS
KEKUANAO'A ST
Waiakea Pond
STATE BUILDING
CAFE 100
HILO SHOPPING CENTER
TYKE'S LAUNDRY
LANIKAULA ST
UNIVERSITY OF HAWAII AT HILO
PU'AINAKO ST
123
KOMOHANA RD
Wailoa River State Recreation Area
BAYFRONT HWY
KAMEHAMEHA AVE
COUNTY BUILDING
KAIKO'O MALL
KINO'OLE ST
ULULANI ST
KAPI'OLANI ST
POLICE STATION
MOHOULI ST
KUKUAU ST
PONAHAWAI ST
SEE "DOWNTOWN HILO" MAP
SCENIC OVERLOOK
'Ale'ale'a Point
THE BAY HOUSE B&B
WILD GINGER INN
DOLPHIN BAY HOTEL
19
Wainaku
Wailuku River
SHIPMAN HOUSE B&B
SCHOOL
WATERFALL INN B&B
WAIANUENUE AVE
RAINBOW FALLS
Wailuku River State Park
To The Old Hawaiian B&B
HILO MEDICAL CENTER
KAUMANA DR
20
To Holmes' Sweet Home B&B
To Inn at Kulaniapia Falls
Kaiwiki
To Lihi Kai and Hale Kai Hawaii B&B
0 2 mi
0 2 km
Onekahakaha Beach County Park
ONEKAHAKAHA
KEOKEA
ARNOTT'S LODGE
HILO TROPICAL GARDENS
KALANI ANA'OLE AVE
ANDREWS AVE
James Kealoha Beach County Park
LOKO WAKA POND
SEASIDE RESTAURANT
Keaukaha
LOKOAKA
NENE
MAUREEN'S B&B
KIOEA
KOLEA
KOLOA
Leleiwi Beach County Park
RICHARDSON OCEAN CENTER
OEOE
'UWA'U
AT THE BEACH WITH FRIENDS

plenty to keep a traveler busy for a number of days. First, spend time exploring the natural beauty of the city and close by botanical gardens, its bay and beaches, and the pretty waterfalls only a few minutes from downtown. Both Rainbow Falls and the potholed riverbed of Boiling Pots are very photogenic, and perhaps best when there's plenty of rain to make them perform at their best. Take an hour or two to walk under the giant banyan trees that canopy Banyan Drive, stroll through the relaxing Lili'uokalani Gardens, and walk the bridge to Coconut Island for a perfect view of the bay and waterfront with snow-capped Mauna Kea as a backdrop. While you are out that way, continue on down Kalaniana'ole Avenue for a morning or afternoon in the water at one of the small beaches along the Keaukaha strip. Hilo is an old town. Reserve a morning or afternoon for a walking tour of town, viewing its well-kept historical buildings, and then spend a few hours at both the Pacific Tsunami Museum, where you will learn about the brutal waters that destroyed much of Hilo's bayfront, and the Lyman Mission House and Museum, where the life of early missionaries to Hawaii comes alive. A bit farther afield is the Pana'ewa Rainforest Zoo, also good for a couple of hours to view tropical animals in a natural environment, and the opportunity to see some of the thick and luxuriant forest cover that surrounds the city. For exploration from Hilo, it's a hour's drive down to the steamy Puna Coast, about the same up to the stark lava lands of Hawaii Volcano National Park or along the wet and wonderful Hamakua Coast to time-lost Waipi'o Valley, but a bit longer for a trek to the top of the Mauna Kea to see the astronomical observatories and experience a sunset from the heights.

Sights

Before the shift of tourism to the dry side of the island, Hilo was the Big Island's major visitor destination. This old town and steamy tropical port still holds many attractions for those willing to look, from missionary homes to forest waterfalls, and landscaped tropical gardens to diminutive beaches with great snorkeling options.

DOWNTOWN

Lyman Museum and Mission House

The Lyman Museum and Mission House (276 Haili St., 808/935-5021, www.lymanmuseum.org, 9:30 A.M.–4:30 P.M. Mon.–Sat., $10 adults, $8 seniors, $3 children 6–17) lies a few short blocks above downtown Hilo. Guided tours of the Lyman Mission House next door are included with museum admission and are given five times a day, on the hour 10 A.M.–3 P.M., by experienced and knowledgeable docents who relate many intriguing stories about the mission house and its occupants.

The Lyman Museum is a modern three-story building. The first-floor Earth Heritage Gallery holds a mineral and rock collection that's rated one of the best in the entire country, and by far the best in Polynesia. These displays are the lifelong collection of Orlando Lyman, the great-grandson of the original Lymans. A collection of seashells from various parts of the world is also on display, as are some rarely seen land snail shells of Hawaii. Other exhibits explain the geology and volcanology of the island, and a section is dedicated to the flora and fauna of Hawaii. Upstairs is the Island Heritage Gallery, where a replica of a Hawaiian thatched house is displayed. Nearby are Hawaiian tools and other artifacts of daily life. Precontact displays give way to kimonos from Japan, a Chinese herbal medicine display, and other displays showing artifacts

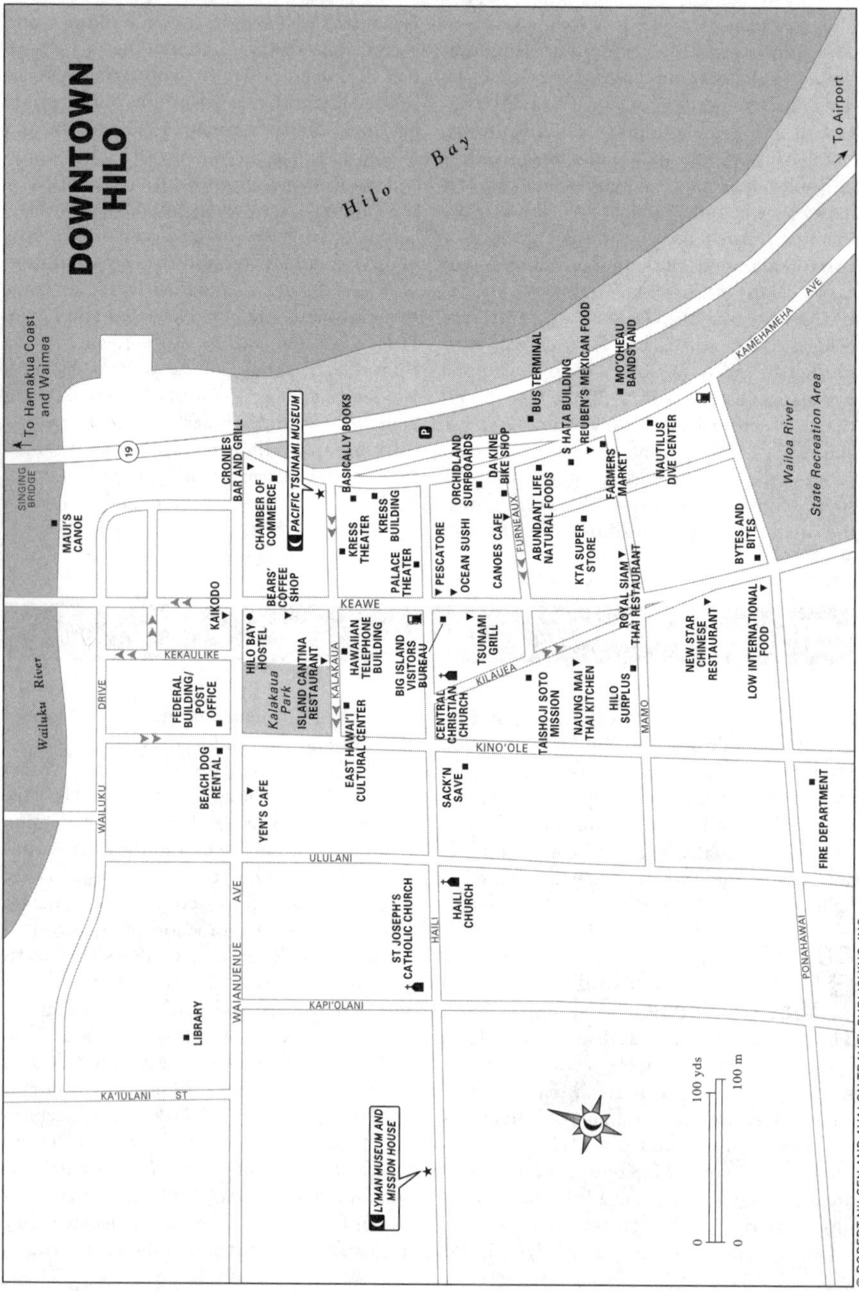
DOWNTOWN HILO
Hilo Bay
To Hamakua Coast and Waimea
To Airport
SINGING BRIDGE
19
MAUI'S CANOE
Wailuku River
CRONIES BAR AND GRILL
CHAMBER OF COMMERCE
PACIFIC TSUNAMI MUSEUM
BASICALLY BOOKS
KRESS THEATER
KRESS BUILDING
PALACE THEATER
BEARS' COFFEE SHOP
KAIKODO
HILO BAY HOSTEL
KEAWE
KEKAULIKE
DRIVE
WAILUKU
FEDERAL BUILDING/ POST OFFICE
BEACH DOG RENTAL
YEN'S CAFE
Kalakaua Park
ISLAND CANTINA RESTAURANT
KALAKAUA
HAWAIIAN TELEPHONE BUILDING
EAST HAWAI'I CULTURAL CENTER
BIG ISLAND VISITORS BUREAU
PESCATORE
OCEAN SUSHI
ORCHIDLAND SURFBOARDS
DA KINE BIKE SHOP
CANOES CAFE
FURNEAUX
TSUNAMI GRILL
CENTRAL CHRISTIAN CHURCH
KILAUEA
KINO'OLE
SACK'N SAVE
TAISHOJI SOTO MISSION
ABUNDANT LIFE NATURAL FOODS
BUS TERMINAL
S HATA BUILDING
REUBEN'S MEXICAN FOOD
MO'OHEAU BANDSTAND
KAMEHAMEHA AVE
FARMERS' MARKET
KTA SUPER STORE
ROYAL SIAM THAI RESTAURANT
NAUNG MAI THAI KITCHEN
HILO SURPLUS
MAMO
NAUTILUS DIVE CENTER
BYTES AND BITES
NEW STAR CHINESE RESTAURANT
LOW INTERNATIONAL FOOD
Wailoa River State Recreation Area
FIRE DEPARTMENT
ULULANI
HAILI
HAILI CHURCH
ST JOSEPH'S CATHOLIC CHURCH
WAIANUENUE AVE
LIBRARY
KAPI'OLANI
PONAHAWAI
KA'IULANI ST
LYMAN MUSEUM AND MISSION HOUSE
100 yds
100 m
0
0

of Filipino, Portuguese, and Korean heritage. The Shipman Collection is a display of Chinese art, with a fine grouping of ceramic and jade pottery and statuary from the last three centuries with a few pieces as old as 2,000 years. Periodic special exhibits are shown in other galleries. Saying good-bye is a bust of Mark Twain, carved from a piece of the very monkeypod tree he planted in Wai'ohinu in 1866. The museum is educational and worth some time, and the gift shop at the entrance a good place to look for authentic Hawaiian products and books.

The preserved New England–style homestead of David and Sarah Lyman, Congregational missionaries who built it in 1839, is the oldest frame building still standing on the Big Island. In 1856, a second story was added, which provided more room and a perfect view of the harbor. In 1930, Haili Street was extended past the home, and at that time the Wilcox and Lyman families had the house turned parallel to the street. The building is now on the National and State Registers of Historic Places.

The Lyman Mission House opened as a museum in 1931. The furniture is authentic "Sandwich Isles" circa 1850. Some of the furniture has come from other missionary homes, although many pieces belonged to the original occupants. The floors and doors are deep, luxurious koa. The main door is a "Christian door," built by Hilo Boarding School students. The top panels form a cross and the bottom depicts an open Bible. One room was used as a schoolroom/dayroom where Mrs. Lyman taught arithmetic, mapmaking, and proper manners. The dining room holds an original family table set with Blue Willow china. Some of the most interesting exhibits are of small personal items like a music box that still plays and a collection of New England autumn leaves that Mrs. Lyman had sent over to show her children what that season was like. Upstairs are bedrooms that were occupied by the Lyman children. Mrs. Lyman kept a diary and faithfully recorded eruptions, earthquakes, and tsunami. Scientists still refer to it for some of the earliest recorded data on these natural disturbances. The master bedroom has a large bed with pineapples carved into the bedposts, crafted by a ship's carpenter who lived with the family for about eight months. The bedroom mirror is an original, in which many Hawaiians received their first surprised look at themselves. A nursery holds a cradle used by all eight children. Broad and spacious, the attic holds more furniture and tools and allows a glimpse of how this amazing house was constructed. It's obvious that the Lymans did not live luxuriously, but they were comfortable in their island home.

Pacific Tsunami Museum

Hilo suffered a devastating tsunami in 1946 and another in 1960. Both times, most of the waterfront area of the city was destroyed, but the 1930 Bishop National Bank building survived, owing to its structural integrity. Appropriately, the Pacific Tsunami Museum (130 Kamehameha Ave., 808/935-0926, www.tsunami.org, 9 A.M.–4 P.M. Mon.–Sat., $7 adults, $6 seniors, and $2 students.) is now housed in this fine art deco structure and dedicated to those who lost their lives in the devastating waves that raked the city. The museum has numerous permanent displays, an audio-visual room, computer linkups to scientific sites, and periodic temporary exhibitions. While there is general scientific information, what's perhaps the most moving feature of this museum are the photographs of the last two terrible tsunamis that struck the city and the stories retold by the survivors of those events. Stop in for a look. It's well worth the time. Other permanent displays of photos relating to the tsunamis are hung in the Kress Building farther down Kamehameha Avenue and on the lower level of Wailoa Center.

Downtown Walking Tour

Start your tour of Hilo by picking up a pamphlet/map entitled *Walking Tour of Historic Downtown,* free at the Hawaii Visitors Bureau office and many restaurants, hotels, and shops. This self-guiding pamphlet takes you down the main streets and back lanes where you discover the unique architecture of Hilo's glory days. On the median strip between the Bayfront Highway and Kamehameha Avenue is a bandstand and main city bus terminal. The **Mo'oheau Bandstand** is all that's left of the dozens of structures that lined the ocean side of Kamehameha Avenue before the 1946 tsunami. Miraculously, this structure survived. The bandstand is sometimes used by the Hawai'i County Band for concerts and for other community events. A **tourist information kiosk** near the bandstand and bus stop has brochures and maps to dispense about the city.

The majority of the vintage buildings have been restored, and the architecture varies from the early 20th century Kress (1932), S. Hata Building (1912), and First Trust Building (1908) to the Zen Buddhist Taishoji Soto Mission and Central Christian Church. Older is the Lyman House (1839) and nearby the New England–style Haili Congregational Church (1859; congregation founded in 1824). A remarkable building is the **Old Police Station** (1932), located at 141 Kalakaua St., opposite Kalakaua Park. On the National and State Registers of Historic Places and Buildings, this old colonial structure is now the home of the East Hawai'i Cultural Center. Next door to the old police station is the **Hawaiian Telephone Building** by C.W. Dickey, a well-known practitioner of the Hawaiian Regional Style. Notice the hipped roof, a typical feature of this style, and the colorful tiles.

Set aside for public use by King Kalakaua himself, **Kalakaua Park** is a grassy area overseen by a huge banyan tree, a midtown oasis. A seated statue of King David Kalakaua, the Merrie Monarch, takes center stage. Across Waianuenue Avenue is the solid and stately **Federal Building** with its offices and downtown post office. This stone structure dates from 1917.

A short walk up Waianuenue Avenue brings you to the **Hilo Public Library.** Sitting at the entrance are two large stones. The larger is called the **Naha Stone,** known for its ability to detect any offspring of the ruling Naha clan.

© ROBERT NILSEN

statue of King Kalakaua in Kalakaua Park in downtown Hilo

The test was simple: Place a baby on the stone, and if the infant remained silent, he or she was Naha; if the baby cried, he or she wasn't. It is believed that this 7,000-pound monolith was brought from Kaua'i by canoe and placed near Pinao Temple in the immediate vicinity of what is now Wailuku Drive and Keawe Street. Kamehameha the Great supposedly fulfilled a prophecy of "moving a mountain" by budging this stone. The smaller stone is thought to be an entrance pillar of the Pinao Temple. Just behind the library is the Wailuku River. Pick any of its bridges for a panoramic view down to the sea. Often, local fishermen try their luck from the Wailuku's grassy banks. The massive, overgrown boulder sitting near the river's mouth is known as **Maui's Canoe.** During the tsunami of 1946, the railroad bridge that crossed the river at bay's edge was torn from its base like a weak Tinker Toy construction. The metal bridge that crosses the river today is known as the Singing Bridge because the mesh that creates the roadway hums or "sings" as rubber tires spin across it.

Around Banyan Drive

If your Hilo hotel isn't situated along Banyan Drive, go there. This bucolic horseshoe-shaped road skirts the edge of the Waiakea Peninsula that sticks out into Hilo Bay. Lining the drive is an almost uninterrupted series of **banyan trees** forming a giant canopy, while the fairways and greens of the Naniloa Country Club golf course take up the center of the tiny peninsula. Skirting its edge are the Lili'uokalani Gardens, a concentration of hotels, and Reed's Bay. This peninsula was once a populated residential area, an offshoot of central Hilo. Like much of the city, it was destroyed during the tsunami of 1960. Park your car at one end and take a stroll through this park-like atmosphere. The four dozen banyans that line this boulevard (the first planted in 1933, the last in 1972) were planted by notable Americans and foreigners, including Babe Ruth, President Franklin D. Roosevelt, King George V, Hawaiian volcanologist Dr. Thomas Jaggar, Hawaiian Princess Kawananakoa, pilot Amelia Earhart, Cecil B. DeMille, and then-senator Richard Nixon. A placard in front of most trees gives particulars. Time has taken its toll here, however, and as grand as this drive once was, it is now a bit overgrown and unkempt in spots, with much of the area needing a little sprucing up.

Lili'uokalani Gardens are formal Japanese-style gardens located along the west end of Banyan Drive. Meditatively quiet, they offer a beautiful view of the bay. Along the footpaths are pagodas, torii gates, stone lanterns, and half-moon bridges spanning a series of ponds and streams. Along one side sits a formal Japanese Tea House where women come to be instructed in the art of the tea ceremony. Few people visit this 30-acre garden, and if it weren't for the striking fingers of black lava and the coconut trees, you could easily be in Japan.

Coconut Island (Moku Ola) is reached by footbridge from a spit of land just outside Lili'uokalani Gardens. It was at one time a *pu'uhonua* (place of refuge) opposite a human sacrificial *heiau* on the peninsula side. Coconut Island has restrooms, a pavilion, and picnic tables shaded by tall coconut trees and ironwoods. It's been a favorite picnic spot for decades; kids often come to jump into the water from stone abutments here, and older folks come for a leisurely dip in the cool water. The only decent place to swim in Hilo Bay, it also offers the best panorama of the city, bay, and Mauna Kea beyond.

© ROBERT NILSEN

the best public park in Hilo is Lili'uokalani Gardens

Wailoa River State Recreation Area

To the east of downtown is **Waiakea Pond,** a brackish lagoon where people often fish. The Wailoa River State Recreation Area, which encompasses the lagoon, is a 132-acre preserve set along both sides of this spring-fed pond. City residents use this big broad area for picnics, pleasure walks, informal get-togethers, fishing, and launching boats. On the eastern side are picnic pavilions and barbecue grills. Arching footbridges cross the river connecting the halves. Stop at the **Wailoa Center** on the western side for tourist information and cultural displays (open weekdays only). The walls in the upstairs gallery of this 10-sided building are used to display works of local artists and cultural/historic exhibits, changed on a regular basis. On the lower level hang astonishing pictures of the 1946 and 1960 tsunamis that washed through the city. The Wailoa Center sits in a broad swath of greenery, an open, idyllic park-like area that used to be a cramped bustling neighborhood known as Shinmachi. It, like much of the city, was almost totally destroyed during the tsunami of 1960. Nearby stands the **Tsunami Memorial** to the residents of this neighborhood who lost their lives in that natural disaster. Also close by is the county **Vietnam War Memorial,** dedicated to those who died fighting that war, and a **statue of King Kamehameha I,** a new version of that which graces the town of Kapa'au at the northern tip of the island. Park at the Wailoa Center on Piopio Street, off Pauahi Street. Additional parking for this landscaped area is on the western side along Park Street at the end of Pi'ilani Street.

East of Waiakea Pond and across Manono Street you'll see **Ho'olulu County Park,** with the Civic Center Auditorium, numerous athletic stadiums. This is the town's center for organized athletic events, large cultural festivals, the yearly Merrie Monarch dance festival, and the annual county fair.

FARTHER AFIELD

Rainbow Falls and Boiling Pots

A few miles out of town, heading west on Waianuenue Avenue, are two natural spectacles within Wailuku River State Park that are definitely worth a look, open 7 A.M.–6:30 P.M. A short way past Hilo High School a sign directs you to Rainbow Falls, a most spectacular yet easily visited natural wonder. You'll look down on a circular pool in the river below that's almost 100 feet in diameter; cascading into it is a lovely waterfall. The 80-foot falls deserve their name because as they hit the water below, their mists throw flocks of rainbows into the air. Underneath the falls is a huge cavern, held

fishing on Waiakea Pond

A near-perfect waterfall, Rainbow Falls is Hilo's finest.

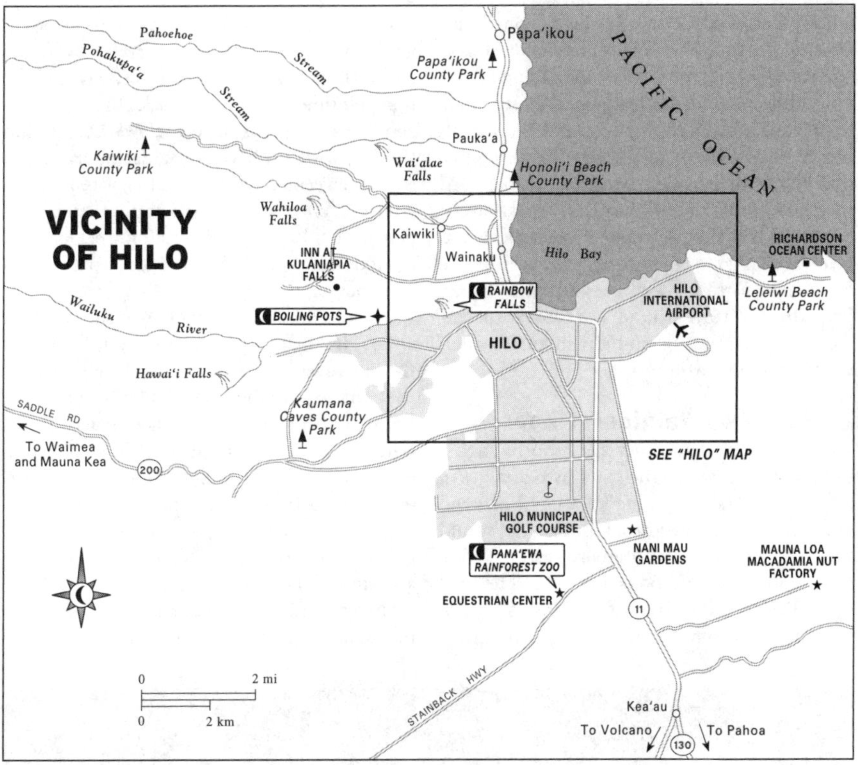

by legend to be the abode of Hina, mother of the god Maui. Most people are content to look from the vantage point near the parking lot, but if you walk to the left, you can take a stone stairway to a private viewing area directly over the falls. Here the river, strewn with volcanic boulders, pours over the edge. Follow the path for a minute or so along the bank to a gigantic banyan tree and a different vantage point. The falls may be best seen in the morning when the sunlight streams in from the front.

Follow Waianuenue Avenue for two more miles past Hilo Medical Center to the heights above town. A sign to turn right onto Pe'epe'e Falls Street points to Boiling Pots. Few people visit here. Follow the path from the parking lot past the toilets to an overlook. Indented into the riverbed below is a series of irregularly shaped depressions that look as though a peg-legged giant left his peg prints in the hot lava. Seven or eight resemble naturally bubbling whirlpool tubs as river water cascades from one into the next. This phenomenon is best after a heavy rain. Turn your head upriver to see **Pe'epe'e Falls,** a gorgeous, five-spouted waterfall. Although signs warn you not to descend to the river—it's risky during heavy rains—locals hike down to the river rocks below to sunbathe and swim in pools that do not have rushing water.

Kaumana Cave

In 1881, Mauna Loa's tremendous eruption discharged a huge flow of lava. The river of lava crusted over, forming a tube through which molten lava continued to flow. Once the eruption ceased, the lava inside siphoned out, leaving the tube now called Kaumana Cave. The cave is only four miles out of downtown Hilo along Route 200, clearly marked at a curve in the road. Oddly enough, it is posted as a fallout shelter. Follow a steep staircase down into a gray hole (actually a skylight of this cave) draped with green ferns and brightened by wildflowers. Smell the scent of the tropical vegetation. You can walk only a few yards into the cave before you'll need a strong flashlight and sturdy shoes. It's a thrill to turn around and look at the entrance, where blazing sunlight shoots through the ferns and wildflowers.

Pana'ewa Rainforest Zoo

Not many travelers can visit a zoo in such a unique setting, where the animals virtually live in paradise. The 150 animals at this 12-acre zoo are endemic and introduced species that would naturally live in such an environment. While small and local, the zoo is a delight. The road to the Pana'ewa Rainforest Zoo (808/959-9233, www.hilozoo.com, 9 A.M.–4 P.M. daily, closed Christmas and New Year's Day) is a trip in itself, getting you back into the country. Follow Route 11 south past mile marker 4 until you see the sign pointing right up Stainback Highway to the zoo. Near the zoo is the **Pana'ewa Equestrian Center,** with a full-size horse racing track. On a typical weekday, you'll have the place much to yourself. The zoo, operated by the county Department of Parks and Recreation, does feedings around 9 A.M. and 3:15 P.M., and the petting zoo activities happen around 1:30 P.M., so you may want to be around for them. Admission is free, although donations to the nonprofit Friends of the Pana'ewa Zoo, which runs the gift shop at the entrance, are appreciated. Here you have the feeling that the animals are not "fenced in" so much as you are "fenced out." The collection of about 75 species includes ordinary and exotic animals from around the world. You'll see pygmy hippos from Africa, a rare white Bengal tiger named Namaste, a miniature horse and steer, Asian forest tortoises, water buffalo, monkeys, and a wide assortment of birds like pheasants and peacocks. The zoo hosts many

Namaste, resting in the afternoon heat

endangered animals indigenous to Hawaii like the *nene,* Laysan duck, Hawaiian coot, *pueo,* Hawaiian gallinule, and even a feral pig in his own stone mini-condo. There are some great iguanas and mongooses, lemurs, and an aviary section with exotic birds like yellow-fronted parrots and blue and gold macaws. The back central area is a tigers' playground; a tall fence marks this rather large area where the tiger still rules his domain. It's got its own pond and tall grasses that make the tigers feel at home. The zoo makes a perfect side trip for families and will certainly delight the little ones.

Mauna Loa Macadamia Nut Factory

Mauna Loa Macadamia Nut Factory (808/966-8618, www.maunaloa.com, 8:30 A.M.–5 P.M. daily) is located several miles south of Hilo off Route 11, nearly to Kea'au. Head down Macadamia Road for about three miles, through the 2,500-acre plantation, until you come to the visitors center. Inside is an informative free video explaining the development and processing of macadamia nuts in Hawaii. Walkways outside the windows of the processing center and chocolate shop let you view the process of turning these delicious nuts into tantalizing gift items, but this is best viewed from August through January when most of the processing is done. Then return to the snack shop for macadamia nut goodies like ice cream and cookies, and the gift shop for samples and an intriguing assortment of packaged macadamia nut items.

MACADAMIA NUTS

Hawaii produces about 40 percent of the world's supply of macadamia nuts, and the majority of the state's crop is raised on the Big Island. About one million macadamia nut trees produce these tasty nuts at the Mauna Loa Macadamia Nut property outside Hilo, with a larger property producing nuts in South Kona. Smaller growers raise this crop at different locations on the Big Island, as well as on Moloka'i, O'ahu, and Kaua'i.

A native of Australia, macadamia nut trees were first brought to Hawaii and planted in Honoka'a in 1881 by the British agriculturist W. H. Purvis. One of these trees is still bearing! A number of these trees were again introduced to Hawaii in 1921 for study but failed to produce an acceptably significant and even-quality product. However, W. Pierre Naquin, then manager of the Honoka'a Sugar Co., thought the nut might have some potential and started the first commercial nut farm in 1924. After years of grafting and experimentation on the island of O'ahu, over half a dozen varieties of the tree proved to yield acceptable nuts, and this led to large-scale commercial ventures in the 1950s. Macadamia nut trees can grow to about 40 feet tall, branch out to about the same width, and have dark green leaves. Trees require at least five years before they begin to produce nuts, and perhaps five to 10 additional years before they are in full production. Once mature, they can produce for years. Trees flower at different times over many months and produce nuts most of the year. This requires harvesting on a periodic basis. While some nuts are shaken from the trees, most fall naturally and are picked up from the ground. The nuts have a leathery skin that breaks open to reveal a very hard brown shell. This shell is cracked open to give forth the fruit itself, a light-colored, crisp and creamy orb about the size of a marble. In larger commercial ventures, the nuts are collected, dried, cracked, and sorted mechanically, while small-time growers may do some of this work by hand. Many of the nuts are roasted and salted, but some are set aside to be put into a brittle, glazed with various concoctions, or dipped in chocolate. Additionally, the nuts are often added to sauces, desserts, pastries, and confections. Some now are pressing the nut for its oil. Macadamia nuts contain mostly monounsaturated fat and traces of several minerals. Its high burn and smoke temperature makes it great for cooking and its smooth texture is appropriate for lighter foods.

While you're here, step out back and take a self-guided tour of the small garden, where many introduced trees and plants are identified.

GARDENS

Aside from the gardens listed below, there are two botanical gardens just a short way north up the Hamakua Coast. These are the Hawaii Tropical Botanical Garden, the best and most luxuriant of the botanical gardens on the island, and the World Tropical Botanical Gardens.

Hilo Forestry Arboretum

Along Kilauea Avenue, between Lanikaula and Kawili Streets, the Department of Natural Resources, Division of Forestry maintains the Hilo Forestry Arboretum (8 A.M.–3 P.M. Mon.–Fri., closed weekends and holidays; no charge). This arboretum and tree nursery contains many of the trees present in Hawaii, including indigenous and imported specimens. Have a look at the diagram map of the grounds in the office before you head out back for a self-guided tour. The map attempts to name the trees by matching them with points on the map as you pass by, instead of referring to signs on each specimen. The trees are magnificent, and you will have this quiet area virtually to yourself. Originally the site was an animal quarantine station operated by the Territory of Hawaii; the 19.4 acres of the arboretum were established in 1920 by Brother Mathias Newell. Brother Newell was a nurseryman employed by the Catholic boys' school in Hilo. At that time the Division of Forestry was already actively introducing plant species from all over the world. For the 40 years between 1921 and 1961 the department was engaged in the development and maintenance of arboretums consisting primarily of plant species from Australia and Africa. Arboretum sites ranged from sea level to Mauna Kea. Plant materials were exchanged, and thousands of breadfruit cuttings were exported. Over 1,000 different tree species and 500 different fruit trees were field-tested. Here at the Hilo Arboretum over 1,000 trees were planted. A few trees such as the paper bark and some pines are more than 50 years old. Presently a small number of timber species are grown for reforestation purposes. Essentially the Hilo site is utilized for the propagation of rare and endangered plant species, for research, and for experimental pursuits.

Nani Mau Gardens

Nani Mau Gardens (421 Makalika St., 808/959-3500, 9 A.M.–4:30 P.M. daily, $10 adult, $5 children ages 4–10, plus $5 adult or $3 children for an optional tram tour) is the largest in Hilo and touring these spectacular displays is well worth a few hours. The gardens consist of 20 sculpted acres. More than a botanical garden, Nani Mau is a "floral theme park" designed as a tourist attraction. Walks throughout the garden are very tame but very beautiful; umbrellas are provided during rainy weather, which adds its own dripping, crystalline charm to the experience. Plants are labeled in English, Latin, and Japanese. The gardens are a huge but ordered display of flowers, flowering trees, and shrubbery. The wildly colored plumage of tropical birds here and there competes with the colors of the exotic blooms. The gardens are broken off into separate areas for hibiscus, anthurium, orchid, gardenia, and bromeliad, along with a Japanese garden, a fruit orchard, and stands of bamboo, palms, and other trees. It also features floral sculptures, a small reflective pond, and an assortment of flowers and shrubs laid out in geometric patterns. The Nani Mau Restaurant provides a cafeteria-style lunch only, 10:30 A.M.–1:30 P.M., and the tourist shop is exactly like a Japanese omiyagi (souvenir) shop. No wonder, since it's owned by ethnic Japanese, and most of the tour buses coming here are filled with Japanese visitors. If you enjoy a clean outdoor experience surrounded by magnificent flowers, this is the place.

Hilo Tropical Gardens

Established in 1948 and apparently the oldest botanical garden on the island, Hilo Tropical Gardens (1477 Kalaniana'ole Ave., 808/969-9873, $2 adults for a self-guided tour and free for children) is back to life after a number of

© ROBERT NILSEN
Nani Mau Gardens

years of neglect. A thick profusion of tropical plants greet you as you enter this garden and a maze of walkways leads through its somewhat overgrown grounds. The garden is compact, so it's not overwhelming. It should take no more than 20 minutes, and some of the plants are marked so you know what you're looking at. Among the many are a host of anthuriums and orchids. Aside from the flowers, here and there along the walkways are pools in lava sinks and a hidden lava tube or two. Enter through the gift shop, where you can find flowers, lei, gifts, and crafts, all of which can be shipped for you. When you're finished, stop next door for a scoop of Hilo Homemade Ice Cream.

BEACHES

If you define a beach as a long expanse of white sand covered by a thousand sunbathers and their beach umbrellas, then Hilo doesn't have any. If a beach, to you, can be a smaller, more intimate affair where a good number of tourists and families can spend the day on pockets of sand between fingers of black lava, then Hilo has a few. Hilo's beaches are small and rocky—perfect for keeping crowds away. The best beaches all lie to the east of the city along Kalaniana'ole Avenue, an area known as the Keaukaha Strip, which runs six miles from downtown Hilo to its dead end at Leleiwi Point. Not all beaches are clearly marked, but even those are easily spotted by cars parked along the road.

Hilo Bayfront Park is a thousand yards of gray-black sand that narrows considerably as it runs west from the Wailoa River toward downtown. At one time it went all the way to the Wailuku River and was renowned throughout the islands for its beauty, but commercialism of the waterfront ruined it. By 1960, so much sewage and industrial waste had been pumped into the bay that it was considered a public menace, and then the great tsunami came. Reclamation projects created the Wailoa River State Recreation Area at the east end, and shorefront land became a buffer zone against future inundation. Few swimmers come to the beach because the water is cloudy and chilly, but the sharks don't seem to mind! The bay is perfect spot for canoe races, and many local teams come here to train. Notice the judging towers and canoe sheds of local outrigger canoe clubs. In the early 1800s, King Kamehameha I reputedly had 800 canoes made and launched from this beach for an assault on Kaua'i to bring that distant island under his control. The armada never made it, but eventually Kaua'i came under the great king's influence by diplomatic means. Toward the west end, near the mouth of the Wailuku River, surfers catch long rides during the winter months, entertaining spectators. There is public parking along the eastern half near the canoe clubs or at the Wailoa river mouth where the fishing boats dock.

Reeds Bay Beach Park is a largely undeveloped area on the east side of the Waiakea Peninsula. Technically part of Hilo Bay, the water is notoriously cold because of a constantly flowing freshwater spring, hence the name Ice Pond, at its innermost end. Mostly frequented by fishermen and locals having a good time on weekends and holidays, some sailors park their private boats here.

Keaukaha Beach at **Carlsmith Beach County Park,** located on Puhi Bay, is the first in a series of beaches as you head east on Kalaniana'ole Avenue. Look for Baker Avenue and pull off to the left into a rough parking area. This is a favorite spot with local people, who swim at Cold Water Pond, a spring-fed inlet at the head of the bay. A sewage treatment plant fronts the western side of Puhi Bay. Much nicer areas await you just up Kalaniana'ole Avenue.

Onekahakaha Beach County Park has it all: safe swimming, small white-sand beach, lifeguards, and amenities. Turn left onto Onekahakaha Road and park in the lot of Hilo's favorite family beach. Swim in the large, sandy-bottomed pool protected by a manmade breakwater. Outside the breakwater the currents can be fierce, and drownings have been recorded. Walk east along the shore to find an undeveloped area of the park with many small tidal pools. Beware of sea urchins.

James Kealoha Beach County Park, also known locally as Four Mile Beach, is next; people swim, snorkel, and fish here, and during winter months it's a favorite surfing spot. A large grassy area is shaded by trees and a picnic pavilion. Just offshore is an island known as Scout Island because local Boy Scouts often camp there. This entire area was known for its fishponds, and inland, just across Kalaniana'ole Avenue, is the 60-acre Loko Waka Pond. This site of ancient Hawaiian aquaculture is now a commercial operation that raises mullet, trout, catfish, perch, tilapia, and others; you'll find the Seaside Restaurant here.

Leleiwi Beach County Park lies along a lovely residential area carved into the rugged coastline. This park, with its parking lot, lifeguard, three pavilions, trees, and rock wall, is a favorite local spot for scuba divers. The shore here is open to the ocean, and currents may be strong. Plentiful sealife makes this a good snorkeling spot. Adjacent is Richardson Ocean Park, known locally as **Richardson's Beach Park.** Richardson Ocean Center is located here. A seawall skirts the shore, and a tiny cove with a black-sand beach is the first in a series. This is a terrific area for snorkeling, with plenty of marinelife, including *honu* (green sea turtles). Walk east to a natural lava breakwater. Behind it are pools filled and flushed by the surging tide. The water breaks over the top of the lava and rushes into the pools, making natural whirlpool tubs. This is one of the most picturesque swimming areas on the island.

Going north out of Hilo a few miles brings you to **Honoli'i Beach County Park.** Turn right onto Nahala Street, then left onto Kahoa, and follow it around until you see cars parked along the road. The water is down a steep series of steps, and while the black-sand beach is not much appreciated for swimming, it is known as one of the finest surfing spots on this side of the island.

Entertainment

Hilo doesn't have a lot of nightlife, but neither is it a morgue. Entertainment here is not generally organized for tourists but for townsfolk and consists mostly of periodic cultural activities and such things as movies and live entertainment at local bars and lounges.

Music Scene

One of the best places for weekend music and dancing, and quick easy food every night of the week except Sunday is the large and lively **Cronies Bar and Grill** (808/935-5158, 11 A.M.–2 A.M. daily), at the corner of Waianuenue and Kamehameha Avenues. Hamburgers, sandwiches, and *pu pu,* with a handful of more expensive entrées, are on the menu, and Cronies offers a full complement of drinks. On Friday and sometimes other nights of the week there's live music. Belly up to the bar for weekday happy hour specials 4–7 P.M., toss some darts at the electronic dartboard, or use the billiard table in the back while the music plays up front.

If you're looking for a night out in the Banyan Drive area, try **Shooter's** (121 Banyan Drive, 808/969-7069, 11 A.M.–3 A.M.). Shooter's is a bar and restaurant where you can dance several nights a week. DJ music ranges from reggae to rock to rap depending upon the crowd and the night, with live music ($5 cover) a couple times a month. The cavernous interior is like a giant rumpus room with cement floors, neon beer signs, and TVs at every angle; the decor is industrial chic. Don't be put off by the atmosphere, which can seem a bit stark and hard at first glance. Shooter's is friendly, has security, and boasts that "there hasn't been one confrontation since the day we opened." That's nice!

Wai'oli Lounge (808/935-9361, 5–9 P.M.) at the Hilo Hawaiian Hotel offers live contemporary Hawaiian music or karaoke every evening. Even though the lounge itself is rather bare, it overlooks the bay and offers the prettiest setting in town for an evening cocktail. Down the street at the **Naniloa Hotel** (808/969-3333), karaoke is offered 8 P.M.–closing most evenings at its downstairs cocktail lounge. **Uncle Billy's Fish and Steakhouse** (808/935-0861) at the Hilo Bay Hotel has a free hula show nightly 6–7:30 P.M. for its dinner patrons, while **Harrington's** (808/961-4966, 7:30–10:30 P.M.) offers its guests live jazz, contemporary, or Hawaiian music Thurs.–Saturday.

Movie Theaters

To catch a flick, try the **Prince Kuhio Stadium Cinemas** (808/961-3456) at the Prince Kuhio Plaza, with nine screens and tickets for $8 adult or $5 senior and student. Downtown in the refurbished Kress Building is the newer four-screen **Kress Cinemas** (808/935-6777), where tickets cost only $1.

The renovated **Palace Theater** (38 Haili St., 808/934-7777, www.hilopalace.com) shows art films, is the venue of the yearly Hawaii International Film Festival, and hosts periodic live performances. Here you have stadium seating, a proscenium stage, and wonderful old murals. If you're into art deco buildings and old cinemas, make this a stop. Movies are generally shown Fri.–Tues. at 7:30 P.M., except Sun., when the show is at 2:30 P.M.; movie tickets are $6 adult and $4 seniors and students. Other performances may be at different times and ticket prices vary.

Art and Cultural Events

East Hawai'i Cultural Center (808/961-5711, www.ehcc.org, 10 A.M.–4 P.M. Mon.–Sat.) is a nonprofit organization that supports local arts and hosts varying festivals, performances, and workshops throughout the year, here and at other locations on the island. It also hosts Shakespeare in the Park performances by a local repertory group that stages, directs, designs, and enacts Shakespearean plays under the large banyan tree in Kalakaua Park across the street during the month of July. If you're in Hilo at this time, it shouldn't be missed. Monthly juried and non-juried art exhibits are shown on the main floor gallery; a venue for various performing artists is upstairs. The bulletin board is always filled with announcements of happenings in the local art scene. Stop in as there is always something of interest on the walls, and because this organization is worthy of support. The Big Island Dance Council, Hawai'i Concert Society, Hilo Community Players, and Bunka No Izumi are all member groups.

Shopping

Like most modern American cities, Hilo has suffered from a shift in business from its downtown core to strip malls and later to larger, suburban shopping malls. Even so, the city has managed to maintain a reasonably thriving business district along its main waterfront road and adjacent streets that is of interest to visitors.

Shopping Malls

Hilo has the best general-purpose shopping on the island. **Prince Kuhio Plaza** (10 A.M.–9 P.M. weekdays, 9:30 A.M.–7 P.M. Saturday, 10 A.M.–6 P.M. Sunday), at E. Pu'ainako and Kanoelehua, is the island's largest shopping mall with over 75 shops. It's basically an indoor covered mall with the addition of several large detached buildings. Jewelry shops, fashion and shoe stores, music and books, sporting goods, fast-food restaurants, and large department stores like Sears and Macy's make this a one-stop shopping experience. Here too you'll find Longs Drugs, a Safeway grocery store, and a Hilo Hattie store in separate buildings. Like its sister shops around the state, **Hilo Hattie** (808/961-3077, 8:30 A.M.–6 P.M.) has a great selection of clothing, food, and gift items, at good prices. Stop here for an introduction of what you might find available on the island.

Across Maka'ala street is the newer **Waiakea Center** with a Borders Books and Music, Island Naturals natural food store, Hilo Bay Cafe, Wal-Mart, and Office Max. These two malls together make the greatest concentration of Hilo shopping.

The strip mall **Pu'ainako Town Center** is located a little farther up Kanoelehua Avenue (Rt. 11) and on the other side of the street, with lots of small shops, a Sack 'n Save Market, KTA Superstore, and one local fast-food outlet after another.

The older and smaller **Hilo Shopping Center,** located closer to downtown along Kilauea Avenue at the corner of Kekuanao'a Street, is much smaller and older but is still full of local shops and some excellent inexpensive restaurants.

Downtown Shops

If you're looking for a simple yet authentic gift or souvenir try the **Lyman Museum gift shop,**

ALOHAWEAR

A grand conspiracy in Hawaii adhered to by everyone – tourist, traveler, and resident – is to "hang loose" and dress casually. Best of all, alohawear is just about all you'll need for comfort and virtually every occasion. The classic mu'umu'u is large and billowy, and aloha shirts are made to be worn outside the pants. The best of both are made of cool cotton or silk and often designed in bright-colored floral patterns or island scenes. Rayon is a natural fiber that isn't too bad, but polyester is hot, sticky, and not authentic. *Holomu* are mu'umu'u fitted at the waist with a flowing skirt to the ankles. They are not only elegant, but perfect for "stepping out."

which also has an excellent collection of books on Hawaiian subjects.

Phoenix Rising (35 Waianuenue Ave., 808/934-7353, 9 A.M.–6 P.M. weekdays, 9 A.M.–4 P.M. Sat.) is a classy, eclectic little shop that sells all sorts of expensive but very nice arts and craft items, gifts, furniture, home accessories, jewelry, and a small selection of silk and natural fiber clothing. Perhaps a hand-painted silk tie for him or a Japanese *tansu* chest for her is just the piece you're looking for.

Sig Zane Design (122 Kamehameha Ave., 808/935-7077, www.sigzane.com, 9 A.M.–5 P.M. weekdays, 9 A.M.–4 P.M. Sat.) is a unique shop on the island. Here, owner and designer Sig Zane creates distinctive island wearables in Hawaiian/tropical designs. Sig's wife, Nalani, who helps in the shop, is a *kumu hula* who learned the intricate dance steps from her mother, Edith Kanakaole, a legendary dancer who has been memorialized with a local tennis stadium that bears her name. You can get shirts, dresses, and pareu, as well as affordable T-shirts, *hapi* coats, and even futon covers. The shelves also hold leather bags, greeting cards, and accessories.

After having moved down to Kamehameha Avenue, business at **Fabric Impressions** (206 Kamehameha Ave., 808/961-4468) has picked up. Stop here for bulk fabric, sewing accessories, quilt supplies, and quilts. Sewing classes and quilting workshops are also offered on a regular basis.

Dreams of Paradise (808/935-5670, 10 A.M.–9 P.M., from 9 A.M. on Wed. and Sat., from 11:30 A.M. on Sun.), is an art gallery located in the restored S. Hata Building. Artists showcased in the gallery specialize in the flora and fauna of Hawaii, produce fine koa furniture, offer distinctive acrylic paintings, catch the sun in stained glass renditions of breadfruit, lotus blossoms, and various Hawaiian flowers, and create sculptures and renditions of animal life. Also of interest in the S. Hata building are Kipuka Smoke Shop for cigars, Bugado's Fine Woods for turnings, carvings, boxes, and furniture, and a Black Pearl jewelry shop.

Caravan Town (194 Kamehameha Ave., 808/934-9580) is one of the most interesting junk stores in Hilo. The shelves hold an internationally eclectic mix of merchandise that includes pendulum clocks, plaster Greek goddesses, luggage, and paper lanterns. Also, the shop specializes in over-the-counter Chinese herbs and medicines purportedly effective for everything from constipation to impotence. Other antique, collectible, and gift shops along this street worth a look are the **Pink Elephant Thrift Shop** (808/935-4095), **The Most Irresistible Shop in Hilo** (808/935-9644), and the venerable old **Oshima's.**

An intriguing and offbeat shop full of natural fiber clothing, textiles, jewelry, and art and handicrafts from Hawaii, Asia, and Africa is **Perfect Harmony** (276 Keawe St., 808/934-0333).

Bookstores

Hilo has some excellent bookstores. **Basically Books** (160 Kamehameha Ave., 808/961-0144 or 800/903-6277, www.basicallybooks.com, 9 A.M.–5 P.M. Mon.–Sat., 10 A.M.–3 P.M. Sun.) is downtown and has a good selection of Hawaiiana, out-of-print books, and an unbeatable selection of maps and charts. You can get anywhere you want to go with these nautical charts, road maps, and topographical maps, including sectionals for serious hikers. The store also features a very good selection of travel books, and flags from countries throughout the world. Owner and proprietress Christine Reed can help you with any of your literary needs. The owners also publish books about Hawaii under their Petroglyph Press name. Occupying the same shop is **Old Town Printers,** in business since 1962, selling stationery, office supplies, postcards, and a terrific selection of calendars.

At the Prince Kuhio Plaza, **Waldenbooks** (808/959-6468, 10 A.M.–9 P.M. weekdays, 9:30 A.M.–7 P.M. Sat., 9:30 A.M.–6 P.M. Sun.) is one of the city's two large and well-stocked chain bookstores.

The largest bookstore in Hilo is **Borders Books and Music** (808/933-1410, 9 A.M.–9 P.M. Sun.–Thurs., 9 A.M.–10 P.M. Fri. and

Sat.), at the Waiakea Center, across Maka'ala Street from the Prince Kuhio Plaza. Borders has tens of thousands of hardcover and paperback books, full Hawaiiana and travel sections, plenty of road maps, and over a dozen newspapers from around the world. Readings, music performances, book and CD signings, and other special events are scheduled throughout the month. If browsing makes you thirsty, stop for a snack at the shop's Cafe Espresso.

Recreation

While Hilo is not the main activity hub of the island, it does offer a variety of recreational opportunities and a good price advantage, particularly for helicopter and van tours. While you won't flock here for outdoor sports, if you're here, you can find plenty to do.

Surfing

If you're thinking about buying or renting a surfboard, looking for a boogie board or surfwear, or just want to find out about surfing conditions in the area, stop by **Orchidland Surfshop** (262 Kamehameha Ave., 808/935-1533, www.surfolhawaii.com). Check its website for surf reports, conditions, and weather forecast. Established in 1972 and run by an avid surfer, this is the granddaddy of surf and water sports stores in Hilo. Surfboard rentals usually run about $20 a day. Surfing is not as big on this island as on the others, but one surfing spot close to town that does draw a fair number of enthusiasts when the waves are right is Honoli'i Cove, about four miles north of the Singing Bridge.

Snorkeling and Scuba

Like surfing, snorkeling is not big in Hilo, but the best sights are at and near Richardson's Beach Park out in the Leleiwi section of town. In Hilo, go to Nautilus Dive Center for snorkel gear rental ($6 a day).

The **Nautilus Dive Center** (382 Kamehameha Ave., 808/935-6939, derooy@gte.net, www.nautilusdivehilo.com, 9 A.M.–4 P.M. Mon.–Sat.), owned and operated by certified instructor William DeRooy, is one of the longest-established dive companies on the Hilo side. This full-service dive center offers guided dives at lower prices than on the more frequented Kona side. But don't be fooled, the Hilo side has some very good diving. Three- to five-day PADI certification is a very reasonable $440 for private lessons, and one-tank introductory shore dives are $85, including transportation. Boat dives can be arranged. New and used dive gear, scuba rental equipment, and snorkel gear rental are also available. DeRooy is willing to provide information over the phone for anyone coming to the Hilo side to dive or snorkel. He updates you on ocean conditions and suggests spots compatible with your ability. Bill is a font of information about the Big Island's water sports and shares it in the true *aloha* spirit. Definitely stop in!

Biking

Aside from the few accommodations in town that have bikes to use or rent, your best bet for two-wheel rental transportation in town is **Mid Pacific Wheels** (1133-C Manono St., 808/935-6211, 9 A.M.–6 P.M. Mon.–Sat., 11 A.M.–5 P.M. Sun.). Mid-range mountain bikes rent for $20 a day, helmet included, but a bike rack or lock is extra. Reduced rates for longer than five-day rentals.

For recycled bicycles, sales and repair, stop and talk with the owner of **Da Kine Bike Shop** (12 Furneaux Lane, 808/934-9861, noon–6 P.M. Mon.–Sat.), just a few steps from Kamehameha Avenue in downtown Hilo. Nothing is new here, but you might find a bike to cruise the beach or tackle a muddy mountain trail. If you plan on using a bike for a while but don't need it when you leave the island, you can buy a bike and sell it back later, based on a specified depreciation value. Bikes are usually available, except perhaps when the university starts a new semester.

The **Hilo Bike Hub** (318 E. Kawila, 808/961-4452) is perhaps the best shop in town for sales and service of quality mountain bikes and accessories. This shop is heavy into the mountain biking scene, including the Big Island Mountain Biking Association, and has information about all the island races and where to bike on-road or off-road on the island.

Golf

Hilo is not known for great golf; the rain and dearth of money and luxury resorts keeps the best courses elsewhere. Yet even here you can swing your irons. The only county-maintained golf course on the island is located high above downtown Hilo. **Hilo Municipal Golf Course** (340 Haihai St., 808/959-7711), is a 6,325-yard, par-71 undulating course with mostly parallel fairways where nonresidents can golf for $29 weekdays and $34 weekends. There are reduced rates for state and island residents. Cart rental is separate, and rental clubs are available. This is definitely a local course but it does provide some challenge. Call ahead for tee times.

Occupying the center of the Waiakea Peninsula and surrounded by Banyan Drive is the **Naniloa Golf Course** (808/935-3000). Maintained by the Naniloa hotel, this small nine-hole course is a par 35 over a flat 2,875 yards; $30 for two times around on weekends or $25 during the week. Electric or pull carts and clubs are extra. It's an easygoing place where lots of people come to learn and practice.

TOURS

Adventure Tours

Arnott's Hiking Adventures (98 Apapane Rd., 808/967-7097, www.arnottslodge.com/activity.html) offers a variety of hiking adventures to visitors looking for more of an adventure than an ordinary group tour offers. While the tours offered do change periodically, several have remained popular. They include a hike to the lava flow at Hawai'i Volcanoes National Park, a waterfall and valleys hike, and the sunset and stargazing trek to the top of Mauna Kea. These are full eight-hour trips—some longer—and the very reasonable costs are $50–60 for those staying at Arnott's Lodge in Hilo and $80–90 for others. Each trip takes only as many as the van will carry and goes only when the weather is cooperative. Some restrictions on age and physical condition apply, so be sure to check with the staff at Arnott's Lodge, or check out the website for the current list of adventures.

Helicopter Tours

With its spotless safety record and large operation, **Blue Hawaiian Helicopters** (808/961-5600 in Hilo, 808/886-1768 in Waikoloa, 800/786-2583, www.bluehawaiian.com) operates several A-Star helicopters from the Hilo heliport and additional A-Star and Eco-star helicopters from the Waikoloa Heliport on the Kona side. From Hilo, 45-minute flights for $198 take in the active volcanic flow, black-sand beaches, and other regions of the tropical southeastern corner of the island. Blue Hawaiian also offers flights on Maui and Kaua'i.

Flying out of the Hilo Airport in a four-passenger Hughes 500 and six-passenger Bell 407 helicopters is **Tropical Helicopters** (808/961-6810, www.tropicalhelicopters.com). Tropical is a small company that gives personal attention to passengers. Its popular 40-minute volcano flight runs $132. An expanded 50-minute flight runs the same basic route but gives you additional flight over waterfalls in the Hilo area for $157. The ultimate "Feel the Heat" flight, $180, takes you for an up-close look at the volcano activity—with the doors off! Other combination flights and charters are options. Check in at the main airport terminal.

Leaving from the Hilo Airport main terminal building, **Paradise Helicopters** (808/969-7392, www.paradisehelicopters.com) flies the same type of machines as Tropical Helicopters and does much the same routing, as they too concentrate on the volcano. Its "Doors Off" tour is $215 and the volcano and waterfalls tour runs $185.

Safari Helicopters (808/969-1259 or 800/326-3356, www.safariair.com) flies from the Hilo Heliport. Flights from Hilo run 45 minutes and 60 minutes, $149–209, and concentrate on the volcano and nearby waterfalls. Safari uses air-conditioned A-Star craft. This is a reputable company with a good reputation, and pilots give you a memorable flight. Safari also flies on Kaua'i.

Sunshine Helicopters (808/969-7501 or 800/469-3000, www.sunshinehelicopters.com) also offers a 45-minute volcano viewing flight from the Hilo Airport for $190.

Fixed-Wing Air Tours

For a small and intimate plane, with wings above the windows, try **Island Hopper** (808/969-2000), which offers flights from both the Hilo and Kona Airports. Volcano and waterfall tours for $139 and a circle-island flight for $199 go from Hilo in a three-passenger plane, while the longer circle-island tours from Kona are $249 in a five-passenger plane.

Accommodations

Accommodations in Hilo are hardly ever booked up, and they're reasonably priced. Sounds great, but some hotels have "gone condo" to survive while others have simply shut their doors, so there aren't as many choices as there once were. During the Merrie Monarch Festival in April, the entire town is booked solid! The best hotels are clustered along Banyan Drive, with a few gems tucked away on the city streets. There are no luxury hotels in Hilo.

BANYAN DRIVE HOTELS $50-100

The low-slung **Hilo Seaside Hotel** (126 Banyan Way, 808/935-0821 or 800/560-5557, www.sand-seaside.com) is owned by the Hawaiian Kimi family. Like the others in this small island chain, it's clean and well kept and has Polynesian-inspired decor with a 1960s or 1970s feel. On the property is Coconut Grill, which serves basic Japanese and American breakfasts and dinners. Room prices are $88 standard, $100 superior garden view, $110 deluxe pool view, and $110 garden kitchenette; third person charge is $10, and breakfast is included for all but the standard rooms. Add approximately $25 for a room/car package. Ask about off-season, AAA, and AARP rates, or book online and save. Each room has a lanai, air-conditioner, ceiling fan, television, and small refrigerator, and there is a coin laundry facility on premises. The grounds are laid out around a well-tended central courtyard garden, and the pool is secluded and away from the street; to the front, a large koi pond lies in another garden. At this family-style hotel, the friendly staff goes out of its way to make you feel welcome. Located across from the Ice Pond, this is a good choice for a moderate price at a convenient location.

Uncle Billy's Hilo Bay Hotel (87 Banyan Dr., 808/935-0861 or 800/442-5841 in Hawaii, 800/367-5102 Mainland, www.unclebilly.com) is sandwiched between two larger hotels on the Waiakea Peninsula. The Hilo Bay's blue metal roof and white louvered shutters, along with the lobby's rattan furniture and thatched longhouse theme are pure 1950s Polynesian Hawaii. Definitely have a look. There is free parking and a small guest pool at the shoreline. This is a no-frills establishment that aims for the economy Mainland business traveler and interisland visitor, but all rooms are clean and air-conditioned with a TV and phone. Rooms run $84–94, studio kitchenettes $94–104—good value for the money, but don't expect anything too plush or luxurious. Numerous discounts are available, so be sure to ask. The in-house Fish and Steakhouse restaurant serves reasonably priced food for breakfast, dinner, and Sunday brunch, and a free hula show is presented every evening at 6 P.M.; lunch is served in the Pineapple Lounge off the lobby. Uncle Billy's General Store, where you can buy everything from beer to sundries and ice cream to resortwear, is part of the complex. Uncle Billy's has a strong local feel. The staff members have spirit and heart and do their best to make your stay a pleasant one.

$100-150

Hawaii Naniloa Hotel (93 Banyan Dr., 808/969-3333 or 800/442-5845 in Hawaii, 800/367-5360 Mainland and Canada, www.naniloa.com) is a 325-room hotel that looks out on Hilo Bay. Rates start at $110 for garden view, $132 for partial ocean view, and $154 for ocean-view rooms; suites are available for $209–264. The Naniloa offers air-conditioning and a TV in all rooms, but only the higher-end rooms have balconies. Other amenities include hotel parking, the Sandalwood and Ting Hao restaurants, a lounge, periodic entertainment at the Crown Room ballroom, a small gift shop, self-service laundry, and two pools. The original hotel dates back more than 60 years and over the years built a fine reputation for value and service. Unfortunately, the Naniloa has grown tired and has gotten a bit raggedy around the edges. It has a million-dollar location but is in need of attention to bring back the high standard that it once maintained. Still, it's very popular for locals traveling between the islands and still a bargain compared to many of the hotels on the Kona side.

$150-250

The **Hilo Hawaiian Hotel** (71 Banyan Dr., 808/935-9361 or 800/367-5004 Mainland and Canada, www.castleresorts.com/HHH) occupies the most beautiful grounds of any hotel in Hilo. From the vantage of the hotel's colonnaded veranda, you overlook formal gardens, Coconut Island, and Hilo Bay. Designed as a huge arc, the hotel's architecture blends well with its surroundings and expresses the theme set by the bay, that of a long, sweeping crescent. While neat, clean, well maintained, and with all necessary amenities, the hotel still has somewhat of a 1970s feel. If you want flash and glamour, try one of the new resorts on the Kona side. However, for down-home quality with a touch of class in Hilo, you can't do better than the Hilo Hawaiian. Prices at this property run $135–165 for a standard room, $155–185 for a superior, $185–205 for an ocean-view room, and $200–405 for suites and kitchettes; all rooms have a/c, phone, and cable color TV, plus there's a swimming pool on the property. Guest services include a gift shop, launderette, free parking, and a front-desk safety deposit box. The Queen's Court restaurant, Wai'oli Lounge, and the Tranquil Waters day spa are all on the property for guests' convenience. This is the best accommodation Hilo has to offer.

HOTELS NEAR DOWNTOWN

$50-100

Dolphin Bay Hotel (333 'Iliahi St., 808/935-1466 or 877/935-1466, john@dolphinbayhotel.com, www.dolphinbay-hilo.com) is a sparkling little gem—simply the best hotel bargain in Hilo, one of those places where you get more than you pay for. It sits on a side street in the Pu'u'eo section of town at the north end of Hilo Bay. John Alexander, the owner/manager, is at the front desk nearly every day. He's a font of information about the Big Island and will happily dispense advice on how to make your day trips fulfilling. The hotel was built by his father, who spent years in Japan, and you'll be happy to discover this influence when you sink deep into the *ofuro*-type tubs in every room. All 18 units have small but sufficient modern kitchens. There are no telephones in the rooms but there is a pay phone in the lobby. Rates for two people are $79 for a standard room, $89 for a superior room, $109 for a one-bedroom, and from $129 for a two-bedroom fully furnished unit; additional guests $10 each per night. Weekly rates can be arranged. The more deluxe units upstairs have open-beamed ceilings and lanai and, with three spacious rooms, feel like apartments. No swimming pool or a/c here, but there are color TVs and fans with excellent cross ventilation. The grounds and housekeeping are immaculate. No meals are provided because of the kitchens, but hotel guests can partake of free bananas, papayas, and other exotic fruits found in hanging baskets in the lobby, as well as free coffee. Walking the short path down to the stream in the morning from the parking lot in the back is a great pick-me-up to start the day. Make reservations, because everyone who has found the Dolphin Bay comes back again and again.

The Wild Ginger Inn (100 Pu'u'eo St., 808/935-5556 or 899/882-1887, www.wildgingerinn.com) is a bubble-gum pink and vibrant green plantation-style hotel from the 1950s, so don't expect the floors to be level or everything to be spotless. It's located a short two blocks from the northern edge of downtown, a few steps from the Dolphin Bay Hotel. An open-air lobby leads to a corridor veranda overlooking the thick greenery of the garden, with a small view of the bay in the distance. A double hammock and vintage rattan chairs in the lobby are for your relaxation. Each of the more than 30 rooms—very basic but reasonably clean—has a private bathroom and ceiling fan, but no telephones. Room rates run $55 for a garden-level room with a double bed; $65 for a room on the main level with a king-size bed, television, and a small refrigerator; and $80–90 for the more spacious suites. Discounts are available for longer stays. Every morning, fruit, juice, and pastries are put out for guests. The inn is completely nonsmoking. Internet access and laundry facilities are available to guests. With new owners in 2005 came new paint, upgraded bathrooms, some new carpet, curtains, needed structural repairs, and a garden makeover, but the plantation style has been kept.

BED-AND-BREAKFASTS

B&Bs are located here and there around town. Several are strung along the highway north of town, a number are out toward Richardson's Beach Park, and a handful are scattered above town in residential pockets.

$50–100

Accepting paying guests for a couple decades and others before that, Amy Gamble Lannan's **Lihi Kai** bed-and-breakfast (30 Kahoa Road, 808/935-7865) is a treasure and the longest running B&B in town. This sedate, contemporary-style house sits on the edge of a cliff just north of town and has a million-dollar view of Hilo Bay; it's less than two miles north of the Singing Bridge. Guests of the two rooms share a bathroom and partake with Amy of a filling breakfast of fruit, pastries, and coffee to start the day. A small swimming pool occupies part of the yard. While Lihi Kai is a treasure, Amy is the jewel. Full of life and love, with a witty sense of humor, she can offer you insight on where to eat, what to see, how to get around, and where to find adventure. Rooms are $65 a night plus $5 a night for less than three nights. Cash or personal check, please; no credit cards. Because the house is so close to the cliff edge, she's reluctant to take children under age eight. Make reservations well in advance, as her guests return again and again.

Holmes' Sweet Home B&B (107 Ko'ula St., 808/961-9089, fax 808/934-0711, homswhom@gte.net, www.hilohawaiibandb.com) is the residence of John and Charlotte Holmes. On a quiet residential cul-de-sac high above town (more than 700 feet in elevation) with a view of Hilo Bay and the city lights, this B&B provides two comfy rooms priced $80–95 that feature a private entrance to a common room, guest refrigerator and microwave, and private bathrooms. A tropical continental breakfast is included.

The first place out along the Keaukaha strip is **Maureen's Bed and Breakfast** (1896 Kalaniana'ole Ave., 808/935-9018 or 800/935-9018, info@maureenbnb.com, www.maureenbnb.com). Surrounded by landscaped lawns and koi ponds, this B&B was built in 1932 from redwood and cedar brought from the Mainland. With its high-ceilinged living room, arched windows and doors, balconies, and a Japanese tearoom, it has plenty of charm in an East-meets-West kind of way. Comfortable and pleasingly decorated, the five rooms rent for $60–110 and have semi-private baths. A filling breakfast is always included. This is a bargain and an all-around good place.

$100-150

A short way past the Singing Bridge, take the first right turn to get to **The Bay House B&B** (42 Pukihae St., 808/961-6311 or 888/235-8195, bigbayhouse@excite.com, www.bayhousehawaii.com). This modern house with its three plush guest rooms sits on the cliff over Hilo Bay, as close as you can get to downtown Hilo. Rooms run $120 a night and each has a king-size or queen-size bed, private bath, television, telephone, and oceanside lanai; from each you can watch the cruise ships come and go from port or the full moon shining on the bay. Island-inspired decorations bring out the individual color and character of each room. Guests share a common entrance room with books, magazines, and refrigerator, and receive a breakfast of fruit, juice, pastries, coffee, and other goodies you can have at your leisure when you wake up. Set even closer to the edge of the cliff is a hot tub, perfect for a starry-night soak. The Bay House is comfortable, clean, and quiet.

Set on a bluff overlooking the ocean just over two miles north of town is **Hale Kai Hawaii Bed and Breakfast** (111 Honoli'i Pali, 808/935-6330, stay@hakekaihawaii.com, www.halekaihawaii.com). This modern house has a small pool and hot tub. A sitting room with refrigerator, books, and television is shared, but each of the four rooms has its own entrance and bath and looks out over the ocean. Room rates run $115–130 a night with the suite at $140, two nights minimum, and this includes a sit-down, homemade breakfast.

Not far from Richardson's Beach Park is **At the Beach with Friends** (369 Nene St., 808/934-8040, beach@hilo.net, www.bed-and-breakfast-hilo-hawaii.com), a contemporary bed-and-breakfast that's built in a garden next to one of the area's many anchialine ponds. The three guest rooms, in a separate part of the house nearest the pond, have their own entrance, yet are connected to the common room where a continental breakfast is served each morning. Room rates are $130–150.

Located on 22 acres of macadamia nut and tropical fruit orchards, upstream and on the north side of Boiling Pots, with views over Hilo and the ocean, and with the 120-foot Kulaniapia Waterfall on the property, is **The Inn at Kulaniapia Falls** (808/935-6789 or 866/935-6789, www.waterfall.net). This contemporary-style B&B features four large second-story suites in its main house, all with private, granite-tiled baths and covered balconies; two suites face the ocean, two face inland. The room rate is $109 double, with $20 for an additional guest, and an expanded continental breakfast of tropical fruits, pastries, and coffee comes with an egg dish. Guests share the first-floor common room, a blend of island-style and Japanese motifs, and can use the kitchen and a barbecue grill. Additionally, the newer, three-floor, one-bedroom Pagoda House on property is also for rent at $200–250 a night. About four miles upland over a paved road—turn at Amau'ulu Road just north of the Wailuku River and follow the signs—only the sound of the waterfall and the birds disturb the quiet.

Located in a quiet, older residential neighborhood just a stroll from Boiling Pots State Park is **The Old Hawaiian B&B** (1492 Wailuku Dr., 808/961-2816 or 877/961-2816, ironwood@flex.com, www.thebigislandvacation.com). This renovated and updated home has two rooms, each accessed by separate entrances off the back lanai, from where there's a short walk through the yard to a river overlook. The large Sunrise Room at $110 has a sunken tub and is a good value. The smaller Bamboo

Room at $80 is more intimate. A simple continental breakfast is served on the lanai.

$150-250

Shipman House Bed and Breakfast Inn (131 Ka'iulani St., tel./fax 808/934-8002 or 800/627-8447, innkeeper@hilo-hawaii.com, www.hilo-hawaii.com) is the grandest B&B in all Hawaii. This Victorian house is one of the few such grand houses in Hawaii and was once the home of the Shipman family, one of the most prominent Big Island landowners, and now presided over by a Shipman descendent. The main house offers three guest rooms with antique beds, private bath, and stately views through enormous windows. Other guests will

SHIPMAN HOUSE

A house can have presence, and, if it's brushed by magic like the Tin Man in *The Wizard of Oz,* it can even attain a heart. The Shipman House was a purchase motivated by love and occupied by a large, dynamic family. The Shipman House, known locally as "the Castle," perched on five verdant acres high above Hilo, has such a heart.

After a quarter century on the Mainland, Barbara Ann Andersen, great-granddaughter of William H. "Willie" Shipman, the original owner, returned with her children and her husband Gary to restore to its former grandeur the residence where she spent her childhood summers, Easters, and Christmases. The house was figuratively stripped to its petticoats and outfitted in grand style.

To appreciate the Shipman House fully, you must know its history, which goes back as far as the first tall ships that arrived from New England bearing the missionaries and their faith to the old kingdom. The first members of the family to reside in Hawaii were the Rev. William C. Shipman and his wife Jane, who arrived in the 1850s. The Rev. Shipman died young, leaving Jane alone and in need of a means to support herself and their three children; she accomplished this by opening a Hawaiian girls' boarding school in Hilo. Later she met and married Mr. William H. Reed, a famous engineer responsible for most of Hilo's bridges and for whom, by strange coincidence, "Reed's Island," the section of Hilo where the mansion sits, was named.

One of the boys, William H. "Willie" Shipman, married Mary Melekahuia Johnson, one of the young Hawaiian ladies at his mother's school. Mary was descended from the ruling *ali'i.* Willie originally determined to study medicine, but one day his stepfather, Mr. Reed, made him an offer he couldn't refuse, saying, "Son, if you will give up medicine and take up the study of business, I'll give you a ranch to run." Willie knew a good opportunity when he saw it, and over the years he became one of the largest landholders on the Big Island, founding W. H. Shipman, Ltd.

Around the turn of the 20th century, Mary often implored Willie to take her for a drive, which would invariably pass by a lovely home being built on Ka'iulani Street. Holding his hand and looking into his eyes she would ask, "Willie, won't you buy me that house?" and he would reply, "I can't. The Wilsons own it." Finally, one day as they passed the house, Mary asked once again, but this time Willie smiled and said, "Yes, my dear. It's been ours for 30 days." They moved into the house in April 1901.

Mary was a dear friend of Hawaii's last queen, Lili'uokalani, who would visit at the Shipman house whenever she was in Hilo. While there the queen would preside over simple but elegant "poi luncheons," always seated at the place of honor at the huge round koa dining room table, where she could look out the bay windows at Hilo below. After lunch, Lili'uokalani would slip away to the library to clandestinely savor a fine cigar.

To arrive at the Castle, ascend Waianuenue Avenue to Ka'iulani Street. There, turn right, cross the bridge, veer left, and you'll see the Shipman House on the rise. The wraparound lanai was a necessity even for well-to-do lodge in the Cottage, a separate building on the grounds, originally built for the express purpose of accommodating visitors. The Cottage contains two spacious bedrooms, each with queen-size bed, window seats, and private bath. Both rooms have private entrances, ceiling fans, and a small refrigerator. This is strictly a no-smoking establishment and a "no TV zone," and children are not encouraged, as there are so many antiques in the house and a steep ravine outside. Room rates are $205–225 single or double; $25 per extra person, add $25 for a single-night stay. The library is open to guests, along with use of the 1912 Steinway piano whose keys were once tickled by Lili'uokalani, and you can look around the

families, who, like all Hawaii residents, spent a great deal of time outdoors. The broad landing provides a wonderful view of Hilo and the sea in the distance, with wildflowers and tangled greenery cascading into a tropical bowl at your feet. Two stained glass windows, encircled by a laurel wreath, the classic sign of a congenial home, greet you on entering. The Double Parlor, the first floor of the rounded three-story Tower that caps the home, is magnificent. Everywhere is glass – old-fashioned, handmade curved glass – its mottled and rippled texture giving a surrealistic twist to the panorama.

Pad along on the burnished fir flooring past koa-wainscoted walls to enter the dining room, where an enormous dining table and *pune'e* (movable couch) are still very functional. The back area of the home is called the conservatory, really the center of the home for day-to-day life, where the family took their meals. Just off it is a solarium and the butler's pantry, next to an Otis in-home elevator, installed in the 1930s and probably Hilo's first. Here, too, is a bedroom, formerly reserved for guests like Jack London and his wife Charmian. The peaceful library, waiting to engulf an afternoon reader within its impressive 12-foot ceilings, is warmed by a brick fireplace with a koa mantel and is fringed by built-in koa bookcases.

Ascend the central staircase to the second floor, where once upon a time a ballroom adorned in white wallpaper with twinkling stars swayed with dancing and music; nowadays part has been converted into a bedroom. At the back near the elevator, a window opening to a catwalk led to a small room built over the water tank. That room served as grandfather Willie's "office," his haven from the clamor of 10 children! In the back corner is a second bedroom. A spiral staircase ascends to the attic, where a "canvas room" was the children's dormitory. A large, freestanding credenza holds hats and antique clothing. Also in the attic is the entrance to the tower, a wine barrel of a room with wraparound windows.

Shipman House is once again one of the finest homes in all Hawaii in which to spend a quiet and elegant visit.

© ROBERT NILSEN

"the Castle"

house on your own in those areas where the doors are open. On Wednesday evenings, a hula class is held on the lanai and guests can participate. Breakfast, served 7:45–9 A.M. (earlier upon request, and special diets are accommodated), is an expanded continental with homemade cereals, assorted local fruits (there are 20 varieties of fruit trees on the property), fruit juices, Kona coffee, yogurt, fruit bread, muffins, popovers, or cinnamon rolls. Check in is 3–6 P.M., and checkout is at 10 A.M. The Shipman House is on both the State and National Registers of Historic Places.

Located a bit farther up Reed's Island is the **Waterfall Inn Bed and Breakfast** (240 Ka'iulani St., 808/969-3407 or 888/808-4456, info@waterfallsinn.com, www.waterfallsinn.com). Perched on the cliff overlooking the Wailuku River, this house is the stately Thomas Guard House from 1916, also on the National Register of Historic Places. Lovingly preserved for appreciative guests, this spacious and eminently comfortable house hints at the grandeur of families of position from the early 1900s. Four upstairs bedrooms have been turned into guest rooms that run $140–190 a night, two-night minimum. Filled with old-style charm and kept in the spirit of the era, yet each room has a separate bathroom and has been updated with telephone, television, and mini-refrigerator. A sit-down continental breakfast is served 7:30–9 A.M. in the sunroom and makes a nourishing start to the day.

HOSTELS

Arnott's Lodge (98 Apapane Rd., 808/969-7097, mahalo@arnottslodge.com, www.arnottslodge.com) is a reasonably priced budget accommodation—safe, clean, and friendly—that offers most everything a traveler might expect while on the road. Follow Kamehameha Avenue east until it turns into Kalaniana'ole Avenue; in about five minutes you'll see a lighted yellow sign pointing seaward to Arnott's. Those without private transportation can be picked up by a free shuttle service operating 8 A.M.–7:30 P.M., with outbound departures set at 8 A.M., 12:30 P.M., and 5:30 P.M. A ride downtown or to the airport costs only $2, or $3 round-trip. Arnott's also offers inexpensive expeditions that are some of the best guided tours on the island. Other services are coin laundry, pay telephones, reasonable Internet access, safe storage of valuables and backpacks at no cost, low-cost use of bicycles, and an inexpensive continental breakfast. Dormitory bunks—male, female, and co-ed—at $20 are spotlessly clean and cooled by cross ventilation and ceiling fans. Single rooms with bath, kitchen, and living room shared with one other room are $42; a double room with the same setup is $52. With private baths, the singles and doubles run $67. A self-contained suite with two bedrooms, one with a double bed and the other with twins, includes a bathroom, kitchen, and living room for $130 for up to five people; each additional person is $15. All room charges are inclusive of tax, and stays are limited to seven days. Check-in is until 8 P.M.; late check-in is $5 extra, and no check-in after 10 P.M. Camping on the lawn with your own tent is an option for $10 per person. Leisure time can be spent in a large entertainment area, where you can watch one of a huge selection of videos. A covered lanai with picnic tables has barbecue grills for your convenience, and to the side is a lanai platform built in a tree. Arnott's is an excellent hostel/lodge offering a quality, hassle-free stay with an international clientele.

Hilo Bay Hostel (101 Waianuenue Ave., 808/933-2771, www.hawaiihostel.net) is perfectly situated to be close to downtown Hilo. Occupying a former hotel that was built in 1913, the hostel has kept much of the old charm but brought in modern amenities. The wide staircase leads up from the street level to the common room, lit through its high ceiling by large skylights. Check in at the office and settle in for a comfortable stay. Clean, well-kept, and well-run, the hostel has a kitchen for everyone to use, and outdoor garden, Internet access, storage lockers, and an information board to help you decide what to see and where to go. Quiet time starts at 10 P.M. Dorm rooms run $18, while a private room is $48 and a private room with its own bathroom is $58. You're in the heart of town here, so it's just a stroll to restaurants, coffee shops, and the bay.

Food

Hilo is the largest city on the island and supports plenty of restaurants. While a number of upscale, nouveau cuisine establishments are making a go of it in town, by far the majority of eateries in Hilo are humble shops selling local foods. Restaurants here represent the variety of people who have made Hawaii their home, so ethnic foods from Europe and Asia abound. The following is a sampling of what's available by area.

DOWNTOWN

Local Style

If you want to eat anything but uninspired "American standard" in Hilo after 9 P.M., go to **Nori's Saimin and Snacks** (688 Kino'ole St., 808/935-9133, 10:30 A.M.–3 P.M. Mon., 10:30 A.M.–3 P.M. and 4 P.M.–midnight Tues.–Sat., 10:30 A.M.–10 P.M. Sun.), stuck away and hard to spot (but worth it) in a little strip business across from the bowling alley. Here you can have a totally "island experience" in a humble, honest restaurant that specializes in authentic "local grinds." Inside, where the service is slow but friendly, are plywood bench seat booths and Formica tables, and the "that's what you really look like" glow of fluorescent lighting. Boiling pots hold saimin of all sorts, which is generously ladled into steaming bowls and topped with fresh vegetables. Also on the menu are plate lunches with a scoop of macaroni salad, and a variety of Chinese, Japanese, and Korean dishes. Two people can eat until they waddle at Nori's for about $15. There's no atmosphere, but the food is authentic and good.

All trips to Hilo must include a brief stop at **Low International Food** (808/969-6652, 9 A.M.–8 P.M. daily except Wed.), long occupying the corner of Kilauea and Ponahawai Streets, where *everyone* comes for the unique bread. Some of the more fanciful loaves are made from taro, breadfruit, guava, mango, passion fruit, coconut, banana, pumpkin, and cinnamon. The so-you-want-to-taste-it-all rainbow bread is a combination of taro, guava, and sweet bread. Loaves cost around $6, and arrangements can be made to ship them anywhere in the country. Breakfast, lunch, and dinner plates, most under $7, range from the shrimp black bean to grilled mahimahi, *lau lau,* and Korean chicken. Choose a table under the pavilion and enjoy your picnic in downtown Hilo.

Hawaiian Regional

Modern and chic with a black-and-white checkerboard floor, linen on the tables, an open-air kitchen, a high ceiling with ceiling fans, and the calming effect of ferns and flowers, is **Café Pesto** (308 Kamehameha Ave., 808/969-6640, 11 A.M.–9 P.M., until 10 P.M. Fri.–Sat.) in the historic S. Hata Building. One of Hilo's fine established restaurants, it offers affordable gourmet food in an open, airy, and unpretentious setting that looks out across the avenue to the bay. Pizzas from the 'ohi'a wood–fired oven can be anything from a simple cheese pie for $8.50 to a large Greek or chili-grilled shrimp pizza for $18; you can also create your own. Lunchtime features sandwiches, calzones, and pasta. For dinner, try an appetizer like Asian Pacific crab cakes or sesame-crusted Hamakua goat cheese. Heartier appetites will be satisfied with the main dinner choices, mostly $15–28, which might be mango-glazed chicken, island seafood risotto, or a combination beef tenderloin and tiger prawns with garlic mashed potatoes. Follow this with a warm coconut tart, liliko'i cheesecake, or crème brûlée and you'll be set for the evening. Café Pesto also has a brass-railed bar where you can order caffe latte or a fine glass of wine to top off your meal in one of the best island-cuisine restaurants in Hilo.

Often considered the best restaurant in town, and certainly the fanciest, is **Kaikodo** (60 Keawe St., 808/961-2558, 11 A.M.–2:30 P.M. Mon.–Sat., 10:30 A.M.–2:30 P.M. Sun., 5–9:30 P.M. daily, until 10 P.M. Fri. and Sat.), located at the corner of Keawe Street and Waianuenue Avenue in what was the historic Toyama Building, and previous to that, the First Trust Building. With first-rate decor and Chinese and Japanese touches, the restaurant offers a sophisticated menu for the most discriminating diner. Lunch offerings might be a tapioca-crusted ono burger or pork *lau lau,* while dinner brings such entrées as gomashio-seared ahi, togarashi-grilled rib eye, or shrimp pasta. Expect most entrées in the $20–27 range. Sushi is also available, as is a *pu pu* menu through the afternoon. Save room for triple berry cobbler or hot lava cake for dessert, a cordial, or after dinner wine.

Italian

Sicilian fishermen would feel right at home at **Pescatore** (235 Keawe St., 808/969-9090, 11 A.M.–2 P.M. and 5:30–9 P.M.) for some of the finest Italian pasta and panini sandwiches in Hilo. The building has had multiple uses over the years and, as part of its colorful past, served as a house of ill repute. It is now a wood-paneled room with high-backed, red velvet armchairs and formally set tables with white linens. Italian-style chandeliers, lace curtains, and koa trim add to the elegance. When the Italian in you desires antipasti, minestrone soup, cioppino classico alla pescatore, gamberetti Alfredo, or any number of other seafood dishes, head for Pescatore. Many dinner entrées run $16–25. While the main entrées are worthy in and of themselves, Pescatore is known for its ahi carpaccio appetizer and double chocolate truffle and homemade macadamia nut amaretto bread pudding desserts. You can't go wrong here, the best Italian place in town.

Mexican

Reuben's Mexican Food (336 Kamehameha Ave., 808/961-2552, 11 A.M.–9 P.M. Mon.–Fri., noon–9 P.M. Saturday) will enliven your palate with its zesty dishes. The interior has the feel of Old Mexico with its bright murals and collection of sombreros and piñatas. Mariachi music wafts through the room, and you better like it because Pancho Villa is keeping an eye on you from the wall! The lengthy menu is reasonable, mostly $9.50–13, with selections like carne asada, steak tacos, chicken flautas, crab enchiladas, and a vegetarian bean chili verde burrito. All are served with beans and rice, and the portions are huge. The bar has a large selection of Mexican, American, and European *cerveza,* but Reuben's is most famous for its margaritas—more than one will get you acting like a human chimichanga. *¡Olé!*

Set adjacent to Kalakaua Park is **Island Cantina Restaurant** (110 Kalakaua St., 808/969-7009, 11 A.M.–9 P.M. daily). Small and intimate, this restaurant is more sophisticated and has more of an American Southwest flavor than Reuben's. On the menu are fajitas, tacos, tamales, enchiladas, and burritos, blackened pork chops, and fish and steak meals, many in the $11–15 range. Dining is made more enjoyable each evening with live music during dinner.

Japanese

Tsunami Grill and Tempura (250 Keawe St., 808/961-6789, 11 A.M.–2 P.M. and 5–9 P.M. Mon.–Sat.) Like many of the restaurants in town, the Tsunami Grill has its own loyal local clientele. While it's short on decor, the food is excellent and the prices are unbeatable. You'll walk away stuffed on traditional Japanese food like gyoza, udon, soba, katsu, tempura, donburi, and saimin, or bento for about $9.

For food of the raw variety, head across the street to **Ocean Sushi** (239 Keawe St., 808/961-6625, 10 A.M.–2 P.M. and 4:30–9 P.M. Mon.–Sat.), Tsunami Grill's sister shop. Ocean Sushi has a laundry list of possibilities on its menu, both traditional and contemporary, where most sushi and rolls run $4.50 or less. Also on the menu are the more expensive sushi boxes and sashimi platters. BYOB OK, no corkage fee.

Chinese

The **New Star Chinese Restaurant** (172 Kilauea Ave, 808/934-8874, 10 A.M.–9 P.M. except Tuesday) is where to head if you want to eat with "the people." The servings are generous and for $8 you can fill up. This large restaurant is clean, the service is friendly, and the dining experience, while certainly not fancy, is definitely authentic. Takeout available.

Thai

The tiny **Naung Mai Thai Kitchen** (86 Kilauea Ave., 808/934-7540, 11–2 P.M. Mon.–Fri., 5–8:30 P.M. Mon.–Thurs., 5–9 P.M. Fri. and Sat.) puts out some of the best Thai food in the state at very reasonable prices. Although nicely decorated, people come for the flavors and fresh ingredients. It has a reputation for spicy foods and is perhaps best known for its pad Thai and spring rolls. Once you try it, you'll want to go back, but go early as the half dozen tables and booths tend to fill up fast. BYOB OK, no corkage fee.

Very clean and down-home proud, the **Royal Siam Thai Restaurant** (70 Mamo St., 808/961-6100, 11 A.M.–2 P.M. Mon.–Sat. and 5–9 P.M. daily) serves up tasty Thai treats. Appetizers and soups include crispy Thai noodle and coconut chicken soup. Entrées range from simple fried rice dishes and curries to meat dishes and seafood selections, mostly in the $7–11 range. There are specials nightly. Vegetarian selections are numerous and portions are large. This little restaurant gets good reviews even if the food is not extraordinary.

Vietnamese

Yen's Café (235 Waianuenue Ave., 808/933-2808, 10:30 A.M.–8 P.M. Mon.–Sat.) is a little hole-in-the-wall-type place with bright lights and Formica table booths, but the food is much better than the surroundings. Try *pho,* a traditional hot noodle soup, grilled shrimp rice plate, or squid in black bean sauce. More recognizable dishes, like kung pao shrimp, ginger chicken, or beef fried rice are also on the menu, with most dishes under $7.

Coffee Shop

Bears' Coffee (106 Keawe, 808/935-0708, 6:30 A.M.–5 P.M. Mon.–Sat., 7:30 A.M.–noon Sun.) is an upscale coffee shop renowned for its breakfasts, but coffee is available in the morning even before they start up the grill. Bears' features Belgian waffles (made from malted flour), bagels, and an assortment of egg dishes. Lunch is hearty deli sandwiches of turkey, pastrami, chicken fillet, tuna, or ham, along with "designer" bagels and salads. You can get most anything for under $5. Beverages include Italian sodas, homemade lemonade, and a large selection of coffee, cappuccino, and caffe latte. All are perfect with desserts like carrot cake, Bears' brownies, cheesecake, and pies. A great place to relax, read the morning paper, check out the Teddy Bears on the wall, or watch Hilo life go by from the sidewalk bistro tables.

Bakery

The specialty of **O'Keefe & Sons** (374 Kino'ole St., 808/934-9334, 6 A.M.–5 P.M. Mon.–Fri., 6 A.M.–3 P.M. Sat.) is artisan bread, but it's also a favorite lunch spot for downtown office workers who stop by for a tasty sandwich made from freshly baked loaves. Rolls, buns, cakes, and a variety of pastries are also available.

Sweet Treats

Places for a refreshing scoop of ice cream downtown are **Tropical Dreams Ice Cream** (9 A.M.–6 P.M. Mon.–Thurs., 9 A.M.–9:30 P.M. Fri.–Sat.), at the refurbished Kress Building along Kamehameha Ave., and **Hilo Homemade Ice Cream** (41 Waianuenue Ave. 808/933-1520, noon–6 P.M. Mon.–Sat., noon–5 P.M. Sun.). Hilo Homemade Ice Cream also has a shop at Hilo Tropical Gardens along Kalaniana'ole Avenue on the way to the beaches.

Hilo Seed and Snacks (15 Waianuenue Ave., 808/935-7355, 9 A.M.–5 P.M. weekdays, 9 A.M.–2 P.M. Sat.) and **Kilauea Preserve Center** (187 Kilauea Ave., 808/935-8360) sell authentic crackseed. If you've never tried this unique island snack, here's your opportunity.

NEAR BANYAN DRIVE

American

Ken's House of Pancakes (1730 Kamehameha Ave., 808/935-8711) is a place to get a good

American meal for a good price. The food is nothing to write home about, but the breakfasts are filling, and the lunches and dinners are just what you'd expect. Everyone knows and loves Ken's. Open 24 hours every day of the year, it's conveniently located near Banyan Drive.

Queen's Court Restaurant (808/935-9361) at the Hilo Hawaiian Hotel on Banyan Drive offers a nightly buffet. Throughout the week, buffets include a prime rib and crab buffet Monday–Thursday, a legendary seafood buffet on Friday, and a Hawaiian seafood buffet

HAWAIIAN FOOD AND ISLAND TREATS

Hawaiian cuisine, the oldest in the islands, consists of wholesome, well-prepared, and delicious foods. All you have to do on arrival is notice the size of some of the local boys (and women) to know immediately that food to them is indeed a happy and serious business. An oft-heard island joke is that "local men don't eat until they're full; they eat until they're tired." Many Hawaiian dishes have become standard fare at a variety of restaurants, eaten at one time or another by anyone who spends time in the islands, but the best still is served at local-style restaurants. Hawaiian food in general is called *kaukau;* cooked food is *kapahaki,* and something broiled is called *ka'ola.* Any of these prefixes on a menu will let you know that Hawaiian food is served. Usually inexpensive, it will definitely fill you and keep you going.

TRADITIONAL FAVORITES

In old Hawaii, although the sea meant life, and indeed a great variety of fish and other seafood was eaten, many more people were involved in cultivating beautifully tended garden plots of taro, sugarcane, breadfruit, and various sweet potatoes *('uala)* than with fishing. They husbanded pigs – a favorite for the *imu* oven – and barkless dogs *('ilio),* and they prized *moa* (chicken) for their feathers and meat but found eating the eggs repulsive. Their only farming implement was the *'o'o,* a sharpened hardwood digging stick.

The Hawaiians were the best farmers of Polynesia, and the first thing they planted was taro, a tuberous root created by the gods at the same time humans were created. This main staple of the old Hawaiians was pounded into poi. Every lu'au will have poi, a glutinous purple paste. It comes in liquid consistencies referred to as one-, two-, or three-finger poi. The fewer fingers you need to eat it, the thicker it is. Poi is one of the most nutritious carbohydrates known, but people unaccustomed to it find it bland and tasteless. Some of the best, fermented for a day or so, has an acidic bite. Poi is made to be eaten *with* something, but locals who love it pop it in their mouths and smack their lips. Those unaccustomed to it will suffer constipation if they eat too much.

While poi fell out of favor during the middle of the 20th century, it is once again becoming popular, and several sizable factories are now producing poi for sale. Waipi'o Valley is a big poi-producing region on the Big Island. You

PHOTO COURTESY OF HVCB/HAWAII TOURISM JAPAN

poi

on Saturday and Sunday. All are very good and would give the finest restaurants a run for their money. The buffets run about $30. The dining room is grand in a 1970s sort of way, with large windows overlooking Hilo Bay. Sunday champagne brunch is more of the same quality. Make reservations, especially on seafood night, because the Hilo Hawaiian attracts many Hilo residents who love great food. Breakfast is served 6:30–9:30 A.M. daily. Lunch runs 11:15 A.M.–1:15 P.M. and is à la carte except Wednesday and Friday, when buffets are also featured.

can find plastic containers of this food refrigerated in many supermarkets and local food stores. In addition, deep-fried slices of taro root, plain or spiced, are now packaged and sold like potato chips.

A favorite dessert is *haupia,* a custard made from coconut that is found at most social gatherings. Like a tiny meal in a pouch, *laulau* is a package of meat, fish, and veggies wrapped in *ti* leaves and baked or steamed. *Poke* is a seafood salad made with a variety of seafood, seaweed, and onions that's frequently found on traditional island menus and more and more in fish markets or deli sections of supermarkets. Hawaii even has a festival dedicated to the innovative creation of this dish. One of its ingredients is *limu,* a generic term for edible seaweed that has been gathered as a garnish since precontact times. Many people still gather *limu* from the shoreline and eat it as a salad or mix with ground *kukui* nuts and salt as a relish. There's no other seaweed except *limu* in Hawaii. Because of this, the heavy, fishy-ocean smell that people associate with the sea (but is actually that of seaweed) is absent in Hawaii.

A favorite Hawaiian snack is *'opihi,* small shellfish (limpets) that cling to rocks. *'Opihi* are cut from the shell and eaten raw by all peoples of Hawaii. Those who gather them always leave some on the rocks for the future. *'A'ama* are the ubiquitous little black crabs that you'll spot on rocks and around pier areas. For fun, local fishermen try to catch them with poles, but the more efficient way is to throw a fish head into a plastic bucket and wait for the crabs to crawl in and trap themselves. The 'a'ama are about as big as two fingers and make delicious eating.

A traditional liquor made from *ti* root is *'okolehao.* It literally means "iron bottom," from the iron blubber pots used to ferment it.

ISLAND TREATS

Certain finger foods, fast foods, and island treats are unique to Hawaii. Here are some of the best and most popular.

Pronounced as in "Winnie the Pooh Pooh," and originally the name of a small shellfish, *pu pu* is now a general term that has come to mean hors d'oeuvres or any finger food. These can be anything from crackers to cracked crab. Often, they're given free at lounges and bars and can even include chicken drumettes, fish kabobs, and tempura. At a good display of them you can have a free meal.

A sweet of Chinese origin, **crackseed** can be any number of preserved and seasoned fruits and seeds. Favorites include coconut, watermelon, pumpkin seeds, mango, plum, and papaya. Distinctive in taste, they take some getting used to but make great trail snacks. They are available in all island markets. Also look for dried fish (cuttlefish) on racks, usually near the crackseed. Nutritious and delicious, it makes a great snack.

Shave ice, a real island institution, makes the Mainland "snow cone" melt into insignificance. Special machines literally shave ice to a fluffy consistency. It's mounded into a paper cone and your choice from dozens of exotic island syrups is generously poured over it. Get a straw and spoon and just slurp away.

Taro chips are like potato chips but made from the taro root. If you can find them fresh, buy a bunch, as they are mostly available packaged.

Two sweets from the Portuguese, *malasadas* are holeless doughnuts and *pao dolce* is sweet bread. Sold in island bakeries, they're great for breakfast or as treats.

Continental

Harrington's (135 Kalaniana'ole Ave., 808/961-4966, 11 A.M.–2 P.M. and 5:30–9:30 P.M. daily) is a longtime institution in town that overlooks the Ice Pond at Reed's Bay. A sunset cocktail or dinner is enhanced with the melodic strains of live jazz, contemporary, or Hawaiian music playing softly in the background on the weekends. The continental cuisine of mostly steak and seafood features appetizers like seafood chowder, mushroom tempura, and escargot in casserole. Although the eggplant parmigiana is vegetarian, other mostly meat entrées include prawns scampi, scallops chardonnay, calamari meunière, thinly sliced Slavic steak (the house specialty), prime rib au jus, and chicken teriyaki go for $16–24. A simpler lunch menu runs mostly under $15. Much appreciated by locals, the menu hasn't changed much since the 1970s. While not inspired, Harrington's turns out eminently pleasing food in a pleasant, convivial atmosphere.

Japanese

Nihon Restaurant (123 Lihiwai St., 808/969-1133, 11 A.M.–1:30 P.M. and 5–9 P.M. Mon.–Sat.), a second-story establishment raised up on pilings and overlooking both Lili'uokalani Gardens and the bay, presents authentic Japanese meals, an excellent sushi bar, and combination dinners along with cultural and artistic displays. What you get here is like what you'd expect from a restaurant in Japan, although somewhat Americanized, with most everything under $19.

Chinese

Ting Hao Mandarin Chinese Restaurant (808/935-8888) at the Naniloa Hotel on Banyan Drive has an emphasis on seafood but does the usual long list of meat and vegetarian dishes as well. Most are under $13, except for the abalone, lobster, and crab dishes, which go for more than $30. If you are staying in the Banyan Drive area, this is a convenient and deserving restaurant.

Thai

Sombat's Fresh Thai Cuisine (808/969-9336, 10:30 A.M.–2 P.M. and 5–9 P.M. weekdays, Sat. 5–9 P.M.) is one of those places that begs for appreciative diners because the food is so tasty. Located in the Waiakea Kai Plaza, near the intersection of Kamehameha and Kanoelehua Avenues, Sombat's is somewhat out of the way but worth the trip. Sombat infuses all her creations with the freshest of herbs and spices, many of which she grows herself, and uses organic produce when available. Dinner dishes run mostly $9–14 and include flat noodle with broccoli and black sauce, green curry with eggplant and basil, and seafood with green bean and red curry sauce.

AROUND TOWN

Local Style

Named after the famous all-Japanese fighting battalion that predated even the famous "442," the **Cafe 100** (969 Kilauea Ave., 808/935-8683, 6:45 A.M.–8:30 P.M. Mon.–Thurs., until 9:30 P.M. Fri.–Sat.) is a Hilo institution. The Miyashiro family has been serving food at its indoor-outdoor restaurant here since the late 1950s. Although the loco moco, a cholesterol atom bomb containing a hamburger and egg atop rice smothered in gravy, was invented at Hilo's Lincoln Grill, the Cafe 100, serving it since 1961, has actually patented this belly-buster and turned it into an art form. There are the regular loco moco, teriyaki loco, spam loco, hot dog loco, oyako loco, and for the health conscious, the mahi loco. So, if your waistline, the surgeon general, and your arteries permit, this is *the* place to have one. With few exceptions, they cost $7 or less. Breakfast choices include everything from bacon and eggs to coffee and doughnuts, while lunches feature beef stew, salmon mixed plate, and fried chicken, or an assortment of sandwiches from teriyaki beef to good old BLT. Make your selection and sit at one of the picnic tables under the veranda to watch the people of Hilo go by.

Another favorite of locals and visitors is **Don's Grill** (485 Hinano St., 808/935-9099,

10:30 A.M.–9 P.M. daily except Monday, from 10 A.M. Sat. and Sun.). This American/Hawaiian family-style basic restaurant is known for a good square meals at reasonable prices. Inside find wood-trimmed blue Formica tables in a very modern yet functionally tasteful setting with additional seating in the solarium. Here you find everything from saimin to sandwiches and fish to rotisserie chicken. Most entrées run $7–12.

Natural Foods

For quick food on the run, stop by **Island Naturals** natural food grocery for something from their hot bar at $6.99 a pound, or order a sandwich or other such item off the menu for $5–7. This is some of the best quick, tasty, and wholesome food in town.

Hawaiian Regional

Located in the Waiakea Center, **Hilo Bay Café** (808/935-4939, 11 A.M.–9 P.M. Mon.–Sat., 5–9 P.M. Sun.) is a convenient location for shoppers, but as it's associated with Island Naturals natural food store, it's also a great place for healthy, wholesome food. Decorated in a decidedly modern style, the Hilo Bay Café has an easy-going, welcoming feel. Lunch might be slow-cooked pork barbecue rubs, crispy spanakopita, or a grilled portobello mushroom sandwich. The dinner menu offers such items as homemade ravioli, coconut-crusted tofu kabobs, potato-crusted fresh fish, and grilled New York pepper steak. Most lunches run $8–10, with evening entrées in the $10–18 range, so this won't be a wallet buster.

Seafood

The Seaside Restaurant (1790 Kalaniana'ole Ave., 808/935-8825, 5–8:30 Tues.–Thurs., 5–9 P.M. Fri.–Sat.) appropriately named, is located across from the ocean out along the Keaukaha strip at a fish farm operation. If you want, have a look at the ponds before you head in for your meal. About a dozen varieties of freshwater and saltwater fish are available on the menu in a number of preparations, and a few steak, chicken, and pasta selections are also available. For fish, come to the Seaside, where most dinners range $18–26. All dinners come complete with salad, vegetables, and rice. This is a popular place with locals—there's been a restaurant here since before WWII—so make a reservation.

South Asian

Situated in a small strip mall at the intersection of Lanikaula and Kilauea Streets, the tiny **Akmal's** (808/969-7479, 11 A.M.–2 P.M. Tues.–Sat., 5 P.M.9 P.M. Mon.–Sat.) offers authentic curry, tandoori, and vegetarian dishes, plus such delicacies as samosa, lamb korma, and chicken vindaloo. Most entrées are under $14. With just four tables, you get attention; Akmal's aims to please.

Sweet Treats

All you folks with that affinity for chocolate will certainly be pleased by the **Big Island Candies** factory and gift shop (585 Hinano St., 808/935-8890 or 800/935-5510, www.bigislandcandies.com, 8:30 A.M.–5 P.M.). Stop by to look through the glass at the delicacies being produced and choose your favorite off the many shelves of possibilities. Hawaiian macadamia nut shortbread cookies, chocolate-dipped shortbread, macadamia nut biscotti, golden macadamia nut brownies, and macadamia nut caramel clusters only start the selections. This store also sells coffee and Hilo Homemade ice cream. You can even peruse the offerings and order off the Web.

Brewery

Hilo has its own microbrewery, the **Mehana Brewing Company** (275 E. Kawili St., 808/934-8211, www.mehana.com, 8 A.M.–5:30 P.M. Mon.–Fri., 10 A.M.–5:30 P.M. Sat.). A small operation—about 1,200 barrels a year—and in business since 1996, this microbrewery crafts five varieties of light beer with no preservatives, brewed especially for the tropical climate. Stop at the small tasting room/logo shop for a sample or gift any day except

Sunday. If it's not too busy, someone may show you around.

FOOD MARKETS

For groceries and general food supplies try: **KTA Super Store** downtown at 321 Keawe Ave. (808/935-3751) or in the Pu'ainako Town Center (808/959-9111); **Safeway** (111 E. Pu'ainako, 808/959-3502); or **Sack 'n Save** at Pu'ainako Town Center (808/959-5831) or downtown at 250 Kino'ole (808/935-3113).

Since 1977, **Abundant Life Natural Foods** (292 Kamehameha Ave., 808/935-7411, 8:30 A.M.–7 P.M. weekdays, from 7 A.M. Wed. and Sat., 10 A.M.–5 P.M. Sunday) has been doing business in downtown Hilo. The store's shelves are stocked with an excellent selection of fresh fruits and veggies, bulk foods, cosmetics, vitamins, and herbs, and the bookshelves cosmically vibrate with a selection of tomes on metaphysics and new-age literature. The store's kitchen puts out daily specials of smoothies, soup, salads, sandwiches, and *bento,* most for under $6.

In the Waiakea Center next to Borders Books is **Island Naturals** market and deli (808/935-5533, 8 A.M.–8 P.M. Mon.–Sat., 9 A.M.–7 P.M. Sun.). Fresh fruit and produce line the shelves, as do packaged, refrigerated, frozen, and bulk natural foods, plus personal care items, supplements, vitamins, and minerals. The deli has ready-to-order foods, a hot bar, and premade items. You'll get wholesome healthy foods here at this full-service shop, with a good vibe from people who care about what they sell.

Fish Market

Suisan Fish Market (93 Lihiwai St., 808/935-9349, 8 A.M.–5 P.M. Mon.–Fri., 8 A.M.–4 P.M. Sat.) is as close to the harbor as you can get for fresh fish and they have as good a selection as anyone in town. A window counter to the side of the building is open early for avid anglers who come to try their luck along the water near the harbor and in the adjacent park.

Farmers Market

On Wednesday and Saturday mornings, stop by the corner of Kamehameha Avenue and Mamo Street for the **Hilo Farmers Market,** perhaps the best farmers market on the island. This is a lively affair, great for local color, where you can get healthy locally grown produce and bouquets of colorful flowers at bargain prices. Across the street at The Market Place and also a few steps up the road under the big tents are more vendors selling flowers, arts and crafts, and other gift items.

© ROBERT NILSEN

One of the best on the island, Hilo Farmers Market is the place to look for fresh fruits and vegetables.

Information and Services

Tourist Information

Good sources of local maps and helpful brochures are the **Big Island Visitors Bureau** (250 Keawe, 808/961-5797, 8 A.M.–noon and 1–4:30 P.M. Mon.–Fri.) at the corner of Keawe and Haili Streets, the **Chamber of Commerce** (106 Kamehameha Ave., 808/935-7178, 8 A.M.–4 P.M. Mon.–Fri.) and the **tourist information kiosk** at the bus terminal (8:30 A.M.–4:30 P.M. Mon.–Fri., 9 A.M.–1 P.M. Sat.).

Emergencies and Health

Hilo Medical Center (1190 Waianuenue Ave., 808/974-4700) has both outpatient services and a 24-hour emergency room. Just up the street is a **Kaiser Permanente** clinic (1292 Waianuenue Avenue, 808/934-4000). Alternately, try **Hilo Urgent Care Center** (45 Mohouli, 808/969-3051, 9 A.M.–9 P.M. Mon.–Fri., 10 A.M.–4 P.M. Sat. and Sun.).

For pharmacies, try **Shiigi Drug** (333 Kilauea Ave., 808/935-0001) at the Kaiko'o Mall, **Longs Drugs** (555 Kilauea Ave., 808/935-3357), and the **KTA Super Store** pharmacy (50 E. Pu'ainako, 808/959-8700).

Post Office

The **Hilo Main Post Office** (1299 Kekuanao'a, 8 A.M.–4:30 P.M. weekdays, 8:30 A.M.–12:30 P.M. Sat.) is an efficiently run, modern post office, clearly marked on the access road to the airport. It is extremely convenient for mailings prior to departure. A downtown postal station (154 Waianuenue Ave., 8 A.M.–4 P.M. weekdays, 12:30–2 P.M. Sat.) is located in the federal building across from Kalakaua Park.

Banks

All the state's big banks have branches in Hilo. Try **City Bank** (333 Kilauea, 808/935-6844) at Kaiko'o Mall, **Central Pacific Bank** (525 Kilauea Ave., 808/935-5251), **Bank of Hawaii** (120 Pauahi St., 808/935-9701), **First Hawaiian Bank** (1205 Kilauea Ave., 808/969-2211), or **American Savings Bank** (100 Pauahi St., 808/935-0084).

Libraries and Schools

The **Hilo Public Library** (300 Waianuenue Ave., 808/933-8888, 11 A.M.–7 P.M. Tues. and Wed., 9 A.M.–5 P.M. Thurs. and Sat., 10 A.M.–5 P.M. Fri.) is a few short blocks above downtown.

The **University of Hawaii at Hilo** (200 W. Kawili, 808/974-7311, http://hilo.hawaii.edu), is a branch of the state university system and has a strong Hawaiian language program. The **Hawaii Community College** (808/974-7311, http://hawaii.hawaii.edu), associated with the university but on a separate campus a short distance away, is a more skills-focused facility.

Internet Access

Bytes and Bites (223-A Kilauea Ave, 808/935-3520, 10 A.M.–10 P.M. daily) is your Internet connection to the world at $2.50 for 15 minutes or $8 an hour, and for faxing, scanning, office programs, games, and computer instruction—drinks and snacks, too. Find it at the corner of Ponahawai across from Low International bakery and restaurant.

On the corner of Waianuenue and Kino'ole, across from the Federal Building, **Beach Dog Rental** (808/961-5207, 8 A.M.–10 P.M. daily) offers Internet access at similar rates.

A number of accommodations around town also offer inexpensive Internet services. Try Arnott's Lodge or the Hilo Bay Hostel.

Laundry

Try **Tyke's Laundromat** (1454 Kilauea Ave., 808/935-1093, 6 A.M.–10 P.M.) offers do-it-yourself and drop-off service in a clean, well-run facility just up from the Hilo Shopping Center.

Getting Around

Hele-On Bus

The county-operated Hele-On bus runs within Hilo and to various towns around the island, but on infrequent schedules. The Hilo bus terminal is located downtown next to the Mo'oheau Bandstand on the median strip between the Bayfront Highway and Kamehameha Avenue. For more information, contact the county Mass Transit Agency (808/961-8744, www.co.hawaii.hi.us/mass_transit/transit_main.htm).

One city bus route runs eight times a day from downtown Hilo, past the Kaiko'o mall to the Prince Kuhio Plaza. Another bus runs five times a day on a more circuitous route between downtown and the Prince Kuhio Plaza, going by way of the university. Twice in the morning, buses connect the Banyan Drive area to downtown Hilo and to the Prince Kuhio Plaza. Intra-city buses run only on weekdays.

Outside of Hilo, buses run once a day on weekdays to/from Oceanview, five times a day on weekdays and once on Saturday to/from Pahoa, four times a day on weekdays to/from Honoka'a, four times a day to/from Waimea, three times a day to/from the North Kohala resorts, and once a day Monday–Saturday to/from South Kona, via Honoka'a, Waimea, Waikoloa, and Kailua-Kona.

As of October 2005, the county has instituted "no-fare" rides for all bus routes on the island, so all Hele-On bus transportation is free.

Taxi

There are nearly two dozen taxi companies in town. When in need of a ride, try one of the following. **A-1 Bob's Taxi** (808/959-4800), **Anuenue Taxi** (808/895-8294), **Hilo Harry's Taxi** (808/935-7091), or **Percy's** (808/969-7060). You can get most anywhere in town or to/from the airport for under $13. Farther afield, you might expect about $50 to Pahoa, $75 to Volcano, and $100 to Honoka'a.

Motorcycles

Big Island Harley-Davidson Rentals (200 Kanoelehua Ave #106, 808/934-9090, www.bigislandHDrentals.com) is an authorized Harley rental center. Big Harleys here rent for $125 for an 8:30 A.M.–5:30 P.M. day or $155 for 24 hours. Half-day rates of $100 and two-day rates of $250 are also available. Each rental requires a $2,000 insurance deposit. Riders must be 23 years old, have a motorcycle endorsement on their license, and wear eye protection. Helmets are available if you want them but are not required.

PUNA

The Puna district, south of Hilo on the southeast coast, was formed from rivers of lava spilling from Mauna Loa and Kilauea again and again over the last million years or so, and continues to be the most volcanically active part of the island today. The molten rivers stopped only when they hit the sea, where they fizzled and cooled, forming a chunk of semi-raw land that bulges into the Pacific—marking the state's easternmost point at **Cape Kumukahi.** These titanic lava flows have left phenomenal reminders of their power. The earth here is raw, rugged, and jagged. It has not yet had sufficient time to age and smooth. Black lava flows streak the land and grudgingly give over to green vegetation. On the coast, cliffs stand guard against the relentless sea, and here and there lava tubes punctuate the coastline, leaving telltale signs of the mountains' might. Yet, the greatest of these features is the rift zone, where rupture lines dart out like streamers from a volcano's central crater. It is here along this zone that the unstable ground has slumped away and fallen into the ocean in great cataclysmic landslides and later settled to create benches of lowlands and the present coastline. It is along this rift zone that the mountain still shows its volatility, for the current active lava flow is disgorging from vents along this line.

Pahoa is the major town in this region. It was at one time the terminus of a rail line that took commodities and people to Hilo. This was timber country and later sugarcane land, but since the mills have closed, it's turned to producing acres of anthuriums and papayas. Down the hill from town, Lava Tree State

HIGHLIGHTS

Lava Tree State Monument: One of the most unusual remnants of a lava flow is a mold of an encased tree trunk; this monument offers numerous examples (page 250).

Kapoho Tidepools: There are not many sand beaches along the Puna coast, but these are perhaps the best representatives of this seashore phenomenon in the Puna district, not to mention a great place to snorkel (page 254).

Puala'a Thermal Spring: For a relaxing dip in a heated natural pool you can do no better than to make a stop here (page 255).

End of the Road: Over the years, lava from the mountains has left its mark on Puna in many different ways. The best place to see a recent lava flow up close is at the End of the Road, where it has hardened over road and village and added new land to the seashore and is creating a new black-sand beach (page 257).

The Painted Church: Escaping the danger of onrushing molten lava, Star of the Sea Catholic church was moved from Kalapana to its new location above the coast at Kaimu (page 258).

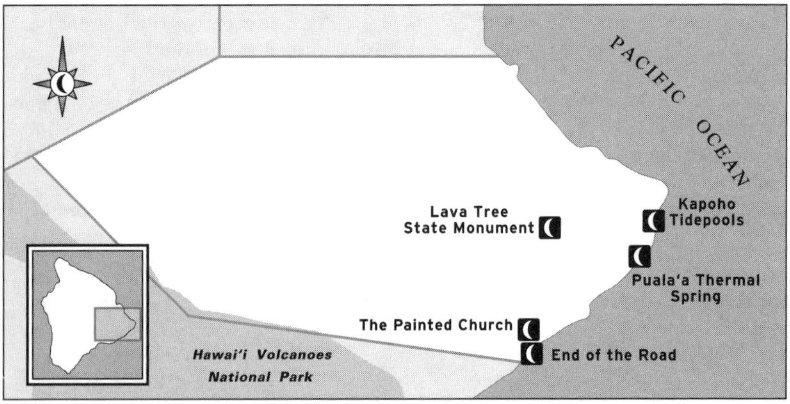

LOOK FOR TO FIND RECOMMENDED SIGHTS, ACTIVITIES, DINING, AND LODGING.

Monument was once a rainforest whose giant trees were covered with lava, like hot dogs dipped in batter. The encased wood burned, leaving a hollow stone skeleton. You can stroll through this lichen-green rock forest before you head farther east into the brilliant sunshine of the coast. Roads take you past a multitude of anthurium and papaya farms, oases of color in a desert of solid black lava. A lighthouse sits atop Cape Kumukahi, and to the north an ancient trail passes beaches where almost no one ever goes.

Southward is a string of popular beaches. You can camp, swim, surf, or just play in the water to your heart's delight, but realize that there are few places to stop for food, gas, or supplies. Also along the coast you can visit natural areas where the sea tortured the hot lava into caves, tubes, arches, and even a natural hot bath. Hawai'i Volcanoes National Park's

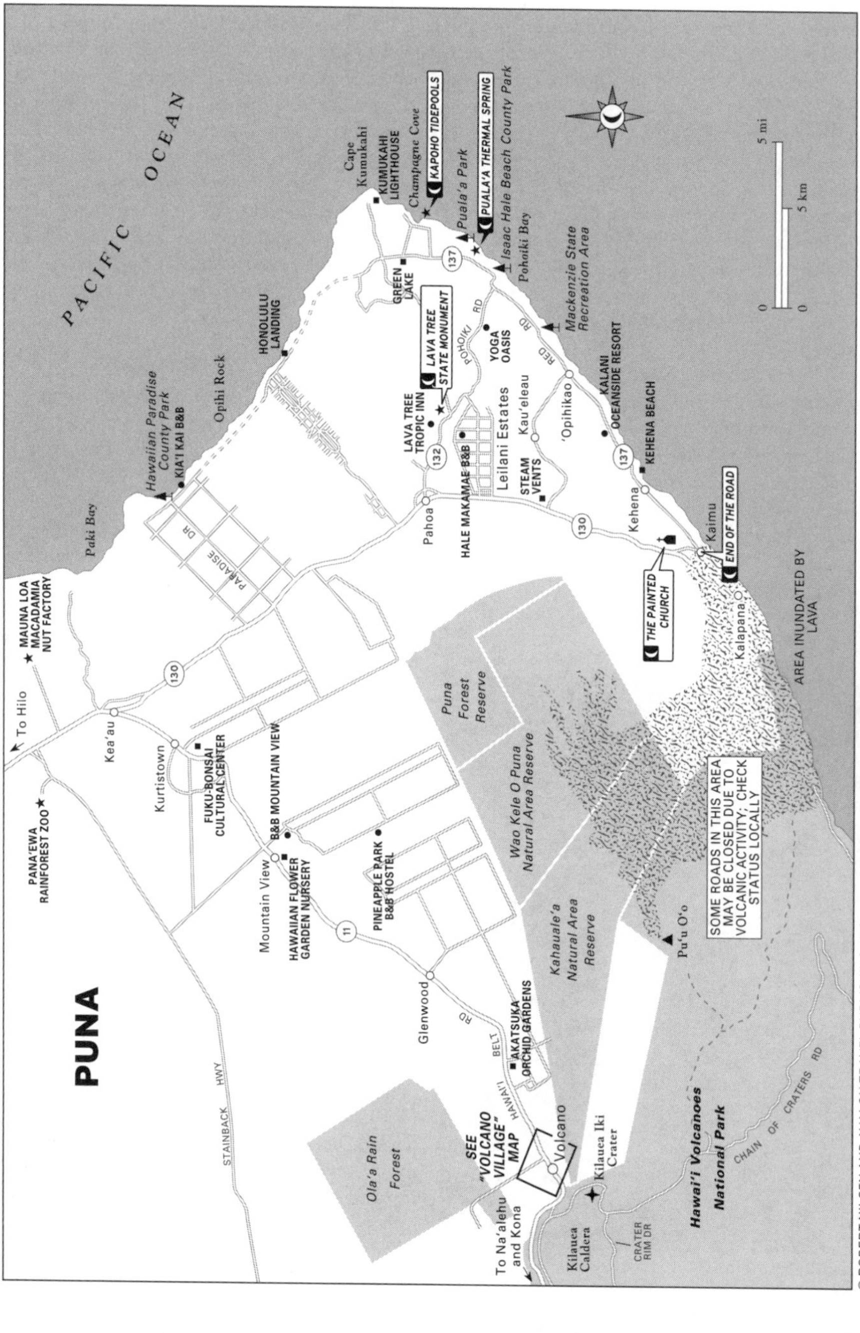
PUNA
PACIFIC OCEAN
Cape Kumukahi
KUMUKAHI LIGHTHOUSE
Champagne Cove
KAPOHO TIDEPOOLS
Puala'a Park
PUALA'A THERMAL SPRING
Isaac Hale Beach County Park
Pohoiki Bay
Mackenzie State Recreation Area
GREEN LAKE
LAVA TREE STATE MONUMENT
HONOLULU LANDING
POHOIKI RD
YOGA OASIS
RED RD
KALANI OCEANSIDE RESORT
KEHENA BEACH
LAVA TREE TROPIC INN
Leilani Estates
Kau'eleau
'Opihikao
Opihi Rock
Hawaiian Paradise County Park
KIA'I KAI B&B
Paki Bay
PARADISE DR
HALE MAKAMAE B&B
STEAM VENTS
Pahoa
Kehena
Kaimu
END OF THE ROAD
THE PAINTED CHURCH
Kalapana
AREA INUNDATED BY LAVA
MAUNA LOA MACADAMIA NUT FACTORY
To Hilo
Kea'au
Kurtistown
FUKU-BONSAI CULTURAL CENTER
B&B MOUNTAIN VIEW
Puna Forest Reserve
Wao Kele O Puna Natural Area Reserve
SOME ROADS IN THIS AREA MAY BE CLOSED DUE TO VOLCANIC ACTIVITY; CHECK STATUS LOCALLY
PANA'EWA RAINFOREST ZOO
Mountain View
HAWAIIAN FLOWER GARDEN NURSERY
PINEAPPLE PARK B&B HOSTEL
Kahauale'a Natural Area Reserve
Pu'u O'o
Glenwood
AKATSUKA ORCHID GARDENS
HAWAI'I BELT RD
STAINBACK HWY
SEE "VOLCANO VILLAGE" MAP
Volcano
Ola'a Rain Forest
Kilauea Iki Crater
Hawai'i Volcanoes National Park
CHAIN OF CRATERS RD
To Na'alehu and Kona
Kilauea Caldera
CRATER RIM DR
0 5 mi
0 5 km
11
130
132
137

eastern end covers the southwestern corner of the Puna district. The park's visitors center that used to stand just before the beginning of Chain of Craters Road burned down in the summer of 1989 when lava surged across the road, severing this eastern gateway to the park and causing an old Catholic church to be moved to a new location. This road is still closed and will undoubtedly remain so until the current volcanic activity ceases, so there is no park access from this side. Yet, raw lava flows and new black-sand beaches are there to be explored.

The **Hawaii Belt Road** (Rt. 11) is a corridor cutting through the center of Puna, running uphill straight toward the town of Volcano. Cutting through well-established villages, this road passes some of the largest and best-known flower farms in the state, and on both sides of this highway are scattered residential subdivisions. Back in these hills, a few enterprising gardeners grow "Puna Butter" *pakalolo,* a significant, though illegal, economic force in the region.

© ROBERT NILSEN

lava tree molds

On the border of Puna and the Ka'u district to the south are the village of **Volcano,** where you will find accommodations, restaurants, and shopping, and the entrance to Hawai'i Volcanoes National Park. Here at the park, the goddess Pele resides at Kilauea Caldera, center of one of the world's most active volcanoes. The Hawaii Belt Road continues southwest through the park and into Ka'u, the southernmost district of the Big Island, and, rounding the bottom of the island, travels up into Kona.

PLANNING YOUR TIME

Visitors with few days on the island often bypass the coastal Puna region on their way to or from Kilauea Volcano. While there are few sights to see along the Hawai'i Belt Road itself in upland Puna, the town of Pahoa and the Puna coast is worth exploring. Highway 130 and its offshoot 132 take you down into the heart of tropical Puna to either end of the coast road. Spend at least a day making a circular route along these roads, or stay and spend a few days letting the area soak in. It's the coast and coastal periphery that really capture the essence of Puna. It's here that old-time Hawaii still has a presence. The warm and humid tropical coastal region calls for travelers to slow down, appreciate the sights, and tune into the forces that have shaped this land. Perhaps start at Cape Kumukahi, the easternmost point of the state of Hawaii, where lava has pushed into the ocean and where its blackness stands in marked contrast to the verdant hillsides above. Push down the coast, stopping at tidepools, thermal ponds, lonely state parks, and isolated black-sand beaches until you are stopped by recent lava that has cut roads that once ran farther west. There at these barricades of solid pahoehoe, contemplate the destructive nature of a lava flow and understand that entire villages have been buried here, but also realize that the regenerative process of life is an ongoing and shifting affair in these parts. Return up the highway past steam vents to relax for an evening at one of the fine restaurants in Pahoa, before heading on to other destinations.

Southeast Coast

The most enjoyable area in the Puna district is the southeast coast, with its beaches and points of natural and historical interest. It is an easy-going, steamy, tropical region, one of the most typically old Hawaiian on the island. If you take Route 130 south from Kea'au, in about 11 miles you reach Pahoa. Like Kea'au, Pahoa is primarily a crossroads. You can continue due south on Route 130, passing a series of steam vents, to the seaside village of Kaimu, beyond where Route 130 used to join coastal Route 137 at Kalapana and feed into Chain of Craters Road, before much of this area was buried by lava flows.

You might go directly east from Pahoa along Route 132. This lovely, tree-lined country road takes you past Lava Tree State Monument, which shouldn't be missed, and then continues to the coast, intersecting Route 137 and terminating at Cape Kumukahi. Route 137 continues north and in short order plunges into a forest of trees; the road turns into a rugged and rutted dirt lane that is often full of potholes and pools of water. Proceed with caution, as this stretch is not kind to low-slung rental cars. If you continue, you will pass secluded private property and as-yet-undeveloped county park land and pop out on the other side at the bottom of the Hawaiian Shores Estates subdivision, which cascades down the hill from Pahoa. You're better off to turn south and enjoy other sights of the coast.

If this seems *too* far out of the way, head down Pohoiki Road where it branches just past the Lava Tree State Monument. Soon you bypass a controversial geothermal power station, pass through a section of huge mango trees that line both sides of the road (be careful when they drop fruit, as this can cause the roadway to become slippery), then reach the coast at Isaac Hale Beach County Park. From there, Route 137 heads southwest down the coast to Kaimu, passing the best Puna beaches en route. Fortunately for you, this area of Puna is one of those places where no matter which way you decide to go, you really can't go wrong.

PAHOA

You can breeze through this "one-street" town, but you won't regret stopping if even for a few minutes. A raised wooden sidewalk passing

ANTHURIUM

Originally a native of Central America, the anthurium was introduced into Hawaii in 1889 by Samuel M. Damon, an English missionary. Damon discovered that Hawaii's climate and volcanic soil made an ideal environment for this exotic flower. Over the years since then, anthurium production has turned into a million-dollar export industry with all the major growers located on the Big Island. Anthuriums grow on a tall stalk as a glossy and heart-shaped flower bract, with a yellowish flower spike arising from the stalk at the bract's base, and accompanied by large shiny green leaves. The most common anthurium has dark red bracts about the size of the palm of a hand, but they have been bred in a variety of colors, from lily white to green, purple, and black, and from silver dollar size to as big as a plate.

DIANA LASICH HARPER

false-front shops is fun to walk along to get a feeling of the early 20th century. Yet, a revitalized 1960s counterculture element thrives in town along with the workaday local population. The shops here are an eclectic mix of food vendors, restaurants, and craft and clothing stores. The rest of town is a bit more utilitarian with a lumberyard, supermarkets, gas stations, a church, schools, police and fire departments, post office, a free-use Olympic-size swimming pool, and the island's oldest movie theater. In recent years, the town has expanded somewhat to include Pahoa Marketplace, a new business complex on the edge of town just as you enter from Kea'au. At one time Pahoa boasted *the* largest sawmill in America. Its buzz saw ripped 'ohi'a railway ties for the Santa Fe and other railroads. It was into one of these ties that the golden spike uniting the East and West coasts of the Mainland was supposedly driven. Many local people earned their livelihood from 'ohi'a charcoal that they made and sold all over the island until it was made obsolete by the widespread use of kerosene and gas introduced in the early 1950s. Pahoa's commercial heart went up in flames in 1955. Along the main street was a tofu factory that had a wood-fired furnace. The old fellow who owned the factory banked his fires as usual before he went home for the night. Somehow, they got out of control and burned all the way down to the main alley dividing the commercial district. The only reason the fire didn't jump the alley was because a papaya farmer happened to be around and had a load of water on the back of his truck, which he used to douse the buildings and save the town.

Pahoa is attempting to protect and revitalize its commercial center and bring new life to vintage buildings like the Akebono Theater, where special-performance live theater now plays. Pahoa has one of the highest concentrations of old buildings still standing in Hawaii that are easily accessible. Although the center of town has been bypassed by a new road, make sure to enter the town and stroll along its main street.

To replace timber and sugar, Pahoa is in the process of becoming a major anthurium growing area. As you get close to Pahoa, coming from Kea'au, you'll see black shade cloth draping anthurium nurseries, sheltering magnificent specimens of the usually red flowers, plus plenty of white, green, and even black anthuriums. Papaya are also grown here in large quantities and at a number of farms located below town toward the coast.

COQUI

One of the most recent infestations of non-native species in the state is that of the coqui, a tiny frog with a loud voice that's originally from Puerto Rico. The area around Lava Tree State Park has been hit especially hard by these obnoxious amphibians, and at night the noise they make, "Ko Kee" (hence their name), is truly and thunderously amazing. Other areas on the Big Island, such as at Volcano Village, as well as locations on all the other main islands, have had verified infestations. While attempts have been made to eradicate these tiny amphibians, there has not been much sustained success. In Lava Tree State Monument, the understory vegetation has been buzzed in hopes of eliminating their preferred environment. These frogs, including related species from other Caribbean nations that have also entered Hawaii, grow up to two inches long and are usually brown or green in color. They are a danger to native species, as they eat insects that native birds rely upon, and may serve as a food source for rats and mongooses that are currently pest species for the state.

Lava Tree State Monument

In 1790, slick, fast-flowing pahoehoe lava surged through this 'ohi'a forest, covering the tree trunks from the ground to about a 12-foot level. The moisture inside the trees cooled the lava, forming a hardened shell. At the same time, tremors and huge fissures cracked the earth in the area. When the eruption ended, the still-hot lava drained away through the fissures, leaving the encased tree trunks standing like sentinels, only to burn away later. The floor of the forest is so smooth in some areas that the lava seems like asphalt. Each lava tree has its own personality; some resemble totem poles, and it doesn't take much imagination to see old, craggy faces staring back at you. Many still stand, while others have tumbled to the ground where you can look inside their pipe-like structure. The most spectacular part of the park is near the entrance. Immense trees loom over cavernous cracks *(puka)* in the earth and send their roots, like stilled waterfalls, tumbling down into them. A 20-minute walk around this park makes a pleasant stop on your journey. To get to Lava Tree, take Route 132 east from Pahoa and on about three miles through a tree tunnel of towering albizia trees to the well-marked entrance on the left. Drinking water is not available, but toilets are.

Vacation Rentals

Right on the main drag as you enter town, across from the Pahoa Village Center, is **Island Paradise Inn** (808/990-0234 or 808/959-9070, www.vrbo.com/vrbo/23179.htm). This set of renovated plantation-era houses up to 30 individuals in its studios and cottages. Rates are $39.50 a night for a one-room suite or $49.50 for a two-room house; three nights minimum. These units have bathrooms and efficiency kitchens and all that you'll need for a home away from home.

Bed-and-Breakfasts

There are a number of bed-and-breakfasts in the general Pahoa area. One in the Leilani Estates just south of town is **Hale Makamae Bed and Breakfast** (13-3315 Makamae St., 808/965-9090, info@bnb-aloha.com, www.bnb-aloha.com). Set in a nicely landscaped lawn, surrounded by a thick jungle of vegetation is a modern house that has one small studio with a queen-size bed for $65, and two larger suites with queen-size beds and kitchenettes for $90–110 a night; two nights minimum. Each unit has a private bath and private entrance, and all look out over the back garden where flowers will delight your eyes and birds will call out in melodies from the surrounding forest. A continental breakfast is served each morning in the breezeway, a great start for a day of exploration in the area.

Lava Tree Tropic Inn (14-355 Puna Rd., 808/965-7441, information@lavatreetropicinn.com, www.lavatreetropicinn.com) is located directly behind the Lava Tree State Monument in a fruit and nut orchard. Somewhat formal in appearance because of the European furniture and accents, this inn is actually very relaxed and casual in a real Hawaii way, with chickens and cats roaming the yard. Four rooms and a suite on the upper level of the main house are rented. The suite, with its own private bathroom, runs $125 a night; the rooms, $75–95, share bathrooms. All guests sit down to a breakfast of fruits and homemade bread and muffins. In the common room are plenty of books for reading and music to listen to, and one evening each week a jazz session is hosted at the B&B. Your host will gladly offer suggestions for food in town or activities in the area.

Located on the ocean at the bottom of the Hawaiian Paradise Park subdivision is **Kia'i Kai Bed and Breakfast** (808/982-9256 or 888/542-4524, inkeeper@hawaii-ocean-retreat.com, www.hawaiian-ocean-retreat.com). Kia'i Kai offers one room and one suite with private bathrooms for $95–125, and a two-bedroom cottage with full kitchen for $155 a night. Breakfasts are included. During the day, hang out on the patio and watch turtles or whales, use the hot tub and lap pool at water's edge, or explore the area's many scenic sights.

Food

Nearly all restaurants in town are only a few steps from each other. As close to the center of town as you can get is **Luquin's Mexican Restaurant** (808/965-9990, until 9 P.M. daily), a reasonably priced Mexican restaurant that offers the usual enchiladas, burritos, tacos, combination platters, and Mexican and American breakfasts, most in the $6–8 range but with some up to $15. Some say it's the best on the island. Margaritas are a house specialty at the cantina. You'll be hard pressed to find a seat at this local favorite on Friday or Saturday evenings.

Paolo's Bistro (333 Pahoa Rd., 808/965-7033, 5:30–9 P.M. Tues.–Sun., a Tuscan Italian restaurant, is the place for fine dining in town. Soft romantic lighting, lace curtains over the windows, candles on the tables, and fine Italian music in the background set the mood, and Paolo himself may wander through the dining room to greet his guests. Start with an appetizer, like a bowl of minestrone soup or fresh mozzarella antipasto, and follow that with ravioli with spinach and ricotta or pasta with prawns. Other entrées might be fresh fish, chicken Marsala, cioppino, or pasta puttanesca, mostly in the $11–21 range, and there are always desserts like tiramisu or strawberries marinated in chardonnay. To round out the meal, have a cup of espresso or a caffe latte. Paolo's serves only homemade pasta and sauces like your *madre* would have made, so this wonderfully tasty food is worth the extra cost. Paolo's is small and intimate, with a few tables inside and out on the back garden, so call to reserve a seat. It's okay to bring your own bottle if you care for wine with dinner.

Next door to Paolo's is **Ning's Thai Cuisine** (808/965-7611, noon–3 P.M. and 5–8:30 P.M. Mon.–Sat.). This small eatery serves memorable Thai food with a fine blend of herbs and spices. Your mouth will not be disappointed. Using local organic ingredients, menu choices include tofu summer rolls, Po Tak seafood soup, and a variety of rice, noodle, seafood, and curry dishes, most in the $8–11 range.

Clemente's (808/965-0055, 11 A.M.–2 P.M. and 5–9 P.M.), just beyond the main walkway in town, is a newer fine dining Italian restaurant that draws its guests from the entire surrounding area. Get your meal started with zuppa pomodoro or some antipasti and move on to pesca marinara, veal saltimbocca, or chicken piccata. Expect traditional preparations for these entrées, which run mostly $15–27. Everyone says that the food is great, the service is good, but it's expensive for funky little Pahoa.

Right in the center of town is **Boogie Woogie Pizza** (808/965-5575, 11 A.M.–10 P.M. Mon.–Sat.). Eat in or takeout, Boogie Woogie does specialty pizzas and you can create your own from their list of ingredients. They run $10–$20, depending on the size.

If you are looking for something more local, head to **Ludi's** (808/965-5599, 9 A.M.–7 P.M. Mon.–Sat.) for Filipino and local grinds.

In the Pahoa Marketplace at the northern entrance to town, you'll find the **Aloha Outpost Cafe** (808/965-8333, 6 A.M.–8 P.M. Mon.–Sat., 7 A.M.–6 P.M. Sun.) for breakfast, soup, sandwiches, coffee, ice cream, and Internet service.

Markets

The old standby in town is the **Pahoa Cash and Carry Store** (808/965-8216, 6 A.M.–9 P.M. weekdays, 7 A.M.–8 P.M. Sat., 8 A.M.–7 P.M. Sun.) on the main drag. This compact shop has all you'll need for groceries, sundries, deli items, and drinks somewhere along its narrow isles.

The longtime establishment **Pahoa Natural Groceries** (808/965-8322, 7:30 A.M.–7:30 P.M. Mon. –Sat., 7:30 A.M.–6 P.M. Sun.) is in a newer building on a side street just off the main drag. The store specializes in organic food items and is one of the finest health food stores on the Big Island. It has an excellent selection of fresh veggies, organic bulk grains, packaged natural foods, herbs and minerals, a hot food table ($5.99/pound), and a very good bakery selection. There's a kitchen on the premises, so the food is not only healthful but very fresh.

You'll also find two farmers markets in town. **Caretakers of Our Land** (7:30 A.M.–noon Sat.), happening at Sacred Heart Catholic Church at the south end of town, is the more typical of these markets, with a variety of food and flowers. Right in the center of town at the Akebono Theater parking lot is the **Akebono Farmers Market** (8 A.M.–1 P.M. Sun.).

More a combination farmers market and flea market, **Maku'u Farmers Market** (6 A.M.–3 P.M. Sun.) is held along Route 130 between Kea'au and Pahoa near mile marker 8. It's very popular—look for the signs and the crowds.

Services

There are **gas stations** just as you enter Pahoa from Kea'au and near the highway on the south end of town.

In the Pahoa Village Center, set along the main road as you enter town, are **Suds 'N Duds** laundry (808/965-2621), where you can clean your clothes, and the **Pahoa Pharmacy** (808/965-7535) for all your health needs.

ALONG THE COAST

All of Puna's beaches, parks, and campgrounds lie along coastal Route 137 stretching for 20 miles from Kumukahi to Kaimu. Route 137 is also called Kapoho-Kalapana Beach Road or simply the "Red Road" because of its distinctive crushed red lava rock color—now mostly covered by black asphalt. Surfers, families, transients, even nude-sunbathing "buffs" have their favorite spots along this southeast coast. For the most part, swimming is possible, but be cautious during high tide. There is plenty of sun, snorkeling sites, and good fishing, and the campgrounds are almost always available.

© ROBERT NILSEN

The Red Road carries visitors down the steamy Puna Coast.

Cape Kumukahi

It's fitting that Kumukahi means "First Beginning" since it is the easternmost point of Hawaii and was recognized as such by the original Polynesian settlers. Follow Route 132 past Lava Tree State Monument for about 10 miles to the coast, where a lighthouse (really, just a skeletal beacon tower) sits like an exclamation point on clinker lava. Along the way, get an instant course in volcanology: You can easily chart the destructive and regenerative forces at work on Hawaii. At the five-mile marker you have a glimpse of the lava flow of 1955. Tiny plants give the lava a greenish cast, and shrubs are already eating into it, turning it to soil. Papaya orchards grow in the raw lava of an extensive flat basin. The contrast between the black, lifeless earth and the vibrant green trees is startling. Farther on is the lava flow of 1960, and you can see at a glance how different it was from the flow of five years earlier. In the center of the flatland near the coast rises a cinder cone, a caldera of a much older mini-volcano unscathed by the modern flows; it is gorgeous with lush vegetation. This is Kapoho Crater, sometimes called Green Mountain. On private property, this low volcanic cone is thickly covered in trees and has a small natural lake in its caldera known as Green Lake.

When Route 132 intersects Route 137, continue straight ahead down the unpaved washboard-like road for about two miles to the Cape Kumukahi Lighthouse. People in these parts swear that on the fateful night in 1960 when the nearby village of Kapoho was consumed by the lava flow, an old woman (a favorite guise of Madame Pele) came to town begging for food and was turned away by everyone. She next went to the lighthouse asking for help and was cordially treated by the lighthouse keeper. When the flow was at its strongest, it came within yards of the lighthouse and then miraculously split, completely encircling the structure but leaving it

PUNA

Champagne Cove

unharmed as the flow continued out to sea for a considerable distance.

Champagne Cove

From the lighthouse, you can walk over lava to the ocean or turn south and follow the rough track for about 30 minutes—vehicles with high clearance only, if you drive in—to Champagne Cove where you can swim and snorkel with turtles. Because the cove is protected only by a small sandbar, be watchful of the waves on days when there is rough water. This cove fronts some of the homes in the Kapoho Beach Lots subdivision. Be mindful of and stay off private property. The black-sand and -rock beach adjacent to Champagne Cove is used by local anglers. Notice the olivine color in the lava that predominates here.

Kapoho Tidepools

Although the old village of Kapoho was covered by lava a few short decades ago, a new community has been rebuilt to take its place. This new village has a mixture of retirees, working-class families, and vacation rentals. The section closest to the lighthouse is the gated community of Kapoho Beach Lots; adjacent to the south is the smaller and public-access area of Vacationland. You can snorkel in the tidepools along the coast fronting Vacationland. Remember that this is a quiet rural community with pride in its coastal environment, so be respectful when you visit. Turn onto Kapoho Kai Drive and head down into this small development, bearing left at the end. Park off the roadway where it's marked Reef Parking. It's only a short walk seaward before these pools become apparent. Wear shoes, as the lava is sharp. Best at high tide or when the tide is coming in, the pools provide good snorkeling in a safe environment. Several hundred yards of this oceanfront have been designated the Wai'opae Tidepools Marine Life Conservation District in 2003, and no commercial fishing or guided tours may take place here.

© ROBERT NILSEN
lagoon at Kapoho

Puala'a Thermal Spring

Back on Route 137, continue south under the dense tree cover. Between mile markers 10 and 11, just after the road narrows, you come upon **Puala'a Park,** also known as Ahalanui. Quietly opened by the County of Hawai'i on July 4, 1993, this lovely, 1.3-acre park was an ancient fishing village where a few families still maintain homes. The park features a sand-bottom pond that's been formed into a pool, often referred to as Warm Pond or Millionaire's Pond, that is thermally heated to a perfect temperature. Step in and relax in its soothing warmth. Some people use the pond to do watsu, a type of in-water massage. The swimming is safe except during periods of very high surf, when ocean water washes in over the outer cement wall. The park is perfect for families with young children. The pond is now watched over by a lifeguard, and toilets have been set up for your convenience. The new parking area is open 7 A.M.–7 P.M.; otherwise park across the street in the old lot.

Isaac Hale Beach County Park

You can't miss this beach park (often referred to as Pohoiki) located on Pohoiki Bay at the junction of Route 137 and Pohoiki Road. Just look for a jumble of boats and trailers parked under the palms. At one time Pohoiki Bay served the Hawaiians as a canoe landing, then it later became the site of a commercial wharf for the Puna Sugar Company. It remains the only boat launching area for the entire Puna Coast, used by pleasure boaters and commercial fishermen. Due to this dual role, it's often very crowded. Amenities include a pavilion, restrooms, and a picnic area; potable water is not available. Camping is permitted with a county permit. Experienced surfers dodge the rip current in the center of the bay. Pohoiki Bay is also one of the best scuba and snorkel sites on the island, but you do have to watch out for the surfers. Within walking distance of the salt-and-pepper beach is another thermal spring in a lava sink surrounded by lush vegetation. It's popular with tourists and residents alike and

Bathing in the warmth of the thermal pool at Puala'a Thermal Spring is a relaxing and soothing experience.

provides a unique and relaxing way to wash away sand and salt. To find it, face away from the sea and go to the left along a small but well-worn path that leads between the water and a beach house. Be sure to ask permission if someone is around. The pools are warm, small, and tranquil. Harmless, tiny brine shrimp nibble at your toes while you soak.

MacKenzie State Recreation Area

This state park was named for forest ranger A. J. MacKenzie, highly regarded throughout the Puna district. He was killed in the area in 1938. The park's 13 acres sit among a cool grove of ironwoods originally planted by MacKenzie. A portion of the old King's highway, scratched out by prisoners in the 19th century as a form of community service, bisects the area. In the past, many people who first arrived on the Big Island hung out at MacKenzie until they could get their start. Consequently, the park received its share of hard-core types, which has earned it a reputation for rip-offs. It's rather deserted and not particularly well looked after now; you can hardly drive in without bottoming out your car. If you're camping, take precautions with your valuables. Even the state admits it's not very safe. The entire coastline along MacKenzie is bordered by low but rugged black-lava sea cliffs. Swimming is dangerous, but the fishing is excellent. Be extremely careful when walking along the water's edge, especially out on the fingers of lava; over the years, people have been swept away by freak waves. Within the park is a skylight of a collapsed lava tube, one end of which exits at the sea cliff and the other a stone's throw inland and across the road. Take a flashlight and be careful if you venture inside. MacKenzie Park is located along Route 137, two miles south of Pohoiki. Picnic facilities are available, but there is no drinking water. A state permit is required for overnight camping.

Kehena Beach

Pass the tiny village of 'Opihikao, where

Kama'ili Road drops down from Route 130 to the Red Road. 'Opihikao was a major town along this coast in the 1800s but has faded away into quaint quietude. Just beyond this community the close canopy of trees opens, the road becomes wider, and the vistas broaden. Here are picture postcard coastal scenes as good as any on the island. Cross over two sections of the 1955 lava flow and soon you come upon Kehena Beach. Kehena is actually two pockets of black-sand beach below a low sea cliff. Entrance to the beach is marked only by a scenic pulloff at mile marker 19, about four miles south of 'Opihikao. At one time Kehena was very popular, and a stone staircase led down to the beach. In 1975 a strong earthquake jolted the area, breaking up the stairway and lowering the beach by three feet. Now access is via a well-worn path, but make sure to wear sneakers because the lava is rough. The ocean here is dangerous, and often pebbles and rocks whisked along by the surf can injure your legs. Once down on the beach, head north for the smaller patch of sand, because the larger patch is open to the sea and can often be awash in waves. The black sand is hot, but a row of coconut palms provides shade. The inaccessibility of Kehena makes it a favorite "no-hassle" nude beach with many "full" sunbathers congregating here.

End of the Road

Just near the lava-inundated village of Kalapana, Routes 130 and 137 come to an abrupt halt where Madame Pele has repaved the road with lava. At the end of the line near the village of Kaimu you come to barricades. Unfortunately, the lava flows beyond here have completely covered the very popular Kaimu Beach Park (also known as Black Sand Beach), Harry K. Brown Beach Park, the national park's Puna visitors center, 13th-century **Waha'ulu Heiau,** the old community of Kalapana, and a number of older Hawaiian village sites. There is no entrance into the national park from this side. **Chain of Craters Road** is still open, but only *within* the park and from the other end.

Volcanic activity has ceased in the Kaimu

Lava flows cut the Puna coastal road.

area and the lava solidified. You can safely walk the short distance over the lava to the ocean. At the end of the road, head straight toward the water and in 15 minutes you are there. The new beach is seaward about a quarter mile from where Kaimu Beach Park used to be. Now, raw and rugged lava meets the sea and is slowly being turned into black sand once again.

In August 2001, the mayor allowed a road to be plowed from the end of Route 130 toward the lava flow for a better view of the activity. Many island people applauded this effort to open access to the inundated area of Kalapana, but the road was closed in March 2002 when part of the new access route was destroyed by additional lava flow. This road has been graded and opened again to local traffic only.

The Painted Church

Star of the Sea Catholic Church (9 A.M.–5 P.M. daily) is a small but famous structure better known as The Painted Church. Originally located near Kalapana, this church was in grave danger of being overrun by a lava flow. An effort to save the historic church from the lava was mounted, and it has been moved to a location along Route 130, just above Kaimu. A brief history of the area asserts that the now-inundated Kalapana was a spiritual magnet for Roman Catholic priests. Old Spanish documents support evidence that a Spanish priest, crossing the Pacific from Mexico, actually landed very near here in 1555. Father Damien, famous priest of the Moloka'i Leper Colony, established a grass church about two miles north and conducted a school when he first arrived in the islands in 1864. The present church dates from 1928, when Father Everest Gielen began its construction. Like an inspired (but less talented) Michelangelo, this priest painted the ceiling of the church, working mostly at night by oil lamp. Father Everest was transferred to Lana'i in 1941, and the work wasn't completed until 1964, when George Heidler, an artist from Atlanta, Georgia, came to Kalapana and decided to paint the unfinished altar section. The artwork itself can only be described as gaudy but

Star of the Sea Catholic Church, interior view

WAHA'ULA HEIAU

Waha'ula Heiau (Temple of the Red Mouth) radically changed the rituals and practices of the relatively benign Hawaiian religion by introducing the idea of human sacrifice. The 13th century marked the end of the frequent comings and goings between Hawaii and the "Lands to the South" (Tahiti), beginning the isolation that would last 500 years until Captain Cook arrived. Unfortunately, this last influx of Polynesians brought a rash of conquering warriors carrying ferocious gods who lusted for human blood before they would be appeased. Pa'ao, a powerful Tahitian priest, supervised the building of Waha'ula and brought in a new chief, Pili, to strengthen the diminished *mana* of the Hawaiian chiefs due to their practice of intermarriage with commoners. Waha'ula became the foremost *luakini* (human sacrifice) temple in the island kingdom and held this position until the demise of the old ways in 1819. Not at all grandiose, the *heiau* was merely an elevated rock platform smoothed over with pebbles.

Waha'ula lay along the coast road near the eastern end of Hawai'i Volcanoes National Park. This entire area is now completely inundated by recent lava flows. Until 1997, the *heiau* itself was a small island in a sea of black lava that miraculously escaped destruction, but in August of that year lava oozed over these 700-year-old walls and filled the compound. Madame Pele has taken back her own.

sincere. The colors are wild blues, purples, and oranges. The ceiling is adorned with symbols, portraits of Christ, the angel Gabriel, and scenes from the Nativity. Behind the altar, a painted perspective gives the impression that you're looking down a long hallway at an altar that hangs suspended in air. The church is definitely worth a few minutes.

Steam Vents

Along Route 130, about halfway between Pahoa and Kaimu, look for a small, unobtrusive sign that reads Scenic Overlook. Pull off and walk about 75 yards toward the sea until you find four nontoxic steam vents. Low mounds of lava with warm steam issuing from cracks in the earth, they are used by many local people as natural saunas. People come here to climb into the openings and relax in the warmth. On occasion, these vents will be overused, garbage is left around, or the surrounding area soiled as a toilet, but by and large they provide a wonderful natural experience. Do your best to keep the area clean and uncluttered for others who follow.

Vacation Rentals

For vacation rental homes at Kapoho, contact **A Piece of Paradise** (P.O. Box 1314, Pahoa, HI 96778, 808/965-1224, www.apoParadise.com). A Piece of Paradise has numerous properties in the oceanfront gated community of Kapoho Beach Lots. Each is completely furnished with full kitchen and living areas and located close enough to the ocean and tidepools to lull you to sleep at night. The most intimate of these is a one-bedroom cottage which rents for $115 a night, while others are two- and three-bedroom homes at $150–195 a night; three nights minimum. One of the best is the Lagoon House, a modest 1950s beach house with an exceptional location, having been built overlooking one of the ponds, "the only warm-water aquarium in the area," and next to Champagne Cove. This three-bedroom house is great for families and romantic couples. Light, breezy, comfortable, with a full kitchen and modern bathroom, this house is owned by the niece of Ray Bolger, the scarecrow of *The Wizard of Oz* fame. Perhaps the cream of the crop is Shangri-La, a more modern property with ponds that has three bedrooms in two open and airy buildings. Good for up to six guests, Shangri-La runs $250 a night. If you desire the seclusion and quietude of a restful oceanside vacation, check with A Piece of Paradise for your reservation.

For a house to rent in Kaimu, contact **Kaimu Bay Vacation Rentals** (808/878-6682, fax

808/878-3204, kaufman@maui.net). Located at the end of the road, across from new lava and near the new black-sand beach, this basic contemporary island-style house has a kitchen, living area, with two bedrooms and a bath upstairs and an additional bedroom and bath downstairs, television, phone, and laundry facilities. Rent runs $129 a night for the two bedrooms or $139 for the entire house; weekly rates are available.

Retreat Centers

The embracing arms of the Puna rainforest surround you as you make your way down the driveway to the quiet and secluded **Yoga Oasis** retreat center (808/965-8460 or 800/274-4446, info@yogaoasis.org, www.yogaoasis.org). Set on 26 acres of forest, with plenty of fruit and nut trees and numerous stands of bamboo, this yoga center and alternative accommodation offers yoga retreats, cooking workshops, and eco-adventure tours. While you can come for the accommodation only, the optional morning yoga classes are a treat. The seclusion is perfect for those who just want a little time to themselves, but the location offers easy access to coastal Puna sights and restaurants in Pahoa, and it is close enough to both Hilo and Hawai'i Volcanoes National Park for easy day trips. Private rooms with shared bath in the main building and the very basic cedar cabin run $75 single or $100 double. Tucked into the jungle are the secluded Coconut and Pine cabins with their private bathrooms and showers. These are $125 single or $145 double a night, with two nights minimum. Tent camping in the meadow, with bathroom and shower use in the main building, is also an option at $35 for one person or $60 for a couple. Room rates include the morning yoga class (8–10 A.M.) and a vegetarian brunch. Healthy, homemade vegetarian dinners run $15–20, while massage, cooking classes, eco-tours, and other activities are added features at additional cost. Yoga workshops and classes are held in the screened and vaulted, spring-floor exercise room on the upper level of the main building. Yoga Oasis is a solar-powered facility and there are no televisions or phones in the rooms, but phone lines at the main building are available for telephone and Internet use.

Kalani Oceanside Resort (RR 2 Box 4500, Pahoa, HI 96778, 808/965-7828 or 800/800-6886, reservations@kalani.com, www.kalani.com) is a nonprofit, international conference and holistic retreat center, a haven where people come when they truly want to step aside for a time. The entrance is located a few miles east of Kaimu on Route 137 between mile markers 17 and 18, on the mountain side of the road. Look for a large Visitors Welcome sign and proceed uphill until you see the office and sundries shop. Depending upon the yearly schedule, a variety of activities include massage, hula, meditation, yoga, lei-making, *lau hala*–weaving, and hikes, for men, women, couples, and families, gay or straight. The grounds have a botanical atmosphere, with a rain-fed swimming pool (clothing optional after 3 P.M.), a watsu pool, hot tub, whirlpool tub, assembly studios, classrooms, cottages, and cedar lodges with kitchen facilities. Kalani is not an oceanfront property, and only some rooms have an ocean view over the trees. Rates are $60 single for a dorm room with shared bath, $105 single and $110 double for a private room with shared bath, $125 single and $135 double for a private room with private bath, $135 single and $155 double for a guest cottage, and $210 single and $240 double for the tree house. Rates are $10 higher from November through the end of April. You can also camp for $20 a night (families pay less per person for camping). A blown conch shell calls you to breakfast at 8 A.M., lunch at noon, and dinner at 6 P.M. (nonguests welcome). The meals cost $11, $12, and $22 respectively, with a meal ticket pre-purchased at the office. Food is served from the buffet line in the open-air dining hall, and fruits and vegetables from the property are used when possible. The generator (and hence the lights) goes off at 11 P.M., but candles are provided for night owls. Kalani is not for everyone, but if you are looking for unpretentious peace and quiet, healthful food, and inner development, this is one place you may find it.

Food

Right where the roads ends you'll find **Verna's Kalapana Drive In** for quick and easy local eats. Have yourself a plate lunch, loco moco, or burger, fries, and a drink, before you head out for the short jaunt over the lava to the water. Usually open until 5 P.M., this is a favorite lunch spot for tour buses that bring guests to view the new lava and beach.

Along the Hawai'i Belt Road

For ages, Hawaiians traveled between the large population centers of Ka'u and Hilo. Those unable to go by sea headed over the shoulder of Kilauea. Today, the Hawaii Belt Road highway roughly follows this route in an uncharacteristically straight path. Along this road, and placed at near equal distances between Hilo and Volcano, are several small towns that are little more than way stops for travelers. Because of its proximity to the national park, only Volcano offers visitors the amenities and comforts they expect.

KEA'AU

Kea'au is the first town south of Hilo on Route 11, and although pleasant enough, it's little more than a Y in the road. Before the sugar mill closed in 1984, this was a bustling town with great swaths of the surrounding land in cane. Kea'au and the numerous subdivisions that have mushroomed on both sides of the highway running to Pahoa and up to Volcano have become bedroom communities to Hilo. Route 130 heads southeast from here to the steamy south coast, while Route 11 heads southwest and passes through the mountain villages of Kurtistown, Mountain View, Glenwood, and Volcano at approximately 10-mile intervals, then enters Hawai'i Volcanoes National Park. The Belt Road, although only two lanes, is straight, well surfaced, and scrupulously maintained. When heading to the Puna coast, it's easiest now to take the Kea'au Bypass Road around the east side of town, right past the old sugar mill, so you don't get bogged down going through town.

At the junction of Route 11 (Hawai'i Belt Road) and Route 130 is **Kea'au Shopping Center,** a small shopping mall with a handful of shops, a landerette, several restaurants, a bank, post office, police station, and a gas station that basically is the town center.

Food

For a congenial environment, try **Charley's Bar and Grill** (808/966-7589, 11 A.M.–2 A.M. Wed.–Sat., 11 A.M.–midnight Sun.–Tues.) for a cool one or a light meal. Stop for sandwiches, burgers, pasta, and a few other lunch and dinner entrées. Several nights a week there are live bands and dancing (cover charge), and on other evenings you can still sing along to the karaoke music, shoot pool, or throw darts. This is the only place in town for a relaxing evening out.

Lemongrass Restaurant (808/982-8558, 10 A.M.–9 P.M. Mon.–Sat., noon–9 P.M. Sun.), a simple unadorned Vietnamese and Thai restaurant in the Kea'au Shopping Center, serves ethnic foods in filling portions with hardly anything more than $8.

Verna's Drive In (808/966-9288), facing Route 130 near the shopping center, is an inexpensive local takeout restaurant where you can fill up on loco moco and plate lunches, or standard American breakfasts and hamburgers.

Markets

Also in the shopping center is **Kea'au Natural Foods** (808/966-8877, 8:30 A.M.–8 P.M. Mon.–Fri., 8:30 A.M.–7 P.M. Sat., 9:30 A.M.–5 P.M. Sun.) with a large stock of organic food items, herbs, and grains but no juice or snack bar. However, pre-made sandwiches from the deli case are always available. Have a look at the bulletin board for information on alternative happenings in the community.

Puna Fresh Foods (7 A.M.–10 P.M. Mon.–Sat., 7 A.M.–9 P.M. Sun.) is the town's full-service grocery store.

The **Kea'au Market** is a daily outdoor marketplace at the intersection in town where you can pick up fresh vegetables and flowers, or a quick bite to eat at one of the food stalls.

MOUNTAIN TOWNS

Kurtistown

Near the highway in what might be considered the center of town are the post office, B. J.'s 76 Service Station, and the **J. Hara Store,** the best-stocked store on the highway for sundries and groceries, as well as fishing and hunting supplies.

Just south of there, down 'Ola'a Road is the **Fuku-Bonsai Cultural Center** (808/982-9880, 8 A.M.–4 P.M. Mon.–Sat., sales@fukubonsai.com, www.fukubonsai.com). This institution is a combination nursery, mail-order shop, bonsai display garden, and bonsai exhibition center. It is also the nonprofit Mid-Pacific Bonsai Foundation's Hawaii State Bonsai Repository. Have a walk through the garden and marvel at the miniature trees and plants demonstrating Japanese, Chinese, and Hawaiian styles, and note the similarities and differences. There are some 200 specimens in formal exhibition. Inside are educational displays of tools, techniques, and more plants. Diminutive plants can be purchased in the shop to carry away, or they can be shipped anywhere in the country. For anyone interested in raising bonsai or simply looking at these wonderfully sculpted plants, this is a worthy stop.

Just over two miles up the road is the **Dan De Luz's Woods** showroom (808/968-6607), which displays all sorts of turned wooden bowls, small wood boxes, and other small objects made of tropical island woods. With such a variety, one look here gives you a good sense of the types of wood grown on the island. Dan and his staff turn most of the bowls here and finish them either here or at their shop in Waimea. If you're at all hungry as you buzz through, stop at the adjacent **Koa Shop Kaffee and Restaurant** (7 A.M.–7:30 P.M. except Tues.).

Look for a vintage plantation house painted blue a short ways beyond and on the opposite side of the highway. This is **Tinny Fisher's Antique Shop** (808/968-6011). What started as "yard sale treasures" turned into a unique curio, antiques, and collectibles shop. The shop has all kinds of antiques and collectibles from Asia and Hawaii, including glass balls, Asian furniture, jewelry, and glassware galore. Tinny's also features a good Hawaiiana collection, with artifacts from the ancient days like *kukui* nut lamps, poi pounders, and stone knives.

Mountain View

Mountain View is a village of nurseries specializing in anthuriums. Many of them sport signs and some invite you to look around. **Hawaiian Flower Gardens Nursery** (808/968-8255 or 877/434-0555), open daily except Sunday, is one. There you can learn a little about the history of these fancy exotic flowers and see all sizes and colors. This is the home of the Toyama Red Anthurium, but they come in all shades from stark white to green and deep purple, and sizes from delicate tiny petals and those as big as a spade. Several other nurseries that not only grow but ship these lovely flowers are **Albert Isa Nursery,** P.O. Box 17, Mt. View, HI 96771, 808/968-6125; and **Hale Ohia Gardens,** P.O. Box 1042, Mt. View, HI 96771, 808/968-8631. For mail-order flowers, prices generally range $35–75 plus shipping costs, depending upon the mix.

Bed & Breakfast Mountain View (808/968-6868 or 888/698-9896, fax 808/968-7017, info@bbmtview.com, www.bbmtview.com) is owned and operated by Jane and Linus Chao, both internationally known artists. The couple's inspired artwork graces the home. A residence and artist studio, this B&B lies just outside the village of Mountain View along S. Kulani Road, on a landscaped four-acre parcel with a marvelous view north to Mauna Kea. The spacious guest rooms are modern in all amenities and equipped with king-size, queen-size, or twin beds; two have private bathrooms, two others share. Everyone has use of the common room for reading, TV, or simply appreciating the fine view. A full breakfast is served each morning in the dining room, and each day the offering is different. Room rates run $55–95 daily. For peace and serenity and inspiration of the artistic soul, there is no better place than Bed & Breakfast Mountain View.

Farther into this labyrinth of roads south of Mountain View is **Pineapple Park B&B Hostel** (11-3489 Pikake, 808/968-8170 or 877/865-2266, ppark@aloha.net, www.pineapple-park.com). This is country living in modern style. A bed in the bunkroom runs $25 a night; a private room is $85. These rooms share kitchen and bath facilities and have use of the common room where there's television and Internet access. No breakfast is provided. Checkout is before 10 A.M., check-in until 7 P.M., and quiet time after 10 P.M. This is a smoke-free environment. There is no public transportation nearby, so you'll need your own.

Along the highway is a mini-mart, a post office, gas station, and **Verna's Too Drive In** (808/968-8774) serving plate lunches, sandwiches, burgers, and shakes throughout the day. As you pass through, take a minute to explore the short side road into the village itself. It seems that every house has a garden of ferns, flowers, and native trees. On this old road through the village is **Mt. View Bakery** (808/968-6353, 7:30 A.M.–noon Mon., Tues, and Thurs., 7:30 A.M.–1:30 P.M. Sat.), home of the famous stone cookies—have them with milk!

Glenwood

Located between mile markers 19 and 20, this town offers a gas station and **Hirano's General Store** for a few basic provisions.

Guided tours of the **Kazumura Cave,** reputedly the longest lava tube system in the world, are offered by Rob Ratkowski (808/967-7208). Tours can be arranged for those who just want to have a quick look to two-mile-long jaunts for the experienced spelunker. These underground adventures travel through the undeveloped lava tube for a raw glimpse of the bowels of Mother Nature. Call for times and pricing. Alternately, **Volcano Cave Adventures** (808/968-0763) also offers unpretentious personalized tours into a rainforest cave starting at $25 per person, minimum of two.

A few minutes beyond town you pass **Akatsuka Orchid Gardens** (808/967-8234 or 888/967-6669, open 8:30 A.M.–5 P.M., daily except major holidays, www.akatsuka-orchid.com). If tour buses don't overflow the parking lot, stop in for a look at how orchids are grown. In the covered showroom, an incredible variety of orchids are on display and for sale, and neat little souvenirs are sold in the gift shop. Akatsuka ships cut flowers and potted orchids anywhere in the country.

Volcano Village

You shouldn't miss taking a ride through the village of Volcano, a beautiful old settlement with truly charming houses and cottages outlined in ferns. Follow the signs off the main highway near mile marker 26 to the Old Volcano Highway, which is the main drag through the village. Tiny one-lane roads, many newly paved and smoother than they ever were, lace this community, which sits virtually atop one of the world's undeniable "power spots." This is a heavily forested area with no sidewalks or streetlights. Lighting is generally subdued, so it can be very dark at night. At about 4,000 feet, it gets surprisingly cool and, of course, it often rains—over 150 inches a year. Summer daytime temperatures average 75°F, around 65°F in winter. At night it drops to 55°F in summer and into the 40s or lower in winter. The fog rolls in

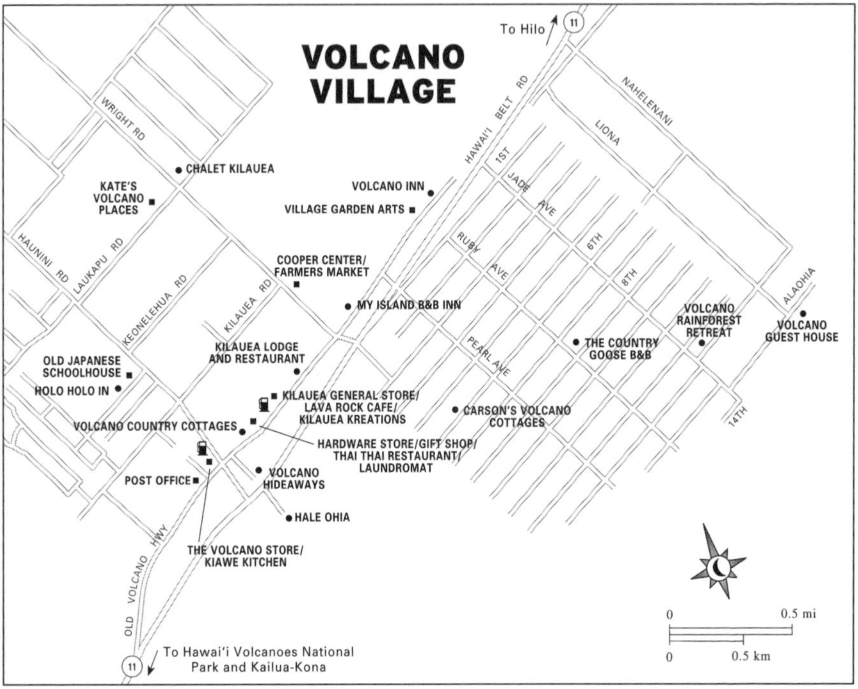

most late afternoons, obscuring distant views but bestowing on the village an otherworldly charm. The area is so green and so vibrant that it appears surrealistic. With flowers, ferns, and trees everywhere, it is hard to imagine a more picturesque village in all of America. But even in this little parcel of paradise, things are changing, if slowly. Volcano Village is home to about 1,500 people and boasts two general stores, a hardware store, two small gift shops/galleries, a post office, a farmers market, a winery, several restaurants, an abundance of accommodations, several artists' studios, and newer and larger subdivisions south of the highway.

SIGHTS

Volcano Golf and Country Club

What's most amazing about this course is where it is. Imagine! You're teeing off atop an active volcano surrounded by one of the last pristine forests in the state. At the right time of year, the surrounding 'ohi'a turn scarlet when they are in bloom. The fairways are carved from lava, while in the distance Mauna Loa looms. Hit a poor shot and you can watch your ball disappear down a steam vent. Just kidding—you're not that close! The course began more than 80 years ago when a group of local golfers hand-cleared three "greens," placing stakes that served as holes. Later this was improved to sand greens with tin cans for holes, and after an eruption in 1924 blanketed the area with volcanic ash that served as excellent fertilizer, the grass grew and the course became a lush green. After World War II the course was extended to 18 holes, and a clubhouse was added. Finally, Jack Snyder, a well-known course architect, redesigned the course to its present par-72 layout. The course is located just north of the Belt Road, about two miles west of the park entrance. Turn on Pi'i Mauna Drive, sometimes called Golf Course

Road. Contact the clubhouse (808/967-7331, www.volcanogolfshop.com) for more information and tee times. After a round of golf, stop for lunch at the clubhouse restaurant.

Volcano Winery

About one mile beyond the golf course at the end of Pi'i Mauna Road and off to your left are the buildings of the Volcano Winery (808/967-7772, 10 A.M.–5:30 P.M. daily, www.volcanowinery.com). This is the only winery on the Big Island and the southernmost in the United States. It's a hands-on operation where everything is done manually. Because the land is at an elevation of about 4,000 feet, the patented Symphony grape (a combination of grenache gris and muscat of Alexandria grapes) is grown to take best advantage of the climatic conditions, which are similar to those in Oregon and Washington. About 14 acres of this rough countryside are currently being cultivated with grapes, producing about 7,000 cases of wine per year, while another 10 acres have been planted in half a dozen other varieties to see if they too will produce acceptable wine. Bottled are dry and semi-dry wines, and three wine and fruit blends including guava chablis, jaboticaba chablis, and a macadamia honey wine. A local favorite, the jaboticaba blend is made with a Brazilian fruit of that name; the honey "wines" are made without any grapes. All bottles cost $13–16 apiece. No tours of the winery are available, but have a sip at the glass-covered koa bar and maybe you'll want to purchase a bottle for later in the evening or a six-bottle case to share with friends when you get home. There also is a small boutique on the premises selling T-shirts, jewelry, *kukui* nut leis, postcards, and other gift items.

ACCOMMODATIONS

There are a great number of accommodations in and around Volcano Village. While most are near the heart of the village, several are located in the fern forests south of the highway and a few are located around the golf course about two miles west of town. Most are bed-and-breakfasts, some are vacation homes where you take care of your own meals, and there is one hostel. These places run from budget and homey to luxurious and elegant, but most are moderate in price and amenities. Some of these establishments also act as agents for other rental homes in the area, so your choices are many. See also the *Volcano House* listing in the *Hawai'i Volcanoes National Park* chapter for a room within the park.

Hostel

Volcano has a hostel, and a fine one it is! Although a modern structure, this all-wood forest house is an old-style place with a comforting, traditional hostel feel. **Holo Holo In** (19-4036 Kalani Honua Rd., 808/967-7950, fax 808/967-8025, holoholo@interpac.net, www.enable.org/holoholo) snuggles under the towering trees in a residential area of the village, next to the old Japanese schoolhouse. Owned, operated, and built by Satoshi Yabuki, a world traveler himself when he was younger, the hostel is open to receive guests 4:30–9 P.M. and check guests out 6:30–9 A.M. Having taken guests for over a dozen years, this hostel has been an AYH member for about half that time. On the downstairs level is a huge kitchen with all needed appliances and utensils and a library of books and information. You are more than welcome to cook, but please clean up after yourself. Here too are a laundry facility and a sauna ($4 per person per use), plus Internet access. Upstairs are the men's and women's dorms and the TV room, and there are bathrooms up and down. Rates are $18 per person for the dorm ($16 for AYH members), or $45 per couple for the two private rooms (each can sleep four, so good for a small family) that share a bathroom. Please bring your own sheets or there will be a nominal extra charge. This is a great little accommodation at a bargain price—a real find.

Vacation Rentals

Conveniently located near stores and restaurants are the three units of **Volcano Hideaways** (P.O. Box 611, Volcano, HI 96785; 808/985-8959, todd@volcanovillage.net, www.volcanovillage.net). Oma's Hapu'u Hideaway is a modern semi-A-frame mountain house of cedar that's great for a family. Here you have all you need: a full kitchen, living room, bathroom, two bedrooms downstairs, one with bunks that's great for kids, and a master bedroom loft upstairs. The house comes with TV and VCR and phone. It's a cozy place that goes for $125 a night. The owners live across the street in a plantation house, and in the rear is The Maid's Quarters, a self-contained cottage with full kitchen, living room tiled with marble, fireplace, spacious bedroom, completely updated bathroom, and a hot tub. This is a lovely place, just right for a romantic couple. This cottage runs $115 a night. Next door is the refurbished Haunani House. Also good for a family, it has three bedrooms, two baths, a full kitchen, living room with gas fireplace, washer and dryer, and television, and rents for $135 a night. All three are good value for the money. Each has a two-night minimum with a fifth night free; $15 for each additional person over two. No breakfast is served.

Bed-and-Breakfasts, $50-100

A bed-and-breakfast with an excellent reputation is **My Island Bed and Breakfast Inn** (19-3896 Volcano Rd., 808/967-7216, fax 808/967-7719, myisland@ilhawaii.net, www.myislandinnhawaii.com). The main house, the oldest in the village, is a New England–style three-level house from 1886 that was the Lyman family summer home for many years. Rooms in this building rent for a reasonable $55–70 single to $70–85 double; some share a bathroom. A few steps away are two garden units that go for $80–105. A fully furnished vacation house on the property, plus five other vacation homes in the village and up near the golf course, go for $145 double with an extra charge for additional guests; two nights minimum. All guests are served a world-class breakfast each morning in the main house. Spend some time in the exquisite seven-acre flower garden here, as it is a wonderful extra benefit to this property.

Located on the downhill side of the highway, the **Country Goose Bed and Breakfast** (P.O. Box 597, Volcano, HI 96785, 808/967-7759 or 800/238-7101 Mainland, fax 808/985-8673, cgoose@interpac.net, www.countrygoose.com) is a very pleasant place with lots of knickknacks on the walls. The knotty pine walls, open-beamed ceiling, and decor all say easy country living. Comfortable and homey, rooms include private baths and entrances, and the common room is open to all guests. Everyone is served a hearty country-style breakfast each morning in the dining room. Nestled under 'ohi'a trees and ferns, half a mile from the highway, this little place is quiet. The gracious owner, Joan Earley, has built herself a fine retreat here and loves to share it with others who love the area. Rooms rent for $90 a night for two, for two nights or more, with an extra $10 for a third person. Joan also represents several one-, two-, and three-bedroom rental homes in the village and out near the golf course that are available for nightly ($135–220), weekly, or longer stays.

Owned and operated by Bonnie Goodell, **Volcano Guest House** (P.O. Box 6, Volcano, HI 96785, 808/967-7775 or 866/886-5226, fax 808/985-7056, innkeeper@volcanguesthouse.com, www.volcanoguesthouse.com) is a very friendly hideaway on the farthest back road of Mauna Loa Estates subdivision, south of the highway from Volcano Village. Each fully furnished unit on property is designed as a self-sufficient unit where guests are guaranteed peace and quiet on a lovely six-acre homesite. The two-story guest home is bright and airy. Enter into a combo living room, kitchen, and dining area, with twin beds in a bedroom. Upstairs is a sleeping area with two twin beds and a queen-size bed. Futons can sleep even more. In the main house, a one-bedroom apartment called Claudia's Place has its own entrance and bathroom. It's completely handicapped-accessible and will sleep up to three. Upstairs in the main house is a separate unit with two bedrooms, one with a queen-size bed and the other with two twins, a bathroom, kitchenette, and views out over the forest. Two newer units called the Twins have been built down the drive. They are mirror footprints of each other and face one another across a covered patio. The Twins are also fully accessible and each has a living room, kitchen, queen-size and twin beds, and sleeps up to four. Bring your own food if you want to cook dinners, but there are always breakfast goodies at the entrance to the house, which you can have anytime you wish. The Volcano Guest House is environmentally friendly, there are laundry facilities on-site, and it's a kid-friendly place. The rate for Claudia's Place and the Upstairs is $85, $95 for either of the Twins, and $105 for the cottage, plus $15 for each additional adult, $10 for kids. Two nights minimum, with the seventh night at no charge. Sometimes Bonnie will allow a one-night stay, but there is a $20 surcharge. Any of the rooms at Volcano Guest House are excellent value for the money.

Bed-and-Breakfasts, $100-150

Kate's Volcano Places (P.O. Box 159 Volcano, HI 96785, 808/967-7990 or 877/967-7990, kathryn@volcanoplaces.com, www.volcanoplaces.com) is a winner! A pleasant, homey, and cozy place, the cottage is a modern reconstruction with full attention to detail that combines Western cabin and Scandinavian styles with a touch of the Orient. One large room, this cottage has a king-size bed, separate bathroom, and full kitchen equipped with all conveniences and stocked with supplies. Up front, the reconditioned island-style Kahi Malu house has two bedrooms, one bathroom, and a full kitchen; the living room, amazingly, is solid koa. Like the cottage, it provides all modern conveniences. Set back farther on the same property is the newer one-bedroom, all-wood luxurious Nohea cottage. Off the central sitting room is a full kitchen, beyond the sliding glass doors is the bedroom, and in the bathroom are twin showers with massage heads. The house and two cottages are set toward the back of the village and are very quiet and private. At a separate location, the three-bedroom Hiiaka house from 1939 is surrounded by a large yard. This house is perfect for a family of up to eight with its huge living room and fireplace, full kitchen, and three bedrooms. Rental rates are $95 for the cottage, $135 for Kahi Mahi, $240 for Nohea, and $150 for Hiiaka, and this includes breakfast goodies stocked in the refrigerator for each morning. For information and reservations, contact Kathryn Grout.

Volcano Country Cottages (P.O. Box 545, Volcano, HI 96785, 808/967-7960 or 888/446-3910, aloha@volcanocottages.com, www.volcanocottages.com) are conveniently located in the heart of the village at one of its oldest homes. Available are the Ohelo Berry Cottage for $95 for one night and the two-bedroom Artist's House for $120; $15 for each additional person beyond two. Perfect for a couple, the studio cottage is a cozy one-room affair with kitchenette, bathroom, room heater, and covered entry that snuggles into the back vegetation. Each morning, a filling and tasty breakfast of fruits and baked goods is left for you to have at your leisure. Set closer to the front of the property under towering tsugi trees, the Artist's House contains a full kitchen (also stocked with morning treats), a woodstove, and washer and dryer. It sleeps four comfortably and up to four more on pull-out futons. Newest are the two one-bedroom, hardwood-floor cottages built at the back of this thickly vegetated lot. Each has a full kitchen, sitting room, and covered lanai and rents for $120 a night. For use by all guests, the hot tub sits behind the main house in the fern forest. This is a gracious place, one of peace and tranquility.

Follow a private mountain lane for a few minutes into an enchanted clearing where the artwork of a meticulous Japanese garden surrounds a New England gabled and turreted home and its attendant cottages of red-on-brown rough-cut shingles. Once the hideaway of the Dillinghams, an old and influential *kama'aina* family, **Hale Ohia** (P.O. Box 758, Volcano, HI 96785, 808/967-7986 or 800/455-3803, fax 808/967-8610, reservations@haleohia.com, www.haleohia.com) is now owned and operated by Michael D. Tuttle, who purchased the property after falling in love at first sight. The main house holds the Dillingham Suite, $129 per night, with its own sitting room, bath, and covered lanai. Simple and clean, with hardwood floors and wainscoted walls, the home is the epitome of country elegance and Hawaiian style. Adjacent in the main house, occupying one bedroom and a big bath, is the Master Suite for $119. Hale Ohia Cottage, once the gardener's residence, has two stories. Stained-glass windows with a calla lily-and-poppy motif add a special touch, while the low ceilings are reminiscent of the captain's quarters on a sailing ship. The first floor rear has a full kitchen and a covered lanai complete with barbecue grill that makes it perfect for evening relaxation. Narrow stairs lead to a full bath located on the first landing, and the upstairs opens into a bright and airy parlor and adjacent bedrooms that can sleep five comfortably, $159. Occupying the bottom floor front of the Ohia Cottage are the Iiwi and Camellia suites, $95–109, which are wheelchair-accessible and can be combined for larger groups. Hale Lehua, once a private study, is secluded down its own lava footpath and rents for $139. The interior is cozy with fireplace, bamboo and wicker furniture, self-contained bathroom, covered lanai, and partial kitchen. More rustic yet more romantic and secluded is the Ihilani Cottage at $159. Newest of the units is Cottage #44—created from a water tank! The round redwood tank has been turned into the bedroom, and attached to it in a newly built structure are the living room, efficiency kitchen, bathroom with shower and whirlpool tub, and covered lanai. This cute little unit is a treasure and rents for $179. To make your stay even more delightful, room rates include an "extended" continental breakfast, and guests are welcome to immerse themselves in the bubbling whirlpool tub that awaits under a canopy of Japanese cedars and glimmering stars. No TV and no smoking, but there is an on-site phone in the wisteria-covered gazebo.

Located at the end of Old Volcano Road on the lower end of town, **Volcano Inn** (808/967-7293 or 800/997-2292, fax 808/985-7349, volcano@volcanoinn.com, www.volcanoinn.com) has four rooms in its main building and other rooms at a second building only a minute away. The main three-story house is of modern design, with a common room and huge dining room where complimentary self-serve breakfasts are available to all guests 7–9 A.M. Rooms run $105–130, $20 less for single occupants. Each has a private entrance and bath, TV and VCR, refrigerator, and coffeemaker. Internet access is free to guests. The Guest House at Pali Uli has three rooms at $99–125, with a detached studio cottage for $136. The inn also operates horseback riding tours. Inquire about what's currently offered.

Deep in the fern forest, **Carson's Volcano Cottages** (P.O. Box 503, Volcano, HI 96785, 808/967-7683 or 800/845-5282, www.carsonscottage.com) offers one B&B room in the main house, but by far the nicer accommodations are in the detached cottages. The suite in the main house is located upstairs and runs $130 a night. The cottage accommodations all have private baths, entrances, and decks, and the garden has a hot tub for everyone to use. The one-acre property is naturally landscaped with ʻohiʻa and ferns, and moss-covered sculptures of Balinese gods peek through the foliage. Nick's Cabin #19, $130 double, a miniature plantation house with corrugated roof and woodstove, has a mini-kitchen and a bath with a skylight—rustic country charm. The three-room cottage, $115 per room, has vaulted ceilings and queen-size beds, and rooms decorated in Hawaiian Monarchy, Oriental, and tropical floral styles. Leaded glass windows open to a private porch. An extended continental breakfast is provided for all guests in their dining room. You'll be comfortable in front of the living room fireplace or enjoying the evening sky from the hot tub. Also rented are three other one- and two-bedroom, fully furnished cottages nearby that run $140–170 and a seaside retreat down in Kapoho.

Bed-and-Breakfasts, $150-250

Kilauea Lodge (P.O. Box 116, Volcano Village, HI 96785, 808/967-7366, fax 967-7367, stay@kilauealodge.com, www.kilauealodge.com), owned and operated by Lorna and Albert Jeyte, is the premier restaurant and lodge atop Volcano, as well as one of the very best on the island. The solid stone and timber structure was built in 1938 as a YMCA camp and functioned as such until 1962, when it became a "mom and pop operation." It faded into the ferns until Lorna and Albert revitalized it in 1987, opening in 1988. The lodge is a classic, with a vaulted, open-beamed ceiling. A warm and cozy "international fireplace" dating from the days of the YMCA camp is embedded with stones and plaques from all over the world. An assortment of rooms, ranging $140–160 and including a complete breakfast for all guests in the restaurant, are located in three adjacent buildings on the property, and there is a hot tub for guests in the rear garden. The brooding rooms of Hale Maluna, the original guesthouse section, were transformed into bright, cozy, and romantic suites. Each room has a bathroom with vaulted 18-foot ceilings and a skylight, a working fireplace, queen-size or twin beds, and swivel rocking chair. A separate one-bedroom cottage, set in the ferns to the side, features a gas fireplace (central heat too), a queen-size bed, private bath, and small living room with queen-size pull-out sofa. In 1991, Kilauea Lodge opened the Hale Aloha building with seven new units around a commodious common room where you can read and snooze by a crackling fire. All rooms in this building are spacious, with vaulted ceilings and tastefully furnished with wicker furniture, white curtains, and fluffy quilts to keep off the evening chill. Many are hung with original artwork by Gwendolyn O'Connor. One downstairs room is handicapped accessible. Check-in is 3–5 P.M. at the office; after that, check in at the restaurant. The Kilauea Lodge provides one of the most *civilized* atmospheres in Hawaii in one of its most powerful natural areas. The combination is hard to beat.

Just up the road from the Kilauea Lodge is the cute little two-bedroom cottage, **Tutu's Place.** Built in 1929 by Uncle Billy of hotel chain fame for "tutu" (grandma), it was bought several decades later by the Warner family. Mr. Warner was a minister and was involved in Hawaiian politics. His wife, Ruth Warner, lived in the cottage for 30 years until it was bought in 1995 by Lorna Larson-Jeyte, the owner of the Kilauea Lodge, who used to visit as a child. Although it's been completely refurbished, people in the know say that the cottage is still imbued with the spirit of Ruth Warner. It's done in a theme of rattan and koa, with a fireplace in the living room, a full kitchen, and a wonderful little bathroom. For a small place, it has a surprisingly roomy feel. The rate is $175 for two people, including breakfast at the Kilauea Lodge, plus $20 for each additional person. To make reservations, call the Kilauea Lodge, and ask for Tutu's Place.

Embraced within the arms of ferns, ʻohiʻa, and bamboo are the three cottages of **Volcano Rainforest Retreat** (808/985-8696 or 800/550-8696, volrain@bigisland.net, www.volcanoretreat.com), a luxury accommodation for discriminating guests wanting privacy for their stay in the rainforest. Constructed in an open style of cedar and redwood, these handcrafted buildings are warm and welcoming and rich in color and detail, and have plenty of windows that look out onto the encircling forest. Hale Kipa (Guest Cottage) has a cozy living room with full kitchen and sleeping loft, perfect for a couple or small family. The six-sided Hale Hoʻano (Sanctuary), the smallest and with the most obvious Japanese influence, has the benefit of an outdoor ofuro tub and shower, and is conducive to meditation and spiritual enrichment. The octagonal Hale Nahele (Forest House) is one large room with an attached full bath, efficiency kitchen and sitting area, and covered lanai—just right for a cozy couple. Each has a small heater for those rare chilly nights. Rates are $200, $124 single/$140 double, $170 a night, respectively; discounts for three nights or longer. The newest addition is the cedar-shingle Bamboo Guest House at $260 a night. This exquisite one-bedroom vacation rental has a full kitchen and dining area, sitting room under clerestory windows, and a relaxing bath with outdoor ofuro tub. All units are stocked with breakfast foods to have at your leisure. The Volcano Rainforest Retreat gets a gold star! For information and reservations or for couple's and meditation retreats offered on property, contact the owners, Peter and Kathleen Golden.

Peeking from the *hapu'u* fern forest in a manicured glen is **Chalet Kilauea** (998 Wright Rd., 808/967-7786 or 800/937-7786, fax 808/967-8660 or 800/577-1849, reservations@volcano-hawaii.com, www.volcano-hawaii.com), where you will be cordially accommodated by owners Lisha and Brian Crawford and their staff. Downstairs there's an outdoor lounge area, and a black-and-white checkerboard dining room where wrought-iron tables sit before a huge picture window. A three-course candlelight breakfast is served here every morning. Enter the second level of the main house to find a guest living room where you can while away the hours playing chess, listening to a large collection of CDs, or gazing from the wraparound windows at a treetop view of the surrounding forest, ferns, and impeccable grounds. Beyond the koi pond in the garden, a freestanding gazebo houses an eight-person hot tub available 24 hours a day. The main house, called The Inn at Volcano, is known for elegance and luxury. It holds four suites and two theme rooms, $139–399, including the Oriental Jade Room, Out of Africa Room, Continental Lace Suite, and the Treehouse Suite. An adjacent "cabin" is the Hapu'u Suite. It has a fireplace in the cozy living room but perhaps its best feature is the master bathroom, which looks out onto the back garden.

Chalet Kilauea also has many other accommodations in Volcano Village. Lokahi Lodge has four rooms that run $99–149, or $590 for a group of up to 14 people. For those on a tighter budget, the Volcano Bed and Breakfast rents rooms for $49–69 and still has plenty of common space. The entire house can be rented for $293 a night and can sleep 13. In addition, several vacation homes dotted here and there about town in the secluded privacy of the forest are available for $139–379. Whatever your price range and whatever your needs, Chalet Kilauea will have something for you, and breakfast is an option at most accommodations.

FOOD

Volcano Village has a surprising diversity of restaurant options that range from inexpensive to gourmet.

Local Style

Situated behind the Kilauea General Store is **Volcano's Lava Rock Cafe** (808/967-8526, 7:30 A.M.–9 P.M. Tues.–Sat., 7:30 A.M.–4 P.M. Sun., 7:30 A.M.–5 P.M. Mon.), the most local of the eateries in the village. Start your day with eggs, griddle items, or loco moco. For lunch you can get a plate lunch, burger, or sandwich, along with sides, fountain drinks, and coffee. Dinners are a bit heartier with the likes of teriyaki chicken and New York steak, and almost everything is under $12, except for a few of the meat dishes that run up to $18.50. While not gourmet, you get plentiful portions at a good price in pleasant surroundings—and there's even Internet access.

You can get away from the crowds and have a satisfying breakfast or lunch at **Volcano Country Club Restaurant** (808/967-8228), at the golf course clubhouse. The green and white interior complements the fairways, which can be seen through the surrounding plate glass windows. A fireplace fills the center of this country kitchen–style room. For breakfast choose omelettes, hotcakes, or other standard American fare. Lunch selections include hearty sandwiches, salads, and burgers, as well as local favorites like teriyaki beef, saimin, or loco moco. Many stop by just for the Portuguese bean soup. Most everything on the menu is under $9.

Thai

Located to the side of the hardware store, **Thai Thai Restaurant** (808/967-7969, 5–9 P.M. daily, takeout only after 8:30 P.M.). This restaurant puts out food that will transport you to the Orient. It has established a good reputation in town for tasty food and large portions. Start with an appetizer (some as big as entrées) like deep-fried tofu or chicken satay. Traditional soups and salads come next, followed by curries or stir-fried selections, most of which can be made with your choice of shrimp, chicken, beef, or pork. Other entrées are garlic and pepper shrimp, ginger chicken and eggplant and basil. Almost everything on the menu is in the $10–16 range.

Italian

Adjacent to The Volcano Store is **Kiawe Kitchen** (808/967-7711, noon–2:30 P.M. and 5:30–9:30 P.M. Thurs.–Tues.), a specialty restaurant for gourmet pizza, pasta, and meat dishes. The tomato-red walls, wood lattice ceiling, granite-top tables, and long bench along the wall all point to an unusual place. Besides that, the kitchen has a wood-fired pizza oven. Although the menu changes somewhat each night, you might expect, aside from the various pizzas, a wood-fired roast lamb sandwich, linguine and clams, rib eye steak, or penne alla puttanesca. The pizza runs around $14 and other entrées $15–24.

Continental

The **Kilauea Lodge Restaurant** (808/967-7366, 5:30–9 P.M. nightly) is an extraordinary restaurant serving gourmet continental cuisine—the premier restaurant in Volcano Village. Reservations are a must. A large fireplace dominates one side of the room with an inviting couch at its front. A warm, welcoming, and homey place, the Kilauea Lodge Restaurant has fine dining in an unpretentious setting. A very friendly and professional staff serves the excellent food prepared by Albert, the owner, and his kitchen help. Although the menu changes a bit every night, you'll start off with fresh bread studded with sunflower and sesame seeds. Appetizers such as baked mushroom caps stuffed with crab and cheese will titillate your palate, or try the baked brie cheese, a specialty. Entrées, ranging mostly $19–37, include soup, salad, and vegetables. The menu is strong on the meats, with its heavy German influence, but vegetarians will be delighted with their options too. Dinner features seafood Mauna Kea (succulent pieces of seafood served atop a bed of fettuccine), paupiettes of beef (prime rib slices rolled around herbs and mushrooms in a special sauce), German sausage plate, lamb Provençal, chicken Tuscany, and a number of more unusual items such as venison, duck à l'orange, and hasenpfeffer (braised rabbit). Always a great choice, the catch of the day is blackened, broiled, or sautéed with a savory sauce. There are always nightly specials and each dish is infused with herbs and pungent seasonings. To match any meal, you can select from the extensive wine list, which includes a special reserve section. Desserts are wonderful, and the meal can be topped off with a cup of Irish or Italian coffee. Expensive, consistently great quality, this is a place for a wonderful evening out.

Café

Around the side and behind The Volcano Store is **JP's Volcano Cafe** (5 A.M.–4 P.M.) This quick-serve café has eggs, pancakes, and local favorites for breakfast and plate lunches, sandwiches, salads, and soup for lunch, plus lots of coffee all day long, with little on the menu over $7. Seating is outside under the awning.

Pizza

If you're looking strictly for takeout, try **Big O's Pizza** (808/985-9995, 4:30–8:30 P.M. Tues.–Sat., 4–6:30 P.M. Sun.–Mon.). The basic 12-inch, thick-crust pie here runs $12.50 with each topping at 50 cents. Call in your order and pick it up at the Kilauea General Store; count on about 30 minutes to make.

Markets

The Volcano Store (808/967-7210, 5 A.M.–7 P.M. daily), also called the "upper store," sells a good selection of basic foods and groceries, and general dry goods items, tropical flowers, a few camping supplies, camera film, and gasoline. For events happening around the village, see the community bulletin board on the wall outside. There is an ATM inside, public telephone booths out front in the parking lot, and a few steps away is the post office.

Just down the road is **Kilauea General Store** (808/967-7555, 7 A.M.–7:30 P.M. daily, until 7 P.M. on Sunday), also called the "lower store." Although it's not as well stocked as a full grocery store, it does have select food items, including some fresh fruit, a deli case, a good selection of beer and wine, postcards, rental videos, an ATM, and an excellent community bulletin board. The Kilauea General Store also sells gasoline.

A **farmers market** (8–11 A.M. Sun.) sells local produce, fruit, flowers, baked goods, soups and other prepared foods, used books, and other items. It's located along Wright Road at the Cooper Center. Come early for the food. This is a wonderful community event. Don't miss it.

SHOPPING

In a separate building behind the Kilauea General Store is **Kilauea Kreations** (808/967-8090, 9:30 A.M.–5:30 P.M. daily), a shop that carries gifts, crafts, and art by local artists. Perhaps best of what they have is wonderfully colorful quilts, quilting and sewing supplies, and materials.

Local artist Ira Ono has opened the **Village Garden Arts** gallery (808/985-8979, 10 A.M.–4 P.M. Tues.–Sat., www.volcanogardenarts.com) to display his own fine contemporary creations and those of other local artists, as well as to create studio space. Displayed are ceramic and clay figures and masks, oil paintings, stone sculptures, wood art, and collages. Inside are the gallery and gift shop, while outside you'll find sculptures on the lawn, a greenhouse, and a nature trail through the yard. Find this gallery at the lower end of Old Volcano Road.

Located in the Volcano Village Center is **Volcano True Value Hardware** (808/967-7969, 7:30 A.M.–5 P.M. daily) for all your home and yard needs, as well as some camping supplies.

For arts and crafts by local artists and souvenirs (mostly imported), have a look at the **Village Art Store** above the hardware store.

INFORMATION AND SERVICES

Out front of the hardware store is a small **tourist information center** (9 A.M.–5 P.M. daily), where you can pick up maps and brochures, as well as information about restaurants and accommodations.

The **post office,** (7:30 A.M.–3:30 P.M. Mon.–Fri., 11 A.M.–noon Sat.) is located in the upper part of the village near The Volcano Store.

There are no banks in Volcano Village, but there are ATM machines at the Kilauea General Store and at the Volcano Store.

For **Internet** access, check at the Lava Rock Cafe.

Volcano Wash and Dry (8 A.M.–7 P.M.) sits behind the hardware store, where you can buy soap for the washing machines.

Gas is available from both the The Volcano Store and Kilauea General Store.

KA'U AND HAWAI'I VOLCANOES NATIONAL PARK

Ka'u is a broad strip at the southern end of the Big Island. It swaths the south flank of Mauna Loa, stretching from Kilauea Caldera in the east to South Point and beyond to the community of Ocean View in the west. Much of it is raw and rugged land, lava of recent age, while the remainder is open grassland, rangeland, and the thick forests on the higher mountain slopes. Ka'u was sugar country and large tracts grew cane for decades. Sugar was the economic powerhouse of the district, but sugar is now gone. Ranching, also a vital element in the Ka'u economy for decades, still remains. A relative backwater, Ka'u has struggled since the demise of its sugar industry, but macadamia nuts and coffee are taking hold in its place. The vast majority of Hawai'i Volcanoes Nation Park lies within the district of Ka'u, and even that which spreads over the western end of Puna is more like the rough lava lands of Ka'u than the steamy lowlands of its neighbor. One major road runs through Ka'u, the Hawaii Belt Road, Route 11. All the towns of Ka'u—and that is all that Ka'u has—lie along this road, but off it run a few smaller byways that take you into the backcountry. The national park is the big draw for Ka'u, but it also has good examples of plantation towns, several rare and unique natural sites, and plenty of space to slow down and enjoy the scenery. Ka'u has the longest undeveloped coastline in the state. While this region has been hit hard by the economic downturn of the past decade, it is now, like the rest of the state, experiencing a period of development and there is some movement to preserve this pristine shoreline for its natural, historical, and cultural value.

© ROBERT NILSEN

HIGHLIGHTS

Hawai'i Volcanoes National Park Visitors Center: There are many wonderful places to visit at Volcanoes National Park, but the first place you should stop is the visitors center (page 283).

Thomas A. Jaggar Museum: For greater insight into the dynamics of the volcano and what you might experience as you travel through the park, make a stop here (page 287).

Halema'uma'u Crater: This is the mythical home of the Hawaiian goddess Pele and the center of Kilauea Caldera. It is perhaps the easiest and most appropriate spot to peer into the heart of the mountain (page 287).

Thurston Lava Tube: To glimpse a fine example of how lava travels underground, visit the easily accessible tube (page 290).

Chain of Craters Road: Providing a great introduction to the park, the road takes you from the Kilauea Caldera down the mountain past small craters, and across older lava flows. It also travels over the edge of the *pali* to the ocean and the new land created by the recent and ongoing active lava flows (page 290).

Punalu'u Black Sand Beach: This is a favorite of locals and one of the few spots on the island to see hawksbill and green sea turtles. They love to swim in the current of the bay and bask on the warm black sand (page 302).

South Point: A place of cultural and historical importance, this is the southernmost tip of the island and country. It is here that Polynesian voyagers may have landed first when exploring from their lands to the south (page 306).

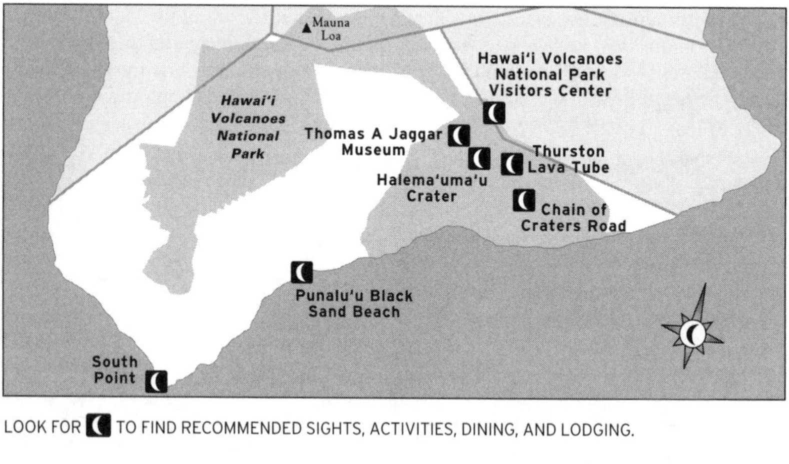

LOOK FOR ☾ TO FIND RECOMMENDED SIGHTS, ACTIVITIES, DINING, AND LODGING.

PLANNING YOUR TIME

Some 2.5 million people visit Hawai'i Volcanoes National Park each year. You should be one. While some people visit the park as part of a day trip on their way through to Kona or Hilo, give it more time. Plan to spend the night (or two) in Volcano or Pahala so you'll be close by rather than travel hours just to get there. The perfect place to start your time at the park is at the visitors center. There you get an introduction to this wonderfully dynamic location. A drive along Crater Rim Drive, with stops at major sites, will keep you busy for a day. Another day can be spent along the Chain of Craters Road and at other sites in the park. For those who desire a more up-close look at the park, get out of your car and hike some of the many park trails. A number can be traversed in less than two hours, but for the diehard, several trails require multiple days of hiking. While the park is the major drawing card for Ka'u, don't fail to spend at least one day in the rest of the region. Pull off into Pahala, one of the best examples of a sugar plantation town. Dip down to the ocean to catch sight of turtles swimming in the bay off Punalu'u black-sand beach or stop to check out the unique Honu'apo seashore ponds. The 12-mile side trip down South Point Road brings you to Ka Lae, the southernmost point of the island, and a three-mile hike from there brings you to a green-sand beach. Ka'u has many wonderful sites, but you have to work a bit to get to them. Pahala, Na'alehu/Wai'ohinu, and Ocean View all have accommodations and food, so there is no need to hurry through.

Hawai'i Volcanoes National Park

Hawai'i Volcanoes National Park (HVNP) is an unparalleled experience in geological grandeur. The upper end of the park is the summit of stupendous Mauna Loa, the most massive mountain on earth. Mauna Loa Road branches off Hwy. 11 and ends at a foot trail for the hale and hearty who trek to the 13,679-foot summit. The park's heart is **Kilauea Caldera,** almost three miles across, 400 feet deep, and encircled by 11 miles of **Crater Rim Drive.** At the park **visitors center** you can give yourself a crash course in geology while picking up park maps, information, and backcountry camping permits. Nearby is **Volcano House,** Hawaii's oldest hotel, which has hosted a steady stream of adventurers, luminaries, royalty, and heads of state ever since it opened its doors in the 1860s. Just a short drive away is a pocket of indigenous forest, providing the perfect setting for a bird sanctuary. In a separate detached section of the park is **'Ola'a Forest,** a pristine wilderness area of unspoiled flora and fauna.

Crater Rim Drive circles Kilauea Caldera past steam vents, sulfur springs, and tortured fault lines that always seem on the verge of gaping wide and swallowing. On the way you can peer into the maw of **Halema'uma'u Crater,** home of the fire goddess, Pele, and you'll pass **Hawaiian Volcano Observatory** (not open to public), which has been monitoring geologic activity since the turn of the 20th century. Adjacent to the observatory is the **Thomas A. Jaggar Museum,** an excellent facility where you can educate yourself on the past and present volcanology of the park. An easy walk is **Devastation Trail,** a paved path across a desolate cinder field where gray, lifeless trunks of a suffocated forest lean like old gravestones. Within minutes is **Thurston Lava Tube,** a magnificent natural tunnel *"leid"* by amazingly vibrant fern grottoes at the entrance and exit.

The southwestern section of the park is dominated by the **Ka'u Desert,** not a plain of sand but a semi-arid slope of lava flow, cinder, scrub bushes, and heat that's been defiled by the windblown debris and gases of Kilauea Volcano and fractured by the sinking coastline. It is a desolate region, an area crossed by a

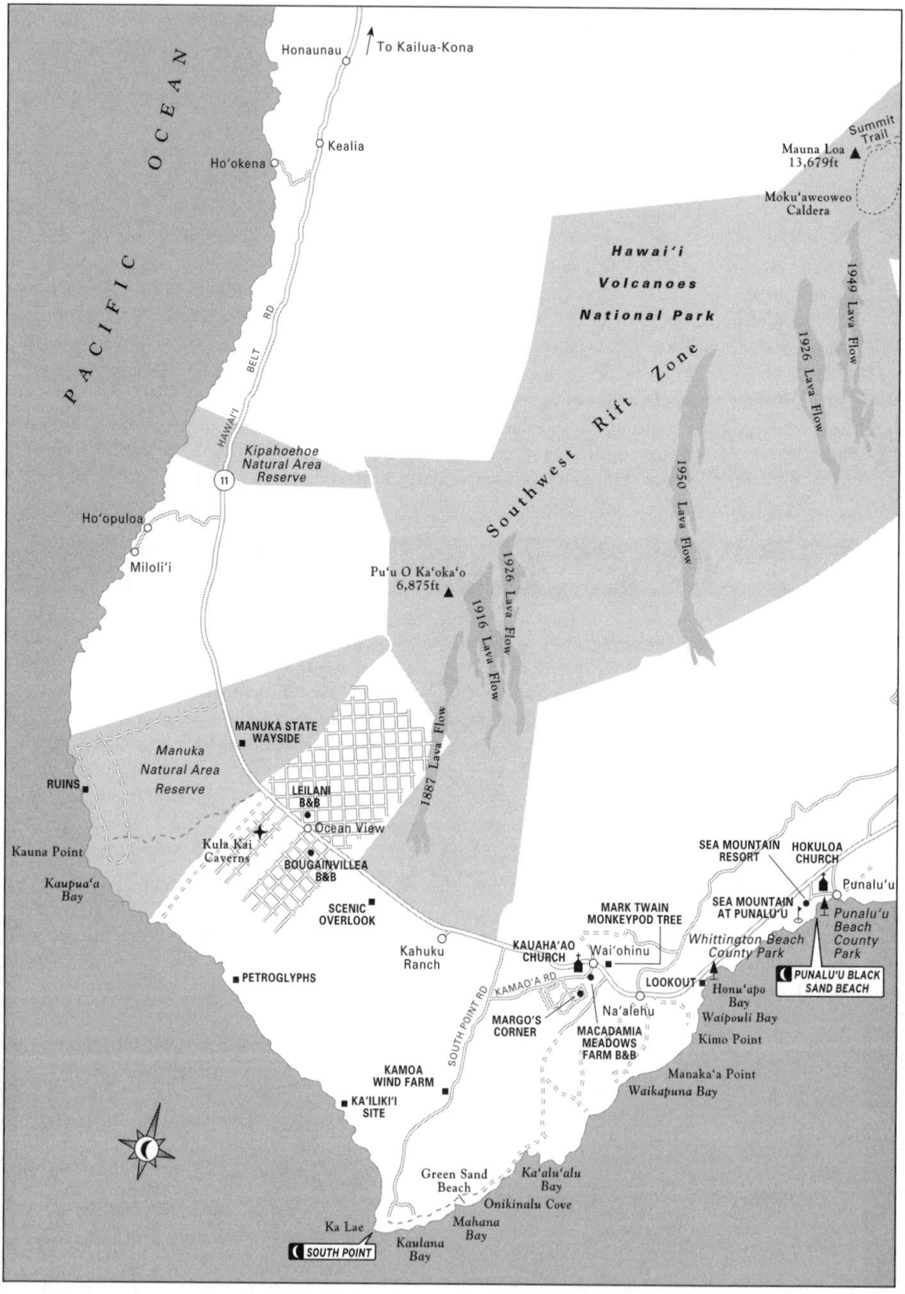
To Kailua-Kona
Honaunau
Kealia
Ho'okena
PACIFIC OCEAN
HAWAI'I BELT RD
11
Kipahoehoe Natural Area Reserve
Ho'opuloa
Miloli'i
Hawai'i Volcanoes National Park
Southwest Rift Zone
Summit Trail
Mauna Loa 13,679ft
Moku'aweoweo Caldera
1949 Lava Flow
1926 Lava Flow
1950 Lava Flow
Pu'u O Ka'oka'o 6,875ft
1926 Lava Flow
1916 Lava Flow
1887 Lava Flow
MANUKA STATE WAYSIDE
Manuka Natural Area Reserve
RUINS
LEILANI B&B
Ocean View
Kula Kai Caverns
BOUGAINVILLEA B&B
Kauna Point
Kaupua'a Bay
SCENIC OVERLOOK
Kahuku Ranch
PETROGLYPHS
SOUTH POINT RD
KAMAO'A RD
KAUAHA'AO CHURCH
Wai'ohinu
MARK TWAIN MONKEYPOD TREE
MARGO'S CORNER
MACADAMIA MEADOWS FARM B&B
Na'alehu
LOOKOUT
SEA MOUNTAIN RESORT
HOKULOA CHURCH
Punalu'u
SEA MOUNTAIN AT PUNALU'U
Whittington Beach County Park
Punalu'u Beach County Park
PUNALU'U BLACK SAND BEACH
Honu'apo Bay
Waipouli Bay
Kimo Point
Manaka'a Point
Waikapuna Bay
KAMOA WIND FARM
KA'ILIKI'I SITE
Green Sand Beach
Ka'alu'alu Bay
Onikinalu Cove
Mahana Bay
Ka Lae
SOUTH POINT
Kaulana Bay

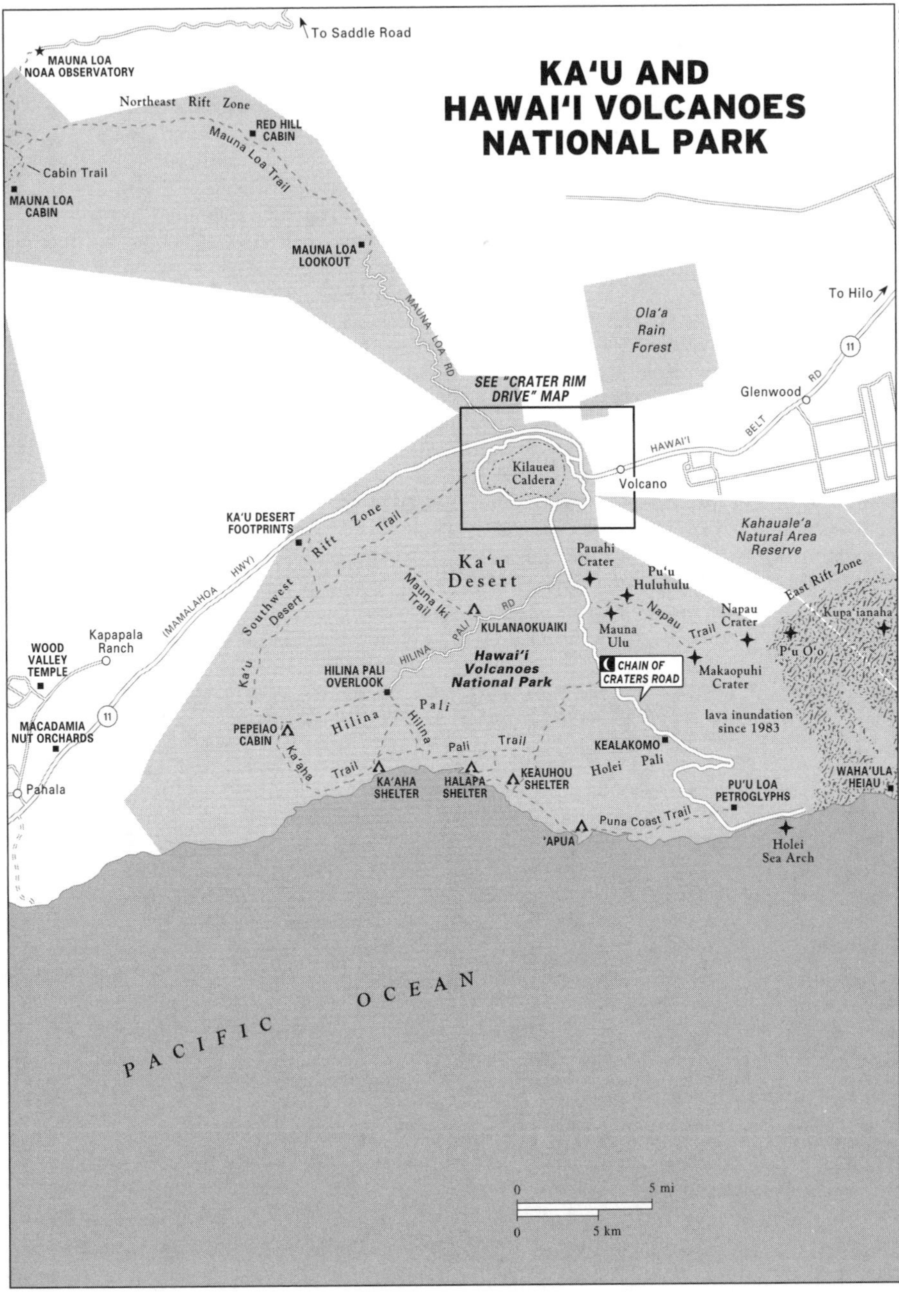
KA'U AND HAWAI'I VOLCANOES NATIONAL PARK
To Saddle Road
MAUNA LOA NOAA OBSERVATORY
Northeast Rift Zone
RED HILL CABIN
Mauna Loa Trail
Cabin Trail
MAUNA LOA CABIN
MAUNA LOA LOOKOUT
MAUNA LOA RD
Ola'a Rain Forest
To Hilo
11
SEE "CRATER RIM DRIVE" MAP
Glenwood
HAWAI'I BELT RD
Kilauea Caldera
Volcano
KA'U DESERT FOOTPRINTS
Rift Zone Trail
Kahauale'a Natural Area Reserve
Pauahi Crater
Ka'u Desert
Pu'u Huluhulu
East Rift Zone
(MAMALAHOA HWY)
Southwest Desert
Mauna Iki Trail
Napau Trail
Napau Crater
Kupa'ianaha
Kapapala Ranch
KULANAOKUAIKI
Mauna Ulu
Pu'u O'o
WOOD VALLEY TEMPLE
Ka'u
HILINA PALI RD
Hawai'i Volcanoes National Park
CHAIN OF CRATERS ROAD
Makaopuhi Crater
HILINA PALI OVERLOOK
Pali
Hilina
lava inundation since 1983
MACADAMIA NUT ORCHARDS
PEPEIAO CABIN
Ka'aha Trail
Hilina Pali Trail
KEALAKOMO
Holei Pali
Pahala
KA'AHA SHELTER
HALAPA SHELTER
KEAUHOU SHELTER
PU'U LOA PETROGLYPHS
WAHA'ULA HEIAU
Puna Coast Trail
'APUA
Holei Sea Arch
PACIFIC OCEAN
0
5 mi
0
5 km

few trails that are a challenge even to the sturdy and experienced hiker. Most visitors, however, head down the **Chain of Craters Road,** first through the 'ohi'a and fern forests, then past numerous secondary craters and down the *pali* to the coast where the road ends abruptly at a hardened flow of lava and from where visitors can glean information about current volcanic activities from the small ranger station and try to glimpse the current volcanic activity in the distance.

The indomitable power of Volcanoes National Park is apparent to all who come here. Mark Twain, enchanted by his sojourn through Volcanoes in the 1860s, quipped, "The smell of sulfur is strong, but not unpleasant to a sinner." Amen, brother! Wherever you stop to gaze, realize that you are standing on a thin skin of cooled lava in an unstable earthquake zone atop one of the world's most active volcanoes.

Established in 1916 as the 13th U.S. national park, Hawai'i Volcanoes National Park now covers 520 square miles. Based on its scientific and scenic value, the park was named an International Biosphere Reserve by UNESCO in 1980 and given World Heritage Site status in 1987 by the same organization, giving it greater national and international prestige. This is one of the top visitor attractions in the state.

Admission to the park is $10 per vehicle (good for multiple entries over a seven-day period), $20 for an annual permit, $5 per bicycle or hiker, and free to those 62 and over with a Golden Age, Golden Eagle, or Golden Access passport. These "passports" are available at the park headquarters and are good at any national park in the United States. For information about the park, write to Hawai'i Volcanoes National Park, P.O. Box 52, Hawaii National Park, HI 96718-0052; call 808/985-6000 for a recorded message; or visit www.nps.gov/havo.

Eruptions

The first white man atop Kilauea was Rev. William Ellis, who scaled it in 1823. Until the 1920s, the floor of the caldera was exactly what people thought a volcano would be: a molten lake of lava. Then the forces of nature changed,

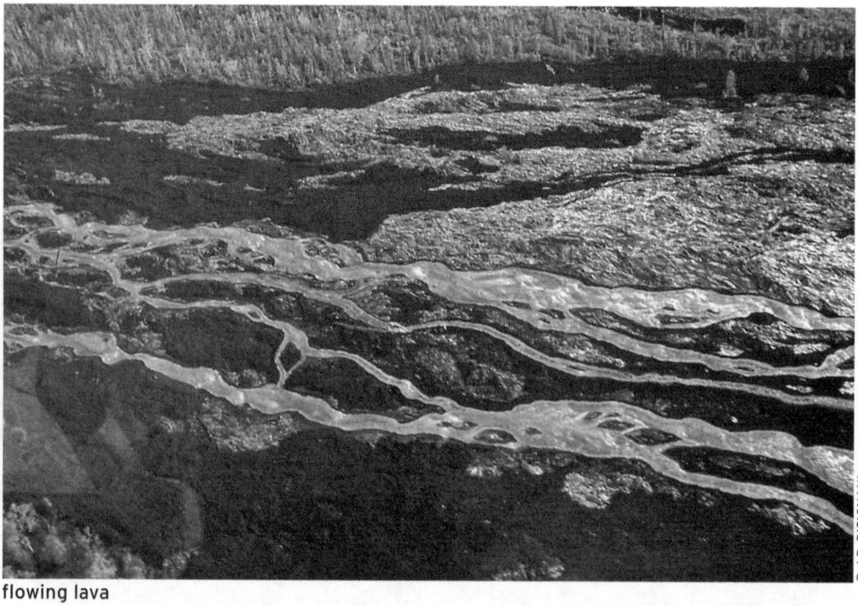

© J.D. BISIGNANI

flowing lava

and the fiery lava subsided and hardened over. Today, Kilauea is called the only "drive-in" volcano in the world, and in recent years it has been one of the most active, erupting almost continuously since 1983 at vents along its eastern fault. When it begins gushing, the result is not a nightmare scene of people scrambling away for their lives, but just the opposite; people flock *to* the volcano. Most thrill-seekers are in much greater danger of being run over by a tour bus hustling to see the fireworks than of being entombed in lava. The volcanic action, while soul-shakingly powerful and not really predictable, is almost totally safe. The Hawaiian Volcano Observatory has been keeping watch since 1912, making Kilauea one of the best-understood volcanoes in the world. The vast volcanic field is creased by rift zones, or natural pressure valves. When the underground magma builds up, instead of *kaboom!* as in Mount St. Helens, it bubbles to the surface like a spring and gushes out as a river of lava. Naturally, anyone or anything in its path would be burned to a cinder, but scientists routinely walk within a few feet of the still-flowing lava to take samples and readings. In much the way canaries detected mine gas, longtime lava observers pay attention to their ears. When the skin on top begins to blister, they know they are too close. The lava establishes a course that it follows much like an impromptu mountain stream caused by heavy rains.

VOLCANO ACTIVITY

For current information on volcano activity in the area, check the Hawaiian Volcano Observatory "Volcano Watch" website (http://hvo.wr.usgs.gov/volcanowatch). Related volcano and earthquake information for the Big Island is also available from the USGS Hawaiian Volcano Observatory (http://hvo.wr.usgs.gov) and from the Hawaii Center for Volcanology website (www.soest.hawaii.edu/GG/HCV/kilauea); or by calling 808/985-6000 for the Park Service's recorded message. Should there be any major increase in activity, local radio stations give up-to-the-minute news.

This does not mean that the lava flows are entirely benign, or that anyone should visit the area during an eruption without prior approval by the Park Service. When anything is happening, the local radio stations give up-to-the-minute news, and the Park Service provides a recorded message at 808/985-6000. In 1790 a puff of noxious gases was emitted from Kilauea and descended on the Ka'u Desert, asphyxiating a rival army of Kamehameha's that just happened to be in the area. Eighty people died in their tracks. In 1881 a flow of lava spilled toward undeveloped Hilo and engulfed an area within today's city limits. In 1942, a heavy flow came within 12 miles of the city. Still, this was child's play in comparison with the unbelievable flow of 1950. Luckily, this went down the western rift zone where only scattered homes were in its path. It took no lives as it disgorged well over 600 million cubic yards of magma that covered 35 square miles! The flow continued for 23 days and produced seven huge torrents of lava that sliced across the Belt Road in three different areas. At its peak, the lava front traveled six miles per hour and put out enough material to pave an eight-lane freeway twice around the world. In 1960, a flow swallowed the town of Kapoho on the east coast. In 1975, an earthquake caused a tsunami to hit the southeast coast, killing two campers and sinking a section of the coast by three feet.

The most recent—and very dramatic—series of eruptions that spectacularly began on January 3, 1983, has continued virtually unabated ever since, producing more than one cubic kilometer of lava. Magma bubbled to the surface about two miles away from Pu'u O'o. The gigantic fissure fountained lava and formed Pu'u O'o Cinder Cone, at its largest some 800 feet high and almost 1,000 feet across. Over a 3.5-year period, there were 47 episodic eruptions from this vent. On July 20, 1986, a new fissure broke upon the surface at Kupa'ianaha just outside the park in a nature reserve and formed a lava lake about one acre in surface size and 180 feet deep. At the end of April 1987 all activity suddenly stopped and the lava drained from the lake and tube system, allowing scientists to accurately gauge the depth. About three weeks later, it started up again when lava poured back into the lake, went through the tube system, and flowed back down to the ocean.

More episodic eruptions followed; from that point the flow turned destructive and started taking homes. It flowed about seven miles to the coast through tubes and on the surface, wiping out Kapa'ahu, parts of Kalapana, and most of the Royal Gardens Subdivision, with more than 180 homes incinerated. In May 1989 it moved into the national park proper, and on June 22, it swallowed the park visitors center at Waha'ula. Since 1992, lava has been flowing into the ocean within the park. Unexpectedly, in January 1997 the dramatic activity shifted two miles westward to the Napau Crater, where lava erupted in spouts of fire and flows, and Pu'u O'o ceased spewing. Since February 1997, the majority of activity moved back to Pu'u O'o Cinder Cone, where there has been a continual shift of vent locations on the west and southwestern flanks and constant renewed activity inside the crater, with lava reaching and entering the ocean at various points from 2002 until the present. Until 1997, remote Waha'ula Heiau was spared, but in August of that year lava inundated and buried the sacred spot. The destruction has caused more than $61 million worth of damage. Many of the homesteaders in the worst areas of the flow were rugged individualists and back-to-nature alternative types who lived in homes that generally had no electricity, running water, or telephones. The homes were wiped out. Some disreputable insurance companies with legitimate policyholders tried to wiggle out of paying premiums for lost homes, although the policies specifically stipulated loss by lava flow. The insurance companies whined that the 2,200°F lava never really touched some of the homes, and therefore they were exonerated from covering the losses. Their claims were resoundingly repudiated in the courts, and people were paid for their losses.

At its height, the output of lava was estimated at 650,000 cubic yards per day, which is equal to 55,000 truckloads of cement, enough to cover a football field 38 miles high. Since this activity started in 1983, it has averaged 300,000–600,000 cubic yards a day (that's over two billion cubic yards!), covered 45 square miles of land, added 570 acres of new land to the park and greater acreage to the areas outside the park, and buried about 13 miles of the Chain of Craters Road. For a history of the park's volcanic activity plus up-to-the-minute reports on current activity, see http://hvo.wr.usgs.gov, or check at the park visitors center. Related information is also available at www.soest.hawaii.edu/GG/HCV.

Mauna Loa

At 13,679 feet, this magnificent mountain is a mere 117 feet shorter than its neighbor Mauna Kea, which is the tallest peak in the Pacific, and by some accounts, tallest in the world. Measured from the sea floor, 18,000 feet beneath the sea, it would top even Mount Everest. Mauna Loa is the most massive mountain on earth, containing some 19,000 cubic miles of solid, iron-hard lava, and it's estimated that this titan weighs more than California's entire Sierra Nevada mountain range! In fact, Mauna Loa (Long Mountain), at 60 miles long and 30 miles wide, occupies the entire southern half of the Big Island, with Hawai'i Volcanoes National Park merely a section of its great expanse.

The summit of Mauna Loa, with its mighty **Moku'aweoweo Caldera** and a broad swath of wilderness on the flank of the mountain rising up to it from Kilauea Caldera, are all within park boundaries. Mauna Loa's oval-shape Moku'aweoweo Caldera is more than three miles long and 1.5 miles wide and has vertical walls towering 600 feet. At each end is a smaller round pit crater. From November to May, if there is snow, steam rises from the caldera. This mountaintop bastion is the least visited part of the park, and in a sense the most separate. In order to visit there you have to hike. An expansion of the park in the early 2000s, encompassing an area that drapes the Southwest Rift Zone of Mauna Loa in Ka'u, added about 40 percent more acreage to the park, but this land is also very remote and still largely inaccessible. Plans for future use of this area include opening up several hundred miles of trails and jeep tracks to hiking and perhaps other activities as well as creating additional campsites and cabins, but these uses will undoubtedly take years to facilitate.

Kilauea Caldera

Many sights of Hawai'i Volcanoes National Park are arranged one after another along **Crater Rim Drive.** Most of these sights are the "drive-up" variety, but plenty of major and minor trails lead off here and there.

Expect to spend a full day atop Kilauea to take in all the sights, and never forget that you're on a rumbling volcano where a misstep or loss of concentration at the wrong moment can lead to severe injury or even death. Try to arrive early with a picnic lunch to save time and hassles. Kilauea Caldera, at 4,000 feet, is about 10°F cooler than the coast. It's often overcast, and there can be showers. Wear walking shoes and bring a sweater or windbreaker. Binoculars, sunglasses, and a hat will also come in handy.

Small children, pregnant women, and people with respiratory ailments should note that the fumes from the volcano can cause problems. Stay away from sulfur vents and don't overdo it, and you should be fine.

Hiking and Biking

There are over 150 miles of hiking trails within the park. One long trail heads up the flank of Mauna Loa to its top; a spiderweb of trails loops around and across Kilauea Caldera and into the adjoining craters; and from a point along the Chain of Craters Road, another trail heads east toward the source of the most recent volcanic activity. But by far the greatest number of trails, and those with the greatest total distance, are those that cut through the Ka'u Desert and along the barren and isolated

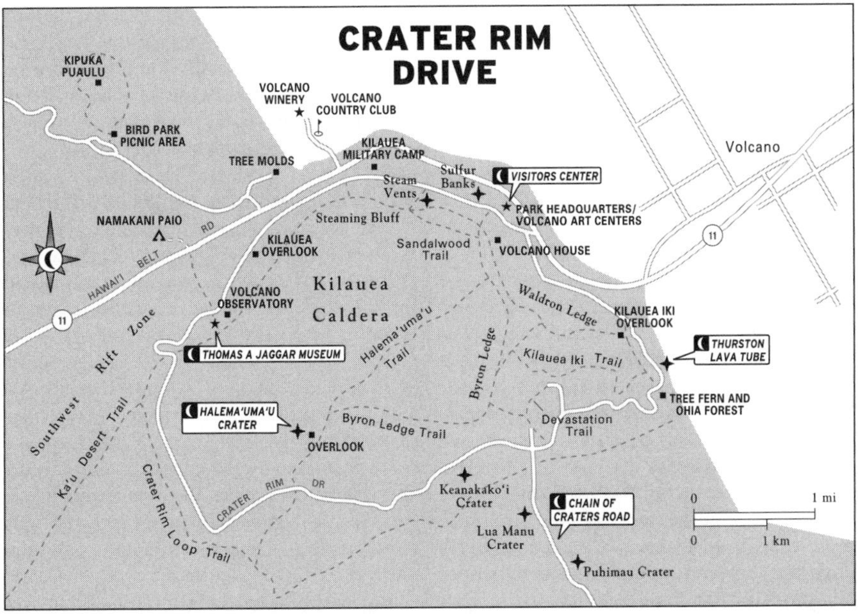

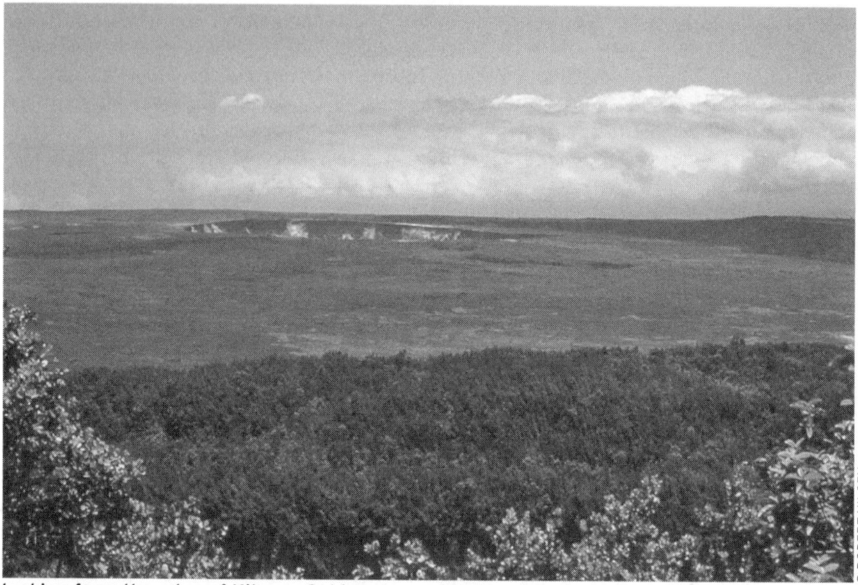

© ROBERT NILSEN

looking from the edge of Kilauea Caldera toward Halema'uma'u crater in the distance

coast. Many have shelters, and trails that require overnight stays provide cabins or primitive campsites.

Because of the possibility of an eruption or earthquake, it is *imperative* to check in at park headquarters, where you can pick up current trail information and excellent maps. In fact, a hiking permit is required for most trails outside the Crater Rim Drive area and the stretch along the coast beyond the end of Chain of Craters Drive. Pick up your free permit no more than one day in advance. When hiking, wear long pants and closed-toe shoes or boots. Much of the park is hot and dry, so carry plenty of drinking water. Wear a hat, sunscreen, and sunglasses, but don't forget rain gear because it often rains in the green areas of the park. Stay on trails and stay away from steep edges, cracks, new lava flows, and any area where lava is flowing into the sea.

If you will be hiking along the trails in the Kilauea Caldera, the free park maps are sufficient to navigate your way. To aid with hikes elsewhere, it's best to purchase and use larger and more detailed topographical maps. Two that are readily available and of high quality are the *Hawai'i Volcanoes National Park* by Trails Illustrated and the Earthwalk Press's *Hawai'i Volcanoes National Park Recreation Map.*

Biking is permitted in the park on paved roads, paved sections of the Crater Rim Trail, and on some dirt trails. Check with the rangers at the visitors center for specifics.

Visit the Volcano by Helicopter

A very dramatic way to experience the awesome power of the volcano is to take a helicopter tour. The choppers are perfectly suited for the maneuverability necessary to get an intimate bird's-eye view. The pilots will fly you over the areas offering the most activity, often dipping low over lava pools, skimming still-glowing flows, and circling the towering steam clouds rising from where lava meets the sea. When activity is really happening, tours are jammed, and prices, like lava fountains, go sky-high. Remember, however, that these tours are increasingly resented by hikers and anyone else trying to have a quiet experience, and that new regulations might limit flights over the lava area. Also, these tours are not without danger, as helicopters have crashed near lava flows during commercial sightseeing flights. Nonetheless, if you are interested, contact one of the helicopter companies located in Hilo or Kona. Alternately, fixed-wing plane tour companies also offer flights over the volcano area from both Hilo and Kona.

Protect the Park

Everything in the park—flora and fauna, rocks, buildings, trails, etc.—is protected by federal law. Be respectful and do not carry anything away with you! Do not climb on any ancient rock structures and do not deface any petroglyph carvings. The ***nene,*** Hawaii's state bird, is endangered. By feeding these birds, visitors have taught them to stand in parking lots and by the roadside. What appears to be a humane and harmless practice actually helps kill these rare birds. Being run over by automobiles has become the leading cause of death of adult birds in the park. Please look, but do not try to approach, feed, or harass the *nene* in any way.

VISITORS CENTER AREA

Visitors Center

The best place to start is at the visitors center (808/985-6000, daily 7:45 A.M.–5 P.M.) and Park Headquarters. The turn-off is clearly marked along Hwy. 11 at mile marker 30. By midmorning it's jammed, so try to be an early bird. The center is well run by the National Park Service, which offers a free film about geology and volcanism, with tremendous highlights of past eruptions and plenty of detail on Hawaiian culture and natural history. It runs every hour on the hour starting at 9 A.M. Free ranger-led tours of the nearby area are also given on a regular basis, and their start times and meeting places are posted near the center's front doors. Also posted are After Dark in the Park educational interpretive program activities, held two or three times a month at 7 P.M. on Tuesday evenings. A self-guided natural history museum gives more information about the geology of the area, with plenty of exhibits on flora and fauna. You will greatly enrich your visit if you take a half-hour tour of the

© ROBERT NILSEN

Nene are sometimes spotted in Hawai'i Volcanoes National Park.

museum, even though more volcano-specific information is available at the state-of-the-art Thomas A. Jaggar Museum a few minutes up the road. Before you head down the road, get a drink of water and use the public bathroom.

For safety's sake, anyone hiking to the backcountry *must* register with the rangers at the visitors center, especially during times of eruption. Do not be foolhardy! There is no charge for camping, and rangers can give you up-to-the-minute information on trails, backcountry shelters, and cabins. Trails routinely close due to lava flows, tremors, and rock slides. The rangers cannot help you if they don't know where you are. Many day trails leading into the caldera from the rim road are easy walks that need no special preparation. The backcountry trails can be very challenging, and detailed maps (highly recommended) are sold at the center along with special-interest geology and natural history publications prepared by the Hawaii Natural History Association.

HAWAI'I VOLCANOES NATIONAL PARK HIKING TRAILS

AROUND KILAUEA CRATER

The **Crater Rim Loop Trail** begins at Volcano House and parallels Crater Rim Drive. Hiking the entire 11.5 miles takes a full day, but you can take it in sections as time and energy permit. It's a well-marked and well-maintained trail, mostly paved or cinder; all you need are proper clothing, water, and determination. For your efforts, you'll get an up-close view of all of the sights outlined along Crater Rim Drive plus other views and vistas.

Halema'uma'u Trail provides some of the best scenery for the effort. It begins at park headquarters and descends into Kilauea Caldera, running about 2.5 miles to the Halema'uma'u Crater pit and crossing lava fields that are only 20-25 years old. Circle back via the Byron Ledge Trail, about three miles long, or arrange to be picked up at the Halema'uma'u parking area on the south side of the Crater Rim Drive.

Kilauea Iki Trail begins at the Thurston Lava Tube parking lot or at the Kilauea Iki Overlook. One of the most popular and picturesque and easiest hikes in the park, this four-mile trail generally takes two hours round-trip and passes over the floor of Kilauea Iki Crater, which was a sea of lava in 1959 when an exceedingly tall spume of lava spouted from the crater rim, creating the most spectacular show the volcano has performed in memory. Start by taking the section of the Crater Rim Trail that follows the rim of the Kilauea Iki Crater, then branch west and descend the western edge of the crater wall. From there it's back across the crater floor, where you pass the spouting site and adjacent ash hill, and a zigzag up the eastern side. Or do it in the reverse. If conditions are right, the cracked and buckled floor of the pit might steam as you walk across. It's easy to link up with the Byron Ledge Trail near the west end of this loop, from where you can walk into Halema'uma'u Caldera or back to park headquarters.

On the south side of Kilauea Iki Crater, the one-mile-long **Devastation Trail** links Pu'u Pua'i Overlook and the Devastation Trail parking area, from where there is a link trail to the Byron Ledge Trail on the Kilauea Caldera rim.

A shorter hike that takes you along the north edge of the rim and back via the Sulphur Banks is the **'Iliahi (Sandalwood) Trail,** a hike of just over one mile round-trip. Along this hike, you're not only treated to the sights and sounds of trees and birds, but also to the mysteries of steam vents, faults, and cracks.

Alternately, go left out of Volcano House and follow the **Earthquake Trail,** a section of the Crater Rim Loop Trail, along **Waldron Ledge.** The easy trail takes you along a paved section of the old Chain of Craters Road that was damaged by a 6.6 magnitude earthquake in 1983. Sections of the road are buckled, and parts have slid down the edge of the rim.

For those who are not traveling by rental car, the public Hele-On bus stops once a day in front of the visitors center Monday–Friday. There are no scheduled stops on weekends. Pick-up for the bus going *to* Hilo is at 8 A.M. Coming *from* Hilo, the bus leaves at 2:40 P.M. from the Mo'oheau Bus Terminal downtown and arrives at the park visitors center about 3:45 P.M.

Volcano House

Have you ever dreamed of sleeping with a goddess? Well, you can cuddle up with Pele by staying at Volcano House. If your plans don't include an overnight stop, go in for a look. Sometimes this is impossible, because not only do tour buses from the Big Island disgorge here, but tour groups are flown in from Honolulu as well. A stop at the lounge provides refreshments and a tremendous view of the crater. Volcano House still has the feel of a country inn. This particular building dates from the 1940s, but the site has remained the

KA'U DESERT AND COASTAL TRAILS

Ka'u Desert Trail starts along Crater Rim Drive about one mile past the Jaggar Museum and heads southwest into the desolation. It runs for about six miles before it meets the Mauna Iki Trail. The **Mauna Iki Trail** heads east, crossing a 1974 flow to connect with the Hilina Pali Road at Kulanaokuaiki Campground. You'll have to follow rock cairns some of the way. Another access to the Ka'u Desert Trail starts along Route 11, between mile markers 37 and 38 and passes the Ka'u Desert Footprints on the way. The Ka'u Desert Trail continues south and swings around to the east, passing Pepeiao Cabin after more than seven miles, on the way to the Hilina Pali Overlook. From the cabin, **Ka'aha Trail** heads down to and along the coast to Ka'aha Shelter, a distance of six miles, where it meets a trail coming down from the overlook. The trail continues up and along the coastal *pali*, dipping down to the Halape shelter after six miles. From Halape, the **Puna Coast Trail** mostly parallels the coast, passing Keauhou shelter and 'Apua Point campsite before it meets the Chain of Craters Road near the petroglyph site. At the shelters, rain catchment tanks provide drinking water. In 1975, an earthquake rocked this area, generating a tsunami that killed two campers at Halape; more than 30 others had to be helicoptered to safety. Hiking in the Ka'u Desert requires full hiking and camping gear. Bring plenty of water.

ON MAUNA LOA

The 17-mile hike to the summit of Mauna Loa is the most grueling in the park. The trailhead (6,662 feet) is at the lookout at the end of the pavement of Mauna Loa Road. Hikers in excellent condition can make the summit in three days round-trip, but four would be more comfortable. There is a considerable elevation gain, so expect freezing weather even in summer and snow in winter. Altitude sickness can also be a problem. En route you pass through *nene* country, with a good chance to spot these lava-adapted geese. Fences keep out feral goats, so remember to close gates after you. The first cabin is at Red Hill (10,035 feet) and the second is on the rim of Moku'aweoweo Caldera (13,250 feet) at the mountaintop. Water is from roof catchments and should be boiled. The two-mile-long **Cabin Trail** runs along the south rim of the summit caldera, while the 2.5-mile **Summit Trail** slips along the north rim to the highest point. The 3.5-mile **Observatory Trail** will also get you to the summit from the Mauna Loa NOAA Atmospheric Observatory on the north slope, but you must ascend via the Saddle Road. The summit treats you to a sweeping panorama that includes the great majority of the Big Island and Haleakala on Maui.

same since a grass hut was perched on the rim of the crater by a sugar planter in 1846. He charged $1 a night for lodging. A steady stream of notable visitors has come ever since: almost all of Hawaii's kings and queens dating from the middle of the 19th century, as well as royalty from Europe. Mark Twain was a guest, followed by Franklin Roosevelt. Most recently, a contingent of astronauts lodged here and used the crater floor to prepare for walking on the moon. In 1866 a larger grass hut replaced the first, and in 1877 a wooden hotel was built. It is now the Volcano Art Center and has been moved just across the road. In 1885, an expansion added 14 rooms and the dining room, and 35 more rooms were constructed in the mid-1920s. An accident caused the hotel to burn down in 1940, but it was rebuilt the next year as the main building that stands today. In 1962, an additional wing was added.

The person who owned and operated Volcano House the longest was George Lycurgus, who took over management of the hotel in 1895. His son, Nick, followed him and managed the hotel until 1969. From 1977 until 1986, the hotel was managed by the Sheraton hotel chain, but since 1986, the hotel has once again been under local management as a concessionaire to the Park Service.

Volcano Art Center Gallery

Art and history buffs should walk across the street to the Volcano Art Center Gallery (808/967-7565, 9 A.M.–5 P.M. daily except Christmas), which is the original 1877 Volcano House, Hawaii's oldest hotel, where you get to see some fine arts and crafts. A new show featuring one of the many superlative island artists is presented monthly, and there are always ongoing demonstrations and special events. Artworks on display are in a variety of media, including canvas, paper, wood, glass, metal, ceramic, fiber, and photographs. There is also a profusion of less expensive but distinctive items like posters, cards, and earthy basketry made from natural fibers collected locally. One of the functions of the art center is to provide interpretation for the national park. All of the 300 or so artists who exhibit here do works that in some way relate to Hawaii's environment and culture. Volcano Art Center is one of the finest art galleries in the entire state, boasting works from the best the islands have to offer. Definitely make this a stop.

As a community-oriented organization, the Volcano Art Center sponsors classes and workshops in arts, crafts, and language; an Elderhostel program; the Kilauea Volcano Wilderness Runs; and a season of performing arts, which includes musical concerts, hula, dance performances, and stage plays. Some involve local performers, while others headline visiting artists. Performances, classes, and workshops take place at the Kilauea Theater at the military camp, at the hula platform within the park, or in town at the Art Center campus building. Tickets for performances are sold individually at local outlets or you can buy a season ticket. For current information and pricing, call the Volcano Art Center office (808/967-8222, www.volcanoartcenter.org) or check out its website for what's happening.

CRATER RIM DRIVE

There are so many intriguing nooks and crannies to stop at along Crater Rim Drive that you'll have to force yourself to be picky if you intend to cover the park in one day. Crater Rim Drive is a circular route; it matters little which way you proceed. Take your choice, but the following sights are listed counterclockwise beginning from the park visitors center. Along this road you will travel from a tropical zone into desert, then through a volcanic zone before returning to lush rainforest. The change is often immediate and differences dramatic. Keep this in mind as you travel around the caldera. Remember that the Jaggar Museum closes at 5 P.M., so be sure to get around to that point with time enough to allow yourself to appreciate what it has to offer.

Sulphur Banks

You can easily walk to Sulphur Banks from the visitors center along a 10-minute paved trail. Your nose will tell you when you're close.

Alternately, walk the 0.7-mile trail from the Steam Vent parking lot. A Boardwalk now fronts a major portion of this site. As you approach these fumaroles, the earth surrounding them turns a deep reddish-brown, covered over in yellowish-green sulfur. The rising steam is caused by surface water leaking into the cracks where it becomes heated and rises as vapor. Kilauea releases hundreds of tons of sulfur gases every day. This gaseous activity stunts the growth of vegetation. And when atmospheric conditions create a low ceiling, the gases sometimes cause the eyes and nose to water. The area is best avoided by those with heart and lung conditions.

Steam Vents

Within a half mile you'll come to Steam Vents, which are also fumaroles, but without sulfur. The entire field behind the partitioned area steams. The feeling is like being in a sauna. There are no strong fumes to contend with here, just other tourists. A short hike from here leads to the Crater Rim Trail, where you can view the Steaming Bluff, which is more pronounced when the temperature is cooler, such as early in the morning.

Kilauea Military Camp is located beyond the vents and is not open to the public except for community events at the theater. The camp serves as an R&R facility for active duty and retired military personnel, and certain other government employees.

Kilauea Overlook

Some distance beyond the Kilauea Military Camp is Kilauea Overlook, as good a spot as any to get a look into the caldera, and there are picnic tables near the parking lot. Here too is **Uwekahuna (Wailing Priest) Bluff,** where the *kahuna* made offerings of appeasement to Pele. A Hawaiian prayer commemorates their religious rites. Unless you're stopping for lunch or making your own (appropriate) offering, it's perhaps better to continue on to the observatory and museum, where you not only have the view outside but get a scientific explanation of what's happening around you.

Thomas A. Jaggar Museum

The **Hawaiian Volcano Observatory** (http://hvo.wr.usgs.gov) has been keeping tabs on the volcanic activity in the area since the turn of the 20th century. The actual observatory is filled with delicate seismic equipment and is closed to the public, but a lookout nearby gives you a dentist's view into the mouth of Halema'uma'u Crater (House of Ferns), Pele's home. Steam rises and you can feel the power, but until 1924 the view was even more phenomenally spectacular: a lake of molten lava. The lava has since crusted over and the floor is again black. Scientists do not predict a recurrence in the near future, but no one knows Pele's mind. This is a major stop for all passing tourists and tour buses. Information plaques in the immediate area tell of the history and volcanology of the park. One points out a spot from which to observe the perfect shield volcano form of Mauna Loa—most times too cloudy to see. Another reminds you that you're in the middle of the Pacific, an incredible detail you tend to forget when atop these mountains.

A wonderful addition to the national park is located next door to the observatory and offers a fantastic multimedia display of the amazing geology and volcanology of the area. The state-of-the-art Thomas A. Jaggar Museum (808/985-6049, 8:30 A.M.–5 P.M. daily, admission free) complete with a miniseries of spectacular photos on movable walls, topographical maps, inspired paintings, and video presentations. The expert staff constantly upgrades the displays to keep the public informed on the newest eruptions. The 30–45 minutes it takes to explore the teaching museum will enhance your understanding of the volcanic area immeasurably. Do yourself a favor and visit this museum before setting out on any explorations, and stop at the book and gift shop for something to take home. Drinking water and bathrooms are available here.

Halema'uma'u Crater

A string of interesting stops follows the observatory. One points out the Ka'u Desert, an inhospitable lava plain studded with a few scraggly plants. Next comes the **Southwest Rift,** a

© ROBERT NILSEN

Offerings to Pele are still sometimes left at Halema'uma'u Crater.

series of cracks running from Kilauea's summit to the sea. You can observe at a glance that you are standing directly over a major earthquake fault. Dated lava flows follow in rapid succession until you arrive at Halema'uma'u Overlook parking lot. A well-maintained cinder trail to the overlook is only 0.25-mile long and gives an up-close view of the crater. The area is rife with fumaroles leaking sulfur dioxide and should be avoided by those with respiratory problems. At the end you're treated to a full explanation of Halema'uma'u. Until this crater crusted over after an explosion in 1942, Halema'uma'u could be seen as a red glow and sometimes as a fabulous display of spouting lava from the Volcano House Hotel. From here, two trails make tracks across the caldera floor to the far side and back to park headquarters. Farther along the road is a spot that was once an observation point that caved in. You won't take the ground under your feet for granted!

Keanakako'i Crater

Keanakako'i Overlook is set on the rim of the diminutive crater of the same name. This was a prehistoric adze quarry from which superior stone was gathered to make tools. It was destroyed by a flow in 1877. If that seems in the remote past, realize that you just crossed a section of road that was naturally paved over with lava from a "quickie" eruption in 1982!

Devastation Trail

Most visitors hike along the half-mile Devastation Trail, which could aptly be renamed Regeneration Trail. The half mile it covers is fascinating, one of the most-photographed areas in the park. It leads across a field devastated by a tremendous eruption from **Kilauea Iki** (Little Kilauea) in 1959, when fountains of lava shot 1,900 feet into the air. The area was once an 'ohi'a forest that was denuded of limbs and leaves, then choked by black pumice and ash. The vegetation has regenerated since then, and the recuperative power of the flora is part of an ongoing study. Blackberries, not indigenous to Hawaii, are slowly taking over. The good news is that you'll be able to pick and eat blackberries as you hike along the paved trail, but the rangers are waging a mighty war against them. Notice that many of the trees have sprouted aerial roots trailing down from the branches: this is total adaptation to the situation, as these roots don't normally

MADAME PELE AND KILAUEA

The goddess Pele is an irascible old dame. Perhaps it's because she had such a bad childhood. All she wanted was a home of her own where she could house her family and entertain her lover, a handsome chief from Kaua'i. But her sea goddess sister, Namakaokaha'i, flooded her out wherever she went after Pele seduced her husband, and the pig god, Kamapua'a, ravished Pele for good measure. So Pele finally built her love nest at Halema'uma'u Crater at the south end of Kilauea Caldera. Being a goddess obviously isn't as heavenly as one would think, and whenever the pressures of life get too much for Pele, she blows her stack. These tempestuous outbursts made Pele one of the most revered gods in the Hawaiian pantheon because her presence and might were so easily felt.

For a thousand years Pele was appeased by offerings of pigs, dogs, sacred *'ohelo* berries (her favorite), and now and again an outcast man or two (never women) who would hopefully turn her energy from destruction to more comfortable pursuits. Also, if Pele was your family's personal goddess, your remains were sometimes allowed to be thrown into the fire pit as a sign of great respect. In the early 1820s, the Chieftess Keopuolani, an ardent convert to Christianity, officially challenged Pele in an attempt to topple her like the other gods of old. Keopuolani climbed down into Pele's crater and ate the sacred *'ohelo* berries, flagrantly violating the ageless *kapu*. She then took large stones and defiantly hurled them into the fire pit below while bellowing, "Jehovah is my God. It is He, not Pele, that kindled these flames."

Yet today, most residents, regardless of background, have an inexplicable reverence for Pele. The Volcano Post Office receives an average of three packages a week containing lava rocks taken by tourists as souvenirs. Some hold that Pele looks upon these rocks as her children and taking them from her is kidnapping. The accompanying letters implore the officials to return the rocks because ever since the offender brought them home, luck has been bad. The officials take the requests very seriously, returning the rocks with the customary peace offering. Many follow-up thank you letters have been written to express relief that the bad luck has been lifted. There is no reference in Hawaiian folklore to this phenomenon, although Hawaiians did hold certain rocks sacred. Park rangers will tell you that the idea of "the bad-luck rocks" was initiated a few decades back by a tour bus driver who became sick and tired of tourists getting his bus dirty by piling aboard their souvenirs. *Voilà!* Another ancient Hawaiian myth! Know, however, that the rocks in Hawai'i Volcanoes National Park are protected by federal law, much meaner and more vindictive than Pele.

Pele is believed to take human form. She customarily appears before an eruption as a ravishing beauty or a withered old hag, often accompanied by a little white dog. She expects to be treated cordially, and it's said that she will stand by the roadside at night hitching a ride. After a brief encounter, she departs and seems to mysteriously evaporate into the ether. Kindness on your part is the key; if you come across a strange woman at night, treat her well – it might not help, but it definitely won't hurt.

appear. As you move farther along the trail, tufts of grass and bushes peek out of the pumice. Then the surroundings become totally barren and look like the nightmare of a nuclear holocaust.

Thurston Lava Tube

If the Devastation Trail produced a sense of melancholy, the Thurston Lava Tube, otherwise called Nahuku, makes you feel like Alice walking through the looking glass. Inside is a fairy kingdom. As you approach, the expected signboard gives you the lowdown on the geology and flora and fauna of the area. Take the five minutes to educate yourself. The paved trail starts as a steep incline, which quickly enters a fern forest. All about you are fern trees, vibrantly green, with native birds flitting here and there. As you approach the lava tube, it seems almost manmade, like a perfectly formed tunnel leading into a mine. Ferns and moss hang from the entrance, and if you stand just inside the entrance looking out, it's as if the very air is tinged with green. If there were such things as elves and gnomes, they would surely live here. The walk through takes about 10 minutes, undulating through the narrow passage. At the other end, the fantasy world of ferns and moss reappears, and the trail leads back, past public restrooms, to the parking lot.

© ROBERT NILSEN

Thurston Lava Tube entrance

CHAIN OF CRATERS ROAD

The Chain of Craters Road that once linked the park with Kalapana village on the coast was severed by an enormous lava flow in 1995 and can now only be driven to where the flow crosses the road beyond the Holei Sea Arch. Remember that the volcanic activity in this area is unpredictable, and that the road can be closed at a moment's notice. As you head down the road, every bend—and they are uncountable—offers a panoramic vista. There are numerous pull-offs; plaques provide geological information about past eruptions and lava flows. The grandeur, power, and immensity of the forces that have been creating the earth from the beginning of time are right before your eyes. Although the road starts off in the ʻohiʻa forest, it opens to broader views and soon cuts diagonally across the *pali* to reach the littoral plain. Much of this section of the road was buried under lava flows from 1969 to 1974. When the road almost reaches the coast, look for a roadside marker that indicates the Puna Coast Trail. Just across the road is the Puʻu Loa Petroglyph Field trailhead. The lower part of the road is spectacular. Here, blacker-than-black sea cliffs, covered by a thin layer of green, abruptly stop at the sea. The surf rolls in, sending up spumes of seawater. In the distance, steam billows into the air where the lava flows into the sea. At road's end you will find a barricade and an information hut staffed by park rangers throughout the afternoon and into the evening. Read the information and heed the warnings. The 20-mile drive from atop the volcano to the barricade takes about 30 minutes and drops 3,700 feet in elevation.

While hiking to the lava flow is not encouraged, park staff do not stop you from venturing out. They warn you of the dangers and the reality ahead. Many visitors do make the hike (it may be more than three miles one-way), but there is no trail. The way is over new and rough lava that tears at the bottom of your shoes. Many hike during the day, but if you go in the evening when the spectacle is more apparent, a flashlight with several extra batteries is absolutely necessary. To hike there and back could take three to four hours. If you decide to hike, bring plenty of water. There is no shade or water along the way, and the wind often blows along this coast. Do not hike to or near the edge of the water, as sections of lava could break off without warning. Depending upon how the lava is flowing, it may or may not be worth the effort. When the lava is flowing, it is often possible to see the reddish glow at night from the end of the road, but you probably won't see much that's distinguishable unless you use high-power binoculars. When the lava is putting on a good show, there could be several hundred cars parked along the road that stretch back for over a mile, so expect a bit of a walk before you even get to the ranger station to start the hike over the lava.

Craters

As you head down Chain of Craters Road you immediately pass a number of depressions for which the road is named. First on the right side is **Lua Manu Crater,** a deep depression now lined with green vegetation. Farther is **Puhimau Crater.** Walk the few steps to the viewing stand at the crater edge for a look. Many people come here to hear the echo of their voices as they talk or sing into this pit. Next comes **Ko'oko'olau Crater,** then **Hi'iaka Crater** and **Pauahi Crater.** Just beyond is a turnoff to the east, which follows a short section of the old road. This road ends at the lava flow, and from here a trail runs as far as **Napau Crater.**

The first mile or more of the Napau Trail takes you over lava from 1974, through forest *kipuka,* past lava tree molds, and up the treed slopes of **Pu'u Huluhulu.** From this cone you have a view down on Mauna Ulu, from which the 1969–74 lava flow disgorged, and east toward **Pu'u O'o** and the currently active volcanic vents, some seven miles distant. Due to the current volcanic activity farther along the

lava entry point, with explosive molten lava and gaseous steam

© ROBERT NILSEN

steam and escaping gases on newly hardened lava

rift zone, you will need a permit to day hike beyond Pu'u Huluhulu; the trail itself may be closed depending upon where the volcanic activity is taking place. However, the trail does continue over the shoulder of Makaopuhi Crater to the primitive campsite at Napau Crater, passing more cones and pit craters, lava flows, and sections of rainforest. A four-hour ranger-led hike out this way runs on Wednesday afternoon only. It's popular and limited to a dozen people, so call to reserve a place at 808/985-6017.

Roadside Sights

For several miles, Chain of Craters Road traverses lava that was laid down about 40 years ago; remnants of the old road can still be seen in spots. There are long stretches of smooth pahoehoe lava interspersed with flows of clinker 'a'a. Here and there, a bit of green pokes through a crack in the rock, bringing new life to this stark landscape. Everywhere you look, you can see the wild "action" of these lava flows, stopped in all their magnificent forms. At one vantage point on the way is **Kealakomo,** a picnic overlook where you have unobstructed views of the coast. Stop and enjoy the sight before proceeding. Several other lookouts and pull-offs have been created along the road to call attention to one sight or another. Soon the road heads over the edge of the *pali* and diagonally down to the flats, passing sections of the old road not covered by lava. Stop and look back and realize that most of the old road has been covered by dozens of feet of lava, the darkest of the dark.

The last section of road runs very close to the edge of the sea, where cliffs rise up from the pounding surf. Near the end of the road is the **Holei Sea Arch,** a spot where the wave action has undercut the rock to leave a bridge of stone. This is small but a dramatic sight. Enjoy the scene, but don't lean too far out trying to get that perfect picture!

Pu'u Loa Petroglyphs

The walk out to Pu'u Loa Petroglyphs is delightful, highly educational, and takes less than one hour. The trail, although it traverses solid lava, is discernible. The tread of feet over

© ROBERT NILSEN

Holei Sea Arch

© ROBERT NILSEN

ropey pahoehoe lava

the centuries has smoothed and discolored the rock. As you walk along, note the *ahu,* traditional trail markers that are piles of stone shaped like little Christmas trees. Most of the lava field leading to the petroglyphs is undulating pahoehoe and looks like a frozen sea. You can climb bumps of lava, 8–10 feet high, to scout the immediate territory. Mountainside, the *pali* is quite visible and you can pick out the most recent lava flows—the blackest and least vegetated. As you approach the site, the lava changes dramatically and looks like long strands of braided rope.

The petroglyphs are in an area about the size of a soccer field. A wooden walkway encircles most of them and helps to ensure their protection. A common motif of the petroglyphs is a circle with a hole in the middle, like a doughnut; you'll also see designs of men with triangular-shaped heads. Some rocks are entirely covered with designs, while others have only a symbolic scratch or two. These carvings are impressive more for their sheer numbers than the multiplicity of design. If you stand on the walkway and trek off at the two o'clock position, you'll see a small hill. Go over and down it, and you will discover even better petroglyphs that include a sailing canoe about two feet high. At the back end of the walkway a sign proclaims that Pu'u Loa meant Long Hill, which the Hawaiians turned into the metaphor "Long Life." For countless generations, fathers would come here to place pieces of their infants' umbilical cords into small holes as offerings to the gods to grant long life to their children. Concentric circles surrounded the holes that held the umbilical cords. The entire area, an obvious power spot, screams in utter silence, and the still-strong *mana* is easily felt.

The Big Island has the largest concentration of petroglyphs in the state, and this site holds its greatest number. One estimate puts the number at 28,000!

OTHER PARK AREAS

Hilina Pali Road

About two miles down the Chain of Craters Road, the Hilina Pali Road shoots off to the southwest over a narrow roughly paved road all the way to the end at **Hilina Pali Lookout**—

about nine miles. Soon after you leave the Chain of Craters Road the vegetation turns drier and you enter the semi-arid Ka'u Desert. The road picks its way around and over old volcanic flows, and you can see the vegetation struggling to maintain a foothold. On the way you pass the Mauna Iki trailhead, Kulanaokuaiki Campground, and former Kipuka Nene Campground—closed to help the *nene* recover their threatened population. You should see geese here, but please leave them alone and definitely don't feed them. The road ends right on the edge of the rift, with expansive views over the benched coastline, from the area of current volcanic flow all the way to South Point. From here, one trail heads down the hill to the coast while another pushes on along the top of the cliff and farther into the dry landscape. At the *pali* lookout is a pavilion and restrooms, but no drinking water. This is not a pleasure ride, as the road is rough, but it is passable. For most it probably isn't worth the time, but for those looking for isolation and a special vantage point, this could be it.

Ka'u Desert Footprints

An entry to the Ka'u Desert Trail starts about eight miles south of the park entrance along Route 11, between mile markers 37 and 38. It's a short 20-minute hike from this trailhead to the Ka'u Desert Footprints. The trek across the small section of desert is fascinating, and the history of the footprints makes the experience more evocative. The trail is only 1.6 miles round-trip, but allow at least an hour, mostly for observation. The predominant foliage is *'ohi'a* that contrasts with the bleak surroundings—the feeling throughout the area is one of foreboding. You pass a wasteland of 'a'a and pahoehoe lava flows to arrive at the footprints. A metal fence in a sturdy pavilion surrounds the prints, which look as though they're cast in cement. Actually they're formed from pisolites: particles of ash stuck together with moisture, which formed mud that hardened like plaster. Eroded and not very visible, the story of these footprints is far more exciting than the prints themselves.

In 1790 Kamehameha was waging war with Keoua over control of the Big Island. One of Keoua's warrior parties of approximately 80 people attempted to cross the desert while Kilauea was erupting. Toxic gases descended upon them, and the warriors and their families were enveloped and suffocated. They literally died in their tracks, but the preserved footprints, although romanticism would have it otherwise, were probably made by a party of people who came well after the eruption or perhaps at some time during a previous eruption. This unfortunate occurrence was regarded by the Hawaiians as a direct message from the gods proclaiming their support for Kamehameha. Keoua, who could not deny the sacred signs, felt abandoned and shortly thereafter became a human sacrifice at Pu'ukohola Heiau, built by Kamehameha to honor his war god, Kuka'ilimoku.

Mauna Loa Road

About 2.5 miles west of the park entrance on the Belt Road, Mauna Loa Road turns off to the north. This road will lead you to the Tree Molds and a bird sanctuary, as well as to the trailhead for the Mauna Loa summit trail. As an added incentive, a minute down this road leaves 99 percent of the tourists behind.

Tree Molds is an ordinary name for an extraordinary place. Turn right off Mauna Loa Road soon after leaving the Belt Road and follow the signs for five minutes. This road runs in to the tree molds area and loops back onto itself. At the loop, a signboard explains what occurred here. In a moment, you realize that you're standing atop a lava flow, and that the scattered potholes were entombed tree trunks, most likely the remains of a once-giant koa forest. Unlike at Lava Tree State Monument, where the magma encased the tree and flowed away, the opposite action happened here. The lava stayed put while the tree trunk burned away, leaving the 15- to 18-foot-deep holes. While the "sights" of this site may not excite some visitors, realizing what happened here and how it happened is an eye-opener.

Kipuka Puaulu is a sanctuary for birds and nature lovers who want to leave the crowds behind, just under three miles from Route 11 up Mauna Loa Road. The sanctuary is an island atop an island. A *kipuka* is a piece of land that is surrounded by lava but has not been inundated by it, leaving the original vegetation and land contour intact. A few hundred yards away, small scrub vegetation struggles, but in the sanctuary the trees form a towering canopy a hundred feet tall. The first sign takes you to an ideal picnic area called Bird Park, with cooking grills; the second, 100 yards beyond, takes you to Kipuka Puaulu Loop Trail. As you enter the trail, a bulletin board describes the birds and plants, some of the last remaining indigenous fauna and flora in Hawaii. Please follow all rules. The dirt trail is self-guided, and pamphlets describing the stations along the way may be dispensed from a box near the start of the path. The loop is only one mile long, but to really assimilate the area, especially if you plan to do any bird-watching, expect to spend an hour minimum. It doesn't take long to realize that you are privileged to see some of the world's rarest plants, such as a small, nondescript bush called *'a'ali'i*. In the branches of the towering 'ohi'a trees you might see an *'elepaio* or an *'apapane,* two birds native to Hawaii. Common finches and Japanese white eyes are imported birds that are here to stay. There's an example of a lava tube, a huge koa tree, and an explanation of how ash from eruptions provided soil and nutrients for the forest. Blue morning glories have taken over entire hillsides. Once considered a pest and aggressively eradicated, they have recently been given a reprieve and are now considered good ground cover—perhaps even indigenous. When you do come across a native Hawaiian plant, it seems somehow older, almost prehistoric. If a precontact Hawaiian could come back today, he or she would recognize only a few plants and trees seen here in this preserve. As you leave, listen for the melodies coming from the treetops and hope the day never comes when no birds sing. To hear the birds at their best, come in early morning or late afternoon.

Mauna Loa Road continues westward and gains elevation for approximately 10 miles. It passes through thick forests of lichen-covered koa trees, cuts across **Kipuka Ki,** and traverses the narrow **Ke'amoku Flow.** At the end of the pavement, at 6,662 feet, you will find a parking area and lookout. If the weather is cooperating, you'll be able to see much of the mountainside; if not, your field of vision will be much restricted. A trail leads from here to the summit of Mauna Loa. It takes two long and difficult days to hike. Under no circumstances should it be attempted by novice hikers or those unprepared for cold alpine conditions. At times, this road may be closed due to extreme fire conditions.

'Ola'a Forest

Off Route 11 close to Volcano Village, turn on Wright Road (or County Road 148) heading toward Mauna Loa. On a clear morning you can see the mountain dead ahead. Continue for approximately three miles until you see a barbed-wire fence. The fence is distinctive because along it you'll see a profusion of *hapu'u* ferns that are in sharp contrast to the adjacent ranch property. The area is laced with cracks and lava tubes. Most are small ankle twisters, but others can open up under you like a glacial crevasse. Here is a true example of a quickly disappearing native forest. What's beautiful about an endemic forest is that virtually all species coexist wonderfully. The ground cover is a rich mulch of decomposing ferns and leaves, fragrant and amazingly soft.

Although open to the public, entrance to this area is *not* encouraged. There are no maintained trails, no well-recognized and marked trailheads, and no services whatsoever. It's a thick, dense forest that provides no easy visible clues to direction or location, and the park offers no maps of the forest to visitors. While there are some hunting trails that lace the area, they are not user-friendly and it's very easy to get lost. If you get lost and if no one knows you're in there, it could be life-threatening. If you do venture in, bring a compass, a cell phone, plenty of water, warm clothing, and rain gear. Leave your name and telephone number with someone on the outside and set aside a time to contact that person. Also, be aware that you may be trampling native species or inadvertently introducing alien species. The Park Service is trying to bring the area back to its native Hawaiian rainforest condition through eradication of alien plants and elimination of feral pigs.

ACCOMMODATIONS

If you intend to spend the night atop Kilauea, your choices of accommodations are few and simple. Volcano House provides the only hotel, but also available are cabins, one campground, and a handful of tent campsites along the hiking trails. For military personnel, lodging is offered at the Kilauea Military Camp.

Cabins and Camping

The main campground in Volcanoes, **Namakani Paio,** clearly marked off Route 11, is situated in a stately eucalyptus grove. There is no charge for tent camping and no reservations are required. It's first-come, first-served. There are cooking grills by each campsite, but no wood or drinking water is provided. While there are toilets, there are no shower facilities for those camping and hiking within the park, so make sure you're with people who like you a whole bunch. Ten small **cabins** are available here through Volcano House. Each accommodates four people and costs $40 single or double, $8 each for a third or fourth person. A $12 refundable key deposit gives access to the shower and toilet, and a $20 refundable deposit gets you linens, soap, towels, and a blanket (extra sleeping bag recommended). Each cabin contains one double bed and two single bunk beds and an electric light, but no electrical outlets. Outside are a picnic table and barbecue grill, but you must provide your own charcoal and cooking utensils. Check in at Volcano House after 3 P.M. and check out by noon. There is a half-mile hiking trail from the campground entrance to the Jaggar Museum.

There are also camping spaces and restrooms at **Kulanaokuaiki,** located halfway down Hilina Pali Road. As at Namakani Paio, these are on a first-come, first-served basis. No reservations are

© ROBERT NILSEN

cabins at Namakani Paio

required and no fee is charged. As it sits in the middle of this arid desert, it's hot, dry, and has little shade. No drinking water is provided.

For backcountry overnight camping, apply at the Kilauea Visitors Center (7:45 A.M.–4:45 P.M.) for a free permit no earlier than the day before you plan to hike. Camping is permitted only in established sites and at trail shelters. No open fires are permitted. Carry all the drinking water you will need, and carry out all that you take in.

Volcano House

If you decide to lodge at **Volcano House** (P.O. Box 53, Hawai'i Volcanoes National Park, HI 96718, 808/967-7321, fax 808/967-8429, volcanohouse@hawaiiantel.net, www.volcanohousehotel.com), don't be frightened away by the daytime crowds. They disappear with the sun. In the late 1980s, Volcano House went through a slow renovation and once again shines as what it always has been: a quiet country inn. The 42 rooms are comfy but old-fashioned. Who needs a pool or TV when you can look out your window into a volcano caldera? To the left of the reception area indoors, a crackling fireplace warms you from the chill in the mountain air, and this fire has burned virtually nonstop since the early days of the hotel. In front of the fireplace are stuffed leather chairs and a wonderful wooden rocker. Paintings and vintage photographs of the Hawaiian kings and queens of the Kamehameha line and magnificent photos of eruptions of the mountain hang on the walls. The hotel, operated by a *kama'aina* family, is an authorized concession of the park. Room rates are main building with crater view $200–225, non-crater view $170; Ohia Wing standard room $95, garden view $125; $15 extra for each additional person. No charge for children 12 and under occupying the same room as their parents. Rooms include koa wood furniture, Hawaiian quilted comforters, a telephone, and room heater, and each has a private bath or shower. Efficiently run, the hotel has a restaurant, lounge, two gift shops, 24-hour front desk service, maid service, and safe-deposit boxes. Besides that, you could hardly get closer to the crater if you tried.

Kilauea Military Camp

One mile west of the park entrance, within the park boundary, is the Kilauea Military Camp (KMC at Kilauea Volcano, A Joint Services Recreation Center, Attn: Reservations, Crater Rim Drive, Hawai'i Volcanoes National Park, HI 96718, 808/967-8333, reservations@kmc-volcano.com, www.kmc-volcano.com). Offering rooms and meals, this facility is open to active duty and retired military personnel, civilian employees of the Department of Defense, and their families. Available are dormitory rooms, one-, two-, and three-bedroom cottages, and apartments. Services include a lounge bar, recreation facility, tennis courts, athletic fields, a general store, post office, launderette, and gas station—all for guests only. Open to the public are the theater, which hosts community events, and a bowling alley with state-of-the-art equipment and its snack bar (3–10 P.M.). Tours of the island can be arranged for guests by the front office staff, and shuttle pick-up (for a fee) from the Hilo airport can also be arranged with advance notice.

FOOD

Volcano House Restaurant (7–10:30 A.M., 11 A.M.–2 P.M., and 5:30–9 P.M.) offers an American standard breakfast buffet for about $8 adults and $5 children, and a lunch buffet, $14 adult or $9 per child, that's often terribly crowded because of tour buses. If there are too many tour buses parked outside during the lunch hour, give it a miss and try later. Dinner starts with appetizers like sautéed mushrooms and a fruit platter. It moves on to entrées like seafood linguine, scampi, New York steak, catch of the day, and roast prime rib, the specialty, and a number of specials. Most entrées run $15–22. A children's menu is also available with dishes under $8. The quality is good, portions large, and the prices reasonable; reservations are recommended. More than the quality of food, however, the view out the big picture window over the caldera is worth the price.

For a nightcap, **Uncle George's Lounge** (4:30–9 P.M.), just beyond the main entry, is a perfect spot to relax and watch the crater disappear into the dark.

During the day, when your little tummy starts grumbling and you don't want to sit down to a big meal, head for the hotel's **Snack Bar** (9 A.M.–5 P.M.) to appease it.

SHOPPING

If you are after an exquisite piece of art, a unique memento, or an inexpensive but distinctive souvenir, be sure to visit the **Volcano Art Center Gallery** (808/967-7565, 9 A.M.–5 P.M. daily). It's a treat.

The hotel has two gift shops, the **Curio Shop,** near the entrance, and the **Crater View Gallery,** overlooking the crater, that carry a wide assortment of tourist gifts, crafts, postcards, film, souvenirs, and a selection of logowear. Both are open 7 A.M.–7:15 P.M.

Along the road, the small **Jaggar Museum gift shop** carries a fine selection of books and gifts relating to Hawaii's natural environment.

Ka'u

The Ka'u district is as simple and straightforward as the broad, open face of a country gentleman. It's not boring, and it does hold pleasant surprises for those willing to look. Formed from the massive slopes of Mauna Loa, the district presents some of the most ecologically diverse land in the islands. The bulk of it stretches 50 miles from north to south and almost 30 miles from east to west, tumbling from the snowcapped mountains through the cool green canopy of highland forests. Nearer the coast above Ninole, Punalu'u, and Na'alehu are a series of lower tabletop mountains that are older and have rocks somewhat similar to the Kohala Mountains at the north end of the island, so this area has some good rich, deep soil. The domain of sugar until 1996, its middle elevations now support stands of macadamia nut trees, eucalyptus, koa, and coffee. At lower elevations it becomes pastureland of belly-deep grass ending in blistering-hot black sands along the coast that are encircled by a necklace of foamy white sea. Much has been scored by recent lava flows and shaken by powerful earthquakes—the worst in 1868. At the bottom of Ka'u is **Ka Lae** (South Point), the southernmost tip of Hawaii and the southernmost point in the United States. It lies at a latitude 500 miles farther south than Miami and 1,000 miles below Los Angeles. Ka Lae was probably the first landfall made by the Polynesian explorers on the islands, and the entire area, particularly the more watered coastal spots, seems to have been heavily populated by early immigrants. A variety of archaeological remains support this belief.

Most people dash through Ka'u on the Hawaii Belt Road, heading to or from Volcanoes National Park. Its main towns, **Pahala** and **Na'alehu,** are little more than pit stops. The Belt Road follows the old Mamalahoa Trail where, for centuries, nothing moved faster than a contented man's stroll. Ka'u's beauties, mostly tucked away down secondary roads, are hardly given a look by most unknowing visitors. If you take the time and get off the beaten track, you'll discover black- and green-sand beaches, turtles basking on the shore, Wild West rodeos, a Tibetan Buddhist temple, and an electricity farm sprouting windmill generators. The upper slopes and broad pasturelands are the domain of hunters, hikers, and *paniolo,* who still ride the range on sure-footed horses. In Ka'u are sleepy former

KA'U SHORELINE

The 80 miles of coastline in Ka'u form the longest undeveloped shoreline in the state. Along this coast are numerous archaeological and historical sites, and the shoreline is also one of largely undisturbed beauty and uniqueness. While sugar reigned for decades are the economic powerhouse of the region, Ka'u slipped back into a semi-somnambulant state following its demise. Ka'u has always been the "backwaters" of the island, and few seemed to see its potential or worth. While one small development, the Seamount at Punalu'u, has been around for years, there is concern by many in the area that the rapidly rising value of land on the Big Island will bring unwanted development to Ka'u, as it has done to the rest of the island. Before any major development occurs, some residents and lawmakers have proposed that an evaluation of the natural, cultural, and historical significance of this coastal area be done in order to determine if it – or parts of it – is worthy of being designated a national shoreline or incorporated into the existing Hawai'i Volcanoes National Park.

plantation towns that don't even know how quaint they are, and beach parks where you can count on finding a secluded spot to pitch a tent. The majority of Ka'u's pleasures are accessible by standard rental car, but many secluded coastal spots can be reached only by four-wheel drive. Those willing to abandon their cars and hike the sparsely populated coast or interior of Ka'u are rewarded with areas unchanged and untouched for generations. Time in Ka'u moves slowly, and *aloha* still forms the basis of day-to-day life.

PAHALA

Some 22 miles southwest of Volcano is Pahala, clearly marked off Route 11. The Hawaii Belt Road flashes past this town, but if you drive into it, you'll find one of the best-preserved examples of a classic sugar town in the islands. Not long ago, the hillsides around Pahala were blanketed by fields of cane and dotted with camps of plantation workers. It was once gospel that sugar would be king in these parts forever, but the huge mill is gone, and the background whir of a modern macadamia nut–processing plant now breaks the stillness. Change is afoot in Ka'u, just like everywhere in Hawaii. Sugar land has been sold, mostly in big chunks. Some may develop their land into ranches or residential areas, while smaller plots are being turned into farms. At least 40 farms now produce Ka'u coffee in hillside plantations above Pahala; while not as well known as Kona coffee, it's gaining a reputation for itself.

With 1,500 people, Pahala has the largest population in the district, even though some people left with the closing of the mill. In town you'll find the basics—a gas station, district hospital, schools, small shopping center, post office, several churches and temples, a Bank of Hawaii office, a small launderette, grocery store, and restaurant. The town itself is well kept with neat rows of workers' homes and is worth the drive through to glimpse a bit of old Hawaii.

Wood Valley Temple

Also known as Nechung Dorje Drayang Ling, or Immutable Island of Melodious Sound, the Wood Valley Temple (P.O. Box 250, Pahala, HI 96777, 808/928-8539, fax 808/928-6271, nechung@aloha.net, www.nechung.org) is true to its name. This simple vermilion and yellow Tibetan Buddhist temple sits like a sparkling jewel surrounded by the emerald-green velvet of its manicured grounds, which are scented by an aromatic stand of majestic eucalyptus trees. The grounds, like a botanical garden, vibrate with life and energy.

The Buddha gave the world essentially 84,000 different teachings to pacify, purify, and develop the mind. In Tibetan Buddhism there are four major lineages, and this temple, founded by Tibetan master Nechung Rinpoche, is a classic synthesis of all four. Monks, lama, and scholars from different schools of Buddhism are periodically invited to come and lecture as resident teachers. The Dalai Lama came in 1980 to dedicate the temple and graced the temple once again in 1994 when he addressed an audience here of more than 3,500 people. Programs vary, but people genuinely interested in Buddhism come here for meditation and soul-searching as well as for peace, quiet, relaxation, and direction. Morning and evening services at 7 A.M. and 6 P.M. are led by the Tibetan monk in residence, and a Saturday Buddhist philosophy class runs 2–5 P.M. Formal classes and retreats depend upon which guest teacher is in residence and some require registration and a fee.

Buddhists strive to become wise and compassionate people. The focus of the temple is to bring together all meditation and church groups in the community. Plenty of local Christian and Buddhist groups use the nonsectarian facilities. Any group that is spiritually, socially, and community oriented and that has a positive outlook is welcome. Wood Valley Temple can't promise nirvana, but it can point you to the path.

The retreat facility is called the Tara Temple and at one time housed a Japanese Shingon Mission in Pahala. When the Shingon sect moved to a new facility in Kona, this building was abandoned and given to Wood Valley Temple. A local contractor moved it to its present location in 1978, cranked it up one story, and built dormitories underneath. The grounds, hallowed and consecrated for decades, already held a Nichiren temple, the main temple here today, that was dismantled in 1919 at its original location and rebuilt on its present site to protect it from lowland flooding.

If you wish to visit, please do so on weekends and be respectful, as this is a retreat center. For those staying, either as guests or as part of a program, rates at the retreat facility are private room single $50, double room $75; bunk in the dorm $35, with use of a large communal kitchen and shared bath. Meals are not provided. All require a two-night minimum stay or a $10 surcharge for only one night. Weekly discounts and group rates are available. Definitely call or write to make reservations and get directions.

© ROBERT NILSEN

Wood Valley Temple

Shopping

On the outskirts of town in an old bank building next to the former theater and just beyond where the mill used to stand, is **Pahala Plantation Store** (808/928-9811, 8 A.M.–6 P.M. daily). This shop carries gifts, souvenirs, some artwork, Ka'u coffee, snacks, T-shirts, and books, and it is the check-in office for the Pahala Plantation Cottages.

Recreation

Hawaiian Wa'akaulua Adventures (808/938-5717, kiko@waakaulua.com, www.waakaulua.com) offers a unique sailing adventure on a traditional-style, 28-foot-long, 50-year-old, double-hull Hawaiian sailing canoe. Captain Kiko takes four to six individuals on sailing trips that can be arranged for any number of launch sites around the island. Rates are $75 per person for a three-hour trip. Sailing on this canoe is an opportunity not only to get out paddling on the water but also to learn about Hawaiian history and culture. Call Hawaiian Wa'akaulua Adventures to arrange a trip and location. It will be an experience you won't forget.

Vacation Rentals

When the sugar mill closed, many people left Pahala and the surrounding area. The town slumped but never disappeared. It has hung on and has slowly managed to infuse life back into itself. Recently, travelers have started to discover what a peaceful area of the island this is and what a fine example Pahala is of a former plantation community. To cater to the traveling public and to provide accommodations for those visiting the volcano, **Pahala Plantation Cottages** (P.O. Box 940, Pahala, HI 96777, 808/928-9811, mahalo@aloha.net, www.pahala-hawaii.com) offers a number of vacation rental accommodations in town, including the renovated seven-bedroom, four-bath plantation manager's house, which rents for $500 a night or $85 a room. Because it has a huge dining room, living room, sitting room, and library, a fully functional kitchen, broad wraparound lanai, and a large yard, it's also perfect for functions, group events, meetings, reunions, and seminars. Other nearby renovated and spacious one- to four-bedroom plantation cottages, with their original wooden floors and high ceilings, period pieces, and antiques, run $85–185 a night and are sizable enough for a family. As each has a full kitchen, no meals are provided, and some amenities include laundry facilities, cable television, VCRs, and computer access. The renovation of these plantation homes has been the work of Julie Neal and friends. Check-in (2–6 P.M.) is at the Pahala Plantation Store. For information and reservations, contact Pahala Plantation Cottages. You'll be glad you did.

Hale O Honu (888/823-5717, www.houseoftheturtle.com) lies in the embracing arms of Wood Valley. This three-bedroom home has two bathrooms, a full kitchen and laundry facilities. There's even a screened outdoor gazebo where you can barbecue and eat your evening meal while listening to the sounds of the forest and watching the incredible show in the night sky. Set in this peaceful neighborhood in a quiet section of the island, Hale O Honu certainly provides the setting for a calm and uninterrupted stay, yet is close to sites like green sea turtles on Punalu'u black-sand beach, South Point and its green-sand beach, and Hawai'i Volcanoes National Park. Rental rates are $125 a night, two nights minimum, or $850 for a week, plus a $75 cleaning fee.

Food

The well-known Tex Drive In of Honoka'a has a branch in Pahala called **Tex Pahala** (808/928-8200, 7 A.M.–8 P.M. Mon.–Sat., 7 A.M.–6 P.M. Sun.), so now you're able to get excellent quality local food and hot *malasadas* at a reasonable price in Ka'u. Expect to find wraps, meat and fish burgers, sandwiches, and plates like Korean chicken and curry stew, with little on the menu over $8.

Located in the center of town, **Mizuno's Superette** (808/928-8101, 6 A.M.–7 P.M. Mon.–Fri., 7 A.M.–5 P.M. Sat., 8 A.M.–noon Sun.) is the place to head for groceries, sundries, and other such supplies.

PUNALU'U

Along the coast just south of Pahala are the small former communities of Punalu'u and Ninole. Punalu'u was an important port during the sugar boom of the 1880s and even had a railroad. Notice the tall coconut palms in the vicinity, and the fishpond behind the beach, both unusual for Ka'u. Punalu'u means Diving Spring, so named because freshwater springs can be found on the floor of the bay. Native divers once paddled out to sea, then dove with calabashes they filled with freshwater from the underwater springs. This was the main source of drinking water for the region.

Ninole Cove is less than a mile down the coast from Punalu'u. What was Ninole is now home to the **Sea Mountain Resort and Golf Course,** built in the early 1970s by a branch of the C. Brewer Company. Ninole Cove has a rocky shoreline and the remains of Ka'ie'ie Heiau sit on the bluff south of the beach.

The string of flat-topped hills in the background is the remains of volcano cones that became dormant about 100,000 years ago. In sharp contrast with them is **Lo'ihi Seamount,** 20 miles offshore and about 3,000 feet below the surface of the sea. This very active submarine volcano is steadily building and should reach the surface in just a few tens of thousands of years.

Punalu'u Black Sand Beach

Punalu'u Beach County Park (turn near mile marker 56) is a county park with full amenities and is famous for its black-sand beach. Here you'll find a pavilion, bathrooms, showers, drinking water, telephone, and open camping area (permit required). During the day there are plenty of tourists around, but at night the beach park empties, and you virtually have it to yourself. Punalu'u boasts some of the only safe swimming on the south coast, but that doesn't mean that it can't have its treacherous moments. Head for the northeast section of the black-sand beach near the boat ramp. Stay close to shore because a prevailing rip current lurks just outside the bay. Hawaiian green sea turtles bask in the warm black sand, and hawksbill

© ROBERT NILSEN

Turtles love Punalu'u Black Sand Beach as much as humans do.

turtles use this beach for building their nests and are often seen swimming in the bay. When they're around, please give them plenty of room and don't harass them—it's the law.

A few gift shops have seen set up at the back of the beach, and a *kaukau* wagon often parks there, offering island sandwiches, shave ice, cold drinks, and snacks.

Capping the low hill overlooking Punalu'u Bay is **Hokuloa Church,** which houses a memorial to Henry Opukaha'ia, the Hawaiian most responsible for encouraging the first missionaries to head to Hawaii to save his people from damnation. Punalu'u was his birth village; his grave overlooks Kealakekua Bay in Kona. Hokuloa Church is a tiny, open-sided stone structure with six short pews. From this hilltop site, you have good views onto both Punalu'u and Ninole bays. A rough gravel road up the hill can be found directly across from the beach park entrance.

Kawa Beach

Between Punalu'u and Honu'apo is Kawa Beach: no signs, no road, just a path leading through the sparse coastal vegetation to the water. Kawa Beach is a black pebble beach, mixed with some black and green sand; it is perhaps best known as an ancient surfing spot. Locals try the water here when the waves are right and even hold a yearly surfing competition to see who's the best in the region. Overlooking the north end of the beach on a low bluff is the large Ke'eku Heiau. Of uncertain origin, it may have been a luakini *heiau* where human sacrifice took place.

Golf

The **Sea Mountain at Punalu'u Golf Course** (808/928-6222) is a 6,416-yard, 18-hole, par-72 course designed by Jack Snyder. As it's set right on the coast, the winds can be strong and usually blow across the fairways, creating challenging play. Greens fees are $36.50 weekdays and $39.50 weekends for guests, $46.50 and $49.50, respectively, for visitors; clubs are available to rent. The clubhouse offers morning coffee at 7 A.M., serves a limited menu of sandwiches and *pu pu* 10 A.M.–2 P.M., and has a full bar that's open later.

Vacation Rentals

Sea Mountain at Punalu'u (P.O. Box 460, Pahala, HI 96777, 808/928-6200, fax 808/928-8075, www.viresorts.com) is a time-share condominium that also rents available units to the general public on a nightly basis when available. Options include studio, one-bedroom, and two-bedroom units at $110–250, depending on the time of year. The Land Company in Na'alehu, which manages several units in this complex, usually rents its units cheaper. Because of its rural location, Sea Mountain can offer secluded accommodations for reasonable prices. Your condo unit will be a low-rise, Polynesian-inspired bungalow with a steep shake roof. The standard units, all tastefully furnished, offer remote color TVs, full kitchens, full baths, ceiling fans, and a lanai. The resort itself has a small swimming pool and spa pool, laundry facilities, four unlit tennis courts, and a golf course. Although the units vary, all are furnished in island theme, typically with rattan couches and easy chairs. The feeling throughout the well-tended resort is a friendly, home-away-from-home atmosphere. Outside your door are the resort's fairways and greens, backdropped by the spectacular coast. If you're after peace and quiet, Sea Mountain is hard to beat.

NA'ALEHU AND WAI'OHINU

Between Punalu'u and Na'alehu, the coastal area is majestic; stretching into the aqua-blue sea is a tableland of black lava with waves crashing against it in a surrealistic seascape that seems to go on forever. Past Whittington Beach County Park, the road heads up the hill to Na'alehu. On the way up the hill, pause at the lookout, enjoy the seascape, and consider that only the tiny specks of the South Pacific islands are between here and Antarctica! If that starts a chill on your shoulders, also know that Ka'u is the warmest region of the island, and

Na'alehu hit 100 degrees in 1931, the highest temperature recorded in the state.

Na'alehu bills itself as the southernmost town in the United States. It is, but aside from the few shops and restaurants in town, it doesn't have much going for it. It does, however, have a nice drive through the center of town. Check out the overhanging monkeypod trees that form a magnificent living tunnel in front of some of the former plantation managers' homes as you pass through on Route 11. Every Fourth of July, a down-home rodeo is held in town for all the amateur riders of the district. Come and enjoy. Na'alehu is a former sugar town, but it still maintains a small downtown business area, has a post office, and supports a gas station.

Less than two miles up the road, a tall church steeple welcomes you to the small town of Wai'ohinu. There's nothing remarkable about this village, except that as you pass through you'll be seeing an example of the real Hawaiian country lifestyle as it exists today. Wai'ohinu was an important agricultural region in centuries past, and King Kamehameha even had personal land here. Just before the well-marked Shirakawa Motel on the *mauka* side of the road is the **Mark Twain Monkeypod Tree.** Unfortunately, this—Wai'ohinu's only claim to fame, except for its undisturbed peace and quiet—blew down in a heavy windstorm in 1957. Part of the original trunk, carved into a bust of Twain, is on display at the Lyman Museum in Hilo. A shoot from the original trunk has grown to become a sizable descendant of the town's original attraction.

Whittington Beach County Park

Three miles north of Na'alehu is a county park with full amenities and camping with county permit, but no drinking water. This park is tough to spot from the road because it's not clearly marked. Before the hill going up to Na'alehu you'll see a bridge at the bottom. Turn seaward and proceed down the access road. The park is never crowded. Here you'll encounter some old ruins from the turn of the 20th century when Honu'apo Bay was an important sugar port. A rail line from the Ka'u cane lands terminated here for shipment of raw sugar to be processed elsewhere. Cattle were shipped from here as well. Before the sugar era, Honu'apo area was a sizable Hawaiian settlement. On the park's north flank is an area of ponds, tidepools, and palm trees, a spot sometimes used by anglers and families for a day at the ocean. Due to community effort, some 200 acres of this adjacent land will hopefully be added as parkland (rather than be developed as million-dollar homesites ringing the ponds under coconut trees) to keep this coastal location natural and undeveloped, as it's one of the few like it along the coast.

Entertainment

The **Na'alehu Theater** (808/929-9133) is a large building along the highway in the center of town. It's a classic old-time theater that was the hub of entertainment during the plantation days. Now it's usually open on Fridays for movies and has been a venue of the Hawaii International Film Festival. Call for what's showing. During the day, it's open as a mini-museum, displaying a small assortment of movie- and theater-related items, and as a small snack shop.

Shopping

Located across from the gas station in Na'alehu is **Jackie's Plantation House,** which carries art, collectibles, and apparel.

You can pick up supplies and buy gas at the **Wong Yuen Store** (808/929-7223, 8 A.M.–7 P.M. Mon.–Sat., 8 A.M.–6 P.M. Sun.) in Wai'ohinu.

Accommodations

The **Shirakawa Motel** (P.O. Box 467, Na'alehu, HI 96772, tel./fax 808/929-7462, info@shirakawamotel.com, www.shirakawamotel.com) in Wai'ohinu is a small, clean, comfortable, "hang loose bruddah" motel where your peace and quiet are guaranteed. The Shirakawa has been open since 1928. The original two-story hotel has now been converted to the home of the retired second-generation owners. Their son now runs the dozen-room, dark green, red roof motel, which consists of clean and utilitarian single-story detached buildings to the side. Prices are a reasonable $43 single or $45 double for a standard room, $50 single or $55 double for a kitchenette, and $65 for a kitchenette with one bedroom. Extra person rollaways are $10. No credit cards.

Macadamia Meadows Farm B&B (P.O. Box 756, Na'alehu, HI 96772, 808/929-8097 or 888/929-8118, innkeeper@macadamiameadows.com, www.macadamiameadows.com) is set, as you might expect, in the middle of an eight-acre working macadamia nut farm along Kama'oa Road, a short hop west of the Wong Yuen Store in Wai'ohinu. But this is more than just a B&B. With the full-size tennis court, swimming pool, and basketball half-court, it seems like a mini-resort. The huge main house, with open kitchen, dining and living areas, and wraparound lanai, looks out on the back lawn and nut trees. Upstairs in the main house are the Volcano Room with its queen-size sleigh bed for $79 and smaller Hawaiian Room at $69. These share a bathroom and can be combined to make a two-bedroom suite for $129. Downstairs is the Macadamia Room with its queen-size bed and lanai for $89. In the detached building, once the nut processing plant, are two more rooms. The Papakalea Room with its queen-size bed and private bath runs $89. Next door is the Punalu'u Room at $129; it has a queen-size canopy bed and queen-size sofa sleeper. The extra charge for a rollaway sleeper for more than a couple is $15 adult and $10 children. All rooms have private entrances and television. A hearty and taste-tempting breakfast is served to all guests, and the owners will gladly show you around the farm and introduce you to the world of nut farming.

Margo Hobbs of **Margo's Corner** (P.O. Box 447, Na'alehu, HI 96772, 808/929-9614, info@margoscorner.com, www.margoscorner.com) can accommodate you in a strikingly original Rainbow Cottage for $85. This pentagonal guesthouse sports a queen-size bed and private bath with shower. Brightly painted outside, it's also a rainbow of cheery colors on the inside. Two nights minimum is preferred. Down in the cool basement, the Adobe Suite, with its private bath and sauna, sleeps up to six people with a queen-size futon in the living area and two raised beds in the bedroom. It rents for $125 a night double and $25 for each additional person; two nights minimum. Touring bicyclists and backpackers can camp for $25 per person in the yard among Norfolk pines; a shared shower is available. Rates include full gourmet vegetarian dinners and breakfast every day; much of the food comes from the organic vegetable garden out back. Appreciated by all who stay, an after-dinner performance of East Indian raga music is put on by one of the hosts. No smoking and no excessive drinking, please. For your extra food needs, Margo's maintains a small but well-stocked health food store that's open in the afternoon. Margo's is about halfway between Wai'ohinu and the South Point Road, just south of Kama'oa Road in the Discovery Harbor subdivision. Call for exact directions and reservations. Margo's is a "lesbian, gay, bisexual, transgender safespace," but gladly open to all.

The Land Office Property Management Division (808/939-7368 or 800/359-6089, www.hawaii-vacation-rental.biz) at the Na'alehu Shopping Center manages many rental properties in the Ka'u region. They are a good source for vacation homes and condos in this area that might meet your needs.

Food

Whereas all the accommodations seem to be in Wai'ohinu, all the food seems to be in Na'alehu. In the center of town at the main intersection, a large, easily spotted sign marks the **Punalu'u Bake Shop and Visitor Center** (808/929-7343 or 866/366-3501, www.punaluubakeshop.com, 9 A.M.–5 P.M. daily except Christmas and New Year's Day). The bake shop, tempting with all kinds of pastries, is especially known for its *pao dolce* (sweet bread). Head past viewing windows to the retail shop for baked goods, sandwiches, plate lunches, ice cream, coffee, cold drinks, and a smattering of souvenirs. Punalu'u sweet bread is well known throughout the island. It makes a good gift if you're visiting friends and can be mail ordered to anywhere in the country. The cool and pleasing gardens here make a fine rest stop for the long stretches through this part of the island.

For a quick sandwich or full meal try the **Hana Hou** restaurant (808/929-9717, 8 A.M.–3 P.M. Mon.–Wed., 8 A.M.–8 P.M. Thurs.–Sun.). Tidy and clean, this restaurant has a menu of typical island cuisine at reasonable prices, with most breakfasts under $6 and lunches and dinners under $10. The Friday special is king crab and steak, while the Saturday special is prime rib. Hana Hou does its own baking, so check out the pies and baked goods. Look for the big "Eat" sign across from the shopping center in the center of town.

Shaka Restaurant (808/929-7404, 10 A.M.–9 P.M.) is on the Wai'ohinu side of the center of town. This eatery is clean and well run, with tapa patterns on the tablecloths and chair cushions. Extensive breakfast and lunch menus feed hungry folks during the day; in the evening your choices include grilled chicken fillet, baby back ribs, fresh catch, New York steak, and veggie stir-fry. Meals come with soup and a dinner salad, and a kids' menu helps keep the prices down for families. Friday brings live evening entertainment and a prime rib special. It's not gourmet by any means, but you won't go away hungry or disappointed. Shaka has the only bar in town.

For quick eats on the go, head for **Ka'alaiki Lunch Shop** (6:30 A.M.–3 P.M. daily) at the baseball park parking lot. This little walk-up place serves full breakfasts, hearty sandwiches, and other island favorites—takeout only—and you'd be hard pressed to spend more than $5 on any meal.

Markets

Na'alehu Shopping Center is along the road in the center of town. In the small complex you'll find the small but full-service **Island Market** grocery store (808/929-7527, 8 A.M.–7 P.M. Mon.–Sat., 9 A.M.–6 P.M. Sun.).

If you are in town on Saturday morning, stop by the **farmers market** at the theater.

SOUTH POINT

South Point is a triangular nub of land that *is* the southern tip of the Big Island. This land sweeps down in gentle gradient from the fertile grasslands along the highway to the ocean, and is raked by winds that blow across its slope, bending tree and bush to the west. Its eastern edge is low and rocky with long stretches of sand dunes and even a green-sand beach. Its west edge is dominated by a sheer cliff that drops precipitously into deep waters rich with fish. It's here that the first Hawaiians may have landed on their perilous journey from the islands to the south, before spreading out to dominate and master all the islands in this island chain. There is archaeological evidence

© ROBERT NILSEN

fishing at South Point

of ancient habitation and usage at South Point but still much speculation abounds as to the actual role it played in those early years of discovery and colonization. In any case, South Point remains a place of mystic and cultural importance for Hawaiians.

Ka Lae

The Hawaiians simply called this Ka Lae (The Point). Some scholars believe Polynesian sailors made landfall here as early as A.D. 150, and that their amazing exploits became navigating legend long before colonization began. A paved, narrow, but passable road branches off from Route 11 approximately six miles west of Na'alehu, and it drops directly south for 12 miles to land's end. Luckily the shoulders are firm, so you can pull over to let another car go by. Car-rental agencies may warn against using this road, but their fears are unfounded. You proceed through a flat, treeless area of rangeland for cattle and horses. Suddenly, incongruously, huge mechanical windmills appear, beating their arms against the sky. This is the **Kamoa Wind Farm.** Notice that this futuristic experiment at America's most southern point uses windmills made in Japan by Mitsubishi! The trees here are bent over by the prevailing wind, demonstrating the obviously excellent wind-power potential of the area. However strong the potential, the wind can also be a liability. You will notice that some windmills have been damaged by winds that were too strong, while others have rusted in disuse. Plans are to cut the number of these windmills, replacing them with machines that are many times as efficient.

Farther along, you enter countryside controlled by the Hawaiian Homelands agency, some of which you are forbidden to enter. While you are not welcome on the land, you do have the right to remain on the road. Here the road splits left and right; go right until road's end, where you'll find a parking area usually filled with the pickup trucks of local fishermen. Walk to the cliff and notice attached ladders that plummet straight down to where fishing boats can anchor. Local skippers moor their boats here and bring supplies and their catch up and down the ladders, or transfer loads via rope. Nearby is a tall white structure with a big square sign turned sideways like a diamond and a navigational light on its top. It marks the true **South Point,** the southernmost tip of the United States and registered historical landmark. Directly below this marker is an ancient *heiau,* and at water's edge are holes curiously carved into some rocks. These are reputed to be **anchor points** used by early Hawaiians to secure their canoes to shore by long ropes while the current carried them a short way offshore. In this manner, they could fish without being swept away. Usually, a few people are line-fishing from the point, and today fishermen use floats or tiny boats to carry only their lines out to sea. The *ulua,* tuna, and *ahi* fishing is renowned throughout this area. The fishing grounds here have always been extremely fertile, and thousands of shell and bone fishhooks have been found throughout the area. Scuba divers say that the rocks off South Point are covered with broken fishing line that the currents have woven into wild macramé. Survey the mighty Pacific and realize that the closest continental landfall is Antarctica, 7,500 miles to the south.

Back where the road Ys, follow the road left and pass a series of WWII barrack foundations being reclaimed by nature. This road, too, leads to a parking area and small Hawaiian Homelands office and information center where you pay a few bucks to park. Out front stands a short statue of a native Hawaiian wrapped in chains, symbolic of their situation as a disenfranchised people in their own land. Beyond is Kaulana boat ramp (*kaulana* means boat landing) where a few seaworthy craft are bobbing away at their moorings and still farther is the trail to Green-Sand Beach.

When the Kona winds blow out of the South Pacific, South Point takes it on the chin. The weather should always be a consideration when you visit. In times past, any canoe caught in the wicked currents was considered lost. Even today, only experienced boaters brave South Point, and only during fine weather.

There is no official camping or facilities of any kind at South Point, but plenty of boat owners bivouac for a night to get an early start in the morning. The lava flow in this area is quite old and grass-covered, and the constant winds act like a natural lawn mower.

Green Sand Beach

The trail to Green Sand Beach starts near the boat ramp at Kaulana Bay. Head east from there past the gate. All along are remnants of precontact habitation, including the remains of a *heiau* foundation. Unfortunately, all-terrain and four-wheel drive vehicles have made tracks through the dunes along this coastal strip, degrading the environment and disturbing the land. If you walk for three miles, you'll come to Papakolea, better known as Green Sand Beach, at Mahana Bay. The lava in this area contains olivine, a green semiprecious stone that weathered into sand-like particles distributed along the beach. You're walking into the wind going there, and it can be strong, but it's not generally a rough go—there's no elevation gain to speak of. The lava in the area is 'a'a, weathered and overlaid by thick ground cover. An ancient eruption deposited 15–18 feet of ash right here, and the grasses grew.

About three miles on, you see what is obviously an eroded cinder cone at the edge of the sea. Peer over the edge to have a peek at the beach with its definite green tinge. This is the only beach along the way, so it's hard to mistake. Green Sand Beach definitely lives up to its name, but don't expect emerald green. It's more like a dull army olive green. Getting down to it can be treacherous. Around the side of the cove, you'll be scrambling over tough lava rock, and you'll have to make drops of four to five feet in certain spots—or you could slide down the sand at the back end. Once you get over the lip of heavy-duty rock, the trail down is not so bad. When you begin your descent, notice overhangs, almost like caves, where rocks have been piled up to extend them. These rocked-in areas make great shelters, and you can see remnants of recent campfires in spots perfect for a night's bivouac. Down at the beach, be very aware of the wave action. The currents can be wicked here, and you should only enter the water on very calm days. No one is around to save you, and you don't want to wind up as flotsam in Antarctica.

OCEAN VIEW

Before you get to Ocean View, you have a sense of what the area is like when you stop at the highway scenic lookout spot near mile marker 75 and view the strong black lava flows that fill the horizon. Ocean View is often referred to as the largest subdivision in the state. In fact, it is a conglomeration of five subdivisions that is several miles wide and that pushes up the mountain about six miles and down toward the ocean another three. The highest lots are at about 5,000 feet. This unincorporated town of self-sufficient individuals who don't want to be bothered by anyone has been carved out of rough volcanic rubble with an overlay of trees and bush. While not the most scenic, it is attractive in its own untamed way. If you're curious, have a drive through.

Services are located in two small shopping centers that flank the highway. Above the highway in the Ocean View Town Center, you'll find an Ace Hardware, the Ocean View Pizzaria, the Kahuku Market, and gas pumps. Below the highway in the Pohue Plaza are a second gas station, the post office, the full-service Ocean View Market, Desert Rose Cafe, and a launderette. Down the road a piece is Mister Bell's Restaurant and sports bar. Aside from house lots and a community center, there's not much else here. This area was hit hard by the downturn in the state economy during the 1990s, and often people had to drive long distances to get work—if they could find it at all. Now the area seems to be growing in a slow and steady manner, but people still have a long distance to commute.

There frankly is little to do in Ocean View itself if you are a visitor, but as there are few lights and little air pollution, this is one of the greatest locations for stargazing in the islands without going up to the top of the mountain.

Kula Kai Caverns

The newest and perhaps most curious offering of this region is the Kula Kai Caverns (808/929-7539, www.kulakaicaverns.com). In contrast to the Ka'eleku Caverns on Maui, which are about 30,000 years old, the Kula Kai Cavern system—13 miles of tunnel have been surveyed—is a mere baby at about 1,000 years old. A tour underground here gives you a look at the bowels of the largest mountain in the world, once used for shelter and as a place to collect water in this region of low rainfall. Like other lava tubes in the world, the Kula Kai Caverns shows fine examples of lava shelves, pillars, lava balls, and other customary lava formations. As these interconnected tubes are so close to the surface in some spots, roots of 'ohi'a trees have penetrated the ceiling of the cave and hang like hairy tendrils. The inside cave temperature averages 68°F year round. An easy 30-minute interpretive Walking Tour ($15 for adults and $8 for kids) leads through the lighted section of the caverns. The more rigorous two-hour Spelunking Tour ($65, age eight and above) takes you deeper into the maze. For those who really love being underground, the Maelstrom Cave Tour keeps you down for about three hours and runs $95 per person. All tours are intended to be an educational and cultural experience. More than to just have a look, it's preferable to learn of the island's volcanic history and how lava tubes form and how they have been used by humans. Other cave tours can be arranged, depending upon your interest and skill level, and all tours are given by prior arrangement only. Long pants and closed-toe shoes are required; gloves, knee pads, hard hats, and lights are provided.

Manuka State Wayside

The Manuka State Wayside is about three miles west of the commercial area in Ocean View and just inside the Ka'u district. This restful wayside has restrooms, a pavilion, and a two-mile trail through a native and introduced forest, all of which lies within the Manuka Natural Area Reserve. The forested slopes above Manuka provide ample habitat for introduced, and now totally successful, colonies of wild pigs, pheasants, and turkeys. Shelter camping (no tents) is allowed on the grounds. This is an excellent rest or picnic stop, but bring your own drinking water. Within a couple of miles, you're in South Kona, heading up the coast past the world's largest single-owner macadamia nut farm, toward Captain Cook and Kailua.

Bed-and-Breakfasts

Bougainvillea Bed and Breakfast (P.O. Box 6045, Ocean View, HI 96737, tel./fax 808/929-7089 or 800/688-1763, peaceful@interpac.net, www.bougainvilleabedandbreakfast.com) has views of the ocean and South Point. As this B&B is located in Ocean View, the landscape for many will be stark, but the inn is quiet and romantic, with fine landscaping all around. Each of the four rooms has a private entrance and bath, while guests share the swimming pool, hot tub, barbecue area, TV, and the game and video library. There is nothing out here to block your view, so at night there is unbeatable stargazing! As your sightseeing options are limited in Ocean View, your gracious hosts Martie and Don Nitsche gladly offer suggestions for activities and can make arrangements for you. A full nutritious homemade breakfast—different each day—is served every morning. Rooms are $75 single or $85 double; $15 for an extra person; two-night minimum. You can't go wrong at this clean and commodious inn.

Located only a short way above the highway, **Leilani Bed and Breakfast** (92-8822 Leilani Parkway, Ocean View, HI 96737, 808/929-7101, fax 939-7136, leilanibnb@fastnethi.com, www.whenworkisplay.com) is set among three lava tube openings. The rambling lava rock house has three bedrooms, two fit for couples and one that could take a couple with two kids. Decorated in tropical designs, each room has its own bathroom but the outdoor hot tub is shared by all. Room rates are $75–85 per night. A covered courtyard separates the guest rooms from the rest of the house, and it's here that a large continental breakfast is served each morning.

Food

Ocean View Pizzaria (808/929-9677, 11 A.M.–7 P.M. Sun.–Thurs., until 8 P.M. Fri.–Sat.) is located in the shopping center above the highway. While the focus is pizza (smalls run $11, large pies go for $13, extra cost for the toppings of your choice), you can also get a salad, hot and cold sandwiches, and even a few baked goods freshly made on-site.

The Desert Rose Cafe (808/939-7673, 7 A.M.–8 P.M. daily) sits down below the highway in the Pohue Plaza. Advertised as "the southernmost café in the USA," the Desert Rose has a Southwest theme and is open for three meals a day. Expect eggs and scrambles for breakfast, sandwiches and burgers for lunch, and a variety of fish and red meat entrées, like Tex-Mex chicken, shrimp scampi, charbroiled pork chop, or Cajun-crusted *ono,* in the $15–20 range for dinner. This small eatery puts out fine nutritious food and is the best in town.

Located just west of the commercial center and just above the highway, **Mister Bell's** restaurant (808/929-7447, 7 A.M.–9 P.M. daily) serves an American-style breakfast, sandwiches and plates lunches for lunch, and a variety of more substantial meals for dinner, with most dinner entrées running $10–15. Clean and spartan with its linoleum floors, lattice-work ceiling, and blue walls, it is the most traditional of the town's restaurants. Dine in or takeout. The attached sports bar is open throughout the evening and is the only such place in town.

Markets

Located in the Pohue Plaza below the highway, the **Ocean View Market** (808/929-9843, 7:30 A.M.–7:45 P.M. Mon.–Sat., 8 A.M.–6 P.M. Sun.) is the town's only full-service grocery store.

Kahuku Country Market (808/929-9011, 5 A.M.–8 P.M. Mon.–Fri., 6 A.M.–8 P.M. Sat.–Sun.), in the Ocean View Town Center, has a variety of basic foods, sundries, beer, and wine; gasoline is available out front.

A few steps away is the **Anuenue Natural Foods Deli and Bakery** (808/929-7550, 9 A.M.–5:30 P.M. Mon.–Fri., 9 A.M.–5 P.M. Sat., 11 A.M.–4 P.M. Sun.). Not only does this shop carry fresh baked goods, it also has a surprisingly good, although limited, selection of packaged foods, fresh fruits and vegetables, and hot soup, as well as vitamins, minerals, and supplements.

BACKGROUND

The Land

GEOGRAPHY

The Big Island is the southernmost and easternmost of the Hawaiian Islands—it is also the largest. This island dwarfs all the others in the Hawaiian chain at 4,028 square miles and growing. It accounts for about 63 percent of the state's total landmass; the other islands could fit within it two times over. With 266 miles of coastline, the island stretches about 95 miles from north to south and 80 miles from east to west. Cape Kumukahi is the easternmost point in the state, and Ka Lae (The Point) is the southernmost point in the country.

Science and *The Kumulipo* oral history differ sharply on the age of the Big Island. Scientists say that Hawai'i is the youngest of the islands, being a little over one million years old; the chanters claim that it was the first "island-child" of Wakea and Papa. It is, irrefutably, closest to the "hot spot" on the Pacific floor, evidenced by Kilauea's frequent eruptions. The geology, geography, and location of the Hawaiian Islands, and their ongoing drifting and building in the middle of the Pacific, make them among the most fascinating pieces of real estate on earth. The Big Island is the *most* fascinating of them all—it is unique.

Separating the Big Island from Maui to the northwest is the 'Alenuihaha Channel, which at about 30 miles wide and over 6,800 feet

© ROBERT NILSEN

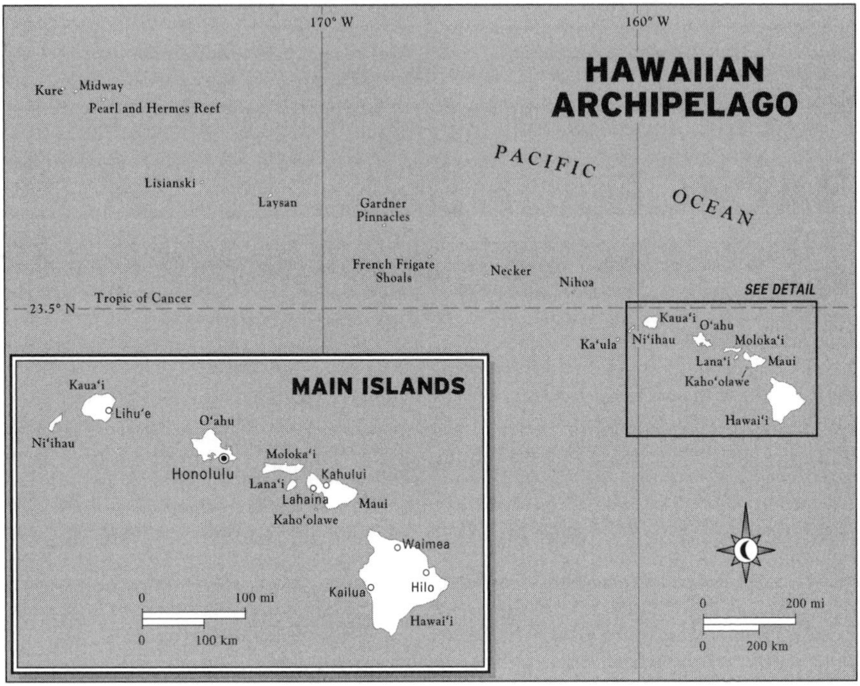

deep, is the state's second widest and second deepest channel.

The Mountains

The tremendous volcanic peak of **Mauna Kea** (White Mountain), located in north-central Hawai'i, has been extinct for over 3,500 years. Its seasonal snowcap earns Mauna Kea its name and reputation as a good skiing area in winter. Over 18,000 feet of mountain below sea level rise straight up from the ocean floor—making Mauna Kea over 31,000 feet tall, almost 3,000 feet taller than Mount Everest; some consider it the tallest mountain in the world. At 13,796 feet above sea level, it is without doubt the tallest peak in the Pacific. Near its top, at 13,020 feet, is **Lake Waiau,** the highest lake in the state and third-highest in the country. Mauna Kea was obviously a sacred mountain to the Hawaiians, and its white dome was a welcome beacon to seafarers. On its slope is the largest adze quarry in Polynesia, from which high-quality basalt was taken to be fashioned into prized tools. The atmosphere atop the mountain, which sits mid-Pacific far from pollutants, is the most rarefied and cleanest on earth. The clarity makes Mauna Kea a natural for astronomical observatories. The complex of telescopes on its summit is internationally staffed and provides data to scientists around the world.

The **Kohala Mountains** to the northwest are the oldest and rise only to 5,480 feet at Kaunu o Kaleiho'ohei peak. This section looks more like the other Hawaiian Islands, with deep gorges and valleys along the coast and a forested interior. As you head east toward Waimea from Kawaihae on Route 19, for every few miles you travel you pick up about 10 inches of rainfall per year. This becomes obvious as you begin to pass little streams and rivulets running from the mountains.

Mount Hualalai, at 8,271 feet, is the backdrop to Kailua-Kona. It's home to many of the Big Island's endangered birds and supports many of the region's newest housing developments. Just a few years ago, Mount Hualalai was thought to be extinct, since the last time it erupted was in 1801. It is now known that within the last 1,000 years, the mountain has erupted about every two or three centuries. In 1929 it suffered an earthquake swarm, which means that a large movement of lava inside the mountain caused tremors. USGS scientists now consider Mount Hualalai only dormant and very likely to erupt at some point in the future. When it does, a tremendous amount of lava is expected to pour rapidly down its steep sides. From the side of this mountain grows the cone Pu'u Wa'awa'a. At 3,967 feet, it's only slightly shorter than the very active Kilauea on the far side of Mauna Loa. Obsidian is found here, and this is one of the few places in Hawaii where this substance has been quarried in large quantities.

Even though **Mauna Loa** (Long Mountain) measures a respectable 13,679 feet, its height isn't its claim to fame. This active volcano, 60 miles long by 30 wide, comprises 19,000 cubic miles of lava, making it the densest and most massive mountain on earth. In 1950, a tremendous lava flow belched from Mauna Loa's summit, reaching an astonishing rate of 6,750,000 cubic yards per hour. Seven lava rivers flowed for 23 days, emitting over 600 million cubic yards of lava that covered 35 square miles. There were no injuries, but the villages of Ka'apuna and Honokua were partially destroyed along with the Magoo Ranch. Its last eruption, in 1984, was small by comparison yet created fountaining inside the summit crater and a "curtain of fire" along its eastern rift.

The lowest of the island's major peaks, **Kilauea** rises only to 4,078 feet. Its pragmatic name means "The Spewing," and it's the world's most active volcano. In the last hundred years, it has erupted on the average once every 11 months. The Hawaiians believed that the goddess Pele inhabited every volcano in the Hawaiian chain, and that her home is now Halema'uma'u Crater in Kilauea Caldera. Kilauea is the most scientifically watched volcano in the world, with a permanent observatory built right into the crater rim. When it erupts, the flows are so predictable that observers run toward the mountain, not away from it! The flows, however, can burst from fissures far from the center of the crater in areas that don't seem "active." This occurs mainly in the Puna district. In 1959, Kilauea Iki crater came to life after 91 years, and although the flow wasn't as massive as others, it did send blazing fountains of lava 1,900 feet into the air. Kilauea has been continuously active since 1983, with eruptions occurring at least once a month and expected to continue. Most activity has been from a vent below Pu'u O'o crater. You might be lucky enough to see this phenomenon while visiting.

Island Builders

The Hawaiians worshiped Madame Pele, the

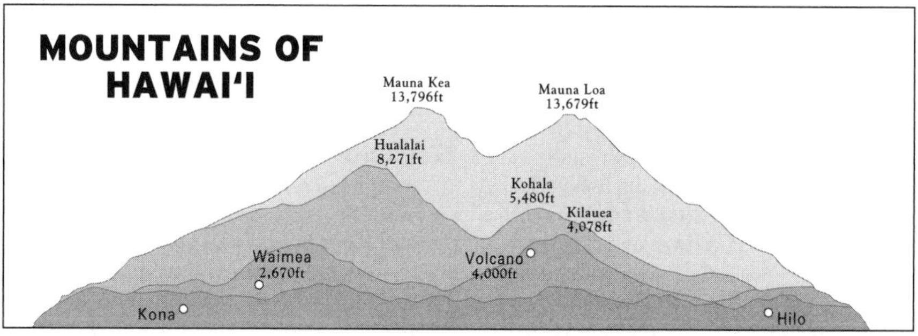

fire goddess whose name translates equally well as Volcano, Fire Pit, or Eruption of Lava. When she was angry, she complained by spitting fire, which cooled and formed land. Volcanologists say that the islands are huge mounds of cooled basaltic lava surrounded by billions of polyp skeletons that have formed coral reefs. The Hawaiian Islands are shield volcanoes that erupt gently and form an elongated dome much like a turtle shell. The Big Island is a perfect example of this. Once above sea level, its tremendous weight sealed the fissure below. Eventually the giant tube that carried lava to the surface sunk in on itself and formed a caldera, as evidenced atop Kilauea. More eruptions occur periodically, and they cover the already existing island like frosting on a titanic cake. Wind and water took over and relentlessly sculpted the raw lava into deep crevices and cuts that became valleys. The most dramatic of these scars occur as the numerous gulches and valleys on the northeast side of the Big Island. Because of less rain and runoff, the west side is smoother, more uniform, and much less etched.

Lava

Lava flows in two distinct types, for which the Hawaiian names have become universal geological terms: **'a'a** and **pahoehoe.** They're easily distinguishable in appearance, but chemically they're the same. 'A'a is extremely rough and spiny and will quickly tear up your shoes if you do much hiking over it. Also, if you have the misfortune to fall down, you'll immediately know why they call it 'a'a. Pahoehoe, a billowy, rope-like lava resembling burned pancake batter, can mold into fantastic shapes. Examples of both types of lava are frequently encountered on various hikes throughout the Big Island. Other lava oddities you may spot are peridots (green, gemlike stones called Pele's Diamonds); clear, feldsparlike, white cotton candy called "Pele's hair"; and gray lichens known as Hawaiian snow covering the older flows. For a full account of recent lava flows and eruptions, see the Hawai'i Volcanoes National Park chapter. As it is relatively young, the Big Island has had less time than the other islands in the chain to be broken down by the forces of wind and rain. Yet, even here, there are areas, particularly in the north on the slopes of the Kohala Mountains, where a thick layer of soil sustains lush grasses and vegetation.

BIG ISLAND QUICK FACTS

Hawai'i has three fitting nicknames: the Big Island, the Volcano Island, and the Orchid Island. It's the youngest, most southerly, and largest island in the Hawaiian chain. At 4,028 square miles, the Big Island is more than twice as large as the other main Hawaiian Islands put together. The island is about 95 miles from north to south, slightly less from east to west with some 266 miles of coastline. Cape Kumukahi is the state's easternmost point, and South Point is the southernmost location in the United States. Hawai'i is about 30 miles across the 'Alenuihaha Channel from Maui. The county seat of Hilo is approximately 220 miles southeast of Honolulu.

Hawai'i is made up of five volcanic peaks: two extinct, two of which are considered dormant, and Kilauea, which been continually active since 1983. At 13,796 feet, Mauna Kea is the tallest mountain in the state as well as the entire Pacific Ocean. Its twin, Mauna Loa, is only slightly shorter at 13,677 feet.

The Big Island has 149,000 residents. As such, it has the second largest island population, but because of its size, it has the smallest population density.

Its color is red, the island flower is the red 'ohi'a lehua, and the island lei is fashioned from the lehua blossom.

Tsunami

Tsunami is the Japanese word for tidal wave. It ranks up there with the worst of them in sparking horror in human beings. But if you were to count up all the people in Hawaii who have been swept away by tidal waves in the last 50 years, the toll wouldn't come

© ROBERT NILSEN
hillside of 'a'a and pahoehoe lava within Hawai'i Volcanoes National Park

close to those killed on bicycles in only a few Mainland cities in just five years. A Hawaiian tsunami is actually a seismic sea wave generated by an earthquake or underwater landslide that could easily have originated thousands of miles away in South America or Alaska. Some waves have been clocked at speeds up to 500 mph. The safest place during a tsunami, besides high ground well away from beach areas, is out on the open ocean, where even an enormous wave is perceived only as a large swell. A tidal wave is only dangerous when it is opposed by land. The Big Island has been struck with the two worst tidal waves in Hawaii's modern history. A giant wave smashed the islands on April 1, 1946, and swept away 159 people and over 1,300 homes. Hilo sustained most of these losses, but Waipi'o Valley was washed clean, devastating the community there, and the schoolyard at Laupahoehoe Point was awash in water, dragging 20 schoolchildren and a teacher to their deaths. On May 23, 1960, Hilo again took the brunt of a wave that rumbled through its business district, killing 61 people.

Earthquakes

These rumblings are also a concern in Hawaii and offer a double threat because they can generate tsunamis. If you ever feel a tremor and are close to a beach, get as far away as fast as possible. The Big Island, because of its active volcanoes, experiences hundreds of technical earthquakes, although 99 percent can only be felt by very delicate equipment. In the last two decades, the Big Island has experienced about one earthquake a year in the range of 5.0–6.0 on the Richter scale, which account for about 60 percent of all quakes of that magnitude in the state. The last major quake on the Big Island occurred in late November 1975, reaching 7.2 on the Richter scale and causing many millions of dollars' worth of damage in the island's southern regions. The only loss of life occurred when a beach collapsed and two people from a large camping party drowned. Like the other islands, the Big Island has an elaborate warning system against natural disasters. You will notice loudspeakers high atop poles along many beaches and coastal areas; these warn of tsunamis, hurricanes, and earthquakes. The loudspeakers are tested at 11 A.M. on the first working day of each month. All island telephone books contain a civil defense warning and procedures section with which you should acquaint yourself—note the maps showing which areas traditionally have been inundated by tsunamis, and what procedures to follow in case an emergency occurs.

Beaches and Ponds

The Big Island takes the rap for having poor beaches—this isn't true! They are certainly few and far between, but many of them are spectacular. Hawai'i is big and young, so distances are greater than on other islands, and the wave action hasn't had enough time to grind much new lava and coral into sand. The Kona and South Kohala coast beaches, along with a few nooks and crannies around Hilo, are gorgeous. Each of the large valleys along the rugged North Kohala Coast, Waipi'o, Waimanu, and Pololu, has a long beach of gray sand. Harder to get to, these beaches have a greater reward because of their isolation. The beaches of Puna and Ka'u are of incredible black sand, a few only years old, and the southern tip of the island has a hidden green sand beach or two enjoyed only by those intrepid enough to get to them.

Just north of the Kona Airport is Makalawena, a beautiful white-sand beach. Inland is its associated wetland pond, one of the most important on the Big Island. Other coastal ponds on the Kona side are located in Kaloko-Honokohau National Historical Park, just north of the Honokohau Harbor, at Kiholo Bay, and at the Kona Village, Waikoloa, and Mauna Lani resorts. On the Hilo side, the most well known, perhaps, are the ponds in Lili'uokalani Park in Hilo and at Kapoho in Puna.

CLIMATE

The average temperature around the island varies between 72 and 78°F. Summers raise the temperature to the mid-80s and winters cool off to the low 70s. Both Kona and Hilo maintain a year-round average of about 74°F, and the South Kohala Coast is a few degrees warmer. As usual, it's cooler in the higher

GREEN FLASH

Nearly everyone who has visited a tropical island has heard of the "green flash" – but few have seen it. Some consider the green flash a fable, a made-up story by those more intent on fantasy than reality. But the green flash is real. This phenomenon doesn't just happen on tropical islands; it can happen anywhere around the midriff of the earth where an unobstructed view of the horizon is present, but the clear atmosphere of a tropical island environment does seem to add to its frequency. The green flash is a momentary burst of luminescent green color that happens on the horizon the instant the sun sets into the sea. If you've seen the green flash you definitely know; there is no mistaking it. If you think you saw something that might have been green but just weren't sure, you probably didn't see it. Try again another day.

The green flash requires a day where the atmosphere is very clear and unobstructed by clouds, haze, or air pollutants. Follow the sun as it sinks into the sea. Be careful not to look directly at the sun until it's just about out of sight. If the conditions are right, a green color will linger at the spot that the sun sets for a fraction of a second before it, too, is gone. This "flash" is not like the flash of a camera, but more a change of color from yellow to green – an intense green – that is instantaneous and momentary.

However romantic and magical, this phenomenon does have a scientific explanation. It seems that the green color is produced as a refraction of the sun's rays by the thick atmosphere at the extreme low angle of the horizon. This bending of the sun's light results in the green spectrum of light being the last seen before the light disappears.

Seeing the green flash is an experience. Keep looking, for no matter how many times you've seen it, each time is still full of wonder and joy.

elevations, and Waimea sees most days in the mid-60s to low 70s, while Volcano maintains a relatively steady 60°F. Atop Mauna Kea, the temperature rarely climbs above 50°F or dips below 30°F, while the summit of Mauna Loa is about 10 degrees warmer. The lowest recorded temperature on the Big Island (and for the state) was 1°F at the Mauna Kea summit in January 1970, while the highest ever recorded was in April 1931 at Pahala in Ka'u—a scorching (for Hawaii) 100°F.

Altitude drops temperatures about three degrees for every 1,000 feet; if you intend to visit the mountain peaks of Mauna Loa and Mauna Kea (both over 13,000 feet), expect the temperature to be at least 30 degrees cooler than at sea level. On occasion, snows atop Mauna Kea last well into June, with nighttime temperatures at or below freezing.

The Big Island is indeed big—and tall. With its arid desert regions, tropical rainforests, temperate upland areas, and frigid alpine slopes, the island has 11 of 13 climatic zones.

Precipitation

Weather-wise, the Big Island's climate varies not so much in temperature but precipitation. Hawai'i has some of the wettest and driest coastal areas in the islands. The line separating wet from dry can be dramatic. Waimea, for example, has an actual dry and wet side of town, as if a boundary line split the town in two! Kona and Hilo are opposites. The Kona Coast is almost guaranteed to be sunny and bright, receiving as little as 15 inches of rainfall per year but with an average of 28 inches. Both Kona and the Ka'u Desert to the south are in the rain shadow of Mauna Loa, and most rain clouds coming from east to west are pierced by its summit before they ever reach Kona. Hilo is wet, with predictable afternoon and evening showers that make the entire town blossom. Though this reputation keeps many tourists away, the rain's predictability makes it easy to avoid a drenching while exploring the town. Hilo gets an average of 128 inches of rainfall per year, with a record of 153.93 inches set in 1971. It also holds the dubious honor of being the town with the most rainfall recorded by the National Weather Service in a 24-hour period—a drenching 22.3 inches in February 1979.

"So Good" Weather

The ancient Hawaiians had words to describe climatic specifics such as rain, wind, fog, and even snow, but they didn't have a general word for weather. The reason is that the weather is just about the same throughout the year and depends more on where you are on any given island than what season it is. The Hawaiians did distinguish between *kau* (the drier and warmer summer months of May–October with reliable trade winds from the northeast) and *ho'oilo* (the cooler and wetter winter months of November–April with more erratic winds), but this distinction included social, religious, and even navigational factors, far beyond a mere distinction of weather variations.

The Trade Winds

Temperatures in the 50th state are both constant and moderate because of the trade winds, a breeze from the northeast that blows at about 5–15 miles per hour. These breezes are so prevailing that the northeast sides of the islands are always referred to as **windward,** regardless of where the wind happens to blow on any given day. You can count on the trades to be blowing an average of 300 days per year, hardly missing a day during summer, and occurring half the time in winter. While usually calm in the morning, they pick up during the heat of the afternoon, then weaken at night. Just when you need a cooling breeze, there they are, and when the temperature drops at night, it's as if someone turned down a giant fan.

The trade winds are also a factor in keeping down the humidity. They will suddenly disappear, however, usually in winter, and might not resume for a few weeks. The tropic of Cancer runs through the center of Hawaii, yet the latitude's famed oppressively hot and muggy weather is joyfully absent in the islands. Honolulu, on the same latitude as sweaty Hong Kong and Havana, has an acceptable 60–75 percent daily humidity factor.

Kona Winds

Kona means leeward in Hawaiian, and when the trades stop blowing, these southerly winds often take over. To anyone from Hawaii, "kona wind" is a euphemism for bad weather, for it brings in hot, sticky air. Luckily, kona winds are most common October–April, when they appear roughly half the time. The temperatures drop slightly during the winter so these hot winds are tolerable, and even useful for moderating the thermometer. In the summer they are awful, but luckily—again—they hardly ever blow during this season.

A kona storm is another matter. These subtropical low-pressure storms develop west of the Hawaiian Islands, and as they move east they draw winds up from the south. Usual only in winter, they can cause considerable damage to crops and real estate. There is no real pattern to kona storms—some years they come every few weeks while in other years they don't appear at all.

Severe Weather

With all this talk of ideal weather, it might seem as if there isn't any bad. Read on. When a storm does hit an island, conditions can be bleak and miserable. The worst storms occur in

HURRICANE FACTS

A **tropical depression** is a low-pressure system or cyclone with winds below 39 mph. A **tropical storm** is a cyclone with winds 39-73 mph. A **hurricane** is a cyclone with winds over 74 mph. These winds are often accompanied by torrential rains, destructive waves, high water, and storm surges.

The National Weather Service issues a **Hurricane Watch** if hurricane conditions are expected in the area within 36 hours. A **Hurricane Warning** is issued when a hurricane is expected to strike within 24 hours. The state of Hawaii has an elaborate warning system against natural disasters. You will notice loudspeakers high atop poles along many beaches and coastal areas; these warn of tsunami, hurricanes, and earthquakes. These sirens are tested briefly at the beginning of each month. As the figures below attest, property damage from recent hurricanes has been great but the loss of life has, thankfully, been minimal.

MAJOR HURRICANES SINCE 1950

Name	Date	Islands Affected	Damages
Hiki	August 1950	Kaua'i	1 death
Nina	December 1957	Kaua'i	–
Dot	August 1959	Kaua'i	$5.5 million
Fico	July 1978	Big Island	–
'Iwa	November 1982	Kaua'i, O'ahu	1 death; $234 million
Estelle	July 1986	Maui, Big Island	$2 million
'Iniki	September 1992	Kaua'i, O'ahu	8 deaths; $1.9 billion

the fall and winter and often have the warped sense of humor to drop their heaviest rainfalls on areas that are normally quite dry. It's not unusual for a storm to dump more than three inches of rain an hour; this can go as high as 10 inches, making Hawaiian rainfalls some of the heaviest on earth.

Hawaii has also been hit with some walloping hurricanes in the last few decades. There haven't been many, but they've been destructive. The vast majority of hurricanes originate far to the southeast off the Pacific coasts of Mexico and Latin America; some, particularly later in the season, start in the midst of the Pacific Ocean near the equator south of Hawaii. Hurricane season is generally considered June–November. Most hurricanes pass harmlessly south of Hawaii, but some, swept along by kona winds, strike the islands. The most recent and destructive was Hurricane ʻIniki, which battered the islands in 1992, killing eight people and causing nearly $2 billion in damage. It had its greatest effect on Niʻihau, the Poʻipu Beach area of Kauaʻi, and the leeward coast of Oʻahu.

Flora and Fauna

The Mystery of Migration

Anyone who loves a mystery will be intrigued by the speculation about how plants and animals first came to Hawaii. Most people's idea of an island paradise includes swaying palms, dense mysterious jungles ablaze with wildflowers, and luscious fruits just waiting to be plucked. In fact, for millions of years the Hawaiian chain consisted of raw and barren islands where no plants grew and no birds sang. Why? Because they are geological orphans that spontaneously popped up in the middle of the Pacific Ocean. The islands, more than 2,000 miles from any continental landfall, were therefore isolated from the normal ecological spread of plants and animals. Even the most tenacious travelers of the flora and fauna kingdoms would be sorely tried in crossing the mighty Pacific. Those that made it by pure chance found a totally foreign ecosystem. They had to adapt or perish. The survivors evolved quickly, and many plants and birds became so specialized that they were limited not only to specific islands in the chain but to habitats that frequently consisted of a single isolated valley. It was as if after traveling so far, and finding a niche, they never budged again. Luckily, the soil of Hawaii was virgin and rich, the competition from other plants or animals was nonexistent, and the climate was sufficiently varied and nearly perfect for most growing things.

The evolution of plants and animals on the isolated islands was astonishingly rapid. A tremendous change in environment, coupled with a limited gene pool, accelerated natural selection. For example, many plants lost their protective thorns and spines because there were no grazing animals or birds to destroy them. Before settlement, Hawaii had no fruits, vegetables, coconut palms, edible land animals, conifers, mangroves, or banyans. The early Polynesians brought 27 varieties of plants that they needed for food and other purposes. About 90 percent of plants on the Hawaiian Islands today were introduced after Captain Cook first set foot here. Tropical flowers, wild and vibrant as we know them today, were relatively few. In a land where thousands of orchids now brighten every corner, there were only four native varieties, the least in any of the 50 states. Today, the indigenous plants and animals have the highest rate of extinction anywhere on earth. By the beginning of the 20th century, native plants growing below 1,500 feet in elevation were almost completely extinct or totally replaced by introduced species. The land and its living things have been greatly transformed by humans and their agriculture. This inexorable process began when

heliconia

Hawaii was the domain of its original Polynesian settlers, then greatly accelerated when the land was inundated by Western peoples.

The indigenous plants and birds of the Big Island have suffered the same fate as those of the other Hawaiian Islands; they're among the most endangered species on earth and disappearing at an alarming rate. There are some sanctuaries on the Big Island where native species still live, but they must be vigorously protected. Do your bit to save them; enjoy but do not disturb.

FLORA

Introduced Plants

Hawaii's indigenous and endemic plants, flowers, and trees are both fascinating and beautiful, but, unfortunately, like everything else that was native, they are quickly disappearing. The majority of flora considered exotic by visitors was introduced either by the original Polynesians or by later white settlers. The Polynesians who colonized Hawaii brought foodstuffs, including coconuts, bananas, taro, breadfruit, sweet potatoes, yams, and sugarcane. They also carried along gourds to use as containers, *'awa* to make a basic intoxicant, and the *ti* plant to use for offerings or to string into hula skirts. Non-Hawaiian settlers over the years have brought mangoes, papayas, passion fruit, pineapples, and the other tropical fruits and vegetables associated with the islands. Also, most of the flowers, including protea, plumeria, anthuriums, orchids, heliconia, ginger, and most hibiscus, have come from every continent on earth. Tropical America, Asia, Java, India, and China have contributed their most beautiful and delicate blooms. Hawai'i is blessed with national and state parks, gardens, undisturbed rainforests, private reserves, and commercial nurseries that offer an exhaustive botanical survey of the island. The following is a sampling of the common native and introduced flora that add dazzling color and exotic tastes to the landscape.

Native Trees

Koa and 'ohi'a are two indigenous trees still seen on the Big Island. Both have been greatly reduced by the foraging of introduced cattle and goats, and through logging and forest fires. The **koa,** a form of acacia, is Hawaii's finest native tree. It can grow to over 70 feet high and has a strong, straight trunk that can measure more than 10 feet in circumference. Koa is a very quick-growing legume that fixes nitrogen

koa tree

in the soil. It is believed that the tree originated in Africa, where it was very damp. It then migrated to Australia, where it was very dry, which caused the elimination of leaves so all that was left were bare stems that could survive in the desert climate. When koa came to the Pacific islands, instead of reverting to the true leaf, its leaf stem just broadened into sickle-shaped, leaflike foliage that produces an inconspicuous, pale-yellow flower. When the tree is young or damaged it will revert to the original feathery, fernlike leaf that evolved in Africa millions of years ago. The koa does best in well-drained soil in deep forest areas, but scruffy specimens will grow on poorer soil. The Hawaiians used koa as the main log for their dugout canoes, and elaborate ceremonies were performed when a log was cut and dragged to a canoe shed. Koa wood was also preferred for paddles, spears, and even surfboards. Today it is still considered an excellent furniture wood. Although fine specimens can be found in the reserve of Hawai'i Volcanoes National Park, loggers elsewhere are harvesting the last of the big trees.

The **'ohi'a** is a survivor and therefore the most abundant of all the native Hawaiian trees. Coming in a variety of shapes and sizes, it grows as miniature trees in wet bogs or as 100-foot giants on cool, dark slopes at higher elevations. This tree is often the first life in new lava flows. The 'ohi'a produces a tuftlike flower—usually red, but occasionally orange, yellow, or white, the latter being very rare and elusive—that resembles a natural pompon. The flower was considered sacred to Pele; it was said that she would cause a rainstorm if 'ohi'a blossoms were picked without the proper prayers. The flowers were fashioned into lei that resembled feather boas. The strong, hard wood was used to make canoes, poi bowls, and especially temple images. 'Ohi'a logs were also used as railroad ties and shipped to the Mainland from Pahoa. It's believed that the golden spike linking rail lines between the U.S. East and West Coasts was driven into a Puna 'ohi'a log when the two railroads came together in Ogden, Utah.

© ROBERT NILSEN
'ohi'a lehua blossom

LOUISE FOOTE
'ohi'a tree

Ferns

If you travel to Hawai'i Volcanoes National Park you will find yourself deep in an amazing tropical rainforest. This unique forest exists because of the 120 inches of annual rainfall, which turns the raw lava into a lush forest. Besides stands of 'ohi'a and koa, you'll be treated to a primordial display of ferns. All new fronds on ferns are called "fiddleheads" because of the way they unfurl and resemble the scrolls of violin heads. Fiddleheads were eaten by Hawaiians during times of famine. The most common ferns are *hapu'u,* a rather large tree fern, and *'ama'uama'u,* a smaller type with a more simple frond. A soft, furry growth around the base of the stalks is called *pulu.* At one time *pulu* was collected for stuffing mattresses, and a factory was located atop Volcanoes. But *pulu* breaks down and forms a very fine dust after a few years, so it never became widely accepted for mattresses.

At high altitudes, young ferns and other plants will often produce new growth that turns bright red as protection against the sun's ultraviolet rays. You'll see it on new foliage before it hardens. Hawaiians called this new growth *liko.* Today, people still make lei from *liko* because it has so many subtle and beautiful colors. 'Ohi'a *liko* is a favorite for lei because it is so striking.

PAKALOLO

In the 1960s and 1970s, mostly *haole* hippies from the Mainland began growing marijuana *(pakalolo),* usually in the more remote sections of the islands, such as Puna on Hawai'i and around Hana on Maui. They discovered what legitimate planters had known for centuries: plant a broomstick in Hawaii, treat it right, and it'll grow. *Pakalolo,* after all, is only a weed, and it grows in Hawaii like wildfire.

The locals quickly got into the act when they realized that they, too, could grow a "money tree." As a matter of fact, they began resenting the *haole* usurpers, and a quiet and sometimes dangerous feud has been going on ever since. Much is made of the viciousness of the backcountry "growers" of Hawaii, as in other areas of the states. There are tales of booby traps and armed patrols guarding plants in the hills, but mostly it's a cat-and-mouse game between the authorities and the growers.

If you, as a tourist, are tramping about in the forest and happen upon someone's "patch," don't touch anything. Just back off and you'll be okay. Pot has one of the largest monetary turnovers of any crop in the islands and, as such, is now considered a major source of agricultural revenue, albeit illicit and underground.

Other Flora

The Hawaiians called the **prickly pear cactus** *panini,* which translates as "very unfriendly," undoubtedly because of the sharp spines covering the flat, thick leaves. The cactus is typical of those found in Mexico and the southwestern United States. It was introduced to Hawaii before 1810 and established itself coincidentally with the cattle brought in at the time; *panini* is very common in North Kohala, especially on the Parker Ranch lands. It is assumed that Don Marin, a Spanish advisor to Kamehameha I, was responsible for importing the plant. Perhaps the early *paniolo* (cowboy) felt lonely without it. The *panini* can grow to heights of 15 feet and is now considered a pest but nonetheless looks as if it belongs. It develops small and delicious pear-shaped fruits. Hikers who decide to pick the fruit should be careful of small, yellowish bristles that can burrow under the skin and irritate. An attempt is being made to control the cactus in *paniolo* country. *El gusano rojo,* the red worm found in the bottom of Mexican tequila, has been introduced to destroy the plant. It burrows into the cactus and eats the hardwood center, causing the plant to wither and die.

More species of **lobelia** grow in Hawaii than anywhere else in the world. A common garden flower elsewhere, it grows to tree height in Hawaii. You'll see some unique species covered with hair or with spikes. The lobelia flower is tiny and resembles a miniature orchid with curved and pointed ends, like the beak of the native *i'iwi.* This bird feeds on the flower's nectar; it's obvious that both evolved in Hawaii together and exhibit the strange phenomenon of nature mimicking nature.

The Big Island has more species of **gesneriad,** the African violet family, than anywhere else on earth. Many don't have the showy flowers that you normally associate with African violets but have evolved into strange species with huge, fuzzy leaves.

BIG ISLAND BOTANICAL GARDENS

The **Hilo Forestry Arboretum** (8 A.M.–3 P.M. Mon.–Fri., closed weekends and holidays; no charge), located in Hilo along Kilauea Avenue between Lanikaula and Kawili Streets, is maintained by the Department of Natural Resources, Division of Forestry. The site is used for the propagation of rare and endangered plant species, for research, and for experimental pursuits. This arboretum contains examples of most of the trees present in Hawaii, including indigenous and imported specimens.

Nani Mau Gardens (421 Makalika St., 808/959-3500, 9 A.M.–4:30 P.M. daily, $10 adult, $5 children ages 4–10, plus $1 adult or $3 children for an optional tram tour) is a 20-acre garden in Hilo featuring separate areas for hibiscus, anthurium, orchid, gardenia, bromeliad, and other tropical plants. This is the showiest garden on the island, a large, tame, and beautiful display. Plants are labeled.

The **Hilo Tropical Gardens** (1477 Kalaniana'ole Ave., 808/969-9873, $2 adult for a self-guided tour and free for children) is the oldest botanical garden on the island, established in 1948. This garden is small and a bit overgrown in its profusion of plants – lots of anthuriums and orchids.

Hawaii Tropical Botanical Garden (808/964-5233, www.hawaiigarden.com, 9 A.M.–5 P.M. daily, adults $15, children 6–16 $5) are a few miles north of Hilo. Here you are in the middle of a tamed tropical rainforest jungle, walking along one mile of manicured paths among more than 2,000 different species of trees and plants. If you were to choose one "natural" garden to visit on the island, this would be it.

The **World Tropical Botanical Gardens** (808/963-5427, www.worldbotanicalgardens.com, 9 A.M.–5:30 P.M. Mon.–Sat., $9.50 adults or $5 for teens, $2.50 kids 5–12) near Honomu on the Hamakua Coast, is a garden in the making. While the plan is to cultivate some 30,000 species, arranged in evolutionary groupings, only small sections are open to the public. The impressive three-tier Umauma Waterfall is on the property.

Amy B. H. Greenwell Ethnobotanical Garden (808/323-3318, www.bishopmuseum.org/exhibits/greenwell/greenwell.html, 8:30 A.M.–5 P.M. Mon.–Fri., suggested donation $4, $5 for a guided tour on Wed. and Fri. at 1 P.M.), is located along Rte. 11, between the communities of Kealakekua and Captain Cook in South Kona. This 12-acre interpretive ethnobotanical garden has indigenous Hawaiian plants, Polynesian introduced plants, and Hawaiian medicinal plants. The garden has remnants of the Kona field system, which dates from precontact times.

The **Sadie Seymour Botanical Gardens** (808/329-7286, www.konaoutdoorcircle.org, 9 A.M.–5 P.M. daily, free for self-guided tours) sits up above the coast in Kailua-Kona. Its plantings are grouped by areas of the world on nearly a dozen terraces. Small but well landscaped, this garden is a quiet retreat in the otherwise dry and hot upper Kona area. **Kealakowa'a Heiau,** an ancient sacred site dedicated to blessing canoes, is on the property.

Specializing in plants that thrive in the arid zone, **Pua Mau Place** (10 Ala Kahua Dr., 808/882-0888, www.puamau.org, 9 A.M.–4 P.M. daily, $10 adults, $8 seniors and students) has an appropriate spot in the dry hills just north of Kawaihae in Kohala. Opened in 2000, it's still young but full of promise.

© ROBERT NILSEN

one reason the Big Island is also known as the Orchid Island

The ***pu'ahanui,*** meaning "many flowers," is Hawaii's native hydrangea; it is common in the upland forests of the Big Island.

Tropical Rainforests

When it comes to pure and diverse natural beauty, the United States is one of the finest pieces of real estate on earth. As if purple mountains' majesty and fruited plains weren't enough, it even received a tiny, living emerald of tropical rainforest. A tropical rainforest is where the earth takes a breath and exhales pure sweet oxygen through its vibrant green canopy. Located in the territories of Puerto Rico and the Virgin Islands and in the state of Hawaii, the rainforests of the United States make up only one-half of 1 percent of the world's total, and they must be preserved. The U.S. Congress passed two bills in 1986 designed to protect the unique biological diversity of its tropical areas, but their destruction has continued unabated. The lowland rainforests of Hawaii, populated mostly by native 'ohi'a, are being razed. Landowners slash, burn, and bulldoze them to create more land for cattle and agriculture and, most distressingly, for wood chips to generate electricity! Introduced wild boars gouge the forest floor, exposing sensitive roots and leaving tiny, fetid ponds where mosquito larvae thrive. Feral goats roam the forests like hoofed locusts and strip all vegetation within reach. Rainforests on the higher and steeper slopes of mountains have a better chance, as they are harder for humans to reach. One unusual feature of Hawaii's rainforests is that they are "upside down." Most plant and animal species live on the forest floor, rather than in the canopy as in other forests.

Almost half of the birds classified in the United States as endangered live in Hawaii, and almost all of these make their homes in the rainforests. We can only lament the passing of the rainforests that have already fallen to ignorance, but if this ill-fated destruction continues on a global level, we will be lamenting our own passing. We must nurture the rainforests that remain, and, with simple enlightenment, let them be.

BIRDS

One of the great tragedies of natural history is the continuing demise of Hawaiian birdlife. Perhaps only 15 original species of birds remain of the more than 70 native families that thrived before the coming of humans. Since the arrival of Captain Cook in 1778, 23 species have become extinct, with 31 more in danger. And what's not known is how many species were wiped out before white explorers arrived. Experts believe that the Hawaiians annihilated about 40 species, including seven species of geese, a rare one-legged owl, ibis, lovebirds, sea eagles, and honeycreepers—all gone before Captain Cook arrived. Hawaii's endangered birds account for 40 percent of the birds officially listed as endangered or threatened by the U.S. Fish and Wildlife Service. In the last 200 years, more than four times as many birds have become extinct in Hawaii as in all of North America. These figures unfortunately suggest that a full 40 percent of Hawaii's endemic birds no longer exist. Almost all of O'ahu's native birds are gone, and few indigenous Hawaiian birds can be found on any island below the 3,000-foot level.

Native birds have been reduced in number because of multiple factors. The original Polynesians helped wipe out many species. They altered large areas for farming and used fire to destroy patches of pristine forests. Also, bird feathers were highly prized for making lei, for featherwork in capes and helmets, and for the large *kahili* fans that indicated rank among the *ali'i.* Introduced exotic birds and the new diseases they carried are another major reason for reduction of native bird numbers, along with predation by the mongoose and rat—especially upon ground-nesting birds. Bird malaria and bird pox were also devastating to the native species. Mosquitoes, unknown in Hawaii until a ship named the *Wellington* introduced them at Lahaina in 1826 through larvae carried in its water barrels, infected most native birds, causing a rapid reduction in birdlife. Feral pigs rooting deep in the rainforests knock over ferns and small trees, creating fetid pools in which mosquito larvae thrive. However, the most damaging factor by far is the assault upon native forests by agriculture and land developers. The vast majority of Hawaiian birds evolved into specialists. They lived in only one small area and ate a very limited number of plants or insects, which once removed or altered soon killed the birds.

You'll spot birds all over the Big Island, from the coastal areas to the high mountain slopes. Some are found on other islands as well, but the indigenous ones listed below are found only or mainly on the Big Island. Every bird listed is either threatened or endangered.

Hawaii's Own

The ***nene,*** or Hawaiian goose, deserves special mention because it is Hawaii's state bird and is making a comeback from the edge of extinction. The *nene* is found only on the slopes of Mauna Loa, Hualalai, and Mauna Kea on the Big Island, in Haleakala Crater on Maui, and at a few spots on Moloka'i and Kaua'i. It was extinct on Maui until a few birds were returned there in 1957, but some experts maintain that the *nene* lived naturally only on the Big Island. *Nene* are raised at the Wildfowl Trust in Slimbridge, England, which placed the first birds at Haleakala; and at the Hawaiian Fish and Game Station at Pohakuloa, along the Saddle Road on Hawai'i. By the 1940s, fewer than 50 birds lived in the wild. Now approximately 125 birds live on Haleakala and 500 on the Big Island. Although the birds can be raised successfully in captivity, their life in the wild is still in question.

PHOTO COURTESY OF HVCB/RON DAHLQUIST

the *nene* bird of Hawai'i

The *nene* is believed to be a descendant of the Canadian goose, which it resembles. Geese are migratory birds that form strong kinship ties, mating for life. It's speculated that a migrating goose became disabled, and along with its loyal mate, remained in Hawaii. The *nene* is smaller than its Canadian cousin, has lost a great deal of webbing in its feet, and is perfectly at home away from water, often foraging and nesting on rugged and bleak lava flows, although it also lives in coastal regions and on grassy mountainsides.

Good places to view *nene* are in Hawai'i Volcanoes National Park at Kipuka Nene, Summit Caldera, Devastation Trail, and Volcanoes Golf Course, at dawn and dusk. The birds gather at the golf course because they love to feed on grasses. The places to view them on the Kona side are Pu'ulani, a housing development north of Kailua-Kona; or Kaloko Mauka, another housing development on the slopes of Mount Hualalai. At the top of the road up Mount Hualalai is a trail, also a good place to see the *nene.* Unfortunately, as the housing developments proliferate and the residents invariably acquire dogs and cats, the *nene* will disappear. The *nene* is a perfect symbol of Hawaii: let it be, and it will live.

The **Hawaiian crow,** or *alala,* is reduced to fewer than 12 birds living on the slopes of Hualalai and Mauna Loa above the 3,000-foot level. It looks like the common raven but has a more melodious voice and, sometimes, dull brown wing feathers. The *alala* breeds in early spring, and the greenish-blue, black-flecked eggs hatch from April to June. It is extremely nervous while nesting, and any disturbance will cause it to abandon its young.

The **Hawaiian hawk** *('io)* primarily lives on the slopes of Mauna Loa and Mauna Kea below 9,000 feet. It travels from there to other parts of

BOB RACE

Hawaiian hawk (*'io*)

the island and can often be seen kiting in the skies over Hawai'i Volcanoes National Park, upland from Kailua-Kona, and in remote spots like Waimanu Valley. This noble bird, the royalty of the skies, symbolized the *ali'i*. The *'io* population was once dwindling, and many scientists feared that the bird was headed for extinction. The hawk exists only on the Big Island for reasons that are not entirely clear. The good news is that the *'io* is making a dramatic comeback, also for reasons still unclear. Speculation is that it may be gaining resistance to some diseases, including malaria, or that it may have learned how to prey on the introduced rats, or even that it may be adapting to life in macadamia nut groves and other alternate habitats.

The ***'akiapola'au,*** a honeycreeper, is a five-inch yellow bird hardly bigger than its name. It lives mainly on the eastern slopes in 'ohi'a and koa forests above 3,500 feet. It has a long, curved upper beak for probing and a smaller lower beak that it uses woodpecker-fashion. The *'akiapola'au* opens its mouth wide, strikes the wood with its lower beak, and then uses the upper beak to scrape out any larvae or insects. Listen for the distinctive rapping sound to spot this melodious singer. The *'akiapola'au* can be seen at the Hakalau National Wildlife Refuge and along the Pu'u O'o Volcano Trail from Hawai'i Volcanoes National Park. It's estimated that only about 1,000 of these birds, one of the rarest of the island's rare winged creatures, are left.

In addition, two other endangered birds of the Big Island are the ***koloa maoli,*** a duck that resembles the mallard, and the slate gray or white ***'alae ke'oke'o*** coot.

Marine Birds

Two coastal birds that breed on the high slopes of Hawaii's volcanoes and feed on the coast are the **Hawaiian dark-rumped petrel** (*'ua'u*) and the **Newell's shearwater** (*'a'o*). The *'ua'u* lives on the barren high slopes and craters, where it nests in burrows or under stones. Breeding season lasts from mid-March to mid-October. Only one chick is born and nurtured on regurgitated squid and fish. The *'ua'u* suffers heavily from predation. The *'a'o* prefers the forested slopes of the interior. It breeds April–November and spends its days at sea and nights inland. Feral cats and dogs reduce its numbers considerably. In addition, the *ae'o* Hawaiian black-necked stilt has become endangered.

Forest Birds

The following birds are found in the upland forests of the Big Island. The ***'elepaio*** is found on other islands but is also spotted in Hawai'i Volcanoes National Park. This long-tailed (often held upright), five-inch brown bird (appearance can vary considerably) can be coaxed to come within touching distance of the observer. Sometimes it will sit on lower branches above your head and scold you. This bird was the special *amakua* (personal spirit) of canoe builders in ancient lore. Fairly common in the rainforest, it is basically a flycatcher.

The ***'amakihi*** and ***'i'iwi*** are endemic birds not endangered at the moment. The *'amakihi* is one of the most common native birds; yellowish green, it frequents the high branches of the 'ohi'a, koa, and sandalwood looking for insects, nectar, or fruit. It is less specialized than most other Hawaiian birds, the main reason for its continued existence. The *'i'iwi* is a bright red honeycreeper with a salmon-colored, hooked bill. It's found on Hawai'i in the forests above 2,000 feet. It too feeds on a variety of insects and flowers. The *'i'iwi* is known for its harsh voice that sounds like a squeaking hinge, but it is also capable of a melodious song. The *'i'iwi* can be spotted at the top of Kaloko Mauka; at Powerline Road, which goes south off the Saddle Road; and at Pu'u O'o Trail in Hawai'i Volcanoes National Park.

The ***'apapane*** is abundant on Hawai'i, especially atop Volcanoes, and, being the most common native bird, it's the easiest to see. It's a chubby, red-bodied bird about five inches long with a black bill, legs, wing tips, and tail feathers. It's quick and flitty and has a wide variety of calls and songs, from beautiful warbles to mechanical buzzes. Its feathers were sought by Hawaiians to produce distinctive capes and helmets for the *ali'i*.

The **Hawaiian thrush** *('oma'o)* is a fairly common bird found above 3,000 feet in the windward forests of Hawai'i. This eight-inch gray bird is a good singer, often seen perching with distinctive drooping wings and a shivering body. The *'oma'o* is probably descended from Townsend's solitaire. The best place to look for it is at the Thurston Lava Tube in Hawai'i Volcanoes National Park, where you can see it doing its baby-bird shivering-and-shaking act. A great mimic, it can sound like a cat or even like an old-fashioned radio with stations changing as you turn the dial. A good place to see the *'oma'o* is along Powerline Road, off the Saddle Road.

The **'akepa** is a four- to five-inch bird. The male is a brilliant orange to red; the female a drab green and yellow. It is found mainly on Hualalai and in windward forests. In ornithological and environmental circles, the *'akepa, 'akiapola'au,* and **Hawaiian creeper** are lovingly referred to as the Big Three, as they are the rarest of the rare birds of the island and a true joy to spot.

The six-inch, bright yellow ***palila*** is found only on Hawai'i in the forests of Mauna Kea above 6,000 feet. It depends exclusively upon *mamane* trees for survival, eating its pods, buds, and flowers.

OTHER HAWAIIAN ANIMALS

Hawaii had only two indigenous mammals, the monk seal or *'ilio holu i ka uaua* (found mostly in the Northwestern Islands) and the hoary bat (found primarily on the Big Island); both are threatened and endangered. The rest of the Big Island's mammals are transplants. But like anything else, including people, that has been in the islands long enough, they take on characteristics that make them "local." There are no native amphibians, reptiles, ants, termites, or cockroaches. These have all been imported.

The following animals are found primarily on the Big Island. The **Hawaiian hoary bat** *('ope'ape'a)* is a cousin of the Mainland bat, a strong flier that made it to Hawaii eons ago and developed its own species. Its tail has a whitish coloration, hence its name. Small populations of the bat are found on Maui and Kaua'i, but the greatest numbers of them are on the Big Island, where they have been spotted even on the upper slopes of Mauna Loa and Mauna Kea. The hoary bat has a 13-inch wingspan. Unlike other bats, it is a solitary creature, roosting in trees. It gives birth to twins in early summer and can often be spotted over Hilo and Kealakekua Bays just around sundown.

The **feral dog** *('ilio)* is found on all the islands but especially on the slopes of Mauna Kea, where packs chase feral sheep. Poisoned and shot by local ranchers, their numbers are diminishing. Black dogs, thought to be more tender, are still eaten in some Hawaiian and Filipino communities.

The **feral sheep** is an escaped descendant of animals brought to the islands by Captain Vancouver in the 1790s, and of merinos brought to the island later and raised for their exceptional woolly fleece. It exists only on the Big Island, on the upper slopes of Mauna Loa, Mauna Kea, and Hualalai; by the 1930s, its numbers topped 40,000 head. The fleece is a buff brown, and its two-foot-wide curved horns are often sought as hunting trophies. Feral sheep are responsible for the overgrazing of young *mamane* trees, necessary to the endangered bird *palila*. In 1979, a law was passed to exterminate or remove the sheep from Mauna Kea so the native *palila* could survive.

Mouflon sheep were introduced to Lana'i and Hawai'i to cut down on overgrazing and serve as trophy animals. This Mediterranean sheep can interbreed with feral sheep to produce a hybrid. It lives on the upper slopes of Mauna Loa and Mauna Kea. Unfortunately, its introduction has not been a success. No evidence indicates that the smaller family groups

Donkey Crossing signs warn of the seldom seen, but often heard, Kona nightingales.

of mouflon cause less damage than the herding feral sheep, and hunters reportedly don't like the meat as much as feral mutton.

The **feral donkey,** better known as the "Kona nightingale," came to Hawaii as a beast of burden. Domesticated donkeys are found on all islands, but a few wild herds still roam the Big Island along the Kona Coast, especially near the exclusive Kona Village Resort at Ka'upulehu.

Feral cattle were introduced by Captain Vancouver, who gave a few domesticated head to Kamehameha; immediately a *kapu* (taboo) against killing them went into effect for 10 years. The lush grasses of Hawaii were perfect and the cattle flourished; by the early 1800s they were out of control and were hunted and exterminated. Finally, Mexican cowboys were brought to Hawaii to teach the locals how to be range hands. From this legacy sprang the Hawaiian *paniolo.*

Most people hardly pay attention to flies, unless one lands on their plate lunch. But geneticists from throughout the world, and especially from the University of Hawaii, make a special pilgrimage to the Volcano area of the Big Island and to Maui just to study the native **Hawaiian drosophila.** This critter is related to the fruit fly and housefly, but there are hundreds of unique native species. The Hawaiian ecosystem is very simple and straightforward, so geneticists can trace the evolutionary changes from species to subspecies through mating behavior. The scientists compare the species between the two islands and chart the differences. Major discoveries in evolutionary genetics have been made through these studies.

MARINELIFE

The **humpback whale,** known in Hawaii as *kohola,* migrates to Hawaiian waters yearly, arriving in late December and departing by mid-May. While whales can be seen anywhere around the Big Island, some of the best places to view them are along the South Kona Coast, especially at Keauhou, Kealakekua Bay, and Ka Lae (South Point), with many sightings off the Puna Coast around Isaac Hale Beach Park, and from the luxury resorts of the South Kohala area.

Hawai'i Volcanoes National Park stretches from the top of Mauna Kea all the way down to

CORAL

Whether you're an avid scuba diver or a novice snorkeler, you'll become aware of Hawai'i's underwater coral gardens and grottoes whenever you peer at the fantastic seascapes below the waves. Coral in Hawaii grows in many shapes, sizes, and colors, like it does elsewhere in the world. Although there is plenty of it, the coral in Hawaii doesn't do as well as in more equatorial areas because the water is too wild and not quite as warm. Hawaii has some 400,000 acres of coral and each island is surrounded by unconnected stretches of coral reef. Most is of the hard coral type as opposed to the soft coral or sponge varieties. Coral looks like a plant fashioned from colorful stone, but it's the skeleton of tiny animals, zoophytes, which need algae in order to live. Coral grows best in water that is quite still, where the days are sunny, and where the algae can thrive.

Coral can be fragile. Please do your part to protect these underwater gardens by not stepping on it, breaking off pieces, or dragging anything across it. Look but don't touch! Many of Hawaii's reefs have been dying in the last 20 years, and no one seems to know why. Pesticides and fertilizers used in agriculture have been pointed to as a possible cause, but other major concerns for coral health are algae bloom and the resultant smothering of coral, erosional runoff of silt from the land, abuse by humans engaging in recreational activities, and even oil from skin and sun block.

the sea. It is here, around Apua Point, that three of the last known nesting sites of the very endangered **hawksbill turtle** *(honu 'ea)* are found. This creature has been ravished in the Pacific, where it is ruthlessly hunted for its shell, which is made into women's jewelry, especially combs. It is illegal to bring items made from turtle shell into the United States, but the hunt goes on.

While they can be seen more often, **green sea turtles** *(honu)* are also endangered. Periodically, they haul themselves up on a beach to rest and warm up. This is normal and they are OK, even when their mottled green shell begins to turn a bit dusky white. Leave them alone in or out of the water; don't disturb or get too close to them. They'll return to the water when they are good and ready.

Billfish

Although these magnificent game fish live in various South Sea and Hawaiian waters, catching them is easiest in the clear, smooth waters

Green sea turtles sun themselves on many Big Island beaches.

off the Kona Coast. The billfish—swordfish, sailfish, marlin, and *a'u*—share two distinctive common features: a long, spearlike or swordlike snout and a prominent dorsal fin. The three main species of billfish caught here are the blue, striped, and black marlin. Of these three, the **blue marlin** is the leading game fish in Kona waters. The blue has tipped the scales at well over 1,000 pounds, but the average fish weighs in at 300–400 pounds. When alive, this fish is a striking cobalt blue, but death brings a color change to slate blue. It feeds on skipjack tuna; throughout the summer, fishing boats look for schools of tuna as a tip-off to blues in the area. The **black marlin** is the largest and most coveted catch for blue-water anglers. This solitary fish is infrequently found in the banks off Kona. Granddaddies can weigh 1,800 pounds, but the average is a mere 200. The **striped marlin** is the most common commercial billfish, a highly prized food served in finer restaurants and often sliced into sashimi. Its coloration is a remarkable royal blue. It leaps spectacularly when caught, giving it a great reputation as a fighter. The striped marlin is smaller than the other marlins, so a 100-pounder is a very good catch.

History

The Big Island plays a significant role in Hawaii's history. A long list of "firsts" occurred here. Historians generally believe (backed up by the oral tradition) that the Big Island was the first in the Hawaiian chain to be settled by the Polynesians. Hawai'i is geographically the closest island to Polynesia; Mauna Loa and especially Mauna Kea, with its white summit, present easily spotted landmarks. Psychologically, the Polynesian wayfarers would have been very attracted to Hawai'i as a lost homeland. Compared to Tahiti and most other South Sea islands (except Fiji), it's huge. It *looked* like the promised land. Some may wonder why the Polynesians chose to live atop an obviously active volcano and not bypass it for a more congenial island. The volcanism of the Big Island is comparatively gentle; the lava flows follow predictable routes and rarely turn killer. The animistic Hawaiians would have been drawn to live where the godly forces of nature were so apparent. The mana (power) would be exceptionally strong, and therefore the *ali'i* would be great. Human sacrifice was introduced to Hawai'i at Waha'ula Heiau in the Puna district in the 13th century, and from there *luakini* (human-sacrifice temples) spread throughout the islands.

THE ROAD FROM TAHITI

The Great Navigators

No one knows exactly when the first Polynesians arrived in Hawaii, but the great "deliberate migrations" from the southern islands seem to have taken place A.D. 500–800, though anthropologists keep pushing the date backward in time as new evidence becomes available. Even before that, however, it's reasonable to assume that the first people to set foot on Hawaiian soil were probably fishermen, or perhaps defeated warriors whose canoes were blown hopelessly northward into unfamiliar waters. They arrived by a combination of extraordinary good luck and an uncanny ability to sail and navigate without instruments, using the sun by day and the moon and rising stars by night. They could feel the water and determine direction by swells, tides, and currents. The movements of fish and cloud formations were also utilized to give direction. Since their arrival was probably an accident, they were unprepared to settle on the fertile but uncultivated lands, having no stock animals, plant cuttings, or women. Forced to return southward, many undoubtedly lost their lives at sea, but a few wild-eyed stragglers must have made it home to tell tales of a paradise to the north

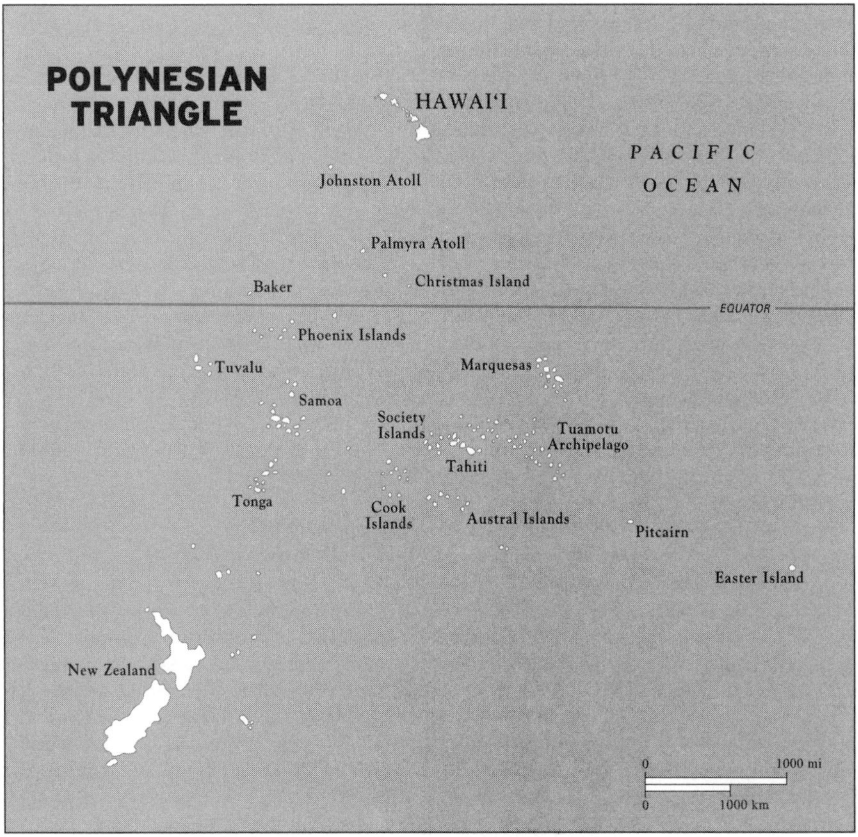

where land was plentiful and the sea bounteous. This is affirmed by ancient navigational chants from Tahiti, Moorea, and Bora Bora, which passing from father to son revealed how to follow the stars to the "heavenly homeland in the north." Possibly a few migrations followed, but it's known that for centuries there was no real reason for a mass exodus, so the chants alone remained and eventually became shadowy legend.

Where They Came From

It's generally agreed that the first planned migrations were from the violent cannibal islands that Spanish explorers called the Marquesas, 11 islands in extreme eastern Polynesia. The islands themselves are harsh and inhospitable, breeding a toughness into these people that enabled them to withstand the hardships of long, unsure ocean voyages and years of resettlement. Marquesans were a fiercely independent people whose chiefs could rise from the ranks because of bravery or intelligence. They must have also been a savage-looking lot. Both men and women tattooed themselves in complex blue patterns from head to foot. The warriors carried massive, intricately designed ironwood war clubs and wore carved whale teeth in slits in their earlobes that eventually stretched to the shoulders. They shaved the sides of their heads with sharks' teeth, tied their hair in two topknots that looked like horns, and rubbed their heavily muscled and tattooed bodies with scented coconut oils. Their cults worshiped mummified ancestors; the bodies of warriors of defeated neighboring tribes were consumed. They were masters at building great double-hulled canoes launched from huge canoe sheds. Two hulls were fastened together to form a catamaran, and a hut in the center provided shelter in bad weather. The average voyaging canoe was 60–80 feet long and could comfortably hold an extended family of about 30 people. These small family bands carried all the staples they would need in the new lands.

The New Lands

For five centuries the Marquesans settled and lived peacefully on the new land, as if Hawaii's *aloha* spirit overcame most of their fierceness. The tribes coexisted in relative harmony, especially since there was no competition for land. Cannibalism died out. There was much coming and going between Hawaii and Polynesia as new people came to settle for hundreds of years. Then, it appears that in the 12th century a deliberate exodus of warlike Tahitians arrived and subjugated the settled islanders. They came to conquer. This incursion had a terrific significance on the Hawaiian religious and social system. Oral tradition relates that a Tahitian priest, Pa'ao, found the mana of the Hawaiian chiefs to be low, signifying that their gods were weak. Pa'ao built a *heiau* at Waha'ula on the Big Island, then introduced the warlike god Ku and the rigid *kapu* system through which the new rulers became dominant. Voyages between Tahiti and Hawaii continued for about 100 years, and Tahitian customs, legends, and language became the Hawaiian way of life. Then suddenly, for no recorded or apparent reason, the voyages discontinued and Hawaii returned to total isolation.

The islands remained forgotten for almost 500 years until the indomitable English seaman, Capt. James Cook, sighted O'ahu on January 18, 1778, and stepped ashore at Waimea on Kaua'i two days later. At that time Hawaii's isolation was so complete that even the Polynesians had forgotten about it. On an earlier voyage, Tupaia, a high priest from Raiatea, had accompanied Captain Cook as he sailed throughout Polynesia. Tupaia demonstrated his vast knowledge of existing archipelagoes throughout the South Pacific by naming over 130 islands and drawing a map that included the Tonga group, the Cook Islands, the Marquesas, and even tiny Pitcairn, a rock in far eastern Polynesia where the mutinous crew of the *Bounty* found solace. In mentioning the Marquesas, Tupaia said, *"he ma'a te ka'ata,"* which means "food is man" or simply "Cannibals!" But remarkably absent from Tupaia's vast knowledge was the existence of Easter Island, New Zealand, and Hawaii.

The next waves of people to Hawaii would be white, and the Hawaiian world would be changed quickly and forever.

THE WORLD DISCOVERS HAWAII

The late 18th century was an extraordinary time in Hawaiian history. Monumental changes seemed to happen all at once. First, Captain James Cook, a Yorkshire farm boy fulfilling his destiny as the all-time greatest Pacific explorer, found Hawaii for the rest of the world. For better or worse, it could no longer be an isolated Polynesian homeland. For the first time in Hawaiian history, a charismatic leader, Kamehameha, emerged, and after a long civil war he united all the islands into one centralized kingdom. The death of Captain Cook in Hawaii marked the beginning of a long series of tragic misunderstandings between whites and natives. When Kamehameha died in 1819, the old religious system of *kapu* came to an end, leaving the Hawaiians in a spiritual vortex. Many takers arrived to fill the void: missionaries after souls, whalers after their prey and a good time, traders and planters after profits and a home. The islands were opened and devoured like ripe fruit. Powerful nations, including Russia, Great Britain, France, and the United States, yearned to bring this strategic Pacific jewel under their own influence.

The 19th century brought the demise of the Hawaiian people as a dominant political

THE *KUMULIPO*

The great genealogies, finally compiled in the late 1800s by order of King Kalakaua, were collectively known as *The Kumulipo, A Hawaiian Creation Chant,* basically a Polynesian account of Genesis. Other chants related to the beginning of this world, but the *Kumulipo* sums it all up and is generally considered the best. The chant relates that after the beginning of time, there is a period of darkness. The darkness, however, mysteriously brims with spontaneous life; during this period plants and animals are born, as well as Kumulipo, the man, and Po'ele, the woman. In the eighth chant darkness gives way to light and the gods descend to earth. Wakea is "the sky father" and Papa is "the earth mother," whose union gives birth to the islands of Hawaii. First born is Hawai'i, followed by Maui, then Kaho'olawe. Apparently, Papa becomes bushed after three consecutive births and decides to vacation in Tahiti. While Papa is away recovering from postpartum depression and working on her tan, Wakea gets lonely and takes Ka'ula as his second wife; she bears him the island-child of Lana'i. Not fully cheered up, but getting the hang of it, Wakea takes a third wife, Hina, who promptly bears the island of Moloka'i. Meanwhile, Papa gets wind of these shenanigans, returns from Polynesia, and retaliates by taking up with Lua, a young and virile god. She soon gives birth to the island of O'ahu. Papa and Wakea finally decide that they really are meant for each other and reconcile to conceive Kaua'i, Ni'ihau, Ka'ula, and Nihoa. These two progenitors are the source from which the *ali'i* ultimately traced their lineage, and from which they derived their god-ordained power to rule. Basically, there are two major genealogical families: the Nanaulu, who became the royal *ali'i* of O'ahu and Kaua'i; and the Ulu, who provided the royalty of Maui and Hawai'i.

One well-known translation of *The Kumulipo* was done in 1951 by Martha Beckwith; previously, one had been done by Queen Lili'uokalani. The best sources of information in English on Hawaiian myth and legend are Martha Beckwith's *Hawaiian Mythology* and the monumental three-volume opus *An Account of the Polynesian Race,* compiled by Abraham Fornander from 1878 to 1885. Fornander, after settling in Hawaii, married an *ali'i* from Moloka'i and had an illustrious career as a newspaperman, Maui circuit judge, and finally Supreme Court justice. For years Fornander sent scribes to every corner of the kingdom to listen to the elder *kupuna.* They returned with firsthand accounts, which he dutifully recorded.

force in their own land and with it the end of Hawaii as a sovereign monarchy. An almost bloodless yet bitter military coup followed by a brief Hawaiian Republic ended in annexation by the United States. As the United States became completely entrenched politically and militarily, a new social and economic order was founded on the plantation system. Amazingly rapid population growth occurred with the importation of plantation workers from Asia and Europe, which yielded a unique cosmopolitan blend of races like nowhere else on earth.

By the dawning of the 20th century, the face of old Hawaii had been altered forever; the "sacred homeland in the north" was hurled into the modern age. The attack on Pearl Harbor saw a tremendous loss of life and brought Hawaii closer to the United States by a baptism of blood. Finally, on August 21, 1959, after five years as a "territory," Hawaii officially became the 50th state of the United States.

Captain Cook Sights Hawaii

In 1776 Capt. James Cook set sail for the Pacific from Plymouth, England, on his third and final expedition into this still largely unexplored region of the world. On a fruitless quest for the fabled Northwest Passage across the North American continent, he sailed down the coast of Africa, rounded the Cape of Good Hope, crossed the Indian Ocean, and traveled past New Zealand, Tasmania, and the

Friendly Islands (where the "friendly" natives hatched an unsuccessful plot to murder him). On January 18, 1778, Captain Cook's 100-foot flagship HMS *Resolution* and its 90-foot companion HMS *Discovery* sighted O'ahu. Two days later, they sighted Kaua'i and went ashore at the village of Waimea. Though anxious to get on with his mission, Cook decided to make a quick sortie to investigate this new land and reprovision his ships. He did, however, take time to remark in his diary about the close resemblance of these newfound people to others he had encountered as far south as New Zealand and marveled at their widespread habitation across the Pacific.

The first trade was some brass medals for a mackerel. Cook also stated that he had never before met natives so astonished by a ship, and that they had an amazing fascination with iron, which they called *ko'i,* Hawaiian for "adze." There is even some conjecture that a Spanish ship under one Captain Gaetano had landed in Hawaii as early as the 16th century, trading a few scraps of iron that the Hawaiians valued even more than Europeans valued gold.

It was also noted that the Hawaiian women gave themselves freely to the sailors with the apparent good wishes of the island men. This was actually a ploy by the *kahuna* to test if the newcomers were gods or men—gods didn't need women. These sailors proved immediately mortal. Cook, who was also a physician, tried valiantly to keep the 66 men (out of 112) who had measurable cases of venereal disease away from the women. The task proved impossible as women literally swarmed the ships; when Cook returned less than a year later, it was logged that signs of VD were already apparent on some natives' faces.

Cook was impressed with the Hawaiians' swimming ability and with their well-bred manners. They had happy dispositions and sticky fingers, stealing any object made of metal, especially nails. The first item stolen was a butcher's cleaver. An unidentified native grabbed it, plunged overboard, swam to shore, and waved his booty in triumph. The Hawaiians didn't seem to care for beads and were not at all impressed with a mirror. Cook provisioned his ships by trading chisels for hogs, while common sailors gleefully traded nails for sex. Landing parties were sent inland to fill casks with freshwater. On one such excursion a Mr. Williamson, who was eventually drummed out of the Royal Navy for cowardice, unnecessarily shot and killed a native. After a brief stop on Ni'ihau, the ships sailed away, but both groups were indelibly impressed with the memory of each other.

COURTESY OF HAWAII STATE ARCHIVES
Captain James Cook

Cook Returns

Almost a year later, when winter weather forced Cook to return from the coast of Alaska, his discovery began to take on far-reaching significance. Cook had named Hawaii the Sandwich Islands, in honor of one of his patrons, John Montague, the Earl of Sandwich. On this return voyage, he spotted Maui on November 26, 1778. After eight weeks of seeking a suitable harbor, the ships bypassed it, but not before the coastline was duly drawn by Lieutenant William Bligh, one of Cook's finest and most trusted officers. (Bligh would find his own drama almost 10 years later as commander of the infamous HMS *Bounty.*) The *Discovery* and *Resolution* finally found safe anchorage at Kealakekua Bay on the Kona Coast of the Big Island. It is very lucky for history that on board was Mr. Anderson, ship's chronicler, who left a handwritten record of the strange and tragic events that followed. Even more important were the drawings of John Webber, ship's artist, who rendered invaluable impressions in superb drawings and etchings. Other noteworthy men aboard were George Vancouver, who would lead the first British return to Hawaii after Cook's death and introduce many fruits, vegetables, cattle, sheep, and goats; and James Burney, who would become a long-standing leading authority on the Pacific.

By all accounts Cook was a humane and just captain, greatly admired by his men. Unlike many supremacists of that time, he was known to have a respectful attitude toward any people he discovered, treating them as equals and recognizing the significance of their cultures. Not known as a violent man, he would use his superior weapons against natives only in an absolute case of self-defense. His hardened crew had been at sea facing untold hardship for almost three years; returning to Hawaii was truly like reentering paradise.

A strange series of coincidences sailed with Cook into Kealakekua Bay on January 16, 1779. It was *makahiki* time, a period of rejoicing and festivity dedicated to the fertility god of the earth, Lono. Normal *kapu* days were suspended and willing partners freely enjoyed each other sexually, as well as dancing, feasting, and the islands' version of Olympic games. It was long held in Hawaiian legend that the great god Lono would return to earth. Lono's image was a small wooden figure perched on a tall, mastlike crossbeam; hanging from the crossbeam were long, white sheets of tapa. Who else could Cook be but Lono, and what else could his ships with their masts and white sails be but his sacred floating *heiau?* This explained the Hawaiians' previous fascination with his ships, but to add to the remarkable coincidence, Kealakekua Harbor happened to be considered Lono's private sacred harbor. Natives from throughout the land prostrated themselves and paid homage to the returning god. Cook was taken ashore and brought to Lono's sacred temple, where he was afforded the highest respect. The ships badly needed fresh supplies so the Hawaiians readily gave all they had, stretching their own provisions to the limit. To the sailors' delight, this included full measures of the *aloha* spirit.

The Fatal Misunderstanding

After an uproarious welcome and generous hospitality for over a month, it became obvious that the newcomers were beginning to overstay their welcome. During the interim a seaman named William Watman died, convincing the Hawaiians that the *haole* were indeed mortals, not gods. Watman was buried at Hikiau Heiau, where a plaque commemorates the event to this day. Incidents of petty theft began to increase dramatically. The lesser chiefs indicated it was time to leave by "rubbing the Englishmen's bellies." Inadvertently many *kapu* were broken by the Englishmen, and once-friendly relations became strained. Finally, the ships sailed away on February 4, 1779.

After plying terrible seas for only a week, *Resolution*'s foremast was badly damaged. Cook sailed back into Kealakekua Bay, dragging the mast ashore on February 13. The natives, now totally hostile, hurled rocks at the sailors. Orders were given to load muskets with ball; firearms had previously only been loaded with shot and a light charge. Confrontations increased when some Hawaiians stole a small boat and Cook's men set after them, capturing the fleeing canoe which held an *ali'i* named Palea. The English treated him roughly; to the Hawaiians' horror, they even smacked him on the head with a paddle. The Hawaiians then furiously attacked the mariners, who abandoned the small boat.

Cook Goes Down

Next the Hawaiians stole a small cutter from the *Discovery* that had been moored to a buoy and partially sunk to protect it from the sun. For the first time, Captain Cook became furious. He ordered Captain Clerk of the *Discovery* to sail to the southeast end of the bay and stop any canoe trying to leave Kealakekua.

Cook then made a fatal error in judgment. He decided to take nine armed mariners ashore in an attempt to convince the venerable King Kalani'opu'u to accompany him back aboard ship, where he would hold him for ransom in exchange for the cutter. The old king agreed, but his wife prevailed upon him not to trust the *haole.* Kalani'opu'u sat down on the beach to think while the tension steadily grew.

Meanwhile, a group of sailors fired upon a canoe trying to leave the bay, and a lesser chief, No'okemai, was killed. The crowd around Cook and his men reached an estimated 20,000, and warriors outraged by the killing of the chief armed themselves with clubs and protective straw-mat armor. One bold warrior advanced on Cook and struck him with his *pahoa* (dagger). In retaliation, Cook drew a tiny pistol lightly loaded with shot and fired at the warrior. His bullets spent themselves on the straw armor and fell harmlessly to the ground. The Hawaiians went wild. Lieutenant Molesworth Phillips, in charge of the nine sailors, began a withering fire; Cook himself slew two natives.

Overpowered by sheer numbers, the sailors headed for boats standing offshore, while Lieutenant Phillips lay wounded. It is believed that Captain Cook, the greatest seaman ever to enter the Pacific, stood helplessly in knee-deep water instead of making for the boats because he could not swim! Hopelessly surrounded, he was knocked on the head, then countless warriors passed a knife around and hacked and mutilated his lifeless body. A sad Lieutenant King lamented in his diary, "Thus fell our great and excellent commander."

The Final Chapter

Captain Clerk, now in charge, settled his men and prevailed upon the Hawaiians to return Cook's body. On the morning of February 16 a grisly piece of charred meat was brought aboard: the Hawaiians, according to their custom, had afforded Cook the highest honor by baking his body in an underground oven to remove the flesh from the bones. On February 17 a group of Hawaiians in a canoe taunted the mariners by brandishing Cook's hat. The English, strained to the limit and thinking that Cook was being desecrated, finally broke. Foaming with blood-lust, they leveled their cannons and muskets on shore and shot anything that moved. It is believed that Kamehameha the Great was wounded in this flurry, along with four *ali'i,* and 25 *maka'ainana* (commoners) were also killed. Finally, on February 21, 1779, the bones of Captain James Cook's hands, skull, arms, and legs were returned and tearfully buried at sea. A common seaman, one Mr. Zimmerman, summed up the feelings of all who sailed under Cook when he wrote, "... he was our leading star." The English sailed next morning after dropping off their Hawaiian girlfriends who were still aboard.

THE UNIFICATION OF OLD HAWAII

Hawaii was already in a state of political turmoil and civil war when Cook arrived. In the 1780s the islands were roughly divided into three kingdoms: venerable Kalani'opu'u ruled Hawai'i and the Hana district of Maui; wily and ruthless warrior-king Kahekili ruled Maui, Kaho'olawe, Lana'i, and later O'ahu; and Kaeo, Kahekili's brother, ruled Kaua'i. War ravaged the land until a remarkable chief, Kamehameha, rose and subjugated all the islands under one rule. Kamehameha initiated a dynasty that would last for about 100 years, until the independent monarchy of Hawaii forever ceased to be.

To add a zing to this brewing political stew, Westerners and their technology were beginning to come in ever-increasing numbers. In 1786, Captain Jean-François de La Pérouse and his French exploration party landed in what's now La Pérouse Bay in South Maui, foreshadowing European attention to the islands. In 1786 two American captains, Portlock and Dixon, made landfall in Hawaii. Also, it was known that a fortune could be made on the fur trade between the Pacific Northwest and Canton, China; stopping in Hawaii could make the trip feasible. After this was reported, the fate of Hawaii was sealed.

COURTESY OF HAWAII STATE ARCHIVES

King Kamehameha

Hawaii under Kamehameha was ready to enter its "golden age." The social order was medieval, with the *ali'i* as knights owing their military allegiance to the king, and the serf-like *maka'ainana* paying tribute and working the lands. The priesthood of *kahuna* filled the posts of advisors, sorcerers, navigators, doctors, and historians. This was Polynesian Hawaii at its apex. But like the uniquely Hawaiian silversword plant, the old culture blossomed and, as soon as it did, began to wither. Ever since, all that was purely Hawaiian has been supplanted by the relentless foreign influences that began bearing down upon it.

Young Kamehameha

The greatest native son of Hawaii, Kamehameha was born under mysterious circumstances in the Kohala district on the Big Island, probably in 1753. He was royal born to Keoua Kupuapaikalaninui, the chief of Kohala, and Kekuiapoiwa, a chieftess from Kona. Accounts vary, but one claims that before his birth, a *kahuna* prophesied that this child would grow to be a "killer of chiefs." Because of this, the local chiefs conspired to murder the infant. When Kekuiapoiwa's time came, she secretly went to the royal birthing stones near Mo'okini Heiau and delivered Kamehameha. She entrusted her baby to a manservant and instructed him to hide the child. He headed for the rugged and remote coast around Kapa'au. Here Kamehameha was raised in the mountains, mostly by men. Always alone, he earned the nickname "the lonely one."

Kamehameha was a man noticed by everyone; there was no doubt he was a force to be reckoned with. He had met Captain Cook when the *Discovery* unsuccessfully tried to land at Hana on Maui. While aboard, he made a lasting impression, distinguishing himself from the multitude of natives swarming the ships by his royal bearing. Lieutenant James King, in a diary entry, remarked that Kamehameha was a fierce-looking man, almost ugly, but that he was obviously intelligent, observant, and very good-natured. Kamehameha received his early military training from his uncle Kalani'opu'u, the great king of Hawai'i and Hana who fought fierce battles against Alapa'i, the usurper who stole his hereditary lands. After regaining Hawai'i, Kalani'opu'u returned to his Hana district and turned his attention to conquering all of Maui. During this period young Kamehameha distinguished himself as a ferocious warrior and earned the nickname of "the Hard-shelled Crab," even though old Kahekili, Maui's king, almost annihilated Kalani'opu'u's army at the sand hills of Wailuku.

When the old king neared death, he passed on the kingdom to his son Kiwala'o. He also, however, empowered Kamehameha as the keeper of the family war god Kuka'ilimoku: Ku of the Bloody Red Mouth, Ku the Destroyer. Oddly enough, Kamehameha had been born not 500 yards from Ku's great *heiau* at Kohala, and he had heard the chanting and observed the ceremonies dedicated to this fierce god from his first breath. Soon after Kalani'opu'u died, Kamehameha found himself in a bitter war that he did not seek against his two cousins, Kiwala'o and his brother Keoua, with the island of Hawai'i at stake. The skirmishing lasted nine years until Kamehameha's armies met the two brothers at Moku'ohai in an indecisive battle in which Kiwala'o was killed.

The result was a shaky truce with Keoua, a much-embittered enemy. During this fighting, Kahekili of Maui conquered O'ahu, where he built a house of the skulls and bones of his adversaries as a reminder of his omnipotence. He also extended his will to Kaua'i by marrying his half-brother to a high-ranking chieftess of that island. A new factor would resolve this stalemate of power—the coming of the *haole.*

The Olowalu Massacre

In 1790 the American merchant ship *Ella Nora,* commanded by Yankee captain Simon Metcalfe, was looking for a harbor after its long voyage from the Pacific Northwest. Following a day behind was the *Fair American,* a tiny ship sailed by Metcalfe's son Thomas and a crew of five. Simon Metcalfe, perhaps by necessity, was a stern and humorless man who would allow no interference. While his ship was anchored at Olowalu, a beach area about five miles east of Lahaina on Maui, some natives slipped close in their canoes and stole a small boat, killing a seaman in the process. Metcalfe decided to trick the Hawaiians by first negotiating a truce and then unleashing full fury upon them. Signaling he was willing to trade, he invited canoes of innocent natives to visit his ship. In the meantime, he ordered that all cannons and muskets be readied with scatter shot. When the canoes were within hailing distance, he ordered his crew to fire at will. Over 100 people were slain; the Hawaiians remembered this killing as "the Day of Spilled Brains." Metcalfe then sailed away to Kealakekua Bay and in an unrelated incident managed to insult Kameiamoku, a ruling chief, who vowed to annihilate the next *haole* ship that he saw.

Fate sent him the *Fair American* and young Thomas Metcalfe. The little ship was entirely overrun by superior forces. In the ensuing battle, the mate, Isaac Davis, so distinguished himself by open acts of bravery that his life alone was spared. Kameiamoku later turned over both Davis and the ship to Kamehameha. Meanwhile, while harbored at Kealakekua, the senior Metcalfe sent John Young to reconnoiter. Kamehameha, having learned of the capture of the *Fair American,* detained Young so he could not report, and Metcalfe, losing patience, marooned his own man and sailed off to Canton. (Metcalfe never learned of the fate of his son Thomas and was later killed with another son while trading with Native Americans along the Pacific coast of the United States.) Kamehameha quickly realized the significance of his two captives and the *Fair American* with its brace of small cannons. He appropriated the ship and made Davis and Young trusted advisors, eventually raising them to the rank of chief. They would all play a significant role in the unification of Hawaii.

Kamehameha the Great

Later in 1790, supported by the savvy of Davis and Young and the cannons from the *Fair American* (which he mounted on carts), Kamehameha invaded Maui, using Hana as his power base. The island's defenders under Kalanikupule, son of Kahekili, who was lingering on O'ahu, were totally demoralized, then driven back into the death trap of the 'Iao Valley of Maui. There, Kamehameha's forces annihilated them. No mercy was expected and none given, although mostly commoners were slain with no significant *ali'i* falling to the victors. So many were killed in this sheer-walled, inescapable valley that the battle was called *ka pani wai,* which means "the Damming of the Waters"—literally with dead bodies.

While Kamehameha was fighting on Maui, his old nemesis Keoua was busy running amok back on Hawai'i, again pillaging Kamehameha's lands. The great warrior returned home flushed with victory, but in two battles he could not subdue Keoua. Finally, Kamehameha had a prophetic dream in which he was told that Ku would lead him to victory over all the lands of Hawaii if he would build a *heiau* to the war god at Kawaihae. Even before the temple was finished, old Kahekili attempted to invade Waipi'o, Kamehameha's stronghold. But Kamehameha summoned Davis and Young, and with the *Fair American* and an enormous fleet of war canoes defeated Kahekili at Waimanu. Kahekili had no choice but to accept the indomitable Kamehameha as the king of Maui, although he himself remained the administrative head until his death in 1794.

Now only Keoua remained in the way, and he would be defeated not by war, but by the great mana of Ku. While Keoua's armies were crossing the desert on the southern slopes of Kilauea, the fire goddess Pele trumpeted her disapproval and sent a huge cloud of poisonous gas and mud-ash into the air. It descended upon and instantly killed the middle legions of Keoua's armies and their families. The footprints of this ill-fated army remain to this day outlined in the mud-ash as clearly as if they were deliberately encased in wet cement. Keoua's intuition told him that the victorious mana of the gods had swung to Kamehameha and that his own fate was sealed. Kamehameha sent word that he wanted Keoua to meet with him at Ku's newly dedicated temple in Kawaihae. Both knew that Keoua must die. Riding proudly in his canoe, the old nemesis came gloriously outfitted in the red-and-gold feathered cape and helmet signifying his exalted rank. When he stepped ashore he was felled by Kamehameha's warriors. His body was ceremoniously laid upon the altar along with 11 others who were slaughtered and dedicated to Ku, of the Maggot-Dripping Mouth.

Increasing Contact

By the time Kamehameha had won the Big Island, Hawaii was becoming a regular stopover for numerous ships seeking the lucrative sandalwood trade with China. In February 1791, Captain George Vancouver, still seeking the Northwest Passage, returned to Kealakekua where he was greeted by a throng of 30,000.

The captain at once recognized Kamehameha, who was wearing a Chinese dressing gown that he had received in tribute from another chief who in turn had received it from the hands of Cook himself. The diary of a crew member, Thomas Manby, relates that Kamehameha, missing his front teeth, was more fierce-looking than ever as he approached the ship in an elegant double-hulled canoe propelled by 46 rowers. The king invited all to a great feast prepared for them on the beach. Kamehameha's appetite matched his tremendous size. It was noted that he ate two sizable fish, a king-sized bowl of poi, a small pig, and an entire baked dog. Kamehameha personally entertained the English by putting on a mock battle in which he deftly avoided spears by rolling, tumbling, and catching them in midair, all the while hurling his own spear a great distance. The English reciprocated by firing cannon bursts into the air, creating an impromptu fireworks display. Kamehameha requested from Vancouver a full table setting, with which he was provided, but his request for firearms was prudently denied.

Captain Vancouver became Kamehameha's trusted advisor and told him about the white man's form of worship. He even interceded for Kamehameha with his headstrong queen, Ka'ahumanu, and coaxed her from her hiding place under a rock when she sought refuge at Pu'uhonua O Honaunau. The captain gave gifts of beef cattle, fowl, and breeding stock of sheep and goats. The ship's naturalist, Archibald Menzies, was the first *haole* to climb Mauna Kea; he also introduced a large assortment of fruits and vegetables. The Hawaiians were cheerful and outgoing, and they showed remorse when they indicated that the remainder of Cook's bones had been buried at a temple close to Kealakekua. John Young, by this time firmly entrenched in Hawaiian society, made no request to sail away with Vancouver. During the next two decades of Kamehameha's rule, the French, Russians, English, and Americans discovered the great whaling waters off Hawaii. Their increasing visits shook and finally tumbled the ancient religion and social order of *kapu*.

Finishing Touches

After Keoua was laid to rest, it was only a matter of time until Kamehameha consolidated his power over all of Hawaii. In 1794 the old warrior Kahekili of Maui died and gave O'ahu to his son, Kalanikupule, while Kaua'i and Ni'ihau went to his brother Kaeo. In wars between the two, Kalanikupule was victorious, though he did not possess the grit of his father nor the great mana of Kamehameha. He had previously murdered a Captain Brown, who had anchored in Honolulu, and seized his ship, the *Jackal.* With the aid of this ship, Kalanikupule now determined to attack Kamehameha. However, while en route, the sailors regained control of their ship and cruised to the Big Island to inform and join with Kamehameha. An army of 16,000 was raised and sailed for Maui, where they met only token resistance, destroyed Lahaina, pillaged the countryside, and subjugated Moloka'i in one bloody battle.

The war canoes sailed next for O'ahu and the final showdown. The great army landed at Waikiki, and though defenders fought bravely, giving up O'ahu by the inch, they were steadily driven into the surrounding mountains. The beleaguered army made its last stand at Nu'uanu Pali, a great precipice in the mountains behind present-day Honolulu. Kamehameha's warriors mercilessly drove the enemy into the great abyss. Kalanikupule, who hid in the mountains, was captured after a few months and sacrificed to Ku, the Snatcher of Lands, thereby ending the struggle for power.

Kamehameha put down a revolt on Hawai'i in 1796. The king of Kaua'i, Kaumuali'i, accepted the inevitable and recognized Kamehameha as supreme ruler without suffering the ravages of a needless war. Kamehameha, for the first time in Hawaiian history, was the undisputed ruler of all the islands of "the heavenly homeland in the north."

Kamehameha's Rule

Kamehameha was as gentle in victory as he was ferocious in battle. Under his rule, which lasted until his death on May 8, 1819, Hawaii enjoyed a peace unlike any the warring islands had ever known. The king moved his royal court to Lahaina, where in 1803 he built the "Brick Palace," the first permanent building of Hawaii. The benevolent tyrant also enacted the "Law of the Splintered Paddle." This law, which protected the weak from the exploitation of the strong, had its origins in an incident of many years before. A brave defender of a small overwhelmed village had broken a paddle over Kamehameha's head and taught the chief—literally in one stroke—about the nobility of the commoner.

However, just as Old Hawaii reached its golden age, its demise was at hand. The relentless waves of *haole* innocently yet determinedly battered the old ways into the ground. With the foreign ships came prosperity and fanciful new goods after which the *ali'i* lusted. The *maka'ainana* were worked mercilessly to provide sandalwood for the China trade. This was the first "boom" economy to hit the islands, but it set the standard of exploitation that would follow. Kamehameha built an observation tower in Lahaina to watch for ships, many of which were his own, returning laden with riches from the world at large.

In the last years of his life Kamehameha

© ROBERT NILSEN

Kamehameha I spent much of the last years of his life in Kona near Ahu'ena Heiau.

returned to his beloved Kona Coast, where he enjoyed the excellent fishing renowned to this day. He had taken Hawaii from the darkness of warfare into the light of peace. He died true to the religious and moral *kapu* of his youth, the only ones he had ever known, and with him died a unique way of life. Two loyal retainers buried his bones after the baked flesh had been ceremoniously stripped away. A secret burial cave was chosen so that no one could desecrate the remains of the great chief, thereby absorbing his mana. The tomb's whereabouts remains unknown, and disturbing the dead remains one of the strictest *kapu* to this day. The Lonely One's kingdom would pass to his son, Liholiho, but true power would be in the hands of his beloved but feisty wife Ka'ahumanu. As Kamehameha's spirit drifted from this earth, two forces sailing around Cape Horn would forever change Hawaii: the missionaries and the whalers.

MISSIONARIES AND WHALERS

The year 1819 was of the utmost significance in Hawaiian history. It marked the death of Kamehameha, the overthrow of the ancient *kapu* system, the arrival of the first "whaler" in Lahaina, and the departure of Calvinist missionaries from New England determined to convert the heathen islands. Great changes began to rattle the old order to its foundations. With the *kapu* system and all of the ancient gods abandoned (except for the fire goddess Pele of Kilauea), a great void was left in the souls of the Hawaiians. In the coming decades Hawaii, also coveted by Russia, France, and England, was finally consumed by America. The islands had the first American school, printing press, and newspaper *(The Polynesian)* west of the Mississippi. Lahaina, in its heyday, became the world's greatest whaling port, accommodating over 500 ships of all types during its peak years.

The Royal Family

Maui's Hana district provided Hawaii with one of its greatest queens, Ka'ahumanu, born in 1768 in a cave within walking distance of Hana Harbor. At the age of 17 she became the third of Kamehameha's 21 wives and eventually the love of his life. At first she proved totally independent and unmanageable and was known to openly defy her king by taking numerous lovers. Kamehameha placed a *kapu* on her body and even had her attended by horribly deformed hunchbacks in an effort to curb her carnal appetites, but she continued to flout his authority. Young Ka'ahumanu had no love for her great, lumbering, unattractive husband, but in time (even Captain Vancouver was pressed into service as a marriage counselor) she learned to love him dearly. She in turn became his favorite wife, although she remained childless throughout her life. Kamehameha's first wife was the supremely royal Keopuolani, who so outranked even him that the king himself had to approach her naked and crawling on his belly. Keopuolani produced the royal children Liholiho and Kauikeaouli, who became King Kamehameha II and III, respectively. Just before Kamehameha I died in 1819 he appointed Liholiho his successor, but he also had the wisdom to make Ka'ahumanu the *kuhina nui,* or queen regent. Initially, Liholiho was weak and became a drunkard. Later he became a good ruler, but he was always supported by his royal mother Keopuolani and by the ever-formidable Ka'ahumanu.

Kapu Is *Pau*

Ka'ahumanu was greatly loved and respected by the people. On public occasions, she donned Kamehameha's royal cloak and spear and, so attired and infused with the king's mana, she demonstrated that she was the real leader of Hawaii. For six months after Kamehameha's death, Ka'ahumanu counseled Liholiho on what he must do. The wise *kuhina nui* knew that the old ways were *pau* (finished) and that Hawaii could not hope to function in a rapidly changing world under the *kapu* system. In November 1819, Ka'ahumanu and Keopuolani prevailed upon Liholiho to break two of the oldest and most sacred *kapu* by eating with women and by allowing women to eat

COURTESY OF HAWAII STATE ARCHIVES

the great Queen Ka'ahumanu, by ship's artist Louis Choris from the Otto Von Kotzebue expedition, circa 1816

previously forbidden foods such as bananas and certain fish. Heavily fortified with strong drink and attended by other high-ranking chiefs and a handful of foreigners, Ka'ahumanu and Liholiho ate together in public. This feast became known as 'Ai Noa (Free Eating). As the first morsels passed Ka'ahumanu's lips, the ancient gods of Hawaii tumbled. Throughout the land, revered *heiau* were burned and abandoned and the idols knocked to the ground. Now the people had nothing but their weakened inner selves to rely on. Nothing and no one could answer their prayers; their spiritual lives were empty and in shambles.

Missionaries

Into this spiritual vortex sailed the brig *Thaddeus* on April 4, 1820. It had set sail from Boston on October 23, 1819, lured to the Big Island by Henry Opukaha'ia, a local boy born at Napo'opo'o in 1792. Coming ashore at Kailua-Kona, the Reverends Bingham and Thurston were granted a one-year trial missionary period by King Liholiho. They established themselves on the Big Island and O'ahu and from there began the transformation of Hawaii. The missionaries were people of God, but also practical-minded Yankees. They brought education, enterprise, and most importantly, unlike the transient seafarers, a commitment to stay and build. By 1824, the new faith had such a foothold that Chieftess Keopuolani climbed to the fire pit atop Kilauea and defied Pele. This was even more striking than the previous breaking of the food *kapu,* because the strength of Pele could actually be seen. Keopuolani ate forbidden *'ohelo* berries and cried out, "Jehovah is my God." Over the next decades the governing of Hawaii slipped away from the Big Island and moved to the new port cities of Lahaina on Maui and, later, Honolulu.

Rapid Conversions

The year 1824 also marked the death of Keopuolani, who was given a Christian burial. She had set the standard by accepting Christianity, and a number of the *ali'i* had followed the queen's lead. Liholiho had sailed off to

England, where he and his wife contracted measles and died. Their bodies were returned by the British in 1825, on the HMS *Blonde* captained by Lord Byron, cousin of *the* Lord Byron. During these years, Ka'ahumanu allied herself with Reverend Richards, pastor of the first mission in the islands, and together they wrote Hawaii's first code of laws based upon the Ten Commandments. Foremost was the condemnation of murder, theft, brawling, and the desecration of the Sabbath by work or play. The early missionaries had the best of intentions, but like all zealots they were blinded by the single-mindedness that was also their greatest ally. They weren't surgically selective in their destruction of native beliefs. *Anything* native was felt to be inferior, and they set about wiping out all traces of the old ways. In their rampage they reduced the Hawaiian culture to ashes, plucking self-will and determination from the hearts of a once-proud people. More so than the whalers, they terminated the Hawaiian way of life.

The Early Seamen

A good portion of the common seamen of the early 19th century came from the dregs of the Western world. Many a whoremongering drunkard had awoken from a stupor and found himself on the pitching deck of a ship, discovering to his dismay that he had been "pressed into naval service." For the most part these sailors were a filthy, uneducated, lawless rabble. Their present situation was dim, their future hopeless, and they would live to be 30 if they were lucky and didn't die from scurvy or a thousand other miserable fates. They snatched brief pleasure in every port and jumped ship at every opportunity, especially in an easy berth like Lahaina. They displayed the worst elements of Western culture, which the Hawaiians naively mimicked. In exchange for *aloha* they gave drunkenness, sloth, and insidious death by disease. By the 1850s the population of native Hawaiians tumbled from the estimated 300,000 reported by Captain Cook in 1778 to barely 60,000. Common conditions such as colds, flu, venereal disease, and sometimes smallpox and cholera devastated the Hawaiians, who had no natural immunities to these foreign ailments. By the time the missionaries arrived, *hapa haole* children were common in Lahaina streets.

The earliest merchant ships to the islands were owned or skippered by lawless opportunists who had come seeking sandalwood after first filling their holds with furs from the Pacific Northwest. Aided by *ali'i* hungry for manufactured goods and Western finery, they raped Hawaiian forests of this fragrant wood so coveted in China. Next, droves of sailors came in search of whales. The whalers, decent men at home, left their morals back in the Atlantic and lived by the slogan "no conscience east of the Cape." The delights of Hawaii were just too tempting for most.

Two Worlds Tragically Collide

The 1820s were a time of confusion and soul-searching for the Hawaiians. When Kamehameha II died the kingdom passed to Kauikeaouli (Kamehameha III), who made his lifelong residence in Lahaina. The young king was only nine years old when the title passed to him, but his power was secure because Ka'ahumanu was still a vibrant *kuhina nui*. The young prince, more so than any other, was raised in the cultural confusion of the times. His childhood was spent during the very cusp of the change from old ways to new, and he was often pulled in two directions by vastly differing beliefs. Since he was royal born, he was bound by age-old Hawaiian tradition to mate and produce an heir with the highest-ranking *ali'i* in the kingdom. This mate happened to be his younger sister, Princess Nahi'ena'ena. To the old Hawaiian advisors, this arrangement was perfectly acceptable and encouraged. To the increasingly influential missionaries, incest was an unimaginable abomination in the eyes of God. The problem was compounded by the fact that Kamehameha III and Nahi'ena'ena were drawn to each other and were deeply in love. The young king could not stand the mental pressure imposed by conflicting worlds. He became a teenage alcoholic too royal to be restrained by anyone in the kingdom, and his bouts of drunkenness and womanizing were both legendary and scandalous.

Meanwhile, Nahi'ena'ena was even more pressured because she was a favorite of the missionaries, baptized into the church at age 12. She too vacillated between the old and the new. At times she was a pious Christian; at others she drank all night and took numerous lovers. As the prince and princess grew into their late teens, they became even more attached to each other and hardly made an attempt to keep their relationship from the missionaries. Whenever possible, they lived together in a grass house built for the princess by her father.

In 1832, the great Ka'ahumanu died, leaving the king on his own. In 1833, at the age of 18, Kamehameha III announced that the "regency" was over and that all the lands in Hawaii were his personally, and that he alone was the ultimate law. Almost immediately, however, he decreed that his half-sister Kina'u would be "premier," signifying that he would leave the actual running of the kingdom in her hands. Kamehameha III fell into total drunken confusion, until one night he attempted suicide. After this episode he seemed to straighten up a bit and mostly kept a low profile. In 1836, Princess Nahi'ena'ena was convinced by the missionaries to take a husband. She married Leleiohoku, a chief from the Big Island, but continued to sleep with her brother. It is uncertain who fathered the child, but Nahi'ena'ena gave birth to a baby boy in September 1836. The young prince survived for only a few hours, and Nahi'ena'ena never recovered. She died in December 1836 and was laid to rest in the mausoleum next to her mother, Keopuolani, on the royal island in Mokuhina Pond in Lahaina. After the death of his sister, Kamehameha III became a sober and righteous ruler. Often seen paying his respects at the royal mausoleum, he ruled longer than any other king, until his death in 1854.

The Missionaries Prevail

In 1823, the first mission was established in Lahaina, Maui, under the pastorate of Reverend Richards and his wife. Within a few years, many of the notable *ali'i* had been, at least in appearance, converted to Christianity. By 1828 the cornerstones for Waine'e Church, the first stone church on the island, were laid just behind the palace of Kamehameha III. The struggle between missionaries and whalers centered on public drunkenness and the servicing of sailors by native women. The normally God-fearing whalers had signed on for perilous duty that lasted up to three years, and when they anchored in Lahaina they demanded their pleasure. The missionaries were instrumental in placing a curfew on sailors and prohibiting native women from boarding ships, which had become customary. These measures certainly did not stop the liaisons between sailor and *wahine,* but they did impose a modicum of social sanction and tolled the end of the wide-open days. The sailors were outraged; in 1825 the crew from the *Daniel* attacked the home of the meddler, Reverend Richards. A year later a similar incident occurred. In 1827, confined and lonely sailors from the whaler *John Palmer* fired their cannons at Reverend Richards' newly built home.

Slowly the tensions eased, and by 1836 many sailors were regulars at the Seamen's Chapel adjacent to the Baldwin home. Unfortunately, even the missionaries couldn't stop the pesky mosquito from entering the islands through the port of Lahaina. The mosquitoes arrived from Mexico in 1826 aboard the merchant ship *Wellington.* They were inadvertently carried as larvae in the water barrels and democratically pestered everyone in the islands from that day forward, regardless of race, religion, or creed.

Foreign Influence

By the 1840s Honolulu was becoming the center of commerce in the islands; when Kamehameha III moved the royal court there from Lahaina, the ascendant fate of the new capital was guaranteed. In 1843, Lord Paulet, commander of the warship *Carysfort,* forced Kamehameha III to sign a treaty ceding Hawaii to the British. London, however, repudiated this act, and Hawaii's independence was restored within a few months when Queen Victoria sent

Admiral Thomas as her personal agent of good intentions. The king memorialized the turn of events by a speech in which he uttered the phrase, *"Ua mau ke e'a o ka 'aina i ka pono"* ("The life of the land is preserved in righteousness"), now Hawaii's motto. The French used similar bullying tactics to force an unfavorable treaty on the Hawaiians in 1839; as part of these heavy-handed negotiations they exacted a payment of $20,000 and the right of Catholics to enjoy religious freedom in the islands. In 1842 the United States recognized and guaranteed Hawaii's independence without a formal treaty, and by 1860 over 80 percent of the islands' trade was with the United States.

The Great Mahele

In 1840, Kamehameha III ended his autocratic rule and instituted a constitutional monarchy. This brought about the Hawaiian Bill of Rights, but the most far-reaching change was the transition to private ownership of land. Formerly, all land belonged to the ruling chief, who gave wedge-shaped parcels called *ahupua'a* to lesser chiefs to be worked for him. The commoners did all the real labor, their produce heavily taxed by the *ali'i.* The fortunes of war, the death of a chief, or the mere whim of a superior could force a commoner off the land. The Hawaiians, however, could not think in terms of "owning" land. No one could *possess* land; one could only *use* land; its ownership was a strange, foreign concept. (As a result, naive Hawaiians gave up their lands for a song to unscrupulous traders, which remains a basic and unrectified problem to this day.) In 1847 Kamehameha III and his advisors separated the lands of Hawaii into three groupings: crown land (belonging to the king), government land (belonging to the chiefs), and the people's land (the largest parcels). In 1848, 245 *ali'i* entered their land claims in the *Mahele Book,* assuring them ownership. In 1850 the commoners were given title in fee simple to the lands they cultivated and lived on as tenants, not including house lots in towns. Commoners without land could buy small *kuleana* (farms) from the government at 50 cents per acre. In 1850, foreigners were also allowed to purchase land in fee simple, and the ownership of Hawaii from that day forward slipped steadily from the hands of its indigenous people.

KING SUGAR

It's hard to say just where the sugar industry began in Hawaii. The Koloa Sugar Plantation on the southern coast of Kaua'i successfully refined sugar in 1835. Others tried, and one success was at Hana, Maui, in 1849. A whaler named George Wilfong hauled four blubber pots ashore and set them up on a rocky hill in the middle of 60 acres he had planted in sugar. A team of oxen turned "crushing rollers" and the cane juice flowed down an open trough into the pots, under which an attending native kept a roaring fire burning. Wilfong's methods of refining were crude but the resulting high-quality sugar turned a neat profit in Lahaina. The main problem was labor. The Hawaiians, who made excellent whalers, were basically indentured workers. They became extremely disillusioned with their contracts, which could last up to 10 years. Most of their wages were eaten up by manufactured commodities sold at the company store, and it didn't take long for them to realize that they were little more than slaves. At every opportunity they either left the area or just refused to work.

Imported Labor

The **Masters and Servants Act of 1850,** which allowed importation of laborers under the contract system, ostensibly guaranteed an endless supply of cheap labor for the plantations. Chinese laborers were imported but were too enterprising to remain in the fields for a meager $3 per month. They left as soon as opportunity permitted and went into business as small merchants and retailers. In the meantime, Wilfong had sold out, releasing most of the Hawaiians previously held under contract, and his plantation fell into disuse. In 1860 two Danish brothers, August and Oscar Unna, bought land at Hana to raise sugar. They solved the labor problem by importing Japanese laborers, who were extremely hardworking and easily managed. The workday lasted 10 hours, six days a week, for a salary of $20 per month plus housing and medical care. Plantation life was very structured, with stringent rules governing even bedtimes and lights out. A worker was fined for being late or for smoking on the job. The workers had great difficulty functioning under these circumstances, and improvements in benefits and housing were slowly gained.

Sugar Grows

The demand for "Sandwich Island Sugar" grew as California became populated during the gold rush and increased dramatically when the American Civil War demanded a constant supply. The only sugar plantations on the Mainland were small plots confined to the Confederate states, whose products would hardly be bought by the Union and whose fields, later in the war, were destroyed. By the 1870s it was clear to the planters, still mainly New Englanders, that the United States was their market; they tried often to gain closer ties and favorable tariffs. The Americans also planted rumors that the British were interested in annexing Hawaii; this put pressure on the U.S. Congress to pass the long-desired **Reciprocity Act,** which would exempt sugar from import duty. It finally passed in 1875, in exchange for U.S. long-range rights to the strategic naval port of Pearl Harbor, among other concessions. These agreements gave increased political power to a small group of American planters whose outlooks were similar to those of the post-Civil War South, where a few powerful whites were the virtual masters of a multitude of dark-skinned laborers. Sugar was now big business, and the Hana district alone exported almost 3,000 tons per year. All of Hawaii would have to reckon with the "sugar barons."

Changing Society

The sugar plantation system changed life in Hawaii physically, spiritually, politically, and economically. Now boatloads of workers came not only from Japan but from Portugal, Germany, and even Russia. The white-skinned workers were most often the field foremen *(luna).* With the immigrants came new religions, new animals and plants, unique cuisines, and a plantation language known as pidgin, or better yet, *da' kine.* Many Asians and, to a lesser extent, the other groups—including the white plantation owners—intermarried with Hawaiians. A new class of people properly termed "cosmopolitan" but more familiarly and aptly known as "locals" was emerging. These were the people of multiple race backgrounds who couldn't exactly say *what* they were but it was clear to all just *who* they were. The plantation owners became the new "chiefs" of Hawaii who could carve up the land and dispense favors. The Hawaiian monarchy was soon eliminated.

A KINGDOM PASSES

The Beginning of the End

Like the Hawaiian people themselves, the Kamehameha dynasty in the mid-1800s was dying from within. King Kamehameha IV (Alexander Liholiho) ruled 1854–1863; his only child died in 1862. He was succeeded by his older brother Kamehameha V (Lot Kamehameha), who ruled until 1872. With his passing, the Kamehameha line ended. William Lunalilo, elected king in 1873 by popular vote, was of royal, but not Kamehameha, lineage. He died after only a year in office, and, being a bachelor, left no heirs. He was succeeded by David Kalakaua, known far and wide as the "Merrie Monarch," who made a world tour and was well received wherever he went. He built 'Iolani Palace in Honolulu. He was personally in favor of closer ties with the United States and helped push through the Reciprocity Act. Kalakaua died in 1891 and was replaced by his sister Lydia Lili'uokalani, last of the Hawaiian monarchs.

The Revolution

When Lili'uokalani took office in 1891, the native population was at a low of 40,000, and she felt that the United States had too much influence over her homeland. She was known to personally favor the English over the Americans. She attempted to replace the liberal constitution of 1887 (adopted by her pro-American brother)

COURTESY OF HAWAII STATE ARCHIVES

Queen Lili'uokalani

with an autocratic mandate in which she would have had much more political and economic control of the islands. When the McKinley Tariff of 1890 brought a decline in sugar profits, she made no attempt to improve the situation. Thus, the planters saw her as a political obstacle to their economic growth; most of Hawaii's American planters and merchants were in favor of a rebellion. She would have to go! A central spokesperson and firebrand was Lorrin Thurston, a Honolulu publisher who, with a central core of about 30 men, challenged the Hawaiian monarchy. Although Lili'uokalani rallied some support and had a small military potential in her personal guard, the coup was ridiculously easy—it took only one casualty. Captain John Good shot a Hawaiian policeman in the arm and that did it. Naturally, the conspirators could not have succeeded without some solid assurances from a secret contingent in the U.S. Congress as well as outgoing president Benjamin Harrison, who favored Hawaii's annexation. Marines from the *Boston* went ashore to "protect American lives," and on January 17, 1893, the Hawaiian monarchy came to an end.

The provisional government was headed by Sanford B. Dole, who became president of the Hawaiian Republic. Lili'uokalani surrendered not to the conspirators but to U.S. ambassador John Stevens. She believed that the U.S. government, which had assured her of Hawaiian independence, would be outraged by the overthrow and would come to her aid. Incoming president Grover Cleveland *was* outraged, and Hawaii wasn't immediately annexed as expected. When queried about what she would do with the conspirators if she were reinstated, Lili'uokalani said that they would be hung as traitors. The racist press of the times, which portrayed the Hawaiians as half-civilized, bloodthirsty heathens, publicized this widely. Since the conspirators were the leading citizens of the land, the queen's words proved untimely. In January 1895 a small, ill-fated counterrevolution headed by Lili'uokalani failed, and she was placed under house arrest in 'Iolani Palace. Officials of the republic insisted she use her married name (Mrs. John Dominis) to sign the documents forcing her to abdicate her throne. She was also forced to swear allegiance to the new republic. Lili'uokalani went on to write *Hawaii's Story* and the lyric ballad "Aloha O'e." She never forgave the conspirators and remained "queen" to the Hawaiians until her death in 1917.

Annexation

The overwhelming majority of Hawaiians opposed annexation and desired to restore the monarchy. But they were prevented from voting by the new republic because they couldn't meet the imposed property and income qualifications—a transparent ruse by the planters to control the election. Most *haole* were racist and believed that the "common people" could not be entrusted with the vote because they were childish and incapable of ruling themselves. The fact that the Hawaiians had existed quite well for 1,000 years before white people even reached Hawaii was never considered. The Philippine theater of the Spanish-American War also prompted annexation. One of the strongest proponents was Alfred

Mahon, a brilliant naval strategist who, with support from Theodore Roosevelt, argued that the U.S. military must have Hawaii in order to be a viable force in the Pacific. In addition, Japan, victorious in its recent war with China, protested the American intention to annex, and in so doing prompted even moderates to support annexation for fear that the Japanese themselves coveted the prize. On July 7, 1898, President McKinley signed the annexation agreement, and this "tropical fruit" was finally put into America's basket.

MODERN TIMES

Hawaii entered the 20th century totally transformed from what it had been. The old Hawaiian language, religion, culture, and leadership were all but gone; Western dress, values, education, and recreation were the norm. Native Hawaiians were now unseen citizens who lived in dwindling numbers in remote areas. The plantations, new centers of social order, had a strong Asian flavor; more than 75 percent of their workforce was Asian. There was a small white middle class, an all-powerful white elite, and a single political party ruled by that elite. Education, however, was always highly prized, and by the turn of the 20th century all racial groups were encouraged to attend school. By 1900, almost 90 percent of Hawaiians were literate (far above the national norm), and schooling was mandatory for all children ages six to 15. Intermarriage was accepted, and there was a mixing of the races like nowhere else on earth.

The military became increasingly important to Hawaii. It brought in money and jobs, dominating the island economy. The Japanese attack on Pearl Harbor, which began U.S. involvement in World War II, bound Hawaii to America forever. Once the islands had been baptized by blood, the average Mainlander felt that Hawaii was American soil. A movement among Hawaiians to become part of the Union began to grow. They wanted a real voice in Washington, not merely a voteless delegate as provided under their territory status. Hawaii became the 50th state in 1959, and the jumbo-jet revolution of the 1960s made it easily accessible to growing numbers of tourists from all over the world.

Pearl Harbor Attack

On the morning of December 7, 1941, the Japanese carrier *Akagi,* flying the battle flag of the famed Admiral Togo of the Russo-Japanese War, received and broadcast over its PA system island music from Honolulu station KGMB. Deep in the bowels of the ship a radioman listened for a much different message, coming thousands of miles from the Japanese mainland. When the ironically poetic message "east wind rain" was received, the attack was launched. At the end of the day, 2,325 U.S. servicemen and 57 civilians were dead; 188 planes were destroyed; 18 major warships were sunk or heavily damaged; and the United States was in the war. Japanese casualties were ludicrously light. The ignited conflict would rage for four years until Japan, through the bombings at Nagasaki and Hiroshima, was vaporized into total submission. At the end of hostilities, Hawaii would never again be considered separate from America.

Statehood

A number of economic and political reasons explain why the ruling elite of Hawaii desired statehood, but, put simply, the vast majority of people who lived there, especially after World War II, considered themselves Americans. The first serious mention of making "The Sandwich Islands" a state was in the 1850s under President Franklin Pierce, but it wasn't taken seriously until the monarchy was overthrown in the 1890s. For the next 50 years statehood proposals were made repeatedly to Congress, but there was stiff opposition, especially from the southern states. With Hawaii a territory, an import quota system beneficial to Mainland producers could be enacted on produce, especially sugar. Also, there was prejudice against creating a state in a place where the majority of the populace was not white.

During World War II, Hawaii was placed under martial law, but no serious attempt to intern the Japanese population was made, as in California. There were simply too many

Japanese, and many went on to gain the respect of the American people with their outstanding fighting record during the war. Hawaii's own 100th Battalion became the famous 442nd Regimental Combat Team, which gained notoriety by saving the Lost Texas Battalion during the Battle of the Bulge and went on to be *the* most decorated battalion in all of World War II. When these GIs returned home, no one was going to tell them that they were not loyal Americans. Many of these AJAs (Americans of Japanese Ancestry) took advantage of the GI Bill and received higher educations. They were from the common people, not the elite, and they rallied grassroots support for statehood. When the vote finally occurred, approximately 132,900 voted in favor of statehood, with only 7,800 votes against. Congress passed the Hawaii State Bill on March 12, 1959, and on August 21, 1959, President Eisenhower announced that Hawaii was officially the 50th state.

Government and Economy

GOVERNMENT

The major difference between the government of the state of Hawaii and those of other states is that it's "streamlined," and in theory more efficient. There are only two levels of government: the state and the county. With no town or city governments to deal with, considerable bureaucracy is eliminated. Hawaii, in anticipation of becoming a state, drafted a constitution in 1950 and was ready to go when statehood came. Politics and government are taken seriously in the Aloha State, which consistently turns in the best national voting record per capita. For example, in the first state elections, 173,000 of 180,000 registered voters voted—a whopping 94 percent of the electorate. In the election to ratify statehood, hardly a ballot went uncast, with 95 percent of the voters opting for statehood. The bill carried in every island of Hawaii except Ni'ihau, where most of the people (total population 250 or so) were of relatively pure Hawaiian blood. When Hawaii became a state, Honolulu became its capital. Since statehood, the legislative and executive branches of state government have been dominated by the Democratic Party. Breaking a 40-year Democratic hold on power and becoming the first woman to hold the position, former Maui mayor and Republican Linda Lingle was elected as governor of Hawaii in 2002. Hawaii is represented in the U.S Congress by two senators, currently Daniel K. Inouye (D) and Daniel K. Akaka (D), and two representatives, currently Neil Abercrombie (D) and Ed Case (D).

County of Hawai'i

Elected in 2000, the mayor of the county of Hawai'i is Harry Kim, Democrat. The mayor is assisted by an elected county council consisting of nine members, one from each council district around the island. Hilo is the county seat.

Of the 25 State Senatorial Districts, Hawai'i County is represented by three. The First District takes in the whole northern section of the island: the Hamakua Coast, Mauna Kea, North and South Kohala, and part of North Kona. The Second District is mainly Hilo and its outlying area. The Third comprises Puna, Ka'u, South Kona, and most of North Kona. Hawai'i County has six of 51 seats in the State House of Representatives. For information on Hawai'i County see www.hawaii-county.com.

ECONOMY

Hawaii's mid-Pacific location makes it perfect for two prime sources of income: tourism and the military. Tourists come in anticipation of endless golden days on soothing beaches, while the military is provided with the strategic position of an unsinkable battleship. Each economic sector nets Hawaii billions of dollars annually, money that should keep flowing smoothly and even increase in the foreseeable future. Tourism alone reaps over $11 billion. These revenues remain mostly aloof from the normal ups and downs of the Mainland U.S. economy. Also contributing to the state revenue are, in descending proportions, manufacturing, construction, and agriculture (mainly sugar and pineapples). As long as the sun shines and the balance of global power requires a military presence, the economic stability of Hawaii is guaranteed.

Tourism

The first hotel in Hawai'i was the **Volcano House,** which overlooked Kilauea Crater and was built in 1866. Today, over 3,000 island residents are directly employed by the hotel industry, and many more indirectly serve the tourists. Of the slightly more than 9,500 hotel and condo rooms, the greatest concentration is in the Kona-Kohala area. While it varies every year, the hotel occupancy rate on the Big Island hovers around 70 percent, up substantially from the slow 1990–early-2000 figures. Hawai'i receives about 1.2 million tourists annually, about 23,500 on any given day. Of the major islands, it ranks third in number of annual visitors, following O'ahu and Maui.

Hilo and the east side traditionally were where tourists went when they visited the Big Island. By and large, that's where the people were and that's where the facilities were built. Few people ventured out beyond this enclave, and traveling was not so easy. There was a hotel in Kailua, but fewer people lived there and the infrastructure was not as sophisticated. In the mid-1960s, luxury resorts started to be built on the sunny Kohala and Kona Coasts, and condominiums followed soon after. Tourists loved the sun and began to flock to the west side. Slowly it built up, then rapidly, and now the Kona-Kohala Coast has far eclipsed the Hilo side as the preferred vacation spot on this island, with nearly three times as many visitors as the wet side.

Agriculture

The Big Island's economy is the state's most agriculturally based. Over 5,000 farmhands, horticultural workers, and *paniolo* work the land to produce about one-third of the state's vegetables and melons, over 75 percent of the total fruit production, 95 percent of the papaya, 75 percent of the bananas, 95 percent of the avocados, and 50 percent of the guavas. Much of the state's taro is also produced on the Big Island, principally in the Waipi'o Valley and along the Hamakua Coast, and ginger production has become a major economic factor with more than six million pounds grown annually. The Big Island also produces some 50 million pounds of macadamia nuts yearly, about 90 percent of the total amount grown in the state. While that's a respectable number, it's less than half the world's total. Hawai'i used to have the only commercial coffee plantations in the country, but now coffee is grown on all the major Hawaiian islands. Due to the increased interest in gourmet Kona coffee, the coffee industry's share in the economy of the island is increasing, and the Big Island grows about three million

Coffee has been grown in Kona for more than 175 years.

PURESTOCK
coffee "cherries"

pounds of coffee every year. More than 350 horticultural farms produce the largest number of orchids and anthuriums in the state, leaving the Big Island awash in color and fragrance. Other exotic flowers and foliage are also a growing concern. In the hills, entrepreneurs raise *pakalolo* (marijuana), which has become the state's most productive although illicit cash crop.

Hawai'i used to be the state's largest sugar grower, with over 150,000 acres in cane. These commercial fields produced four million tons of refined sugar, 40 percent of the state's output. The majority of sugar land was along the Hamakua Coast, long known for its abundant water supply. At one time, the cane was even transported to the mills by water flumes. Other large pockets of cane fields were found on the southern part of the island in Ka'u and Puna, as well as at the northern tip in North Kohala. With the closing of the last mill in 1996, sugar is no longer grown commercially on the island. Still, small entrepreneurial farms grow it on greatly reduced acreage. The big cane trucks have ceased to roll, and the few remaining smokestacks stand in silent testimony to a bygone era.

The upland Kona district is a splendid area for raising coffee; it gives the beans a beautiful tan. Lying in Mauna Loa's rain shadow, the district gets dewy mornings followed by sunshine and an afternoon cloud shadow. Kona coffee has long been accepted as gourmet quality and is sold in the better restaurants throughout Hawaii and in fine coffee shops around the world. It's a dark, full-bodied coffee with a rich aroma. Approximately 600 small farms produce nearly $15 million a year in coffee revenue. Few, however, make it a full-time business. The production of Kona coffee makes up only about one-tenth of 1 percent of the coffee grown around the world. The rare bean is often blended with other varietals. When sold unblended it is quite expensive. With its similar climactic conditions, the district of Ka'u has also begun to grow coffee, albeit it much smaller quantities. While not yet well known, Ka'u coffee has gained a loyal following.

Hawai'i's cattle ranches produce over five million pounds of beef per year, 50 percent of the state's total. More than 450 independent ranches are located on the island, with total acreage of over 650,000 acres, but they are dwarfed both in size and production by the massive Parker Ranch, which alone has 175,000 acres and is about half the size of O'ahu. While beef is the largest player in the livestock market, pork, dairy products, eggs, poultry, sheep, goats, bees, and honey also are components, and together constitute perhaps half of the island's livestock revenues.

Military

On average, about 60 military personnel are stationed on the Big Island at any one time, with about the same number of dependents. Most of these people are attached to the enormous Pohakuloa Military Reserve in the center of the island; a lesser number are at a few minor installations around Hilo, Kailua, and at Kilauea Volcano.

Land Ownership

Hawai'i County comprises over 2.5 million acres. Of this total, the state controls about 800,000 acres, mostly forest preserves and undeveloped land; the federal government has large acreage in the Hawai'i Volcanoes National Park, Pohakuloa Military Training

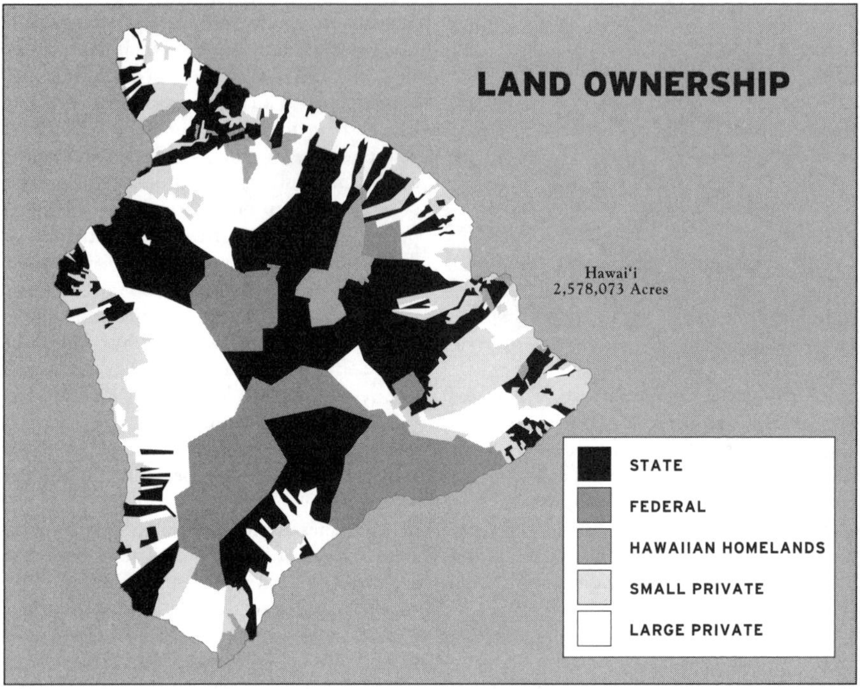

Area, and Hakalau Forest National Wildlife Refuge. Large landowners control most of the rest except for about 116,000 acres of Hawaiian Homelands. The major large landowners are the Bishop Estate, Parker Ranch, and the Samuel Damon Estate.

People

Nowhere else on earth can you find such a kaleidoscopic mixture of people as in Hawaii. Every major race is accounted for, and over 50 ethnic groups are represented throughout the islands, making Hawaii the most racially integrated state in the country. Its population of 1.2 million includes some 80,000 permanently stationed military personnel and their dependents. Until the year 2000, when California's white population fell below 50 percent, Hawaii was the only U.S. state where whites were not the majority. About 56 percent of Hawaiian residents were born there, 26 percent were born on the U.S. Mainland, and 18 percent are foreign-born.

The population has grown steadily in recent times, but fluctuated wildly in the past. In 1876, it reached its lowest ebb, with only 55,000 permanent residents. This was the era of large sugar plantations; their constant demand for labor was the primary cause for importing various peoples from around the world and led to Hawaii's racial mix. World War II saw the population swell from 400,000 to 900,000. Most of the 500,000 military personnel left at war's end, but many returned to settle after getting a taste of island living.

Hawai'i Population Figures

With 149,000, the Big Island has the second-largest island population in Hawaii, just over 12 percent of the state's total. However, it has the least population density of the main islands, with about 37 people per square mile; two-thirds urban, one-third rural. The Hilo area has the largest population with 47,000 residents, followed by North and South Kona with about 37,000, Puna at 31,000, South Kohala at 13,000, and the Hamakua Coast, North Kohala, and Ka'u each between 6,000 and 8,000. Within the last dozen years, the areas of Puna and South Kohala have experienced the greatest increases in population. There is no ethnic majority on the Big Island; population numbers include 32 percent Caucasian, 28 percent mixed, 27 percent Asian, 11 percent Hawaiian, and 2 percent other.

THE HAWAIIANS

The study of the native Hawaiians is ultimately a study in tragedy because of their near demise as a viable people. When Captain Cook first sighted Hawaii in 1778, there were an estimated 300,000 natives living in relative harmony with their ecological surroundings; within 100 years a scant 50,000 demoralized and dejected Hawaiians existed almost as wards of the state. Today, although more than 240,000 people claim varying degrees of Hawaiian blood, experts say that fewer than 1,000 are pure Hawaiian, and this might be stretching it.

It's easy to see why people of Hawaiian lineage could be bitter over what they have lost, being strangers in their own land now, much like Native Americans. The overwhelming majority of "Hawaiians" are of mixed heritage, and the wisest take the best from all worlds. From the Hawaiian side comes simplicity, love of the land, and acceptance of people. It is the Hawaiian legacy of *aloha* that remains immortal and adds that special elusive quality that *is* Hawaii.

Polynesian Roots

The Polynesians' original stock is muddled and remains an anthropological mystery, but it's believed that they were nomadic wanderers who migrated from both the Indian subcontinent and Southeast Asia through Indonesia, where they learned to sail and navigate on protected waterways. As they migrated they honed their sailing skills until they could take on the Pacific, and as they moved, they absorbed people from other cultures and races until they had coalesced into what we now know as Polynesians.

Abraham Fornander, still considered a major authority on the subject, wrote in his 1885 *Account of the Polynesian Race* that he believed the Polynesians started as a white (Aryan) race that was heavily influenced by contact with the Cushite, Chaldeo-Arabian civilization. He estimated their arrival in Hawaii at A.D. 600, based on Hawaiian genealogical chants. Modern science seems to bear this date out, although it remains skeptical about his other surmises. According to others, the intrepid Polynesians who actually settled Hawaii are believed to have come from the Marquesas Islands, 1,000 miles southeast of Hawaii. The Marquesans were cannibals and known for their tenacity and strength, attributes that would serve them well. Tahitians and other islanders arrived several hundred years later, creating a mix even in Polynesian blood.

The Caste System

Hawaiian society was divided into rankings by a strict caste system determined by birth, and from which there was no chance of escaping. The highest rank was the *ali'i*—the chiefs and royalty. The impeccable genealogies of the *ali'i* were traced back to the gods themselves, and the chants *(mo'o ali'i)* were memorized and sung by professionals (called *ku'auhau*) who were themselves *ali'i*. Rank passed from both father and mother, and custom dictated that the first mating of an *ali'i* be with a person of equal status.

A *kahuna* was a highly skilled person whose advice was sought before any major project was undertaken, such as building a house, hollowing a canoe log, or even offering a prayer. The *mo'o kahuna* were the priests of Ku and Lono, and they were in charge of praying and following rituals. They were very powerful *ali'i* and kept strict secrets and laws concerning their various functions.

Besides this priesthood of *kahuna,* there were other *kahuna* who were not *ali'i* but commoners. The two most important were the healers *(kahuna lapa'au)* and the black magicians *(kahuna 'ana'ana),* who could pray a person to death. The *kahuna lapa'au* had a marvelous pharmacopoeia of herbs and spices that could cure over 250 diseases common to the Hawaiians. The *kahuna 'ana'ana* could be hired to cast a love spell over a person or cause his or her untimely death. They seldom had to send out a reminder for payment!

The common people were called the *maka'ainana,* "the people of land"—farmers, artisans, and fishermen. The land they lived on was owned by the *ali'i,* but they were not bound to it. If the local *ali'i* was cruel or unfair, the *maka'ainana* had the right to leave and reside on another's lands. The *maka'ainana* mostly loved their local *ali'i* much like a child loves a parent, and the feeling was reciprocal. *Maka'ainana* who lived close to the *ali'i* and could be counted on as warriors in times of trouble were called *kanaka no lua kaua,* "a man for the heat of battle." They were treated with greater favor than those who lived in the backcountry, *kanaka no hi'i kua,* whose lesser standing opened them up to discrimination and cruelty. All *maka'ainana* formed extended families called *'ohana* who usually lived on the same section of land, called *ahupua'a.* Those farmers who lived inland would barter their produce with the fishermen who lived on the shore, and thus all shared equally in the bounty of land and sea.

A special group called *kauwa* was a landless, untouchable caste confined to living on reservations. Their origins were obviously Polynesian, but they appeared to be descendants of castaways who had survived and become perhaps the aboriginals of Hawaii before the main migrations. It was *kapu* for anyone to go onto *kauwa* lands, and doing so meant instant death. If a human sacrifice was needed, the *kahuna* would simply summon a *kauwa,* who had no recourse but to mutely comply. To this day, to call someone *kauwa,* which now supposedly means only servant, is still considered a fight-provoking insult.

Kapu and Day-to-Day Life

Occasionally there were horrible wars, but mostly the people lived quiet and ordered lives based on a strict caste society and the *kapu* system. Famine was known, but only on a regional level, and the population was kept in check by birth control, crude abortions, and the distasteful practice of infanticide, especially of baby girls. The Hawaiians were absolutely loving and nurturing parents under most circumstances and would even take in a *hanai* (adopted child or oldster), a lovely practice that lingers to this day.

A strict division of labor existed among men and women. Men were the only ones permitted to have anything to do with taro: this foodstuff was so sacred that there were a greater number of *kapu* concerning taro than concerning man himself. Men pounded poi and served it to the women. Men also were the fishermen and the builders of houses, canoes, irrigation ditches, and walls. Women tended to other gardens and shoreline fishing and were responsible for making tapa cloth. The entire family lived in the common house called the *hale noa.*

Certain things were *kapu* between the sexes. Primarily, women could not enter the *mua* (men's eating house), nor could they eat with men. Certain foods, such as pork, coconut, red fish, and bananas, were forbidden to women, and it was *kapu* for a man to have intercourse before going fishing, engaging in battle, or attending a religious ceremony. Young boys lived with the women until they underwent a circumcision rite called *pule ipu.* After this was performed, they were required to keep the *kapu* of men. A true Hawaiian settlement required a minimum of five huts: the men's eating hut; women's menstruation hut; women's eating hut; communal sleeping hut; and prayer hut. Without these five separate structures, Hawaiian "society" could not happen, since the *i'a kapu* (forbidden eating between men and women) could not be observed.

Ali'i could also declare a *kapu* and often did so. Certain lands or fishing areas were temporarily made *kapu* so that they could revitalize. Even today, it is *kapu* for anyone to remove all the *'opihi* (a type of limpet) from a rock. The great King Kamehameha I even placed a *kapu* on the body of his notoriously unfaithful child bride, Ka'ahumanu. It didn't work! The greatest *kapu (kapu moe)* was afforded to the highest ranking *ali'i:* anyone coming into their presence had to prostrate themselves. Lesser ranking *ali'i* were afforded the *kapu noho:* lessers had to sit or kneel in their presence. Commoners could not let their shadows fall upon an *ali'i,* nor enter an *ali'i*'s house except through a special door. Breaking a *kapu* meant immediate death.

The Causes of Decline

Less than 100 years after Captain Cook's arrival, King Kalakaua found himself with only 48,000 Hawaiian subjects. Wherever the king went, he would beseech his people, *"Ho'oulu lahui"*—"Increase the race"—but it was already too late. It was as if nature herself had turned her back on these once-proud people. Many of their marriages were barren, and in 1874, when only 1,400 children were born, a full 75 percent died in infancy. The Hawaiians could do nothing but watch as their race faded from existence.

The ecological system of Hawaii has always been exceptionally fragile, and this included its people. When the first whites arrived they found a great people who were large, strong, and virile. But when it came to fighting off the most minor diseases, the Hawaiians proved as delicate as hothouse flowers. To exacerbate the situation, the Hawaiians were totally uninhibited toward sexual intercourse between willing partners, and they engaged in it openly and with abandon. Unfortunately, the sailors who arrived were full of syphilis and gonorrhea. The Hawaiian women brought these diseases home, and, given the nature of Hawaiian society at the time, the diseases spread like wildfire. By the time the missionaries came in 1820 and helped to halt the unbridled fornication, they estimated the native population at only 140,000—less than half of what it had been—only 40 years after initial contact! In the next 50 years measles, mumps, influenza, and tuberculosis further ravaged the people. Furthermore, Hawaiian men were excellent sailors, and it's estimated that during the whaling years at least 25 percent of all able-bodied Hawaiian men sailed away, never to return.

But the coup de grace that really ended the Hawaiian race as such was that racial newcomers to the islands were attracted to the Hawaiians and the Hawaiians were in turn attracted to them. With so many interracial marriages, the Hawaiians literally bred themselves out of existence. By 1910, there were still twice as many full-blooded Hawaiians as mixed-bloods, but by 1940 mixed-blooded Hawaiians were the fastest-growing group, and full-blooded the fastest declining.

Hawaiians Today

Many of the Hawaiians who moved to the cities became more and more disenfranchised. Their folk society stressed openness and a giving nature but downplayed the individual and the ownership of private property. These cultural traits made them easy targets for users and schemers until they finally became either apathetic or angry. Most surveys reveal that although Hawaiians number only 13 percent of the population, they account for almost 50 percent of the financially destitute families and also about half of all arrests and illegitimate births. Ni'ihau, a privately owned island, is home to about 160 pure-blooded Hawaiians, representing the largest concentration of them, per capita, in the islands. The Robinson family, which owns the island, restricts visitors to invited guests only.

The second-largest concentration is on Moloka'i, where 2,700 Hawaiians, living mostly on 40-acre *kuleana* of Hawaiian Home Lands, make up 40 percent of that island's population. The majority of mixed-blooded Hawaiians, 240,000 or so, live on O'ahu, where they are particularly strong in the hotel and entertainment fields. People of Hawaiian extraction are still a delight to meet, and anyone so lucky as to be befriended by one long regards this friendship as the highlight of his or her travels. The Hawaiians have always given their *aloha* freely to all the peoples of the world, and it is we who must acknowledge this precious gift.

THE CHINESE

Next to Yankees from New England, the Chinese are the oldest migrant group in Hawaii, and their influence has far outshone their meager numbers. They brought to Hawaii, along with their individuality, Confucianism, Taoism, and Buddhism, although many have long since become Christians. The Chinese population, at 56,000, makes up only 5 percent of the state's total, and the vast majority reside on O'ahu. As an ethnic group they account for the least amount of crime, the highest per capita income, and a disproportionate number of professionals.

The First Chinese

No one knows his name, but an unknown Chinese immigrant is credited with being the first person in Hawaii to refine sugar. This Asian wanderer tried his hand at crude refining on Lana'i in 1802. Fifty years later the sugar plantations desperately needed workers, and the first Chinese brought to Hawaii under the newly passed Masters and Servants Act were 195 coolies from Xiamen, who arrived in 1852. These conscripts were contracted for three to five years and given $3 per month plus room and board. This was for 12 hours a day, six days a week, and even in 1852 these wages were the pits. The Chinese almost always left the plantations the minute their contracts expired. They went into business for themselves and promptly monopolized the restaurant and small-shop trades.

The Chinese Niche

Although many people in Hawaii considered all Chinese ethnically the same, they were actually quite different. The majority came from Guangdong Province in southern China. They were two distinct ethnic groups: the Punti made up 75 percent of the immigrants, and the Hakka made up the remainder. In China, they remained separate from each other, never mixing; in Hawaii, they mixed out of necessity. For one thing, hardly any Chinese women came over at first, and the ones who followed were at a premium and gladly accepted as wives, regardless of ethnic background. The Chinese were also one of the first groups who willingly intermarried with the Hawaiians, from whom they gained a reputation for being exceptionally caring spouses.

The Chinese accepted the social order and kept a low profile. For example, during the turbulent labor movements of the 1930s and 1940s in Hawaii, the Chinese community produced not one labor leader, radical intellectual, or left-wing politician. When Hawaii became a state, one of the two senators elected was Hiram Fong, a racially mixed Chinese. Since statehood, the Chinese community has carried on business as usual as they continue to rise both economically and socially.

THE JAPANESE

Most scholars believe that (inevitably) a few Japanese castaways floated to Hawaii long before Captain Cook arrived, and they might have introduced the iron with which the islanders seemed to be familiar before white explorers arrived. The first official arrivals from Japan were ambassadors sent by the Japanese shogun to negotiate in Washington; they stopped en route at Honolulu in March 1860. But it was as plantation workers that the Japanese were brought en masse to the islands. A small group arrived in 1868, and mass migration started in 1885.

In 1886, because of famine, the Japanese government allowed farmers mainly from southern Honshu, Kyushu, and Okinawa to emigrate. Among these were members of Japan's little-talked-about untouchable caste, called *eta* or *burakumin* in Japan and *chorinbo* in Hawaii. They gratefully seized this opportunity to better their lot, an impossibility in Japan. The first Japanese migrants were almost all men. Between 1897 and 1908 migration was steady, with about 70 percent of the immigrants being men. Afterwards, migration slowed because of a "gentlemen's agreement," a euphemism for racism against the "yellow peril." By 1900 there were over 60,000 Japanese in the islands, constituting the largest ethnic group.

AJAs, Americans of Japanese Ancestry

Parents of most Japanese children born before World War II were *issei* (first generation), who considered themselves apart from other Americans and clung to the notion of "we Japanese." Their children, the *nisei,* or second generation, were a different matter altogether. In one generation they had become Americans, and they put into practice the high Japanese virtues of obligation, duty, and loyalty to the homeland; that homeland was now unquestionably the United States. After Pearl Harbor was bombed, the FBI kept close tabs on the Japanese community, and the menace of the "enemy within" prompted the decision to place Hawaii under martial law for the duration of the war. It has since been noted that not a single charge of espionage or sabotage was ever reported against the Japanese community in Hawaii during the war.

AJAs as GIs

Although Japanese had formed a battalion during World War I, they were insulted by being considered unacceptable American soldiers in World War II. Some Japanese Americans volunteered to serve in labor battalions, and because of their flawless work and loyalty, it was decided to put out a call for a few hundred volunteers to form a combat unit. Over 10,000 signed up! AJAs formed two distinguished units in World War II: the 100th Infantry Battalion and later the 442nd Regimental Combat Team. They landed in Italy at Salerno and even fought from Guadalcanal to Okinawa. They distinguished themselves by becoming the most decorated unit in American military history.

The AJAs Return

Many returning AJAs took advantage of the GI Bill and received college educations. The "Big Five" corporations for the first time accepted former AJA officers as executives, and the old order was changed. Many Japanese became involved with Hawaiian politics, and the first elected to Congress was Daniel Inouye, who had lost an arm fighting in World War II. Hawaii's past governor, George Ariyoshi, elected in 1974, was the country's first Japanese American to reach such a high office. Most Japanese, even as they climb the economic ladder, tend to remain Democrats.

Today, one out of every two political offices in Hawaii is held by a Japanese American. In one of those weird quirks of fate, it is now the Hawaiian Japanese who are accused by other ethnic groups of engaging in unfair political practices—nepotism and reverse discrimination. Many of these accusations against AJAs are undoubtedly motivated by jealousy, but the AJAs' record in social fairness issues is not without blemish; true to their custom of family loyalty, they do stick together.

There are now 290,000 people in Hawaii of Japanese ancestry (and another 100,000 of mixed Japanese blood), nearly one-quarter of the state's population. They are the least likely of any ethnic group in Hawaii to marry outside of their group—especially the men—and they enjoy a higher-than-average standard of living.

CAUCASIANS

White people have a distinction separating them from all other ethnic groups in Hawaii: they are lumped together as one. You can be anything from a Protestant Norwegian dockworker to a Greek Orthodox shipping tycoon, but if your skin is white, in Hawaii you're a *haole.* What's more, you could have arrived at Waikiki from Missoula, Montana, in the last 24 hours, or your *kama'aina* family can go back five generations, but, again, if you're white, you're a *haole.*

The word *haole* has a floating connotation that depends upon the spirit in which it's used. It can mean everything from a derisive "honky" or "cracker" to nothing more than "white person." The exact Hawaiian meaning is clouded, but some say it meant "a man of no background," because white men couldn't chant a genealogical *koihonua* telling the Hawaiians who they were. The word eventually evolved to mean "foreign white man" and, today, simply "white person."

White History

Next to Hawaiians themselves, white people have the oldest stake in Hawaii. They've been there as settlers in earnest since the missionaries of the 1820s and were established long before any other migrant group. From the 19th century until statehood, old *haole* families owned and controlled mostly everything, and although they were generally benevolent, philanthropic, and paternalistic, they were also racist. They were established *kama'aina* families, many of whom made up the boards of the Big Five corporations or owned huge plantations and formed an elite social circle that was closed to the outside. Many managed to find mates from among close family acquaintances.

Their paternalism, which they accepted with grave responsibility, at first only extended to the Hawaiians, who saw them as replacing their own *ali'i.* Asians were considered primarily instruments of production. These supremacist attitudes tended to drag on in Hawaii until quite recent times and are today responsible for the sometimes sour relations between white and nonwhite people in the islands. Today, all white people are resented to a certain degree because of these past acts, even though they personally were in no way involved.

White Plantation Workers

In the 1880s the white landowners looked around and felt surrounded and outnumbered by Asians, so they tried to import white people for plantation work. None of their schemes seemed to work out. Europeans were accustomed to a much higher wage scale and better living conditions than were provided on the plantations. Although only workers and not considered the equals of the ruling elite, they still were expected to act like a special class. They were treated preferentially, which meant higher wages for the same jobs performed by Asians. Some of the imported workers included: 600 Scandinavians in 1881; 1,400 Germans 1881–1885; 400 Poles 1897–1898; and 2,400 Russians 1909–1912. Many proved troublesome, like the Poles and Russians, who staged strikes after only months on the job. Many quickly moved to the Mainland. A contingency of Scots, who first came as mule skinners, did become successful plantation managers and supervisors. The Germans and Scandinavians were well received and climbed the social ladder rapidly, becoming professionals and skilled workers.

The Depression years, not as economically bad in Hawaii as in the continental United States, brought many Mainland whites seeking opportunity, mostly from the South and the West. These new people tended to be even more racist toward brown-skinned people and Asians than the *kama'aina haole,* and they made matters worse. They also competed more intensely for jobs. The racial tension generated during this period came to a head in 1932 with the infamous Massie Rape Case, in which five local men were accused on circumstantial evidence of raping the wife of a naval officer. The five were finally acquitted, but Thomas Massie and his mother-in-law, with the assistance of several others, killed one of the boys. Found guilty at their trial, these whites served just one hour for the murder, and this is considered one of the greatest miscarriages of justice in American history.

The Portuguese

The last time anyone looked, Portugal was still attached to the European continent, but for some anomalous reason the Portuguese weren't considered *haole* in Hawaii for the longest time. About 12,000 arrived between 1878 and 1887, and another 6,000 came between 1906 and 1913. Accompanied during this period by

8,000 Spanish, they were considered one and the same. Most of the Portuguese were illiterate peasants from Madeira and the Azores, and the Spanish hailed from Andalusia. They were very well received, and because they were white but not *haole,* they made a perfect "buffer" ethnic group. Committed to staying in Hawaii, they rose to be skilled workers—the *luna* class on the plantations. However, they de-emphasized education and became very racist toward Asians, regarding them as a threat to their job security.

By 1920, the 27,000 Portuguese made up 11 percent of the population. After that they tended to blend with the other ethnic groups and weren't counted separately. Portuguese men tended to marry within their ethnic group, but a good portion of Portuguese women married other white men and became closer to the *haole* group, while another large portion chose Hawaiian mates and grew further away. Although they didn't originate pidgin English (see *Language* in this chapter), the unique melodious quality of their native tongue did give pidgin that certain lilt it has today. Also, the ukulele was closely patterned after the *cavaquinho,* a Portuguese stringed folk instrument.

The White Population

Today Caucasians make up the largest racial group in the islands at about 25 percent of the population. With mixed white blood, that number jumps to nearly 40 percent. They are spread evenly throughout Kaua'i, O'ahu, Maui, and the Big Island, with much smaller percentages on Moloka'i and Lana'i. On the Big Island, there are concentrations in Hilo, North Kona, South Kohala, and Waimea. In terms of pure numbers, the white population is the fastest growing in the islands because most people settling in Hawaii are white Americans predominantly from the West Coast.

FILIPINOS AND OTHERS

The Filipinos who came to Hawaii brought high hopes of amassing personal fortunes and returning home as rich heroes; for most it was a dream that never came true. Filipinos had been American nationals ever since the Spanish-American War of 1898 and as such weren't subject to immigration laws that curtailed the importation of other Asian workers at the turn of the 20th century. The first to arrive were 15 families in 1906, but a large number came in 1924 as strikebreakers. The majority were illiterate peasants called Ilocanos from the northern Philippines; about 10 percent were Visayans from the central cities. The Visayans were not as hardworking or thrifty but were much more sophisticated. From the first, Filipinos were looked down upon by all the other immigrant groups and were considered particularly uncouth by the Japanese. The value they placed on education was the least of any group, and even by 1930 only about half could speak rudimentary English, the majority remaining illiterate. They were billeted in the worst housing, performed the most menial jobs, and were the last hired and first fired.

One big difference between Filipinos and other groups was that the men brought no Filipino women to marry, so they clung to the idea of returning home. In 1930 there were 30,000 men and only 360 women. This hopeless situation led to a great deal of prostitution and homosexuality; many of these terribly lonely bachelors would feast and drink on weekends and engage in their gruesome but exciting pastime of cockfighting on Sundays. When some did manage to find wives, their mates were inevitably part Hawaiian. Filipino workers continued to be imported, although sporadically, until 1946, so even today there are a few old Filipino bachelors who never managed to get home, and the Sunday cockfights remain a way of life.

The Filipinos constitute 14 percent of Hawaii's population, some 170,000 individuals, with almost 75 percent living on O'ahu. Some 275,000 are of mixed Filipino blood. Many visitors to Hawaii mistake Filipinos for Hawaiians because of their dark skin, and this is a minor irritant to both groups. Some streetwise Filipinos even claim to be Hawaiians, because being Hawaiian is "in" and goes over well with the tourists, especially the young women tourists. For the most part, these people are hardworking, dependable laborers who do tough work for little recognition. They remain low on the social totem pole and have not yet organized politically to stand up for their rights.

Other Groups

About 10 percent of Hawaii's population is a conglomerate of other ethnic groups. Of these, one of the largest and fastest growing is Korean, with 25,000 people. About 8,000 Koreans came to Hawaii from 1903 until 1905, when their government halted emigration. During the same period about 6,000 Puerto Ricans arrived, and today about 30,000 consider themselves a Puerto Rican mix. There were also two attempts made in the 1800s to import other Polynesians to strengthen the dying Hawaiian race, but they were failures. In 1869 only 126 central Polynesian natives could be lured to Hawaii, and from 1878 to 1885 2,500 Gilbert Islanders arrived. Both groups became immediately disenchanted with Hawaii. They pined away for their own islands and departed for home as soon as possible.

Today, however, 16,000 Samoans have settled in Hawaii, and with more on the way they are one of the fastest-growing minorities in the state. For unknown reasons, Samoans and native Hawaiians get along extremely poorly and have the worst racial tensions and animosity of any groups. The Samoans ostensibly should represent the archetypal Polynesians that the Hawaiians are seeking, but it doesn't work that way. Samoans are criticized by Hawaiians for their hot tempers, lingering feuds, and petty jealousies. They're clannish and are often the butt of "dumb" jokes. This racism seems especially ridiculous, but that's the way it is.

Just to add a bit more exotic spice to the stew, there are about 22,000 blacks, 3,500 Native Americans, 4,000 Tongans, 7,000 other Pacific Islanders, and 8,000 Vietnamese refugees living on the islands.

Culture

RELIGION

The Lord saw fit to keep His island paradise secret from humans for a few million years, but once we finally arrived we were awfully thankful. Hawaii sometimes seems like a floating tabernacle; everywhere you look there's a church, temple, shrine, or *heiau*. The islands are either a very holy place, or there's a powerful lot of sinning going on that would require so many houses of prayer. Actually, it's just America's "right to worship" concept fully employed in microcosm. All the peoples who came to Hawaii brought their own forms of devotion. The Polynesian Hawaiians praised the primordial creators, Wakea and Papa, from whom their pantheon of animistically inspired gods sprang. To a modern world these old gods would never do. Unfortunately for the old gods, there were too many of them, and belief in them was looked upon as superstition, the folly of semicivilized pagans. So the famous missionaries of the 1820s brought Congregational Christianity and the "true path" to heaven.

Inconveniently, the Catholics, Mormons, Reformed Mormons, Adventists, Episcopalians, Unitarians, Christian Scientists, Lutherans, Baptists, Jehovah's Witnesses, Salvation Army, and every other major and minor denomination of Christianity that followed in their wake brought their own brands of enlightenment and never quite agreed with each other. Chinese and Japanese immigrants established the major sects of Buddhism, Confucianism, Taoism, and Shintoism. Allah is praised, the Torah is chanted in Jewish synagogues, and nirvana is available at a variety of Hindu temples. If the spirit moves you, a Hare Krishna devotee will be glad to point you in the right direction and give you a "free" flower for only a dollar or two. If the world is still too much with you, you might find peace at a Church of Scientology, or meditate at a Kundalini yoga institute, or perhaps find relief at a local assembly of Baha'i. Anyway, rejoice, because in Hawaii you'll not only find paradise, you may even find salvation.

Hawaiian Beliefs

The Polynesian Hawaiians worshiped nature. They saw its forces manifested in a multiplicity of forms to which they ascribed godlike powers, and they based daily life on this animistic philosophy. Handpicked and specially trained storytellers chanted the exploits of the gods. These ancient tales, kept alive in a special oral tradition called *mo'olelo,* were recited only by day. Entranced listeners encircled the chanter; in respect for the gods and in fear of their wrath, they were forbidden to move once the tale was begun. This was serious business, during which a person's life could be at stake. It was not like the telling of *ka'ao,* which were simple fictions, tall tales, and yarns of ancient heroes related for amusement and to pass the long nights. Any object, animate or inanimate, could be a god. All could be infused with mana, especially a dead body or respected ancestor.

'Ohana had personal family gods called *'aumakua* on whom they called in times of danger or strife. There were children of gods called *kupua* who were thought to live among humans and were distinguished either for their beauty and strength or for their ugliness and terror. It was told that processions of dead *ali'i,* called "Marchers of the Night," wandered through the land of the living, and unless you were properly protected it could mean death if they looked upon you. There were simple ghosts known as *akua lapu* who merely frightened people. Forests, waterfalls, trees, springs, and a thousand forms of nature were the manifestations of *akua li'i,* "little spirits" who could be invoked at any time for help or protection. It made no difference who or what you were in old Hawaii; the gods were ever-present and took a direct and active role in your life.

Behind all of these beliefs was an innate sense of natural balance and order. It could be interpreted as positive-negative, yin-yang, plus-minus, life-death, light-dark, whatever, but the main idea was that everything had its opposite. The time of darkness when only the gods lived was *po.* When the great gods descended to the earth and created light, this was *ao* and humanity was born. All of these *mo'olelo* are part of *The Kumulipo,* the great chant that records the Hawaiian version of creation. From the time the gods descended and touched the earth at Ku Moku on Lana'i, the genealogies were kept. Unlike the Bible, these included the noble families of female as well as male *ali'i.*

Heiau and Idols

A *heiau* is a Hawaiian temple. The basic *heiau* was a masterfully built and fitted rectangular stone wall that varied in size from about as big as a basketball court to as big as a football field. Once the restraining outer walls were built, the interior was backfilled with smaller stones and the top dressing was expertly laid and then rolled, perhaps with a log, to form a pavementlike surface. All that remains of Hawaii's many *heiau* are the stone platforms or walls. The buildings upon them, made from perishable wood, leaves, and grass, have long since disappeared.

Some *heiau* were dreaded temples where human sacrifices were made. Tradition says that this barbaric custom began at Waha'ula Heiau on the Big Island in the 12th century and was introduced by a ferocious Tahitian priest named Pa'ao. Other *heiau,* such as Pu'uhonua o Honaunau, also on the Big Island, were temples of refuge where the weak, widowed, orphaned, and vanquished could find safety and sanctuary.

The Hawaiian people worshiped gods who took the form of idols fashioned from wood, feathers, or stone. The eyes were made from shells, and until these were inlaid, the idol was dormant. The hair used was often human hair, and the arms and legs were usually flexed. The mouth was either gaping or formed a wide figure-eight lying on its side, and more likely than not was lined with glistening dog teeth. Small

THE STRIFES OF MAUI

Of all the heroes and mythological figures of Polynesia, Maui is the best known. His "strifes" are like the great Greek epics, and they make excellent tales of courage and action that elders loved to relate to youngsters around the evening fire. Maui was abandoned by his mother, Hina of Fire, when he was an infant. She wrapped him in her hair and cast him upon the sea where she expected him to die, but he lived and returned home to become her favorite. She knew then that he was a born hero and had strength far beyond that of ordinary mortals. His first exploit was to lift the sky. In those days the sky hung so low that humans had to crawl around on all fours. A seductive young woman approached Maui and asked him to use his great strength to lift the sky. In fine heroic fashion, the big boy agreed, if the beautiful woman would euphemistically "give him a drink from her gourd." He then obliged her by lifting the sky, and he might even have made the earth move for her once or twice.

The territory of humanity was small at that time. Maui decided that more land was needed, so he conspired to "fish up islands." He descended into the land of the dead and petitioned an ancestress to fashion him a hook from her jawbone. She obliged and created the mythical hook, *Manai ikalani*. Maui then secured a sacred *'alae* bird, which he intended to use for bait, and bid his brothers to paddle him far out to sea. When he arrived at the deepest spot, he lowered *Manai ikalani*, baited with the sacred bird, and his sister, Hina of the Sea, placed it into the mouth of "Old One Tooth," who held the land fast to the bottom of the waters. Maui then exhorted his brothers to row but warned them not to look back. They strained at the oars with all their might and slowly a great land mass arose. One brother, overcome by curiosity, looked back, and when he did so, the land shattered into all of the islands of Polynesia.

Maui still desired to serve humanity. People were without fire, the secret of which was held by the sacred *'alae* birds, who learned it from Maui's far-distant mother. Hina of Fire gave Maui her burning fingernails, but he oafishly kept dropping them into streams until all had fizzled out and he had totally irritated his generous progenitor. She pursued him, trying to burn him to a cinder; Maui chanted for rain to put out her scorching fires. When she saw that they were being quenched, she hid her fire in the barks of special trees and informed the mud hens where they could be found, but first made them promise never to tell humans. Maui knew of this and captured a mud hen, threatening to wring its scrawny, traitorous neck unless it gave up the secret. The bird tried trickery and told Maui first to rub together the stems of sugarcane, then banana, and even taro. None worked, and Maui's determined rubbing is why these plants have hollow roots today.

Finally, with Maui's hands tightening around the mud hen's gizzard, the bird confessed that fire could be found in the *hau* tree and also the sandalwood, which Maui named *'ili aha* (fire bark) in its honor. He then rubbed all the feathers off the mud hen's head for being so deceitful, which is why their crowns are featherless today.

Maui's greatest deed, however, was in snaring the sun and exacting a promise that it would go slower across the heavens. The people complained that there were not enough daylight hours to fish or farm. Maui's mother could not dry her tapa cloth because the sun rose and set so quickly. She asked her son to help. Maui went to his blind grandmother, who lived on the slopes of Haleakala and was responsible for cooking the sun's bananas, which he ate every day in passing. She told him to personally weave 16 strong ropes with nooses from his sister's hair. Some say these came from her head, but other versions insist that it was no doubt Hina's pubic hair that had the power to hold the sun god. Maui positioned himself with the rope, and as each of the 16 rays of the sun came across Haleakala, he snared them until the sun was defenseless and had to bargain for his life. Maui agreed to free him if he promised to go more slowly. From that time forward the sun moved more slowly and Haleakala (The House of the Sun) became his home.

© ROBERT NILSEN

Some aspects of the old Hawaiian religious culture still remain today, and offerings are still occasionally laid at the base of *heiau* altars, like here at Ke'eku Heiau on Kawa Bay in Ka'u.

figures made of woven basketry were expertly covered with feathers. Red and yellow feathers were favorites taken from specific birds by men whose only work was to roam the forests in search of them.

Ghosts

The Hawaiians had countless superstitions and ghost legends, but two of the more interesting involve astral travel of the soul and the "Marchers of the Night." The soul, *'uhane,* was considered by Hawaiians to be totally free and independent of its body, *kino.* The soul could separate, leaving the body asleep or very drowsy. This disembodied soul *(hihi'o)* could visit people and was considered quite different from a *lapu* or ordinary spirit of a dead person. A *kahuna* could immediately recognize if a person's *'uhane* had left the body, and a special wreath was placed upon the head to protect the person and to facilitate reentry.

If confronted by an apparition, you could test to see if it was indeed dead or still alive by placing leaves of an *'ape* plant upon the ground. If the leaves tore when they were walked upon, the spirit was merely human, but if they remained intact it was a ghost. Or you could sneak up and startle the vision, and if it disappeared it was a ghost. Also, if no reflection of the face appeared when it drank water from an offered calabash, it was a ghost. Unfortunately, there were no instructions to follow once you had determined that you indeed had a ghost on your hands. Maybe it was better not to know! Some people would sprinkle salt and water around their houses, but this kept away evil spirits, not ghosts.

There are also many stories of *kahuna* restoring a soul to a dead body. First they had to catch it and keep it in a gourd. They then placed beautiful tapa and fragrant flowers and herbs about the body to make it more enticing. Slowly, they would coax the soul out of the gourd until it reentered the body through the big toe.

Death Marchers

One inexplicable phenomenon that many people

attest to is *ka huaka'i o ka po,* "Marchers of the Night." This march of the dead is fatal if you gaze upon it, unless one of the marchers happens to be a friendly ancestor who will protect you. The peak time for "the march" is 7:30 P.M.–2 A.M. The marchers can be dead *ali'i* and warriors, the gods themselves, or the lesser *'aumakua.* When the *'aumakua* march there is usually chanting and music. *Ali'i* marches are more somber. The entire procession, lit by torches, often stops at the house of a relative and might even carry him or her away. When the gods themselves march, there is often thunder, lightning, and heavy seas. The sky is lit with torches, and they walk six abreast, three gods and three goddesses. If you get in the way of a march, remove your clothing and prostrate yourself. If the marching gods or *'aumakua* happen to be ones to which you prayed, you might be spared. If it's a march of the *ali'i,* you might make it if you lie face upward and feign death. If you *do* see a death march, the last thing that you'll worry about is lying naked on the ground looking ridiculous.

Missionaries

In Hawaii, when you say "missionaries," it's taken for granted you're referring to the small and determined band of Congregationalists who arrived aboard the brig *Thaddeus* in 1820, and the follow-up groups, called "companies" or "packets," that reinforced them. They were sent from Boston by the American Board of Commissioners for Foreign Missions (ABCFM), which learned of the supposed sad and godless plight of the Hawaiian people through returning sailors and especially through the few Hawaiians who had come to America to study.

The person most instrumental in bringing the missionaries to Hawaii was a young man named Opukaha'ia. He was an orphan befriended by a ship's captain and taken to New England, where he studied theology. Obsessed with the desire to return home and save his people from certain damnation, Opukaha'ia wrote accounts of life in Hawaii that were published and widely read. These accounts were directly responsible for the formation of the Pioneer Company to the Sandwich Islands Missions in 1819. Unfortunately, Opukaha'ia died in New England from typhus the year before they left.

The first missionaries had the straightforward task of bringing the Hawaiians out of paganism and into Christianity and civilization. They met with terrible hostility—not from the natives, but from the sea captains and traders who were very happy with the open debauchery and wanton whoremongering that was status quo in the Hawaii of 1820. Many direct confrontations between these two factions even included the cannonading of missionaries' homes by American sea captains who were denied the customary visits of island women, thanks to meddlesome "do-gooders." The most memorable of these incidents involved "Mad Jack" Percival, the captain of the USS *Dolphin,* who bombed a church in Lahaina to show his rancor. The truth of the situation was much closer to the sentiments of James Jarves, who wrote, "The missionary was a far more useful and agreeable man than his Catholicism would indicate; and the trader was not so bad a man as the missionary would make him out to be." The missionaries' primary aim might have been conversion, but the most fortuitous by-product was education, which raised the consciousness of every Hawaiian, regardless of religious affiliation. In 40 short years Hawaii was considered a civilized nation well on its way into the modern world, and the American Board of Missions officially ended its support in 1863.

Non-Christians

By the beginning of the 20th century, both Shintoism and Buddhism, brought by the Japanese and Chinese, were firmly established in Hawaii. The first official Buddhist temple was Hongpa Hongwanji, established on O'ahu in 1889. All the denominations of Buddhism account for 17 percent of the island's religious total, and there are about 50,000 Shintoists. The Hindu religion has perhaps 2,000 adherents, and the Hindu Temple on Kaua'i is strong and vigorous with one of the largest stone temple structures outside of India. About the same number of Jewish people live throughout Hawaii with only one synagogue, Temple Emanu-El, on O'ahu. The largest number of people in Hawaii (300,000) remain unaffiliated, and about 10,000 people are in new religious movements and lesser-known faiths such as Baha'i and Unitarianism.

LANGUAGE

Hawaii is part of America and people speak English there, but that's not the whole story. If you turn on the TV to catch the evening news, you'll hear "Walter Cronkite" English, unless of course you happen to tune in to a Japanese-language broadcast designed for tourists from that country. You can easily pick up a Chinese-language newspaper or groove to the music on a Filipino radio station, but let's not confuse the issue. All your needs and requests at airports, car-rental agencies, restaurants, hotels, or wherever you happen to travel will be completely understood, as well as answered, in English. However, when you happen to overhear islanders speaking, what they're saying will sound somewhat familiar but you won't be able to pick up all the words, and the beat and melody of the language will be noticeably different.

Hawaii—like New England, the Deep South, and the Midwest—has its own unmistakable linguistic regionalism. All the ethnic peoples who make up Hawaii have enriched the English spoken there with words, expressions, and subtle shades of meaning that are commonly used and understood throughout the islands. The greatest influence on English has come from the Hawaiian language itself, and words such as "aloha," "hula," "lu'au," and "lei" are familiarly used and understood by most Americans.

Other migrant peoples, especially the Chinese, Japanese, and Portuguese, influenced the local dialect to such an extent that the simplified plantation lingo they spoke has become known as "pidgin." A fun and enriching part of the "island experience" is picking up a few words of Hawaiian and pidgin. English is the official language of the state, business, education, and perhaps even the mind; but pidgin is the language of the people, the emotions, and life, while Hawaiian (also an official language of the state, but used "only as provided by law") remains the language of the heart and the soul.

NOTE ON HAWAIIAN DIACRITICS

Aside from the five vowels and seven consonants, written Hawaiian uses two diacritical marks to distinguish spoken sounds. These are the *'okina,* or glottal stop, written as a reverse apostrophe (') before a vowel; and the macron *kahako,* a short line written over a vowel indicating that the vowel is stressed. For technical reasons, the *kahako* is not used in this book. The *'okina* is used in Hawaiian place names, names of historical persons, and ordinary Hawaiian words, where appropriate. It is not used in business names if the business itself does not use this symbol. The name Hawai'i, written with an *'okina* refers to the island of Hawai'i, the Big Island; without the *'okina,* it refers to the entire state. The word Hawaiian, written without the glottal stop, refers to both the Polynesian inhabitants of the islands before Western contact and to those people of all races who currently reside in the state.

Note: Many Hawaiian words are commonly used in English, appear in English dictionaries, and therefore would ordinarily be subject to the rules of English grammar. The Hawaiian language, however, does not pluralize nouns by adding an "s"; the singular and plural are differentiated in context. For purposes of this book, and to highlight the Hawaiian culture, the Hawaiian style of pluralization will be followed for common Hawaiian words. The following are some examples of plural Hawaiian nouns treated this way in this book: *haole* (not *haoles*), *kahuna,* lei, lu'au, and *nene.*

Pidgin

The dictionary definition of pidgin is a simplified language with a rudimentary grammar used as a means of communication between people speaking different languages. Hawaiian pidgin is a little more complicated than that. It had its roots during the plantation days of the 19th century when white owners and *luna* (foremen) had to communicate with recently arrived Chinese, Japanese, and Portuguese laborers. It evolved as a simple language of the here and now, primarily concerned with the necessary functions of working, eating, and sleeping. It has an economical noun-verb-object structure (although not necessarily in that order).

Hawaiian words make up most of pidgin's non-English vocabulary. It includes a good smattering of Chinese, Japanese, and Samoan; the distinctive rising inflection is provided by the melodious Mediterranean lilt of the Portuguese. Pidgin is not a stagnant language. It's kept alive by hip new words introduced by cool people and especially by slang words introduced by teenagers. It's a colorful English, like "jive" spoken by American blacks, and is as regionally unique as the speech of Cajuns in rural Louisiana bayous. *Maka'ainana* of all socio-ethnic backgrounds can at least understand pidgin. Most islanders are proud of it, while some consider it a low-class jargon. The Hawaiian House of Representatives has given pidgin an official sanction, and most people feel that it adds a real local style and should be preserved.

Pidgin is first learned at school, where all students, regardless of background, are exposed to it. The pidgin spoken by young people today is "fo' real" different from that of their parents. It's no longer only plantation talk but has moved to the streets and picked up some sophistication. At one time there was an academic movement to exterminate it, but that idea died away with the same thinking that insisted on making left-handed people write with their right hand. It is strange, however, that pidgin has become the unofficial language of Hawaii's grassroots movement, when it actually began as a white owners' language that was used to supplant Hawaiian and all the languages brought to the islands.

Although hip young *haole* use pidgin all the time, it has gained the connotation of being the language of the nonwhite locals and is part of the "us against them" way of thinking. All local people, *haole* or not, do consider pidgin their own island language and don't really like it when it's used by *malihini* (newcomers). If you're in the islands long enough, you don't have to bother learning pidgin; it'll learn you. There's a book sold all over the islands called *Pidgin to da Max,* written by (you guessed it) a *haole* from Nebraska named Doug Simonson. You might not be able to understand what's being said by locals speaking pidgin (that's usually the idea), but you should be able to *feel* what's being meant.

Hawaiian

The Hawaiian language sways like a palm tree in a gentle wind. Its words are as melodious as a love song. Linguists say that you can learn a lot about people through their language; when you hear Hawaiian you think of gentleness and love, and it's hard to imagine the ferocious side so evident in Hawaii's past. With its many Polynesian root words easily traced to Indonesian and Malay, Hawaiian is obviously from this same stock. The Hawaiian spoken today is very different from old Hawaiian. Its greatest metamorphosis occurred when the missionaries began to write it down in the 1820s, but in the last couple of decades there has been a movement to reestablish the Hawaiian language. Not only are courses in it offered at the University of Hawaii, but there is a successful elementary immersion school program in the state, some books are being printed in it, and more and more musicians are performing it. Many scholars have put forth translations of Hawaiian, but there are endless, volatile disagreements in the academic sector about the real meanings of Hawaiian words. Hawaiian is no longer spoken as a language except on Ni'ihau, and the closest tourists will come to it are in place-names, street names, and words that have become part of common usage, such as aloha and *mahalo.* A few old Hawaiians still speak it at home, and sermons are delivered in Hawaiian at some local churches. Kawaiaha'o

Church in downtown Honolulu is the most famous of these, but each island has its own.

Thanks to the missionaries, the Hawaiian language is rendered phonetically using only 12 letters. They are the five vowels, a-e-i-o-u, sounded as they are in Italian; and seven consonants, h-k-l-m-n-p-w, sounded exactly as they are in English. Sometimes "w" is pronounced as "v," but this only occurs in the middle of a word and always follows a vowel. A consonant is always followed by a vowel, forming two-letter syllables, but vowels are often found in pairs or even triplets. A slight oddity about Hawaiian is the glottal stop called *'okina.* This is an abrupt break in sound in the middle of a word such as "uh-oh" in English and is denoted with a reversed apostrophe ('). A good example is *ali'i;* or even better, the O'ahu town of Ha'iku, which actually means "Abrupt Break."

Pronunciation Key

For those unfamiliar with the sounds of Italian or other Romance languages, the vowels are sounded as follows:

A—in stressed syllables, pronounced as in "ah" (that feels good!). For example, Haleakala is pronounced "hah-lay-AH-kah-LAH."

E—short "e" is "eh," as in "pen" or "dent" (thus *hale* is "HAH-leh"). Long "e" sounds like "ay" as in "sway" or "day." For example, the Hawaiian goose *(nene)* is a "nay nay," not a "knee knee."

I—pronounced "ee" as in "see" or "we" (thus *pali* is pronounced "PAH-lee").

O—pronounced as in "no" or "oh," such as "KOH-uh" (koa) or "OH-noh" (ono).

U—pronounced "oo" as in "do" or "stew"; for example, "KAH-poo" *(kapu)* or "POO-nah" (Puna).

Diphthongs

There are also eight vowel pairs known as "diphthongs" (ae-ai-ao-au-ei-eu-oi-ou). These are the sounds made by gliding from one vowel to another within a syllable. The stress is placed on the first vowel. In English, examples would be s*oi*l and b*ai*l. Common examples in Hawaiian are lei and *heiau.*

Stress

The best way to learn which syllables are stressed in Hawaiian is by listening closely. It becomes obvious after a while. There are also some vowel sounds that are held longer than others; these can occur at the beginning of a word, such as the first "a" in *"'aina,"* or in the middle of a word, like the first "a" in *"lanai."* Again, it's a matter of tuning your ear and paying attention.

When written, these stressed vowels, called *kahako,* occur with a macron, or short line, over them. Stressed vowels with marks are not written as such in this book. No one is going to give you a hard time if you mispronounce a word. It's good, however, to pay close attention to the pronunciation of street names and placenames because many Hawaiian words sound alike and a misplaced vowel here or there could be the difference between getting where you want to go and getting lost.

ARTS OF OLD HAWAII

Since everything in old Hawaii had to be fashioned by hand, almost every object was either a genuine work of art or the product of a highly refined craft. With the "civilizing" of the natives, most of the "old ways" disappeared, including the old arts and crafts. Most authentic Hawaiian art by master craftsmen exists only in museums, but with the resurgence of Hawaiian roots, many old arts are being revitalized, and their legacy lives on in a few artists who have become proficient in them.

Magnificent Canoes

The most respected artisans in old Hawaii were the canoe makers. With little more than a stone adze and a pump drill, they built canoes that could carry 200 people and last for generations—sleek, well proportioned, and infinitely seaworthy. The main hull was usually a gigantic koa log, and the gunwale planks were minutely drilled and sewn to the sides with sennit rope. Apprenticeships lasted for years, and a young man knew that he had graduated when one day he was nonchalantly asked to sit down and eat with the master builders. Small family-sized canoes with outriggers were used for fishing and perhaps carried a spear rack; large oceangoing double-hulled canoes were used for migration and warfare. On these, the giant logs had been adzed to about two inches thick. A mainsail woven from pandanus was mounted on a central platform, and the boat was steered by two long paddles. The hull was dyed with plant juices and charcoal, and the entire village helped launch the canoe in a ceremony called "drinking the sea."

Carving

Wood was a primary material used by Hawaiian craftsmen. They almost exclusively used koa because of its density, strength, and natural luster. It was turned into canoes, woodware, calabashes, and furniture used by the *ali'i.* Temple idols were another major product of woodcarving. Various stone artifacts were also turned out, including poi pounders, mirrors, fish sinkers, and small idols.

ARTS AND CULTURE INFORMATION

East Hawai'i Cultural Council (808/961-5711, www.ehcc.org) publishes *Art Centering,* a monthly newsletter of what's happening artistically and culturally on the Big Island. The publication includes a good monthly calendar of events with listings from exhibit openings to movies. East Hawai'i Cultural Council operates an art gallery and showplace in downtown Hilo. Associated groups are the East Hawai'i Cultural Center, Big Island Dance Council, Hawai'i Concert Society, Hilo Community Players, and Bunka No Izumi.

Volcano Art Center (808/967-8222) promotes visual and performing arts at Volcano and offers community art classes and workshops. The Art Center publishes the *Volcano Gazette,* a monthly newsletter detailing events it sponsors, and operates the Volcano Art Center Gallery in Hawai'i Volcanoes National Park.

Weaving

Hawaiians became the best basket makers and mat weavers in all of Polynesia. *Ulana* (woven mats) were made from *lau hala* (pandanus) leaves. Once split, the spine was removed and the leaves stored in large rolls. When needed they were soaked, pounded, and then fashioned into various floor coverings and sleeping mats. Intricate geometrical patterns were woven in, and the edges were rolled and well fashioned. Coconut palms were not used to make mats in old Hawaii, but a wide variety of basketry was made from the aerial root *'ie'ie.* The shapes varied according to use. Some baskets were tall and narrow, some were cones, others were flat like trays, while many were woven around gourds and calabashes.

Featherwork

This highly refined art was practiced only on the islands of Tahiti, New Zealand, and Hawaii, but the fashioning of feather helmets and idols was unique to Hawaii. Favorite colors were red and yellow, which came only in a very limited supply from a small number of birds such as the *'o'o, 'i'iwi, mamo,* and *'apapane.* Professional bird hunters in old Hawaii paid their taxes to *ali'i* in prized feathers. The feathers were fastened to a woven net of *olona* cord and made into helmets, idols, and beautiful flowing capes and cloaks. These resplendent garments were made and worn only by men, especially during battle, when a fine cloak became a great trophy of war. Featherwork was also employed in the making of *kahili* and lei, which were highly prized by the noble *ali'i* women.

Lei-Making

Any flower or blossom can be strung into a lei, but the most common are orchids or the lovely smelling plumeria. Lei, like babies, are all beautiful, but special lei are highly prized by those who know what to look for. Of the different stringing styles, the most common is *kui*—stringing the flower through the middle or side. Most "airport-quality" lei are of this type. The *humuhumu* style, reserved for making flat lei, is made by sewing flowers and ferns

BIG ISLAND MUSEUMS AND HISTORICAL SOCIETIES

The **Pacific Tsunami Museum** (130 Kamehameha Ave., 808/935-0926, www.tsunami.org, 9 A.M.-4 P.M. Mon.-Sat., $7 adults, $6 seniors, and $2 students.) is housed in the art deco-style First Hawaiian Bank building near the bay front in Hilo. It's dedicated to those who lost their lives in the destructive tidal waves that hit and virtually destroyed the city in 1946 and 1960. Visual displays, video film, and computer links all add to the educational focus of this organization, but most moving are the photographs of these last two terribly destructive tsunami to hit the city.

Lyman Museum and Mission House (276 Haili St., 808/935-5021, 9:30 A.M.-4:30 P.M. Mon.-Sat., $10 adults, $8 seniors, $3 children 6-17) in Hilo was first opened in 1931. The main building is a New England-style missionary home from 1839, the oldest wood frame house on the island. It contains furniture and household goods from Rev. and Mrs. Lyman and other missionary families on the island. In a modern annex are a collection of Hawaiian native and immigrant artifacts and items of daily use in the Island Heritage Gallery and a very fine collection of rocks and minerals in the Earth Heritage Gallery.

Hulihe'e Palace (75-5718 Ali'i Dr., 808/329-1877, www.huliheepalace.com, 9 A.M.-4 P.M. Mon.-Sat. and 10 A.M.-4 P.M. Sun., except major holidays, $6 adults, $4 seniors, $1 students) is a Victorian-style building in downtown Kailua-Kona, one of three royal palaces in the state – and the country. Used by the Hawaiian monarchs until 1916, it now contains countless items owned and used by the royal families. It's a treasure house and well worth a look. Guided or self-guided tours are available.

The **Parker Ranch Historic Homes** (808/885-5433, 10 A.M.-5 P.M. daily, $8.50 adults, $8 seniors, $7 children) are located just west of downtown Waimea. Pu'opelu, the ranch home of the Parker family, is a structure to be appreciated in and of itself, but it also houses artwork of world-prominent European artists, Chinese glass art, and antique furniture collected by Richard Smart, the last of the Parker line. Reconstructed on the grounds is Mana House, the original Parker ranch home from 1847, also open for viewing.

The **Parker Ranch Museum** (808/885-7655, 9 A.M.-5 P.M. daily, adults $6.50, $6 seniors, children $5.50) in the visitors center at the Parker Ranch Shopping Center, is an exhibit of Parker family history and a brief history of ranching and *paniolo* life on the Big Island. Many display items plus a video are offered.

Located in a renovated schoolhouse in Waimea, the **Isaacs Art Center Museum and Gallery** (65-1268 Kawaihae Rd., 808/885-5884, http://isaacsartcenter.hpa.edu, 10 A.M.-5 P.M. Tues.-Sat.) houses an impressive collection of fine art works in many media.

The **Kona Historical Society Museum** (808/323-3222, www.konahistorical.org, 9 A.M.-3 P.M. weekdays, $2 donation) is just south of the town of Kealakekua. Housed in a native stone and lime mortar general store from 1875, this museum has a small collection of glassware and photographs. An archive of Kona-area historical items is housed in the basement and is open by appointment only.

Onizuka Space Center (808/329-3441, www.planet-hawaii.com/astronautonizuka, 8:30 A.M.-4:30 P.M. daily except Thanksgiving, Christmas, and New Year's Day, $3 adults, $1 children) is located at the Kona International Airport. This center is a memorial to Hawaii's first astronaut and a space education facility for adults and children. It includes interactive and static exhibits, models, audiovisual displays, and lots of reading material.

The **Laupahoehoe Train Museum** (36-2377 Mamalahoa Hwy., www.thetrainmuseum.com, 808/962-6300, 9 A.M.-4:30 P.M. weekdays, 10 A.M.-2 P.M. weekends, $4 adult, $3 seniors), located near the Laupahoehoe Lookout, is a small but wonderful view into trains and life along the train line of the Hamakua Coast.

The **Thomas A. Jaggar Museum** (808/985-6049, 8:30 A.M.-5 P.M. daily, admission free) is a state-of-the-art venture with multimedia displays depicting the geology and volcanology of the Kilauea Caldera and entire volcano zone in Hawai'i Volcanoes National Park.

HAWAIIAN LEI

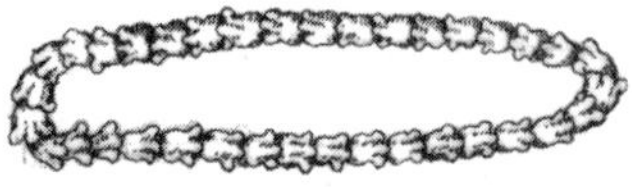

crown

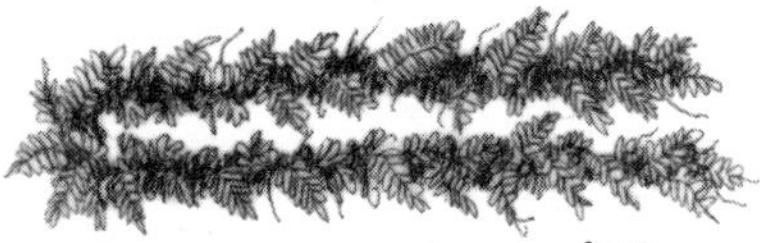

fern

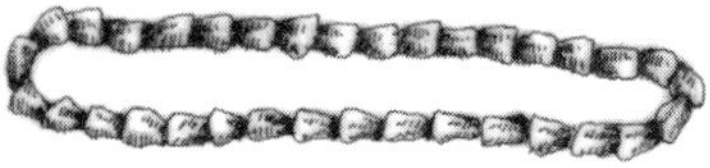

lau hala

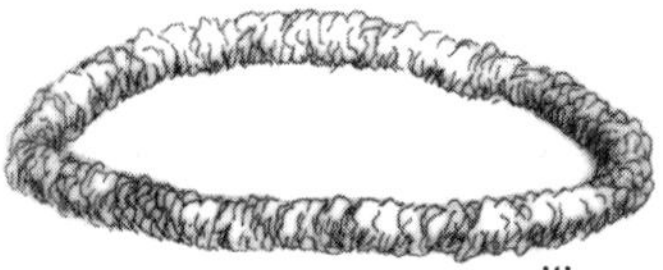

ilima

plumeria

DIANA LASICH HARPE

to a *ti,* banana, or sometimes *hala* leaf. A *humuhumu* lei makes an excellent hatband. *Wili* is the winding together of greenery, ferns, and flowers into short, bouquet-type lengths. The most traditional form is *hili,* which requires no stringing at all but involves braiding fragrant ferns and leaves such as *maile.* If flowers are interwoven, the *hili* becomes the *haku* style, the most difficult and most beautiful type of lei.

Every major island is symbolized by its own lei made from a distinctive flower, shell, or fern. Each island has its own official color as well, though it doesn't necessarily correspond to the color of the island's lei. The island of Hawai'i's lei is made from the red (or rare creamy white or orange) 'ohi'a lehua blossom. The lehua tree grows from sea level to 9,000 feet and produces an abundance of tufted flowers.

Tapa Cloth

Tapa, cloth made from tree bark, was common throughout Polynesia and was a woman's art. A few trees such as the *wauke* and *mamaki* produced the best cloth, but a variety of other types of bark could be utilized. First the raw bark was pounded into a feltlike pulp and beaten together to form strips (the beaters had distinctive patterns that helped make the cloth supple). The cloths were decorated by stamping (a form of block printing) and dyed with natural colors from plants and sea animals in shades of gray, purple, pink, and red. They were even painted with natural brushes made from pandanus fruit, with an overall gray color made from charcoal. The tapa cloth was sewn together to make bed coverings, and fragrant flowers and herbs were either sewn or pounded in to produce a permanent fragrance. Tapa cloth is still available today, but the Hawaiian methods have been lost, and most comes from other areas of Polynesia.

ARTS TO BUY

Referring to Hawaii as "paradise" is about as hackneyed as you can get, but when you specify "artists' paradise" it's the absolute truth. Something about the place evokes art (or at least personal expression) from most people.

The islands are like a magnet: they not only draw artists to them, but they draw art *from* the artists.

The inspiration comes from the astounding natural surroundings. The land is so beautiful yet so raw; the ocean's power and rhythm are primal and ever-present; the riotous colors of flowers and fruit leap from the deep-green jungle background. Crystal water beads and pale mists turn the mountains into mystic temples, while rainbows ride the crests of waves. The stunning variety of faces begging to be rendered suggests that all the world sent delegations to the islands. And in most cases it did! Inspiration is everywhere, as is art, good or bad.

Sometimes the artwork is overpowering in itself and in its sheer volume. Though geared to the tourist's market of cheap souvenirs, there is hardly a shop in Hawaii that doesn't sell some item that falls into the general category of "art." You can find everything from carved monkey-face coconut shells to true masterpieces.

Alohawear

Wild Hawaiian shirts or bright mu'umu'u, especially when worn on the Mainland, have the magical effect of making wearers feel like they're in Hawaii, while at the same time eliciting spontaneous smiles from passers-by. Maybe it's the colors, or perhaps it's just the "vibe" that signifies "party time" or "hang loose," but nothing says Hawaii like alohawear. There are more than a dozen fabric houses in Hawaii turning out distinctive patterns, and many dozens of factories creating their own personalized designs. These factories often have attached retail outlets, but in any case you can find hundreds of shops selling alohawear. Aloha shirts were the brilliant idea of a Chinese merchant in Honolulu, who used to hand-tailor them and sell them to the tourists who arrived by ship in the glory days before World War II. They were an instant success. Mu'umu'u or "Mother Hubbards" were the idea of missionaries, who were appalled by Hawaiian women running about au naturel and insisted on covering their new Christian converts from head to foot. Now the roles are reversed, and it's Mainlanders who come to Hawaii and immediately strip down to as little clothing as possible.

At one time alohawear was exclusively made of cotton or from manmade, natural fiber–based rayon, and these materials are still the best for any tropical clothing. Beware, however: polyester has slowly crept into the market! No material could possibly be worse for the island climate, so when buying your alohawear make sure to check the label for material content. On the bright side, silk also is used and makes a good material but is a bit heavy for some. Mu'umu'u now come in various styles and can be worn for the entire spectrum of social occasions in Hawaii. Aloha shirts are basically cut the same as always, but the patterns have undergone changes; apart from the original flowers and ferns, modern shirts might depict an island scene in the manner of a silk-screen painting. A basic good-quality mu'umu'u or aloha shirt is guaranteed to be worth its price in good times and happy smiles. The connoisseur might want to purchase *The Hawaiian Shirt, Its Art and History* by R. Thomas Steele. It's illustrated with more than 150 shirts that are now considered works of art by collectors the world over.

Scrimshaw

The art of etching and carving on bone and ivory has become an island tradition handed down from the times of the great whaling ships. Examples of this Danish sailors' art date all the way back to the 15th century, but, like jazz, it was really popularized and raised to an art form by Americans—whalers on decade-long voyages from "back east" plying vast oceans in search of great whales. Frederick Merek, who sailed aboard the whaling ship *Susan,* was the best of the breed; however, most sailors only carved on the teeth of great whales to pass the time and have something to trade for whiskey, women, and song in remote ports of call. When sailors, most of whom were illiterate, sent scrimshaw back to family and friends, it was considered more like a postcard than artwork. After the late 1800s, scrimshaw faded from popular view and became a lost art form until it was revived, mostly in Lahaina, during the 1960s. Today, scrimshaw can be found throughout Hawaii, but the center remains the old whaling capital of Lahaina, Maui.

Scrimshaw is used in everything from belt buckles to delicate earrings and even coffee-table centerpieces. Prices go from a few dollars up to thousands and can be found in limited quantities in some galleries and fine art shops around the island.

Woodwork

While the carving and fashioning of old traditional items has by and large disappeared, lathe-turning of wooden bowls and the creation of wooden furniture from native woods is alive and strong. Old Hawaiians used koa almost exclusively because of its density, strength, and natural luster, but koa is becoming increasingly scarce. Costly *milo* and monkeypod, as well as a host of other native woods, are also excellent for turnings and household items and have largely replaced koa. These modern wooden objects are available at numerous shops and galleries. Countless inexpensive carved items are sold at variety stores, such as tikis, hula dancers, or salad servers, but most of these are imported from Asia or the Philippines.

Weaving

The tradition of weaving has survived in Hawaii but is not strong. Older experienced weavers are dying, and few younger ones are showing interest in continuing the craft. The time-tested material of *lau hala* is still the best, although much is now made from coconut fronds. *Lau hala* is traditional Hawaiian weaving from the leaves *(lau)* of the pandanus *(hala)* tree. These leaves vary greatly in length, with the largest over six feet, and they have a thorny spine that must be removed before they can be worked. The color ranges from light tan to dark brown. The leaves are cut into strips one-eighth- to one-inch wide and are then employed in weaving. Any variety of items can be made or at least covered in *lau hala.* It makes great purses, mats, baskets, and table mats. You can still purchase items from bags to a woven hat, and all share the desirable qualities of strength, lightness, and ventilation.

Woven into a hat, it's absolutely superb but should not be confused with a palm-frond hat. A *lau hala* hat is amazingly supple and even when squashed will pop back into shape. A good one is expensive and with proper care will last for years. All *lau hala* should be given a light application of mineral oil on a monthly basis, especially if it's exposed to the sun. For flat items, iron over a damp cloth and keep purses and baskets stuffed with paper when not in use. Palm fronds also are widely used in weaving. They, too, are a great natural raw material, but not as good as *lau hala.* Almost any woven item, such as a beach bag woven from palm, makes a good authentic yet inexpensive gift or souvenir.

Quilts

Along with the gospel and the will to educate, the early missionaries brought skills and machines to sew. Aside from wanting to cover the naked bodies of their new converts, many

PHOTO COURTESY OF HVCB/HAWAII TOURISM JAPAN

quilt with traditional Hawaiian motifs

taught the Hawaiians how to quilt together small pieces of material into designs for the bed. Quilting styles and patterns varied over the years and generally shifted from designs familiar to New Englanders to those more pleasing to Hawaiian eyes, and a number of standard patterns include leaves, fruits, and flowers of the islands. Most Hawaiian-design quilts seen for sale in the islands today are now made in the Philippines under the direction of Hawaiian designers. Because of labor costs, they are far less expensive than any quilt that is actually made in Hawaii.

Paintings

One thing is for sure: like the rest of the Hawaiian Islands, Hawai'i draws painters. Multitudes of painters. Captivated by the island's beauty, color, natural features, and living things, these artists interpret what they see and sense in a dizzying display from realism to expressionism. From immense *pali* cliffs to the tiniest flower petals, and humble workers' homes to the faces of the island people, they are all portrayed. Color, movement, feeling are captured, and the essence of Hawai'i is the result. Galleries and shops around the island display local artists' work, but there is a concentration of galleries in Holualoa above Kailua-Kona. Well-known artists charge a handsome fee for their work, but you can find some exceptional work for affordable prices hidden here and there among the rest.

Gift Items

Jewelry is always an appreciated gift, especially if it's distinctive, and Hawaii has some of the most original. The sea provides the basic raw materials of pink, gold, and black corals that are as beautiful and fascinating as gemstones. Harvesting coral is very dangerous work. The Lahaina beds off Maui have one of the best black coral lodes in the islands, but unlike reef coral, these trees grow at depths bordering the outer limits of a scuba diver's capabilities. Only the best can dive 180 feet after the black coral, and about one diver per year dies in pursuit of it. Conservationists have placed great pressure on the harvesters of these deep corals, and the state of Hawaii has placed strict limits and guidelines on the firms and divers involved.

Puka shells (with small, naturally occurring holes) and *'opihi* shells are also made into jewelry. Many times these items are very inexpensive, yet they are authentic and are great purchases for the price.

Hawaii also produces some unique food items appreciated by most people. Jars of macadamia nuts and butters are great gifts, as are bags of rich, gourmet-quality Kona coffee. Guava, pineapple, passion fruit, and mango are often gift-boxed into assortments of jams, jellies, and spicy chutneys. And for that special person in your life, you can bring home island fragrances in bars of soap and bottles of perfumes and colognes in the exotic scents of gardenia, plumeria, and even ginger. All of the above items are reasonably priced, lightweight, and easy to carry.

HULA

The hula is more than an ethnic dance; it is the soul of Hawaii expressed in motion. It began as a form of worship during religious ceremonies and was only danced by highly trained men. It gradually evolved into a form of entertainment, but in no regard was it sexual. The hula was the opera, theater, and lecture hall of the islands all rolled into one. It was history portrayed in the performing arts. In the beginning an androgynous deity named Laka descended to earth and taught men how to dance the hula. In time the male aspect of Laka departed for the heavens, but the female aspect remained. The female Laka set up her own special hula *heiau* at Ha'ena on the Na Pali Coast of Kaua'i, where it still exists. As time went on, women were allowed to learn the hula. Scholars surmise that men became too busy wresting a living from the land to maintain the art form.

Men did retain a type of hula for themselves called *lua*. This was a form of martial art employed in hand-to-hand combat that evolved into a ritualized warfare dance called *hula ku'i*. During the 19th century, the hula almost vanished because the missionaries considered it vile and heathen. King Kalakaua is generally regarded as having saved it during the 1800s, when he formed his own troupe and encouraged the dancers to learn the old hula. Many of the original dances were forgotten, but some were retained and are performed to this day. Although professional dancers were highly trained, everyone took part in the hula. *Ali'i,* commoners, young, and old all danced.

Hula is art in swaying motion, and the true form is studied rigorously and taken very seriously. Today, hula *halau* (schools) are active on every island, teaching hula and keeping the old ways and culture alive. (Ancient hula is called *hula kahiko,* and modern renditions are known as *hula auana.*) Performers still spend years perfecting their techniques. They show off their accomplishments during the fierce competition of the Merrie Monarch Festival in Hilo every April. The winning *halau* is praised and recognized throughout the islands.

Hawaiian hula was never performed in grass skirts; tapa or *ti*-leaf skirts were worn. Grass skirts came to Hawaii from the Gilbert Islands, and if you see grass and cellophane skirts in a "hula revue," it's not traditional. Almost every major resort offering entertainment or a lu'au also offers a revue. Most times, young island beauties accompanied by proficient local musicians put on a floor show for the tourists. It'll be fun, but it won't be traditional.

A hula dancer has to learn how to control every part of her/his body, including facial expressions, which help to set the mood. The hands are extremely important and provide instant background scenery. For example, if the hands are thrust outward in an aggressive manner, this can mean a battle; if they sway gently overhead, they refer to the gods or to creation; they can easily become rain, clouds, sun, sea, or moon. Watch the hands to get the gist of the story, but as one wise guy said, "You watch the parts you like, and I'll watch the parts I like!" The motion of swaying hips can denote a long walk, a canoe ride, or sexual intercourse. Foot motion can portray a battle, a walk, or any kind of conveyance. The overall effect is multidirectional synchronized movement. The correct chanting of the *mele* is an integral part of the performance. These story chants, accompanied by musical instruments, make the hula very much like opera; it is especially similar in the way the tale unfolds.

THAT GOOD OLD ISLAND MUSIC

The missionaries usually take a beating when it's recounted how much Hawaiian culture they destroyed while "civilizing" the natives. However, they seem to have done one thing right. They introduced the Hawaiians to the diatonic musical scale and immediately opened a door for latent and superbly harmonious talent. Before the missionaries, the Hawaiians knew little about melody. Though sonorous, their *mele* were repetitive chants in which the emphasis was placed on historical accuracy and not on "making music." The Hawaiians, in short, didn't *sing.* But within a few years of the missionaries' arrival, they were belting out good old Christian hymns, and one of their favorite pastimes became group and individual singing.

Early in the 1800s, Spanish *vaqueros* from California were imported to teach the Hawaiians how to be cowboys. With them came guitars and moody ballads. The Hawaiian *paniolo* (cowboys) quickly learned how to punch cows and croon away the long lonely nights on the range. Immigrants who came along a little later in the 19th century, especially from Portugal, helped create a Hawaiian-style music. Their biggest influence was a small, four-stringed instrument called a *braga* or *cavaquinho.* One owned by Augusto Dias was the prototype of a homegrown Hawaiian instrument that became known as the ukulele. "Jumping flea," the translation of ukulele, is an appropriate name devised by the Hawaiians when they saw how nimble the fingers were as they "jumped" over the strings.

King Kalakaua (The Merrie Monarch) and Queen Lili'uokalani were both patrons of the arts who furthered the Hawaiian musical identity at the turn of the 20th century. Kalakaua revived the hula and was also a gifted lyricist and balladeer. He wrote the words to "Hawai'i

PHOTO COURTESY OF HVCB/HAWAII TOURISM JAPAN

ukulele

Pono'i," which became the anthem of the nation of Hawaii and later the state anthem. Lili'uokalani wrote the hauntingly beautiful "Aloha O'e," which is often pointed to as the "spirit of Hawaii" in music. Detractors say that its melody is extremely close to that of the old Christian hymn, "Rock Beside the Sea," but the lyrics are so beautiful and perfectly fitted that this doesn't matter.

Just prior to Kalakaua's reign, a Prussian bandmaster, Captain Henri Berger, was invited to head the fledgling Royal Hawaiian Band, which he turned into a very respectable orchestra lauded by many visitors to the islands. Berger was open-minded and learned to love Hawaiian music. He collaborated with Kalakaua and other island musicians to incorporate their music into a Western format. He headed the band for 43 years, until 1915, and was instrumental in making music a serious pursuit of talented Hawaiians.

Popular Hawaiian Music

Hawaiian music has a unique twang, a special feeling that says the same thing to everyone who hears it: "Relax, sit back in the moonlight, watch the swaying palms as the surf sings a lullaby." This special sound is epitomized by the bouncy ukulele, the falsettos of Hawaiian crooners, and the smooth ring of the "steel" or "Hawaiian" guitar. The steel guitar is a variation originated by Joseph Kekuku in the 1890s. Stories abound of how Joseph Kekuku devised this instrument; the most popular versions say that Joe dropped his comb or pocketknife on his guitar strings and liked what he heard. Driven by the faint rhythm of an inner sound, he went to the machine shop at the Kamehameha Schools and turned out a steel bar for sliding over the strings. To complete the sound he changed the catgut strings to steel and raised them so they wouldn't hit the frets. Voilà!—Hawaiian music as the world knows it today.

The first melodious strains of **slack-key guitar** *(ki ho'alu)* can be traced back to the time of Kamehameha III and the *vaqueros* from California. The Spanish had their way of tuning the guitar, and they played difficult and aggressive music that did not sit well with Hawaiians, who were much more gentle and casual in their manners.

Hawaiians soon became adept at making their own music. At first, one person played the melody, but it lacked fullness. There was no body to the sound. So, as one *paniolo* fooled with the melody, another soon learned to play bass, which added depth. But, players were often alone, and by experimenting they learned that they could get the right hand going with the melody, and at the same time play the bass note with the thumb to improve the sound. Singers also learned that they could "open tune" the guitar to match their rich voices.

Hawaiians believed knowledge was sacred, and what is sacred should be treated with utmost respect—which meant keeping it secret, except from sincere apprentices. Guitar playing became a personal art form whose secrets were closely guarded, handed down only to family members, and only to those who showed ability and determination. When old-time slack-key guitar players were done strumming, they loosened all the strings so no one could figure out how they had had their guitars tuned. If

CHANTS

Until the 1820s, when New England missionaries began a phonetic rendering of the Hawaiian language, the past was kept vividly alive only by the sonorous voices of special *kahuna* who chanted the sacred *mele*. The chants were beautiful, flowing word pictures that captured the essence of every aspect of life. These *mele* praised the land *(mele 'aina)*, royalty *(mele ali'i)*, and life's tender aspects *(mele aloha)*. Chants were dedicated to friendship, hardship, and favorite children. Entire villages sometimes joined together to compose a *mele;* every word was chosen carefully, and the wise old *kahuna* would decide if the words were lucky or unlucky. Some *mele* were bawdy or funny on the surface but contained secret meanings, often bitingly sarcastic, that ridiculed an inept or cruel leader. The most important chants took listeners back into the dim past before people lived in Hawaii. From these genealogies *(koihonua)*, the *ali'i* derived the right to rule, since these chants went back to the gods Wakea and Papa, from whom the *ali'i* were directly descended.

Today, the art of chanting continues but in a manner that is, perhaps, less strict but still serious. It is generally used for cultural events, meetings, and ceremonies where the importance is beyond question. Often the *kahuna* dresses in traditional Hawaiian garb and his resonant voice still casts a spell upon listeners like similar voices have done for generations. Chants also appear on some modern Hawaiian music CDs, so this ancient form is getting a wider hearing.

they were playing, and some interested folks came by who weren't part of the family, the Hawaiians stopped what they were doing, put their guitars down, and put their feet across the strings to wait for the folks to go away. As time went on, more and more Hawaiians began to play slack-key, and a common repertoire emerged.

Accomplished musicians could easily figure out the simple songs, once they had figured out how the family had tuned the guitar. One of the most popular tunings was the "open G." Old Hawaiian folks called it the "taro patch tune." Different songs came out, and if you were in the family and were interested in the guitar, your elders took the time to sit down and teach you. The way they taught was straightforward—and a test of your sincerity at the same time. The old master would start to play. He just wanted you to listen and get a feel for the music—nothing more than that. You brought your guitar and *listened.* When you felt it, you played it, and the knowledge was transferred. Today, only a handful of slack-key guitar players know how to play the classic tunes classically. The best-known and perhaps greatest slack-key player was Gabby Pahinui, with The Sons of Hawaii. He has passed away but left many recordings behind. Another slack-key master was Raymond Kane. None of his students were from his own family, and most were *haole* musicians trying to preserve the classical method of playing.

Hawaiian music received its biggest boost from a remarkable radio program known as *Hawaii Calls.* This program sent out its music from the Banyan Court of Waikiki's Moana Hotel from 1935 until 1975. At its peak in the mid-1950s, it was syndicated on over 700 radio stations throughout the world. In fact, Japanese pilots heading for Pearl Harbor tuned in island music as a signal beam. Some internationally famous classic tunes came out of the 1940s and 1950s. Jack Pitman composed "Beyond the Reef" in 1948; more than 300 artists have recorded it and it has sold well over 12 million records. Other million-sellers include: "Sweet Leilani," "Lovely Hula Hands," "The Cross-eyed Mayor of Kaunakakai," and "The Hawaiian Wedding Song."

By the 1960s, Hawaiian music began to die. Just too corny and light for those turbulent years, it belonged to the older generation and the good times that followed World War II. One man was instrumental in keeping Hawaiian music alive during this period. Don Ho, with his "Tiny Bubbles," became the token Hawaiian musician of the 1960s and early 1970s.

He's persevered long enough to become a legend in his own time, and his Polynesian Extravaganza at the Hilton Hawaiian Village packed visitors in until the early 1990s. He's now at the Waikiki Beachcomber and still doing a marvelous show. Al Harrington, "The South Pacific Man," until his retirement had another Honolulu "big revue" that drew large crowds. Of this type of entertainment, perhaps the most Hawaiian was Danny Kaleikini, the Ambassador of Aloha, who entertained his audience with dances, Hawaiian anecdotes, and tunes on the traditional Hawaiian nose flute.

The Beat Goes On

Beginning in the mid-'70s, islanders began to assert their cultural identity. One of the unifying factors was the coming of age of "Hawaiian" music. It graduated from the "little grass shack" novelty tune and began to include sophisticated jazz, rock, and contemporary rhythms. Accomplished musicians whose roots were in traditional island music began to highlight their tunes with this distinctive sound. The best embellish their arrangements with ukuleles, steel guitars, and traditional percussion and melodic instruments. Some excellent modern recording artists have become island institutions. The local people say that you know the Hawaiian harmonies are good if they give you "chicken skin."

Each year special music awards, **Na Hoku Hanohano,** or Hoku for short, are given to distinguished island musicians. The following are some of the Hoku winners considered by their contemporaries to be among the best in Hawaii: Barney Isaacs and George Kuo, Na Leo Pilimihana, Robi Kahakalau, Kealii Reichel, Darren Benitez, Sonny Kamahele, Ledward Kaapana, Hapa, Israel Kamakawiwio'ole, Amy Hanaiali'i, and Pure Heart. Though most do not perform on the Big Island, if they're playing, don't miss them. Some, unfortunately, are no longer among the living, but their recorded music can still be appreciated.

Past Hoku winners who have become renowned performers include the Brothers Cazimero, who are blessed with beautiful harmonic voices; Krush, highly regarded for their contemporary sounds; The Peter Moon Band, fantastic performers with a strong traditional sound; Henry Kapono, formerly of Kapono and Cecilio; and The Beamer Brothers. Others include Loyal Garner, Del Beazley, Bryan Kessler & Me No Hoa Aloha, George Kahumoku Jr., Olomana, Genoa Keawe, and Irmagard Aluli.

Those with access to the Internet can check out the Hawaiian music scene at one of the following: Hawaiian Music Island (www.mele.com), Nahenahenet (www.nahenahe.net) and Hawaiian Music Guide (www.Hawaii-music.com). While these are not the only Hawaiian music websites, they are a good place to start. For listening to Hawaiian music on the Web, try Kaua'i Community Radio (http://kkcr.org) or Radio Breeze (www.breezeofhawaii.com).

FESTIVALS, HOLIDAYS, AND EVENTS

In addition to all the American national holidays, Hawaii celebrates its own festivals, pageants, ethnic fairs, and a multitude of specialized exhibits. They occur throughout the year—some particular to only one island or locality, others, such as Aloha Festivals and Lei Day, celebrated on all the islands. At festival time, everyone is welcome. Many happenings are annual events while others are onetime affairs. Check local newspapers and the free island magazines for exact dates. Island-specific calendar and event information is also available on the Web (http://events.bigisland.org) for events on Hawai'i.

For additional events of all sorts throughout the state, visit the calendar of events listing on the Hawaii Visitors Bureau website (http://calendar.gohawaii.com) or visit the State Foundation of Culture and the Arts website (www.state.hi.us/sfca), which features arts and cultural events, activities, and programs.

February

The **Waimea Cherry Blossom Festival** showcases ethnic presentations, Japanese cultural events, a parade, and a tea ceremony.

MIXED CUISINE OF HAWAII

Hawaii is a gastronome's Shangri-la, a sumptuous smorgasbord in every sense of the word. The varied ethnic groups that have come to Hawaii in the last 200 years have all brought their own special enthusiasm and culture – and lucky for all, they didn't forget their cook pots, hearty appetites, and exotic taste buds.

The Polynesians who first arrived found a fertile but uncultivated land. Immediately they set about growing taro, coconuts, and bananas, and raising chickens, pigs, fish, and dogs, though the latter was reserved for nobility. Harvests were bountiful, and the islanders thanked the gods with the traditional feast called the lu'au. Most foods were baked in the underground oven *(imu)*. Participants were encouraged to feast while relaxing on straw mats and enjoying the hula and various entertainments. The lu'au is as popular as ever and is a treat that's guaranteed to delight anyone with a sense of eating adventure.

The missionaries and sailors came next, and their ships' holds carried barrels of ingredients for puddings, pies, dumplings, gravies, and roasts – the sustaining "American foods" of New England farms. The mid-1800s saw the arrival of boatloads of Chinese and Japanese peasants, who wasted no time making rice instead of bread the staple of the islands. The Chinese added their exotic spices, cooking complex Sichuan dishes as well as workers' basics like chop suey. The Japanese introduced shoyu (soy sauce), sashimi, boxed lunches *(bento)*, delicate tempura, and rich, filling noodle soups. The Portuguese brought their luscious Mediterranean dishes of tomatoes, peppers, and plump, spicy sausages, nutritious bean soups, and mouthwatering sweet treats like *malasadas* (holeless doughnuts) and *pao dolce* (sweet bread). Koreans carried crocks of zesty kimchi and quickly fired up grills for *pulgogi*, marinated beef cooked over a fire. Filipinos served up their delicious adobo stews of fish, meat, or chicken in a rich sauce of vinegar and garlic.

Recently, Thai and Vietnamese restaurants have been offering their irresistible dishes next door to restaurants serving fiery burritos from Mexico or elegant marsala cream sauces from France. The ocean breezes of Hawaii not only cool the skin but waft with them some of the most delectable aromas on earth, making the taste buds tingle and the spirit soar.

March

The month rumbles in with the **Kona Stampede** at Honaunau Arena, Honaunau, Kona. *Paniolo* provide plenty of action during the full range of rodeo events.

The end of March is dedicated to Prince Kuhio, a member of the royal family and Hawaii's first delegate to the U.S. Congress. **Prince Kuhio Day** is a state holiday honoring the prince, held on March 26, his birthday.

The annual Kona Brewers Festival brings beer makers from around the island to Kona to celebrate the beermaking prowess of the island. Not only are a variety of beers featured, but nonalcoholic brews and food are on tap. Receipts go to nonprofit environmental groups in the islands.

This month also hosts the annual Kona Chocolate Festival (www.konachocolatefestival.com), a celebration of this earthly delight with tastings, concoctions, symposiums, fancy drinks, music, dance, and many other events. The event is held at the Outrigger Keauhou Beach Resort.

April

Wesak, or **Buddha Day,** is on the Sunday closest to April 8 and celebrates the birthday of Gautama Buddha. Ornate offerings of tropical flowers are placed at temple altars throughout Hawaii.

The **Merrie Monarch Festival** in Hilo sways with the best hula dancers that the islands' hula *halau* have to offer. Gentle but stiff competition features hula in both its ancient *(kahiko)* and modern *(auana)* forms. The festival runs for a

Why then was "tourist food" in Hawaii so woeful for so long? Of course, there have always been a handful of fine restaurants, but for the most part the food lacked soul, with even the fine hotels opting to offer second-rate renditions of food more appropriate to large Mainland cities. Surrounded by some of the most fertile and pristine waters in the Pacific, you could hardly find a restaurant offering fresh fish, and it was an ill-conceived boast that even the fruits and vegetables lying limp on your table were "imported." Beginning with a handful of extremely creative and visionary chefs in the early 1980s, who took the chance of perhaps offending the perceived simple palates of visitors, a delightfully delicious new cuisine was born. Based upon the finest traditions of continental cuisine – including, to a high degree, its sauces, pastas, and presentations – the culinary magic of Pacific Rim boldly combines the pungent spices of Asia, the fantastic fresh vegetables, fruits, and fish of Hawaii, and, at times, the earthy cooking methods of the American Southwest. The result is a cuisine of fantastic tastes, subtle yet robust and satiating but health-conscious – the perfect marriage of fresh foods prepared in a fresh way. Now restaurants on every island proudly display menus labeled "Pacific Rim," "Hawaiian Regional," "fusion," or some other such name as a proud sign of this trend. As always, some are better than others, but the general result is that "tourist food" has been vastly improved and everyone benefits. Many of these exemplary chefs left lucrative and prestigious positions at Hawaii's five-diamond hotels and opened signature restaurants of their own, making this fine food much more available and affordable.

In 1998, a new and younger group called Hawaiian Island Chefs came together to further promote the offering of innovative foods made with island-grown produce and the bounty of the sea. In addition, this group aims to influence culinary programs in the state in order to help carry on this fine tradition. With the incredible mix of peoples and cultures in Hawaii, the possibilities are endless, and this new group of chefs intends to shepherd the fusion experience along, while promoting local farming enterprises and more nutritious food for everyone in the process.

week, always starting on Easter Sunday; 2006 was its 43rd year! It's immensely popular with islanders, so hotels, cars, and flights are booked solid. This is the state's most prestigious hula competition. For information refer to the festival website (www.merriemonarchfestival.org) or call the Naniloa Resort (808/935-9168).

Lavaman Triathlon (www.lavamantriathlon.com), 1.5K swim, 40K bike ride, and a 10K run, is a mini "Ironman" race held at the Waikoloa Beach Resort that incorporates other events in the day's festivities.

May

May 1 is May Day to the communist world, but in Hawaii red is only one of the colors when everyone dons a lei for **Lei Day.** Festivities abound throughout Hawaii.

Honoka'a Annual Western Week End at Honoka'a is a fun-filled weekend with a Western theme. It includes a cookout, parade, rodeo, and dance.

The annual **Spring Arts Festival** held at the Wailoa Center in Hilo is a juried art show featuring mixed media artwork by Big Island artists.

The **Annual Keauhou-Kona Triathlon** at Keauhou Bay is open to athletes unable to enter the Ironman and to anyone in good health. Each of its three events is half as long as in the Ironman, and it allows relay-team racing for each grueling segment.

The **Kona Classic Underwater Photography and Art Festival** features the unique and deliriously colorful reef and fish of the Kona Coast. Photo trips, dives, film, and lu'au are some of the events.

June

King Kamehameha Day, June 11, is a state holiday honoring Kamehameha the Great, a Big Island native son, with festivities on all islands. Check local papers for times and particulars. Hilo is hospitable with a *ho'olaule'a* (large, festive party), parades, art demonstrations, entertainment, and contests.

Hilo flashes its brilliant colors with the **Annual Hilo Orchid Society Show** at the Hilo Civic Auditorium, and the **Annual Big Island Bonsai Show,** Wailoa Center, Hilo. Both are sometimes scheduled for April or July. The orchid show has been held for half a century, and the bonsai show for about half that time.

Bon Odori, also called O Bon Festival, the Japanese festival of departed souls, features dances and candle-lighting ceremonies held at numerous Buddhist temples throughout the island. These festivities change yearly and can be held anytime from late June to early August.

The annual **Waikii Music Festival** takes place on the polo field of the Waikii Ranch on the slopes of Mauna Kea. This event offers a variety of local music and dance, crafts, games, and plenty of food.

July

Every year on the weekend closest to July 1, the weeklong **Pu'uhonua O Honaunau National Historical Park Annual Cultural Festival** is held at the national park south of Kealakekua Bay. This free event features traditional Hawaiian arts and crafts, music, dance, and food, and everyone is welcome.

The week of the **Fourth of July** offers the all-American sport of rodeo along with parades. Don't miss the **Parker Ranch Fourth of July Horse Races and Rodeo** in Waimea. The epitome of rodeo by Hawaii's top cowboys is set at the Parker Ranch, one of the largest privately owned ranches in all of America.

The annual **Volcano Wilderness Marathon and Rim Runs,** a truly energetic 26-mile race through the desolate Ka'u Desert, a 10-mile run around the Caldera Crater Rim, and a five-mile run/walk down into and out of the Kilauea Caldera, are held within the Hawai'i Volcanoes National Park and feature over 1,000 participants.

With well-known headliners and newcomers alike, the annual **Big Island Hawaiian Music Festival** is held in Hilo at the UH Hilo Performing Arts Center, sponsored by the East Hawai'i Cultural Center. This weekend event showcases not only slack-key guitar, but also steel guitar, ukulele, and falsetto singing. For information, see the East Hawai'i Cultural Center website (www.ehcc.org) and click on the Hawaiian Music Festival link.

Held in Kona, the **Na Pua 'O Ke Kai** billfish tournament is a daylong fishing event for women.

August

The **Pro-Am Billfish Tournament,** held in the waters off Kona, precedes and is a qualifying meet for the more famous annual **Hawaiian International Billfish Tournament,** held about one week later. A world-renowned tournament and the Big Daddy of them all, the HIBT (808/329-6155, www.konabillfish.com) has been held every year since 1959.

August 17 is **Admission Day,** a state holiday recognizing the day that Hawaii became a state.

On the weekend closest to Admission Day, a royal procession, traditional hula, lei workshops, games, and crafts are on the schedule at the **Hawaiian Cultural Festival** at Pu'ukohola Heiau in Kawaihae.

The **International Festival of the Pacific** features a "Pageant of Nations" in Hilo. Folk dances, complete with authentic costumes from throughout Asia and the Pacific, add a rare excitement to the festivities. Other events include a parade, hula, and food from the Pacific.

Kailua-Kona hosts the annual **Queen Lili'uokalani Outrigger Canoe Race** every Labor Day weekend. Single-hull, double-hull, and one-person events are held over a two-day period. Run between Kailua and Honaunau, this 18-mile race is the longest in the state, with over 2,500 paddlers in competition.

September

In early September don't miss the **Parker Ranch Round-Up Rodeo and Horse Races** at the ranch rodeo arena in Waimea.

The **Hawai'i County Fair** at Hilo is an old-time fair held on the grounds of Hilo Civic Auditorium.

Aloha Festivals (www.alohafestivals.com) celebrate Hawaii's own "intangible quality," *aloha*. This two-month series of several dozen individual festivals includes parades, lu'au, athletic competitions, historical pageants, balls, and various entertainment. The spirit of *aloha* is infectious and all are welcome. Check local papers and tourist literature for happenings near you.

October

When they really "wanna have fun," super-athletes come to the **Ironman Triathlon World Championship** at Kailua-Kona. A 2.4-mile open-ocean swim, followed by a 112-mile bike ride, and topped off with a full 26.2-mile marathon is their idea of a good day. For information, contact the Ironman Office (808/329-0063, www.ironmanlive.com).

Lasting two weekends, the **Hamakua Music Festival** (808/775-3378, www.hamakuamusicfestival.com) features island musicians and those of national fame. While jazz is always scheduled, classical and Hawaiian music are also sometimes performed.

November

Taste the best coffee commercially grown in the United States at the annual **Kona Coffee Cultural Festival** (www.konacoffeefest.com), held in Kailua-Kona and the surrounding area. This festival is the longest-running food festival in the state (36th annual in 2006) and celebrates a product that's been growing in the region for about 175 years. Parades, arts and crafts, ethnic foods, entertainment, and farm tours are part of the festivities.

Celebrating another of the island's agricultural products, the **Taro Festival** is held yearly in Honoka'a.

November 11, **Veterans Day,** is a national holiday celebrated by parades.

The **Hawaii International Film Festival** showcases new and engaging films, mainly from Asian and Pacific Rim countries. On the Big Island, these films show at various theaters around the island. For information, contact the HIFF office (808/528-3456 or 800/752-8193, www.hiff.org).

December

The people of Hilo celebrate a New England Christmas in memory of the missionaries with **A Christmas Tradition,** held at the Lyman Mission House and Museum in Hilo. To get a jump on it, the **Annual Waimea Christmas Parade** is held in Waimea toward the beginning of the month. For those on the Kona side, the down-home **Annual Christmas Parade** runs along Ali'i Drive with floats, music, Christmas music, and Santa.

On **New Year's Eve** hold onto your hat, because they do it up big in Hawaii. The merriment and alcohol flow all over the islands. Firecrackers are illegal, but they go off everywhere. Legal fireworks are also very popular. Beware of hangovers and "amateur" drunken drivers.

ESSENTIALS

Sports and Recreation

CAMPING

The Big Island has the best camping in the state, with more facilities and less competition for campsites than on the other islands. Nearly three dozen parks fringe the coastline and sit deep in the interior; almost half offer camping. The ones with campgrounds are state-, county-, and nationally operated, ranging from remote walk-in sites to housekeeping cabins. All require camping permits—inexpensive for the county and state parks, free for the national parks. Camping permits can be obtained by walk-in application to the appropriate office or by writing ahead. Although there is usually no problem obtaining campsites, when writing, request reservations well in advance, allowing a minimum of one month for letters to go back and forth.

Most campgrounds have pavilions, fireplaces, toilets (sometimes pits), and running water, but usually no individual electrical hookups. Pavilions often have electric lights, but sometimes campers appropriate the bulbs, so it's wise to carry your own. Drinking water is available, but at times brackish water is used for flushing toilets and for showers, so read all signs regarding water. Backcountry shelters have catchment water that needs purification,

but never hike without an adequate supply of your own. Cooking fires are allowed in established fire pits, but no wood is provided. Charcoal is a good idea, or bottled fuel for those hiking. When camping in the mountains, be prepared for cold and rainy weather. Women, especially, should never hike or camp alone, and everyone should exercise precautions against theft, though it's not as prevalent as on the other islands.

County Parks

Permits are required for overnight tent and RV camping at county parks. County parks that allow camping are Isaac Hale in Puna, Kolekole and Laupahoehoe in Hamakua, Kapa'a and Mahukona in North Kohala, Spencer in South Kohala, Ho'okena and Miloli'i in South Kona, and Punalu'u and Whittington in Ka'u. Camping is limited to one week at any one site June–August and to two weeks at any one site for the rest of the year. The permit-issuing office is the Department of Parks and Recreation, County of Hawai'i (101 Pauahi St., Suite 6, Hilo, HI 96720, 808/961-8311, www.hawaii-county.com, 7:45 A.M.–4:30 P.M. Mon.–Fri.). You can pick up your permit in person or have it mailed. If you'll be arriving after hours or on a weekend, have the permits mailed to you. Branch offices (all with reduced hours) are located at the KCAC Permit Office in Kailua-Kona (808/327-3560), the Waimea Community Center in Waimea (808/887-3014), Yano Hall in Captain Cook (808/323-3060), the Na'alehu Clubhouse in Na'alehu (808/939-2510), and in Pahala at the Pahala Community Center (808/928-3102). Fees are adults, $5 per day; children 13–17, $2 per day; youngsters under 12, $1 per day. Pavilions for exclusive use are $25 per day with kitchen, $10 without.

State Parks

Day use of state parks is free, with no permit required, but you will need a permit for tent camping and for cabins. Five consecutive nights is the limit for either camping or cabins at any one site. If you want a permit, at least one week's notice is required regardless of availability. State park permits are issued no more than one year in advance. No permits will be issued without proper identification. You can also write well in advance for permits, which will be mailed to you, but you must include photocopies of identification for each camper over 18. Children under 18 will not be issued a permit, and they must be accompanied by an adult. No reservations are guaranteed without at least a seven-day notice. Include name, address, and telephone numbers of those in the group, number of campers (with ID photocopies), dates of use, and number of tents. Reservations can now be made online. You can pick up your permit at the state parks office (Department of Land and Natural Resources, Division of State Parks, P.O. Box 936, 75 Aupuni St. #204, Hilo, HI 96721, 808/974-6200, www.hawaii.gov/dlnr/dsp, 8 A.M.–3:30 P.M. Mon.–Fri.). Camping is permitted only at Kalopa and MacKenzie State Recreation Areas and Manuka State Wayside, where there is a $5 fee per campsite per night. Forest cabins are located at Kalopa SRA, and A-frame cabins are at Hapuna Beach SRA. The four-person A-frames are a flat $20 per night. The group housekeeping cabins at Kalopa SRA are $55 for up to eight people. When writing for permits, specify exactly which facility you require, for how long, and for how many people. Located along the Saddle Road near Pohakuloa Military Camp, Mauna Kea State Recreation Area is once again open for overnight use of the housekeeping cabins, which range $35–45 for 4–6 people per night, up to five nights.

Hawai'i Volcanoes National Park

For overnight backcountry camping in Hawai'i Volcanoes National Park, permits are required but available free through the park visitors center. Your stay is limited to seven days per campground per year. There are a half dozen walk-in primitive campsites and two trail cabins in the park; you can't reserve them and should expect to share them with other hikers. Applications for camping and hiking are taken only one day in advance. No open fires are permitted.

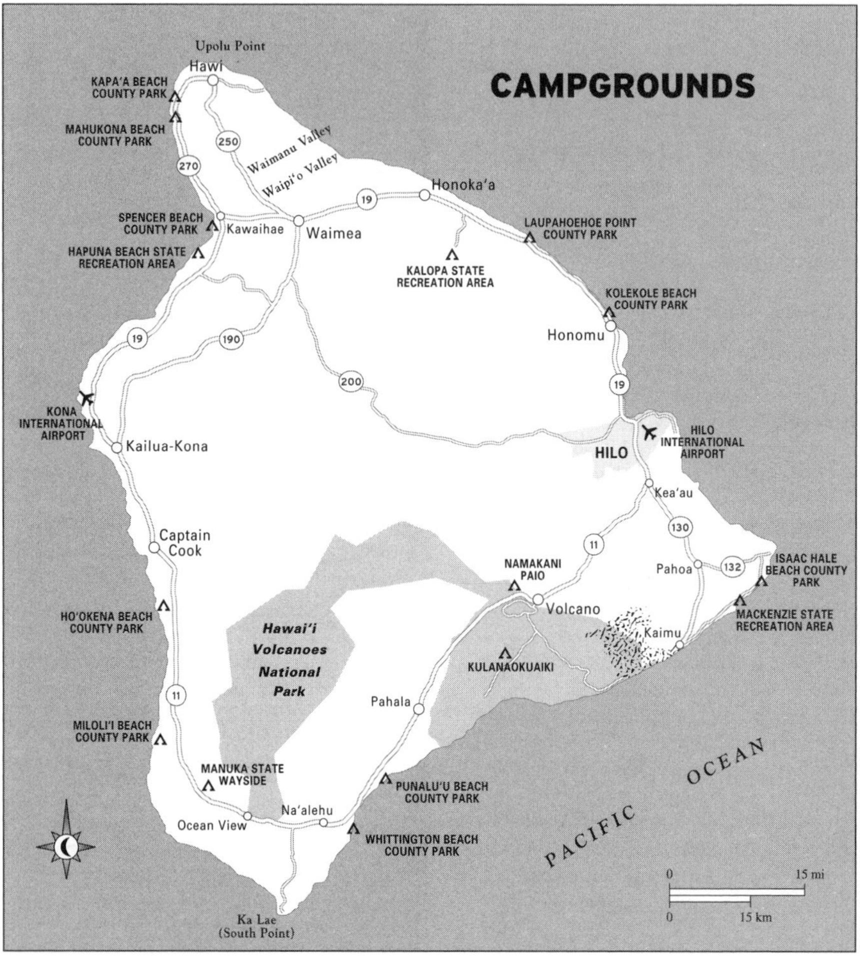

At primitive campsites along the coast, there are three-sided, open shelters that offer a partial covering against the elements. Camping is also available at both Namakani Paio and Kulanaokuaiki drive-in campgrounds, but there are no shower facilities. There is no charge for tent camping at these two campsites, and no reservations are required. For information on camping and hiking in the park, stop by the visitors center or write the park headquarters (Hawai'i Volcanoes National Park, P.O. Box 52, Hawaii National Park, HI 96718, 808/985-6000, 7:45 A.M.–5 P.M. daily). A-frame cabins are provided in the national park at Namakani Paio Campground, and arrangements are made through Volcano House (808/967-7321 or 800/325-3535, www.volcanohousehotel.com) on a first-come, first-served basis. A cooking pavilion has fireplaces, but wood and drinking water are not provided. Each of the 10 small cabins sleeps up to four people and costs $40 single or double, and $8 each for a third or fourth person. Linens, soap, towels, and a blanket are provided, but you would be wise to bring an extra sleeping bag, as it can get cold. Each cabin contains one double bed and two single bunk beds and an electric light, but no electrical outlets. There is a picnic table and barbecue grill for each cabin, but you'll need to bring your own charcoal and cooking utensils. Check in at Volcano House after 3 P.M. and check out by noon.

Waimanu Valley

Camping is also permitted in Waimanu Valley. Apply for a free camping permit from the Division of Forestry and Wildlife (P.O. Box 4849, Hilo, HI 96720, 808/974-4221, 8 A.M.–4 P.M. Mon.–Fri.), no more than one month in advance. Nine campsites are available, each with a fireplace, and three composting toilets are shared among the campers. Camping is limited to seven days and six nights.

HIKING

Hiking on the Big Island is stupendous. There's something for everyone, from civilized short walks at scenic points to exhausting treks to the summit of Mauna Loa. The largest number of trails, and the most outstanding according to many, are laced across Hawai'i Volcanoes National Park. In the north you'll find Waipi'o, Waimanu, and Pololu Valleys. The State Division of Forestry and Wildlife also maintains a number of trails in various locations around the island that cater to all levels of hikers. Check with them for details and maps.

For descriptions of hiking trails discussed in this book, refer to the individual destination chapters.

It's most enjoyable (and safest) to hike with someone—share the experience. If possible, don't hike or camp alone, especially if you're a woman. Don't leave your valuables in your tent, and always carry your money, papers, and camera with you. At the least, let someone know where you are going and when you plan to be back; supply an itinerary and your expected route, then stick to it.

There are many reasons to stay on designated trails—this not only preserves Hawai'i's fragile environment, it also keeps you out of dangerous areas. Occasionally, trails will be closed for maintenance, so stay off those routes. Most

on Halema'uma'u Trail in Kilauea Caldera

trails are well maintained, but trailhead markers are sometimes missing. Look for mileage markers along many park and forest reserve trails to gauge your progress. They are usually metal stakes set about a foot off the ground with numbers indicating the distance from a trailhead. The trails themselves can be muddy, and therefore treacherously slippery.

It's wise to buy and use a trail map and a hiking trail book. Alternatively, you could check general information and trail descriptions on the Division of Forestry and Wildlife's Na Ala Hele—Hawai'i Trail and Access System—website (www.hawaiitrails.com) before planning a hike.

Hikers will want to wear comfortable clothing. Shorts and a T-shirt will suffice on many trails, but long pants and long-sleeved shirts are better where it's rainy and overgrown. Bring a windbreaker or rain gear—it can rain and blow at any time. Wear sturdy walking or hiking shoes that you don't mind getting wet and muddy—it's almost guaranteed on some trails. Sturdy shoes will be imperative on trails over

HELICOPTER TOURS OVER THE BIG ISLAND

Air tours are a great way to see the Big Island, but they are expensive, especially when the volcano is putting on a mighty display. Expect to spend a minimum of $100 for a front-row seat to watch the amazing light show from the air. Other flights run more than $350 per person! Some discounts may be offered seasonally and for booking over the Internet. Kilauea volcano erupting is like winning the lottery for these small companies, and many will charge whatever the market will bear. To get the best view of the volcanic activity, schedule your flight for the morning, no later than 2 P.M. Later, clouds and fog can set in to obstruct your view. While the volcano is the premier focus of these tour companies, some also offer tours up the Hamakua Coast for a view of the sea cliffs, deep valleys, waterfalls, and the North Kohala Mountains, and most do a modified round-island tour that takes in the volcano, east and west coastlines, and Hamakua valleys and waterfalls. Helicopter flights from the Hilo Commuter Terminal are very competitively priced, with savings on volcano tours over the companies operating out of the Kona Commuter Terminal; however, there are more flights out of Kona as there are more tourists on that side. Additionally, flights by Blue Hawaiian Helicopters also leave out of the Waikoloa Heliport, located across the highway from the entrance to Waikoloa Resort at the intersection of Queen Ka'ahumanu Highway and Waikoloa Road.

Everyone has an opinion as to which company offers the best ride, the best narration, or the best service. All the helicopter companies on Hawai'i are reputable – but there have been some accidents. Nearly all pilots have been trained by the military, and most fly five- or six-seat A-Star machines with a few four-passenger Bell JetRangers and Hughes 500s still in use. Most have two-way microphones so you can communicate with the pilot. Each gives a preflight briefing to go over safety regulations and other details. Remember that the seating arrangement in a helicopter is critical to safety. The preflight crew is expertly trained to arrange the chopper so that it is balanced, and with different people of various sizes flying every day, their job is very much like a chess game. This means that the seating goes strictly according to weight. If you are not assigned the seat of your choice, for safety's sake, please do not complain. It's very difficult not to have a fascinating flight, no matter where you sit.

Nearly everyone wants to take photographs of their helicopter tour. Who wouldn't? Here are a few things to consider. Most of the newer helicopters are air-conditioned, which means that the windows don't open, so you might experience glare or some distortion. If you need absolutely clear shots, choose a chopper where the windows open or go with the one that flies with its doors off. Also, if you are the only one taking pictures on a tour and you're seated in the middle of the rear seat, you won't be happy. Ask for a ride in a smaller rig where everyone gets a window seat.

lava. Some very wet spots and stream crossings may be better done in tabi or other water shoes. Your clothes may become permanently stained with mud—a wonderful memento of your trip. Officials and others often ask hikers to pick clinging seeds off their clothes when coming out at the trailhead and to wash off boots so as not to unintentionally transport seeds to nonnative areas.

Always bring food because you cannot, in most cases, forage from the land, and carry plenty of drinking water, at least two quarts per day. Heat can cause your body to lose water and salt. If you become woozy or weak, rest, take salt, and drink water as you need it. Remember, it takes much more water to restore a dehydrated person than to stay hydrated as you go, so take small, frequent sips. No matter how clean it looks, water in most streams is biologically polluted and will give you bad stomach problems if you drink it without purifying it first; either boil it or treat it with tablets. For your part, please don't use the streams as a toilet.

It's always a good idea to wear sunscreen, as the sun can be intense and UV rays penetrate the clouds, and use mosquito repellent—even in paradise pesky bugs abound. Carry a dedicated trash bag and pack out all your garbage.

Many trails are used by hunters of wild boar, deer, or game birds. If you hike in hunting areas during hunting season, you should wear brightly colored or reflective clothing. Often, forest reserve trails have check-in stations at trailheads. Hikers and hunters must sign a logbook, especially if they intend to camp. The comments by previous hikers are worth reading for up-to-the-minute information on trail conditions.

Twilight is short in the islands, and night sets in rapidly. In June, sunrise is around 6 A.M. and sunset 7 P.M.; in December, these occur at 7 A.M. and 6 P.M. If you become lost, find an open spot and stay put; at night, stay as dry as you can. If you must continue, walk on ridges and avoid the gulches, which have more obstacles and make it harder for rescuers to spot you. Do not light a fire. Some forest areas can be very dry and fire could spread easily. Fog is only encountered at the 1,500- to 5,000-foot level, but be careful of disorientation.

Generally, stay within your limits, be careful, and enjoy yourself.

BIKING

With all the triathletes coming to Hawai'i, and all the fabulous, little-trafficked roads, you'd think the island would be great for biking! It can be—in the right area—but it's not guaranteed. Pedaling around the Big Island can be both fascinating and frustrating. If you circle the island, it's nearly 300 miles around on its shortest route. Most pick an area and bike there. Generally, roads are flat or of gradual gradient, making for some relatively easy riding. The major exceptions are the roads from Kailua to Holualoa, Kawaihae to Waimea, from Waimea up over the mountain to Hawi, the Saddle Road, and the road up to the summit of Mauna Kea. Generally, roads are well paved, but the shoulders on secondary highways and back roads are often narrow and sometimes in poor shape. Be especially careful on Mamalahoa Hwy. from Palani Junction south through Holualoa to Honalo and from there south to Honaunau, as there is plenty of traffic and the road is narrow and windy.

You might be better off bringing your own bike, but there are a handful of bike rental shops around the island. Road bikes are great for touring and for a workout along the Kona highways and from Hilo to Volcano. Otherwise, you're better off with a cruiser for pedaling around town or along the beach or a mountain bike that can handle the sometimes poor back-road conditions as well as limited off-road biking possibilities.

Wear a helmet, bring sunglasses, use bike gloves, and wear appropriate bike shoes. If possible, have a bike pump, extra tube, and repair kit with you. Bring plenty of water and snacks. Take a map, but get information from a bike shop for the kind of riding you want to do before you head out.

Trail Guides

For those who desire off-street trails to paved

roads, pick up a copy of the Big Island Mountain Bike Association's off-road, public-access trail guide at either Hawaii Visitors Bureau office or at most bike shops on the island. In addition to an introduction to the organization and safety tips, each trail is briefly described and accompanied by a rudimentary map, directions to the start of the trail, and any additional information that's necessary to complete the ride. The type of ride, length in distance, ride time, elevation change, and level of expertise needed is also listed. Trails vary from flat shoreline jaunts to rugged mountain workouts, for riders from beginners to advanced. Check it out before you ride; this information comes from experienced island riders. For additional information, contact BIMBA (www.bimbahawaii.net).

For mountain biking and trail information on all the major islands, pick up a copy of *Mountain Biking the Hawaiian Islands, 2nd ed.* by John Alford (Ohana Publishing, Honolulu, 877/682-7433, www.bikehawaii.com).

Getting Your Bike to the Big Island

Transporting your bike to Hawai'i from one of the neighbor islands is no problem. All of the interisland carriers will fly it for you for about $20 one-way on the same flight as you take—just check it in as baggage. Bikes must be packed in a box or hard case, supplied by the owner. Handlebars must be turned sideways and the pedals removed or turned in. Bikes go on a space-available basis only—usually not a problem, except, perhaps, during bicycle competitions. In addition, a release of liability for damage may have to be signed before the airline will accept the bike. If you plan ahead, you can send your bike the previous day by air freight, but that is more expensive.

Getting your bike to Hawaii from the Mainland will depend upon which airline you take. Some will accept bicycles as baggage traveling with you (approximate additional charge of $50)—they may or may not have to be broken down and boxed in a bicycle box—while others will only take them as air freight, in which case the rates can be exorbitant.

Organized Multiday Bicycle Tours

Kona's own **Orchid Isle Bicycling** company (P.O. Box 3486, Kailua-Kona, HI 96745, 808/327-0087 or 800/219-2324, oibhawaii@aol.com, www.orchidislebicycling.com) offers four-, six-, and eight-day bike tours throughout the year, either around the island or along the Kona coast. These tours run $1,895–2,495 and include bike rental, food, accommodations, and support services.

Three Mainland-based companies also do multiday bicycle touring. **Backroads** (801 Cedar St., Berkeley, CA 94710, 510/527-1555 or 800/462-2848, goactive@backroads.com, www.backroads.com) goes easy on the environment with its bicycle and multisport trips to the Big Island. Offered several times a year, the six-day circle-island bike tour concentrates on the Kona Coast, Volcano, and North Kohala, and costs $2,998. Backroads also does a six-day multisport trip that takes you into the major scenic areas of the island; it runs $2,998. All on-island arrangements are included.

Bicycle Adventures (P.O. Box 11219, Olympia, WA 98508, 360/786-0989 or 800/443-6060, office@bicycleadventures.com, www.bicycleadventures.com) also organizes road trips around the Big Island, mostly on less-used roads that take in many of the best sights the island offers. The seven-day trip circles the island from the Kona side, with departures throughout the year. Rides average 45 miles a day with overnights planned mostly at inns and small hotels. These all-inclusive tours cover everything you'll need while on the island; the cost is $2,686 plus $148 bike rental.

Getaway Adventures (2228 Northpoint Parkway, Santa Rosa, CA 95407, 707/568-3040 or 800/499-2453, info@getawayadventures.com, www.getawayadventures.com) also offers similar six- and eight-day round-island rides that include swimming, kayaking, and snorkeling. These trips start in Hilo and head around the bottom of the island first. Rates are $1,997 and $2,197, respectively, with a bike rental fee of $130.

The cost of air transportation to/from Hawaii

is not covered in the above rates and is the responsibility of the participant.

GOLF

The Big Island has some of the most beautiful golf links in Hawaii. The Kohala-area courses taken together are considered by some to be the crown jewel of the state's golf options. Robert Trent Jones Sr. and Jr. have both built exceptional courses here. Dad built the Mauna Kea Beach Hotel course, while the kid built his at the Waikoloa Beach Resort. The Mauna Kea course bedevils many as the ultimate challenge. Other big name golf course architects (and players) such as Jack Nicklaus, Arnold Palmer, and Tom Weiskopf have added

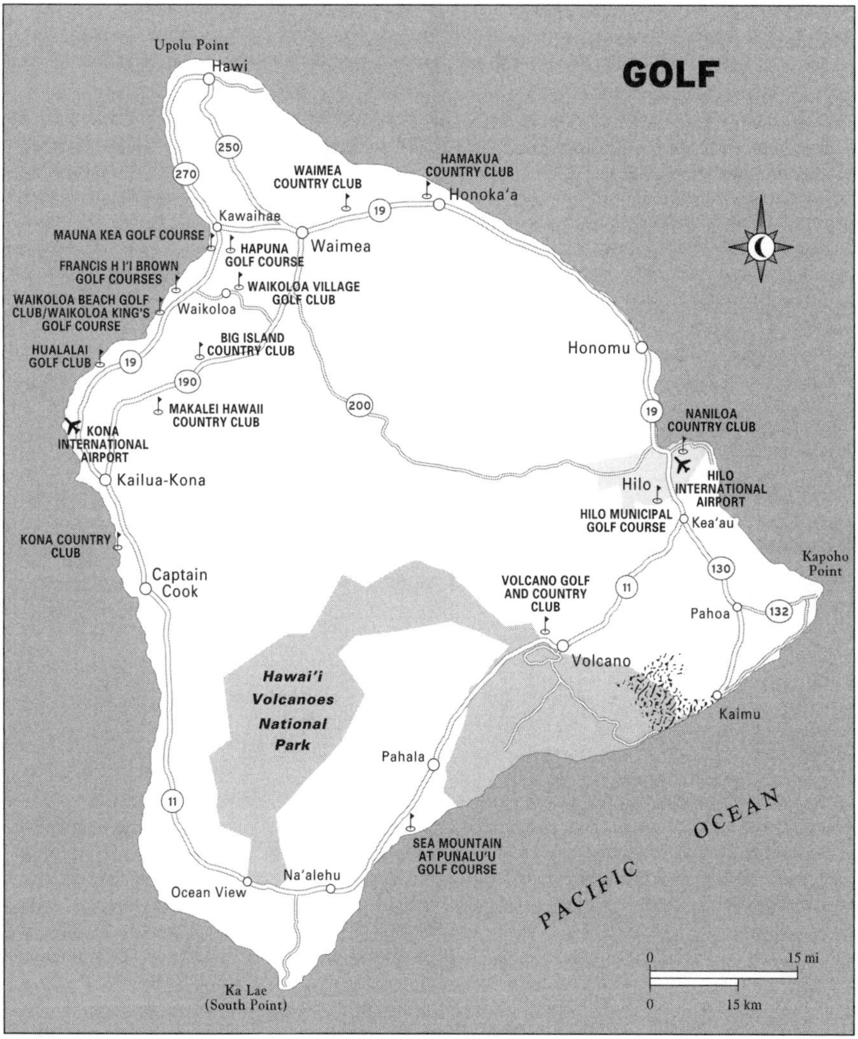

BIG ISLAND GOLF COURSES

COURSE	PAR	YARDS	FEES	CART	CLUBS
Big Island Country Club 71-1420 Mamalahoa Hwy. Kailua-Kona, HI 96740 808/325-5044	72	6,510	$99	incl.	$30
Frances H. I'i Brown Golf Courses					
South Course	72	6,938	$205	incl.	$45
North Course 68-1310 Mauna Lani Dr. Kohala Coast, HI 96743 808/885-6655	72	6,913	$205	incl.	$45
Hamakua Country Club P.O. Box 344 Honoka'a, HI 96727 808/775-7244	33	2,490 (9 holes)	$20	none	none
Hapuna Golf Course 62-100 Kauna'oa Dr. Kohala Coast, HI 96743 808/880-3000 www.Hapunabeachhotel.com/HBP/golf	72	6,534	$145	incl.	$40
Hilo Municipal Golf Course 340 Haihai St. Hilo, HI 96720 808/959-7711	71	6,325	$29-34	$16	$15
Hualalai Golf Club (resort guests and Hualalai homeowners only) 100 Ka'upulehu Dr. Kailua-Kona, HI 96740 808/325-8480	72	6,632	$185	incl.	$60
Kona Country Club					
Mountain Course	72	6,634	$140	incl.	$45
Ocean Course 78-7000 Ali'i Dr. Kailua-Kona, HI 96740 808/322-2595 888/707-4522 www.konagolf.com	72	6,748	$155	incl.	$45
Makalei Hawaii Country Club 72-3890 Hawaii Belt Rd. Kailua-Kona, HI 96740 808/325-6625	72	7,041	$110	incl.	$25

COURSE	PAR	YARDS	FEES	CART	CLUBS
Mauna Kea Golf Course 62-100 Mauna Kea Beach Dr. Kohala Coast, HI 96743 808/882-5400 www.maunakeabeachhotel.com/MKB/golf	72	6,737	$195	incl.	$40
Naniloa Country Club 120 Banyan Dr. Hilo, HI 96720 808/935-3000	35	2,875 (9 holes)	$25-30 (18 holes)	$7.50 (9 holes)	$10
Sea Mountain at Punalu'u Golf Course P.O. Box 190 Pahala, HI 96777 808/928-6222	72	6,416	$47-50	incl.	$25
Volcano Golf and Country Club Pi'i Mauna Dr. Hawai'i Volcanoes National Park, HI 96718 808/967-7331 www.volcanogolfshop.com	72	6,547	$63.50	incl.	$20
Waikoloa Beach Golf Club 1020 Keana Pl. Waikoloa, HI 96738 808/885-6060 877/924-5656 www.waikoloagolf.com	70	6,566	$195	incl.	$50
Waikoloa King's Golf Course 600 Waikoloa Beach Dr. Waikoloa, HI 96738 808/886-7888 877/924-5656 www.waikoloagolf.com	72	6,594	$195	incl.	$50
Waikoloa Village Golf Club 68-1792 Melia St. Waikoloa, HI 96738 808/883-9621	72	6,814	$80	$20	$35
Waimea Country Club 47-5220 Mamalahoa Hwy. Kamuela, HI 96743 808/885-8053 www.waimeagolf.com	72	6,661	$70	$25	$35

their talents here as well. Sometimes the Kohala golf courses are used for tournament play, like the Senior Skins Tournament at the Francis H. I'i Brown South Course. If the Kohala courses are too rich for your blood, there are a few in the Kailua area that are less expensive, or you can play a round in Hilo for $29 and hit nine holes in Honoka'a for $20. How about golfing at Volcano Golf Course, where, if you miss a short putt, you can blame it on an earthquake?

Most golf courses offer lessons. Many have driving ranges, some that are lighted. All except for two have pro shops and clubhouses with a restaurant or snack shop. Greens fees listed in the chart are for Hawaii nonresidents. Most courses offer reduced *kama'aina* rates and discount rates for play that starts later in the day. Be sure to ask about these rates as they often afford substantial savings. Guests of resorts affiliated with a golf course also get reduced greens fees.

Deciding at the last minute to golf? Want a discount rate? Willing to golf where it may not necessarily be your first choice? Try **Stand-by Golf** (808/322-2665 or 888/645-2665), where you can arrange tee times for great savings. Call one day in advance or in the morning on the day you want to play.

For printed information on golf in Hawaii, pick up a copy of *Guide to Golf: Hawaiian Islands* or *Fins and Fairways* magazines, or the newspaper-format *Hawai'i Golf News and Travel.*

Some tipping on golf courses is the norm. A $1 tip to the bag drop attendant is customary, $2 if a bag boy takes your bags from the car, and a couple bucks extra if he cleans your clubs for you.

SNORKELING

Snorkeling is simple and can be enjoyable to anyone who can swim. In about 15 minutes you can be taught the fundamentals of snorkeling—you really don't need formal instructions. Other snorkelers or dive-shop attendants can tell you enough to get you started. Because you can breathe without lifting your head, you get great propulsion from the fins and hardly ever need to use your arms. You can go for much

© ROBERT NILSEN

heading out on a snorkel trip

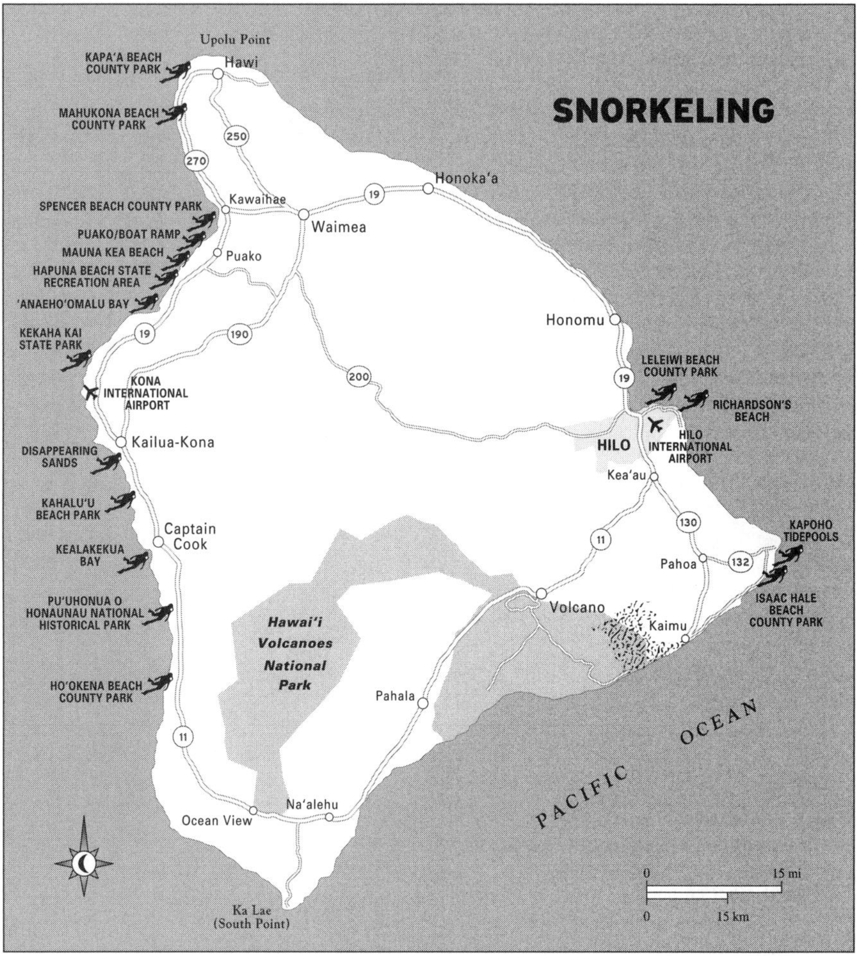

greater distances and spend longer periods in the water than if you were swimming. Experienced snorkelers make an art of this sport, and you, too, can see and do amazing things with a mask, snorkel, and flippers. Don't, however, get a false sense of invincibility and exceed your limitations.

Some hotels and condos have snorkel equipment for guests, but if it isn't free, it will almost always cost more than if you rent it from a snorkel or dive shop. These shops rent snorkel gear at competitive rates; depending upon the quality of gear, snorkel gear rental runs about \$3–9 a day. Sporting goods stores and department stores like Kmart and Wal-Mart also have this equipment for sale; a basic set might run as little as \$20.

Miles of coral reef ring the island, and it's mostly close to shore so you don't have to swim too far out to see coral communities. These are some of the most popular snorkeling sites. Kona: Kekaha Kai State Park, Pawai Bay, Disappearing Sands Beach, Kahalu'u Beach Park, Kealakekua Bay by the Captain Cook monument

REEF FISH

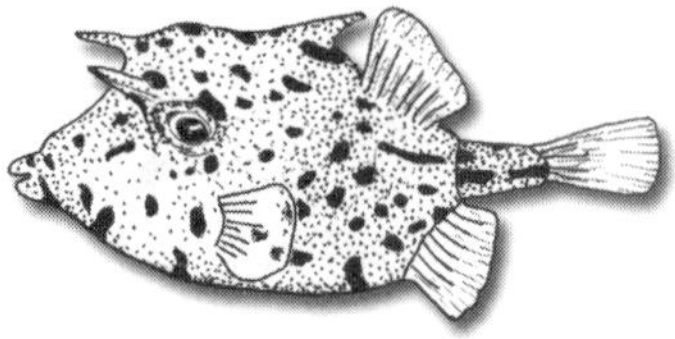

blue-spotted cowfish

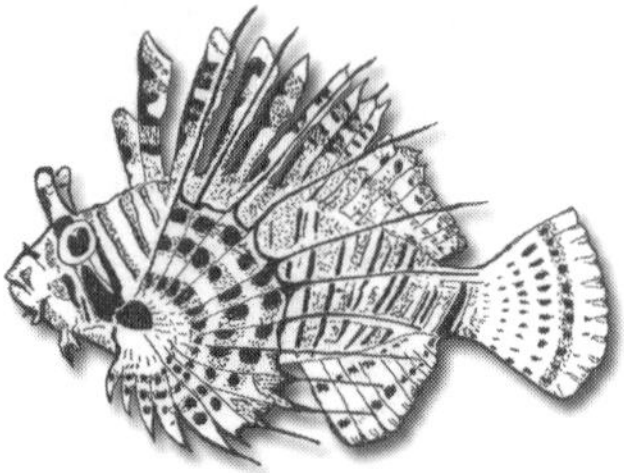

Hawaiian lionfish

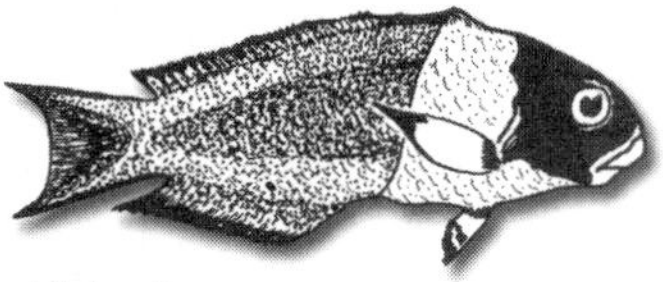

saddleback wrasse

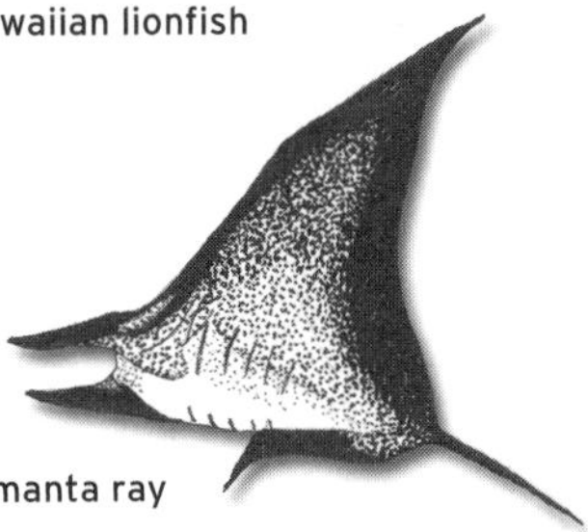

manta ray

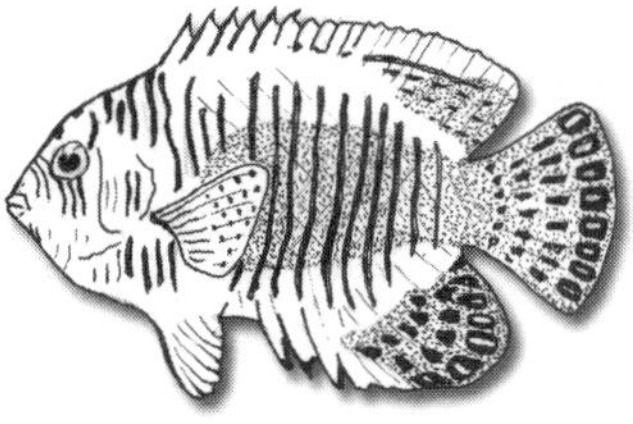

Potter's angelfish

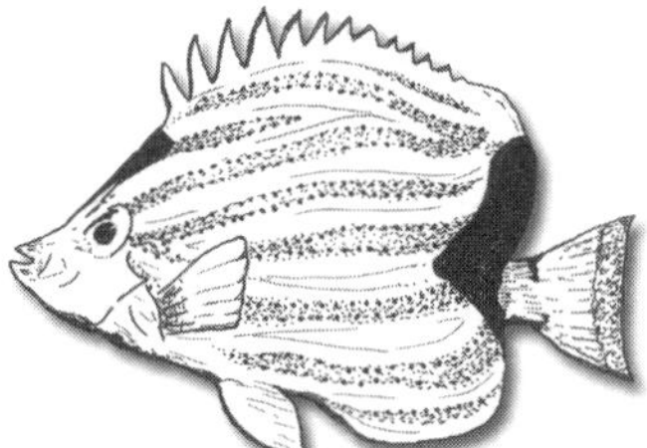

bluestripe butterflyfish

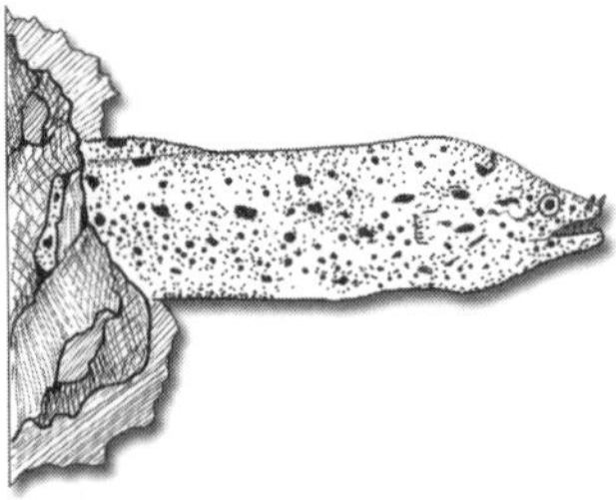

mottled moray

manini

LOUISE FOOTE/DIANA LASICH HARPER

trumpetfish

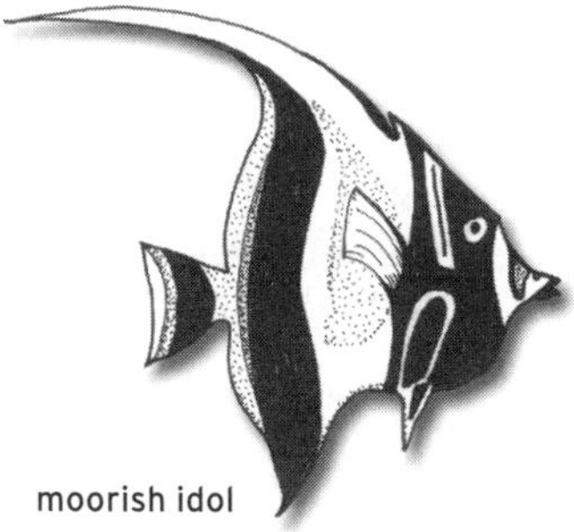

moorish idol

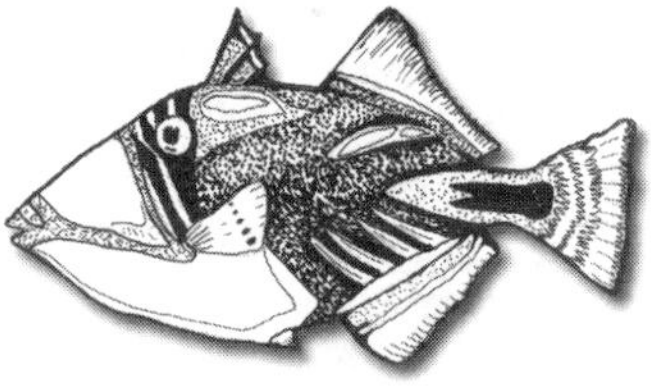

lagoon humu

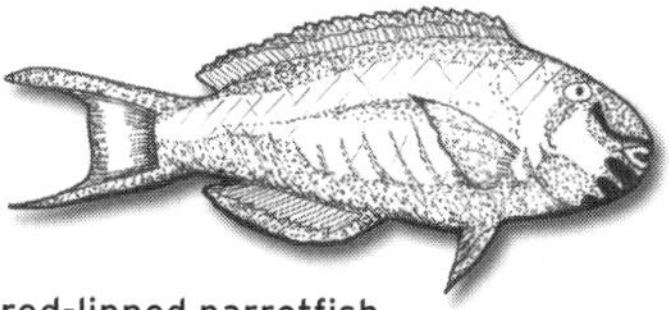

red-lipped parrotfish

threadfin butterflyfish

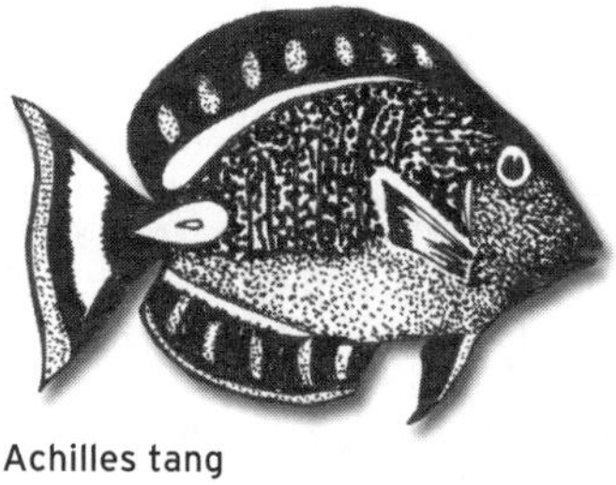

Achilles tang

uhu

LOUISE FOOTE/DIANA LASICH HARPER

(often said to be the best on the island), and at Pu'uhonua O Honaunau in Honaunau Bay. Kohala: 'Anaeho'omalu Beach, Hapuna Beach, Mauna Kea Beach, Puako coastal area, Spencer Beach County Park, Mahukona Beach County Park, and Kapa'a Beach County Park. Hilo: Leleiwi Beach County Park and Richardson's Beach. Puna: Kapoho tidepools and Isaac Hale Beach Park.

Before you put your mask on, however, ask at a snorkel shop about which locations are best for the season and water conditions. Inquire about types of fish and other sea creatures you might expect to see, water clarity, entry points, surf conditions, water current, and parking.

BEACHES

Being the youngest island, Hawai'i has far fewer beaches than any of the other major Hawaiian islands. All but a handful of these shoreline retreats are small affairs, often with volcanic rock intrusions. All beaches are open to the public. Most are accessed through beach parks, but some access is over private property. All hotels and condominiums must by law offer pathway access to beaches they front, and each has some parking set aside for public use.

Generally speaking, beaches and shorelines on the north and west coasts of the island have high surf conditions and strong ocean currents during winter months – use extreme caution – and those on the south and east experience some high surf during the summer months. A few county beaches have lifeguards. At some beaches, flags will warn you of ocean conditions. A yellow flag means use caution. A half-yellow, half-red sign signifies caution because of strong winds. A red flag indicates hazardous water conditions – beach closed, no swimming. In addition, yellow and black signs are sometimes posted at certain beaches to indicate other warnings: dangerous shore break, high surf spot, strong currents, presence of jellyfish, or beach closed.

See specific destination chapters for individual beach descriptions.

SCUBA DIVING

If you think that Hawaii is beautiful above the sea, wait until you explore below. Warm tropical waters that average 75–80°F year-round and coral growth make it a fascinating haven for reef fish and aquatic plantlife. You'll discover that Hawaiian waters are remarkably clear, with excellent visibility. Fish in every fathomable color parade by. Lavender clusters of coral, red and gold coral trees, and over 1,500 different types of shells carpet the ocean floor. In some spots the fish are so accustomed to humans that they'll nibble at your fingers. In other spots, lurking moray eels add the special zest of danger. Sharks and barracuda pose less danger than scraping your knee on the coral or being driven against the rocks by a heavy swell. There are enormous but harmless sea bass and a profusion of sea turtles. All this awaits you below the surface of Hawaii's waters.

Hawai'i has particularly generous underwater vistas open to anyone donning a mask and fins. Those in the know consider the deep diving along the steep drop-offs of Hawai'i's geologically young coastline some of the best in the state. The ocean surrounding the Big Island has not had a chance to turn the relatively new lava to sand, which makes the visibility absolutely perfect, even to depths of 150 feet or more. There's also 60–70 miles of coral belt around the Big Island, which adds up to a magnificent diving experience. Only advanced divers should attempt deep-water dives, but beginners and snorkelers will have many visual thrills inside the protected bays and coves. While most people head to the west (Kona) side, there is very good diving on the east side as well, particularly near Hilo. As always, weather conditions will dictate how the water and underwater conditions will be, so always inquire about sites and conditions with one of the dive shops before you head for the water.

If you're a scuba diver you'll have to show your C Card before local shops will rent you gear, fill your tanks, or take you on a charter dive. Plenty of outstanding scuba instructors will give you lessons toward certification, and they're especially reasonable because of the stiff competition. Prices vary, but you can take a three- to five-day semiprivate certification course including all equipment for about $350–500. Divers unaccustomed to Hawaiian waters should not dive alone regardless of their experience. Most opt for dive tours to special dive grounds guaranteed to please. These vary also, but an accompanied single-tank dive where no boat is involved goes for about $60; expect to spend $90–110 for a two-tank boat dive. Most introductory dives will be about $130. Special charter dives, night dives, and photography dives are also offered. Basic equipment costs $25–35 for the day, and most times you'll only need the top of a wet suit.

KAYAKING

Ocean kayaking has gained much popularity in Hawai'i in the last several years. The state has no whitewater kayaking, and there are no rivers on the Big Island appropriate for river kayaking. Although the entire coastline would offer adventure for the expert kayaker, most people try sections of the west coast near Kealakekua Bay or Puako and east out of Hilo that offer excellent shoreline variation and great snorkeling. Generally speaking, water conditions on the Kona Coast are best in the winter and on the Hilo side are better in the summer.

Be sure to check with the kayak shops to get the latest information about sea conditions, and consider taking one of their organized tours. Tours go to exceptional places, and while they vary, the tours generally run about $65–100 for a half day. See the individual destination chapters for details. Wear a swimsuit or shorts and T-shirt that you don't mind getting wet, and water shoes or sandals. Be sure to take a brimmed hat and sunglasses, put on sunscreen, take a towel and a dry change of clothes (a dry bag is usually provided on tours), and don't forget drinking water and snacks. A windbreaker is recommended for the open ocean.

Kayaks (the sit-upon kind) generally rent for about $25 single or $50 tandem for a day. Most shops want day-rental kayaks back by 5 P.M. Some shops rent carriers to haul the kayak. A few are located near a launch site, but many have shops away from the water so you will

Kealakekua Bay is a favorite spot for snorkelers and kayakers.

have to strap the kayak to a rack and drive to where you want to set in the water.

FISHING

Hawaii has some of the most exciting and productive "blue waters" in all the world. Here you can find a sportfishing fleet made up of skippers and crews who are experienced professional anglers. You can also fish from jetties, piers, rocks, or the shore. If rod and reel don't strike your fancy, try the old-fashioned throw net, or take along a spear when you go snorkeling or scuba diving. There's nighttime torch fishing that requires special skills and equipment, and freshwater fishing in public areas. Streams and irrigation ditches yield introduced trout, bass, and catfish. While you're at it, you might want to try crabbing, or working low-tide areas after sundown hunting octopus, a tantalizing island delicacy.

Deep-Sea Fishing

Hawai'i is positioned well for **deep-sea fishing.** Within eight miles there are waters to depths of 18,000 feet. Most game-fishing boats work the waters on the calmer Kona side of the island. Some skippers, carrying anglers who are accustomed to the sea, will also work the much rougher windward coasts and island channels where the fish bite just as well. Trolling is the preferred method of deep-sea fishing; this is done usually in waters of 1,000–2,000 fathoms (a fathom is six feet). The skipper will either "area fish," which means running in a crisscross pattern over a known productive area, or "ledge fish," which involves trolling over submerged ledges where game fish are known to feed. The most advanced marine technology, available on many boats, sends sonar beeps searching for fish. On deck, the crew and anglers scan the horizon in the age-old Hawaiian tradition, searching for clusters of seabirds feeding on bait fish pursued to the surface by the huge and aggressive game fish. "Still fishing" or "bottom fishing" with hand-lines yields some tremendous fish.

The most thrilling game fish in Hawaiian waters is **marlin,** generically known as "billfish" or *a'u* to the locals. The king of them is the blue marlin, with record catches of well over 1,000 pounds, and these are called "granders." The mightiest caught in the waters off this island was a huge 1,649 pounds—reeled in in 1984. There are also striped marlin and sailfish, which often go over 200 pounds. The best times for marlin are during spring, sum-

SEASICKNESS

Many people are affected by motion sickness, particularly on sailing vessels. If you tend to get queasy, try one of the following to prevent symptoms. Although there are others, oral medications widely available through pharmacies are Dramamine, Bonine, and Triptone. Dramamine and Bonine may cause drowsiness in some people; Triptone seems not to. Although these medications are usually taken just before boarding a ship, they might work better if a half dose is taken the night before and another half dose is taken the morning of your ride. In all cases, however, take medication as prescribed by the manufacturer.

An alternative to medication is Seabands, elastic bands worn around the wrists that put gentle pressure on the inside of the wrist by way of a small plastic button. They are available at pharmacies and at most scuba shops and can be reused until the elastic wears out. Follow directions for best results.

Without medication or pressure bands, you can still work to counter the effects of motion sickness. The night before, try not to eat too much, particularly greasy food, and don't drink alcohol to excess. If your stomach begins to feel upset, try a few soda crackers. If you begin to feel dizzy, focus on the horizon or a mountaintop – something stationary – and try to direct your thoughts to something other than your dizziness or queasiness. With children (and perhaps adults as well), talking about what animal figures they can see in the clouds or how many houses they can spot along the shoreline may be enough to distract them until they begin feeling better.

mer, and fall. The fishing tapers off in January and picks up again by late February. "Blues" can be caught year-round, but, oddly enough, when they stop biting it seems as though the striped marlin pick up. Second to the marlin are **tuna.** *'Ahi* (yellowfin tuna) are caught in Hawaiian waters at depths of 100–1,000 fathoms. They can weigh 300 pounds, but 25–100 pounds is common. There are also *aku* (skipjack tuna) and the delicious *ono,* which average 20–40 pounds. **Mahimahi,** with its high prominent forehead and long dorsal fin, is another strong, fighting, deep-water game fish abundant in Hawaii. These delicious fish can weigh up to 70 pounds.

Shore Fishing

Shore fishing and bait casting yield *papio,* a jack tuna. *Akule,* a scad (locally called *halalu*), is a smallish schooling fish that comes close to shore and is great to catch on light tackle. *Ulua* are shore fish and can be found in tidepools. They're excellent eating, average two to three pounds, and are taken at night or with spears. *'O'io* are bonefish that come close to shore to spawn. They're caught by bait casting and bottom fishing with cut bait. They're bony, but they're a favorite for fish cakes and *poke. Awa* is a schooling fish that loves brackish water. It can grow up to three feet long and is a good fighter; a favorite for throw-netters, it's even raised commercially in fishponds. Besides these there are plenty of goatfish, mullet, mackerel, snapper, sharks, and even salmon.

Freshwater Fishing

Hawaii has only one native freshwater game fish, the *'o'opu.* This goby is an oddball with fused ventral fins. It grows to 12 inches long and is found on all the islands. Introduced species include largemouth and smallmouth bass, bluegill, catfish, *tucunare,* oscar, carp, and tilapia. All of these species are best caught with light spinning tackle or with a bamboo pole and trusty old worm. A catch limit is in effect for eight species of freshwater fish. Freshwater fishing is limited to the **Waiakea Public Fishing Area,** a state-operated facility in downtown Hilo. This 26-acre pond offers a variety of saltwater and brackish-water species. Fishing is usually allowed in most State Forest Reserve Areas. Owners' permission must be obtained to fish on private property.

Charters

By and large, the vast majority of charter fishing boats on the Big Island berth at the Honokohau Harbor just north of Kailua-Kona. A few boats also leave from Keauhou Bay and Kawaihae Harbor on the west side, and some use the river mouth in Hilo. Captains of these vessels invariably have been fishing these waters for years and know where to look for a catch. Rates vary, as do the length of outings (usually four, six, or eight hours) and number of passengers allowed on the boats. Although pricing varies, fishing excursions generally run in the vicinity of $100 a half-day to $200 for a full-day shared charter, and $500 half-day to $900 full-day exclusive charter.

An excellent publication listing some boats and general deep-sea fishing information is *Fins and Fairways* (800/367-8014, www.fishkona.com). This tabloid, published by Capt. Tom Armstrong and available free at newsstands and in hotel and condo lobbies, is filled with descriptions of boats, phone numbers, captains' names, maps, and photos of recent catches. You can also contact **The Hawaiian International Billfish Association** (808/329-6155, www.konabillfish.com) for details on upcoming tournaments and "what's biting and when." Of course, the bar at the Harbor House Restaurant at the Honokohau Marina might be just as easy a place to get quick, reliable, and up-to-the-minute information on how the fish are biting as well as which boats seem to be having the best luck.

Licenses

No license is needed for recreational saltwater fishing. A license is needed for freshwater fishing only. A **Freshwater Game Fishing License** is good for one year, July 1–June 30. Licenses cost $25 for nonresidents; $10 for 7-day tourist use; $20 for 30-day tourist use; $5 for residents over age 15 and active duty military personnel, their spouses, and dependents under age 15; and $3 for children ages 9–15; licenses are free to senior citizens over age 65 and children under age nine when accompanied by an adult with a license. You can pick up a license at sporting goods stores or at the Division of Aquatic Resources (75 Aupuni St., Rm. #204, Hilo, 808/974-6201), or at Honokohau Marina (74-381 Kealakeha Pkwy., Suite L, Kailua-Kona, 808/327-6226). Be sure to ask for the *Hawaii Fishing Regulations* and *Freshwater Fishing in Hawaii* booklets. All game fish may be taken year-round except trout, *'ama'ama, moi,* and certain crustaceans (check specific regulations).

Getting There

With the number of visitors each year approaching seven million—and another several hundred thousand just passing through—the state of Hawaii is one of the easiest places in the world to get to... by plane. About half a dozen large North American airlines (plus additional charter airlines) fly to and from the islands. About twice that number of foreign carriers, mostly from Asia and Oceania, also touch down there on a daily or weekly basis. Hawaii is a hotly contested air market. Competition among carriers is fierce, and this makes for some sweet deals and a wide choice of fares for the money-wise traveler. It also makes for pricing chaos. Airlines usually adjust their flight schedules about every three months to account for seasonal differences in travel and route changes. Before planning a trip to and around the islands, be sure to contact the airlines directly, view the airlines' Internet sites, check well-established Internet travel sites, go through your travel agent for the most current information on routes and flying times, or seek out charter companies as they offer attractive alternatives. Familiarize yourself with the alternatives at your disposal so you can make an informed travel selection.

There are two categories of airlines you can take to Hawaii: **domestic,** meaning American-owned, and **foreign**-owned. An American law, penned at the turn of the 20th century to protect American shipping, says that *only* an American carrier can transport you between two American cities. In the airline industry, this law is still very much in effect. It means, for example, that if you want a round-trip flight between San Francisco and Honolulu, you *must* fly on a domestic carrier. If, however, you are flying from San Francisco to Tokyo, you are at liberty to fly a foreign airline, and you may even have a stopover in Hawaii, but you must continue to Tokyo or some other foreign city and cannot fly back to San Francisco on the foreign airline. Travel agents know this, but if you're planning your own trip, be aware of this fact.

If you fly to Hawaii from a foreign country, you are free to use either an American or foreign carrier.

FLIGHTS TO THE BIG ISLAND

Most island flights in the past landed at Hilo International Airport. With the Kona Coast gaining popularity, all domestic flights from the Mainland have shifted to that side of the island, and the only direct international connection to the Big Island lands there as well. United, American, Northwest, and Aloha Airlines operate nonstop flights to the Big Island from the Mainland.

All other major domestic and foreign carriers fly you to Honolulu and have arrangements with either Hawaiian Airlines or Aloha Airlines for getting you to the Big Island. This sometimes involves a plane change, but your baggage can be booked straight through. If you fly from the Mainland with Hawaiian or Aloha, you have the added convenience of

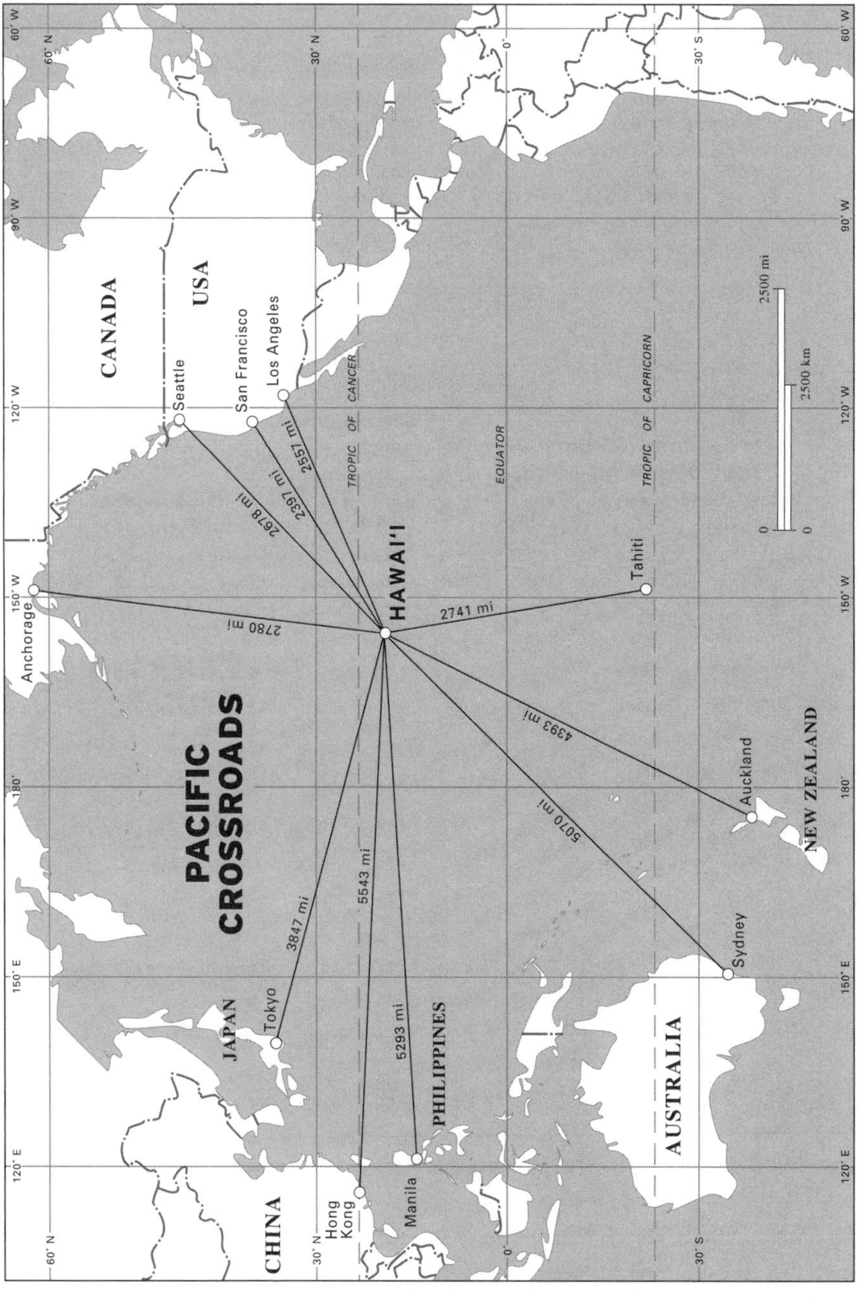
PACIFIC CROSSROADS
CANADA
USA
CHINA
JAPAN
PHILIPPINES
AUSTRALIA
NEW ZEALAND
HAWAI'I
Anchorage
Seattle
San Francisco
Los Angeles
Tahiti
Auckland
Sydney
Tokyo
Manila
Hong Kong
2780 mi
2678 mi
2397 mi
2557 mi
2741 mi
4393 mi
5070 mi
3847 mi
5543 mi
5293 mi
TROPIC OF CANCER
EQUATOR
TROPIC OF CAPRICORN
0
2500 mi
2500 km
60° N
30° N
0°
30° S
60° W
90° W
120° W
150° W
180°
150° E
120° E

FLIGHT TIMES TO HAWAII

Flights from California take about five hours, and a bit longer from the Northwest or Pacific Canada; you gain two hours over Pacific Standard Time when you land in Hawaii (three hours during daylight saving time). From the East Coast it takes about 11 hours, and you gain five hours over Eastern Standard Time.

Flights from Japan take about seven hours, and there is a five-hour difference between the time zones. Travel time between Sydney, Australia, or Auckland, New Zealand, and Hawaii is about nine hours. Sydney and Auckland are ahead of Hawaii time by 20 and 22 hours, respectively.

dealing with just one airline. Several charter airlines also fly to the Big Island nonstop from the Mainland.

Hilo International Airport

The largest airport on the Big Island is Hilo International Airport, which services Hilo and the eastern half of the island. Formerly known as Gen. Lyman Field, it was named after Gen. Albert Kuali'i Brickwood Lyman, the first ethnic Hawaiian to become a Brigadier General (1942) in the U.S. Army. This airport is remarkably close to downtown Hilo. It's a modern facility with full amenities, and its runways can handle jumbo jets. Interisland flights from here connect directly to Kona, Kahului, and Honolulu, from where you can get to any other airport in the state. The two-story terminal has an information center, a restaurant, a number of vendors, restrooms,

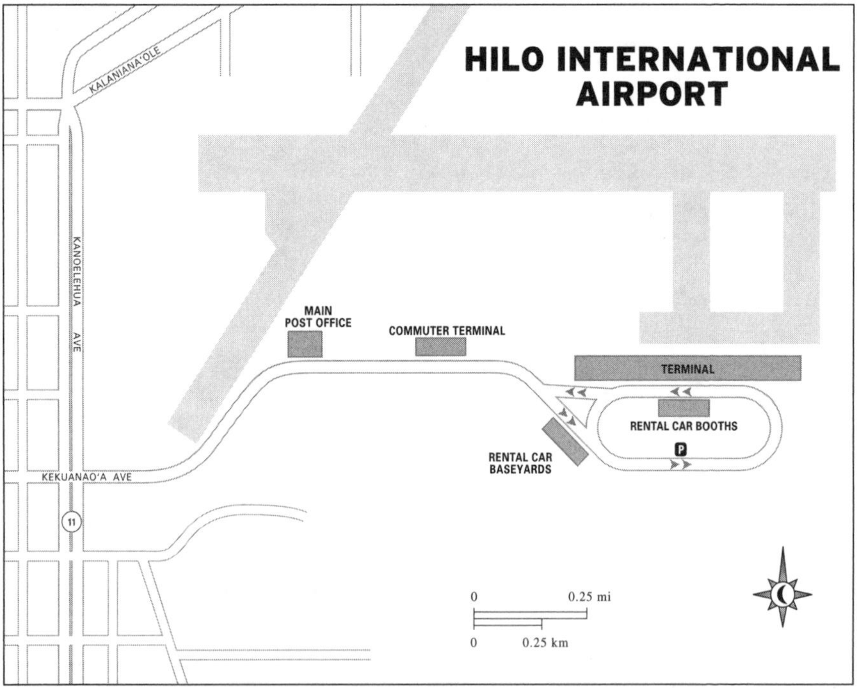

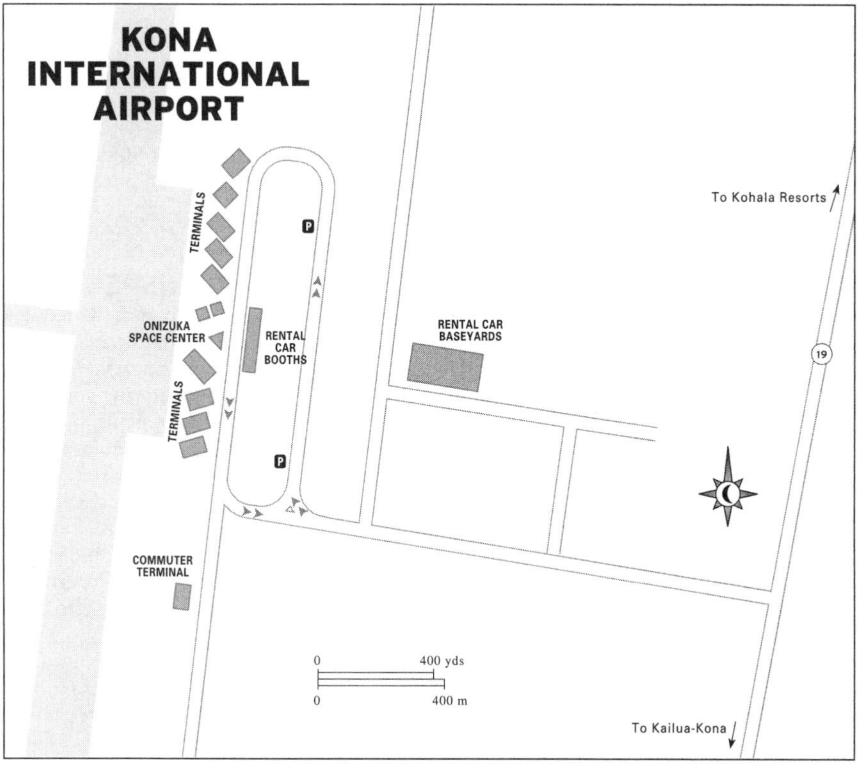

and telephones. There is no bank or money exchange, but a post office is a short way down the approach road. As you look at the terminal building, the departure lounge is in the center beyond the check-in counters and agricultural inspection station. Arrivals are on the right and the arrival area has baggage claim, restrooms, public telephones, and a small tourist information booth that's usually open when flights are arriving. To the left of the departure area are a number of helicopter tour company counters. Major car-rental agencies have booths to the front of the terminal across the traffic lanes. There is no public transportation to or from the airport; a taxi for the three-mile ride to town costs about $13. Public parking is in a large lot behind the car rental booths. Parking fees run $1 for the first half hour, $1 for the second half hour, $1 for each additional hour, and a maximum of $7 per day. Along the airport road, a short way in toward town, is the old commuter terminal building (pay parking), where several helicopter and fixed-wing airplane tour companies have their offices and where you check in for their tours.

Kona International Airport

Kona International Airport is nine miles north of Kailua-Kona and handles the air traffic for Kona, Kohala, and the west side of the island. The Kona Airport is surrounded by fields of black lava. This airport handles a growing amount of air traffic from other island cities and all the Mainland and international flights, eclipsing Hilo as the island's major air transportation hub. Interisland flights arrive from Hilo, Honolulu, and Kahului; Mainland and international flights arrive from San Francisco,

Los Angeles, Seattle, Oakland, and Tokyo. During winter, charter flights also fly in from Vancouver. The terminal is a series of open-sided, nonconnected, Polynesian-style buildings. There are no jetways; everyone boards and deplanes by stairway onto the tarmac. Departures leave near the center of this cluster, where you also find the agricultural inspection station; arrivals come to either end. Most Hawaiian, American, and Japan Air Lines departures are from the left-hand side; Aloha and United Airlines use mostly the right-hand side. American has check-in counters more or less in the center of this line of terminals. Here too are lockers, telephones, restrooms, visitor information booths near both baggage claim areas, various food vendors, lei stands, and other shops. Car-rental agencies have booths across the circle road. The public parking lot is open 5:30 A.M.–9 P.M.; it costs $1 for the first half hour, $1 each hour after that, and $7 maximum for 24 hours. There is no public transportation to the airport. A private cab to your hotel in Kailua-Kona will be $15 or more, greater if going up the Kohala Coast. The commuter terminal just down the road is for helicopter and fixed-wing tourist flight check-in.

Other Airports

Waimea-Kohala Airport is just outside Waimea (Kamuela). There are few amenities and no public transportation into town. Only a few weekly commuter flights are scheduled between Waimea and Honolulu. **Upolu Airport** is a lonely strip on the extreme northern tip of the island, with no facilities whatsoever and no scheduled flights.

VISAS

Entering Hawaii is like entering anywhere else in the United States. Foreign nationals must have a current passport, and most must have a proper visa, an ongoing or return air ticket, and sufficient funds for the proposed stay in Hawaii. A visa application can be made at any U.S. embassy or consular office outside the United States and must include a properly filled out application form, two photos 1.5 inches square, and a nonrefundable fee of $100. Canadians do not need a visa or passport but must have proper identification such as a passport, driver's license, or birth certificate. Visitors from 28 countries do not need a visa to enter the United States for 90 days or less. As this list is amended periodically, be sure to check in your country of origin to determine whether you need a visa for U.S. entry.

AGRICULTURAL INSPECTION

Everyone visiting Hawaii must fill out a "Plant and Animals Declaration Form" and present it to the appropriate official upon arrival in the state. Anyone carrying any of the listed items must have these items inspected by an agricultural inspection agent at the airport. These items include but are not limited to fruits, vegetables, plants, seeds, and soil, as well as live insects, seafood, snakes, and amphibians. For more information on what is prohibited, contact the Hawaii Department of Agriculture, Kona Airport (808/326-1077, www.hawaiiag.org/hdoa).

Remember that before you leave Hawaii for the Mainland, all of your bags are again subject to an agricultural inspection, a usually painless procedure taking only a minute or two. To facilitate your departure, leave all bags unlocked until after inspection. There are no restrictions on beach sand from below the high water line, coconuts, cooked foods, dried flower arrangements, fresh flower lei, pineapples, certified pest-free plants and cuttings, and seashells. However, papayas must be treated before departure. Some restricted items are berries, fresh gardenias, jade vines, live insects and snails, cotton, plants in soil, soil itself, and sugarcane. Raw sugarcane is okay, however, if it is cut between the nodes, has the outer covering peeled off, is split into fourths, and is commercially prepackaged. For any questions pertaining to plants that you want to take to the Mainland, call the US Department of Agriculture, Plant Protection and Quarantine office (808/933-6930 in Hilo, 808/326-1252 in Kona).

Foreign countries may have different agricultural inspection requirements for flights from

Hawaii (or other points in the United States) to those countries. Be sure to check with the proper foreign authorities for specifics.

PETS AND QUARANTINE

Hawaii has a very rigid pet quarantine policy designed to keep rabies and other Mainland diseases from reaching the state. All domestic pets are subject to a **120-day quarantine** (a 30-day quarantine or a newer five-day-or-less quarantine is allowed by meeting certain pre-arrival and post-arrival requirements—inquire), and this includes substantial fees for boarding. Unless you are contemplating a move to Hawaii, it is not feasible to take pets. For complete information, contact the Department of Agriculture, Animal Quarantine Division in Honolulu (99-951 Halawa Valley St., 'Aiea, HI 96701, 808/483-7151).

TRAVEL COMPANIES

Many tour companies advertise packages to Hawaii in large city newspapers every week. They offer very reasonable airfares, car rentals, and accommodations. Without trying, you can get round-trip airfare from the West Coast and a week in Hawaii for $600–700 using one of these companies, with prices invariably more expensive during summer. Some airlines offer great package deals that are hard to beat. United Vacations (800/377-1816, www.unitedvacations.com) by United Airlines is one. The following companies also offer great deals. This list is by no means exhaustive.

A California-based company specializing in Hawaii, **Pleasant Hawaiian Holidays** (800/742-9244, www.pleasantholidays.com) makes arrangements for flights, accommodations, and transportation only. For flights, it primarily uses American Trans Air but also uses select commercial airlines and regularly scheduled flights. Aside from the air connection, Pleasant Hawaiian offers a choice of accommodation levels from budget to luxury, a fly/drive option if you have your own accommodation, and numerous perks, like a flower lei, first morning orientation, service desks at hotels, and coupons and gift certificates. Pleasant Hawaiian is easy to work with and stands behind its services. A deposit is required after booking and there is a time frame for full payment that depends upon when you make your reservation. Fees are assessed for changing particulars after booking, so get apprised of all financial particulars. Most major travel agents work with Pleasant Hawaiian, but you can also contact the company directly.

The California-based tour company **SunTrips** (800/786-8747, www.suntrips.com) runs flights to the four major islands of Hawaii from Oakland, Portland, Seattle, and Denver. It offers flight, accommodation, and/or car rental packages that match any for affordability. Most of its flights use Ryan International or North American airlines. Your price will depend upon your choice of accommodations and type of car. Using both charter and commercial air carriers, SunTrips does not offer assigned seating until you get to the airport. They recommend you get there two hours in advance, and they ain't kidding! This is the price you pay for getting such inexpensive air travel. SunTrips financial regulations are similar to those at Pleasant Hawaiian; be sure to inquire.

STA Travel (800/781-4040 or visit www.statravel.com) is a full-service travel agency specializing in student travel, regardless of age. Those under 26 do not have to be full-time students to get special fares. Through STA, bona fide students can get an International Student Identification Card (ISIC), which often gets you discount fares and fees, and anyone can get a Hostelling International card. Older independent travelers can avail themselves of services; although they are ineligible for student fares, STA works hard to get you discounted or budget rates. Many tickets issued by STA are flexible, allowing changes with no penalty, and are open-ended for travel up to one year. Aside from airfares, STA also books accommodations and packages. STA has some 300 offices around the world. STA also maintains Travel Help, a service available at all offices designed to solve all types of problems that may arise while traveling. STA is a well-established travel agency with an excellent and well-deserved reputation.

Getting Around

BY AIR

Getting to and from the Big Island via the other islands is easy and convenient. The only effective way for most visitors to travel between the Hawaiian Islands is by air. Luckily, Hawaii has excellent air transportation that boasts one of the industry's safest flight records. All interisland flights have a no-smoking regulation. Items restricted on flights from the Mainland and from overseas are also restricted on flights within the state. Baggage allowances are the same as anywhere, except that due to space constraints, carry-on luggage on the smaller prop planes may be limited in number and size. The longest direct interisland flight in the state, 214 miles, is between Honolulu to Hilo and takes about 45 minutes. Hawaiian and Aloha have competitive prices, with interisland flights at about $100 each way.

Note: Although every effort has been made for up-to-date accuracy, remember that schedules are constantly changing. The following should be used only as a point of reference. Please call the airlines listed below for their current schedules.

Hawaiian Airlines

Contact Hawaiian Airlines (www.hawaiianair.com) in Hilo (808/935-0858) or Kona (808/326-1214). The majority of flights to the Big Island with Hawaiian Airlines run between Honolulu and Kona; about a dozen flights (about 40 minutes) are spread throughout the day from approximately 5:15 A.M. to 8 P.M. One of these flights stops at Kahului, Maui. A similar schedule applies to Hilo, but with slightly fewer flights each day. All other Hawaiian Airlines flights originating in Hilo

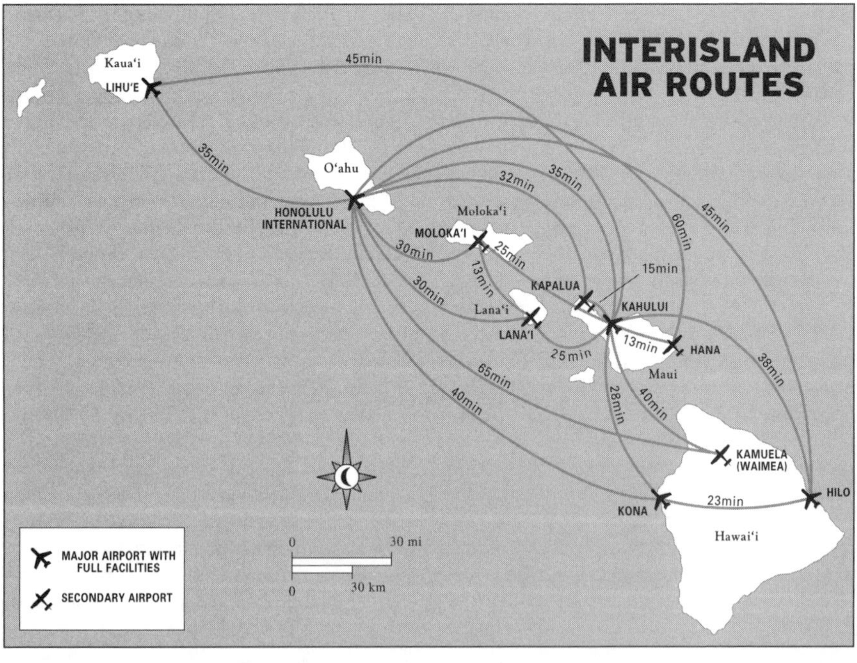

or Kona go through Kahului or Honolulu. Hawaiian Airlines uses Island Air as a commuter link to the smaller island airports and partners with Alaska Airlines, American Airlines, Continental Airlines, and Northwest Airlines.

Aloha Airlines

Aloha Airlines (808/935-5771 on the Big Island, www.alohaair.com) also services the Big Island with flights to/from the neighboring islands. Its 14 daily Honolulu-Kona runs start at 5:30 A.M., with the last at 7:10 P.M.; about one dozen Honolulu-Hilo flights depart throughout the day, 5:30 A.M.–6:55 P.M. Connecting through Honolulu, there are 7–10 daily flights to Lihu'e, Kaua'i, from Kona and Hilo. Aloha also flies a couple of times a day from both Kona and Hilo direct to Kahului, Maui, and once a day between Hilo and Kona. Aloha Airlines uses Island Air as a commuter link to the smaller island airports and partners with United Airlines.

Island Air

A subsidiary of Aloha Airlines, **Island Air** (800/652-6541 in Hawaii, 800/323-3345 nationwide, www.islandair.com) connects both Kona and Hilo to Kahului, Maui.

Pacific Wings

This carrier (808/873-0877, www.pacificwings.com) is a local and reputable commercial airline that seems to fill the gaps that the bigger airlines often miss. On the Big Island, it only services the Waimea Airport on regularly scheduled flights.

BY SEA

In 2001, following the terrorist attacks on the Mainland and a dramatic dip in numbers of travelers to the Hawaiian Islands, American Hawaii Cruises stopped all interisland cruise service within the Hawaiian Islands. This company had operated seven-day cruises to four of the islands for years.

In December 2001, Norwegian Cruise Lines (800/327-7030 or 888/625-4292, www.ncl.com), a subsidiary of Star Cruises PLC of Malaysia, began running a weekly seven-day round-trip cruise that went throughout the Hawaiian Islands with a leg down to Fanning Island and back. Now under the name NCL America, it offers a 10-day Hawaii and Fanning Island trip on *Norwegian Wind.* In addition, *Pride of Aloha* and *Pride of America* (newly christened in June 2005) run seven-day round-trip cruises to the four main islands,

© ROBERT NILSEN

cruise ship off Kailua-Kona

DRIVING TIPS

Wear your seat belt – it's the law! Police keep an eye out for miscreants and often ticket those who do not use their restraints. Not wearing a seat belt is a primary offense in Hawaii, meaning officers can pull you over for not wearing a seat belt even if you are not breaking any other laws. Protect your small children as you would at home with car seats – either bring one from home or rent one from a car rental company.

The mile markers are great for pinpointing sights and beaches. The lower number on these small signs is the highway number, so you can always make sure that you're on the right road.

In most cases, you'll only get one key for your rental car. Don't lock it inside. If you do, call AAA (or other auto emergency service that you may have) and ask for assistance. Failing that, a local locksmith can open your car for a fee or the rental car agency can send out a second key by taxi, but both of these options can get quite pricey.

Gas prices in Hawaii are above the national average, sometimes by as much as 30-40 cents a gallon. Prices may be a few cents per gallon more expensive in communities that are more distant from the main population centers.

Many people on the roads in Hawaii are tourists and can be unsure about where they're going. Slow down, be aware, and drive defensively.

In Hawaii, drivers don't generally honk their horns except to say hello or signal an emergency. It's considered rude, and honking to hurry someone might earn you a knuckle sandwich. Hawaiian drivers reflect the climate: they're relaxed and polite. Often on smaller roads, they'll brake to let you turn left when they're coming at you. They may assume you'll do the same, so be ready, after a perfunctory turn signal from another driver, for him or her to turn across your lane. The more rural the area, the more apt this is to happen. Don't expect it in the large cities.

Respect Do Not Enter and Private Property signs – *Kapu* means the same thing. Stay off cane haul roads. These, too, are on private property.

Car rental companies state that their cars are not to be driven off paved roads – read your policy. This seems absolutely ridiculous for 4WD vehicles, but it may be true nonetheless. When a road is signed for 4WD only, assume that's the case for a good reason. With some exceptions, car rental companies prohibit you from taking their rental vehicles across the Saddle Road or down South Point Road.

Speed limits change periodically along the highways of Hawai'i. Police routinely check the speed of traffic by use of radar equipment. Be aware of this so you don't go home with more than a suntan. Unlike on the other islands, there are long stretches of open road on the Big Island. On some of these, you may become mesmerized by the road and unconsciously increase your speed. Pay attention.

Like the other islands, the Big Island is afflicted by rush hour traffic. This is most pronounced in Kailua from the airport south to town. To a lesser degree, traffic on the highway coming north from South Kona into Kailua, the highway from Kea'au and Pahoa into Hilo, and the road through Waimea can also be heavy. To help alleviate some traffic congestion, bypass roads have been constructed around Kea'au and Pahoa, and across the back of Hilo.

There are a few emergency call boxes along the highways of the Big Island that are connected directly to an emergency response network. These telephones are to be used strictly for emergency calls when you have car trouble. They are in yellow boxes on tall poles topped by small solar panels.

making stops at Nawiliwili Harbor on Kaua'i, Honolulu on O'ahu, Kahului on Maui, and both Kona and Hilo on the Big Island. From summer 2006, *Pride of Hawaii* will be added to the fleet for these Hawaii-only routes. The itineraries of these ships differ somewhat, with some spending more time in port and others more time at sea. All the ships begin their journey at Honolulu; however, you may also start your trip on Maui for interisland routes. For specific information on routes, itineraries, and pricing, contact the company directly or work through a travel agent.

BY LAND

The most common way to get around Hawai'i is by rental car. The abundance of agencies keeps prices competitive. Hawai'i also has limited public bus service, expensive taxis, and reasonable bicycle, motorcycle, and moped rentals. Hitchhiking, while illegal on the Big Island, is still used by some to get around.

Highway Overview

Getting around the Big Island is fairly easy. There is one main highway called the Hawai'i Belt Road (also called Mamalahoa Highway) that circles the island, one cross-island highway called the Saddle Road, and a few other highways and secondary roadways. The Hawai'i Belt Road is known by different numbers in various sections around the island, and this may lead to some confusion. Connecting Kailua-Kona and Hilo around the south end, the number is Highway 11. Major roads that lead off of it are Napo'opo'o Road, which runs down to Kealakekua Bay; Ke Ala O Keawe Road to Pu'uhonua O Honaunau National Historical Park; South Point Road, which drops down to the southernmost tip of the island; Chain of Craters Road, which leads through Hawai'i Volcanoes National Park to the lava-covered littoral Puna Coast; and Kea'au-Pahoa Road (Highway 130) from Kea'au to the hinterland of Puna. In Puna, Kapoho-Pahoa Road (Highway 132) and Kapoho-Kalapana Beach Road (Highway 137) make a circle with Highway 130 from Pahoa, down along the shore, and back again.

Going north from Kailua-Kona, the Hawai'i Belt Road (Highway 190), which starts off for the first few miles as Palani Road, cuts across the upper slopes of the volcanoes to Waimea. Slicing through coffee country, as part of the Belt Road, is Highway 180. From Honalo, Route 11 heads down toward Kailua, first as Kuakini Highway, which itself makes a tangent into town, and then continues as Queen Ka'ahumanu Highway. Heading north from Kailua, Queen Ka'ahumanu Highway becomes Route 19. In Kawaihae, it turns uphill to Waimea, becoming Kawaihae Road. In Waimea, Highways 19 and 190 merge, and Highway 19 becomes the designation as the Hawai'i Belt Road continues along and down the Hamakua Coast back to Hilo. Connecting Highway 19 and Highway 190 through the town of Waikoloa is Waikoloa Road. In Honoka'a, Highway 240 leaves the Belt Road and runs north to the edge of Waipi'o Valley. North Kohala is cut by two roads. Akoni Pule Highway (Highway 270) runs along the coast up and around the tip as far as the Pololu Valley. Connecting this road and the town of Waimea is the Kohala Mountain Road (Highway 250). Off-limits to most rental cars, the Saddle Road (Highway 200) rises to about 6,500 feet between the tall peaks of Mauna Loa and Mauna Kea, making a shortcut between Hilo and Waimea or the Kohala Coast. From along the Saddle Road, four-wheel drive roads lead up to the observatories atop Mauna Kea and nearly to the top of Mauna Loa.

Rental Cars

Rental car options in Hawaii are as numerous as anywhere in the United States, from a subcompact to a full-size luxury land yacht. The most numerous seem to be compact cars and midsize sedans, but convertibles and four-wheel drive jeeps are very popular, and some vans and SUVs are also available. Nearly all have automatic transmissions and air-conditioning. Generally, you must be 21 years old; a few agencies will rent to 18-year-olds, while some require you to be 25 for certain vehicles. Those ages 21–24 will usually be charged an extra fee, which may be significant.

If you're traveling during the peak seasons of Christmas, Easter, or summer, absolutely reserve your car in advance. If you're going off-peak, you stand a very good chance of getting the car you want at a price you like once you land in the islands. You can get some sweet deals. To be on the safe side, and for your own peace of mind, it's generally best to book ahead.

All major car rental companies in Hawaii use flat rate pricing, which provides a fixed daily rate and unlimited mileage. Most car companies, local and national, offer special rates and deals, like AAA discounts. These deals are common, but don't expect rental companies to let you know about them. Make sure to inquire. The basic rates aren't your only charges, however. On top of the actual rental fee, you must pay an airport access fee, airport concession fee, state tax, and a road tax surcharge—in total, an additional 25–30 percent.

Most companies have child seats available for rent on a daily basis, $5 a day or $40–50 maximum, and can install right- or left-hand controls for handicapped drivers. Agencies generally require 48–72 hours' advance notice to install hand controls.

Most car companies charge you a fee if you rent the car in Hilo and drop it off in Kona, and vice versa. Agencies prohibit their vehicles from being used on the Saddle Road and are prejudiced against the spur road leading to South Point. The road to the top of Mauna Kea is a four-wheel-drive-only road. Heed the signs, not so much for going up, but for needed braking power coming down. Avis and Harper allow you to drive the Saddle Road, and Harper rents four-wheel drives for the Mauna Kea and Mauna Loa roads. No way whatsoever should you attempt to drive down to Waipi'o Valley in a regular car! The grade is unbelievably steep, and only a four-wheel drive can make it. Put simply, you have a good chance of being killed if you try it in a car.

Car Rental Agencies

The following are major firms represented at both the Hilo and Kona Airports. Kona numbers begin with a "3" while Hilo numbers start with a "9."

Dollar (800/800-4000, www.dollarcar.com) has an excellent reputation and very competitive prices. Dollar rents mostly Chrysler vehicles: sedans, Jeeps, and convertibles. Great weekly rates, and all major credit cards accepted.

Alamo (808/961-3343, 808/329-8896 or 800/327-9633, www.goalamo.com) has good weekly rates and mostly GM cars.

National (808/935-0891, 808/329-1674 or 800/227-7368, www.nationalcar.com) features GM and Nissan cars and accepts all major credit cards.

Avis (808/935-1290, 808/327-3000 or 800/321-3712, www.avis.com) features late-model GM cars as well as most imports and convertibles.

Budget (800/527-0700, www.budget.com) offers competitive rates on a variety of late-model Ford and Lincoln-Mercury cars and specialty vehicles.

Hertz (808/933-2566, 808/329-3566, or 800/654-3011, www.hertz.com) is competitively priced with many fly/drive deals. Hertz features Ford vehicles.

Thrifty (866/450-5101 or 800/367-2277, www.thrifty.com) uses mostly Chrysler vehicles.

Some years ago, local companies abounded, but today only one has survived with any significance. At **Harper** (808/969-1478 or 800/852-9993, www.harpershawaii.com) in Hilo, you can rent a car, truck, seven- to 15-passenger van, RV, or four-wheel drive for driving up to Mauna Kea. Good competitive rates.

Hele-On Bus

The county of Hawai'i maintains the Mass Transit Agency, known throughout the island as the Hele-On Bus. For information, schedules, and fares contact the Mass Transit Agency (25 Aupuni St., Hilo, 808/961-8744, open 7:45 A.M.–4:30 P.M. Mon.–Fri., www.co.hawaii.hi.us/mass_transit/transit_main.htm).

The main bus terminal is in downtown Hilo at Mo'oheau Park, just at the corner of Kamehameha Avenue and Mamo Street. The Hele-On Bus system now has a mostly modern fleet of large buses that are clean and comfortable. The Hele-On operates approximately 6 A.M.–6 P.M. Mon.–Fri., depending on the run, except for the route to Kona and Kohala, which also operates Saturdays, and the route from North Kohala to the Kohala resorts, which operates daily. There are a number of intra-Hilo routes with additional intercity routes to points around the periphery of the island, but these all operate on a very limited schedule, sometimes only once a day. If you're in a hurry then definitely forget about taking the bus, but if you want to meet the people of Hawai'i, there's no better way. Large items like surfboards, boogie boards, and bicycles are not allowed.

As of October 2005, the county has instituted "no-fare" rides for all bus routes on the island, so all Hele-On bus transportation is currently free.

There are four basic intercity routes connecting to Hilo. One—the longest bus route—goes from Kealia, south of Captain Cook, all the way to Hilo on the east coast via Kailua-Kona, Waikoloa, Waimea, and the Hamakua Coast. Operating Mon.–Sat., this journey covers 110 miles in just over four. Additional intra-Kona buses run just between Kealia and Kailua on weekdays. You can take the southern route from the Ocean View post office through Ka'u, Na'alehu, and Hawai'i Volcanoes National Park to Hilo. This trip takes just 2.5 hours. A third route to Hilo runs from Pahoa through Kea'au, while the fourth starts in Waimea then proceeds down the coast through Honoka'a and Honomu to Hilo. In the Kohala district, a daily bus runs every weekday morning from Kapa'au through Hawi to the various Kohala resorts and returns in the late afternoon.

Taxis

Both the Hilo and Kona Airports always have taxis waiting for fares. Fares are regulated. From Hilo's airport to downtown costs about $12, to the Banyan Drive hotels about $8. From the Kona Airport to hotels and condos along Ali'i Drive in Kailua fares run $20–35, north to Waikoloa Beach Resort they run about $45, and fares are approximately $65 as far north as the Mauna Kea Resort. Obviously, a taxi is no way to get around if you're trying to save money. Most taxi companies, both in Kona and Hilo, also run sightseeing services for fixed prices. In **Kona** try Kona Airport Taxi (808/329-7779), Paradise Taxi (808/329-1234), or C&C Taxi (808/329-6388). In **Hilo** try Hilo Harry's Taxi (808/935-7091), A-1 Bob's Taxi (808/959-4800), or Percy's Taxi (808/969-7060).

An alternative in the Kona area is **SpeediShuttle** (808/329-5433 or 877/521-2085, www.speedishuttle.com). Operating 7 A.M.–10 P.M. daily, SpeediShuttle runs multi-seat vans, so its prices are cheaper per person the more people you have riding. It also would be appropriate if you have lots of luggage. Sample rates for a shared taxi from the Kona Airport are $23 to downtown Kailua-Kona, $32 to the south end of Kailua and the Keauhou area, and $36 for a ride up to Waikoloa Beach Resort. For a single rider, fares can be three times as much. SpeediShuttle has a courtesy phone at the airport for your convenience. Reservations a day ahead are not necessary but may be helpful to get a ride at the time you want.

Hitchhiking

The old thumb works on the Big Island about as well as anywhere else. Though hitchhiking is technically illegal, the police seem to have much more important things to pay attention to than going after those just trying to get down the road. Stay off the roadway, be low-key, but make your intentions known. Your best chance may be being picked up by a visiting or local *haole.* Sometimes locals in pickup trucks will stop to give you a ride for short distances. Women *should not* hitch alone! Some people hitchhike rather than take the Hele-On Bus not so much to save money but to save time! It's a good idea to check the bus schedule (and routes), and set out about 30 minutes before the scheduled departure. If you don't have good luck hitching a ride, just wait for the bus to come along and hail it. It'll stop.

Tips for Travelers

ACCOMMODATIONS: POINTS TO CONSIDER

Finding suitable accommodations on the Big Island is never a problem. The 10,000-plus rooms available at the island's 450 properties have the lowest annual occupancy rate of any in the islands at about 60 percent. With some 4,500 rooms, a concentration of the state's greatest luxury resorts are within minutes of each other on the Kohala Coast. All are superb, with hideaway "grass shacks," exquisite art collections as an integral part of the grounds, picture-perfect gardens, world-ranked golf courses, and perfect beaches. Kona has roughly 3,500 fine, reasonably priced hotel rooms strung along Ali'i Drive from Kailua to Keauhou. Interspersed among the big hotels are smaller hotels, condominiums, and time-shares with homey atmospheres and great rates. Hilo has about 1,300 rooms and you can get some of the best bargains on the island. For a real treat, head to Hawai'i Volcanoes National Park and stay at one of the vacation rentals or bed-and-breakfasts tucked away there, or at Volcano House, where raw nature has thrilled kings, queens, and luminaries for well over a century. You can comfortably stay in the cowboy town of Waimea, find a place in a pass-through town like Captain Cook, or try a self-growth, yoga, or meditation retreat in Puna or Ka'u. The rest are scattered around the island in small villages from Na'alehu in the south to Hawi in the north, where you can almost count on being the only off-island guest.

Hotels

Even with the wide variety of other accommodations available, most visitors, at least first-timers, tend to stay in hotels. Hotels come in all shapes and sizes, from 10-room, family-run affairs to high-rise giants. Most readily available and least expensive is a bedroom with bath. Some hotels have suites, and some of the more economical places also offer kitchenettes. Check-in is usually 3 P.M., checkout most often is noon. Like anywhere in the world, all hotels have some amenities, and some hotels have all of them. If you need something in particular, be sure to check directly with the hotel or view its website. A few hotels have purposefully created an environment without phones, TVs, or entertainment centers so that you can get plugged into your surroundings and stay disconnected from other distractions. Hawaiian hotels have also made a concerted effort to offer a variety of cultural activities for their guests to educate and bring the place closer to home.

Every year Hawaiian hotels welcome in the New Year by hiking their **rates** by about 10 percent. Because of the tough competition, rates are competitive, even with the 11.4 percent tax (7.25 percent accommodations tax, plus 4.16 percent general excise tax) added on. The basic daily rate is almost always geared toward double occupancy; many hotels will add an additional charge for extra persons up to a certain number. Plenty of hotels offer the family plan, which allows children, usually 17 and under, to stay in their parents' room free if they use the existing beds. Only a very limited number of hotels offer the American plan, where breakfast and dinner are included with the night's lodging. Discounts of various sorts are offered, but these vary by hotel. Some of the typical discounts are AAA, AARP, car and room, room and breakfast, fifth-night free, *kama'aina* (state resident), and Internet rates. In all cases, ask about other-than-published rates because this information won't necessarily be volunteered. In addition to regular hotel charges and taxes, some luxury hotels and resorts now charge a "resort fee," usually around $15, that is used to offset a variety of amenities and parking costs.

While some hotels have a single basic rate throughout the year, most have a tiered pricing policy based on times of the year. This often translates as regular- and value-season rates (which may be referred to differently at different hotels), while some also include holiday rates. While the difference between "high season" and "low season" is less distinct than it used to be, Hawaii's **peak season** still runs from just before Christmas until after Easter and then again throughout the summer, when rooms are at a premium. Value-season rates, when rooms are easier to come by, are often about 10 percent below the regular rate.

In Hawaiian hotels you always pay more for a good **view.** Terms vary slightly, but usually "oceanfront" means your room faces the ocean and your view is mostly unimpeded. "Ocean view" is more vague. It could be a decent view, or it could require standing on the dresser and craning your neck to catch a tiny slice of the sea sandwiched between two skyscrapers. "Garden view" means just that, and "mountain view" may mean that you have a view of a mountain or simply that you have a view away from the ocean. Rooms are designated and priced upward with garden view or mountain view being the least expensive, then ocean view and oceanfront rooms. Suites are invariably larger and more expensive, and these usually get the best locations and views.

Note: Prices listed in the travel chapters are based on a standard published rate, double occupancy, without taxes or other charges added, unless otherwise noted.

SHOES OFF

Whether it's that the old Hawaiians didn't wear shoes, the mild climate, which encourages people to go barefoot, the custom of many Asian immigrants to Hawaii to remove their shoes when going indoors, or for some other reason altogether, it's a custom in Hawaii to take your shoes off when entering someone's house. This holds true for B&Bs, condos, and vacation rentals, but not for hotels. This custom, plus the weather, makes wearing rubber thongs (slippahs) or similar slip-on shoes most popular.

But beware the Slipper Dog. Every neighborhood has one, and they always strike in the middle of the night. Because of the custom of no shoes inside, a pile of slippers invariably graces the entrance to most homes, somewhat like a freeform sculpture or cosmic artificial plant. In the morning, a slipper or two – but never two from the same pair – are missing. Instantly resignation and recognition set in. Slipper Dog! So, if you see a local person, or even a tourist, walking down the street a bit lopsided wearing one pink size-9 slipper and one black size-12 slipper, you will be observing at close hand a victim of the Slipper Dog.

Condominiums

The main qualitative difference between a condo and a hotel is in amenities. At a condo, you're more on your own. You're temporarily renting an apartment, so there won't be any bellhops and rarely a bar, restaurant, or lounge on the premises, though many times you'll find a sundries store. Condos can be studios (one big room), but mostly they are one- or multiple-bedroom affairs with a complete kitchen. Reasonable housekeeping items should be provided. All have sufficient amenities, but remember that the furnishings provided are up to the owner. Maid service might be included on a limited basis (for example, once weekly), or you might have to pay extra for it. Swimming pools are common, and depending on the "theme" of the condo, you can find saunas, weight rooms, hot tubs, and tennis courts.

Condos usually require a minimum stay, most often three days, but seven is also commonplace, and during peak season two weeks isn't unheard of. Generally speaking, studios can sleep two, a one-bedroom place will sleep four, two bedrooms sleep six, and three bedrooms sleep eight. Most have a sleeper couch in the sitting room that folds out into a bed. You can find clean, decent condos for as little as $450 per week, all the way up to exclusive apartments for well over $2,000. Most fall into the $700–1,000 per week range. The method of paying for and reserving a condo is just about the same as for a hotel. However, requirements for deposits, final payments, and cancellation charges are much stiffer than in hotels. Make absolutely sure you fully understand all of these requirements when you make your reservations.

The real advantage of condos is for families, friends who want to share, and especially people on long-term stays, for which you will always get a special rate. The kitchen facilities save a great deal on dining costs, and it's common to find units with their own mini-washers and dryers. To sweeten the deal, many condo companies offer coupons that can save you money on food, gifts, and activities at local establishments. Parking space is ample for guests, and as at hotels, plenty of stay/drive deals are offered.

Vacation Rentals

Vacation rentals are homes or cottages that are rented to visitors, usually for a week or longer. Sometimes shorter rentals can be arranged. These rentals come with all the amenities of condo units, but they are usually freestanding homes. As with condos, meals are not part of the option. Perhaps the best way to locate a vacation rental, at least the first time you visit the island, is through a rental/real estate agent. Accommodations from simple beach homes to luxurious hideaways are put into the hands of rental agents. The agents have descriptions of the properties and terms of the rental contracts, and many will furnish photographs. Be aware that most places, although not all, have out-cleaning fees in addition to the rental rate. When contacting an agency, be as specific as possible about your needs, length of stay, desired location, and how much you're willing to spend. Be aware that during high season, rentals are at a premium; if you're slow to inquire there may be slim pickin's.

Bed-and-Breakfasts

Lodging in private homes called bed-and-breakfasts (B&B) is becoming increasingly fashionable throughout the United States, and Hawaii is no exception, with about 100,000 B&B guests yearly.

The primary feature of bed-and-breakfasts is that every one is privately owned and therefore unique. The range of B&Bs is wide, but most fall into the broad middle living standard in America. Still, the lifestyles of B&B hosts differ, so it's prudent to choose a host family with whom one's lifestyle is compatible if at all possible.

Unlike at a hotel or a condo, you'll usually be staying *with* a host (usually a family), although your room will be private, with private baths and separate entrances quite common. Many B&Bs now also offer separate cottages, and some homes do not have live-in hosts, but the unifying feature is that breakfast is provided. Meals vary as much as B&B styles. They range from a full-blown, sit-down affair with home-cooked meals at a prescribed time to a plate of fruit and pastries with a bottle of juice left in a room refrigerator for you to have whenever you want.

You can make arrangements directly or you might want to go through an agency which acts as a go-between, matching host and guest. Agencies have a description of each B&B they rent for, its general location, the fees charged, and a good idea of the lifestyle of the host family. What the agency will want to know from you is where you want to stay, what type of place you're looking for, your price range, arrival and departure dates, and other items that will help them match you with a place. (Are you single? Do you have children? Are you a smoker? etc.) You, of course, can do all the legwork yourself, but these people know their territory and guarantee their work. They also inspect each B&B and make sure that all have a license and insurance to operate. Most can also arrange discount rental cars and interisland airfares for you.

Make all your arrangement well in advance. You might be lucky and find a place that has an opening on short notice, but give yourself four weeks as a minimum. For holiday travel, three to six months' lead time would not be imprudent. Expect a minimum-stay requirement (three days is common). As with condos, B&Bs have different requirements for making and holding reservations and for payment. Most will hold a room with a credit card deposit or check covering a certain percentage of the total expected bill. Be aware, however, that some B&Bs do not accept credit cards or personal checks, so you must pay in cash, travelers checks, or money orders. Always inquire about the method and type of payment when making your initial inquiries.

Operating strictly for establishments on the Big Island is **Hawaii Island B&B Association,** or HIBBA (info@stayhawaii.com, www.stayhawaii.com), a local organization that monitors its members for quality standards. Its website and brochure lists member accommodations, descriptions, and contact information.

One of the most experienced agencies, **Bed And Breakfast Honolulu (Statewide)** (3242 Kaohinani Dr., Honolulu, HI 96817, 808/595-7533, fax 808/595-2030 or 800/288-4666, www.hawaiibnb.com, rainbow@hawaiibnb.com), owned and operated by Mary Lee and Gene Bridges, began in 1982. Since then, they've become masters at finding the perfect accommodations to match visitors' desires, needs, and pocketbooks. **All Islands Bed and Breakfast** (808/263-2342, fax 808/263-0308 or 800/542-0344, www.all-islands.com, inquiries@all-islands.com) can also match your needs up with numerous homes on the Big Island. **Hawaii's Best Bed and Breakfast** (P.O. Box 485, Laupahoehoe, HI 96764, 808/962-0100, fax 808/962-6360 or 800/262-9912, http://bestbnb.com, reservations@bestbnb.com) has listings all over the state.

Hostels

The Big Island has several very reasonably priced hostels operating at this time. Perhaps the truest hostel experience on the Big Island is at **Holo Holo In** in Volcano (19-4036 Kalani Honua Road, 96785, 808/967-7950, fax 808/967-8025, holoholo@interpac.net, www.enable.org/holoholo).

Both **Arnott's Lodge** (98 Apapane Rd., 808/969-7097, mahalo@arnottslodge.com, www.arnottslodge.com) and **Hilo Bay Hostel** (101 Waianuenue Ave., 808/933-2771, www.hawaiihostel.net) are good options in Hilo. Hilo Bay Hostel is downtown, while Arnott's Lodge is out near beaches to the east of town. Aside from lodgings, Arnott's has tenting space on the lawn and runs wonderful and inexpensive touring excursions.

Pineapple Park B&B Hostel runs one unit south of Kurtistown (11-3489 Pikake, 808/968-8170 or 877/865-2266, ppark@aloha.net, www.pineapple-park.com) and another on the Kona side along the highway in Captain Cook (808/323-2224 or 877/800-3800, fax 808/323-2086, ppark@aloha.net, www.pineapple-park.com).

The **Hotel Honoka'a Club** (P.O. Box 247, Honoka'a, HI 96727, 808/775-0678 or 800/808-0678, www.hotelhonokaa.com) is located in Honoka'a, near Wapi'o Valley.

SERVICES FOR TRAVELERS WITH DISABILITIES

A person with a disability can have a wonderful time in Hawaii; all that's needed is a little preplanning. The key for a smooth trip is to make as many arrangements ahead of time as possible. Tell the transportation companies and hotels you'll be dealing with the nature of your handicap in advance so that they can make arrangements to accommodate you. Bring your medical records and notify medical establishments of your arrival if you'll be needing their services. Travel with a friend or make arrangements for an aide on arrival. Bring your own wheelchair if possible and let airlines know if it is battery-powered; boarding interisland flights often requires steps. Airlines can board you early on special lifts, but they must know that you're coming. Many hotels and restaurants accommodate persons with disabilities, but always call ahead just to make sure.

Information

The Commission on Persons with Disabilities was designed with the express purpose of aiding disabled people. It is a source of invaluable information and distributes some self-help booklets, which are published jointly by the Disability and Communication Access Board and the Hawaii Centers for Independent Living. Any person with disabilities heading to Hawaii should write first or visit the office of Hawaii Centers for Independent Living (414 Kuwili St., #102, Honolulu, HI 96817, 808/522-5400). On Hawai'i, check either Center for Independent Living—East Hawai'i (400 Hualani St., #16D, Hilo, HI 96720, 808/935-3777) or Center for Independent Living—West Hawai'i (81-6627 Mamalahoa Hwy., Ste. B5, Kealakekua, HI 96750, 808/323-2221).

Services

At Hilo Airport, all passengers arrive or leave via a jetway on the second level, and there are escalators, stairs, and some elevators between levels. Baggage claim, bathrooms, and telephones are accessible. Parking is convenient in designated areas. The Kona Airport is all one level. Boarding and deplaning by lift is possible for the disabled. There are no jetways. Bathrooms and telephones are accessible, and there is specially designated handicapped parking.

All rental car agencies can install hand controls on their cars if given enough notice—usually 48–72 hours. Your own state handicap placard will be honored here. Medical help, nurses, and companions can be arranged through the **Center for Independent Living** (808/935-3777 in Hilo or 808/323-2221 in Kona). Doctors are referred by **Hilo Medical Center** (808/974-4700) and the **Kona Community Hospital** (808/322-9311). Medical equipment rentals are available in Hilo from **Apria Healthcare** (808/969-1221), **Rainbow Medical Supply** (808/935-9393), and **Shiigi Drug** (808/935-0001); and in Kona from **Big Island Medical Equipment** (808/323-3313).

ALTERNATIVE WAYS TO THE ISLAND

Ecotours to Hawaii

Sierra Club Trips offers Hawaii trips for nature lovers who are interested in an outdoor experience. Various trips include birding on the Big Island, and kayak and camping trips on Kaua'i. All trips are led by experienced guides and are open to Sierra Club members only ($35 per year to join). For information contact the Sierra Club Outing Department (85 2nd St., 2nd Fl., San Francisco, CA 94105, 415/977-5522, www.sierraclub.org/outings).

Educational Trips

Not a tour company per se, but an educational opportunity, **Elderhostel Hawaii** offers short-term programs on five of the Hawaiian Islands. Different programs focus on history, culture, cuisine, and the environment in association with one of the colleges or universities in the islands. Most programs use hotels for accommodations. For information, contact Elderhostel (11 Avenue de Lafayette, Boston, MA 02111-1746, 877/426-8056, www.elderhostel.org).

PREVENTING THEFT

From the minute you sit behind the wheel of your rental car, you'll be warned not to leave valuables unattended and to lock up your car tighter than a drum. Signs warning about theft at most major tourist attractions help to fuel your paranoia. Many hotel and condo rooms offer safes so you can lock your valuables away and relax while getting sunburned. The majority of theft in Hawaii is of the "sneak thief" variety. If you leave your hotel door unlocked, a camera sitting on the seat of your rental car, or valuables on your beach towel, you'll be inviting a very obliging thief to pad away with your stuff. You'll have to take precautions, but they won't be anything like those employed in rougher areas of the world—just normal American precautions. Hawaii's reputation is much worse than the reality. Besides, Hawaiians are still among the friendliest, most giving, and understanding people on earth.

If you must walk alone at night, stay on the main streets in well-lit areas. Always lock your hotel door and windows and place valuable jewelry in the hotel safe. When you leave your hotel for the beach, there is absolutely no reason to carry all your traveler's checks, credit cards, or a big wad of money. Just take what you'll need for drinks and lunch. If you're uptight about leaving money in your beach bag, stick it in your bathing suit. American money is just as negotiable when damp. Don't leave your camera on the beach unattended. While sightseeing in your shiny new rental car, which immediately brands you as a tourist, again, don't take more than what you'll need for the day. Many people lock valuables away in the trunk, but remember that most good car thieves can "jimmy" it as quickly as you can open it with your key.

Campers face special problems because their entire scene is open to thievery. Most campgrounds don't have any real security, but who, after all, wants to fence an old tent or a used sleeping bag? Many tents have zippers that can be secured with a small padlock. In the end, you must just take what precautions that you can and trust the goodness of others.

Health and Safety

In a survey published some years ago by *Science Digest,* Hawaii was cited as the healthiest state in the United States in which to live. Indeed, Hawaiian citizens live longer than residents anywhere else in America: men to 76 years and women to 82. Lifestyle, heredity, and diet help with these figures, but Hawaii is still an oasis in the middle of the ocean, and germs just have a tougher time getting there. There are no cases of malaria, cholera, or yellow fever. Because of a strict quarantine law, rabies is also nonexistent. On the other hand, tooth decay—perhaps because of a wide use of sugar and the enzymes present in certain tropical fruits—is 30 percent above the national average. Also, obesity and related heart problems and hard drug use—especially "ice"—are prevalent among native Hawaiians. With the perfect weather, a multitude of fresh-air activities, soothing negative ionization from the sea, and a generally relaxed and carefree lifestyle, everyone feels better there. Hawaii is just what the doctor ordered: a beautiful, natural health spa. That's one of its main drawing cards. The food and tap water are perfectly safe, and the air quality is the best in the country.

Handling the Sun

Don't become a victim of your own exuberance. People can't wait to strip down and lie on the sand like beached whales, but the tropical sun will burn you to a cinder if you're silly. The burning rays come through more easily in Hawaii because of the sun's angle, and you don't feel them as much because there's always a cool breeze. The worst part of the day is 11 A.M.–3 P.M. The Big Island lies between 19 and 20 degrees north latitude, not even close to the equator, but it's still over 1,000 miles south of sunny Southern California beaches. Force yourself to go slowly. Don't worry; you'll be able to flaunt your best souvenir, your golden Hawaiian tan, to your green-with-envy friends when you get home. It's better than showing them a boiled lobster body with peeling skin! If your skin is snowflake white, 15 minutes per side on the first day is plenty. Increase by 15-minute intervals every day, which will allow you a full hour per side by the fourth day. Have faith; this is enough to give you a deep golden, uniform tan. If you lie out on the beach, are simply out in the sun during the day, if you're off hiking or kayaking, or have rented a convertible car (an unexpected culprit for sunburn), use sunblock lotion that has greater strength than you use at home—most people recommend SPF 25 or higher—and reapply every couple of hours. If you do burn, try taking aspirin as quickly as you can. No one knows exactly what it does, but it seems to provide some relief. Alternatively, apply a cold compress or aloe juice, but be careful with aloe because it may stain clothing.

Whether out on the beach, hiking in the mountains, or just strolling around town, be very aware of dehydration. The sun and wind tend to sap your energy and your store of liquid. Bottled water in various sizes is readily available in all parts of Hawaii. Be sure to carry some with you or stop at a store or restaurant for a fill-'er-up.

Don't forget about your head and eyes. Use

HAWAIIAN FOLK MEDICINE AND COMMON CURATIVE PLANTS

Hawaiian folk medicine is well developed, and its cures for common ailments have been used effectively for centuries. Hawaiian *kahuna* were highly regarded for their medicinal skills, and Hawaiians were by far some of the healthiest people in the world until the coming of the Europeans. Many folk remedies and cures are used to this day and, what's more, they work. Many of the common plants and fruits that you'll encounter provide some of the best remedies. When roots and seeds and special exotic plants are used, the preparation of the medicine is as painstaking as in a modern pharmacy. These prescriptions are exact and take an expert to prepare. They should never be prepared or administered by an amateur.

Arrowroot, for diarrhea, is a powerful narcotic used in rituals and medicines. **Kava** *(Piper methysticum),* also called *'awa,* is chewed and the juice is spat into a container for fermenting. Used as a medicine for urinary tract infections, rheumatism, and asthma, it also induces sleep and cures headaches. A poultice for wounds is made from the skins of ripe **bananas.** Peelings have a powerful antibiotic quality and contain vitamins A, B, and C, phosphorus, calcium, and iron. The nectar from the plant was fed to babies as a vitamin juice. **Breadfruit** sap is used for healing cuts and as a moisturizing lotion. **Coconut** is used to make moisturizing oil, and the juice was chewed, spat into the hand, and used as a shampoo. **Guava** is a source of vitamins A, B, and C. **Hibiscus** has been used as a laxative. ***Kukui*** nut oil makes a gargle for sore throats and a laxative, plus the flowers are used to cure diarrhea. ***Noni,*** an unappetizing hand grenade-shaped fruit that you wouldn't want to eat unless you had to, reduces tumors, diabetes, and high blood pressure, and the juice is good for diarrhea. **Sugarcane** sweetens many concoctions, and the juice of toasted cane was a tonic for sick babies. **Sweet potato** is used as a tonic during pregnancy and juiced as a gargle for phlegm. **Tamarind** is a natural laxative and contains the most acid and sugar of any fruit on earth. **Taro** has been used for lung infections and thrush, and as a suppository. **Yams** are good for coughs, vomiting, constipation, and appendicitis.

your sunglasses and wear a brimmed hat. Some people lay a towel over their neck and shoulders when hiking and others will stick a scarf under their hat and let it drape down over their shoulders to provide some protection.

Haole Rot

A peculiar condition caused by the sun is referred to locally as *haole* rot. It's called this because it supposedly affects only white people, but you'll notice some dark-skinned people with the same condition. Basically, the skin becomes mottled with white spots that refuse to tan. You get a blotchy effect, mostly on the shoulders and back. Dermatologists have a fancy name for it, and they'll give you a fancy prescription with a very fancy price tag to cure it. It's common knowledge throughout the islands that Selsun Blue shampoo has an ingredient that stops the white mottling effect. Just wash your hair with it and then make sure to rub the lather over the affected areas, and it should clear up.

Bugs

Everyone, in varying degrees, has an aversion to vermin and creepy crawlers. Hawaii isn't infested with a wide variety, but it does have its share. Mosquitoes were unknown in the islands until their larvae stowed away in the water barrels of the *Wellington* in 1826 and were introduced at Lahaina. They bred in the tropical climate and rapidly spread to all the islands. They are a particular nuisance in the rainforests. Be prepared and bring a natural repellent like citronella oil, available in most health stores on the islands, or a commercial product available in groceries and drugstores.

Campers will be happy to have mosquito coils to burn at night as well.

Cockroaches are very democratic insects. They hassle all strata of society equally. They breed well in Hawaii, and most hotels are at war with them, trying desperately to keep them from being spotted by guests. One comforting thought is that in Hawaii they aren't a sign of filth or dirty housekeeping. They love the climate like everyone else, and it's a real problem keeping them under control.

WATER SAFETY

Hawaii has one very sad claim to fame: more people drown here than anywhere else in the world. Moreover, there are dozens of victims yearly with broken necks and backs or with injuries from scuba and snorkeling accidents. These statistics shouldn't keep you out of the sea, because it is indeed beautiful—and benevolent in most cases—and a major reason to go to Hawaii. But if you're foolish, the sea will bounce you like a basketball and suck you away for good. The best remedy is to avoid situations you can't handle. Don't let anyone dare you into a situation that makes you uncomfortable. "Macho men" who know nothing about the power of the sea will be tumbled into Cabbage Patch Kids dolls in short order. Ask lifeguards or beach attendants about conditions, and follow their advice. If local people refuse to go in, there's a good reason. Even experts get in trouble in Hawaiian waters. Some beaches are as gentle as lambs, others, especially on the north coasts during the winter months, are frothing giants.

While beachcombing, or especially when walking out on rocks, never turn your back to the sea. Be aware of undertows (the waves drawing back into the sea). They can knock you off your feet. Before entering the water, study it for rocks, breakers, and reefs. Look for ocean currents, especially those within reefs that can cause riptides when the water washes out a channel. Observe the water well before you enter. Note where others are swimming or snorkeling and go there. When snorkeling, wear a T-Shirt. It may save your back from major sunburn. Don't swim alone if possible, and obey all warning signs. Come in *before* you get tired.

When the wind comes up, get out. Stay out of the water during periods of high surf. High surf often creates riptides that can pull you out to sea. Riptides are powerful currents, like rivers in the sea, that can drag you out. Mostly they peter out not too far from shore, and you

© ROBERT NILSEN

can often see their choppy waters on the surface. If caught in a "rip," don't fight to swim directly against it. You'll lose and only exhaust yourself. Swim diagonally across it, while going along with it, and try to stay parallel to the shore until you are out of the strong pull.

When bodysurfing, never ride straight in; come to shore at a 45-degree angle. Remember, waves come in sets. Little ones can be followed by giants, so watch the action awhile instead of plunging right in. Standard procedure is to duck under a breaking wave. You can survive even thunderous oceans using this technique. Don't try to swim through a heavy froth and never turn your back and let it smash you.

Stay off of coral. Standing on coral damages it, as does breaking it with your hands, and it might give you a nasty infection.

Leave the fish, turtles, and seals alone. Fish should never be encouraged to feed from humans. Green sea turtles and seals are endangered species, and stiff fines can be levied on those who knowingly disturb them. Have a great time looking, but give them space.

Hawaiians want to entertain you, and they want you to be safe. The county, for its part, doesn't put up ocean conditions signs at beaches just to waste money. They're there for your safety. Pay heed. The last rule is, "If in doubt, stay out."

Yikes!

Sharks live in all the oceans of the world. Most mind their own business and stay away from shore. Hawaiian sharks are well fed—on fish—and don't usually bother with unsavory humans. If you encounter a shark, don't panic! Never thrash around because this will trigger its attack instinct. If it comes close, scream loudly.

Portuguese man-of-wars put out long, floating tentacles that sting if they touch you. It seems that many floating jellyfish are blown into shore by winds on the eighth, ninth, and 10th days after the full moon. Don't wash the sting off with freshwater, as this will only aggravate it. Hot saltwater will take away the sting, as will alcohol (the drinking or the rubbing kind), aftershave lotion, and meat tenderizer (MSG), which can be found in any supermarket or Chinese restaurant.

Coral can give you a nasty cut, and it's known for causing infections because it's a living organism. Wash the cut immediately and apply an antiseptic. Keep it clean and covered, and watch for infection.

Poisonous sea urchins, such as the lacquer-black *wana,* can be beautiful creatures. They are found in shallow tidepools and will hurt you if you step on them. Their spines will break off, enter your foot, and burn like blazes. There are cures. Vinegar and wine poured on the wound will stop the burning. If those are not available, the Hawaiian solution is urine. It might seem ignominious to have someone pee on your foot, but it'll put the fire out. The spines will disintegrate in a few days, and there are generally no long-term effects.

Hawaiian reefs also have their share of moray eels. These creatures are ferocious in appearance but will never initiate an attack. You'll have to poke around in their holes while snorkeling or scuba diving to get them to attack. Sometimes this is inadvertent on the diver's part, so be careful where you stick your hand while underwater.

Present in streams, ponds, and muddy soil, **Leptospirosis** is a *freshwater*-borne bacteria, deposited by the urine of infected animals. From two to 20 days after the bacteria enter the body, there is a *sudden* onset of fever accompanied by chills, sweats, headache, and sometimes vomiting and diarrhea. Preventive measures include: staying out of freshwater sources where cattle and other animals wade and drink; not swimming in freshwater if you have an open cut; and not drinking stream water.

MEDICAL SERVICES

Hospitals

On the east side, 24-hour medical help is available from **Hilo Medical Center** (1190 Waianuenue Ave., 808/974-4700). While in Ka'u, seek help from the **Ka'u Hospital** in Pahala (808/928-8331). On the west side, try **Kona Community Hospital** in Kealakekua (79-1019 Haukapila St., 808/322-9311). The **North**

Hawaii Community Hospital in Kamuela (67-1125 Mamalahoa Hwy., 808/885-4444) services the northern part of the island.

Medical Clinics

For minor emergencies and urgent care in Kona, try **Hualalai Urgent Care** (808/327-4357) at the Crossroads Medical Center on Henry Street. In Hilo, try **Hilo Urgent Care Center** (45 Mohouli, 808/969-3051). In Honoka'a, see the **Hamakua Health Center** (808/775-7204).

Pharmacies

Longs Drugs, KTA Super Store, and **Kmart** all have pharmacies.

Others that should meet your needs are: **Village Pharmacy** (808/885-4418) in Waimea, **Hilo Pharmacy** (808/961-9267) along the bay front, **Waikoloa Pharmacy** (808/883-8484) in Waikoloa, **Ka'u Community Pharmacy** (808/928-6252), and **Kamehameha Pharmacy** (808/889-6161) in Kapa'au.

Information and Services

MONEY

Currency

U.S. currency is among the drabbest in the world. It's all the same size, with little variation in color; those unfamiliar with it should spend some time getting acquainted so they don't make costly mistakes. U.S. coins in use are: penny ($0.01), nickel ($0.05), dime ($0.10), quarter ($0.25), half dollar ($0.50), and $1; paper currency is $1, $2 (uncommon), $5, $10, $20, $50, and $100. Bills larger than $100 are not in common usage. Since 1996, new designs have been issued for the $100, $50, $20, $10, and $5 bills. Both the old and new bills are accepted as valid currency.

Banks

Full-service bank hours are generally 8:30 A.M.–4 P.M. Mon.–Thurs. and until 6 P.M. Friday. There are no weekend hours, and weekday hours will be a bit longer at counters in grocery stores and other outlets. All main towns on Hawai'i have one or more banks: Hilo, Kailua-Kona, Waimea, Kealakekua, Honoka'a, Pahoa, Waikoloa, Pahala, and Hawi. Virtually all branch banks have ATMs for 24-hour service, and these can be found at some shopping centers and other venues around the island. ATMs work only when the Hawaiian bank you choose to use is on an affiliate network with your home bank. Of most value to travelers, banks sell and cash travelers checks, give cash advances on credit cards, and exchange and sell foreign currency (sometimes with a fee). Major banks on the Big Island are American Savings Bank, Bank of Hawaii, First Hawaiian Bank, and Central Pacific Bank.

Travelers Checks

Travelers checks are accepted throughout Hawaii at hotels, restaurants, car rental agencies, and most stores and shops. However, to be readily acceptable they should be in U.S. currency. Some larger hotels that frequently have Japanese and Canadian guests will accept their currency. Banks accept foreign-currency travelers checks, but it'll mean an extra trip and inconvenience. It's best to get most of your travelers checks in $20–50 denominations; anything larger will be hard to cash in smaller shops and boutiques, though not in hotels.

Credit Cards

More and more business is transacted in Hawaii using credit cards. Almost every form of accommodation, shop, restaurant, and amusement accepts them. For renting a car they're almost a must. With "credit card insurance" readily available, they're as safe as travelers checks and even more convenient. Write down the numbers of your cards in case they're stolen. Don't rely on them completely, because there are some establishments—many bed-and-breakfasts, for example—that won't accept them or perhaps won't accept the kind you carry.

Taxes

Hawaii does not have a state sales tax, but it does have a general excise tax that runs at about four percent, and this will usually be added to most sales transactions. In addition, there is an accommodations tax of 7.25 percent, so approximately 11.4 percent will be added to your hotel bill when you check out.

COMMUNICATIONS AND MEDIA

Post Office

Normal business hours are 8 A.M.–4:30 P.M. Mon.–Fri., 9 A.M.–1 P.M. Sat., although some branch offices now have slightly different hours, particularly on Saturday. The central post office on Hawai'i is in Hilo, and there are 25 branch post offices in towns around the island. Larger hotels and condominiums also offer limited postal services.

Telephone

The telephone system on the main islands is modern and comparable to any system on the Mainland. Any phone call to a number on that island is a **local call;** it's **long distance** when dialing to another island. As they do everywhere else in the United States, long-distance rates for land lines go down at 5 P.M. and again at 11 P.M. until 8 A.M. the next morning. Rates are cheapest from Friday at 5 P.M. until Monday at 8 A.M. Local calls from public telephones cost $0.50. Public telephones are found at hotels, street booths, restaurants, most public buildings, and some beach parks. It is common to have a phone in most hotel rooms and condominiums, though a service charge is usually collected, even on local calls. Emergency calls are always free. You can "direct dial" from Hawaii to the Mainland and more than 160 foreign countries. Undersea cables and satellite communications ensure top-quality phone service. Toll-free calls are preceded by 800/, 888/, 877/, or 866/; there is no charge to the calling party. Many are listed in this book.

For directory assistance, dial: 411 (local), 1-555-1212 (interisland), area code/555-1212 (Mainland), or 800/555-1212 (toll-free). **The area code for all the islands of Hawaii is 808.**

Newspapers

Major daily newspapers on the Big Island include *Hawaii Tribune-Herald* (www.hilohawaiitribune.com), a Hilo publication, and *West Hawaii Today* (www.westhawaiitoday.com), published in Kona. Both are owned by the same parent company and cost $0.50 daily and $1 on Sunday. Providing it's still happening, an alternative and progressive view on island issues is the *Ka'u Landing,* a monthly out of Ocean View.

Hawaii's two main English-language dailies are the *Honolulu Star Bulletin* (www.starbulletin.com) and the *Honolulu Advertiser* (www.honoluluadvertiser.com). These are also available at stands around the island for $0.75 daily or $2 on Sunday. *USA Today* and other papers with nationwide distribution, as well as some international newspapers, can also be picked up at Borders Books.

Island Radio Stations

More than a dozen and a half radio stations broadcast on the Big Island. Most broadcast only on either the Hilo or Kona side, while a few send signals to both sides. Among the most popular are:

East Side

KIPA 620 AM: Rainbow Radio: easy listening contemporary
KPUA 670 AM: news, talk, and sports
KHLO 850 AM: oldies
KANO 91.1 FM: Hawaii Public Radio, classical, news
KHWI 92.7 FM: rock and roll
KWXX 94.7 FM: island music, light contemporary rock

KBIG 97.9 FM: adult contemporary
KAPA 100.3 FM: Hawaiian

West Side
KIPA 620 AM: Rainbow Radio: easy listening contemporary
KAGB 99.1 FM: Hawaiian
KAOY 1012.5 FM: rock and roll
KLEO106.1 FM: contemporary adult

Libraries

Libraries are located in towns and schools all over the island, with the main branch in Hilo (300 Waianuenue Ave., 808/933-8888). This location can provide information regarding all libraries. In Kailua-Kona, the library (75-140 Hualalai Rd., 808/327-4327) is in the center of town. Check with each individual branch for times and services. Library cards are available free for Hawaii state residents and military personnel stationed in Hawaii, $25 for nonresidents (valid for five years), and $10 for three months for visitors. Free Internet access is available to library cardholders.

Bookstores

For bookstores on the island, see the individual travel chapters for details.

TOURIST INFORMATION

Hawaii Visitors Bureau

The Hawaii Visitors Bureau or HVB (www.gohawaii.com) is a top-notch organization providing help and information to all of Hawaii's visitors. Anyone contemplating a trip to Hawaii should visit a nearby office or check out its website for any specific information that might be required. The Hawaii Visitors Bureau's advice and excellent brochures on virtually every facet of living in, visiting, or simply enjoying Hawaii are free. The material offered is too voluminous to list, but for basics, request individual island brochures, maps, vacation planners (also on the Web at www.hshawaii.com), and an all-island members directory of accommodations, restaurants, entertainment, and transportation. Allow two to three weeks for requests to be answered.

Statewide offices include: **Hawaii Visitors Bureau Administrative Office** (2270 Kalakaua Ave., Suite 801, Honolulu, 808/923-1811), **O'ahu Visitors Bureau** (733 Bishop St., Suite 1872, Honolulu, 808/524-0722 or 877/525-6242, www.visit-oahu.com), **Big Island Hawaii Visitors Bureau, Hilo Branch** (250 Keawe St., Hilo, 808/961-5797 or 800/648-2441, www.bigisland.org), **Big Island Hawaii Visitors Bureau, Kona Branch** (250 Waikoloa Beach Dr., Suite B-15, Waikoloa, 808/886-1655), **Kaua'i Hawaii Visitors Bureau** (4334 Rice St., Suite 101, Lihu'e, 808/245-3971 or 800/262-1400, www.kauaivisitorsbureau.org), and **Maui Hawaii Visitors Bureau** (1727 Wili Pa Loop, Wailuku, 808/244-3530 or 800/525-6284, www.visitmaui.com).

Other Organizations

Two other helpful organizations are the **Moloka'i Visitors Association** (808/553-3876 or 800/800-6367 Mainland, www.molokai-hawaii.com) and **Destination Lana'i** (808/565-7600 or 800/947-4774, www.visitlanai.net).

Additional online information pertaining to the island of Hawai'i can be found at the official County of Hawai'i website (www.hawaii-county.com).

Free Tourist Literature

Free tourist literature and the narrow-format, magazine-style *This Week Big Island, Spotlight's Big Island Gold,* and *Big Island Maps, Beach and Tours,* are available at the airport, many hotels, and most restaurants and shopping centers around the island. They come out monthly or quarterly and contain money-saving coupons, island maps, and information on local events, activities, shopping, and restaurants. The small-format magazine-style *Coffee Times* focuses on cultural and historical topics, while the newspaper-format *Hawai'i Island Journal* concentrates on issues of the day and has a very good island calendar of events section. With a focus on activities and fun things to do, *101 Things to Do on Hawaii the Big Island* is a great resource and also has money-saving coupons.

PHOTO COURTESY OF HVCB/HAWAII TOURISM JAPAN

a stand for newspapers and free papers on the corner of Ali'i Drive

Publications with local orientation are *Kohala Mountain News, Kona Times, Hamakua Times,* and *The Waimea Gazette. Big Island Drive Guide* is available from the car rental agencies and contains tips, coupons, and good maps. The Hawaii AAA *Tourbook* is also very useful. Other publications of interest are the *Big Island Visitor Magazine* and the in-flight magazines of Aloha and Hawaiian Airlines.

Maps

Aside from the simple maps in the ubiquitous free tourist literature, the Big Island Visitors Bureau, Hawaiian Airlines, and other organizations put out folding pocket maps of the island that are available free at the airport and tourist brochure racks around the island. Various Hawai'i island and street maps are available at Borders Books in Hilo and Kailua. Perhaps the best and most detailed of these island maps is the University of Hawai'i Press reference map of Hawai'i, The Big Island. These maps can be found at gift and sundries shops around the island, and at bookshops. If you are looking for detail, the best street map atlas of the Big Island is a two-volume publication by Odyssey Publishing: *The Ready Mapbook of West Hawaii* and *The Ready Mapbook of East Hawaii.*

The Basically Books bookshop in Hilo carries USGS maps, and Kona Marine in Kona carries nautical charts. The state Division of Forestry and Wildlife office in Hilo has map and trail description handouts for trails in the Na Ala Hele state trail system, and the visitors center at Hawai'i Volcanoes National Park carries hiking trail map for park trails.

FILM AND PROCESSING

Photographic film, in print and slide, color and black and white, are all available on the Big Island, but color print film is most widely available. The island's few camera shops carry the widest variety and may be the only ones that carry slide film, but print film can also be found at gift shops, sundries stores, most activity outlets, and general merchandise stores throughout the island. By and large, the cost of film is slightly more expensive in Hawaii than on the Mainland; the cost of developing is roughly the same. There is no camera repair service on the Big Island. Parts and accessories, aside from new camera bodies and their accompanying lenses, are difficult to come by.

For one-hour service print film developing, see **Longs Drug, Kmart,** or one of the independent shops listed in the travel chapters of this book. Slide film is sent to Honolulu to be developed.

LOCAL RESOURCES

Emergencies

For **police, fire, and ambulance** anywhere on the Big Island, dial **911.**

For **nonemergency police** assistance and information, dial 808/935-3311.

Civil Defense: In case of natural disaster such as hurricanes or tsunamis on the Big Island, call 808/935-0031.

Coast Guard Search and Rescue: 800/552-6458.

Sexual Assault Crisis Line: 808/935-0677.

Weather, Marine, and Volcano Reports, and Time of Day

For recorded information on **local island weather,** call 808/961-5582; for the **marine report,** call 808/935-9883; and for **volcano activity,** call 808/985-6000. For time of day, dial 808/961-0212.

Consumer Protection

If you encounter problems finding accommodations or experience bad service or downright rip-offs, try the following: the Chamber of Commerce in Hilo (808/935-7178) or in the Kona/Kohala area (808/329-1758), the Office of Consumer Protection (808/933-0910), or the Better Business Bureau of Hawaii on O'ahu (877/222-6551).

WEIGHTS AND MEASURES

Hawaii, like all of the United States, employs the "English method" of measuring weights and distances. Basically, dry weights are in ounces and pounds; liquid measures are in ounces, quarts, and gallons; and distances are measured in inches, feet, yards, and miles. The metric system is known but is not in general use.

Electricity

The same electrical current is in use in Hawaii as on the U.S. Mainland and is uniform throughout the islands. The system functions on 110 volts, 60 cycles of alternating current (AC). Appliances from Japan will work, but there is some danger that they will burn out, while those requiring the normal European voltage of 220 will not work.

Time Zones

There is no daylight saving time in Hawaii. When daylight saving time is not observed on the Mainland, Hawaii is two hours behind the West Coast, four hours behind the Midwest, five hours behind the East Coast, and 11 hours behind Germany. Hawaii, being just east of the International Date Line, is almost a full day behind most Asian and Oceanian cities. Hours behind these countries and cities are: Japan, 19 hours; Singapore, 18 hours; Sydney, 20 hours; New Zealand, 22 hours; Fiji, 22 hours.

RESOURCES

Glossary

HAWAIIAN

The following list gives you a taste of Hawaiian and provides a basic vocabulary of words in common usage that you are likely to hear. Becoming familiar with them is not a strict necessity, but they will definitely enhance your experience and make talking with local people more congenial. Many islanders spice their speech with certain words and you, too, can use them just as soon as you feel comfortable. You might even discover some Hawaiian words that are so perfectly expressive they'll become regular parts of your vocabulary. Some Hawaiian words have been absorbed into the English language and are found in English dictionaries. The definitions given below are not exhaustive, but are generally considered the most common.

'a'a rough clinker lava. 'A'a has become the correct geological term to describe this type of lava found anywhere in the world.

'ae yes

ahupua'a pie-shaped land divisions running from mountain to sea that were governed by konohiki, local ali'i who owed their allegiance to a reigning chief

aikane friend; pal; buddy

'aina land; the binding spirit to all Hawaiians. Love of the land is paramount in traditional Hawaiian beliefs.

akamai smart; clever; wise

akua a god, or simply "divine"

ali'i a Hawaiian chief or noble

aloha the most common greeting in the islands; can mean both hello and good-bye, welcome and farewell. It can also mean romantic love, affection, or best wishes.

anuenue rainbow

'a'ole no

'aumakua a personal or family god, often an ancestral spirit

auwe alas; ouch! When a great chief or loved one died, it was a traditional wail of mourning.

'awa also known as kava, a mildly intoxicating traditional drink made from the juice of chewed 'awa root, spat into a bowl, and used in religious ceremonies

halakahiki pineapple

halau school, as in hula school

hale house or building; often combined with other words to name a specific place, such as Haleakala (House of the Sun), or Hale Pa'i at Lahainaluna, meaning Printing House

hana work; combined with pau means end of work or quitting time

hanai literally "to feed." Part of the true aloha spirit. A hanai is a permanent guest, or an adopted family member, usually an old person or a child. This is an enduring cultural phenomenon in Hawaii, in which a child from one family (perhaps that of a brother or sister, and quite often one's grandchild) is raised as one's own without formal adoption.

haole a word that at one time meant foreigner but now means a white person or Caucasian

hapa half, as in a mixed-blooded person being referred to as hapa haole

hapai pregnant; used by all ethnic groups when a keiki is on the way

haupia a coconut custard dessert often served at a lu'au

he'enalu surfing

heiau A platform made of skillfully fitted rocks, upon which temporary structures were built as temples and offerings made to the gods.

holomu an ankle-length dress that is much more fitted than a mu'umu'u, and which is often worn on formal occasions

hono bay, as in Honolulu (Sheltered Bay)

honu green sea turtle; endangered

ho'oilo traditional Hawaiian winter that began in November

ho'olaule'a any happy event, but especially a family outing or picnic

ho'omalimali sweet talk; flattery

huhu angry; irritated

hui a group; meeting; society. Often used to refer to Chinese businesspeople or family members who pool their money to get businesses started.

hukilau traditional shoreline fish-gathering in which everyone lends a hand to huki (pull) the huge net. Anyone taking part shares in the lau (food). It is much more like a party than hard work, and if you're lucky you'll be able to take part in one.

hula a native Hawaiian dance in which the rhythm of the islands is captured by swaying hips and stories told by lyrically moving hands. A halau is a group or school of hula.

huli huli barbecue, as in huli huli chicken

i'a fish in general. I'a maka is raw fish.

imu underground oven filled with hot rocks and used for baking. The main cooking method featured at a lu'au, used to steam-bake pork and other succulent dishes. The tending of the imu was traditionally for men only.

ipo sweetheart; lover; girl- or boyfriend

kahili a tall pole topped with feathers, resembling a huge feather duster. It was used by an ali'i to announce his or her presence.

kahuna priest; sorcerer; doctor; skillful person. In old Hawaii kahuna had tremendous power, which they used for both good and evil. The kahuna ana'ana was a feared individual who practiced "black magic" and could pray a person to death, while the kahuna lapa'au was a medical practitioner bringing aid and comfort to the people.

kai the sea. Many businesses and hotels employ kai as part of their name.

kalua means roasted underground in an imu. A favorite island food is kalua pork.

kama'aina a child of the land; an old-timer; a longtime island resident of any ethnic background; a resident of Hawaii or native son or daughter. Hotels and airlines often offer discounts called "kama'aina rates" to anyone who can prove island residency.

kanaka man or commoner; later used to distinguish a Hawaiian from other races. Tone of voice can make it a derisive expression.

kane means man, but actually used to signify a relationship such as husband or boyfriend. Written on a lavatory door it means "men's room."

kapu forbidden; taboo; keep out; do not touch

kaukau slang word meaning food or chow; grub. Some of the best food in Hawaii comes from the kaukau wagons, trucks that sell plate lunches and other morsels.

kauwa a landless, untouchable caste once confined to living on reservations. Members of this caste were often used as human sacrifices at heiau. Calling someone kauwa is still a grave insult.

kava see 'awa

keiki child or children; used by all ethnic groups. "Have you hugged your keiki today?"

kiawe an algaroba tree from South America commonly found in Hawaii along the shore. It grows a nasty long thorn that can easily puncture a tire. Legend has it that the trees were introduced to the islands by a misguided missionary who hoped the thorns would coerce natives into wearing shoes. Actually, they are good for fuel, as fodder for hogs and cattle, and for reforestation, none of which you'll appreciate if you step on one of the thorns or flatten a tire on your rental car!

ko'ala any food that has been broiled or barbecued

kokua help. As in "Your kokua is needed to keep Hawaii free from litter."

kolohe rascal

kona wind a muggy subtropical wind that blows from the south and hits the leeward side of the islands. It usually brings sticky hot weather and one of the few times when air-conditioning will be appreciated.

konane a traditional Hawaiian game, similar to checkers, played with pebbles on a large flat stone used as a board

ko'olau windward side of the island

kukui a candlenut tree whose pods are polished and then strung together to make a beautiful lei. Traditionally the oil-rich nuts were strung on the rib of a coconut leaf and used as a candle.

kuleana homesite; the old homestead; small farms. Especially used to describe the small spreads on Hawaiian Homelands on Moloka'i.

Kumulipo ancient Hawaiian genealogical chant that records the pantheon of gods, creation, and the beginning of humankind

kupuna a grandparent or old-timer; usually means someone who has gained wisdom. The statewide school system now invites kupuna to talk to the children about the old ways and methods.

la the sun. Often combined with other words to be more descriptive, such as Lahaina (Merciless Sun) or Haleakala (House of the Sun).

lanai veranda or porch. You'll pay more for a hotel room if it has a lanai with an ocean view.

lani sky or the heavens

lau hala traditional Hawaiian weaving of mats, hats, etc., from the prepared fronds of the pandanus (screw pine)

lei a traditional garland of flowers or vines. One of Hawaii's most beautiful customs. Given at any auspicious occasion, but especially when arriving or leaving Hawaii.

lele the stone altar at a heiau

limu edible seaweed of various types. Gathered from the shoreline, it makes an excellent salad. It's used to garnish many island dishes and is a favorite at lu'au.

lolo crazy, as in "lolo buggah" (stupid or crazy guy)

lomi lomi traditional Hawaiian massage; also, raw salmon made into a vinegared salad with chopped onion and spices

lua the toilet; the head; the bathroom

luakini a human-sacrifice temple. Introduced to Hawaii in the 13th century at Waha'ula Heiau on the Big Island.

lu'au a Hawaiian feast featuring poi, imu-baked pork, and other traditional foods. Good ones provide some of the best gastronomic delights in the world.

luna foreman or overseer in the plantation fields. They were often mounted on horseback and were renowned for either their fairness or their cruelty. Representing the middle class, they served as a buffer between plantation workers and white plantation owners.

mahalo thank you. Mahalo nui means "big thanks" or "thank you very much."

mahele division. The "Great Mahele" of 1848 changed Hawaii forever when the traditional common lands were broken up into privately owned plots.

mahimahi a favorite eating fish. Often called a dolphin, but a mahimahi is a true fish, not a cetacean.

mahu a homosexual; often used derisively like "fag" or "queer"

maile a fragrant vine used in traditional lei. It looks ordinary but smells delightful.

maka'ainana a commoner; a person "belonging" to the 'aina (land), who supported the ali'i by fishing and farming and as a warrior

makai toward the sea; used by most islanders when giving directions

make dead; deceased

malihini what you are if you have just arrived: a newcomer; a tenderfoot; a recent arrival

malo the native Hawaiian loincloth. Never worn anymore except at festivals or pageants.

mana power from the spirit world; innate energy of all things animate or inanimate; the grace of god. Mana could be passed on from one person to another, or even stolen. Great care was taken to protect the ali'i from having their mana defiled. Commoners were required to lie flat on the ground and cover their faces whenever a great ali'i approached. Kahuna were often employed in the regaining or transference of mana.

manini stingy; tight; a Hawaiianized word taken from the name of Don Francisco Marin, who was instrumental in bringing many fruits and plants to Hawaii. He was known for never sharing any of the bounty from his substantial gardens on Vineyard Street in Honolulu; therefore, his name came to mean "stingy." Also a type of fish.

manuahi free; gratis; extra

mauka toward the mountains; used by most islanders when giving directions

mauna mountain. Often combined with other words to be more descriptive, such as Mauna Kea (White Mountain)

mele a song or chant in the Hawaiian oral tradition that records the history and genealogies of the ali'i

Menehune the legendary "little people" of Hawaii. Like leprechauns, they are said to shun humans and possess magical powers.

moa chicken; fowl

moana the ocean; the sea. Many businesses and hotels as well as places have moana as part of their name.

moe sleep

mo'olelo ancient tales kept alive by the oral tradition and recited only by day

mu'umu'u a "Mother Hubbard," an ankle-length dress with a high neckline introduced by the missionaries to cover the nakedness of the Hawaiians. It has become fashionable attire for almost any occasion in Hawaii.

nani beautiful

nui big; great; large; as in mahalo nui (thank you very much)

'ohana a family; the fundamental social division; extended family. Now often used to denote a social organization with grassroots overtones.

'okolehau literally "iron bottom"; a traditional booze made from ti root. 'Okole means "rear end" and hau means "iron," which was descriptive of the huge blubber pots in which 'okolehau was made. Also, if you drink too much it'll surely knock you on your 'okole.

oli chant not done to a musical accompaniment

'ono delicious; delightful; the best. Ono ono means "extra or absolutely delicious."

'opihi a shellfish or limpet that clings to rocks and is gathered as one of the islands' favorite pu pu. Custom dictates that you never remove all of the 'opihi from a rock; some are always left to grow for future generations.

'opu belly; stomach

pahoehoe smooth, ropy lava that looks like burnt pancake batter. It is now the correct geological term used to describe this type of lava found anywhere in the world.

pakalolo "crazy smoke"; grass; smoke; dope; marijuana

pake a Chinese person. Can be derisive, depending on the tone in which it is used. It is a bastardization of the Chinese word meaning "uncle."

pali a cliff; precipice. Hawaii's geology makes them quite common. The most famous are the pali of Oahu where a major battle was fought.

paniolo a Hawaiian cowboy. Derived from the Spanish español. The first cowboys brought to Hawaii during the early 19th century were Mexicans from California.

papale hat. Except for the feathered helmets of the ali'i warriors of old Hawaii, hats were generally not worn. However, once the islanders saw their practical uses and how fashionable they were, they began weaving them from various materials and quickly became experts at manufacture and design.

pa'u long split skirt often worn by women when horseback riding. In the 1800s, an island treat was watching pa'u riders in their beautiful dresses at Kapi'olani Park in Honolulu. The tradition is carried on today at many of Hawaii's rodeos.

pau finished; done; completed. Often combined into pau hana, which means end of work or quitting time.

pilau stink; bad smell; stench

pilikia trouble of any kind, big or small; bad times

poi a glutinous paste made from the pounded corm of taro, which ferments slightly and has a light sour taste. Purplish in color, it's a staple at lu'au, where it is called "one-, two-, or three-finger" poi, depending upon its thickness.

pono righteous or excellent

pua flower

puka a hole of any size. Puka is used by all island residents, whether talking about a pinhole in a rubber boat or a tunnel through a mountain.

punalua a traditional practice, before the missionaries arrived, of sharing mates. Western seamen took advantage of it, leading to the spread of contagious diseases and eventual rapid decline of the Hawaiian people.

pune'e bed; narrow couch. Used by all ethnic groups. To recline on a pune'e on a breezy lanai is a true island treat.

pu pu an appetizer; a snack; hors d'oeuvres; can be anything from cheese and crackers to sushi. Oftentimes, bars or nightclubs offer them free.

pupule crazy; nuts; out of your mind

pu'u hill, as in Pu'u 'Ula'ula (Red Hill)

tapa a traditional paper cloth made from beaten bark. Intricate designs were stamped in using beaters, and natural dyes added color. The tradition was lost for many years but is now making a comeback, and provides some of the most beautiful folk art in the islands. Also called Kapa.

taro the staple of old Hawaii. A plant with a distinctive broad leaf that produces a starchy root. It was brought by the first Polynesians and was grown on magnificently irrigated plantations. According to the oral tradition, the life-giving properties of taro hold mystical significance for Hawaiians, since it was created by the gods at about the same time as humans.

ti a broad-leafed plant that was used for many purposes, from plates to hula skirts. Especially used to wrap religious offerings presented at the heiau.

tutu grandmother; granny; older woman. Used by all as a term of respect and endearment.

ukulele uku means "flea" and lele means "jumping," so literally "jumping flea" – the way the Hawaiians perceived the quick finger movements used on the banjo-like Portuguese folk instrument called a cavaquinho. The ukulele quickly became synonymous with the islands.

wahine young woman; female; girl; wife. Used by all ethnic groups. When written on a lavatory door it means "women's room."

wai freshwater; drinking water

wela hot. Wela kahao is a "hot time" or "making whoopee."

wiki quickly; fast; in a hurry. Often seen as wiki wiki (very fast), as in "Wiki Wiki Messenger Service."

USEFUL PHRASES

Aloha ahiahi Good evening

Aloha au ia 'oe I love you

Aloha kakahiaka Good morning

Aloha nui loa much love; fondest regards

Hau'oli la hanau Happy birthday

Hau'oli makahiki hou Happy New Year

Komo mai please come in; enter; welcome

Mele kalikimaka Merry Christmas

'Okole maluna bottoms up; salute; cheers; kampai

PIDGIN

The following are a few commonly used words and expressions that should give you an idea of pidgin. It really can't be written properly, merely approximated, but for now, *"Study da' kine an' bimbye it be mo' bettah, brah! OK? Lesgo."*

an' den and then? big deal; so what's next?

auntie respected elderly woman

bad ass very good

bimbye after a while; bye and bye. "Bimbye, you learn pidgin."

blalah brother, but actually only refers to a large, heavy-set, good-natured Hawaiian man

brah all the bros in Hawaii are brahs; brother; pal. Used to call someone's attention. One of the most common words even among people who are not acquainted. After a fill-up at a gas station, a person would say "Tanks, brah."

chicken skin goose bumps

cockaroach steal; rip off. If you really want to find out what cockaroach means, just leave your camera on your beach blanket when you take a little dip.

da' kine a catchall word of many meanings that epitomizes the essence of pidgin. Da' kine is a euphemism for pidgin and is substituted whenever the speaker is at a loss for a word or just wants to generalize. It can mean: you know? watchamacallit; of that type.

geev um give it to them; give them hell; go for it. Can be used as an encouragement. If a surfer is riding a great wave, the people on the beach might yell, "Geev um, brah!"

grinds food

hana ho again. Especially after a concert the audience shouts "hana ho" (one more!).

hele on let's get going

howzit? as in "howzit, brah?" what's happening?

how's it going? The most common greeting, used in place of the more formal "How do you do?"

huhu angry! "You put the make on the wrong da' kine wahine, brah, and you in da' kine trouble if you get one big Hawaiian blalah plenty huhu."

lesgo let's go! do it!

li'dis an' li'dat like this or that; a catch-all grouping especially if you want to avoid details; like, ya' know?

lolo buggah stupid or crazy guy (person). Words to a tropical island song go, "I want to find the lolo who stole my pakalolo."

mo' bettah better, real good! great idea. An island sentiment used to be, "mo' bettah you come Hawaii." Now it has subtly changed to, "mo' bettah you visit Hawaii."

ono number one! delicious; great; groovy. "Hawaii is ono, brah!"

pakalolo literally "crazy smoke"; marijuana; grass; reefer

pakiki head stubborn; bull-headed

pau a Hawaiian word meaning finished; done; over and done with. Pau hana means end of work or quitting time. Once used by plantation workers, now used by everyone.

seestah sister, woman

shaka hand wave where only the thumb and baby finger stick out, meaning thank you, all right!

sleepah slippers, flip-flops, zori

stink face (or stink eye) basically frowning at someone; using facial expression to show displeasure. Hard looks. What you'll get if you give local people a hard time.

swell head burned up; angry

talk story spinning yarns; shooting the breeze; throwing the bull; a rap session. If you're lucky enough to be around to hear kupuna (elders) "talk story," you can hear some fantastic tales in the tradition of old Hawaii.

tanks, brah thanks, thank you

to da max all the way

waddascoops what's the scoop? what's up? what's happening?

Suggested Reading

Many publishers print books on Hawaii. Following are a few that focus on Hawaiian topics. **University of Hawai'i Press** (www.uhpress.hawaii.edu) has the best overall general list of titles on Hawaii. The **Bishop Museum Press** (www.bishopmuseum.org/press) puts out many scholarly works on Hawaiiana, as does **Kamehameha Schools Press** (www.kspress.ksbe.edu). Also good, with a more general-interest list, are **Bess Press** (www.besspress.com), **Mutual Publishing** (www.mutualpublishing.com) and **Petrogylph Press** (www.basicallybooks.com). In addition, a website specifically oriented toward books on Hawaii, Hawaiian music, and other things Hawaiian is **Hawaii Books** (www/hawaiibooks.com).

ASTRONOMY

Bryan, E.H. *Stars over Hawaii.* Hilo, HI: Petroglyph Press, 1977. An introduction to astronomy, with information about the constellations and charts featuring the stars filling the night sky in Hawaii, by month. An excellent primer.

Rhoads, Samuel. *The Sky Tonight—A Guided Tour of the Stars over Hawaii.* Honolulu: Bishop Museum, 1993. Four pages per month of star charts—one each for the horizon in every cardinal direction. Exceptional!

COOKING

Alexander, Agnes. *How to Use Hawaiian Fruit.* Hilo, HI: Petroglyph Press, 1984. A slim volume of recipes using delicious and different Hawaiian fruits.

Beeman, Judy, and Martin Beeman. *Joys of Hawaiian Cooking.* Hilo, HI: Petroglyph

Press, 1977. A collection of favorite recipes from Big Island chefs.

Choy, Sam. *Cooking from the Heart with Sam Choy.* Honolulu: Mutual Publishing, 1995. This beautiful, hand-bound cookbook contains many color photos by Douglas Peebles.

Fukuda, Sachi. *Pupus, An Island Tradition.* Honolulu: Bess Press, 1995.

Margah, Irish, and Elvira Monroe. *Hawaii, Cooking with Aloha.* San Carlos, CA: Wide World, 1984. Island recipes, as well as hints on decor.

Rizzuto, Shirley. *Fish Dishes of the Pacific—from the Fishwife.* Honolulu: Hawaii Fishing News, 1986. Features recipes using all the fish commonly caught in Hawaiian waters (husband Jim Rizzuto is the author of *Fishing, Hawaiian Style*).

CULTURE

Dudley, Michael Kioni. *Man, Gods, and Nature.* Honolulu: Na Kane O Ka Malo Press, 1990. An examination of the philosophical underpinnings of Hawaiian beliefs and their interconnected reality.

Hartwell, Jay. *Na Mamo: Hawaiian People Today.* Honolulu: Ai Pohaku Press, 1996. Profiles 12 people practicing Hawaiian traditions in the modern world.

Heyerdahl, Thor. *American Indians in the Pacific.* London: Allen and Unwin Ltd., 1952. Theoretical and anthropological accounts of the influence on Polynesia of the Indians along the Pacific coast of North and South America. Though no longer in print, this book is fascinating reading, presenting unsubstantiated yet intriguing theories.

Kamehameha Schools Press. *Life in Early Hawai'i: The Ahupua'a.* 3rd ed. Honolulu: Kamehameha Schools Press, 1994. Written for schoolchildren to better understand the basic organization of old Hawaiian land use and its function, this slim volume is a good primer for people of any age who wish to understand this fundamental societal fixture.

Kirch, Patrick V. *Feathered Gods and Fishhooks: An Introduction to Hawaiian Archaeology and Prehistory.* Honolulu: University of Hawai'i Press, 1997. This scholarly, lavishly illustrated, yet very readable book gives new insight into the development of precontact Hawaiian civilization. It focuses on the sites and major settlements of old Hawai'i and chronicles the main cultural developments while weaving in the social climate that contributed to change. A very worthwhile read.

FAUNA

Boom, Robert. *Hawaiian Seashells.* Honolulu: Waikiki Aquarium, 1972. Photos by Jerry Kringle. A collection of 137 seashells found in Hawaiian waters, featuring many found nowhere else on earth. Broken into categories with accompanying text including common and scientific names, physical descriptions, and likely habitats. A must for shell collectors.

Carpenter, Blyth, and Russell Carpenter. *Fish Watching in Hawaii.* San Mateo, CA: Natural World Press, 1981. A color guide to many of the reef fish found in Hawaii and often spotted by snorkelers. If you're interested in the fish that you'll be looking at, this guide will be very helpful.

Denny, Jim. *The Birds of Kauai.* Honolulu: University of Hawai'i Press, 1999. Worthy companion for any birder to the island.

Fielding, Ann, and Ed Robinson. *An Underwater Guide to Hawai'i.* Honolulu: University of Hawai'i Press, 1987. If you've ever had a desire to snorkel/scuba the living reef waters of Hawaii and to be familiar with what you're seeing, get this small but fact-packed book. The amazing array of marinelife found throughout the archipelago is captured in glossy photos with accompanying informative text. Both the scientific and common names of specimens are given. This book will enrich your underwater experience and serve as an easily understood reference guide for many years.

Goodson, Gar. *The Many-Splendored Fishes of Hawaii.* Stanford, CA: Stanford University Press, 1985. This small but thorough "fish-watchers" book includes entries on some deep-sea fish.

Hawaiian Audubon Society. *Hawaii's Birds.* 5th ed. Honolulu: Hawaii Audubon Society, 1997. Excellent bird book, giving description, range, voice, and habits of the over 100 species. Slim volume; good for carrying while hiking.

Hobson, Edmund, and E.H. Chave. *Hawaiian Reef Animals.* Honolulu: University of Hawai'i Press, 1987. Colorful photos and descriptions of the fish, invertebrates, turtles, and seals that call Hawaiian reefs their home.

Kay, Alison, and Olive Schoenberg-Dole. *Shells of Hawai'i.* Honolulu: University of Hawai'i Press, 1991. Color photos and tips on where to look.

Mahaney, Casey. *Hawaiian Reef Fish, The Identification Book.* Planet Ocean Publishing, 1993. A spiral-bound reference work featuring many color photos and descriptions of common reef fish found in Hawaiian waters.

Nickerson, Roy. *Brother Whale, A Pacific Whalewatcher's Log.* San Francisco: Chronicle Books, 1977. Introduces the average person to the life of earth's greatest mammals. Provides historical accounts, photos, and tips on whale-watching. Well-written, descriptive, and the best "first time" book on whales.

Pratt, H.D., P.L. Bruner, and D.G. Berrett. *The Birds of Hawaii and the Tropical Pacific.* Princeton, N.J.: Princeton University Press, 1987. Useful field guide for novice and expert bird-watchers, covering Hawaii as well as other Pacific Island groups.

Pratt, Douglas. *A Pocket Guide to Hawaii's Birds.* Honolulu: Mutual Publishing, 1996. A condensed version of Pratt's larger work with a focus on birds of the state.

Tomich, P. Quentin. *Mammals in Hawai'i.* Honolulu: Bishop Museum Press, 1986. Quintessential scholarly text on all mammal species in Hawaii, with description of distribution and historical references. Lengthy bibliography.

van Riper, Charles, and Sandra van Riper. *A Field Guide to the Mammals of Hawaii.* Honolulu: Oriental Publishing. A guide to the surprising number of mammals introduced into Hawaii. Full-color pages document description, uses, tendencies, and habitat. Small and thin, this book makes a worthwhile addition to any serious hiker's backpack.

FLORA

Kepler, Angela. *Hawaiian Heritage Plants.* Honolulu: University of Hawai'i Press, 1998. A treatise on 32 utilitarian plants used by the early Hawaiians.

Kepler, Angela. *Hawai'i's Floral Splendor.* Honolulu: Mutual Publishing, 1997. A general reference to flowers of Hawaii.

Kepler, Angela. *Tropicals of Hawaii.* Honolulu: Mutual Publishing, 1989. This small-format book features many color photos of nonnative flowers.

Kuck, Lorraine, and Richard Togg. *Hawaiian Flowers and Flowering Trees.* Rutland, VT: Tuttle, 1960. A classic, though no longer in print, field guide to tropical and subtropical flora illustrated in watercolor. A "to the point" description of Hawaiian plants and flowers with a brief history of their places of origin and their introduction to Hawaii.

Merrill, Elmer. *Plant Life of the Pacific World.* Rutland, VT: Tuttle, 1983. This is the definitive book for anyone planning a botanical tour to the entire Pacific Basin. Originally published in the 1930s, it remains a tremendous work, worth tracking down through out-of-print book services.

Miyano, Leland. *Hawai'i, A Floral Paradise.* Honolulu: Mutual Publishing, 1995. Photographed by Douglas Peebles, this large-format book is filled with informative text and beautiful color shots of tropical flowers commonly seen in Hawaii.

Miyano, Leland. *A Pocket Guide to Hawai'i's Flowers.* Honolulu: Mutual Publishing, 2001. A small guide to readily seen flowers in the state. Good for the backpack or back pocket.

Sohmer, S.H., and R. Gustafson. *Plants and Flowers of Hawai'i.* Honolulu: University of Hawai'i Press, 1987. Sohmer and Gustafson cover the vegetation zones of Hawaii, from mountains to coast, introducing you to the wide and varied floral biology of the islands. They give a good introduction to the history and unique evolution of Hawaiian plantlife. Beautiful color plates are accompanied by clear and concise plant descriptions, with the scientific and common Hawaiian names listed.

Teho, Fortunato. *Plants of Hawaii—How to Grow Them.* Hilo, HI: Petroglyph Press, 1992. A small but useful book for those who want their backyards to bloom into tropical paradises.

Wagner, Warren L., Derral R. Herbst, and H. S. Sohner. *Manual of the Flowering Plants of Hawai'i,* revised edition, vol. 2. Honolulu: University of Hawai'i Press in association with Bishop Museum Press, 1999. Considered the Bible for Hawaii's botanical world. Scholarly.

Valier, Kathy. *Ferns of Hawaii.* Honolulu: University of Hawai'i Press, 1995. One of the few books that treat the state's ferns as a single subject.

HEALTH

Gutmanis, June. *Kahuna La'au Lapa'au.* Honolulu: Island Heritage, rev. ed. 2001. Text on Hawaiian herbal medicines: diseases, treatments, and medicinal plants, with illustrations.

McBride, L.R. *Practical Folk Medicine of Hawaii.* Hilo, HI: Petroglyph Press, 1975. An illustrated guide to Hawaii's medicinal plants as used by the *kahuna lapa'au* (medical healers). Includes a thorough section on ailments, diagnosis, and the proper folk remedy. Illustrated by the author, a renowned botanical researcher and former ranger at Hawai'i Volcanoes National Park.

Wilkerson, James A., M.D., ed. *Medicine for Mountaineering and Other Wilderness.* 4th ed. Seattle: The Mountaineers, 1992. Don't let the title fool you. Although the book focuses on specific health problems that may be encountered while mountaineering, it is the best first-aid and general health guide available today. Written by doctors for the layperson to use until help arrives, it is jam-packed with easily understandable techniques and procedures. For those planning extended hikes, it is a must.

HISTORY

Apple, Russell A. *Trails: From Steppingstones to Kerbstones.* Honolulu: Bishop Museum Press, 1965. This "Special Publication #53" is a special-interest archaeological survey focusing on trails, roadways, footpaths, and highways and how they were designed and maintained throughout the years. Many "royal highways" from precontact Hawaii are cited.

Ashdown, Inez MacPhee. *Kaho'olawe.* Honolulu: Topgallant Publishing, 1979. The tortured story of the lonely island of Kaho'olawe by one of the family who owned the island until it was turned into a military bombing target during World War II. It's also a first-person account of life on the island.

Ashdown, Inez MacPhee. *Ke Alaloa o Maui.* Wailuku, HI: Kama'aina Historians Inc., 1971. A compilation of the history and legends connected to sites on the island of Maui. Ashdown was at one time a "lady in waiting" for Queen Lili'uokalani and was later proclaimed Maui's "Historian Emeritus."

Barnes, Phil. *A Concise History of the Hawaiian Islands.* Hilo, HI; Petroglyph Press, 1999. An examination of the main currents of Hawaiian history and its major players, focusing on the important factors in shaping the social, economic, and political trends of the islands. An easy read.

Cameron, Roderick. *The Golden Haze.* New York: World Publishing, 1964. An account of Captain James Cook's voyages of discovery throughout the South Seas. Uses original diaries and journals for an "on the spot" reconstruction of this great seafaring adventure.

Cox, J. Halley, and Edward Stasack. *Hawaiian Petroglyphs.* Honolulu: Bishop Museum Press, 1970. The most thorough examination of petroglyph sites throughout the islands.

Daws, Gavan. *Shoal of Time, A History of the Hawaiian Islands.* Honolulu: University of Hawai'i Press, 1974. A highly readable history of Hawaii dating from its "discovery" by the Western world down to its acceptance as the 50th state. Good insight into the psychological makeup of influential characters who helped form Hawaii's past.

Donohugh, Douglas. *The Story of Koloa: A Kauai Plantation Town.* Honolulu: Mutual Publishing, 2001. A short history of the town of Koloa and its role in the history of sugar in Hawaii, with the addition of a concise history of the islands and a tour through the town today.

Dorrance, William H. and Francis S. Morgan. *Sugar Islands: The 165-Year Story of Sugar in Hawai'i.* Honolulu: Mutual Publishing, 2000. An overall sketch of the sugar industry in Hawaii from inception to decline, with data on many individual plantations and mills around the islands. Definitely a story from the industry's point of view.

Finney, Ben, and James D. Houston. *Surfing, A History of the Ancient Hawaiian Sport.* Los Angeles: Pomegranate, 1996. Features many early etchings and old photos of Hawaiian surfers practicing their native sport.

Fornander, Abraham. *An Account of the Polynesian Race; Its Origins and Migrations, and the Ancient History of the Hawaiian People to the Times of Kamehameha I.* Rutland, VT: C.E. Tuttle Co., 1969. This is a reprint of a three-volume opus originally published 1878–1885. It is still one of the best sources of information on Hawaiian myth and legend.

Free, David. *Vignettes of Old Hawaii.* Honolulu: Crossroads Press, 1994. A collection of short essays on a variety of subjects.

Fuchs, Lawrence. *Hawaii Pono.* Honolulu: Bess Press, 1961. A detailed, scholarly work presenting an overview of Hawaii's history, based upon ethnic and sociological interpretations. Encompasses most socio-ethnological groups from native Hawaiians to modern entrepreneurs. This book is a must for obtaining some social historical background.

Handy, E.S., and Elizabeth Handy. *Native Planters in Old Hawaii.* Honolulu: Bishop Museum Press, 1972. A superbly written, easily understood scholarly work on the intimate relationship of precontact Hawaiians and the *aina* (land). Much more than its title implies, this book should be read by anyone seriously interested in Polynesian Hawaii.

Ii, John Papa. *Fragments of Hawaiian History.* Honolulu: Bishop Museum, 1959. Hawaii's history under Kamehameha I as told by a Hawaiian who actually experienced it.

Joesting, Edward. *Hawaii: An Uncommon History.* New York: W.W. Norton Co., 1978. A truly uncommon history told in a series of vignettes relating to the lives and personalities of the first Caucasians in Hawaii, Hawaiian nobility, sea captains, writers, and adventurers. Brings history to life. Absolutely excellent!

Joesting, Edward. *Kauai: The Separate Kingdom.* Honolulu: University of Hawai'i Press, 1984. The history of Kaua'i through the end of the Hawaiian monarchy. Joesting brings the story of the island to life through the people who shaped it.

Kamakau, S. M. *Ruling Chiefs of Hawaii,* revised edition. Honolulu: Kamehameha Schools Press, 1992. A history of Hawaii from the legendary leader 'Umi to the mid-Kamehameha Dynasty, from oral tales and from a Hawaiian perspective.

Krauss, Robert. *Grove Farm Plantation: The Biography of a Hawaiian Sugar Plantation.* Palo Alto, CA: Pacific Books, 1984. A history of the Grove Farm, the Wilcox family, and the economy of sugar on Kaua'i.

Kurisu, Yasushi. *Sugar Town, Hawaiian Plantation Days Remembered.* Honolulu: Watermark Publishing, 1995. Reminiscences of life growing up on sugar plantations on the Hamakua Coast of the Big Island. Features many old photos.

Lili'uokalani. *Hawaii's Story by Hawaii's Queen.* Reprint, Honolulu: Mutual Publishing, 1990. Originally written in 1898, this moving personal account recounts Hawaii's inevitable move from monarchy to U.S. Territory by its last queen, Lili'uokalani. The facts can be found in other histories, but none provides the emotion or point of view expressed by Hawaii's deposed monarch. This is a must-read to get the whole picture.

McBride, Likeke. *Petroglyphs of Hawaii.* Hilo, HI: Petroglyph Press, 1997. A revised and updated guide to petroglyphs found in the Hawaiian Islands. A basic introduction to these old Hawaiian picture stories.

Nickerson, Roy. *Lahaina, Royal Capital of Hawaii.* Honolulu: Hawaiian Service, 1978. The story of Lahaina from whaling days to present, spiced with ample photographs.

Tabrah, Ruth M. *Ni'ihau: The Last Hawaiian Island.* Kailua, Hawaii: Press Pacifica, 1987. Sympathetic history of the privately owned island of Ni'ihau.

Takaki, Ronald. *Pau Hana: Plantation Life and Labor in Hawaii.* Honolulu: University of Hawai'i Press, 1983. The story of immigrant labor and the sugar industry in Hawaii until the 1920s from the worker's perspective.

INTRODUCTORY

Carroll, Rick, and Marcie Carroll, ed. *Hawai'i: True Stories of the Island Spirit.* San Francisco: Travelers' Tales, Inc., 1999. A collection of stories by a variety of authors that were chosen to elicit the essence of Hawaii and Hawaiian experiences. A great read.

Cohen, David, and Rick Smolan. *A Day in the Life of Hawaii.* New York: Workman, 1984. On December 2, 1983, 50 of the world's top photojournalists were invited to Hawaii to photograph the variety of daily life on the islands. The photos are excellently reproduced, and accompanied by a minimum of text.

Day, A.G., and C. Stroven. *A Hawaiian Reader.* 1959. Reprint, Honolulu: Mutual Publishing, 1984. A poignant compilation of essays, diary entries, and fictitious writings that takes you from the death of Captain Cook through the "statehood services."

Department of Geography, University of Hawai'i, Hilo. *Atlas of Hawai'i.* 3rd ed. Honolulu: University of Hawai'i Press, 1998. Much more than an atlas filled with reference maps, this also contains commentary on the natural environment, culture, and sociology; a gazetteer; and statistical tables. Actually a mini-encyclopedia on Hawai'i.

Michener, James A. *Hawaii.* New York: Random House, 1959. Michener's fictionalized historical novel has done more to inform *and* misinform readers about Hawaii than any other book ever written. A great tale with plenty of local color and information, but read it for pleasure, not facts.

Piercy, LaRue. *Hawaii This and That.* Honolulu: Mutual Publishing, 1994. Illustrated by Scot Ebanez. A 60-page book filled with one-sentence facts and oddities about all manner of things Hawaiian. Informative, amazing, and fun to read.

Steele, R. Thomas: *The Hawaiian Shirt: Its Art and History.* New York: Abbeville Press, 1984.

LANGUAGE

Elbert, Samuel. *Spoken Hawaiian.* Honolulu: University of Hawai'i Press, 1970. Progressive conversational lessons.

Elbert, Samuel, and Mary Pukui. *Hawaiian Dictionary.* Honolulu: University of Hawai'i Press, 1986. The best dictionary available on the Hawaiian language. The *Pocket Hawaiian Dictionary* is a less expensive, condensed version of this dictionary, and adequate for most travelers with a general interest in the language.

Pukui, Mary Kawena, Samuel Elbert, and Esther T. Mookini. *Place Names of Hawaii.* Honolulu: University of Hawai'i Press, 1974. The most current and comprehensive listing of Hawaiian and foreign place-names in the state, giving pronunciation, spelling, meaning, and location.

Schutz, Albert J. *All About Hawaiian.* Honolulu: University of Hawai'i Press, 1995. A brief primer on Hawaiian pronunciation, grammar, and vocabulary. A solid introduction.

MYTHOLOGY AND LEGENDS

Beckwith, Martha. *Hawaiian Mythology.* Reprint, Honolulu: University of Hawai'i Press, 1976. Over 60 years after its original printing in 1940, this work remains the definitive text on Hawaiian mythology. Beckwith compiled this book from many sources, giving exhaustive cross-references to genealogies and legends expressed in the oral tradition. If you are going to read one book on Hawaii's folklore, this should be it.

Beckwith, Martha. *The Kumulipo.* 1951. Reprint, Honolulu: University of Hawai'i Press, 1972. Translation of the Hawaiian creation chant.

Colum, Padraic. *Legends of Hawaii.* New Haven: Yale University Press, 1937. Selected legends of old Hawaii, reinterpreted but closely based upon the originals.

Elbert, S.H., ed. *Hawaiian Antiquities and Folklore.* Honolulu: University of Hawai'i Press, 1959. Illustrated by Jean Charlot. A selection of the main legends from Abraham Fornander's great work, *An Account of the Polynesian Race.*

Kalakaua, His Hawaiian Majesty, King David. *The Legends and Myths of Hawaii.* Edited by R.M. Daggett, with a foreword by Glen Grant. Honolulu: Mutual Publishing, 1990. Originally published in 1888, Hawaii's own King Kalakaua draws upon his scholarly and formidable knowledge of the classic oral tradition to bring alive ancient tales from precontact Hawaii. A powerful yet somewhat Victorian voice from Hawaii's past speaks clearly and boldly, especially about the intimate role of pre-Christian religion in the lives of the Hawaiian people.

Melville, Leinanai. *Children of the Rainbow.* Wheaton, IL: Theosophical Publishing, 1969. A book on higher spiritual consciousness attuned to nature, which was the basic belief of pre-Christian Hawaii. The appendix contains illustrations of mystical symbols used by the *kahuna.* An enlightening book in many ways.

Pukui, Mary Kawena, and Caroline Curtis. *Hawaii Island Legends.* Honolulu: The Kamehameha Schools Press, 1996. Hawaiian tales and legends for pre-teens.

Pukui, Mary Kawena, and Caroline Curtis. *Tales of the Menehune.* Honolulu: The Kamehameha Schools Press, 1960. Compilation of legends relating to Hawaii's "little people."

Pukui, Mary Kawena, and Caroline Curtis. *The Waters of Kane and other Hawaiian Legends* Honolulu: The Kamehameha Schools Press, 1994. Tales and legends for the pre-teen.

Thrum, Thomas. *Hawaiian Folk Tales.* 1907. Reprint, Chicago: McClurg and Co., 1950. A collection of Hawaiian tales from the oral tradition as told to the author from various sources.

Westervelt, W.D. *Hawaiian Legends of Volcanoes.* 1916. Reprint, Boston: Ellis Press, 1991. A small book concerning the volcanic legends of Hawaii and how they related to the fledgling field of volcanism in the early 1900s. The vintage photos alone are worth a look.

NATURAL SCIENCE AND GEOGRAPHY

Carlquist, Sherwin. *Hawaii: A Natural History.* National Tropical Botanical Garden, 1984. Definitive account of Hawaii's natural history.

Clark, John. *Beaches of the Big Island.* Honolulu: University of Hawai'i Press, 1997. Definitive guide to beaches, including many off the beaten path. Features maps and black-and-white photos. Also *Beaches of O'ahu, Beaches of Kaua'i and Ni'ihau,* and *Beaches of Maui County.*

Hazlett, Richard, and Donald Hyndman. *Roadside Geology of Hawai'i.* Missoula, MT: Mountain Press Publishing, 1996. Begins with a general discussion of the geology of the Hawaiian Islands, followed by a road guide to the individual islands offering descriptions of easily seen features. A great book to have in the car as you tour the islands.

Hubbard, Douglass, and Gordon Macdonald. *Volcanoes of the National Parks of Hawaii.* 1982. Reprint, Volcanoes, HI: Hawaii Natural History Association, 1989. The volcanology of Hawaii, documenting the major lava flows and their geological effect on the state.

Kay, E. Alison, comp. *A Natural History of the Hawaiian Islands.* Honolulu: University of Hawai'i Press, 1994. A selection of concise articles by experts in the fields of volcanism, oceanography, meteorology, and biology. An excellent reference source.

Macdonald, Gorden, Agatin Abbott, and Frank Peterson. *Volcanoes in the Sea.* Honolulu: University of Hawai'i Press, 1983. The best reference to Hawaiian geology. Well explained for easy understanding. Illustrated.

Ziegler, Alan C., *Hawaiian Natural History, Ecology, and Evolution.* Honolulu: University of Hawai'i Press. An overview of Hawaiian natural history with treatment of ecology and evolution in that process.

PERIODICALS

Hawaii Magazine. 3 Burroughs, Irvine, CA. This magazine covers the Hawaiian islands like a tropical breeze. Feature articles on all aspects of life in the islands, with special departments on travel, events, exhibits, and restaurant reviews. Up-to-the-minute information, and a fine read.

PICTORIALS

La Brucherie, Roger. *Hawaiian World, Hawaiian Heart.* Pine Valley, CA: Imagenes Press, 1989.

POLITICAL SCIENCE

Bell, Roger. *Last Among Equals: Hawaiian Statehood and American Politics.* Honolulu: University of Hawai'i Press, 1984. Documents Hawaii's long and rocky road to statehood, tracing political partisanship, racism, and social change.

SPORTS AND RECREATION

Alford, John, D. *Mountain Biking the Hawaiian Islands.* Ohana Publishing, 1997. Good off-road biking guide to the main Hawaiian islands.

Ambrose, Greg. *Surfer's Guide to Hawai'i.* Honolulu: Bess Press, 1991. Island-by-island guide to surfing spots.

Ball, Stuart. *The Hiker's Guide to the Hawaiian Islands.* Honolulu: University of Hawai'i Press, 2000. This excellent guide includes 44 hikes on each of the four main islands.

Cagala, George. *Hawaii: A Camping Guide.* Boston: Hunter Publishing, 1994. Useful.

Chisholm, Craig. *Hawaiian Hiking Trails.* Lake Oswego, OR: Fernglen Press, 1989. Also *Kauai Hiking Trails.*

Cisco, Dan. *Hawai'i Sports.* Honolulu: University of Hawai'i Press, 1999. A compendium of popular and little-known sporting events and figures, with facts, tidbits, and statistical information. Go here first for a general overview.

Lueras, Leonard. *Surfing, the Ultimate Pleasure.* Honolulu: Emphasis International, 1984. One of the most brilliant books ever written on surfing.

McMahon, Richard. *Camping Hawai'i: A Complete Guide.* Honolulu: University of Hawai'i Press, 1997. This book has all you need to know about camping in Hawaii, with descriptions of different campsites.

Morey, Kathy. *Hawaii Trails.* Berkeley, CA: Wilderness Press, 1997. Morey's books are specialized, detailed hiker's guides to Hawaii's outdoors. Complete with useful maps, historical references, official procedures, and plants and animals encountered along the way. If you're focused on hiking, these are the best to take along. *Maui Trails, Oahu Trails,* and *Kauai Trails* are also available.

Rosenberg, Steve. *Diving Hawaii.* Locust Valley, NY: Aqua Quest, 1990. Describes diving locations on the major islands as well as the marine life divers are likely to see. Includes many color photos.

Smith, Robert. *Hawaii's Best Hiking Trails.* Kula, Maui, HI: Hawaiian Outdoor Adventures, 1991. Other guides by this author include *Hiking Oahu, Hiking Maui, Hiking Hawaii,* and *Hiking Kauai.*

Sutherland, Audrey. *Paddling Hawai'i,* revised edition. Honolulu: University of Hawai'i Press, 1998. All you need to know about sea kayaking in Hawaiian waters.

Wallin, Doug. *Diving & Snorkeling Guide to the Hawaiian Islands,* 2nd ed. Pisces Books, 1991. A guide offering brief descriptions of diving locations on the four major islands.

Internet Resources

Government

www.hawaii-county.com

The official website of Hawai'i County. Includes, among other items, a county data book, information about parks and camping, and island bus schedules.

www.hawaii.gov

Official website for the state of Hawai'i. Includes information for visitors, on government organizations, on living in the state, business and employment, education, and many other helpful topics.

Tourist Information

www.instanthawaii.com

This site has wide-ranging information about the Big Island and topics pertaining to the state in general. Good for an introduction before you travel.

www.gohawaii.com

This official site of the Hawaii Visitors and Convention Bureau, the state-run tourism organization, has information about all the major Hawaiian islands: transportation, accommodations, eating, activities, shopping, Hawaiian products, an events calendar, a travel planner, as well as information about meetings, conventions, and the organization itself.

www.bigisland.org

The official site of the Big Island Visitors Bureau, a branch of the Hawaii Visitors Bureau, has much the same information as the above website but specific to the island of Hawai'i. A very useful resource.

www.bestplaceshawaii.com

Produced and maintained by H&S Publishing, this first-rate commercial site has general and specific information about all major Hawaiian islands, a vacation planner, and suggestions for things to do and places to see. For a non-governmental site, this is a great place to start a search for tourist information about the state or any of its major islands. One of dozens of sites on the Internet with a focus on Hawaii tourism-related information.

www.konaweb.com

This site offers a multiplicity of tourist information for those wishing to visit or move to the island, information on island living, and an events calendar.

www.alternative-hawaii.com

Alternative source for eco-friendly general information and links to specific businesses, with some cultural, historical, and events information.

www.hawaiiecotourism.org

Official Hawaii Ecotourism Association website. Lists goals, members, and activities and provides links to member organizations and related ecotourism groups.

www.stayhawaii.com

Website for the Hawaii Island Bed and Breakfast Association, Inc., the only island-wide B&B member organization. Lists a majority of the island's registered B&Bs. Some registered B&Bs are not members of this organization.

Chambers of Commerce

www.gohilo.com

Hawaii Island Chamber of Commerce site strong on business and economic issues, particularly relating to the eastern side of the island. Much additional general information.

www.kona-kohala.com

Chamber of Commerce website for west Hawai'i.

Cultural Events

http://calendar.gohawaii.com

For events of all sorts happening throughout the state, visit the calendar of events listing on the Hawaii Visitors Bureau website. Information can be accessed by island, date, or type.

www.hawaii.gov/sfca

This site of the State Foundation of Culture and the Arts features a calendar of arts and cultural events, activities, and programs held throughout the state. Information is available by island and type.

Interisland Airlines

www.hawaiianair.com
www.alohaairlines.com
www.pacificwings.com

These websites for Hawaiian Airlines, Aloha Airlines, and Pacific Wings list virtually all regularly scheduled commercial air links throughout the state.

Music

www.mele.com

Check out the Hawaiian music scene at Hawaiian Music Island, one of the largest music websites that focuses on Hawaiian music, books and videos related to Hawaiian music and culture, concert schedules, Hawaiian music awards, and links to music companies and musicians. Others with broad listings and general interest information are: Nahenahenet, **www.nahenahe.net,** and Hawaiian Music Guide, **www.hawaii-music.com.**

Books on Hawaii

www.uhpress.hawaii.edu

The University of Hawai'i Press website has the best overall list of titles for books published on Hawaiian themes and topics. Other publishers to check for substantial lists of books on Hawaiiana are the Bishop Museum Press, **www.bishopmuseum.org/press/press.html;** Kamehameha Schools Press,

http://kspress.ksbe.edu; Bess Press, **www.besspress.com;** Mutual Publishing, **www.mutualpublishing.com;** and Petrogylph Press, **www.basicallybooks.com.**

Newspapers

www.westhawaiitoday.com
www.hilohawaiitribune.com

Web presence for the newspapers West Hawaii Today, published in Kona, and Hawaii Tribune-Herald, published in Hilo. Good for local and statewide news. Both have the same parent company.

www.starbulletin.com
www.honoluluadvertiser.com

Websites for Hawaii's two main English-language dailies, the Honolulu Star Bulletin and the Honolulu Advertiser, both published in Honolulu. Both have a concentration of news coverage about O'ahu but also cover major news from the neighbor islands.

Museums

www.hawaiimuseums.org

This site is dedicated to the promotion of museums and cultural attractions in the state of Hawai'i with links to member sites on each of the islands. A member organization.

www.bishopmuseum.org

Site of the premier ethnological and cultural museum dedicated to Hawaiian people, their culture, and cultural artifacts.

National Parks

www.nps.gov/havo

This official site of Hawai'i Volcanoes National Park is a wealth of general information about the park. Related sites are **www.nps.gov/puho,** for Pu'uhonua O Honaunau, a restored Hawaiian temple of refuge, and **www.nps.gov/puhe,** for Pu'ukohola Heiau, a restored Hawaiian temple, both national historical sites administered by the National Park Service.

Astronomical Observatories

www.ifa.hawaii.edu

For information about the astronomical observatories and individual telescope installations on the top of Mauna Kea on the Big Island as well as the Onizuka Center for International Astronomy on the mountain's flank, log onto this University of Hawaii Institute for Astronomy website and follow the links from there.

Volcano Information

http://hvo.wr.usgs.gov

For a history of the Kilauea Volcano volcanic activity, plus up-to-the-minute reports on current activity, see this Hawai'i Volcano Observatory website. Related volcanic information is also available at **www.soest.hawaii.edu/GG/HCV.**

Ethnic Hawaiian Affairs

www.oha.org

Official site for the state-mandated organization that deals with native Hawaii-related affairs.

www.reinstated.org

Site of Reinstated Hawaiian Government, one of the organizations of native Hawaiians who are advocating for sovereignty and independence. While there are many independent native Hawaiian rights organizations that are pushing for various degrees of sovereignty or independence for native Hawaiian people, two others are listed below: Kingdom of Hawaii, **www.freehawaii.org;** (another) Kingdom of Hawaii, **www.pixi.com/~kingdom.**

Index

BEACHES

C

D

E

F

FESTIVALS AND EVENTS

H

HEIAU

HIKING

I

JK

MUSEUMS

N

QR

S

WXYZ

Acknowledgments

to Madame Pele and all women of heart

Since the passing of J.D. Bisignani, the original author of *Moon Handbooks Big Island of Hawai'i,* I have taken on the great task of revising this book and others in his series of guides to Hawaii. Joe, you have been an inspiration to me and have laid a solid foundation for the subsequent revisions of these books. Even though you are gone, you've been with me with each word. To you, my good friend, a big thank you.

As always, the staff at Avalon Travel Publishing has been professional in every way. A sincere thank you to every one.

The following individuals require special thanks for their assistance in the revision of this book: Nancy Daniels, Barbara Campbell, Bob Hendrickson, Jim Sergeant, Jackie Horne, Sarah McCowatt, Christine Jimenez, Toni Roberts, John Alexander, Steve Marcotte, Michael Tuttle, Peter Golden, Julie Neal, Charlene Cowan, Leanne Pletcher, Aven Wright-McIntosh, Kathy Lane, and my wife, Linda Nilsen. *Mahalo* to you all.

MAP SYMBOLS

Expressway	Highlight	Airfield	Golf Course
Primary Road	City/Town	Airport	Parking Area
Secondary Road	State Capital	Mountain	Archaeological Site
Unpaved Road	National Capital	Unique Natural Feature	Church
Trail	Point of Interest	Waterfall	Gas Station
Ferry	Accommodation	Park	Lava
Railroad	Restaurant/Bar	Trailhead	Mangrove
Pedestrian Walkway	Other Location	Snorkeling	Reef
Stairs	Campground		Swamp

CONVERSION TABLES

°C = (°F - 32) / 1.8
°F = (°C x 1.8) + 32
1 inch = 2.54 centimeters (cm)
1 foot = 0.304 meters (m)
1 yard = 0.914 meters
1 mile = 1.6093 kilometers (km)
1 km = 0.6214 miles
1 fathom = 1.8288 m
1 chain = 20.1168 m
1 furlong = 201.168 m
1 acre = 0.4047 hectares
1 sq km = 100 hectares
1 sq mile = 2.59 square km
1 ounce = 28.35 grams
1 pound = 0.4536 kilograms
1 short ton = 0.90718 metric ton
1 short ton = 2,000 pounds
1 long ton = 1.016 metric tons
1 long ton = 2,240 pounds
1 metric ton = 1,000 kilograms
1 quart = 0.94635 liters
1 US gallon = 3.7854 liters
1 Imperial gallon = 4.5459 liters
1 nautical mile = 1.852 km

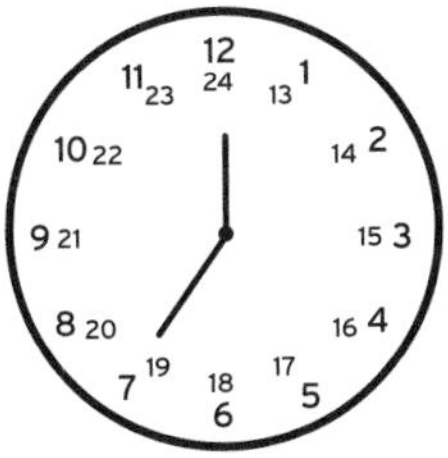

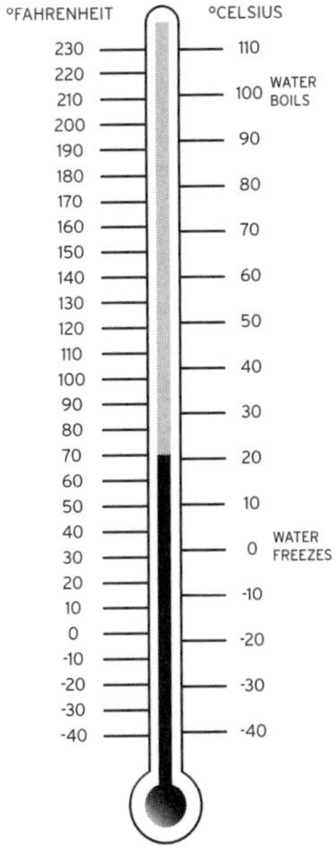

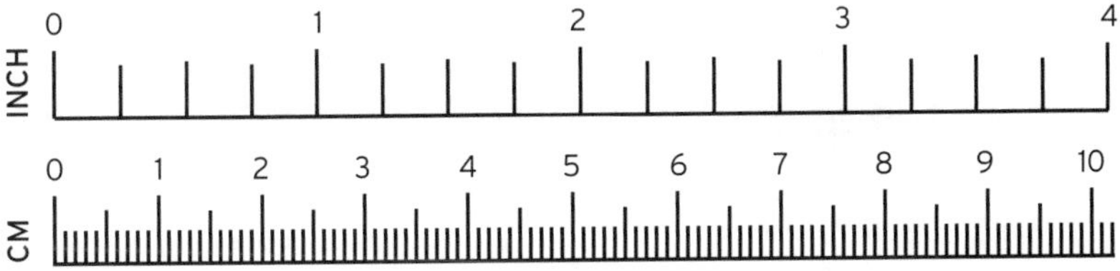

MOON BIG ISLAND OF HAWAI'I
Avalon Travel Publishing
An Imprint of
Avalon Publishing Group, Inc.

1400 65th Street, Suite 250
Emeryville, CA 94608, USA
www.moon.com

Editors: Cinnamon Hearst, Kay Elliot
Series Manager: Kathryn Ettinger
Acquisitions Manager: Rebecca K. Browning
Copy Editor: Valerie Sellers Blanton
Graphics Coordinator: Elizabeth Jang
Production Coordinator: Elizabeth Jang
Cover & Interior Designer: Gerilyn Attebery
Map Editor: Kat Smith
Cartographer: Kat Bennett
Cartograpy Manager: Mike Morgenfeld
Indexer: Judy Hunt

ISBN-10: 1-56691-959-2
ISBN-13: 978-1-56691-959-3
ISSN: 1531-4138

Printing History
1st Edition – 1990
6th Edition – September 2006
5 4 3 2 1

Front cover photo: pink plumeria on banana leaf © Dana Edmunds/Pacific Stock Photography

Title page photo: Kona sunset; © Robert Nilsen

Printed in the United States of America by Malloy

KEEPING CURRENT

If you have a favorite gem you'd like to see included in the next edition, or see anything that needs updating, clarification, or correction, please drop us a line. Send your comments via email to feedback@moon.com, or use the address above.